The Politics of Personal Information

The Politics of Personal Information
Surveillance, Privacy, and Power in West Germany

Larry Frohman

berghahn
NEW YORK • OXFORD
www.berghahnbooks.com

First published in 2021 by
Berghahn Books
www.berghahnbooks.com

© 2021, 2023 Larry Frohman
First paperback edition published in 2023

All rights reserved. Except for the quotation of short passages for the purposes of criticism and review, no part of this book may be reproduced in any form or by any means, electronic or mechanical, including photocopying, recording, or any information storage and retrieval system now known or to be invented, without written permission of the publisher.

Library of Congress Cataloging-in-Publication Data

A C.I.P. cataloging record is available from the Library of Congress
Library of Congress Cataloging-in-Publication Control Number: 2020048774

British Library Cataloguing in Publication Data

A catalogue record for this book is available from the British Library

ISBN 978-1-78920-946-4 hardback
ISBN 978-1-80539-115-9 paperback
ISBN 978-1-80539-361-0 epub
ISBN 978-1-78920-947-1 web pdf

https://doi.org/10.3167/9781789209464

For Young-sun

Contents

List of Illustrations ix

List of Abbreviations x

Acknowledgments xiii

Introduction. Surveillance, Privacy, and Power in the Information Society 1

Part I. Population Registration, Power, and Privacy

Chapter 1
The Federal Population Registration Law, Administrative Power,
and the Politicization of Privacy 37

Part II. Negotiating Communicative Norms in the Computer Age: The Information Question and the Federal Privacy Protection Law, 1970–90

Chapter 2
Rethinking Privacy in the Age of the Mainframe:
From the Private Sphere to Informational Self-Determination 79

Chapter 3
The Legislative Path to the Federal Privacy Protection Law, 1970–77 108

Chapter 4
"Only Sheep Let Themselves Be Counted": The 1983/87 Census Boycotts,
the Census Decision, and the Question of Statistical Governance 135

Chapter 5
Out of the Frying Pan and into the Fire: The Census Decision,
Party Politics, and the Revision of the Federal Privacy Protection Law 177

Part III. The Precautionary Turn: Security, Surveillance, and the Changing Nature of the State

Chapter 6
Paper, Power, and Policing, 1948–72:
The Federal Criminal Police on the Cusp of the Computer Age   209

Chapter 7
The Quest for Security and the Meaning of Privacy: Computers,
Networks, and the Securitization of Space, Place, Movement, and Identity   251

Chapter 8
Mapping the Radical Milieu: Terrorism, Counterterrorism,
and the New Police Surveillance   282

Chapter 9
The Reform of Police Law: *Datenschutz*, the Defense of Law,
and the Debate over Precautionary Surveillance   323

Conclusion   358

Selected Bibliography   367

Index   377

Illustrations

Figure 1.1.	Population information system flowchart.	46
Figure 1.2.	Automation of the population information system in Rhineland-Pfalz.	48
Figure 1.3.	Databases are matters of political concern—and rightly so. They lead to better political decisions.	50
Figure 4.1.	The normalizing power of information technology.	145
Figure 4.2.	The reduction of the individual to an object of technocratic rule.	161
Figure 4.3.	"Man is always the measure."	165
Figure 4.4.	*60 Million Peas.*	167
Figure 6.1.	Wanted persons poster: "Violent Anarchists—the Baader-Meinhof Band" (1970/72).	220
Figure 6.2.	Fingerprint files stored in the stairwell of the Federal Criminal Police (1970).	228
Figure 7.1.	"The new ID card hardly has any drawbacks."	263
Figure 8.1.	Herold's master plan for combatting terrorism.	291
Figure 8.2.	Police officers rushing a mainframe computer to a crime scene.	304
Figure 8.3.	Herold explaining his criminalistic philosophy to Privacy Commissioner Bull.	307

Abbreviations

AdSD	Archiv der sozialen Demokratie
AfS	*Archiv für Sozialgeschichte*
AGG	Archiv Grünes Gedächtnis
AHR	*American Historical Review*
AIfS	Archiv des Instituts für Sozialforschung (Hamburg)
BAK	Bundesarchiv Koblenz
BayHStA	Bayerisches Hauptstaatsarchiv
BDSG	Federal Privacy Protection Law (Bundesdatenschutzgesetz)
Berlin DSB	Berlin Beauftragter für Datenschutz und Informationsfreiheit
BGBl.	*Bundesgesetzblatt*
BKA	Bundeskriminalamt
BMF	Bundesministerium der Finanzen
BMG	Bundesministerium für Gesundheit
BMI	Bundesministerium des Innern
BMJ	Bundesministerium der Justiz
BMJFG	Bundesministerium für Jugend, Familie und Gesundheit
Bulletin	*Bulletin. Presse- und Informationsamt der Bundesregierung*
BVerfGE	Entscheidungen des Bundesverfassungsgerichts
CDU	Christian Democratic Union

CILIP	*CILIP: Bürgerrechte & Polizei*
CR	*Computer und Recht*
CSU	Christian Social Union
DÖV	*Die Öffentliche Verwaltung*
Drs.	Drucksache (Bundestag unless otherwise noted)
DuD	*Datenschutz und Datensicherheit* (later *Datenschutz und Datensicherung*)
DVBl.	*Deutsches Verwaltungsblatt*
DVR	*Datenverarbeitung im Recht*
FAZ	*Frankfurter Allgemeine Zeitung*
FDP	Free Democratic Party
FR	*Frankfurter Rundschau*
GuG	*Geschichte und Gesellschaft*
GVBl.	*Gesetz- und Verwaltungsblatt*
HHStA	Hessisches Hauptstaatsarchiv
Interview…	Interviews with a number of early privacy advocates and privacy commissioners are available at https://www.datenschutzzentrum.de/interviews/.
JMH	*Journal of Modern History*
JZ	*Juristenzeitung*
KJ	*Kritische Justiz*
KritV	*Kritische Vierteljahresschrift für Gesetzgebung und Rechtswissenschaft*
LAB	Landesarchiv Berlin
LKA/LKÄ	Landeskriminalamt/-ämter
NJW	*Neue juristische Wochenschrift*
NRW	Landesarchiv Nordrhein-Westfalen
ÖVD	*Öffentliche Verwaltung und Datenverarbeitung*
PA-DBT	Parlamentsarchiv: Deutscher Bundestag (3114: Innenausschuss)

RDV	*Recht der Datenverarbeitung*
RuP	*Recht und Politik*
SPD	Social Democratic Party
StAH	Staatsarchiv Hamburg
StAF	Stadtarchiv Frankfurt/Main
Sten. Ber.	*Stenographische Berichte* (proceedings of the Bundestag)
StPO	Code of Criminal Procedure (Strafprozessordnung)
SZ	*Süddeutsche Zeitung*
VfZ	*Vierteljahrshefte für Zeitgeschichte*
ZRP	*Zeitschrift für Rechtspolitik*

Acknowledgments

Over the years, many people have served as sounding boards for larger and smaller portions of this project, commiserated with me, and provided support when it was most needed. Although these debts can only be poorly repaid through printed expressions of gratitude, I would nevertheless like to express my thanks to the Ann Arbor Germanists, especially Kathleen Canning, Geoff Eley, Young-sun Hong, Jennifer Jenkins, and Dennis Sweeney, who have adopted me into their extended academic and social family. Karrin Hanshew has been my most important intellectual interlocutor, and special thanks are due to her for her trenchant but constructive comments on the initial version of my chapters on police surveillance. On the other side of the Atlantic, I owe thanks to Heidrun Suhr, Dorothee Wierling, and especially Carola Sachse, who has been a wonderful guide to Berlin gastronomy, and who has never failed to skewer a loose argument. Closer to home, I would like to thank Iona Man-cheong, Kathleen Wilson, Alix Cooper, Janis Mimura, and Ira Livingston, as well as Renate Bridenthal.

I would also like to thank the various agencies that supported the research on which this work is based. A research visit grant from the German Academic Exchange Service helped get the project off the ground. Subsequent work was supported by summer fellowships from the Center for Contemporary History in Potsdam and the National Endowment for the Humanities. A Fulbright Research Fellowship later enabled me to spend a full year at the Center for Contemporary History, where I was associated with their research project on the advent of the digital society. My involvement with the Center made me more sensitive to the role of computerization and sharpened my understanding of the main themes in the historiography of contemporary Germany. I would like to thank the director, Frank Bösch, the members of the computerization group (Rüdiger Bergien, Martin Schmitt, Julia Erdogan, Thomas Kasper, and Janine

Funke), and all of the staff for creating a congenial and extraordinarily stimulating intellectual environment.

I would like to thank Rüdiger Bergien for bravely undertaking the yeoman's task of reading the penultimate—and substantially longer—draft of the completed manuscript. I also owe much to Carl Caldwell and the two anonymous reviewers, whose comments on behalf of Berghahn Books helped make this a stronger and more readable book. I would also like to thank the many archives that I visited for allowing me to exploit their holdings. The archivists there were universally helpful in unearthing materials that proved to be crucial for my research and securing access to many papers that had only recently been acquired by their respective institutions. They also provided indispensable assistance in navigating archival regulations to gain access to their holdings from the 1980s.

Several of the individuals who figure prominently in the pages that follow took time to meet with me during the early stages of this project, and I would like to thank Hans Peter Bull, Spiros Simitis, Maja Stadler-Euler, and Gisela Wild for sharing their thoughts, as well as their offprints and their personal papers, with me and helping me find my way through that thicket of ideas and experiences that collectively shaped German privacy law. Horst Herold, the president of the Federal Criminal Police 1971-81, died in December 2018. Herold's writings and his professional practice were a source of fascination to all, and the object of unbounded hostility for many. But whatever one's attitudes toward Herold, he personified the digital zeitgeist in many respects, and I regret that I was never able to meet with him.

Parts of chapter 1 were originally published as Larry Frohman, "Population Registration, Social Planning, and the Discourse on Privacy Protection in West Germany," *Journal of Modern History* 87 (June 2015): 316–356, © 2015 by The University of Chicago, and earlier versions of chapters 4 and 9 were published in *Archiv für Sozialgeschichte* and the *German Studies Review*, respectively. I would like to thank these journals for publishing my ongoing research and then allowing me to reprint this material.

But my last and most important thanks go to Young-sun Hong, whose support sustained me as I labored to bring this project to a successful conclusion.

Introduction
Surveillance, Privacy, and Power in the Information Society

Surveillance and privacy are two of the primary concepts through which we seek to make sense of modernity and of a world in which virtually all forms of social interaction are digitally mediated. They have already become—and are certain to remain—two of the most contentious issues of our age. In this book I will argue that the two concepts can only be understood in relation to one another and that this relationship is mediated by two interrelated factors: the forms of social and political power that structure information exchange in specific contexts and the power generated by the technologies and bureaucratic routines employed to collect and process this information.

Population surveillance has been theorized in a number of different ways. Many studies have argued in a Weberian vein that the development of bureaucracy has enhanced the power of the modern state by making it possible to identify and mobilize individual members of the population for fiscal, military, and welfare purposes.[1] However, the identification, classification, registration, enumeration, and monitoring of the population—that is, those administrative practices that Pierre-Joseph Proudhon collectively condemned as the essence of "government"[2]—did not simply make all individuals equal before the state. They also opened the way to the individualized care and control of these persons, and both the sociomedical discourses through which these individual differences were theorized and the disciplinary technologies through which such knowledge was deployed have been the privileged objects of Foucauldian studies of surveillance.[3] Surveillance has also been approached from a third influential perspective, whose constitutive insight is that the schemata through

---

Notes for this chapter begin on page 27.

which populations are categorized and classified must be understood as systems of language or representation. This school analyzes the process through which human bodies are abstracted from their physical and social existence and dissolved into discrete data flows, which can then be reassembled to form "data doubles" that can themselves become the targets of political intervention and administrative control. This approach, which takes the database as its paradigm and seeks to illuminate the distinctive features of digital surveillance, has been most systematically developed by the new subdiscipline of surveillance studies.[4]

While the present study draws on both the Weberian and the surveillance studies schools, it has been influenced by three works in particular. James Beniger's *The Control Revolution* (1986) and Alfred Chandler's *The Visible Hand* (1977) both describe the formation and functioning of surveillance and control systems, whose primary objects were material objects and economic processes. These systems functioned through the collection, processing, and application of information, and both authors argue — the one explicitly, the other implicitly — that the consolidation of these systems and the forms of social organization and social control to which they gave rise marked the emergence of the information society. However, the nature of the objects surveilled through these systems did not raise questions regarding personal privacy. By contrast, James Rule's *Private Lives and Public Surveillance* (1974) was the first major work to use such a framework to analyze the large-scale surveillance of individuals by means of records and personal information, the ways in which such systems functioned as a mechanism of social governance and control, and the impact of such surveillance on the personal privacy and civil liberties of the population being surveilled.[5]

In earlier times, the informational needs of the state and business were limited; the available paper-based technologies imposed narrow limits on the amount of personal information that could be collected by large organizations; and, as a result, most of the information that was collected was maintained and processed decentrally and at the local level. In such a world, privacy was conceived primarily as a quality belonging to the intimate, domestic sphere of individuals and families. It seldom arose as a problem in relation to records of personal information, and, even when it did, it was conceived primarily in terms of insuring the security of such data against unauthorized access. However, Rule was writing at the moment when computers were just coming into use as tools for the processing of administrative data, and the specific nature of the privacy problems associated with integrated processing of such information had not yet become clear. The present study can in part be read as a continuation of Rule's account in order to analyze both the growing centrality of personal information as a steering medium, which plays a role comparable to that of money, law, and political power in the governance of the welfare state, and the distinctive ways in which population surveillance and personal privacy were theorized in the age of the mainframe. It represents the first broadly conceived, archivally grounded historical study of population surveillance, privacy law, and the diverse problems posed by the use of personal information for the governance of individuals and populations in Germany (and the European welfare state more generally) since World War II.

The issues that were raised during these years continue to shape public debate. However, my goal in this work is to reach behind both the explosive growth of social media and the internet and the enormous expansion of state surveillance of the digital domain since the early 2000s to the moment of the mainframe in order to understand the origins and import of these controversies.

In the 1970s and 1980s, West Germany was among the most technologically advanced countries in the world, and the country was a pioneer in both the use of the new information and communication technologies for population surveillance and the adoption of privacy protection legislation. This book originated as a study of the cornerstone of this legislative complex: the Federal Privacy Protection Law (Bundesdatenschutzgesetz), which was approved at the turn of 1976/77.[6] However, it quickly evolved into a search for a framework that would make it possible to understand how both the law and the new conception of informational privacy that informed it functioned as a means of resolving the social conflicts generated by new informational practices, new information technologies, and the disruption of the norms that had governed social communication in the bourgeois era. In the chapters that follow, I make two main arguments, one theoretical, the other historical. First, the book is conceived as an intervention into the ongoing debate over the nature of informational privacy as it has been waged in the disciplines of law, philosophy, sociology, and surveillance studies. I argue—most explicitly in the final section of this introduction and in chapter 2, but implicitly throughout the text—that in the 1970s and 1980s West German theorists of informational privacy developed a model for thinking about privacy and power in ways that pointed beyond the liberal, individualist conception of privacy, which, despite its intrinsic theoretical limitations, has been the cornerstone of virtually all thinking on the topic. Second, I use this understanding of the ways in which social and power relations structure information exchange as the framework for my historical account of population surveillance and the evolving meaning of privacy in West Germany.

The politicization of privacy in West Germany and across the Western world at the turn of the 1970s can be understood only in relation to the evolution of the information society. Unfortunately, the existing literature is of limited usefulness in illuminating precisely how this connection is to be made. The grand sociological theories, which have used the concept to theorize the impact of computers and the internet on markets, firm organization, and the social organization of labor, are for the most part relentlessly presentist and technologically determinist.[7] Neither these works nor the growing body of scholarly literature devoted to the history of information, the early—and early modern—information society, the history of libraries, the discipline of information science or documentation, the social circulation of information, the informationalization of labor processes, and the question of information and empire provide useful ways for thinking about the relationship between surveillance and privacy.[8] In the chapters that follow, I argue that surveillance and privacy in the contemporary world can be understood only by focusing on a phenomenon that has been neglected by existing theories of the information society: the systematic use of *personal information*—that is, information pertaining to identified (or identifiable) individuals and their vital, biopolitical activities—as a medium for social governance, the new forms of power generated by control over this information, and the conflicts arising out of its use.

It has become almost a matter of ritual to begin accounts of privacy with a nod to the difficulty, if not the impossibility, of defining the concept, at least in the abstract, and I see no reason to deny myself this pleasure.[9] In the recent literature, privacy has been conceptualized in terms of three dimensions or strands: spatial, decisional, and informational. Informational privacy is the newest of these strands, and in this book I argue that the articulation of this new approach was driven by a growing awareness of the fact that the older concept of the private sphere was incapable of theorizing either the specific problems associated with the routine, bureaucratic collection of personal information or the use of the new information technologies to store, process, and disseminate it.[10]

"Surveillance" is the conceptual label that is most often applied to these informational activities. For example, a 2006 report written by the Surveillance Studies Network for the United Kingdom's information commissioner defined surveillance as the "purposeful, routine, systematic and focused attention paid to personal details, for the sake of control, entitlement, management, influence or protection."[11] This does not differ in any fundamental way from Anthony Giddens's often-cited definition of surveillance as the accumulation, storage, and use of coded information to coordinate populations and superintend the activities of the persons to whom this information pertains.[12] However, by including the encoding of this information in his definition, Giddens highlights the fact that information is never gathered for its own sake, but only in anticipation of how it can be used, and that its meaning is determined by the pragmatic interests of those organizations that define, collect, and control it. This process of encoding, as James Scott has argued, simplifies the infinitely complex structures of the social and natural worlds, and, in so doing, it gives rise to specific "regimes of visibility," accessibility, and governability and naturalizes those forms of knowledge constructed in this way.[13] What both of these definitions have in common is that they argue that surveillance cannot be understood apart from the anticipated use of the information collected in this way to exercise control—that is, power—over the objects of such attention, regardless of whether this power is conceived as a means of care or control.[14] My central claim is that privacy describes a social relation and that it should, therefore, be understood as a means of conceptualizing and contesting both the exchange of information in specific contexts and the forms of social power that structure these exchanges.[15]

Giddens provides a useful set of concepts for thinking about the relationship between information, information processing, and power. In *The Nation-State and Violence*, he begins with the organization, which he defines as "a collectivity in which knowledge about the conditions of system reproduction is reflexively used to influence, shape or modify that system reproduction," and he defines the political in terms of the administrative power of organizations—that is, their capacity to marshal the "authoritative resources" through which dominion is exercised over individuals and their activities.[16] Giddens argues that surveillance is the primary means for the concentration of the authoritative resources involved in the formation of the nation-state and thus the necessary precondition of the administrative power of states, and his characterization of societies that use information in a reflexive manner to control the evolution of organizations and social systems as information societies situates his work in close proximity to those of Beniger, Chandler, and Rule.[17] While Giddens himself shows how official statistics exemplified the reflexive use of information by the nation-state, I argue that personal information, especially that collected by population registries and the police, could be used to govern individuals, populations, and large-scale social processes in ways that aggregate statistical data could not. When approached from this perspective, the history of both information societies and information states can be written in terms of the development of their surveillance capacity—that is, in terms of the development of their ability to collect, aggregate, analyze, disseminate, and apply both personal information and the aggregate statistical information derived from this individualized data to enhance their administrative power and their ability to govern expanding areas of social life and geographical territory in an increasingly intense, continuous, and effective manner.[18]

Giddens also postulated that the rationalization and intensification of each of the four institutional clusterings of modernity that he analyzed in that work gave rise to social movements directed against the consequences of these processes: a labor movement against the power of private property, an ecological movement against the disenchantment and exploitation of nature, a peace movement against violence as a mechanism of internal pacification, and movements seeking to expand democratic participation in order to redress the imbalances of power resulting from the intensification of surveillance.[19] I argue that the politicization of privacy at the turn of the 1970s represented just such a response to the intensification of administrative power. The expansion, bureaucratization, and computerization of population surveillance by both corporations and the state, as well as the new forms of surveillance that developed in conjunction with the modernization of the welfare state, gave rise to a distinctly postindustrial social question, which Horst Herold (SPD)—the president of the Federal Criminal Police (the Bundeskriminalamt) from 1971 to 1981 and one of the chief protagonists of the story to be told below—once called the "information question," which he presciently predicted would dominate public debate in the 1980s.[20] These processes also gave rise to a new form of social politics, which I call the politics of personal information; to new discourses on (informational) privacy, which became the primary means of theorizing the impact of this surveillance; and to a corresponding social movement, which contested these developments and the forms of governance they authorized in the name of both individual autonomy and the collective needs of a democratic society.

Neither the Third Reich nor the Stalinist society that had been constructed on the other side of the intra-German border were ever entirely absent from the minds of those persons who were concerned about these issues, and West German sensibilities with regard to surveillance and privacy were undoubtedly heightened by the experience of these two dictatorships. However, the nature of state surveillance and the political parameters of personal privacy in both of these states was so radically different from that in the Federal Republic that a direct comparison makes little sense.[21]

The citizens of the Federal Republic enjoyed fundamental rights that had been denied during the Third Reich, and the 1970s debate over surveillance and privacy took place within a constitutional framework that had been constructed as the antithesis of Nazi totalitarianism. Even though these debates served at times as a medium for mastering the country's Nazi past, the postwar politics of personal information should be understood less as a response to Nazi rule than as an attempt—common to all Western societies during these years—to theorize both the specific forms of social power generated by new informational practices and technologies and their impact on civil liberties. The rhetorical recourse to Nazism to explain the significance of these new forms of informational power was the product of a transitional moment at which the interested public was still struggling to articulate a new language to express its insights and concerns. Although this rhetoric resonated widely because it expressed an inchoate awareness that these developments were bringing about a secular shift in the informational relations between the individual and both the state and the firm, it contributed little to explaining the actual mechanisms that were driving this process.[22]

In West Germany, the East German Ministry of State Security was invoked much less often than the police or the population technologies of the Nazis as a negative example of state surveillance. There is a certain irony here. Not only was the Stasi much larger than the Gestapo and not only did it directly entangle a much larger proportion of the population in the surveillance of each other; since the early 1970s the Stasi had also made use of computers and other record-keeping technologies that were much more akin to those employed in the Federal Republic than to those available to the Nazis several decades before.[23] Nevertheless, the differences between the political systems of the two German states were reflected in their respective languages of privacy. In the East, "data protection" referred not to the defense of personal privacy and constitutional limitations on state surveillance, but rather to the protection of police files from unauthorized disclosure to outsiders. In view of differences such as these, little is to be learned from a forced comparison of surveillance and privacy in the two states. The more relevant comparisons would be with the very different postwar privacy cultures of the Anglo-American world and Scandinavia, as well as with the other countries of the EU, whose privacy cultures have—despite their different constitutional traditions—converged on the principles codified in the 2016 General Data Protection Regulation. However, these are topics for different studies.

The Argument

Virtually all of the developments to be recounted in the following pages took place within a compact period of time extending from the mid-1960s to the turn of the 1990s. However, the arguments that are developed here cannot be made in a straightforward chronological manner, and the book is instead divided into three thematic parts whose individual arguments can only be fully understood in relation to those made in the other parts. Each part covers the entire period under study here, and the initial chapter of each part reaches back to anchor the narrative in the immediate postwar years. Within each part, the chapters generally proceed in a chronological manner, though the thematic organization of the book leads to some chronological overlap. I have made considerable effort to both minimize redundancies and flag important references between chapters to help the reader follow the connections among the many individual arguments being made here. As we shall see, the point at which all of the separate strands of the argument (population registration in chapter 1, the census boycotts and the reform of privacy law in chapters 4 and 5, and policing in chapters 7 and 9) converge—and then diverge again—is the December 1983 ruling by the Constitutional Court on the legal challenges to the decennial census, which codified a right to privacy or "informational self-determination."

Nothing is easier—and often more misleading—than to make large generalizations about information processing, surveillance, and privacy. To avoid these dangers, I approach the question in a very different way and proceed, instead, by means of a thick description of the information processing methods—including the available media, the associated bureaucratic practices, and the possibilities and limits of data exchange and integration—employed by the population registries and the police. Like Rule's seminal study of large-scale record-keeping systems on the cusp of the computer age, I analyze both the internal dynamics of the population surveillance system being constructed in West Germany at the time (i.e., its individual components and their interaction) and the external power effects of this system. I begin with the manual information processing technologies employed in the postwar years and then examine the crisis of paper-based systems in the age of mass data processing, the specific mechanisms of surveillant control made possible by integrated data processing, and the debates over privacy and power generated by these new ways of using personal information. The logic of privacy protection law discussed in part II cannot be understood without this knowledge.

The contemporary history of the digital age, of the information society, and of the broader social impact of the computer (as opposed to its technological development) is only just now beginning to be written.[24] Although computers vastly expanded the information processing capacity of the state and transformed the ways in which new information was produced from existing data, the computerization of the public administration did not mark a fundamental discontinuity in the history of the West German information society. Rather, it should be seen as one more in a long series of attempts to solve those information processing problems on which state administrative power depended. It is also important to remember that computers are technosocial systems, and that, whatever their functionalities, the questions they raised regarding the distribution of privacy and access rights ultimately remained political ones.[25] Nor should we overlook the extent to which the design and functioning of the computer was itself modeled on the bureaucratic systems developed in the age of paper.[26]

From its founding in 1949 into the second half of the 1960s, the Federal Republic was governed by the conservative Christian Democratic Union (CDU) and its even more conservative sister party, the Bavarian Christian Social Union (CSU). Through most of this period, they were joined by the Free Democratic Party (FDP) as the junior member of the governing coalition. In October 1963, the elderly Konrad Adenauer (CDU) was succeeded as chancellor by Economics Minister Ludwig Erhard (CDU), the corpulent, cigar-chomping architect of the 1948 currency reform. However, in 1966, foreign policy setbacks and differences over economic and fiscal policy led to the breakdown of these postwar political arrangements and the formation of a grand coalition of conservatives and Social Democrats (SPD), headed by Kurt Kiesinger (CDU), which held power from December 1966 until October 1969. While the exclusion of the FDP from the governing coalition represented a mortal threat to the party, the entry of the Social Democrats into the national government for the first time since 1930 was one of the first fruits of the party's efforts to distance itself from Marxism and class struggle and transform itself into a broad-based *Volkspartei*.

The public administration that had been constructed under Adenauer was in important respects ill-suited for meeting the needs of the new state. The routines that governed the postwar administration had been established in an era in which the primary responsibility of the public administration was the maintenance of public order and the rule of law. However, by the end of the 1950s, it was becoming increasingly urgent to modernize the policies and procedures of the federal administration in order to respond to the problems posed by the expanding scope of state social intervention, the resulting need for greater coordination across the different levels of government in the new federal state, and the associated need for more information to manage these processes. The rationalization of office processes and the introduction of new technologies, including electronic data processing, was part of this process,[27] and it was under the grand coalition that plans were first laid for many of the projects that will be discussed in the chapters that follow.

Planning was the master concept in the political discourse of the Federal Republic from the mid-1960s to the mid-1970s. The idea of planning—especially comprehensive or "global" social and economic planning, rather than planning for discrete geographical regions or sectors of social life—had been discredited during the early postwar years by its association with Nazism and, later, communism and centralized state control.

However, by the mid-1960s, planning was coming to be seen as the key to sustaining the postwar economic conjuncture and rationally managing the evolution of complex societies, and it was in conjunction with this new interest in planning that information first emerged as a distinct policy concern for public officials at the federal, state, and local levels.[28]

Erhard's resistance to such planning was an important factor in his fall. A planning staff—which focused on social, rather than economic, planning—was established in the chancellor's office in early 1967, though it played only a minor role under Kiesinger, while the June 1967 Economic Stability and Growth Law marked the breakthrough of Keynesian macroeconomic planning in West Germany.[29] As we shall see below, in 1966 the coordinating body of federal and state police officials called for the creation of a national criminal information system to enhance the crime-fighting efficiency of the police in what was perceived as a period of rapid social and cultural change; in the social policy domain, the Labor Ministry was building a social database for planning purposes and laying the foundation for the computerization of the pension (and later the sickness) insurance funds; in 1968/69 officials in the chancellor's office began preliminary work on plans for a national database system to support their planning efforts; and, at virtually the same moment, administration officials were crafting plans to automate the population registration system.

Part I consists of a single chapter. The first two-thirds of chapter 1 address the postwar history of the population registration system, which was the most important source of personal information for both planning and policing. The plan to automate the local population registries and then to link them together—via a proposed national ID number—to create a national population information system for planning and administrative use was the most important state initiative in the informational domain. It was also the direct catalyst for both the politicization of privacy at the turn of the 1970s and the introduction of the Federal Privacy Protection Law. However, these plans were upset by growing privacy concerns at the very moment that the proposed population information system was assuming new importance for combatting terrorism, and the population registration law that was ultimately adopted by the Bundestag was informed by a privacy logic that was the antithesis of the logic of data integration that had inspired the original vision of a reformed and modernized population identification and information system.

The final third of the chapter turns back to the late 1960s to show how the new concept of informational privacy emerged as a response to the problems raised by the advent of integrated, electronic data processing. The most elemental functionality of such systems was to bring together information whose disclosure may have been appropriate, or even desirable, in one context, but which might take on a different meaning when linked with other information and used in new and unanticipated contexts. The new concept of informational privacy represented a counterconcept to that of data integration, and the initial privacy protection project represented an attempt to theorize and contain two problems associated with integrated information systems: the integration or transparency effect and the perceived loss of control over the disclosure of personal information within such systems. By increasing the informational asymmetry between the data subject and his communicative partners (including the state), both of these effects threatened to predetermine the possibilities of action and self-representation to such a degree that the person could no longer be considered a morally autonomous actor possessing that dignity whose protection was the cornerstone of the West German constitution. This line of thinking, which applied the fundamental rights codified in the country's Basic Law to the new forms of social communication and information exchange that were developing in the 1960s, provided the constitutional fulcrum for the subsequent development of privacy protection law in the Federal Republic. It also serves as the hinge connecting the history of population registration and integrated data processing to that of privacy protection law in part II.

Although plans for the different information or database systems had been set in motion during the Kiesinger administration, they came to fruition under the Social Democratic-Liberal coalition, which governed the country from October 1969 to October 1982. Not only did the new chancellor Willy Brandt (SPD) promise new policies toward East Germany and the communist bloc. He also challenged the legislature to "dare more democracy." However, the preconditions for the comprehensive social reform program through which this promise was to be redeemed were the modernization of the chancellor's office, the cabinet, and the public administration and the establishment of a comprehensive social planning mechanism. The personal information that was to be collected through the reformed population registration system was crucial to both these plans and the information and planning systems being constructed by all of the federal states at the turn of the 1970s.

The SPD was supported in this undertaking by the FDP, whose policies, electorate, and position in the country's party landscape were all changing rapidly in the late 1960s. Since its founding, the party had been an uneasy electoral home for two quite different strands of liberalism: a rather illiberal national liberalism, whose position on the national and German questions placed a number of the party's leaders at the far right of the political spectrum, and a more democratically minded constitutional liberalism that was the heir of the country's prewar progressive tradition.

Until 1966, the party had been held together by a shared commitment to pro-business policies, which reflected the economic and social interests of its main constituents. Although differences with Erhard over tax and budget issues had led the FDP to withdraw from its coalition with the CDU/CSU, at that point the party leadership still considered a coalition with the Social Democrats to be anathema, and after 1966 the party's future remained unclear. But after its exclusion from the government, the FDP began to pivot to the left in conjunction with a shift in the social composition of its constituency, and by the 1969 election the growing influence of the social liberal and civil libertarian wing of the party made a coalition with the Social Democrats appear more natural than it had in the past.[30] This political reorientation was confirmed by the party's 1971 Freiburg program, which provided the intellectual basis for the party's coalition with the Social Democrats, and deputy party chair Hans-Dietrich Genscher, whose own plans for making the public administration more modern and efficient overlapped with those of the SPD, was appointed interior minister in the new cabinet.

The interior ministry was led by liberal politicians through the entire span of the social-liberal coalition. As part of a cabinet reshuffling that followed upon Brandt's resignation in May 1974 and the election of Helmut Schmidt (SPD) as the new chancellor, Genscher became vice-chancellor and foreign minister, and he was succeeded as interior minister by the left-liberal law professor Werner Maihofer, one of the chief authors of the Freiburg Program. Like Genscher, Maihofer strongly supported the modernization of the police. However, Maihofer had the misfortune of serving as interior minister during the peak years of left-wing terrorism. While his continuous involvement in security matters prevented him from playing a major role in the drafting of the Federal Privacy Protection Law, he also incurred the odium of many of his erstwhile supporters for his role in the expansion of police surveillance. His implication in several major surveillance scandals, together with the diminishing influence of the social-liberal wing of the party, led to his resignation in June 1978. He was succeeded by Gerhart Baum, who, as we shall see, was both more sensitive to privacy questions than his predecessor and in a better position to put his convictions into practice.

Part II examines the postwar history of privacy law in West Germany. Although chapter 2 begins in the 1950s, it focuses on the articulation in the 1970s and early 1980s of a new conception of privacy in terms of the role-specific disclosure of information and strategic nonknowledge as a way of containing the transparency effect of data linkages in integrated information systems. The idea of a right to informational self-determination was originally put forth as a remedy to the loss of control over both the flow of personal information and the meaning attributed to it by others, and this right coexisted uneasily with both the information access rights of others and their freedom to ascribe meaning to the information that they obtained in the course of social communication. As we shall see in greater detail in the final part of this introduction, many people have argued that the subjective nature of privacy rights has rendered the concept both incoherent and incapable of theorizing the social power generated by surveillance systems. In contrast, I argue that West German privacy theorists escaped these problems by showing how the individual personality unfolded in and through a reflexive, communicative process, and that they embedded their account of this communicative process in a broader analysis of the social interests and power structures that determined what information had to be disclosed, and what information could be concealed, in specific social roles and contexts.

In the following, I will use the term "privacy advocates" to denote the first generation of legal scholars, administrative scientists, and computer or information scientists who grappled with the problems arising out of the electronic processing of personal information. In contrast to Scott's depiction of a modernizing state riding roughshod over a prostrate civil society, the early privacy protection movement was firmly rooted in the political establishment.[31] Unlike later social movements, which challenged the symbolic codes of industrial modernity, the early privacy protection movement was reformist and committed to working within the existing political system to find a proper balance between privacy and access rights.[32]

Privacy rights always impose limitations on the informational activity of the state, and in this respect it is possible to speak of privacy law (and the freedom of information laws, which were first mooted between the mid-1970s and the mid-1980s) as a mode of democratization and to distinguish it from more authoritarian positions, which privilege the informational prerogatives of the public administration. However, at times privacy legislation was supported by all of the major parties, and it is difficult to put a single social or political label on the early privacy advocates. In the 1970s and 1980s, the central figures in the privacy protection field included Spiros Simitis, the liberal Frankfurt law professor, longtime (1975–91) Hessian privacy commissioner, and the most systematic West German thinker on privacy matters; Hans Peter Bull (SPD), Hamburg law professor, the first federal privacy commissioner, and later interior minister of Schleswig-Holstein; the legal scholar Adalbert Podlech, the author of an influential essay on the constitutional foundations of privacy law, whose academic career was deflected by his sympathy for the anti-authoritarian movement; Wilhelm Steinmüller, one of the founders of the field of legal informatics, the lead author of one of the founding documents of German privacy protection law, and ultimately a radical critic of state population surveillance; Otto Mallmann, the author of an important early monograph on privacy protection and later presiding judge on the Federal Administrative Court; Ulrich Dammann, the author of a number of influential essays on integrated data processing, planning, and privacy and longtime civil servant in the office of the federal privacy commissioner; Reinhard Riegel, who monitored the work of the security agencies for the federal privacy commissioner from 1978 to 1986 and who ultimately ran afoul of the conservative reaction; Ruth Leuze, who as Baden-Württemberg privacy commissioner was one of the most outspoken defenders of privacy rights in the 1980s; Herbert Fiedler, another of the early leading figures in the fields of legal and administrative informatics; Ernst Benda (CDU), federal interior minister (1968–69), the author of an influential 1974 essay on personality profiles and the private sphere, and presiding judge of the Constitutional Court at the time of the census decision; Eggert Schwan (CDU), a maverick conservative civil libertarian, whose warnings regarding the totalitarian character of the security laws proposed by the Kohl administration led to clashes with his party colleagues; and last, but by no means least, Herbert Auernhammer, Ministerialrat in the federal interior ministry and chief author of the Federal Privacy Protection Law.

Most of these men and women had been born between 1934 and 1945. They were about a decade younger than many of the politicians (including Benda and his successors as interior minister) and civil servants (Auernhammer and others whom we shall encounter) who already occupied important positions at the turn of the 1970s. On the other hand, they were slightly older than the generation of 1968, and many of them were already established academics by the time the movement reached its peak.

Its translated name notwithstanding, the Federal Privacy Protection Law, whose legislative history is the focus of chapter 3, was not simply, and not even primarily, a privacy law. Nor was it merely a code of fair information practices designed to ensure the accuracy, completeness, and confidentiality of electronically processed data. Rather, it represented an attempt to codify what were deemed to be socially adequate, substantive norms for information exchange and use. However, the juridification of these communicative practices was fraught with difficulties. The strategic decision—dictated by the reliance on the concept of informational self-determination—to indirectly protect privacy by regulating the processing of personal information made it impossible to specify in the abstract what information was to be considered personal and what uses constituted a misuse of this information. On the other hand, the use of the novel concept of "formatted files" to determine what information was to fall within the scope of the law highlighted the different kinds of power generated by the collection, use, and exchange of this information. Ultimately, the reliance upon a number of elastic formulations to balance between competing interests deferred, rather than resolved, the conflicts on which the concrete meaning of the law depended. These compromises made the early amendment of the law unavoidable, and these reform efforts brought to the surface the systematic differences between the SPD and the FDP regarding the purpose of the law.

Widespread social protest and the rise of left-wing terrorism led to the rapid modernization and expansion of police surveillance capacity in the 1970s, which we will examine in part III, and, from the second half of the decade into the 1980s, the West German public was increasingly polarized by the expansion of state surveillance. All of these concerns coalesced in an entirely unexpected manner around the decennial census scheduled for April 1983. At the turn of that year, a boycott movement sprang up out of nowhere and set in motion a rapid learning process that, within a matter of months, made control over the collection and use of personal information into one of the central political issues of the 1980s and beyond. The impact of these events upon the country's privacy culture is the topic of chapter 4.

Although the protesters frequently compared the census with the population policies of the Nazis, I argue that the protests were a much more direct reaction to the new information technologies than they were to the Nazi past and that the language of the 1983 boycott echoed academic analyses of the ways in which computers were generating novel forms of normalizing, disciplinary power that diminished both the scope for the development of the personality and the freedom of the individual to participate meaningfully in the democratic process.

The 1983 boycott coincided with a major political realignment. Although the reform plans of the social-liberal coalition had originally rested on the optimistic belief that economic planning would make it possible to indefinitely prolong the postwar economic boom, in the fall of 1982 the FDP broke with the SPD over differences in economic policy, but remained in power as the junior partner in a new coalition led by the CDU/CSU.[33] Helmut Kohl (CDU) was elected chancellor in October of that year, and the new balance of political power was confirmed by the February 1983 Bundestag election. Baum was succeeded as interior minister by Friedrich Zimmermann (CSU). Zimmermann was a reactionary who would have been more at home as police minister in the 1870s than he was as interior minister in a democracy, and he contributed greatly to the polarization of the public debate over privacy and security in the 1980s.

The census had been challenged in the courts, as well as in the streets, and, two weeks before the scheduled start of the census, the Constitutional

Court (the Bundesverfassungsgericht) issued a temporary injunction blocking the count until the case had been decided on its merits. This was the first time that the Court had overturned a law that had been properly approved by the Bundestag. This decision stunned the Kohl administration, especially Zimmermann, who had made the suppression of the boycott a measure of both the authority of the state and the administration's ability to govern. In its December 1983 ruling on these challenges, the Constitutional Court codified a right to informational self-determination, which it argued was implicit in the country's constitutional commitment to human dignity and the free development of the personality, and personal data was to be protected as a means of securing these underlying values.

Although the Court overturned those portions of the census law that authorized the use of name-based or reidentifiable census data for administrative purposes, it upheld the census in principle. This set the stage for a second boycott, which was directed against a revised census law. These 1987 events forced the Greens, who had first entered the Bundestag during the 1983 boycott, to reflect on the party's position in the parliamentary system, while their analysis of both the impact of the new information technologies and the ways in which personal information was used to govern modern society became an important, though heretofore overlooked, element of the party's identity.

The census decision forced the federal and state legislatures to revise every major law governing the use of personal information within the public administration. These included the population registration, ID card, and passport laws; the federal statistical, census, microcensus, and archive laws; federal and state laws governing the police and the intelligence agencies; and the Code of Criminal Procedure, the Code of Administrative Procedure,[34] and, of course, the Federal Privacy Protection Law itself. To a surprising degree, these amendments transformed laws that in the past had governed specific domains of social or administrative action into information—that is, access and privacy—laws. This task, which defined to a large extent the domestic political agenda of the Kohl administration in the second half of the 1980s, is the focus of chapters 5, 7, and 9.

Chapter 5, which, like chapter 4, can be fully understood only when read in conjunction with the account of police surveillance in part III, examines both the Court's reasoning in the census decision and the long, arduous process, which stretched from 1977 to 1990, of amending the Federal Privacy Protection Law. The census decision has been hailed as the constitutional cornerstone of privacy rights and condemned as a defective juridical construct. I argue that it was both. There is growing unanimity in the literature that most of the problems of both the decision and subsequent privacy law can be traced to the Court's apparent construction of the right to informational self-determination as a subjective individual right "to determine the conditions under which [one's] personal information shall be disclosed and used."[35] However, it is not clear that the Court actually understood the right in this manner. As I argue in chapter 2, most West German privacy advocates explicitly rejected such an individualist construction of privacy rights, and the Court had access to a body of literature that had shown that the development of the personality was a social, communicative process, which was shaped by the social interests and power relations of the larger society within which it was embedded. Unfortunately, the Court's reasoning in the decision did not systematically integrate this literature or give adequate expression to its own best insights.

Although the ruling codified the new right to informational self-determination, the Court left it to the legislature to balance this right against the collective interest in welfare, security, and the efficiency of the public administration. In the post-1983 debate, the revision of the Federal Privacy Protection Law was linked to a controversial packet of security laws, and the debates over the law governing the Domestic Intelligence Agency (the Bundesamt für Verfassungsschutz) and the reform of state police law (chapter 9) played a central role in defining the concrete meaning of the privacy law. The views of the civil libertarian wing of the FDP, which insisted that individual freedom could be protected only by the limitation of state informational activity, were in many respects quite close to those of the federal and state privacy commissioners. However, the conservative parties espoused a more Hobbesian view and refused to countenance any limitations that they believed would impair the sovereignty of the state and the efficiency of either the security agencies or the civilian administration. Although these differences led to legislative deadlock, which dragged on from 1984 until the end of the decade, the main features of the revised privacy law and the amendments to the other major laws regulating the use of personal information in the federal government—all of which were approved on the eve of reunification—ultimately reflected the priorities of the conservative parties.

In addition to population registration and the healthcare field,[36] policing was the most important domain in which the meaning of privacy was contested and redefined. Part III will focus primarily on the Federal Criminal Police, the most important police agency under the direct control of the federal government and the fulcrum of its efforts to modernize policing. It was during the 1970s that the Federal Criminal Police was transformed from an antiquated agency that played only a subsidiary role in the security sector into one of the most modern, computerized police agencies in the world, surpassed only by the FBI.

In 2004, Klaus Weinhauer argued that it was time to approach terrorism from a broader, specifically historical perspective, which, in contrast to the studies by social and political scientists that had dominated the literature up to that point, would explore the social, cultural, and political dimensions of the phenomenon. However, he warned that this task could only be accomplished by situating such research in relation to a comparably conceived history of "internal security"—that is, in relation to the sociocultural, administrative, and political-parliamentary processes through which the West German understanding of "stateness" was constructed in the confrontation with terrorism.[37] In the intervening years, both parts of this agenda have been realized to a substantial degree—with state actors, counterterrorism, and, more recently, the transnational dimensions of both political violence and policing becoming an integral part of the broader history of West Germany during the 1970s.[38] Part III, which focuses more on the informational infrastructure and practices of the security agencies than on security policy, should be seen as a contribution to this literature.

All West German police laws charge law enforcement with protecting "public security" (öffentliche Sicherheit). But while the parameters of public security are defined by the Criminal Code, internal security (innere Sicherheit) is a political, rather than a legal, concept, whose content and rhetorical thrust vary according to time and place. As we shall see, the internal security regime that was established in the late 1940s was a quintessential product of the Cold War. It was defined almost exclusively by the fear of communist subversion from within, which, it was argued, posed an existential threat to the Federal Republic because it could be exploited to create the opportunity for military aggression from the East, and by a corresponding willingness to limit the civil liberties of those who were perceived as seeking to undermine the country's "free, democratic order." Although the Allies had been concerned primarily with the threat of resurgent Nazism, the reintegration of many former Nazis into the political system and the public administration under Adenauer, along with the deepening Cold War, transformed these exceptional powers into a weapon that was directed almost exclusively against the left. At the end of the 1960s, the Social Democratic-Liberal coalition initially sought to reconceptualize internal security as a social problem that could be combatted by welfarist means as part of its broader project of social and political reform, but these plans were blocked and then overshadowed by the rise of domestic terrorism. As a result, the country's internal security regime remained relatively unchanged until the late 1970s.

Chapter 6 begins with an account of internal security policy, the organization of policing, and a history of the terrorist groups that became the objects of police surveillance in the 1970s. This section provides much of the context needed to understand the arguments made in part III (and, to a lesser degree, parts I and II). The remainder of the chapter describes the entangled history of police information processing and the joint impact of computerization and terrorism on the role of the Federal Criminal Police from the mid-1960s to 1972. Here I argue that the declining effectiveness of the Federal Criminal Police in the 1960s provides a classic illustration of both the process by which the traditional, paper-based information processing systems employed by the agency (and by other public and private organizations involved in the mass processing of personal information) were overwhelmed by the new demands placed on them and the ways in which integrated information systems promised to enhance the administrative power of the state and its ability to govern individuals and populations on a national scale.

However, capturing the gains in efficiency and effectiveness promised by such systems depended not only on automating the Federal Criminal Police itself, but also on building an integrated national criminal information network to link the agency's system with those being developed by the federal states. Work on such a network was stalled through the late 1960s by the institutional rivalries rooted in the federalist structure of the security sector. The January 1972 decision by the Conference of State and Federal Interior Ministers to construct the national criminal information system INPOL (Informationssystem der Polizei) — whose architecture was shaped in decisive ways by the federalist prerogatives of the states — was part of a cluster of security measures adopted between 1971 and 1973 to modernize the Federal Criminal Police, expand the agency's authority, and enable it to better respond to the threats posed by left-wing terrorism.

Chapters 7 and 8 both deal with the period from the early 1970s to the mid-1980s. Chapter 7 takes a more structural approach. It analyzes the build-out of INPOL, its integration with the main population information systems that were being constructed by the civilian administration, and the ways in which this nascent network facilitated the securitization of space, place, movement, and identity. While these developments enabled the state to govern the population in ways that had not been possible before and gave the exchange of data among these offices and agencies a new quality that could not have been foreseen, much less authorized, by legislators in the age of paper, this new surveillance infrastructure and the surveillance practices that it made possible also posed novel privacy problems. These were classic examples of how technological change was forcing the legislature to explicitly renegotiate the parameters of socially acceptable information exchange. Additional privacy concerns were raised by Herold's proposal, which was first mooted at the end of the 1970s, to build a new version of INPOL, which he believed would solve the technical problems that plagued the still-unfinished network and constitute a major step toward the realization of his vision of the police as a fully informationalized, self-optimizing cybernetic system.

The second novel form of administrative power that was the topic of public concern during these decades grew out of the changing ways in which personal information was used to govern the welfare state. Since the end of the 1800s, the threshold for state intervention for welfare, security, and public health purposes had been the existence of a concrete danger. However, beginning in the 1970s, the modernization of the welfare state made it appear more urgent, more economical, and more rational to collect the information that would be needed to identify and preempt deviant behavior at the predelinquent or prepathological stage, before it had become a concrete danger whose occurrence could no longer be forestalled. This line of thinking justified the extension of state surveillance into what the Germans called the logical and chronological *Vorfeld* of concrete dangers. However, neither the potential causes of deviance nor the appropriate means for preventing them could ever be fully known, and the impossibility of perfect knowledge gave rise to two complementary modes of governing an uncertain future.

Chapters 8 and 9 analyze these two modes of governing the future, the forms of surveillance to which they gave rise, and their political import. Chapter 8 takes a chronological approach to the parallel histories of the formation of a counterterrorism surveillance regime centered on the Federal Criminal Police and the development of an array of new surveillance practices to map the radical milieu and track down terrorists, and later organized criminals, who relied on strategies and tactics that could not be defeated using the methods developed to combat "ordinary" crime. This chapter examines the criminalistic rationale for these practices, the ways in which they pushed against the boundaries of liberal police law, the ways in which the concept of privacy was employed to contest this expansion of police surveillance, and the role of these conflicts in determining the concrete meaning of both privacy and its mirror image, internal security.

The impact of these new surveillance practices would have been blunted in the absence of a unified apparatus to collect, analyze, and apply this information, and the chapter shows how terrorism provided the rationale for the grudging, limited, but nevertheless unprecedented centralization of power in the hands of the Federal Criminal Police between 1975 and 1977. However, the inability to prevent a new wave of political violence, the passage of the Federal Privacy Protection Law, the appointment of Baum as interior minister, and a growing sense that this new surveillance apparatus was itself becoming a threat to civil liberties and personal privacy precipitated both a Thermidorian reaction against the surveillance regime that had taken shape since 1975 and a broad public debate over whether the Federal Republic was being transformed into an authoritarian surveillance state (*Überwachungsstaat*).

The census decision forced the states to explicitly authorize, and delimit, the collection and exchange of personal information by the police, and the central point of contention in the reform of state police laws, which is the focus of chapter 9, was the codification of the new surveillance practices. Chapter 9 distinguishes between liberal and illiberal modes of governing an uncertain future, their respective logics of prevention and repression, and the distinctive forms of surveillance that they authorized. The liberal mode of governance, which was exemplified by Herold's conception of the "social sanitary" mission of the police, sought to tame this uncertainty by identifying the natural laws of social deviance and then using this knowledge to deploy (dis)incentives to alter the strategic calculations that led these persons to deviate from social norms. Illiberal governance arose at the limits of this liberal project. It involved the reassertion of sovereign power from within the social domain in order to repress deviant, criminal behavior by those who showed themselves unable or unwilling to respond to such incentives and thus incapable of being governed through freedom. This was the rationality that informed the new forms of surveillance that were to be codified in the reformed police laws of the 1980s.

Contemporary analyses of terrorism and organized crime figured the future as uncertain, unknowable, and threatening, and the search for security involved an open-ended process of risk discovery—that is, a search for "unknown unknowns"(rather than simply the expanded collection of information on known risks), the extension of surveillance further and further into the *Vorfeld*, and the reliance upon tacit knowledge, intuition, and context-based judgment by the security agencies.[39] As such, "precautionary" surveillance and intervention obeyed a dynamic, transgressive logic because they contained no intrinsic limits or criteria that would permit them to be subjected to legal norms or formal procedures. Consequently, there was a constant danger that such activity would hollow out the rule of law in the name of a postliberal security regime in which the distinction between law and exception was progressively obscured.[40]

The codification of these new surveillance practices represented a direct challenge to the basic principles of liberal police law, which had predicated the informational activity of the police on the existence of either a concrete danger or well-founded individual suspicion. Chapter 9 argues that privacy protection law served as the primary means for theorizing the problems arising out of the new police surveillance practices and for defending legal norms and a liberal economy of informational parsimony against the transgressive logic of precautionary surveillance.[41] In this way, I argue, the end of the postwar paradigm of internal security was marked not only by reassertion of civil liberties and privacy rights against the state, but also by the emergence—and partial institutionalization—of an entirely new paradigm that was structured around the logic of precautionary surveillance.

Surveillance and the Political Relevance of Privacy

Any account of privacy will remain little more than an academic exercise unless it succeeds in both explaining the precise nature of the harms entailed by the routine collection of personal information by large organizations and showing how the concept can be used to theorize and contest the administrative power generated by such surveillance.[42] However, many observers are skeptical of such an undertaking, and some critics have gone so far as to claim that the concept of privacy has no analytic purchase or political relevance in contemporary surveillance societies. Privacy, they argue, represents neither the "antidote" to surveillance nor its "ontological antithesis."[43] They attribute the theoretical and political deficiencies of the concept to its subjective nature, to the impossibility of precisely defining its contours, and to the resulting tendency "to reduce surveillance to an individual matter rather than [to see it as] an inherently social concern."[44] In the damning words of John Gilliom, the concept of privacy is "hyper-individualistic, spatial, legalistic, blind to discrimination, and, in the end, simply too narrow to catch the richness of the surveillance experience."[45]

Although such arguments are not without their merits, in the 1970s and 1980s West German privacy advocates approached the question of informational privacy, or what came to be called *Datenschutz* (literally, though not entirely accurately, "data protection" [see chapters 2 and 3]), from a very different perspective. My goal here is to demonstrate the continuing political relevance of these early German reflections on informational privacy by showing that their efforts to think through the problems posed by both bureaucratic population surveillance and the use of the new information technologies to process this data drove a paradigm shift from the idea of a private sphere of seclusion *from* society to a concept of informational self-determination, which theorized both the social and power relations between individuals *in* society and the informational relations to which these social processes give rise. This approach, I argue, enabled them to avoid the contradictions of individualist conceptions of privacy and incorporate into their understanding of privacy an analysis of those forms of power whose ostensible neglect has been adduced by critics as the cause of the political irrelevance of the concept. In this way, privacy became, as Sarah Igo has argued, one of the central salients through which citizenship has been defined in the modern world.[46]

Since the 1960s, George Orwell's *1984* (1949) and Jeremy Bentham's panopticon—as read through the lens of Michel Foucault's *Discipline and Punish* (1975)—have provided the most important frameworks for thinking about surveillance in contemporary society.[47] Orwell's book provided both a powerful language for describing the dangers posed by the invasion of the private sphere and a trove of epithets that could be hurled against the computer and the record-keeping state. However, both the nature of the power generated through physical or observational surveillance in a totalitarian state and the ways in which it shaped individual subjectivity are quite different from that produced by the routine, automated collection of personal information that was the focus of West German privacy theory in the 1970s.

The issue is somewhat more complicated with regard to Foucault.[48] In *Discipline and Punish*, Foucault argued that the correct training of malleable subjects depended on three technologies: hierarchical observation, normalizing judgment, and their combination in the examination, as well as the recording of the results of such examinations in disciplinary writing, which made it possible to classify, form categories, determine averages, and establish norms.[49] However, he never attempted to fit computers, databases, or paper filing systems into the framework that he had constructed in that book, and a substantial literature has grown up around what he left unsaid. A number of authors have argued that the new information technologies have led to the perfection of panoptic surveillance.[50] However, in recent years this position has come under attack from a number of directions. On the one hand, it is not clear whether surveillance in the postwar West (still) functions primarily as a mechanism for disciplining and normalization. For example, Gilles Deleuze has argued that, just as the disciplinary society succeeded the society of sovereignty, so too has the disciplinary society been succeeded by what he called the "society of control," which governs not through the containment and normalization of difference, but rather through the modulation of the individual and the use of difference as a "motivational force."[51]

The other defining characteristic of the panopticon, a unified hierarchy of surveillant visibility, which Foucault deemed essential to spatially fixing the individual objects of surveillance so as to better subject them to normalizing judgment, has also been called into question. Kevin Haggerty and Richard Ericson have argued that we are now witnessing the opportunistic convergence of otherwise discrete state and private-sector surveillance systems to form "surveillant assemblages." These assemblages, they argue, are energized by a range of motives, including control, governance, security, profit, and entertainment; they develop "rhizomatically" without the sovereign center and hierarchical structure that was essential to the disciplinary power of the panopticon; and they extend routine surveillance to populations that were not subject to such monitoring in the past and to nonhuman phenomena.[52]

These reservations regarding the usefulness of panopticism for theorizing the nature of electronic surveillance grow even greater when we look more closely at the structure and functioning of the database. According to Deleuze, the database serves not as a technology for making *in*dividuals, but rather for producing what he calls "dividuals," who are created by the dispersion of the unified subject into the discrete, strategically important attributes or characteristics defined by those who determine the database fields in which this data is registered. This encoding, which is the antithesis of the disciplinary writing that records the progress of the individual toward the norm, makes possible, Deleuze argues, the modulation of individual action—that is, the authorization or denial of access to spaces, rights, and services—along as many dimensions as there are attributes.[53] Thus, even though electronic surveillance in the networked society may be increasingly comprehensive, its logic and political rationality are in many ways the opposite of those of the panopticon, and the differential visibility inherent in the functioning of the database makes it possible to govern individuals and populations by modulating, discriminating among, and "sorting" them in different ways.[54]

The shift from parsing the private sphere to the analysis of the context in which personal information is used has also provided the basis for the work of philosopher and information scientist Helen Nissenbaum, who has defined privacy in terms of the "contextual integrity" of informational practices. Nissenbaum argues that society is comprised of different spheres, or (sub)systems, where people engage in distinct activities, play specific roles, and obey the tacit norms that have evolved in tandem with these practices. Privacy is recognized, she argues, when informational practices conform to those norms that reflect the settled expectations of the community, and it is violated when they deviate from or challenge them.[55] While Nissenbaum's arguments rest on the Burkean presumption that these "settled" practices can provide a norm by which to judge new uses, I argue that these practices can never be fully "integral" because communicative norms are themselves the product of prior political contestation and that, therefore, privacy can only be understood as the provisional outcome of the permanent conflict between the right to information and the right to privacy as it plays out at specific times in specific contexts. Seen in this way, the privacy protection legislation of the 1970s and 1980s represented an attempt to politically renegotiate—in a period of accelerating cultural change, administrative modernization, technological advances, and political polarization—the parameters for the socially adequate exchange of information.

The dominant conception of privacy and privacy rights, which is grounded in a liberal, individualist anthropology, has been subject to numerous criticisms.[56] The most notable, and the most debilitating, of these criticisms focuses on the impossibility of casuistically resolving the antinomies created by the abstract juxtaposition of the private sphere and the public, and of the individual and society. Not only are judgments regarding the privacy or sensitivity of specific information indelibly subjective. The liberal commitment to the neutrality of the state in such matters also means that privacy rights can enjoy only relatively weak procedural protections. Critics have also argued that, to the extent that it represents an interest in preventing others from gaining knowledge of certain matters, the right to privacy amounts to nothing more than a right to conceal, to misrepresent oneself to others, and to manipulate them.[57] Others have argued in similar terms that the privatistic, inner-directed nature of privacy rights is incompatible with both democratic participation and communitarian commitments to the common good.[58]

These individualist foundations have always put the defenders of privacy on the defensive because, when conceived in this way, privacy rights have invariably been found to be of only secondary importance when weighed against other collective interests in information disclosure, such as security, welfare, the efficient functioning of both the public administration and the market, and free speech. Although Priscilla Regan has sought to put privacy rights on a firmer foundation by showing that they have a value to society that cannot be reduced to individual preferences or rights, her work remains grounded in the tradition of liberal privacy rights.[59]

Julie Cohen's *Configuring the Networked Self* (2012) is the most important attempt to shift the language of the debate.[60] Cohen traces all of the contradictions that have bedeviled privacy theory and policy to the attempt to ground privacy rights on the autonomous, presocial self presumed by liberal political theory. She argues that privacy cannot be understood as either a fixed condition or as an attribute such as seclusion or control. Instead, she argues that selfhood is the end product of a communicative, essentially social process, which is shaped by the anticipation of how Others will respond to the demands for social recognition articulated by the self, whose identity takes shape at the interface, and through the interplay, of the individual and the cultural and social systems into which the person is born and socialized. She argues that privacy must be understood as a form of active, creative, playful, tactical, aleatory, and situationally determined "boundary management," which enables the "capacity for self-determination" to develop by sheltering "dynamic, emergent subjectivity from the efforts of commercial and government actors to render individuals and communities fixed, transparent, and predictable."[61] In this way, her focus shifts from subjective rights claims to what she calls the structural conditions for human flourishing—that is, the conditions that are necessary to preserve the space for play and choice in the construction of identity.[62]

While Cohen's arguments point in important ways beyond the liberal paradigm, they are perhaps not as novel as she claims. In the chapters that follow, I will argue that in the 1970s and early 1980s West German privacy theorists had already developed a compelling account of the social nature of privacy. Cohen's shift from subjective rights claims to the exploration of the objective, structural, or systemic preconditions for the preservation of the social space required for boundary management has much in common with German privacy theory, both then and now. However, when Cohen speaks of the development of the self as a process, she does so in rather abstract terms, and, in practice, she does not examine as closely as the more sociologically minded German privacy theorists the ways in which social interests and political power determine which boundary management practices can be employed in specific contexts.

In a central section of her book, Cohen explains that

> choices about privacy are choices about the scope for self-articulation. . . . Choices about privacy are constitutive not simply of civil society, as some privacy theorists would have it, but of a particular type of civil society that prizes particular types of activities and particular types of subjects. . . . Privacy exemplifies a culture's normative, collective commitments regarding the scope of movement, both literal and metaphorical, accorded to its members.[63]

These choices, however, are not made in a vacuum. The process by which new communicative norms were negotiated was an essentially political one, and, as Herold predicted, the information problem became one of the central points of contention in the West German culture wars of the 1970s and 1980s.[64] In the account of population registration, privacy law, and police surveillance in the chapters that follow, I will analyze both the ways in which German privacy theorists understood the potential harms and benefits that would result from giving (or denying) specific parties access to specific kinds of information for specific purposes and the process through which Germans sought to negotiate new collective norms to govern the use of personal information at the dawn of the information society.[65]

Notes

1. Anthony Giddens, *The Nation-State and Violence* (University of California Press, 1987); Christopher Dandeker, *Surveillance, Power and Modernity: Bureaucracy and Discipline from 1700 to the Present Day* (Polity Press, 1990); James Scott, *Seeing Like a State* (Yale University Press, 1998); Jane Caplan and John Torpey, eds., *Documenting Individual Identity: The Development of State Practices in the Modern World* (Princeton University Press, 2001); and John Torpey, *The Invention of the Passport: Surveillance, Citizenship and the State* (Cambridge University Press, 2000). Local, corporate, and ecclesiastical authorities were either bypassed by this process or instrumentalized by the state for its own purposes. See Anton Tantner, *Ordnung der Häuser, Beschreibung der Seelen. Hausnummerierung und Seelenkonskription in der Habsburgermonarchie* (StudienVerlag, 2007).
2. Pierre-Joseph Proudhon, *General Idea of the Revolution in the Nineteenth Century*, trans. John Beverly Robinson (Freedom Press, 1923), 294. Virtually all of these administrative practices or population technologies have their own historiographies, though for obvious reasons they are often entwined with one another. These literatures will be glossed in the appropriate places in the chapters that follow.
3. David Shearer, "Elements Near and Alien: Passportization, Policing, and Identity in the Stalinist State, 1932–1952," *JMH* 76 (2004): 835–81.
4. This argument was first made at length in Mark Poster, *The Mode of Information: Poststructuralism and Social Context* (University of Chicago Press, 1990); see also William Bogard, *The Simulation of Surveillance: Hypercontrol in Telematic Societies* (Cambridge University Press, 1996); Kevin Haggerty and Richard Ericson, "The Surveillant Assemblage," *British Journal of Sociology* 51, no. 4 (December 2000): 605–22; and the journal *Surveillance & Society*. Although there is a fourth school of surveillance studies, which focuses on the political economy of surveillance and information, these works seldom explicitly theorize privacy. The most important exception to this stricture is Shoshana Zuboff, *The Age of Surveillance Capitalism* (PublicAffairs, 2019). For an overview of the different approaches to the study of surveillance, see David Lyon, *Surveillance Society: Monitoring Everyday Life* (Open University Press, 2001), 107–25.
5. Beniger, *The Control Revolution: Technological and Economic Origins of the Information Society* (Harvard University Press, 1986); Chandler, *The Visible Hand: The Managerial Revolution in American Business* (Harvard University Press, 1977); and Rule, *Private Lives and Public Surveillance: Social Control in the Computer Age* (Schocken, 1974). Two other works should also be considered in this context: Kevin Robins and Frank Webster, *Times of the Technoculture. From the Information Society to the Virtual Life* (Routledge, 1999), especially 87–127; and Paul Edwards, *The Closed World: Computers and the Politics of Discourse in Cold War America* (MIT Press, 1996), both of which emphasize the relationship between information, control, and representation, as well as the role of cybernetics in the functioning of the information society.
6. "Gesetz zum Schutz vor Mißbrauch personenbezogener Daten bei der Datenverarbeitung [Law for the protection against the misuse of personal data resulting from its processing]," *BGBl.*, 1977, 201–14.
7. Frank Webster, *Theories of the Information Society*, 2nd ed. (Routledge, 2002); and Webster et al., eds., *The Information Society Reader* (Routledge 2003).
8. These works include, but are by no means limited to, Toni Weller, *Information History: An Introduction* (Chandos, 2008); Alistair Black, Dave Muddiman, and Helen Plant, *The Early Information Society: Information Management in Britain before the Computer* (Ashgate, 2007); David Vincent, *The Culture of Secrecy: Britain 1832–1998* (Oxford University Press, 1998); Vincent, "Government and the Management of Information 1844–2009," in *The Peculiarities of Liberal Modernity in Imperial Britain*, ed. Simon Gunn and James Vernon

(University of California Press, 2011), 165–81; Oz Frankel, *States of Inquiry: Social Investigations and Print Culture in Nineteenth-Century Britain and the United States* (Johns Hopkins University Press, 2006); Alex Wright, *Cataloging the World: Paul Otlet and the Birth of the Information Age* (Oxford University Press, 2014); Markus Krajewski, *Paper Machines: About Cards & Catalogs, 1548–1929* (MIT Press, 2011); Nicholas Popper, "An Information State for Elizabethan England," *JMH* 90 (September 2018): 503–35; Ann Blair, *Too Much to Know: Managing Scholarly Information Before the Modern Age* (Yale University Press, 2011); Randolph C. Head, *Making Archives in Early Modern Europe: Proof, Information, and Political Record-Keeping, 1400–1700* (Cambridge University Press, 2019); Jacob Soll, *The Information Master: Jean-Baptiste Colbert's Secret State Intelligence System* (University of Michigan Press, 2009); Christopher Bayly, *Empire and Information: Intelligence Gathering and Social Communication in India, 1780–1870* (Cambridge University Press, 1996); and Andreas Boes, Tobias Kämpf, and Thomas Lühr, "Von der 'großen Industrie' zum 'Informationsraum.' Informatisierung und der Umbruch in den Unternehmen in historischer Perspektive," in *Vorgeschichte der Gegenwart*, ed. Anselm Doering-Manteuffel et al. (Vandenhoeck & Ruprecht, 2016), 57–78.

9. Colin Bennett and Charles Raab, *The Governance of Privacy: Policy Instruments in Global Perspective* (MIT Press, 2006), xxii–xxiii. Daniel Solove, *Understanding Privacy* (Harvard University Press, 2008), 1, calls privacy a "concept in disarray," and in this book he attempts to reconstruct the concept by arguing that it should be understood as a label that is applied to a number of discrete "privacy problems" that share a family resemblance, but no common core concern.

10. On the three dimensions of privacy, see Beate Roessler, *The Value of Privacy* (Polity, 2004). Part of the reason why Solove, *Understanding Privacy*, concludes that the concept of privacy is in such theoretical disarray is that he lumps together the distinct problems raised by each of these strands, though without being able to fall back on the integrating concept of personality rights that is at the core of German thinking on the topic (chapter 2 below). Roger Clarke, "Information Technology and Dataveillance," *Communications of the ACM* 31, no. 5 (May 1988): 498–512, coined the term "dataveillance" to capture the shift from observational surveillance to the automated surveillance of persons by means of their personal information—that is, "via their records and transactions." Gary Marx's claim that the distinguishing characteristic of the "new surveillance" is the use of technology to "extract or create" information that is not accessible by the unaided senses retains both Clarke's emphasis on technology and his shift in focus from the direct observation of reality to its digital emulation, but does not address the personal nature of this information. See Marx, *Windows into the Soul: Surveillance and Society in an Age of High Technology* (University of Chicago Press, 2016), 20; and Marx, "What's New About the 'New Surveillance'? Classifying for Change and Continuity," *Surveillance & Society* 1, no. 1 (2002): 9–29.

11. David Murakami Wood, ed., *A Report on the Surveillance Society* (Surveillance Studies Network, 2006; https://ico.org.uk/media/about-the-ico/documents/1042390/surveillance-society-full-report-2006.pdf), 4.

12. Giddens, *The Nation-State and Violence*, 2, 14–15. In *Policing the Risk Society* (University of Toronto Press, 1997), 55–56, Richard Ericson and Kevin Haggerty define surveillance as "the bureaucratic production of knowledge about, and risk management of, suspect populations" in order to "efficiently format, and make available, detailed knowledge about people in the hope that it will come in handy in the system's future dealings with them, or, more often, in the dealings other institutions (credit, welfare, insurance, health, education, and so on) might have with them." Although this definition reflects their understanding of the mutation of the police from an institution for the production of social order into one dedicated to the production of knowledge for a compliance regime, the focus of part III of the present book remains individual offenders and the

"hard edge" of crime control, prosecution, and punishment, which plays, they argue, an increasingly residual role in the policing of the risk society.

13. Scott, *Seeing Like a State*; and Leon Hempel, Susanne Krasmann, and Ulrich Bröckling, "Sichtbarkeitsregime: Eine Einleitung," in "Sichtbarkeitsregime—Überwachung, Sicherheit und Privatheit im 21. Jahrhundert," special issue, *Leviathan* 25 (2010): 7–24.

14. The tension between control for solicitude, entitlement, and protection and control for the repression of dangers is one of the central themes of Amy Fairchild, Ronald Bayer, and James Colgrove, *Searching Eyes: Privacy, the State, and Disease Surveillance in America* (University of California Press, 2007); the same point is made in Lyon, *Surveillance Society*, 3; and Sarah Igo, *The Known Citizen: A History of Privacy in Modern America* (Harvard University Press, 2018), especially her discussion of Social Security (55–98).

15. "Privacy protection" and "data protection" (i.e., *Datenschutz*) are not equivalent expressions. The most careful analysis of the relationship between data and privacy protection in European law is Gloria Gonzáles Fuster, *The Emergence of Personal Data Protection as a Fundamental Right of the EU* (Springer, 2014). However, Gonzáles Fuster's terminological inquiry is only able to cleanly distinguish between the two by declining to investigate the concrete nature of the rights that are to be protected by means of the protection of personal data. In contrast, I use the term privacy as a label or umbrella term for these interests and argue that in Germany the privacy of the private sphere and the privacy of personal data or information were both grounded in the same constitutional principles. Conversely, Neil Richards, "Reviewing *The Digital Person*: Privacy and Technology in the Information Age," *Georgetown Law Journal* 94 (2006): 1087–140, argues (1094, 1133–39) that the term privacy is "cognitively limiting," especially with reference to databases and routine data collection, and that, unlike "privacy," "data protection" does not—by definition—make it impossible to focus on the intermediate zone between "private" and "public." However, my definition of privacy as a social relationship shows that the term need not be understood in the manner implied by Richards. My use of "privacy," rather than "data protection" (which, it should be noted, suffers from its own limitations and ambiguities), to define the focus of this book is more than a mere personal preference, and the validity and usefulness of this choice will ultimately depend on the way the content of this concept is fleshed out in the following chapters.

16. Giddens, *The Nation-State and Violence*, 12, 17, 19.

17. Giddens, *The Nation-State and Violence*, 178, 181, 309.

18. Edward Higgs, *The Information State in England* (Palgrave, 2004), popularized the title term of his work. I will use the terms "information society" and "information state" interchangeably to denote a secular social formation whose distinguishing feature is the increasing importance of personal information as a medium of social governance. The body of this book, however, deals primarily with the use of personal information by the state and the public administration. This is partly a matter of choice and partly a result of the available sources. Josh Lauer, *Creditworthy: A History of Consumer Surveillance and Financial Identity in America* (Columbia University Press, 2017), 9–10, 34, 180, argues that the private sector played "the leading role" in the formation of the modern surveillance society. David Lyon, "Situating Surveillance: History, Technology, Culture," in *Histories of State Surveillance in Europe and Beyond*, ed. Kees Boersma et al. (Routledge, 2014), 32–46, notes (41) that "in the longer historical sweep, it is hard to say which came first, state or commercial surveillance. And of course, they may well have been intertwined." Igo makes a similar claim in *The Known Citizen*, 15–16.

19. Giddens, *The Nation-State and Violence*, 310ff.

20. Interview with Herold, "Die Polizei als gesellschaftliches Diagnoseinstrument," in *Die neue Sicherheit. Vom Notstand zur Sozialen Kontrolle*, ed. Roland Appel et al. (Kölner Volksblatt, 1988), 65–92, citation 89.

21. Elizabeth Harvey et al., eds., *Privacy and Private Life in Nazi Germany* (Cambridge University Press, 2019); Paul Betts, *Within Walls: Private Life in the German Democratic Republic* (Oxford University Press, 2010); and Orlando Figes, *The Whisperers: Private Life in Stalin's Russia* (Penguin, 2008), have all argued that the totalitarian state never fully succeeded in politicizing and absorbing the family and its private life, while Andreas Glaeser, *Political Epistemics: The Secret Police, the Opposition, and the End of East German Socialism* (University of Chicago Press, 2011), and Oleg Kharkhordian, *The Individual and the Collective in Russia: A Study of Practices* (University of California Press, 1999), both explore theoretically the dynamic driving state penetration of the private.
22. Recent scholarship has argued that the Gestapo lacked the manpower to actively surveil the general population and that it depended instead on denunciations from a public that was mobilized behind the ideology of a racial national community. See Gisela Diewald-Kerkmann, *Politische Denunziation im NS-Regime oder die kleine Macht der "Volksgenossen"* (J. H. W. Dietz Nachfolger, 1995); Robert Gellately, *The Gestapo and German Society: Enforcing Racial Policy, 1933–1945* (Oxford University Press, 1990); and Klaus-Michael Mallmann and Gerhard Paul, "Allwissend, allmächtig, allgegenwärtig? Gestapo, Gesellschaft und Widerstand," *Zeitschrift für Geschichtswissenschaft* 41 (1993): 984–99. While the introduction to Harvey, *Privacy and Private Life in Nazi Germany*, 25, foregrounds spatial and decisional privacy, I have analyzed the Nazi use of personal information as a surveillance mechanism in Frohman, "Population Registration in Germany, 1842–1945: Information, Administrative Power, and State-Making in the Age of Paper," *Central European History* 53, no. 3 (September 2020): 503–32.
23. Rüdiger Bergien, "Programmieren mit dem Klassenfeind. Die Stasi, Siemens und der Transfer von EDV-Wissen im Kalten Krieg," *VfZ* 67, no. 1 (2019): 1–30; Bergien, "'Big Data' als Vision. Computereinführung und Organisationswandel in BKA und Staatssicherheit (1967–1989)," *Zeithistorische Forschungen* 14 (2017): 258–85; and Christian Booß, "Der Sonnenstaat des Erich Mielke. Die Informationsverarbeitung des MfS: Entwicklung und Aufbau," *Zeitschrift für Geschichtswissenschaft* 60 (2012): 441–57.
24. For Germany, see Frank Bösch, ed., *Wege in die digitale Gesellschaft. Computernutzung in der Bundesrepublik, 1955–1990* (Wallstein, 2018); Armin Nassehi, *Muster. Theorie der digitalen Gesellschaft* (C. H. Beck, 2019); David Gugerli, *Wie die Welt in den Computer kam. Zur Entstehung digitaler Wirklichkeit* (S. Fischer, 2018); Martin Schmitt, Julia Erdogan, Thomas Kasper, and Janine Funke, "Digitalgeschichte Deutschlands. Ein Forschungsbericht," *Technikgeschichte* 83, no. 1 (2016): 33–70; Thomas Kasper, "'Licht im Rentendunkel': Die Computerisierung des Sozialstaats in Bundesrepublik und DDR," dissertation, University of Potsdam, 2018; Bergien, "Programmieren mit dem Klassenfeind"; Corinna Schlombs, *Productivity Machines: German Appropriations of American Technology from Mass Production to Computer Automation* (MIT Press, 2019); Michael Homberg, "Mensch/Mikrochip. Die Globalisierung der Arbeitswelten in der Computerindustrie 1960 bis 2000—Fragen, Perspektiven, Thesen," *VfZ* 66, no. 2 (2018): 267–93; Hannes Mangold, *Fahndung nach dem Raster. Informationsverarbeitung bei der bundesdeutschen Kriminalpolizei, 1965–1984* (Chronos, 2017); Julia Fleischhack, *Eine Welt im Datenrausch. Computeranlagen und Datenmengen als gesellschaftliche Herausforderung in der Bundesrepublik Deutschland (1965–1975)* (Chronos, 2016); and Jürgen Danyel, "Zeitgeschichte der Informationsgesellschaft," *Zeithistorische Forschungen* 9, no. 2 (2012): 186–211.
25. As Shoshana Zuboff, "Big Other: Surveillance Capitalism and the Prospects of an Information Civilization," *Journal of Information Technology* 30 (2015): 75–89, has written (75), "'big data' ... is not a technology or an inevitable technology effect. It is not an autonomous process.... It originates in the social, and it is there that we must find it and know it." Robins and Webster, *Times of the Technoculture*, 91, make a similar point: "The 'Information Revolution' is inadequately conceived ... as a question of technology

Introduction

and technological innovation. Rather, it is better understood as a matter of differential (and unequal) access to, and control over, information resources."

26. Jon Agar, *The Government Machine: A Revolutionary History of the Computer* (MIT Press, 2003).
27. Frieder Günther, "Rechtsstaat, Justizstaat oder Verwaltungsstaat? Die Verfassungs- und Verwaltungspolitik," in *Hüter der Ordnung. Die Innenministerien in Bonn und Ost-Berlin nach dem Nationalsozialismus*, ed. Frank Bösch and Andreas Wirsching (Wallstein, 2018), 381–412, especially 401–2.
28. Gabriele Metzler, *Konzeptionen politischen Handelns von Adenauer bis Brandt. Politische Planung in der pluralistischen Gesellschaft* (Schöningh, 2005); Alexander Nützenadel, *Stunde der Ökonomen. Wissenschaft, Politik und Expertenkultur in der Bundesrepublik, 1949–1974* (Vandenhoeck & Ruprecht, 2005); Michael Ruck, "Ein kurzer Sommer der konkreten Utopie: Zur westdeutschen Planungsgeschichte der langen 60er Jahre," in *Dynamische Zeiten. Die 60er Jahre in den beiden deutschen Gesellschaften*, ed. Axel Schildt (Hamburg, 2000), 362–401; Special issue on planning, *Geschichte und Gesellschaft* 34, no. 3 (2008); Elke Seefried, *Zukünfte. Aufstieg und Krise der Zukunftsforschung, 1945–1980* (De Gruyter, 2015); Seefried and Dierk Hoffmann, eds., *Plan und Planung. Deutsch-deutsche Vorgriffe auf die Zukunft* (De Gruyter 2018); Michel Christian et al., eds., *Planning in Cold War Europe: Competition, Cooperation, Circulations 1950s–1970s* (De Gruyter, 2018); and Larry Frohman, "Network Euphoria, Super-Information Systems, and the West German Plan for a National Database System," *German History* 38, no. 2 (2020): 311–37.
29. Winfried Süß, "'Wer aber denkt für das Ganze?' Aufstieg und Fall der ressortübergreifenden Planung im Bundeskanzleramt," in *Demokratisierung und gesellschaftlicher Aufbruch. Die sechziger Jahre als Wendezeit der Bundesrepublik*, ed. Matthias Frese et al. (Schöningh, 2003), 349–77.
30. On the political realignment of 1969, see Manfred Görtemaker, *Geschichte der Bundesrepublik Deutschland* (C. H. Beck, 1999), 437–525; and, on the reorientation of the FDP, see Heino Kaack, "Die Liberalen," in *Die zweite Republik. 25 Jahre Bundesrepublik Deutschland – eine Bilanz*, ed. Richard Löwenthal and Hans-Peter Schwarz (Seewald Verlag, 1974), 408–32.
31. Scott, *Seeing Like a State*, 4–5.
32. It can be described in much the same terms used by Andrei Markovits and Philip Gorski, *The German Left: Red, Green, and Beyond* (Oxford University Press, 1993), 100–1, to characterize the early 1970s citizens' initiatives.
33. Görtemaker, *Geschichte der Bundesrepublik*, 563–96; and Andreas Wirsching, *Abschied vom Provisorium, 1982–1990* (Deutsche Verlags-Anstalt, 2006), 17–33.
34. The relatively obscure Verwaltungsverfahrensgesetz, which was passed in 1976, codified for federal and state government the principles of administrative law that had developed over the previous century. The law, which had long been opposed by the defenders of a more conservative, étatistic conception of the role of the public administration, was regarded as an important step toward increasing both the transparency of the administration and the legal rights of individual citizens in their interaction with it.
35. BVerfGE 65, 1 (43).
36. I have examined the changing meaning of privacy in the healthcare field in Frohman, "Medical Surveillance and Medical Confidentiality in an Age of Transition: The Debate over Cancer Registration in West Germany," *Social History of Medicine* (forthcoming); and "Redefining Medical Confidentiality in the Digital Era: Healthcare Reform and the West German Debate over the Use of Personal Medical Information in the 1980s," *Journal of the History of Medicine and Allied Sciences* 72, no. 4 (October 2017): 468–99.
37. Weinhauer, "Terrorismus in der Bundesrepublik der Siebzigerjahre. Aspekte einer Sozial- und Kulturgeschichte der Inneren Sicherheit," *AfS* 44 (2004): 219–42; and Weinhauer, "Staatsmacht ohne Grenzen? Innere Sicherheit, 'Terrorismus'-Bekämpfung und

die bundesdeutsche Gesellschaft der 1970er Jahre," in *Rationalitäten der Gewalt. Staatliche Neuordnungen vom 19. bis zum 21. Jahrhundert*, ed. Susanne Krasmann and Jürgen Martschukat (Transkript, 2015), 215–38.
38. Karrin Hanshew, "Beyond Friend or Foe? Terrorism, Counterterrorism and a (Transnational) *Gesellschaftsgeschichte* of the 1970s," *GuG* 42 (2016): 377–403.
39. Christopher Daase and Oliver Kessler, "Knowns and Unknowns in the 'War on Terror': Uncertainty and the Political Construction of Danger," *Security Dialogue* 38 (2007): 411–34; and Ulrich Bröckling, "Prävention: Die Macht der Vorbeugung," in *Gute Hirten führen sanft* (Suhrkamp, 2017), 73–112.
40. Udo Di Fabio, "Sicherheit in Freiheit," *NJW* 61, no. 7 (2008): 421–25; Günter Frankenberg, *Staatstechnik. Perspektiven auf Rechtsstaat und Ausnahmezustand* (Suhrkamp, 2010), 119–23; and Giorgio Agamben, *State of Exception* (University of Chicago Press, 2005), 14.
41. On security as a motif in West German history, see Christoph Wehner, *Die Versicherung der Atomgefahr. Risikopolitik, Sicherheitsproduktion und Expertise in der Bundesrepublik Deutschland und den USA, 1945–1986* (Wallstein, 2017); Martin Diebel, *Atomkrieg und andere Katastrophen. Zivil- und Katastrophenschutz in der Bundesrepublik und Großbritannien nach 1945* (Schöningh, 2017); Martin Geyer, "Security and Risk: How We Have Learned to Live with Dystopian, Utopian, and Technocratic Diagnoses of Security since the 1970s," *Historia 396* 5, no. 1 (2015): 93–134; Special issue on security and the demarcation of historical epochs, *GuG* 38, no. 3 (2012); Christopher Daase et al., eds. *Sicherheitskultur. Soziale und politische Praktiken der Gefahrenabwehr* (Campus, 2012); Eckart Conze, "Sicherheit als Kultur. Überlegungen zu einer 'modernen Politikgeschichte' der Bundesrepublik Deutschland," *VfZ* 53, no. 3 (2005): 357–80; Conze, *Die Suche nach Sicherheit. Eine Geschichte der Bundesrepublik Deutschland von 1949 bis in die Gegenwart* (Siedler, 2009); and "Forum: Surveillance in German History," *German History* 34, no. 2 (2016): 293–314.
42. Neil Richards, "The Dangers of Surveillance," *Harvard Law Review* 126, no. 7 (2013): 1934–65.
43. Dietmar Kammerer, *Bilder der Überwachung* (Suhrkamp, 2008), 14; Bennett, "In Defence of Privacy: The Concept and the Regime," *Surveillance & Society* 8, no. 4 (2011): 485–96 and the forum (497–516) on Bennett's essay. The citations here are from Gilliom, "A Response to Bennett's 'In Defence of Privacy,'" *Surveillance & Society* 8, no. 4 (2011): 500–4, citation 502; and Stalder, "Privacy is Not the Antidote to Surveillance," *Surveillance & Society* 1, no. 1 (2002): 120–24.
44. Lyon, *Surveillance Society*, 4.
45. Gilliom, "A Response to Bennett's 'In Defence of Privacy,'" 501.
46. Igo, *The Known Citizen*.
47. Daniel J. Solove, "Privacy and Power: Computer Databases and Metaphors for Information Privacy," *Stanford Law Review* 53, no. 6 (July 2001): 1393–462; and the discussion of these and other models and metaphors in David Lyon, *The Electronic Eye: The Rise of Surveillance Society* (Polity, 1994).
48. Rob Boyne, "Post-Panopticism," *Economy and Society* 29, no. 2 (May 2000): 285–307; Kevin Haggerty, "Tear Down the Walls: On Demolishing the Panopticon," in *Theorizing Surveillance: The Panopticon and Beyond*, ed. David Lyon (Willan Publishing, 2006), 23–45; David Murakami Wood, "Beyond the Panopticon? Foucault and Surveillance Studies," in *Space, Knowledge and Power: Foucault and Geography*, ed. Jeremy Crampton and Stuart Elden (Ashgate, 2007), 245–63; Greg Elmer, "Panopticon—Discipline—Control," in *Routledge Handbook of Surveillance Studies*, ed. Kirstie Ball et al. (Routledge, 2012), 21–29; Elmer, "A Diagram of Panoptic Surveillance," *New Media & Society* 5, no. 2 (2003): 231–47; and Bart Simon, "The Return of Panopticism: Supervision, Subjection and the New Surveillance," *Surveillance & Society* 3, no. 1 (2005): 1–20.
49. Foucault, *Discipline and Punish: The Birth of the Prison* (Vintage Books, 1979), 170–94.
50. The argument is summarized in Lyon, *The Electronic Eye*, 67–71, 166.

51. Deleuze, "Postscript on the Societies of Control," *October* 59 (Winter 1992): 3–7.
52. Haggerty and Ericson, "The Surveillance Assemblage."
53. Foucault, *Discipline and Punish*, 170; Deleuze, "Postscript on the Societies of Control"; and Haggerty and Ericson, "The Surveillance Assemblage," 619.
54. David Lyon, ed., *Surveillance as Social Sorting: Privacy, Risk and Automated Discrimination* (Routledge, 2002); and Oscar Gandy, *The Panoptic Sort: A Political Economy of Personal Information* (Westview Press, 1993).
55. Nissenbaum, *Privacy in Context: Technology, Policy, and the Integrity of Social Life* (Stanford University Press, 2010), especially 129–57. In her subsequent work, Nissenbaum has paid greater attention to the historicity of informational norms and the power relations that underlie them. See, for example, Nissenbaum, "Contextual Integrity Up and Down the Data Food Chain," *Theoretical Inquiries in Law* 20 (2019): 221–56, especially 226–27, 233–34. There are important similarities between Nissenbaum's arguments and those advanced by Ari Ezra Waldman in *Privacy as Trust: Information Privacy for an Information Age* (Cambridge University Press, 2018), especially his understanding of privacy as a social concept and his jurisprudential argument that the definition of informational privacy in terms of trust in the adherence to context-based informational norms can provide the basis for a robust tort-based defense against the routine violation of these norms.
56. On this liberal "privacy paradigm," see Bennett and Raab, *The Governance of Privacy*, 3–28; and Bennett, "In Defence of Privacy."
57. Richard Posner, "An Economic Theory of Privacy," *Regulation* 2, no. 3 (May/June 1978): 19–26; and Posner, "The Right of Privacy," *Georgia Law Review* 12, no. 3 (Spring 1978): 393–422.
58. Amitai Etzioni, *The Limits of Privacy* (Basic Books, 2000), 203, 215, argues that common goods should most always take precedence over individual privacy.
59. Regan, *Legislating Privacy: Technology, Social Values, and Public Policy* (University of North Carolina Press, 1995), 212–43, argues that privacy is a *common* value, which is shared by all individuals, even though they may differ on the precise nature of privacy rights; that it is a *public* value, which is necessary for the functioning of a democratic society; and that it is an inherently *collective* value because technology and market forces make it impossible for any single person to enjoy privacy rights without securing a minimal degree of privacy for all individuals. These ideas are further developed in Regan, "Privacy and the Common Good: Revisited," in *Social Dimensions of Privacy*, ed. Beate Roessler and Dorota Mokrosinska (Cambridge University Press, 2015), 50–70; Kirsty Hughes, "The Social Value of Privacy, the Right of Privacy to Society and Human Rights Discourse," in *Social Dimensions of Privacy*, 225–43; and Joshua Fairfield and Christoph Engel, "Privacy as a Public Good," in *Privacy and Power: A Transatlantic Dialogue in the Shadow of the NSA-Affair*, ed. Russell A. Miller (Cambridge University Press, 2017), 95–128.
60. Cohen, *Configuring the Networked Self: Law, Code, and the Play of Everyday Practice* (Yale University Press, 2012).
61. Cohen, "What Privacy Is For," *Harvard Law Review* 126, no. 7 (May 2013): 1904–33, citation 1905; and the corresponding passage in Cohen, *Configuring the Networked Self*, 149–50.
62. Cohen, *Configuring the Networked Self*, 223ff.
63. Cohen, *Configuring the Networked Self*, 149.
64. On the 1970s as a period of contestation, see Thomas Mergel, "Zeit des Streits. Die siebziger Jahre in der Bundesrepublik als eine Periode des Konflikts," in *Geschichte denken. Perspektiven auf die Geschichtsschreibung heute*, ed. Michael Wildt (Vandenhoek & Ruprecht, 2014), 224–43.
65. Solove's deconstruction of existing theories of privacy in *Understanding Privacy* results in a series of dualisms, which authorize the empiricist or nominalist taxonomy of pri-

vacy harms that is the heart of his defense of privacy rights. In contrast, I argue that these dualisms can be largely resolved if we follow the early German privacy theorists in viewing privacy as a social relationship, that is, as the outcome of a political process in which contextually based informational norms are being continuously (re)negotiated by individuals and groups, and if we view the individual information privacy harms identified by Solove as different ways in which dignity and the development of the personality are harmed by informational practices that violate these communal norms.

Part I
POPULATION REGISTRATION, POWER, AND PRIVACY

Chapter 1

The Federal Population Registration Law, Administrative Power, and the Politicization of Privacy

At the beginning of *Seeing Like a State*, James Scott writes that "the premodern state was, in many crucial respects, partially blind; it knew precious little about its subjects, their wealth, their landholdings and yields, their location, their very identity." It was, Scott argues, population registries, which, in conjunction with the introduction of surnames and the development of means for pinpointing the location of these persons, first made it possible for state officials to dream of a perfectly legible population.[1] However, population registration can only function in conjunction with both civil registration, which plays an equally essential role in defining the administrative identity of the individuals who make up the population, and the associated practices for identifying the individual members of the population and collecting the necessary information from them.[2] Together, they form a logical and administrative whole, whose components and practices, as well as the forms of power they generate and the privacy questions they raise, will be the focus of this and the following chapters.

The collection of personal information is the sine qua non of diverse political rationalities: sovereign control of territory, the disciplinary fixing of individuals in social and geographical space, and the biopolitical cultivation of populations. However, the extent to which, and the intensity with which, such information can be used for any of these purposes

---

Notes for this chapter begin on page 68.

depends on the ability to collect this information, channel it to the center of the organization where it can be integrated with other information and analyzed, and then return it to the bureaucratic periphery, which is the site of encounter between the state administration and the individual citizen. In their original form, however, population registries simply represented snapshots produced by one-time or periodic censuses conducted for circumscribed purposes, and they were incapable of producing the continuous, individualized knowledge required by the modern state in order to make good on its claims to sovereignty and to fulfill its obligation to promote the welfare and security of its people. What good, for example, does it do to have a registry listing the individual members of a population if the list cannot be kept up to date?—if the state cannot continuously keep track of mobile individuals and make them into the objects of administrative solicitude and control?—if it cannot be assured that every individual is included in the registry, that every individual is counted only once, and that the proper distinctions are made both among citizens and between citizens and others?—if it cannot be assured that all of the information needed by the state for its diverse administrative purposes is collected and made available to the relevant agencies in a complete and timely manner and in actionable form?—and if it cannot be assured that personal information is securely attached to the proper biological individual? Solving these problems—problems where surveillance and information processing were two sides of the same coin—was crucial to the development of the modern state. While Jon Agar has noted that it is important to put the "bureau" back into studies of "bureaucracy," I would suggest that it is equally important to understand the intimate relation between bureau and *kratos*—that is, between information processing technologies and power or authority.[3]

The history of population registration is the key to understanding the relationship between population information, information processing, and state administrative power from the mid-1800s to the present. Population registration regulations, whose roots reach back to at least the 1500s, were originally intended to facilitate the policing of the mobile underclasses. However, the function of population registries changed between the mid-nineteenth and the mid-twentieth centuries. In this era of nationalizing states and imperialist rivalries, state legitimacy and power depended to a greater extent than ever before on the ability to collect information relating to specific individuals and then use this data to mobilize resources and regulate the social and economic domains. Although the population registries never entirely shed their security function, between the 1840s and the 1940s they became the most important source of such population information for the local, and then the national, interventionist state, and the processing of this information became a central source of state administrative power. It was also during this period that population registration, as well as the identification and control practices associated with it, came to be seen as natural attributes of the state—a process that Mara Loveman has characterized, following Pierre Bourdieu, as "the primitive accumulation of symbolic power"—and the associated forms of administrative knowledge came to be seen as natural and self-evident precisely because they made it possible to carry out essential state functions.[4]

I have elsewhere examined the relationship between population registration, information processing, and administrative power from the 1842 Prussian poor law to the end of the Third Reich, and the present chapter will continue this story down to the recent past.[5] The defeat of Nazi Germany brought an end to a phase of intensive innovation in the domain of population registration and related population technologies. The breakup of the centralized national police led to the devolution of the population registries to local authorities in the American and British occupation zones, and occupation authorities nullified those laws that were regarded as distinct products of Nazi ideology. However, the 1938 Reich Population Registration Ordinance did not fall under this ban, and both the military administration and West German officials quickly showed themselves to be more interested in rebuilding the population registration system and extending the ID card requirements instituted since 1938 than in rolling them back. In the early years of the Federal Republic, this gave rise to a lively debate over the relative importance of the security and welfare functions of the registries, the fate and form of the national ID card, and the role of population surveillance in a democratic society.[6]

Until 1945 and beyond, the use of registry information was limited by the reliance on paper as a medium of storage and transition. However, in the 1960s these limits were progressively rolled back by a cluster of technological advances: the development of third-generation computers, which employed integrated circuits and randomly accessible memory, the construction of integrated data processing systems, and the development of new communication technologies, which expanded the space-time scale of administrative power by permitting decentralized, real-time access to the data stored in such systems.[7] At the end of the 1960s, these innovations made it possible to conceive of a plan to computerize the local population registries and link them together to create an integrated population information system for administrative and planning purposes. This plan, however, was predicated on the use of a national ID number to organize data storage and retrieval, link data from different sources to specific individuals, and ensure the unambiguous identification of each member of the population. The introduction of such a number, which had been under consideration since the beginning of the 1960s, became the centerpiece of the draft Federal Population Registration Law (Bundesmeldegesetz), which was proposed in 1971. The authors of this law regarded it as a major step toward the modernization of the public administration and as the culmination of a process—one that they believed had begun with the Reich Population Registration Ordinance—by which the role of the registries as a source of information for the civilian administration had come to rival, if not eclipse, their original security function.[8]

Before 1945, privacy had seldom emerged as an important concern in relation to the population registries. This changed after the end of the war. The debate over the national ID number and the Federal Population Registration Law was the direct catalyst for the politicization of privacy at the turn of the 1970s, and privacy became the language through which the administrative power generated by the use of integrated data processing by the population registries was conceptualized and contested.[9] The Federal Population Registration Law was being debated at the same time as the Federal Privacy Protection Law, and, as we shall see below, the crystallization of a new privacy consciousness in conjunction with this debate led the Bundestag to reject the national ID number and the associated plan for a national population information system. By contrast, the Population Registration Framework Law (Melderechtsrahmengesetz), which was ultimately approved in 1980, was informed by the principles of the new privacy law, and it sought, at least in principle, if not always in practice, to establish an economy of informational parsimony within the public administration rather than to promote the generalized, relatively unrestricted exchange of personal information.

The first two-thirds of this chapter use the Federal Population Registration Law to examine the development of state surveillance capacity and the conflicts surrounding access to information contained in these registries. However, these debates do not directly address the way that privacy was conceptualized at the time. At the turn of the 1970s, all of the federal states (the *Länder*) were developing information and planning systems, and the relationship between planning, integrated data processing, and privacy was much more direct at the state level than was the case at the federal level. In the final section of the chapter, I will focus on developments in the state of Hesse, which in 1970 adopted the world's first computer privacy law.[10] Here I will argue that contemporary efforts to think through the problems resulting from the perceived loss of control over the disclosure and use of personal information in integrated data processing systems led to the reformulation of privacy in terms of a systematic counterlogic to the logic of data integration that had inspired these state-level information and planning systems.

The National ID Number: Multiple Paths to a Unique Identifier

The idea of population enumeration was not peculiarly German. It arose in modern societies in conjunction with both the desire to identify, mobilize, and monitor individual members of the population and the attendant need to develop technologies that would permit record keeping on such a scale. In West Germany, the idea had been in the air since at least the beginning of the 1960s, and the introduction of service numbers by the defense ministry in 1960 and of the pension insurance number in 1964 led the government to again "take up an old plan, which has been discussed for years at the state and federal level."[11] Although interior ministry officials were aware of Nazi experiments with national ID numbers, their initiatives in this area owed more to contemporary needs than to institutional continuities.[12]

As a mechanism for identifying the individual members of a population, the alphanumeric combination of name and date of birth was both less efficient than numbers alone and not sufficiently unique to preclude confusion: thirteen of the most common family names accounted for 5 percent of the total population; a quarter of the male population was denominated by ten personal names; and 5 percent of all men answered to "Hans."[13]

In the first half of the 1960s, a national ID number was regarded both as the key to capturing the efficiencies of integrated data processing and as a solution to the problems caused by the proliferation of enumeration systems as business and each branch and level of government sought to automate their own record-keeping activities. As Ministerialrat Wolf von Dreising, who at the time headed the administrative law and organization department in the interior ministry, explained in 1964, "Advancing automatic data processing is forcing the administration to employ ID numbers. However, in order to avoid placing excessive demands on the citizenry by permitting the introduction of different numbers in different branches of the public administration, it is essential to reach timely agreement on a single ID number."[14] However, official understanding of the purpose of the number would evolve substantially between 1964 and the turn of the 1970s.

The issue was complex, and attitudes were divided along several axes: Who was interested in such a number? For what purpose? How great was this interest? How would the number have to be structured? Who would be responsible for assigning it? At what age?[15] Differences with respect to all of these questions should cast doubt on the idea that population enumeration was somehow inherent in the logic of bureaucratic modernization.

The Bundespost and the Bundesbahn were keenly interested in using such a number to automate payroll for their hundreds of thousands of employees, and the former hoped that a national ID number would substantially reduce the cost of disbursing pension payments, especially if the number were also adopted as the pension number.[16] Although the federal and state finance ministries were also interested in such a number for both the automation of their own payroll systems and the rationalization of the tax administration, for the latter purpose the number had to be structured differently than that being contemplated by the interior ministry. The Federal Criminal Police, on the other hand, did not feel that the number was necessary or useful since it did not engage in the kind of mass data processing that made the number so valuable for other agencies.

It was also argued that a national ID number would bring greater efficiency to the private sector. Although banks and insurance companies engaged in the greatest amount of routine data processing, the Economics Ministry reported that neither was particularly interested in a national ID number, most likely because they had already established their own account numbers. On the other hand, the Committee for Efficient Administration (Ausschuss für Wirtschaftliche Verwaltung) welcomed the national ID number for several reasons: it would rationalize the personnel administration of large and mid-sized firms, make the exchange of information both between branches of the same company and between these firms and the social insurance funds more efficient, and accelerate the broader rationalization of economic life.

The states were also of a divided mind on the issue. While one administrative expert in Hamburg dismissed the idea of an identification number that would be used by all branches of the public administration as an example of administrative perfectionism run amok, the president of the Hamburg police welcomed the idea, but argued that it would have to be flanked both by an obligation to carry the recently introduced national ID card, which would have to bear the ID number, and by the fingerprinting of the entire population to ensure that the physical bearer of the card was in fact the person identified by the number.[17]

There were also complications with local government. Local government was at the forefront of the automation of public administration in the 1960s. By the end of 1967, approximately 120 cities were already using electronic data processing to maintain their population registries and automate a growing number of administrative tasks.[18] Like most federal officials, the Kommunale Gemeinschaftsstelle für Verwaltungsvereinfachung, a professional group devoted to making local government more economical and efficient, regarded the proliferation of isolated systems and their associated identifiers as the most pressing obstacle to further rationalization. However, unlike federal officials, they were less interested in a national ID number than in "ensur[ing] that a uniform ID number [can be] introduced *in each city*" (emphasis added).[19] While a law facilitating the introduction of local ID numbers would have enabled the cities to move ahead with the development of integrated information systems, this would have made it more difficult to later introduce an ID number that could serve as a unique identifier at the national level. Conversely, if the cities were forced to wait for the introduction of a national ID number, the inevitable delays would slow down the introduction of electronic data processing at the local level.

There was also the question of whether the civil registries, the social insurance funds, or the population registries were to be responsible for assigning the numbers. The choice depended in part on the prior decision as to whether the number was to be issued at birth or when the person entered the labor market—a decision that itself depended on determining the primary purpose of the number.[20] Although discussion temporarily ground to a halt in 1966 because the states were unwilling to bear the costs of implementing a national ID number, the looming delay brought new urgency to an old problem. While this situation made it more tempting than ever for the cities to forge ahead with their own ID numbers, this would have made it impossible to solve the problem that von Dreising was coming to see as being of "decisive significance" for the entire project: the unique identification of each and every member of the population.[21]

In late 1967 federal, state, and local tax authorities agreed to introduce what they called a preliminary ID number for their own use. Since such a number would have effectively precluded the later establishment of a single, national ID number, the interior ministry was forced to act, and ministry officials promised to introduce a corresponding law by the summer of 1968.[22] But what ministry officials actually proposed was very different from both what had been discussed in 1964 and from what local government expected and desired.

The plan that was presented in April 1968 still focused on the use of the ID number to capture the efficiencies of integrated data processing. "The possibilities of electronic data processing," it noted, "can only be fully exhausted if a closed system [that is, one that embraced the entire public administration] is constructed, which permits the networking of the individual subsystems and communication between them." However, the most important precondition for the construction of such a network was the unambiguous identification of each and every member of the population. This, in turn, depended on ensuring that every member of the population was enumerated, that no one was assigned more than one number, that no number was assigned to multiple individuals, and that the number itself was permanent and unalterable. The fact that the number was also to make evident the sex of the bearer gave rise to discussions—half bemused, half genuinely perplexed—of what was to be done with the ID numbers of people who underwent sex change operations. Officials also wondered whether or not the inclusion of the date of birth might render the number unacceptable to the female population. Such a network would make it unnecessary for persons to register their departure with local officials whenever they moved. The fact of their settlement would be automatically communicated to the registry office in their previous residence—and the personal information held by the registries would automatically follow them as they moved. In this way, the backwards reporting system that had been established in 1938 would be reconstructed in electronic form. The plan also pushed the logic of efficiency and data integration to its ultimate consequence in anticipating that the national ID number would replace both the pension insurance and tax numbers and serve as the serial number for the national ID card.[23] Although the transparency and accessibility of the population was regarded primarily as the precondition for capturing the efficiencies of integrated data processing, these modernizing ambitions would ultimately prove to be the undoing of the interior ministry plan.

This plan, which was conceived and introduced under the grand coalition, appealed to both the conservative, state-centered worldview of such older civil servants as von Dreising and the more democratically minded, but technocratically oriented members of the younger generation, such as Egon Hölder, who in 1969 would become head of the interior ministry department responsible for organization, rationalization, and automation in the federal government.[24] Within the governing coalition itself, there was both conflict and ample room for collaboration between those technocratic, modernizing civil servants, whose enthusiasm for planning was limited to measures intended to consolidate the existing social order by promoting administrative efficiency and economic growth, and those who hoped that planning would ultimately lead to the transformation of bourgeois society.[25] These shared concerns were also evident in the information and planning systems that were being constructed at the turn of the 1970s in all of the states, including those governed by the conservative parties.

The proposed system would have enhanced the surveillance capacity of the state in three ways: it would have reinstituted the universal backward reporting system that had collapsed at the end of the war;[26] the connection of the national ID number to ID cards and passports would have further intensified the administrative power generated by the state monopoly over the legitimate means of identification, which had been established by the introduction in 1950 of a national ID card;[27] and, as we shall shortly see, the use of the population registration system to create a national population registry would have enhanced the ability of the state to locate specific individuals and bring all relevant administrative information to bear on their governance.

Although the initial draft law proposed a national ID number "for the economical organization of administrative activity and as precondition for integrated data processing in the public administration,"[28] the Kommunale Gemeinschaftsstelle was horrified by the ministry's proposal. Not only would it require the creation at the state and federal level of an expensive and entirely redundant administrative apparatus to issue and administer the numbers; parts of the draft were so controversial, the organization argued, that there was no chance that it would be approved in the foreseeable future. This made the Kommunale Gemeinschaftsstelle regret even more its earlier decision to postpone its own plan for a preliminary ID number. Since most of the requisite information was held at the local level, the organization argued that those communities that had already automated their registries could immediately distribute ID numbers at virtually no additional cost.[29]

In January 1968, the administration had not said precisely what might be done with the information to be held in the proposed state population registries, and in the interim discussion had largely been limited to their role in promoting the efficient use of electronic data processing. This changed at the beginning of 1969, when officials began to argue that the personal information that would have to be collected to assign the ID number could also be used for administrative purposes.[30] By July 1969, the theoretical possibility of using the ID number and population registry data in this way had coalesced into a concrete plan to create an integrated population information or database system (an *integriertes Einwohnerdatenbanksystem* or *Einwohner-Informationssystem*).[31] This transformation and expansion of the purpose of the proposed integrated population information system, whose development coincided with the concretization of the plan to create a national database or database network for social planning purposes, also made it clear that the population registration system could no longer be considered exclusively a matter of policing, and it reflected the fact that the registries were being transformed into a service agency whose responsibility for providing the civilian administration with the population information needed to carry out its tasks could no longer be seen as something secondary or ancillary to its security functions.[32]

This new function, however, did not obviate the original role of the proposed number in enhancing administrative efficiency. In the past, the absence of a unique identifier and the problems involved in combining

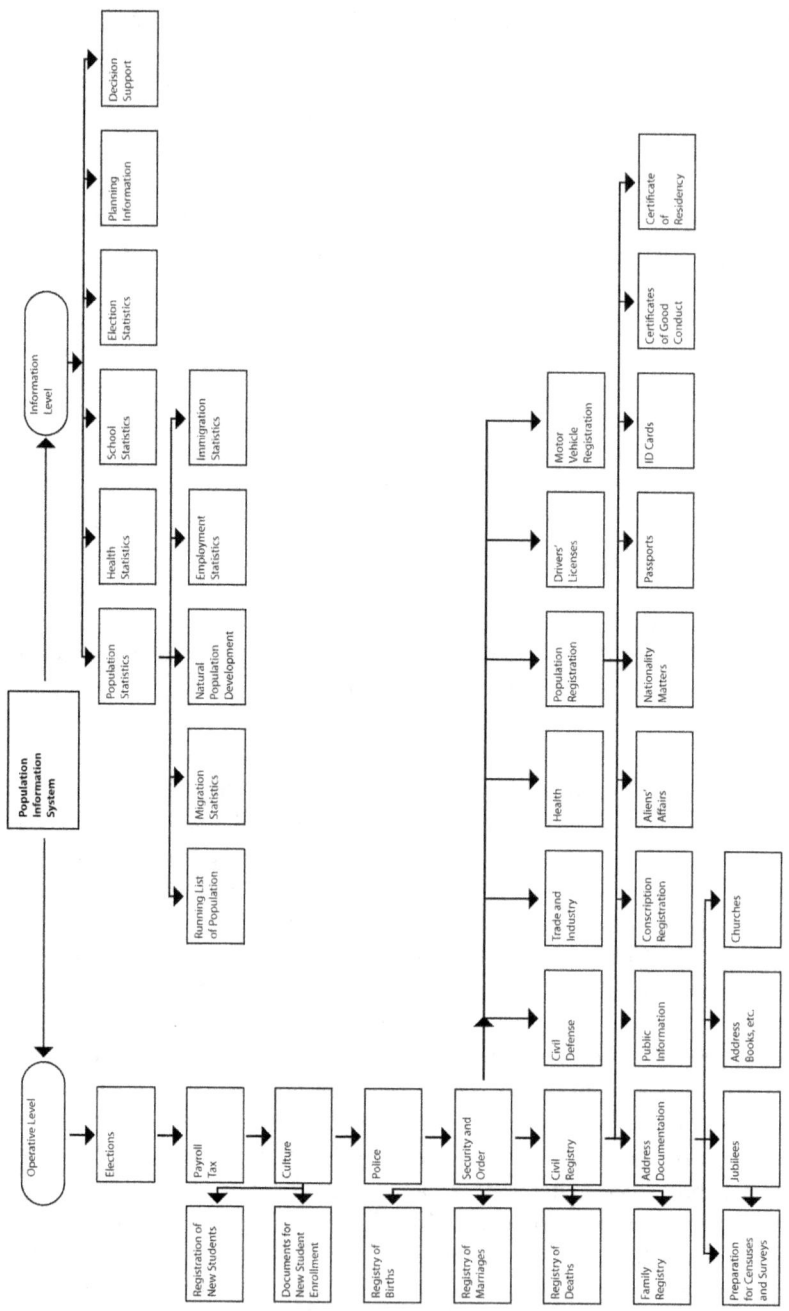

Figure 1.1. Population information system flowchart. Source: Bundesministerium des Innern, ed., *Personenkennzeichen. Meldewesen, Datenverarbeitung, Datenschutz*, (=*betrifft*, vol. 7, 1971), 17.

and synchronizing specialized registries had multiplied the labor and cost involved in collecting the same data in multiple places and keeping it up to date. The magnitude of the problem becomes even clearer once we take account of the fact that—as was widely estimated—registry data on 40 percent of the population had to be updated each year. Ultimately, the local population registries were chosen as the core of the proposed information system because they already held 90 percent of the relevant information and were the primary site at which changes to this information were registered. The ID number promised to enhance the efficiency of the public administration by facilitating the exchange of information among different branches of the administration and eliminating the redundant information collection activities by different offices, while the use of the number as a "universal reference number" to file and retrieve paperwork promised to make the interaction between the public and the administration less burdensome.

The first draft of the Federal Population Registration Law was completed in April 1970, and a revised version was approved by the cabinet in May 1971.[33] The law was explicitly conceived as an information law. Its first article stated that the task of registry officials is "to collect, administer and make available to other offices—unless otherwise specified by law—the personal information on every resident that is needed for the lawful fulfillment of public obligations. The exchange of personal information is to be encouraged and facilitated (*ist zu fördern*)." The law also authorized the exchange of personal information with other branches of the public administration "to the extent that access to this information is necessary to fulfill their responsibilities," a problematic formulation that left it up to the office requesting the data to determine precisely what its responsibilities were and whether the requested information was, in fact, necessary to carry them out.[34] However, as the preamble to the law explained, information exchange within the public administration was to be limited only by the available technology and the information needs of the public administration.[35]

Figure 1.1 shows the many ways in which the information contained in the integrated population information system could be used for administrative and statistical purposes.

This vision was realized to a large degree by the state-level population information system rolled out by Rhineland-Pfalz in 1971. This system, which made use of an identifier constructed according to the same schema as the anticipated national ID number, was the most complex such system in the Federal Republic and the first to make widespread use of telematics.[36] Figure 1.2 shows the lines connecting the main state computer center in Mainz to the state, regional, and local police offices, as well as to

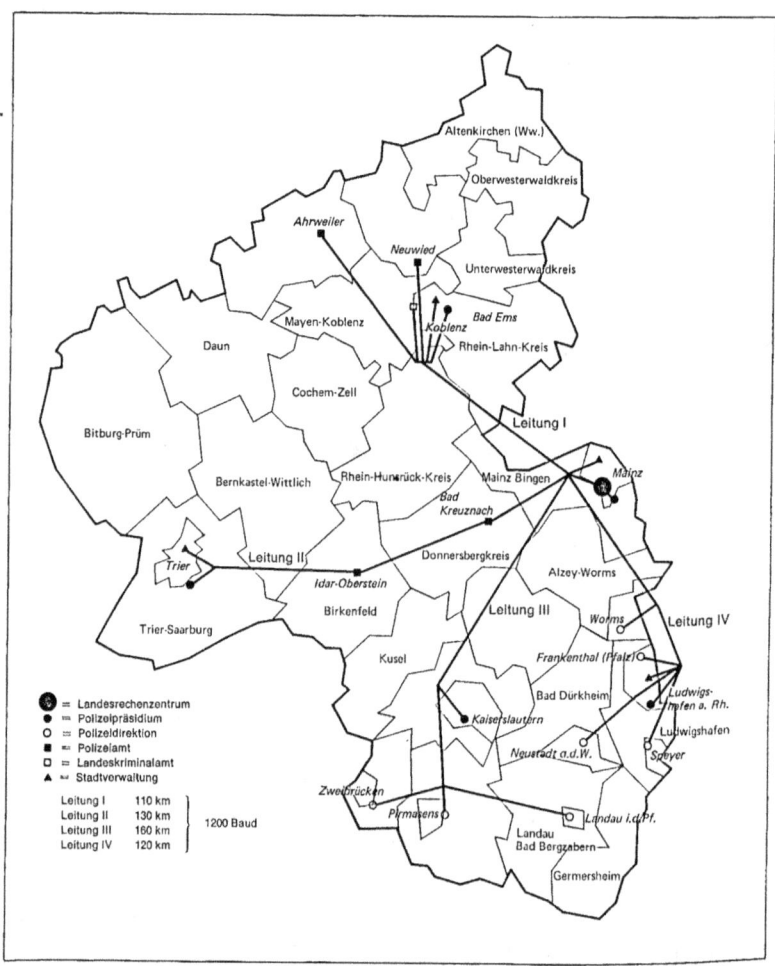

Figure 1.2. Automation of the population information system in Rhineland-Pfalz. Source: Joachim Stöckle, "Die Automation des Einwohnermeldwesens im Rahmen eines Datenfernarbeitungssystems," *IBM-Nachrichten* 21 (October 1971): 899.

selected local government offices. But Rhineland-Pfalz was precocious, and the nationwide automation of the population registries stretched out across the 1970s.

Genscher hoped to begin assigning the ID numbers in 1973. However, from the very beginning the population registration law raised privacy concerns, and the subsequent entanglement of the population registration and privacy protection laws soon revealed this hope to be an illusion.

The New Privacy Consciousness and the Rejection of the National Population Information System

In a 1971 booklet written to generate support for the proposal, the interior ministry explained that the welfare state depended on detailed knowledge of the individual members of the population in order to meet the growing demands placed upon it:

> New services and measures are constantly demanded from the public administration. In every area its tasks become more complex and complicated. The material that forms the basis for mastering these tasks is information regarding conditions in the country and in many cases information pertaining to the circumstances of the citizen. To the same extent that citizens demand individualized services, the administration is forced to obtain individualized data in order to satisfy these demands. This consequence cannot be avoided.[37]

Both the officials who drafted the law and the major computer companies were confident that more information and better technologies for collecting and analyzing it would lead to better government, and the cover illustration of the booklet showed a punched tape, which, as it unwound, gradually morphed into a long parade of people joyously celebrating the promise of the better life that was expected to follow from computerization and rationalization of government (figure 1.3). To sell the idea to the public, the administration pointed out that a number of other countries—ranging from the Benelux and Scandinavian countries to Israel and South Korea—already used such numbers. They even approached East German officials to inquire about the possibility of establishing a common enumeration system in case of future reunification, though nothing ever came of this proposal.[38] In fact, the public initially viewed the ID number quite positively.[39] However, at the turn of the 1970s both public debate and the work of the Bundestag was increasingly shaped by an understanding of the specific issues raised by integrated information systems.

In the spring of 1969, just as the first draft of the law was being circulated, the Bundestag passed a resolution asking that the administration ensure that the use of new information technologies for the collection of personal information by state and local government did not encroach upon the private sphere.[40] The initial draft of the population registration law had stipulated that the processing of personal information should not infringe upon the legitimate privacy concerns (*schutzwürdige Belange*) of the citizenry. However, it did not define these interests or explain why they were important or what would constitute an infringement. In the Bundestag, Genscher initially tried to deflect concerns about the privacy implications of the ID number. He claimed that the linkage of personal in-

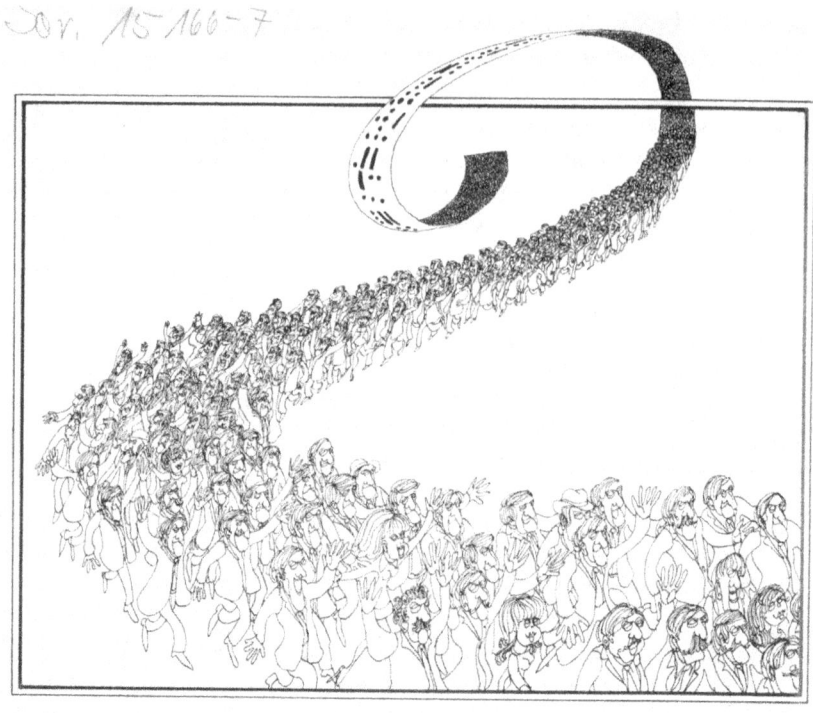

Figure 1.3. Databases are matters of political concern—and rightly so. They lead to better political decisions. Source: Cover image for Bundesministerium des Innern, ed., *Personenkennzeichen. Meldewesen, Datenverarbeitung, Datenschutz* (1971). Artwork by Hans-Georg Rauch.

formation from diverse sources was already possible using manual methods, but that it had simply not been economical to do so in the past. It was computerization, he insisted, not the ID number, that had altered the economics of such linkages. The only real danger to individual privacy was the misuse of the computer—something that could already be prevented through proper safeguards.[41] Despite these disclaimers, representatives from all parties remained concerned about the impact of electronic data processing on the private sphere, and in October 1970 Genscher was forced to agree to introduce a law to protect against the potential privacy harms of the ID number. This was the origin of what would become the Federal Privacy Protection Law, and from this point onward population registration and privacy protection were joined at the hip.[42]

There were several aspects of the population registration law that proved to be particularly thorny. The first related to precisely what information was to be included in the standard personal data record to be maintained by the local population registries. Public attention quickly came to focus on a draft version of a standard record that contained some two hundred fields. Although this was often invoked as an egregious example of bureaucratic "data hunger," a number of the fields were mutually exclusive (e.g., married, widowed, divorced, and so on), while many other fields simply contained the office and file number needed to document other pieces of information (e.g., the civil registry office and entry number in the birth registry needed to document date of birth; that is, they were metadata, rather than data itself). One official later explained in exasperation that a sample had shown that only thirty-two pieces of information were held on average for unmarried persons, "not 200!," and that only forty-eight pieces were held on average for a married man with two children.[43] Nevertheless, the approval at the end of 1974 of this standard data record went some way toward meeting privacy concerns because this exhaustive enumeration served as a bar to the discretionary collection of even more information.[44]

The second had to do with public access to registry information. Here, the draft law essentially codified established practice. It allowed anyone to obtain the name, address, and date at which a person moved into or out of a residence. It also allowed persons to obtain additional information, including the proposed ID number, date and place of birth, previous names and addresses, nationality, occupation and marital status, if they could demonstrate a legitimate interest in it. Conversely, it permitted individuals to block access to this data if they could demonstrate a legitimate interest in doing so. Officials claimed that this graduated access to, and protection of, registry information corresponded to both the practical needs of social and commercial life and the sensitivity of the different kinds of information.[45]

Third, since state population registration laws would have to be amended to implement the federal law, this provided an opportunity to revisit both the hotel registration requirement and the related ID card and carry obligations, all of which had been a matter of dispute in the 1950s.[46] Until this point, security issues had played only a peripheral role in the drafting of the population registration law. However, the May 1972 offensive of the RAF (chapter 6), the arrest of many of the original members of the group in June, and the September attack on the Munich Olympics made terrorism and domestic security the top priority of the administration. It was precisely at this moment that officials first began to speak obliquely of the "security aspects" of the population registration law. By the time that the national criminal information system was approved in January 1972, security officials had become far more interested in the national ID number than they had been in the 1960s, and these considerations ensured that the law became an integral component of the June 1972 Program for the Domestic Security of the Federal Republic.[47]

Public concerns about the privacy implications of the proposed population registry network were also heightened by the expansion of police surveillance in the first half of the 1970s and by uncertainty about the kinds of information that might be contained in such integrated systems. In a 1973 article entitled "100445301111," *Der Spiegel* speculated that the ID number might enable the state to bring together information on income, educational history (including such things as grades, IQ test results, and teacher evaluations), ethnicity and race, criminal history, participation in demonstrations and other political activities, unconfirmed (and unverifiable) accusations, speculation, and subjective judgments by the police and intelligence agencies, psychological dispositions and job skills, reading habits, and vacations, as well as medical and reproductive information and information from labor offices, municipal utilities, motor vehicle registration bureaus, hospitals, schools and universities, and the social insurance funds. The prospect that the ID number might be used in the private sector opened up the possibility that such a system would be able to draw in information from credit reporting agencies, travel agencies, mail order companies, dating and marriage counseling services, and banks. Young women went abroad for abortions for fear that their actions would somehow find their way into police computers and later come back to haunt them. As the jurist Ruprecht Kamlah, the author of an important early study of American privacy law, explained, "The only reason the state is not omniscient is because many of its agencies are unaware of the information possessed by other agencies." What people feared was that the proposed ID number would make it possible to link together "at the push of a button" the discrete pieces of personal information that had been gathered from diverse sources for utterly disparate purposes to form an extremely problematic "profile" of or "dossier" on the individual and then instantaneously disseminate this information to other persons, who could then use it for all kinds of illegitimate and nefarious ends.[48]

These concerns had already been voiced by the *Frankfurter Allgemeine Zeitung*, which in 1969 had observed that one city of 500,000 already maintained 126 manual registers: "Now [the citizen] will have to reckon with the possibility that, by means of a 'central computer' [and the proposed ID number], all of the 126 agencies that maintain these registries will be able to acquire a full mosaic picture of his person." The newspaper warned that such computer networks "could make the person transparent to an unbearable degree."[49]

One of the most penetrating—and hilarious—critiques of such state-sponsored population surveillance came from Diethart Kerbs, at the time a lecturer at the Pädagogische Hochschule in Berlin-Lankwitz. At Christmas 1973, Kerbs distributed a mock questionnaire from an imaginary agency with an ominous-sounding name: the Federal Bureau for the Electronic Registration of Personal Information (Bundesanstalt für datenmäßige Personenerfassung).[50] The directions explained that, according to a recent decision by the Bundestag, every citizen would soon receive an individual control number that would guarantee the total registration—in computer-compatible format—of information pertaining to his or her personal circumstances for the purpose of establishing a Federal Resident Dossier, which would be available to the police and security agencies "at all hours and without delay." The defense of the free, democratic constitutional order, the questionnaire continued in language that was redolent of the categorical assertiveness of the Nazis in security matters, required the "total informational transparency" of each and every citizen. While the optimal control of the individual would be ensured through the complete collaboration of all public and private entities that collected personal information, the flier explained, the corresponding transparency of the state for its citizens would have to take a back seat for the foreseeable future. Persons who opposed the undertaking would, like Jews in the Third Reich, have to wear a cloth "A" (for anarchist) on their clothing, and those who refused would be sent to a work camp.

The questions ranged from the basic (name, address, family members) to the expected (Do you take drugs? Do you own books by Marx, Engels, Lenin, Mao, Brecht, or other authors hostile to the democratic state?) to the playfully subversive (Are you homosexual/heterosexual? If yes, why? If not, why not?). But it also contained a number of questions that had in fact been asked of politically suspect applicants for civil service jobs as a result of the 1972 Radicals Resolution: Do you live in a communal residence (*Wohngemeinschaft*)? Have you ever actively participated in strikes? Did you ever run for student office in college? Are you a member of a political organization? If so, which? Have you ever been the subject of a police investigation? Have you ever hit a police officer? Do you frequently sign resolutions? Have you ever associated with anti-capitalist persons or organizations? If so, which? Many of these questions were intrusive and their answers intrinsically prejudicial (as they were intended to be), and there was ample reason to be concerned about the collection of such information by a state that was fundamentally suspicious of so many of its citizens.

Although there was strong support for privacy legislation in all of the major parties, there were also persistent lines of cleavage within them. Both the FDP and the Christian Democrats had to balance between business wings that were concerned about both the costs of complying with privacy legislation and its implications for the way they did business and those wings of their parties concerned primarily with privacy and civil liberties. The general public did not become broadly interested in the question until later in the decade.

In light of continuing criticism, in May 1974 the Bundestag domestic affairs committee held a public hearing on the draft Federal Privacy Protection Law and the privacy provisions of the Federal Population Registration Law. The testimony at this hearing pitted two important values — efficiency and privacy — against each other. Echoing the interior ministry's 1971 booklet, the Kommunale Gemeinschaftsstelle linked the growing need for personal information to the changing nature of the state and the expanding scope of its activity. "The more that the center of gravity of the tasks for which the administration is responsible is displaced from acts of sovereign control and the protection of individual rights (*Hoheits- und Eingriffsverwaltung*) to the provision of social services and the promotion of individual welfare (*Daseinsvorsorge*)," the organization argued, "the more that increasingly detailed information is required—information that may also reach into the intimate sphere of the citizen." For the cities to fulfill their planning and social service responsibilities, "the unrestricted provision of the personal information required by local government is—to the extent that this information is necessary for the lawful discharge of public functions—indispensable." Ensuring that registry information was not improperly accessed and used, the organization concluded, contributed far more to the protection of the private sphere than the statutory limitation of the information available to the administration.[51]

Others, however, were more critical of the population registration law. Kamlah, for example, complained that it gave registry officials virtually unlimited authority to collect practically any information that might conceivably be needed by any office for one purpose or another. Part of what Kamlah was trying to do was to gain acceptance for the then novel notion that the collection of personal information by the state had to be explicitly authorized by law because it infringed upon the liberty and privacy of the individual and that it could, therefore, no longer be understood as a purely administrative activity that had no impact on the rights of the person. Consequently, he warned that the problems of the public administration "cannot be solved by turning the principles of the rule of law on their heads."[52]

These discussions of the privacy implications of the proposed population information system ultimately moved the Bundestag to make substantial modifications to the draft Federal Population Registration Law.[53] The domestic affairs committee declined to revisit the provision of the law that made the agency requesting personal information responsible for determining the legality of its request. However, in June 1972 the interior ministry decided against including hotel registration and identity verification requirements in the law.[54] In October 1974 ministry officials decided to remove the ID number from the list of data that could be made available to other private individuals. In November 1974 the domestic affairs committee decided to strike the programmatic passage encouraging the exchange of personal information.[55] And the standard record was, as we have seen, ratified at the end of 1974.[56]

The administration expected that these were the last changes that would have to be made in order to secure parliamentary approval and that it was just a matter of waiting until the Federal Privacy Protection Law had been finalized so that both pieces of legislation could be approved by the Bundestag at the same time. However, the most important development did not come until May 1976, when the Bundestag legal affairs committee unexpectedly came out against the law. What sense did it make, the committee asked, to approve a privacy protection law if its stated goals were going to be undermined by the unrestricted exchange and integration of personal information that would follow upon the introduction of a national ID number?[57]

This decision implicitly bundled together concerns about humanism, the invasion of privacy, and efficiency, and the proposed Federal Population Registration Law ultimately faltered because the legislature had grown concerned about the privacy implications of the very data linkage mechanisms on which the promise of the information revolution in government rested.[58] As one official explained in a post mortem, "We have of late become increasingly cognizant of the dangers associated with the ID number, whereas in past years the claims of the federal interior ministry and the states regarding both the rationalizing effect [of the number] and the needs of social planners were, unfortunately, accepted uncritically." This was due, at least in part, he argued, to the fact that the same division of the interior ministry that was responsible for the rationalization and efficiency of the federal administration was also responsible for drafting the law to limit the extent to which the new technology could be used for this purpose. This official suggested that the national ID number was at this point being pursued primarily because of its value for domestic security, and he wondered "whether [further] rationalization in this domain is politically tenable if it leads to the creation of more centralized power, which cannot remain without influence on the rights of the individual and the structure of the administration."[59] Although the administration contested the committee's reasoning, the decision was a political disaster, and interior ministry officials seemed to be at a loss with regard to how to proceed. But the administration had too much invested in the undertaking to simply let it drop, and the wave of terrorist acts that rolled across the country in 1977 (chapter 6) brought security issues to the forefront of public attention—and, in so doing, gave new life to the population registration law.

Retreat from Nirvana: The Population Registration Framework Law

In the winter of 1977-78, the interior ministry circulated a new version of the population registration law. Although it no longer included the national ID number, whose absence appeared to mark the abandonment of the plan to create a national population information system, the law, which had been drafted against the background of the events of German Autumn, sought in a number of ways to enhance the value of the registries for the police and intelligence agencies. It required the states to establish electronic address registries for their respective populations. In addition, not only did it permit the states to store additional information in these registries; it also allowed the interior ministry—with the approval of the Bundesrat—to require the states to include additional information.[60]

These provisions opened the door to the re-creation at the state level of the population information system that had been the heart of the Federal Population Registration Law. Moreover, at that very moment the Bundestag was debating the introduction of a new, machine-readable, counterfeit-proof ID card (chapter 7). If the states had chosen (or been required) to store information on these cards in their address registries, this would have permitted the linkage of the overlapping bodies of information held in the address and ID card registries and enabled the police and the intelligence agencies to use the serial number of the card as an ersatz national ID number to access the state registries. This was one of the flash points in the interlinked debate over the population registration and ID card laws.

Lastly, the draft also included a number of measures to ensure that the police would be better able to determine the actual location of any individual at any time. These included the nationwide introduction of the hotel registration requirement (as well as the identity verification and attendant carry obligations), the reintroduction of the landlord countersignature on the population registration forms of their tenants, and the requirement that persons register with the police whenever they moved out of an apartment.[61] This draft aroused widespread opposition, especially after the Federal Privacy Protection Law went into effect at the beginning of 1978, and Gerhart Baum withdrew it shortly after he became interior minister in June of that year.

Even though the programmatic statement that "the exchange of personal information is to be encouraged and facilitated" had been dropped from the draft law in 1974, the mission of the registries was still defined as "collect[ing], administer[ing], and mak[ing] available to other offices—unless otherwise specified by law—the personal information on every resident needed for the lawful fulfillment of public obligations." A number of influential privacy advocates argued that the only way to limit the linkage and exchange of personal information was to restrict the registries to their traditional responsibilities and prevent them from becoming a multifunctional data pool for the public administration.[62] This was the strategy that was adopted by the Population Registration Framework Law (Melderechtsrahmengesetz), which was approved by the Bundestag in April 1980. This law thus became, together with Book Ten of the Social Insurance Code, the first law to apply the principles of the Federal Privacy Protection Law to a specific domain of data processing in the public administration.[63]

While the main goal of the original version of the population registration law had been to rationalize the public administration, the Population Registration Framework Law gave priority to privacy protection—though with important limitations.[64] The new law charged the population registries with the more narrowly limited responsibility of collecting the information needed to determine the identity and location of the population. Instead of authorizing the collection of all personal information that might be of use to the public administration, the new law exhaustively enumerated the specific pieces of information that the registries were authorized to collect. Although it permitted the registries to collect the information that was required to implement certain federal laws (including elections, taxes, and conscription), it also specified that the information collected to carry out these laws could be used only for these purposes, rather than for general administrative or planning purposes, that this information had to be stored separately from the information the registries collected on their own authority, and that these separate bodies of information could be linked together only to the extent that this was necessary to carry out these supplemental functions. Such compartmentalization was the antithesis of the vision of data integration that had underlain the original version of the Federal Population Registration Law.

The privacy implications of the Population Registration Framework Law were anything but clear. While the law permitted the states to use the registries to collect additional information needed to implement state laws, it did not contain any provisions that would have prevented the states from using this authority to effectively re-create the state-level population or address registries envisioned by earlier versions of the law.[65]

Moreover, although the original administration draft had required the registries to store the serial number of the new ID cards, this requirement was dropped from the final version of the law to ensure that it could not be "misused" as an ersatz national ID number. But the practical impact of this self-denying clause was unclear because many of the states still planned to require the population registries to store the serial number, even though this appeared to violate the intentions of the Bundestag.[66] Lastly, although this law prohibited the use of these serial numbers to access information held in computer databases, it allowed police and prosecutors to use them in precisely this way.[67]

"Sagt die Wahrheit ungeniert, ist am Arsche tätowiert"

The transparency project described in the preceding pages succeeded to a large degree. Even though the administration was forced to abandon its plan for a national population information system, the German population was much more legible to, and accessible by, the state at the end of the period under study here than it had been at the beginning. The automation of the local registries, their integration into state-level information and planning systems, and the expanding statistical information available to state and national governments steadily enhanced the ability of the state to reflexively monitor the activity of the population and make it—both individually and collectively—into the object of systematic control for both welfare and security purposes.

If the devolution of the population registries onto local government after 1945 and the subsequent struggle by the police to regain control over them had originally been little more than an administrative turf war, the census decision gave this dispute a new importance, and the issue was brought to a head in the 1980s by the drafting of a new state population registration law in Berlin in order to implement the changes required by the Population Registration Framework Law. After the census decision, the Berlin legislature asked Ernst Benda, who had retired from the Constitutional Court after the decision had been handed down, to assess the constitutionality of a proposal to reorganize the city's population registry, but to leave it under the overall authority of the police president. In his memorandum, Benda argued that population registration and policing were functionally distinct responsibilities and that, as long as the primary purpose of the police was to protect against and investigate crime, any balancing between privacy and security by the head of that agency would invariably be prejudiced in favor of the latter. Benda insisted that the decision on how best to balance between these conflicting goals was the proper responsibility of elected officials, not such appointed bureaucrats as the police president. The city administration ultimately followed his recommendation in creating a freestanding population registration office. This set in motion a nationwide trend to set up independent population registration offices, which were often rebranded in consumerist, neoliberal terms as "citizens' service bureaus" (*Bürgerämter*).[68]

By the middle of the 1980s, the developments described in the preceding pages were also beginning to leave their mark on German popular culture. One can get a sense of apprehension regarding the looming surveillance state from the rock singer Udo Lindenberg, who in 1985 released a cheeky song in which he parodied the virtues of the national ID number. He described the number as a convenient reminder "in case I forget my name"; it was "both practical and individual" and a perfect way to preserve one's unique identity in a sea of people named "Schmidt, Müller, Udo, Dave or Karl-Heinz." "That's why," the stanza concluded, "I'd rather be called D-4718161." But for all of the playful sarcasm that he poured—to a technomusical rhythm—on the ID number and the claims of greater convenience, in the final line Lindenberg insisted in a darker, more abrupt tone that it was no longer possible to dissemble, camouflage oneself, or evade the eye of the state. Everyone might as well go ahead and tell the truth about his or her administrative identity because—via the ID number and the databases to which it was linked—this information was virtually tattooed on the body: "*sagt die Wahrheit ungeniert, ist am Arsche tätowiert.*"[69]

However, the expansion and intensification of state surveillance was not a one-way process. It also gave rise to a multifaceted social movement that challenged this growth of administrative power in the name of personal privacy. In conjunction with a 2006 reform of the provisions of the Basic Law relating to the federal structure of the state, the federal government was given exclusive authority for the regulation of the population registration system. While the legislation of the 1960s and 1970s had envisioned a network of local population registries, the draft of a new Federal Population Registration Law circulated in 2007 provided for the creation of a centralized, national population registry; it would also have permitted the exchange of information between the registry and a large number of public agencies, including tax authorities, the police, and the intelligence agencies.[70] The effect would have been to create a population information system that was substantially more centralized and integrated than the one envisioned in the 1960s. However, this Christian Democratic proposal provoked strong opposition from both the Social Democrats and the FDP, and the centralist features were dropped from the draft.[71]

In 2012–13 a revised population registration law was finally adopted. The final readings of the law took place on 28 June 2012 as Germany was playing against Italy in the semifinal of the UEFA soccer championship, and the law was approved after a 57-second debate.[72] The most controversial provisions dealt with the use of registry information for commercial purposes. The original administration draft had prohibited the registries from providing basic identifying information if this was to be used for advertising purposes or by commercial information brokers. In the domestic affairs committee, the CDU and FDP pushed through a provision that allowed advertisers and commercial information brokers to obtain this information—including current address and name, which was important for identifying women who changed their names upon marriage—unless the individual opted out on an annual basis. The committee draft also permitted such businesses to use the registries to update information that they already held, though without giving individuals the opportunity to opt out. The administration was publicly embarrassed by both the process and the content of the amendment, and nearly 200,000 persons signed a protest petition under the slogan "My data is not for sale."[73] These objections were taken up by the Bundesrat, and the version that was ultimately approved in February 2013 dropped the conditional opt-out mechanism in favor of an explicit opt-in.[74]

The population registries are not the only large collection of personal information that has been an object of controversy in recent years. In 2009 the Bundestag approved the creation of a database (Elektronisches Entgeltnachweis or ELENA) to collect information on earnings, work history (including illness and work actions), and related social information on the entire economically active population. Widespread public opposition led the Merkel administration to abandon the program only eighteen months after it had begun operation.

But one should be wary of overestimating the limitations placed on police use of population registry information by federal privacy legislation. Although the privacy provisions of the 1980 Population Registration Framework Law prohibited the processing and exchange of personal information in the absence of specific legal authorization, such access was often authorized by other legislation, as we shall see in later chapters, and the limitations on the exchange and use of the personal information contained in the registries ultimately depended less on the protections afforded by the registry law itself than on such related legislation.

The upshot was that, as the civil liberties activist Udo Kauß wrote with respect to the debate over the national ID card law (chapter 7), the explicit prohibition of a central ID card registry "did not . . . prohibit anything that was not already—in another manner, though at the cost of enormous technical effort—a reality in the population registries and the technical infrastructure through which they are connected." As a result, the efforts of the privacy commissioners to prevent the creation of a national registry of personal information amounted to little more than tilting at windmills: "Rightfully endeavoring to prevent the creation of a central population registry, they sought to continue [in the debate over the national ID card] a confrontation that had already been lost in the domain where it should have properly been fought: the field of population registration."[75] In the end, therefore, legislative initiatives that were ostensibly designed to limit state population surveillance tended to authorize access to registry information—at least by some users for some purposes—as much as to restrict it.[76]

Integrated Data Processing and the Birth of Informational Privacy

Computers could store more information than the human mind could ever retain, process this information faster and with greater accuracy, and, at the push of a button, reassemble it in unlimited combinations. Orwell's Big Brother was often invoked to characterize the dangers associated with information systems of such superhuman dimensions. However, as we have seen, the most elemental functionality of integrated data processing was to bring together information that had been disclosed in one context and to make it available for use in new and often unanticipated contexts, and the root of the privacy problem was, I will argue, to be found less in the sheer amount of the information concentrated in such systems or the speed with which it was processed than in this integration effect and the prospect of unrestricted secondary use within such systems.[77]

At the time, the linkage between planning, information, and modernity was so compelling that, at least initially, privacy could hardly be conceived as a problem. Government agencies at every level held vast quantities of information on individual citizens. However, these card files and individual dossiers were organized to meet the administrative, regulatory, and revenue-generating needs of the agency that produced them; information pertaining to specific individuals could not be easily linked across agencies, aggregated and analyzed for planning purposes, or acted upon; and, as a result, each agency created more work for itself and for the public by collecting and maintaining all of the information needed to carry out its own duties. Integrated information systems promised to bring about a revolution in administrative practice: by linking across functional domains the discrete pieces of information pertaining to specific individuals, such systems promised to increase efficiency, reduce the amount of paperwork to be completed by the public, generate new insights and new information, and thereby transform information processing from a bureaucratic and financial burden into a political resource. In the words of a Siemens report describing the integrated information system that the company proposed for the state of Bavaria,

> the great advantages of electronic data processing can only be fully realized when the data and information that are accumulated in the different branches of the public administration are no longer separately registered and processed. Integrated data processing, in which data is stored only once and then made available to all other users, is the decisive factor for the efficient and functional use of such technology.... In such an integrated information system, administrative activity will be carried out, thanks to the practically unlimited capacity to record, process and disseminate information, in such a manner that the results of traditional administration will be generated more rapidly and economically, and a qualitatively new dimension will be brought to the process of decision making at every level of administration.[78]

What glimmered in the eyes of the proponents of such systems was, according to one critic,

> an unimaginably perfect information exchange ... in which every possible notation regarding every citizen inconspicuously comes together, fills up electronic file drawers, and can be called up at any time.... Today, the goal of every bureaucracy can only be—and, in fact, is already—to deposit in a central location all of the information that it has at its disposal and to then have it served back up for *every imaginable purpose* according to its needs. (Emphasis added)[79]

Even as the *Frankfurter Allgemeine Zeitung* warned about the dangers of Big Brother, the newspaper was confident that the new degree of data integration resulting from the introduction of a national ID number would enable planners to formulate a "broad panorama of rationally conceivable developmental possibilities for the needs of man."[80]

This was the informational program of West German high modernism—one that was not without plausibility or appeal. But the information sought by planners was to an overwhelming degree personal information. While many people regarded integrated information systems as the epitome of technological modernity and administrative rationality, others believed that the transparency effect of these linkages and the problems associated with the secondary use of information—that is, with the ability to make information that had originally been disclosed in a specific context for clearly defined purposes available to new users in different contexts "for every imaginable purpose"—represented a palpable threat to personal privacy and individual freedom.

Although it has received little attention, municipal government was a pioneer in the use of the new information technologies in the public administration, and in this area it was generally far ahead of the states, the federal government, and the social insurance funds. Local government offices were the primary point of contact between the citizen and the state; they were responsible for carrying out both their own administrative obligations and the growing number of tasks delegated to them by the state and federal governments; and they were, as a result, the first level of government to face the pressures caused by population growth, increased geographical mobility, the expanding welfare state, and the attendant need to engage in the "mass" processing of routine administrative data. The informational policies of the states depended on, and often sought to promote, the automation of local government because most of the data needed for state-level planning systems was generated by local administrative processes.[81]

By the turn of the 1970s, *Landesdatenbanken-* or *Landesinformationssysteme* were either being planned or constructed—parallel to the reform of the population registries—in every state.[82] Most of the state electronic data processing laws passed at the time established central data processing centers—which were often created within, or as adjuncts to, the state statistical offices—and regional data processing centers for local government. However, the real purpose of these laws was as much to coordinate the exchange of information among local governments, while channeling local data into these state-level systems, as it was to promote the automation of local government.

These laws proved to be unexpectedly controversial because data integration tended to collapse different levels, branches, and geographical regions of government and thereby upset the established constitutional balance of power between the executive and legislative branches, between the minister president and the state ministries, and between state and local government.[83] All of the conflicts over the relative merits of a centralized (Bavaria) or decentralized (North Rhineland-Westphalia, Schleswig-Holstein) organization of public sector data processing also arose in Hesse, where concerns over the loss of control over the information contained in such systems led to the passage of the world's first computer privacy law in 1970.

The Hessian law establishing a central state data processing office was introduced in May 1969.[84] It called for the establishment of both a state Central Data Processing Office (the Hessische Zentrale für Datenverarbeitung) and a set of regional centers to handle the data processing needs of local governments. The basic principle on which all such systems were based was that all of the administratively relevant information pertaining to specific individuals should be collected once and only once (most often the local level, where it was generated) and then stored in a single location, where it could then—thanks to fusion of computing and telecommunications technologies—be made available in up-to-date form on an as-needed basis to all other users, who would thus be in a position both to make use of this information and to update it in the course of their own administrative activity. Finance Minister Albert Osswald (SPD), who in 1969 succeeded Georg August Zinn as minister president, was the driving force behind the project.

There was a widespread fear that the new information and communication technologies would further aggravate existing informational and power asymmetries between the two branches of the government. Alfred Dregger, the head of the opposition CDU in the state, described the data pool to be assembled under the law as a "first-rate bastion of power," and he argued that the regional data processing centers should be communal institutions that operated on behalf of local, not state, government. There were demands that the legislature be given direct access to the information stored in the system; the Hessian League of Cities insisted that the law guarantee the autonomy of local self-government; and it was even proposed that local government be given the right to block the transfer of any of its information that was held in regional data processing centers.[85] But the only major change that was incorporated into the final version of the law was the provision that the constitutional right of local government to self-administration should not be infringed upon by the operation of the Central Data Processing Office.[86]

In contrast to Bavaria and other states, where debate remained focused on the efficient organization of data processing, privacy quickly emerged as a central concern in Hesse. Even before the second reading of the data processing law, the decision had been made to introduce a privacy protection law to counteract the dangers posed by the former.

The nexus between planning, integrated data processing, and privacy was illuminated in an ideal-typical manner in Hesse.[87] As Ulrich Dammann argued at the time, integrated data processing systems were nothing other than vast machines for violating the central principles of privacy protection law. However, the privacy dangers inherent in such systems were much more palpable at the state level, where the build-out of information and planning systems was proceeding apace, where such systems included the personal information generated by administrative processes at the local and state levels, and where it was easier, even without a national ID number, to connect information across functional domains.[88] At the macrolevel, such integration was the precondition for modeling complex, dynamic social processes. But the integration effect had very different implications at the microlevel, where the questions of transparency, power, and control were theorized in terms of personal privacy.[89]

In addition to the constitutional issues noted above, the plan to create a Hessian Central Data Processing Office also raised other concerns. Klaus Bresse, the director of the office, feared that such centers would lead the citizen to see "himself faced with an anonymous robot bureaucracy, whose inner mechanism he cannot comprehend," and he worried that this lack of understanding would transform the latent tension between the citizen and the administration into a general crisis of trust. The debate over both the data processing centers and the proposed privacy protection law was littered with references to Orwell. As one politician wryly noted, not only had the data center law created a Big Brother in the form of the Central Data Processing Office; it had also created—in the form of the regional centers—a series of Little Brothers. However, the most visceral manifestation of this crisis of trust was the sense that individuals were losing control over their personal information because information whose disclosure might have been appropriate or necessary in one context was—without the knowledge of the individual and the ability to control such secondary usage—being made accessible in other contexts, where its involuntary disclosure might be less appropriate, embarrassing, or even harmful. This unease was particularly evident, Bresse explained, in those cases where "the citizen has the feeling that the private matters that he must constantly disclose to the bureaucracy no longer remain in the files of this specific office and of its employees, whom he knows, but are rather broadly disseminated via the channels of data processing or even become public."[90]

One of the best early analyses of the privacy problem and its relation to social planning came from Osswald, who argued that in highly differentiated industrial societies, which were characterized by the increasing interdependence of social systems, the linkage, coordination, and orientation of complex social processes in relation to an overarching plan was the precondition for rational decision-making.[91] The preceding years, he noted, had seen the frenetic application of electronic data processing for the automation of routine administrative tasks. However, building a planning system required that electronic data processing be employed in novel ways because modeling these interdependencies depended on both the linkage of personal information across functional domains and more intensive communication and cooperation among the different departments of the public administration, whose internal structure increasingly emulated the complexity of society itself.[92] Information, he insisted, was becoming just as important as money as a medium for steering social processes. "The reality of the goals and the quality of the decisions that determine the path to their realization," Osswald explained, "depend . . . on the quality of the underlying information . . . . The solution of the information problem [is] the condition faced by every government planning system when it is a question of mastering tasks of the future."[93] While the expanding informational needs of the state were to be met through the new state data processing system, its analytical and prognostic needs were to be met by the Hessian Planning Information and Analysis System, whose mission was to model the complex relations between different social (sub)systems.[94]

Since planning systems displayed an intrinsic tendency toward the total registration of individual, Osswald argued that there was a real danger that the accumulation of so much information in a single system would render the individual citizen even more defenseless against the state and that the transformation of the citizen into the object of manipulation and control by a technocratic bureaucracy would undermine the democratic process.[95] But a privacy protection law was also necessary for a second reason. Echoing Bresse, Osswald explained that, in the past, the public agencies to which the individual had disclosed his personal information as the condition for enjoying public services had possessed only a limited functional and geographic competence; the information that they collected was held only in paper form; and each agency had a more or less proprietary attitude towards its own files. These features ensured a modicum of privacy and served as a bar to the "omniscience" of the state. However, the storage of personal information in integrated information systems inverted this calculus. Now the individual citizen could no longer tell who was accessing his personal information or for what purpose it was being used, while the protections previously offered by the social and geographical proximity between the citizen and the agents of the state were being eroded by the ability to transmit data over large distances. As a result, Osswald concluded, "it has become possible in principle to peer into the private sphere and manipulate the information gained thereby."[96]

If, as David Lyon has argued, "all societies that are dependent on communication and information technologies for administrative and control processes are surveillance societies," then it was precisely at this moment that West Germany was becoming a surveillance society.[97] The question was how to meet the resulting dangers. The administration had originally considered inserting into the data processing center law provisions calling for the appointment of a "trust commissioner" (*Beauftragter für Vertrauensschutz*) to watch over the operation of the system and ensure that personal information, as well as that of local government, was not being used in improper ways. However, administration officials soon concluded that it would be better to address these issues in a separate law, which would be the counterpart of, and a corrective to, the electronic data processing law.

This would ensure that the commissioner would be perceived as independent of the institution that he was supposed to regulate and permit the officeholder to look beyond the confines of the center to monitor all of the possible ways in which the legitimate interests of the individual could be harmed by state data processing.[98]

The privacy protection law that was approved by the Landtag in October 1970 reaffirmed the confidentiality of information used for electronic data processing, guaranteed the right to have incorrect information corrected, and provided for legal recourse in case the individual was injured by unauthorized access. However, the legislative competence of the Landtag was limited, and these protections applied only to data processing within the state administration. The law also created the new post of privacy commissioner (*Datenschutzbeauftragter*). The commissioner was to be independent of the state administration, and the office was charged with monitoring the compliance of the public administration with the law, providing expert opinion on privacy protection, and serving as an ombudsman for the public. This compliance strategy would later be emulated by almost all of the state and federal privacy laws.[99]

But there was a clear disjunction between Osswald's analysis of the political dimensions of the privacy problem and the protections contained in the law. Like the other early data protection measures, the main goal of the Hessian law was to ensure that the personal information that was processed by the government was accurate and that it was protected against unauthorized access, disclosure, and use. In this respect, it was similar to both the recommendations made by the British Younger Committee in 1972 and to the more widely known Code of Fair Information Practices formulated in 1973 by the US Department of Health, Education and Welfare.[100] Such codes represented the minimum consensus around which European and American privacy regulations converged in the early 1970s.[101]

However, the Hessian law did not codify the final purpose principle, and it did not consider the *normal* use of personal information within integrated information systems and the kinds of power that it generated as a problem requiring legislative action. As a result, the law did not attempt to substantively balance privacy and access rights by specifying what information could be collected by state agencies, the conditions under which it could be collected, the conditions under which it could be made available to others, or the uses to which it could be put. Such questions were implicit in the design and operation of integrated information systems. They surfaced immediately in conjunction with the Federal Population Registration Law. And they were the central point of contention in the drafting of the Federal Privacy Protection Law.

Notes

1. James Scott, *Seeing Like a State* (New Haven, 1998), 2, 82.
2. There is a growing literature on identification documents and practices. See Jane Caplan and John Torpey, eds., *Documenting Individual Identity: The Development of State Practices in the Modern World* (Princeton, 2001); Kees Boersma et al., eds., *Histories of State Surveillance in Europe and Beyond* (Routledge, 2014), 133ff.; John Torpey, *The Invention of the Passport: Surveillance, Citizenship and the State* (Cambridge, 2000); Keith Breckenridge, *Biometric State: The Global Politics of Identification and Surveillance in South Africa, 1850 to the Present* (Cambridge University Press, 2014); Ilsen About et al., eds., *Identification and Registration Practices in Transnational Perspective* (Palgrave, 2013); David Lyon, *Identifying Citizens: ID Cards as Surveillance* (Polity, 2009); Colin Bennett and David Lyon, eds., *Playing the Identity Card: Surveillance, Security and Identification in Global Perspective* (Routledge, 2008); Pierre Piazza, *Histoire de la carte nationale d'identité* (Odile Jacob, 2004); and, on the closely related topic of fingerprinting, Simon Cole, *Suspect Identities: A History of Fingerprinting and Criminal Identification* (Harvard University Press, 2001). On civil registration, see Keith Breckenridge and Simon Szreter, eds., *Registration and Recognition: Documenting the Person in World History* (Oxford University Press, 2012); and Gérard Noiriel, "The Identification of the Citizen: The Birth of Republican Civil Status in France," in *Documenting Individual Identity*, ed. Caplan and Torpey, 28–48.
3. Agar, *The Government Machine: A Revolutionary History of the Computer* (MIT Press, 2003), 5.
4. Loveman, "The Modern State and the Primitive Accumulation of Symbolic Power," *American Journal of Sociology* 110, no. 6 (May 2005): 1651–83; Bourdieu, "Rethinking the State: Genesis and Structure of the Bureaucratic Field," in *Practical Reason* (Stanford University Press, 1998), 35–63; and Götz Aly and Karl Heinz Roth, *The Nazi Census: Identification and Control in the Third Reich* (Temple University Press, 2004), 146–47.
5. Frohman, "Population Registration in Germany, 1842–1945: Information, Administrative Power, and State-Making in the Age of Paper," *Central European History* 53, no. 3 (2020): 503–32; "Population Registration, Social Planning, and the Discourse on Privacy Protection in West Germany," *JMH* 87, no. 2 (June 2015): 316–56; and *Poor Relief and Welfare in Germany from the Reformation to World War I* (Cambridge University Press, 2008), chapter 4.
6. I briefly discuss these developments in "Population Registration, Social Planning, and the Discourse on Privacy Protection in West Germany," but am unable to include a more extensive discussion in the present work due to space limitations.
7. Anthony Giddens, *The Nation-State and Violence* (University of California Press, 1987), 2, 14, 172–73. The advent of random access memory replaced the serial, batch processing of records stored on magnetic tape and made it possible to access data on an "online" basis.
8. Drs. VI/2654, 7.
9. In Britain, the 1972 Younger Report declined to propose the codification of a general right of privacy, in part because of administration resistance, in part because of the difficulties involved in defining the concept, but also in part because threats to privacy emanating from the public sector were excluded from the committee's remit, even though many people regarded the potential infringement on civil liberties by the government as a greater threat than interference by business and other individuals. See K. Younger, ed., *Report on the Committee on Privacy* (HMSO, 1972), 1–2, 5; and Kevin Manton, *Population Registers and Privacy in Britain, 1936–1984* (Palgrave, 2019).
10. Although the Hessian law was the first such act, it was quickly followed by comparable legislation in Sweden (1973), the United States (1974), and—across the remainder of the 1970s and 1980s—most of the other members of the expanding Common Market, as well as Canada, New Zealand, and Australia.

11. Trost, Vermerk, Betr.: Bevölkerungskennziffer (29 January 1964), StAH 136-1/447; and BMI to Innenminister/-senatoren der Länder, Betr.: Einführung eines einheitlichen Personenkennzeichens (31 August 1964), BAK B106/45482, Bd. 2. On the pension insurance number and the computerization of the pension insurance system, see Thomas Kasper, "'Licht im Rentendunkel': Die Computerisierung des Sozialstaats in Bundesrepublik und DDR," dissertation, University of Potsdam, 2018.
12. One member of one of the many groups where these ideas were discussed was Kurt Passow, who had been involved in the original experiments with national ID numbers during World War II. See Ausschuss für Wirtschaftliche Verwaltung, Betr.: Verlegung der Sitzung des Fachausssschusses "Einheitliches Personenkennzeichen" (26 February 1965), StAH 136-1/447; and Aly and Roth, *The Nazi Census*, 140.
13. Bundesministerium des Innern, ed., *Personenkennzeichen. Meldewesen, Datenverarbeitung, Datenschutz*, (=*betrifft*, vol. 7, 1971), 6.
14. Ergebnisprotokoll über die Besprechung am 13. Oktober 1964 im BMI . . . , StAH 136-1/447. See also Ergebnis-Protokoll über die Besprechungen am 2. März 1964 im BMI zum Thema "Entwicklung eines einheitlichen Personenkennzeichens," and the minutes of a 13 October 1964 discussion under the same title, both in BAK B106/45482, Bde. 1 and 2 respectively.
15. The following discussion draws on the materials in BAK B106/45482, Bde. 1–3, and StAH 136-1/447.
16. The West German debate over a national ID number can be usefully compared with Sarah Igo's discussion of the early history of the Social Security number in *The Known Citizen: A History of Privacy in Modern America* (Harvard University Press, 2018), 55–98. However, in contrast to the United States, the Germans had long been able to claim membership in the social community constituted by the country's social insurance programs without relying on such a number.
17. Ergebnis-Protokoll über die Besprechung am 13. Oktober 1964 im BMI zum Thema "Entwicklung eines einheitlichen Personenkennzeichens," BAK B106/45482, Bd. 2; Verwaltungsrat Ulrich/A30 to A0, Betr.: Bevölkerungskennziffer (24 February 1964), and Polizeipräsident, Betr.: Bevölkerungskennziffer (22 April 1964), both in StAH 136-1/47.
18. Drs. 6/2654, 8. The idea of using fingerprints—presumably in conjunction with a national ID card—as a universal civilian identifier (as opposed to the older use for the identification of criminals and other marginal or subordinate groups) had already been broached in both England and the United States in 1919. See Cole, *Suspect Identities*, 197; and Edward Higgs, *Identifying the English: A History of Personal Identification 1500 to the Present* (Continuum, 2011), 144–48.
19. Kommunale Gemeinschaftsstelle für Verwaltungsvereinfachung to BMI/von Dreising, Betr.: Einführung eines einheitlichen Personenkennzeichens (2 December 1964), BAK B106/45482, Bd. 2.
20. The brief discussion of the ID number in the Bundestag in January 1965 (4. Wahlperiode, 156. Sitzung [20 January 1965], 7661–62) insured a steady flow of public comment across the remainder of the decade. See the materials in BAK B106/45485, Bd. 1.
21. I B 3/v. Dreising, Vermerk, Betr.: Einheitliches Personenkennzeichen (16 August 1966), BAK B106/45482, Bd. 3.
22. Kommunale Gemeinschaftsstelle für Verwaltungsvereinfachung, Betr.: Zentrale elektronische Datenverarbeitung (27 November 1968), BAK B136/5056.
23. Bundesminister des Innern to oberste Bundesbehörden, Betr.: Einführung eines allgemeinen Personenkennzeichens (2 April 1968), B106/45483, Bd. 5. Interior ministry officials also hoped that this virtual centralization of the population registration system would ultimately lead to its real centralization, though they felt it better to keep quiet about this long-term goal for fear of stirring up opposition to their short-term plans. See V II 3/Hölder, Vermerk, Betr.: Personenkennzeichen (26 January 1968), BAK B106/45483,

Bd. 4. Manton, *Population Registration in Britain*, argues that, through the end of the 1960s, British officials and politicians from all parties were interested less in population registration per se than in the creation of an enumeration system, which would permit record linkages among paper files, and that successive administrations deflected privacy concerns *toward* computers so as to shield the linkages among such paper files, which held far more information than electronic systems, from critical scrutiny.

24. Frieder Günther, "Rechtsstaat, Justizstaat oder Verwaltungsstaat? Die Verfassungs- und Verwaltungspolitik," in *Hüter der Ordnung. Die Innenministerien in Bonn und Ost-Berlin nach dem Nationalsozialismus*, ed. Frank Bösch and Andreas Wirsching (Wallstein, 2018), 381–412, especially 403–4.
25. Michael Ruck, "Ein kurzer Sommer der konkreten Utopie: Zur westdeutschen Planungsgeschichte der langen 60er Jahre," in *Dynamische Zeiten. Die 60er Jahre in den beiden deutschen Gesellschaften*, ed. Axel Schildt (Hamburg, 2000), 362–401, especially 391.
26. This system, which required registry officials in the person's new residence to let their counterparts in the previous legal residence of the newcomer know where the person had actually settled, was essential to keeping track of a mobile population and maintaining a seamless record of the identity and location of individual citizens and residents. The idea of such a universal backward reporting system had been mooted since the turn of the century and was eventually put into practice in the late 1930s. See Frohman, "Population Registration in Germany, 1842–1945."
27. Drs. 1/1032; *Sten. Ber.*, I. Wahlperiode, 71. Sitzung (22 June 1950), 2571–73; 79. Sitzung (26 July 1950), 2913–18; and *BGBl.*, 1950, 807.
28. BMI/Ministerialrat Joachim Hertel to Schleswig-Holstein Ministerium des Innern, Betr.: Einführung eines allgemeinen Personenkennzeichens (3 March 1969), BAK B106/45514, Bd. 1.
29. Kommunale Gemeinschaftsstelle/Jähnig to BMI/Hölder, Betr.: Einheitliches Personenkennzeichen (1 March 1968), BAK B106/45483, Bd. 4; Kommunale Gemeinschaftsstelle to BMI, Betr.: Einführung eines bundeseinheitlichen Personenkennzeichens (9 October 1968), BAK B106/45514, Bd. 1; and Kommunale Gemeinschaftsstelle, Rundschreiben no. 32 (27 November 1968), BAK B136/5056.
30. V II 1/BMI to the other Bundesminister, Betr.: Einführung eines allgemeinen Personenkennzeichens (20 January 1969), BAK B106/45483, Bd. 6.
31. V II 1/Hölder to oberste Bundesbehörden, Betr.: Unterrichtung über den Stand der Vorbereitungen zur Einführung eines Personenkennzeichens (1 July 1969) and the attached memorandum, BAK B106/45483, Bd. 7.
32. Ergebnisprotokoll über die zweite Sitzung des 1. Arbeitsausschusses "Rechtsfragen" am 29. April 1969, BAK B106/45514; and Lothar Beyer, "Der Streit um die Aufgaben des Meldewesens," in *Kommunkationstechnische Vernetzung*, ed. Ralf Bernd Abel et al. (S. Toeche-Mittler Verlag, 1986), 205–41, who also notes (206, 210) this terminological development.
33. Entwurf eines Gesetzes über das Meldewesen (Stand: 15. April 1970), BAK B136/5056. The draft approved by the cabinet was submitted to the Bundestag in May as Drs. VI/2654, and the law was reintroduced with no substantive changes in the following legislative period as Drs. VII/1059.
34. BMI, Ergebnisniederschrift über die Besprechung des Entwurfs eines Gesetzes über das Meldewesen (25 June 1970), BAK B136/5056, explicitly stated that the decision regarding whether to provide information was to be made by the office requesting the information, not registry officials.
35. Drs. VI/2654, 16.
36. Joachim Stöckle, "Die Automation des Einwohnermeldwesens im Rahmen eines Datenfernarbeitungssystems," *IBM-Nachrichten* 21 (October 1971): 897–904; Helmut Kohl, "Das Landesrechenzentrum Rheinland-Pfalz in Mainz," *IBM-Nachrichten* 21 (1971):

862–64; and Klaus Maxeiner et al., "Das Projekt Landesinformationssystem Rheinland-Pfalz—erste IMS-Anwendung im öffentlichen Bereich von Bund und Ländern," *IBM-Nachrichten* 23 (1973): 847–54.
37. Bundesministerium des Innern, *Personenkennzeichen*, 5.
38. See the materials in BAK B106/45493 and 45500, especially Bundesminister des Innern to Bundesminister für Gesamtdeutsche Fragen (September 1968). The fortunes of centralized, electronic population registries and national ID numbers were very different in Scandinavia. See Susanne Bauer, "From Administrative Infrastructure to Biomedical Resource: Danish Population Registries, the 'Scandinavian Laboratory,' and the 'Epidemiologist's Dream,'" *Science in Context* 27, no. 2 (2014): 187–213. In the late 1960s, the East Germans also decided to introduce a national ID number and establish a computerized central population registry, which began operation at the beginning of 1984. This database held different information than its West German counterparts and was used differently by both the civilian administration and the security agencies. See Axel Krapp and Michael Thaten, "Das Zentrale Einwohnerregister unter Datenschutz- und Datensicherheitsaspekten," *RDV* 7, no. 2 (1991): 73–76; and Sven Mörs, Kirsten Paritong-Waldheim, and Martin Schallbruch, *Das Meldewesen in beiden deutschen Staaten und die Neuordnung in Berlin* (TU Berlin, Forschungsberichte des Fachbereichs Informatik, Bericht 91-08).
39. According to Hertel, Betr.: Entwurf eines Gesetzes über das Meldewesen (9 May 1973), BAK B106/96316, a 1972 survey showed that 70 percent of the population approved of the number, 16 percent opposed it, and 14 percent were undecided.
40. *Sten. Ber.*, 5. Wahlperiode, 226. Sitzung (28 March 1969), 12484.
41. Drs. 6/598, 5–6. These points were reiterated in Drs. 6/648, 20–21. The interior ministry had originally sought to dispel these concerns, when it described its plan to the other ministries in V II 1/Hölder to oberste Bundesbehörden, Betr.: Unterrichtung über den Stand der Vorbereitungen zur Einführung eines Personenkennzeichens (1 July 1969) and the attached memorandum, BAK B106/45483, Bd. 7. At the same moment, concerns were being voiced as to whether the questions included in the 1970 census might not intrude improperly into the intimate sphere. See "Vater Staat stellt bald hochnotpeinliche Fragen," *General-Anzeiger* (15 January 1970), and Ministerialrat Wegner to BMI (23 February 1970), both in BAK B106/53348.
42. Drs. 6/1223, Ministerialrat Biederbick, Vermerk: Fragen des Datenschutzes (25 January 1971), BAK B141/60007, and the 1974 correspondence reaffirming the linkage in BAK B106/96320.
43. Joachim Schweinoch in Bundesministerium des Innern, Sachverständigenanhörung zum Melderecht am 20./21.11.1978. Teil A: Stenographisches Wortprotokoll, 221–22, BayHStA Landesdatenschutzbeauftragter/533.
44. On this 200-item standard record, see Niederschrift über die Sitzung der Berichterstattergruppe "Datenschutz-/Meldegesetz" (18 December 1974), Anlage 1, and Niederschrift (12 November 1974), which details the flow of specific pieces of information between the registry office and twenty other agencies and offices, both in BAK B106/96320. A later version was published as "An die zweihundert Daten machen den Bürger aus," *FAZ*, 11 February 1978, 5.
45. Drs. VI/2654, 5, 17.
46. See the correspondence in BAK B106/45446, especially BMI, Zusammenstellung des geltenden Melderechts – Hotelmeldepflicht und Nebenmeldepflicht (22 June 1972).
47. Hertel, Vermerk Betr.: Sicherheitsaspekte des Bundesmeldegesetzes (5 June 1972), Hertel to Genscher, Betr.: Sicherheitsaspekte des Bundesmeldegesetzes (17 June 1972), and the appended talking points for the Innenministerkonferenz, all in BAK B106/45446.
48. "100445301111—Das Schlimmste von King Kong?," *Der Spiegel*, 26 November 1973, 66–87. This concern about how ID numbers and integrated information systems could

facilitate the construction of dossiers and thus denude the individual before those who controlled such databases had aroused sharp opposition since the late 1960s. See Gerd Brüggemann, "Werden die Bürger durch Knopfdruck 'durchsichtig'?" *Die Welt*, 25 June 1969; and "Der große Bruder," *FAZ*, 11 December 1974. Others, however, emphasized the increased efficiency, transparency, accuracy, and accessibility that computers brought to public administration. See Burkart Lutz and Klaus Dill, "Die Verwaltung, der Computer und der Bürger," in *Der Mensch und die Technik*, Beilage to *SZ*, 18 September 1969.
49. Hanno Kühnert, "Tücken der Computer," *FAZ*, 10 June 1969.
50. The questionnaire is found in BAK B106/45484. This was the only public protest against the ID number that had so far come to the attention of state and federal officials.
51. *Datenschutz/Meldegesetz. Sachverständigenanhörung, Gesetzestexte. Aus der öffentlichen Anhörung des Innenausschusses des Deutschen Bundestages vom 6. Mai 1974* (Presse- und Informationszentrum des Deutschen Bundestages, 1974), 204–6.
52. Ibid., 201–2.
53. See the materials in BAK B136/14280.
54. Problem der "Identitätsprüfung" im Melderecht (26 May 1972), and the memorandum by the interior minister (30 June 1972), both in BAK B106/45446. The matter was revisited numerous times. See 61. and 106. Sitzungen des Innenausschusses (22 January 1975 and 2 April 1976), PA-DBT 3114, 7. Wahlperiode, which reaffirmed the decision not to include such a requirement in the federal law, but to allow the states to impose such a requirement if they chose to do so.
55. Niederschrift über die Sitzung der Berichterstattergruppe "Datenschutz-/Meldegesetz" (12 November 1974), BAK B106/96320, Bd. 42; and 61. Sitzung des Innenausschusses (22 January 1975), PA-DBT 3114, 7. Wahlperiode.
56. In addition, in April 1976 the domestic affairs committee voted (106. Sitzung des Innenausschusses [2 April 1976], PA-DBT 3114, 7. Wahlperiode) to prohibit the use of the ID number as a unique identifier by the private sector.
57. Protokoll: 97. Sitzung des Rechtsausschusses (5 May 1976), BAK B141/60025; Auernhammer, Vermerk, Betr.: Sitzung des Rechtsausschusses (5 May 1976), BAK B106/96326; Kurzprotokoll. 111. Sitzung des Innenausschusses (19 May 1976), BAK B106/96325; "Die große Nummer wird nicht gemacht," *Vorwärts* (27 May 1976); and Beyer, "Der Streit um die Aufgaben des Meldewesens," 213–14. As we shall see in chapter 3, this move was a reaction to the decision by the Bundestag domestic affairs committee to retreat from its previous decision to make the protections contained in the draft Federal Privacy Protection Law substantially more rigorous than those contained in the original administration draft.
58. These events trailed similar developments in the United States, where the computerization of Internal Revenue Service operations in the early 1960s led to the new requirement that filers provide Social Security numbers on their tax returns. However, in 1973, a committee appointed by the secretary of health, education and welfare recommended against both the adoption of a national ID number, which "would enhance the likelihood of arbitrary or uncontrolled linkage of records about people," and the expanded use of the Social Security Number for such purposes. U.S. Department of Health Education and Welfare, *Records, Computers and the Rights of Citizens: Report of the Secretary's Advisory Committee on Automated Personal Data Systems* (1973), 108–22, citation 122. The reasoning behind this recommendation (167) was similar to that of the Germans.
59. Regierungsdirektor Großkopf, Grobe Zusammenfassung der Problematik Datenschutz/Personenkennzeichen (17 May 1976), BAK B136/14280.
60. Entwurf: Bundesmeldegesetz und Begründung (Stand: 24. November 1977), BAK B136/14280.
61. According to Kurze Stellungnahme zum Entwurf eines Meldegesetzes, BAK B136/14280, the law would have also required landlords to report vacant apartments.

62. Bundesministerium des Innern, Sachverständigenanhörung zum Melderecht am 20./ 21.11.1978. Teil A, 19–20, 235, and Teil B: Schriftliche Stellungnahmen, 6–7, BayHStA Landesdatenschutzbeauftragter/533.
63. Drs. 8/3825, 4261, and 4333; *Sten. Ber.*, 8. Wahlperiode, 213. Sitzung (23 April 1980), 17136–141, and 225. Sitzung (25 June 1980), 18257–63; *BGBl.* (1980), 1429–36; and Beyer, "Die Streit um die Aufgaben des Meldewesens," 217. On the amendment to the Social Insurance Code, see *BGBl.* (1980), 1469–1502, especially 1484ff.
64. State Secretary Andreas von Schoeler (FDP), *Sten. Ber.*, 8. Wahlperiode, 213. Sitzung (23 April 1980), 17136; and Drs. 8/3825, 12.
65. See Simitis's reasoning in Hessian Drs. 9/4032, 30–36.
66. Paul Laufs (CDU), *Sten. Ber.*, 225. Sitzung (25 June 1980), 18257–58. See the correspondence concerning the model draft state population registration law in BayHStA Landesbeauftragter für den Datenschutz/414, especially the criticism of the proposed inclusion of the serial number by Bavarian privacy commissioner Konrad Stollreither in Aktenvermerk, Betr.: Rohentwurf für ein Landesmeldegesetz (undated).
67. *BGBl.*, 1980, 270.
68. Benda, Gutachtliche Äußerung zu verfassungsrechtlichen Fragen des Entwurfs eines Meldegesetzes für das Land Berlin (28 December 1984), and the minutes of the 14 January 1985 hearing on Benda's memorandum, both in Berlin DSB (No Aktenzeichen, Landesmeldegesetz); and Dietmar Peitsch, "Rechtliche und organisatorische Probleme bei der Ausgliederung der Meldebehörde aus der Berliner Polizei," *Die Polizei* 78, no. 4 (1987): 101–5. On the *Bürgerämter*, see Beyer, "Der Streit um die Aufgaben des Meldewesens," 228–32. Although Benda had no reservations about the population registration system itself, he questioned the constitutionality of two provisions of the registry law that we have repeatedly encountered: the hotel and hospital registration obligations, which he flatly condemned as vestiges of an older police state mentality.
69. See Lindenberg's two-part "Datenbank/D-471 81 61," http://www.udo-lindenberg.de/ datenbank.57851.htm/, http://www.udo-lindenberg.de/d_471_81_61.57826.htm. The line can be translated "[You may as well] tell the whole truth, it is tattooed on your ass."
70. See "Referenenentwurf Meldegesetz," on personal blog of Philip Banse, http://philip banse.de/docs/Referenenentwurf_Meldegesetz.pdf.
71. "Schäubles Einwohneramt," *Taz*, 28 June 2008; and "Schäubles Entwurf fürs zentrale Melderegister entzweit Koalition," *Spiegel Online*, 27 June 2008, https://www.spiegel .de/politik/deutschland/sicherheit-schaeubles-entwurf-fuers-zentrale-melderegister-entzweit-koalition-a-562609.html.
72. *Sten. Ber.*, 17. Wahlperiode, 187. Sitzung (28 June 2012), 22464–470; and Drs. 17/7746 and 17/10158.
73. https://www.vzbv.de/pressemitteilung/meldegesetz-190000-unterschriften-bundes laender-ueberreicht.
74. Drs. 17/12463; *Sten. Ber.*, 17. Wahlperiode, 225. Sitzung (28 February 2013), 27943; and *BGBl.*, 2013, 1084–1103. The law also reintroduced the landlord countersignature—less, at least nominally, for security reasons than to prevent people from falsely claiming a residence that would allow them preferential access to social services.
75. Udo Kauß, "Das neue Ausweissystem—eine Lücke wird geschlossen," in *Der neue Personalausweis*, ed. Jürgen Taeger (Rohwolt, 1984), 41–88, citations 70, 79. The same point is made in Adalbert Podlech, "Die Begrenzung staatlicher Informationsverarbeitung durch die Verfassung angesichts der Möglichkeit unbegrenzter Informationsverarbeitung mittels der Technik," *Leviathan* 12, no. 1 (1984): 85–98, especially 86–87.
76. As this book is going to press, the administration has just resurrected—in modified form—the plan for a national ID number. The draft law (Entwurf eines Gesetzes zur Einführung einer Identifikationsnummer in die öffentlichen Verwaltung und zur Änderung weiterer Gesetze [Stand: 31.7.2020], which is widely available online) proposes

that the tax identification number that was introduced in 2007 be used as a unique identifier for the exchange of personal information across the entire public administration. However, to circumvent both the limitations on data integration imposed by the census decision and the problems resulting from the absence of a national population registry, it calls for the establishment of a complex infrastructure in which current identifying information (and the associated metadata) is held by the tax office and the exchange of personal information is routed through a "registry modernization bureau," which will be responsible for comparing the information held by the tax offices with that held in other registries and then updating the latter on the basis of the former as it passes through this clearinghouse. The privacy commissioners claim that this proposed identity management system, which the government argues is necessary to implement the 2017 e-government law, will endanger privacy rights in a variety of ways, and they argue—as they did with regard to the 1980 Population Registration Framework Law— that the only way to forestall such threats is to limit the use of the tax ID number to the identification of specific individuals.

77. I differ here from Julia Fleischhack, *Eine Welt im Datenrausch. Computeranlagen und Datenmengen als gesellschaftliche Herausforderung in der Bundesrepublik Deutschland (1965– 1975)* (Chronos Verlag, 2016).
78. Siemens, *Bayerisches Informationssystem* (=*Beiträge zur integrierten Datenverarbeitung in der öffentlichen Verwaltung,* vol. 1, 1970), 1–2, 47. This Bavarian system would have linked all communal and private sector databases into a central state information network that was directly subordinate to the state cabinet, and changes in the personal information reported to any office would have been automatically transmitted to all other state offices. Podlech later described this proposal as a "horror vision" that had provided the impetus for privacy protection legislation. See https://www.datenschutzzentrum.de/artikel/932-Interview-mit-Prof.-Dr.-Dr.-Adalbert-Podlech.html at 16:30. An earlier version of the Siemens proposal had described the goal of the system—in terms that were so controversial that they were removed from the second edition—as "the unlimited availability of all information on all inhabitants, both horizontally and vertically," cited by Wilhelm Steinmüller (https://www.datenschutzzentrum.de/artikel/939-Interview-mit-Prof.-Wilhelm-Steinmueller.html at 40:05).
79. Gerhard Fauth, "Macht durch Computer," *Kölner Stadt-Anzeiger* (17 August 1968).
80. "Der große Bruder," *FAZ* (11 December 1974).
81. Jürgen Ostermann, "Automation in der Verwaltung. Realität und Zukunftserwartung," *Die Verwaltung* 3 (1970), 129–58, especially 148–49.
82. Siemens, *Bayerisches Informationssystem,* 5–18, Ulrich Dammann, "Manipulation oder Öffentlichkeitsinformation? Zur Funktion von Planungsinformationssystemen," in *Informationsrechte und Kommunikationspolitik,* ed. Klaus Lenk (Toeche-Mittler, 1976), 137–63, especially 140; Bericht des Jahres 1972 über die Entwicklung der Datenverarbeitung in Berlin, 3, LAB B Rep. 004, no. 449; Maxeiner et al., "Das Projekt Landesinformationssystem Rheinland-Pfalz"; and Werner Ruckriegel, "Elektronische Datenverarbeitung in der Landesverwaltung Nordrhein-Westfalens," *Die Verwaltung* 2 (1969): 445–66.
83. See the discussion of these state laws in Malte von Berg et al., "Die ADV-Organisationsgesetze und Vereinbarungen der Bundesländer," *ÖVD* 2 (1972): 319–29 and 380–85; and Klaus Bresse, "Soll und Haben in der Datenverarbeitung mit Folgerungen für die Zukunft," *ÖVD* 2 (1972): 501–5.
84. The administration's conception of an integrated data processing system is set out in Hessische Zentrale für Datenverarbeitung, ed., *Grosser Hessenplan. Entwicklungsprogramm für den Ausbau der Datenverarbeitung in Hessen* (Wiesbaden, 1970).
85. Hessischer Landtag. 6. Wahlperiode, 51. Sitzung (21 May 1969), 2759–71, especially 2763–64; the petition by the Hessischer Städtetag (16 June 1969), and §22.1 of the un-

titled, undated draft of a proposed amendment to the SPD version, both in HHStA Abt. 502/12130a.
86. *Hess. GVBl.*, 1969, 304–6; and Hessischer Landtag, 6. Wahlperiode, 65. Sitzung (11 December 1969), 3402–09. The failure to secure parliamentary access was the main reason why the CDU did not vote for the law.
87. Hesse was the only state that passed a computer privacy law before the Brandt administration had made clear its intention to introduce a national law. This announcement sidelined other states, which were reluctant to pass their own laws before the parameters of the proposed federal legislation had become clear. For privacy initiatives in other states, see 1. Tätigkeitsbericht des Datenschutzbeauftragten, Hessen Drs. 7/1495; Christoph Mallmann, *Datenschutz in Verwaltungs-Informationssystemen* (Oldenbourg, 1976), 75–79; Referat V III 4/Auernhammer to the Interministerielle Arbeitsgruppe "Datenbanksystem" (26 September 1972), BAK B106/96310; and "Vermerk: Fragen des Datenschutzes" (undated), BAK B141/600079.
88. Dammann, "Manipulation oder Öffentlichkeitsinformation?" 142ff.; and Dammann, "Zur politischen Kontrolle von Planungsinformationssystemen," in *Erfassungschutz. Der Bürger in der Datenbank zwischen Planung und Manipulation*, ed. Helmut Krauch (Deutscher Verlags-Anstalt, 1975), 105–17.
89. The Germans were well aware of the American debate over the proposed National Data Center and made frequent reference to it. See Peter Menke-Glückert, "Datenbanken als Bürgerschreck?" *Der Mensch und die Technik. Beilage der SZ* (18 September 1969); Ulrich Seidel, *Datenbanken und Persönlichkeitsrecht unter besonderer Berücksichtigung der amerikanischen Computer Privacy* (Verlag Dr. Otto Schmidt, 1972), 18, 56–59; Klaus Lenk, "Datenschutz in der öffentlichen Verwaltung," in *Datenschutz. Juristische Grundsatzfragen beim Einsatz elektronischer Datenverarbeitungsanlagen in Wirtschaft und Verwaltung*, ed. Wolfgang Kilian et al. (Athenäum-Verlag, 1973), 15–50, especially 31; and Kölner Arbeitskreis für Wissenschaftliche Beratung der Politik, Arbeitspaper no. 3 . . . Datenbanksystem (7 August 1969), BAK B136/26216.
90. Bresse to Ministerpräsident, Betr.: Entwurf eines Datenschutzgesetzes (10 November 1969), Staatskanzleiaktenzeichen 3v24/051; and Hessischer Landtag, 6. Wahlperiode, 65. Sitzung (11 December 1969), 3404. This and other relevant documents were still held in the Hessian interior ministry at the time I conducted my research summer 2009. Sentiments similar to those expressed by Bresse were also set out in Vermerk zu den vorgesehenen §§22 und 23 über "Vertrauensschutz" . . . (29 July 1969), HHStA Abt. 502/12131b.
91. Osswald, *Der soziale Rechtsstaat als Herausforderung*, especially "Computer im Dienste moderner Gesellschafts- und Sozialpolitik," 35–45, citation 36–37, and "Umfassende Information—ein Mittel zur Stärkung der Demokratie," 46–63. For more extensive discussion of these issues, see Frohman, "Network Euphoria."
92. Osswald, *Der soziale Rechtsstaat als Herausforderung*, 32, 38–39, 51–52; and Ariane Leendertz, "Das Komplexitätssyndrom. Gesellschaftliche 'Komplexität' als intellektuelle und politische Herausforderung," in *Die neue Wirklichkeit. Semantische Neuvermessungen und Politik set den 1970er Jahren*, ed. Leendertz and Wencke Meteling (Campus Verlag, 2016), 93–131.
93. Osswald, *Der soziale Rechtsstaat als Herausforderung*, 55.
94. Ibid., 38–41.
95. Ibid., 60.
96. Ibid., 43.
97. Lyon, *Surveillance Society: Monitoring Everyday Life* (Milton Keynes, 2001), 1.
98. Der Initiativantrag der Fraktion der SPD betreffend dem Entwurf . . . Errichtung der Hessischen Zentrale für Datenverarbeitung . . . wird durch folgenden Abschnitt ergänzt

(26 August 1969), Staatskanzleiaktenzeichen 3v24/051, Vermerk zu den vorgesehenen §§22 und 23 über "Vertrauensschutz" . . . (29 July 1969), HHStA Abt. 502/12131b; and Kabinettvorlage, Betr.: Entwurf eines Datenschutzgesetzes (13 June 1970), HHStA Abt. 502/15164.

99. Hessischer Landtag Drs. VI/3065, 3151, 3376; *Sten. Ber.*, 80. Sitzung (30 September 1970), 4271–72; and *Hess. GVBl.*, 1970, 625–27.

100. *Report on the Committee on Privacy*, 182–84; and Department of Health, Education and Welfare, *Records, Computers and the Rights of Citizens* (1973), xix–xxxv and 41.

101. Colin J. Bennett, *Regulating Privacy: Data Protection and Public Policy in Europe and the United States* (Cornell University Press, 1992), chapter 3; and Viktor Mayer-Schönberger, "Generational Development of Data Protection in Europe," in *Technology and Privacy: The New Landscape*, ed. Philip Agre and Marc Rotenberg (MIT Press, 1997), 219–41.

Part II

NEGOTIATING COMMUNICATIVE NORMS IN THE COMPUTER AGE

The Information Question and the
Federal Privacy Protection Law, 1970–90

Chapter 2

Rethinking Privacy in the Age of the Mainframe
From the Private Sphere to Informational Self-Determination

The starting point for postwar German thinking on privacy was the concept of the private sphere. In its 1957 Elfes decision, the Constitutional Court affirmed the existence of "a sphere for the private fashioning of life..., a final, inviolable domain of human freedom..., which is shielded from the actions of all public power."[1] As the Court later explained in its 1969 microcensus decision, this "interior space" was worthy of constitutional protection because it was the precondition for the "free and self-responsible development of the personality."[2] However, the 1970s debate over computer privacy and privacy protection law began by rejecting the concept of the private sphere, which a 1971 study commissioned by the federal interior ministry dismissed as "obsolete" and "unusable" as the basis for privacy protection legislation.[3]

At the turn of the 1970s, privacy advocates distanced themselves from the concept of the private sphere for three reasons: it was impossible to delimit it; it rested on historical and sociological assumptions that no longer held; and, as noted in the introduction, it was incapable of theorizing either the specific problems associated with the routine, bureaucratic collection of personal information or those arising out of the use of the new information technologies to store, process, and disseminate this information, neither of which could be understood in terms of the "invasion" of the private sphere. While "sphere theory" attempted to spell out

---

Notes for this chapter begin on page 101.

the degree of protection to be afforded to specific kinds of information according to their ostensible degree of intimacy or sensitivity, the advent of integrated information systems shifted the focus from the intrinsic characteristics of this information to conditions of access and the context within which it was used. As part of this process, the language of privacy was reformulated to theorize the problems resulting from the integration effect and the perceived loss of control over personal information inherent in the functioning of such systems.

The distinction between the public sphere and the private was constitutive of modern liberalism,[4] and privacy has often been understood in liberal terms as a subjective right to dispose over one's personal information in a manner akin to property rights. However, the founding figures of German privacy law explicitly criticized this position, and I will argue that the attempts to think through the problems described above drove a paradigm shift from the idea of a private sphere of seclusion *from* society to a theory of informational self-determination that focused on the context in which information was used and the power relations between individuals *in* society that structured this context. They argued that privacy was an informational relationship that was social in nature, that it was politically constructed in ways that emulated the larger structures of action and inequality in society, and that it could, therefore, only be defended—and delimited—on the basis of a comprehensive, critical theory of that society.

The West Germans approached the privacy problem using concepts that derived from their own constitutional tradition and that were, consequently, quite different from those employed in the United States.[5] The West German Basic Law embodies an objective order of values, and the country's constitutional commitment to individual dignity and the development of the personality provides a normative foundation for privacy rights that is absent in the United States. Although the Basic Law enumerates a number of individual protections, the right to the free development of the personality contained in Article 2 functions in a subsidiary manner to protect against unenumerated threats to human dignity. In so doing, it provides—in contrast to the American emphasis on original intent—a mechanism for adapting the law to the changing needs of the modern world. The Constitutional Court, however, has been very reluctant to provide a positive description of dignity. Instead, it has argued in negative terms—both personalist and Kantian—that human dignity is violated whenever the individual is degraded into a "mere object" for others, and between the 1969 microcensus decision and the 1983 census decision the Court repeatedly addressed two questions: Were modern forms of social communication—including the use of the new information technologies—constraining the freedom of the individual to choose how he would represent himself to such an extent that it would render the free development of the personality impossible? If so, what was the best remedy for these dignitarian injuries?

The American constitutional tradition is a distinctly liberal one, whose founding documents sought above all to limit the reach of the state, while leaving citizens largely free to choose how to make use of their liberty. In the United States, the market and the media—that is, property rights, the right to information access, and the right to free speech—constrain privacy to an extent that is inconceivable in Germany. As a result, informational privacy rights remain woefully underprotected in the United States, in large part because they lack a comparable normative, constitutional foundation. In their famous 1890 article "The Right to Privacy," Samuel Warren and Louis Brandeis attempted to import a continental conception of personality rights into the United States and then to establish a constitutional foundation for the idea by grafting it on to Fourth Amendment in Brandeis's famous dissent in *Olmstead v. United States* (1927).[6] However, the graft did not take, and, despite the fragmentary recognition of the right to privacy across the first half of the century, the underlying doctrine of personality rights remained a foreign body in American jurisprudence. William Prosser's influential 1960 reconceptualization of privacy in terms of the invasion of four distinct interests dispensed with any reference to personality rights and thus stripped away any systematic, normative claims as to why privacy should be protected, while the development of media law in the 1960s systematically privileged freedom of speech over privacy rights.[7]

In the shadow of these developments, American privacy law has been shaped by the line of sexual and reproductive rights decisions descending from *Griswold v. Connecticut* (1965). However, in these cases what was really adjudicated under the rubric of "privacy" was decisional autonomy, and they provide little if any support for a theory of informational privacy.[8] The only Supreme Court case to explicitly address these issues is *Whalen v. Roe* (1977). In its ruling in this case, the Court recognized the "threat to privacy implicit in the accumulation of vast amounts of personal information in computerized data banks or other massive government files."[9] However, the Court did not need to expand on these threats in order to decide the case, nor has it subsequently addressed the issues that, in conjunction with personality rights, played a central role in the development of the German understanding of informational privacy. As a result, most American privacy law rests on what Daniel

Solove has called the "secrecy paradigm,"[10] and those privacy rights that do exist survive on the rickety lifeline of penumbras and substantive due process.

The right to the development of the personality is not unlimited. The German dignitarian commitment means that individuals must treat other persons as ends in themselves, not as means, and the political anthropology, or the vision of man and his place in society, embodied in the Basic Law is one of community, solidarity, and mutual respect and recognition. These ideas were first set out in the 1954 Investment Assistance decision. There, the Court explained that "the conception of man on which the Basic Law is based is not that of an isolated, sovereign individual. Rather, the Basic Law has resolved the tension between the individual and the community by privileging the embeddedness of the person in, and his obligations to, the community without, however, diminishing the intrinsic value [of the person]."[11] Although it is not clear whether this argument successfully squared the circle of individual and community, it did give rise to a specifically German understanding of privacy rights, which maintained that the innermost core of the personality enjoyed absolute protection, but that this protection diminished in proportion to the extent to which the actions of the individual moved away from the interior domain and acquired a social dimension. In practice, the Court's broad understanding of this social dimension meant that the scope of the protections accorded to this innermost sphere was defined so narrowly that it lost all jurisprudential relevance, and, in any case, the development of the concept of informational privacy in the 1970s and early 1980s entailed the rejection of this postwar understanding of the privacy problem.

The development of West German constitutional jurisprudence relating to privacy rights was a complicated affair because every attempt to more fully articulate the concept of the private sphere and the protections to be accorded it also revealed the limits of this way of thinking. At the time, the Court was unable to either fully think through the resulting problems or abandon the concept of the private sphere altogether. As we shall see below, it was not until the turn of the 1980s that the Court committed itself to developing a new approach to privacy that did not depend on the concept of the private sphere. This involved the articulation of a new strand of personality rights that theorized the impact on human dignity resulting from the loss of control over personal information. However, the link between personality rights and personal data was not forged by the Court until the census decision, and, even then, it was only partly successful in theorizing the reflexive nature and social dimension of privacy.

The Sociological Critique of the Private Sphere

The historiography of the private sphere consists of two broad narratives that contradict and complement each other. The first tells the story of the separation of state and society and of the formation within this latter domain of the domestic sphere as the specific social location of the private. The second traces the deprivatization of the familial sphere by the emergent welfare state.[12] In the aftermath of Nazi rule, war, and total defeat, the reconstruction of the private, domestic sphere was one of the top priorities of West German politicians, who regarded the penetration of the state into the all-important sphere of social reproduction as one of the hallmarks of communism.[13] Measures to return to the private sphere those forms of domestic labor, such as housekeeping, provisioning, and the preparation and consumption of food, which had historically been regarded as quintessential forms of maternal, caring labor to be performed within the home, but which had acquired a public or communal dimension during the war, were central to the reconstruction of the familial sphere. They played a pivotal role in both demarcating the boundaries of the private and the public and distinguishing West Germany's consumer democracy from both Nazi totalitarianism and the collectivist society that was being established in East Germany.[14] This concern for the sanctity of the familial sphere was reinforced by Catholic social thought, which had a pervasive influence on postwar political and legal theory in West Germany.[15]

Although the public sphere and public opinion were the object of sustained attention in the 1950s and early 1960s by such thinkers as Hannah Arendt, Helmut Schelsky, Reinhart Koselleck, Wilhelm Hennis, and Jürgen Habermas, their accounts proceeded by way of an analysis of what Habermas might have called the structural transformation of the *private* sphere. Unfortunately, I do not have the space to discuss these postwar theories of the private sphere. Nor is this absolutely necessary because at the turn of the 1970s the focus of privacy theorizing shifted from the private sphere to the specific problems raised by routine, bureaucratic collection of personal information for administrative purposes.

This new focus was evident in the study of privacy protection by Otto Mallmann. Drawing on Habermas, Mallmann analyzed the ways in which the bourgeois private sphere was being eroded by mass media and the commercialization of personal information. He concluded that the concerns that had prompted the original call by Warren and Brandeis for a "right to be left alone" were "specifically bourgeois" ones, whose social foundations were rapidly disappearing.[16]

Like Mallmann, Spiros Simitis maintained that the historical linkage of privacy and autonomy in bourgeois society was ceasing to hold, and he argued that both the expansion of the welfare state and the deepening of consumer capitalism were entangling the individual in informational processes that rendered increasingly illusory the notion that the individual was free to determine whether or not to provide public and private sector bureaucracies with the personal information—no matter how banal or how intimate—they required as the condition for helping individuals satisfy their basic needs. "The mesh of social services demanded by the individual," Simitis argued,

> is becoming ever finer, and the number of persons who are dependent on permanent contact with the public administration is becoming ever larger. Each of these services deprivatizes the individual and transforms his person into a sum of details carefully registered [by the state]. The social service state and the demand for total information cannot be separated from one another. Rather, the registration of the individual is the functional precondition for a society that is, to a substantial degree, administered by the state.[17]

For Simitis, individuals were forced to make a Faustian bargain with the state because it was no longer possible to enjoy reasonable and customary rights to essential public goods without first disclosing one's personal information. While the renunciation of the services for which one would otherwise be eligible would be an act of social insanity tantamount to dropping out of the modern world, the expanding control of large organizations over social life was systematically deprivatizing the individual and transforming citizens into transparent, manipulable objects of bureaucratic administration.

Similar tendencies could also be observed in the private sector. Whoever wished to take out a life insurance policy or apply for credit, Simitis noted, was forced to reveal information regarding a domain of experience that could no longer be considered private in any meaningful sense of the term. "This undoubtedly happens against the background of one's own decision," he maintained, "but in reality [it takes place] only in order to enjoy services, which have long counted among the self-evident features of individual existence in industrial society." As was the case with public social services, the notion of voluntary disclosure lost all meaning if this was the only way of insuring against the risks of modern society or taking advantage of the opportunities it presented. In such a situation, "the individual does not at first even pose the question of the exclusiveness of his private sphere. The only thing that interests him are the services on which he depends, services which, however, can only be obtained via the willingness to disclose information."[18] This reasoning led Simitis to the stark conclusion that "privacy no longer exists in late industrial society."[19]

The question, then, was how to conceptualize privacy and its role in modern society? Simitis argued that criticisms of the "misuse" of information failed to grasp the distinctive nature of the problems posed by electronic databases and bureaucratic processes. The real danger, he argued, was to be found in the fact that the new information technologies were generating new forms of informational and social power that were leading to the expansion, intensification, and perfection of social control. Although Simitis was consistently critical of the concept of the private sphere, he still felt that it played a valuable role as a placeholder, which marked—using the constitutional language of personality law—the threshold "that cannot be crossed if information collection and processing are not to fully functionalize the individual and degrade him to a mere object of state and private bureaucracy. . . . A society that declares the private sphere to be superfluous thus abandons all hope for self-determination. The existence of the private sphere is to this extent the fundamental condition for individual freedom."[20]

These concerns were shared by the jurist Klaus Lenk. Like Simitis, Lenk argued that the real problem lay not in the misuse of personal information, but rather in its normal, intended use, and that the issue addressed under the rubric of privacy and its invasion was actually that of social power. As he wrote in 1973, "To define privacy with regard to public administration is equivalent to determining how much and what kind of control . . . of citizens should be conceded to the state." Although many people had argued that privacy played a vital role in diminishing the psychological pressures of the conflicting roles that individuals must fill in modern society, Lenk insisted that such arguments obscured the question of "what social influences determine what happens within this domain." Like Simitis, Lenk argued that the private sphere could serve as a domain of individual seclusion and autonomy only under limited historical conditions. With their passing, "the emphatic concept of the private sphere as the guarantor of a domain, which is the sociological precondition for the formation of autonomous personalities, is thereby exhausted (*ist damit begraben*)." The danger no longer lay, he insisted, in the "curious intrusion of the microcensus into the private sphere," but rather in the transformation of this information into a source of social power and a mechanism for social governance. This, he concluded, required the reformulation of the language of privacy because the concept of the private sphere was incapable of theorizing either the power relations that determined access to personal information or the normalizing effects of their use: "The critical analysis of consumer habits, political orientations, etc.," he concluded, "can no longer be conceptualized in terms of a threat to the private sphere."[21]

The Informational Unity of the State, the Database, and the Status of the Subject

These debates were complicated by a set of distinct, but not unrelated, problems posed by the development of integrated population information systems.

One of the most troubling problems, Wilhelm Steinmüller observed, was that "integrated data processing presumes the existence of an integrated administration," and it was integrated information systems and the new communication technologies that together made it possible for the first time to imagine the entire public administration as a single, unified informational entity.[22] Consequently, a growing number of people worried that integrated information systems would lead to a dangerous concentration of power and radically alter the administrative practices and structures that had served as the bulwark of privacy and the rule of law in the era of manual information processing.[23]

Much of the early legal-political debate on integrated information systems pivoted around the constitutional doctrine of *Amtshilfe*, which required the different departments and levels of government to provide each other with information they needed to carry out their responsibilities. While information had—in the age of paper—only been made available to other agencies on the basis of a case-by-case evaluation of the needs of the office requesting the data, integrated information systems and online connections threatened to eliminate these technological and organizational checks on the exchange of information within the public administration. While integrated data processing tended to promote the informational unity of the public administration, early privacy advocates argued that these problems could only be forestalled, and personal privacy protected, by establishing what came to be called the division of informational powers (*informationelle Gewaltenteilung*), which would block the promiscuous exchange of personal information across administrative boundaries.[24]

While some of the analyses of the impact of integrated information systems by early German privacy advocates were modernist accounts of the logic and consequences of bureaucratic rationalization, others built on the postmodernist conception of databases as mechanisms of representation. Although the accuracy and completeness of information was always a concern, privacy experts argued that multifunctional databases were intrinsically incapable of capturing the complex reality they aspired to model and that, as a result, they invariably deformed the information that was stored in them.[25] As Simitis explained, information was not gathered for its own sake, but rather in anticipation of how it could be used to generate administrative power. These anticipated uses also determined what was to count as "information" because data was only given meaning and transformed into information when it was evaluated in relation to the specific purpose for which it was collected.[26] In short, to use the title of a recent book, he argued that "raw data" was an oxymoron.[27]

More important, the strategic process of defining certain elements of experience as being relevant to the organization collecting this information, abstracting them out of the thick symbolic field in which they were originally embedded, and then fitting this messy, complex reality into the simplified, prefigured discursive space of the database field made it possible to recode these attributes as indicators of such states as normality, truth, delinquency, madness, creditworthiness—and then to use this regime of visibility as the basis of governance and social sorting. For example, since firms were interested in individuals only in their capacity as potential consumers, rather than, say, as voters, churchgoers, or club members, the market researchers they employed disaggregated the individual "into an aggregate of data that are strategically important for the market,"[28] which were then used to construct a profile or representation of the data subject.[29]

The counterpart to the prestructuring of such strategically important information—in the form of database fields—was the neglect of the context within which this information had originally been embedded. While highly formalized schemata ensured that information flowed quickly through any bureaucracy and that it would have the same meaning for all users, this reduction of context tended to alienate the individual from his information. When carried to its logical extreme, Ulrich Dammann argued, the individual would find himself virtually supplanted by the data double to which his real history had been reduced ("*seine zu Daten geronnene Lebensgeschichte*"). This meant, Dammann continued, that

> his actual behavior is contrasted with his profile (*Datenhistorie*) [and then] interpreted and evaluated from this perspective. In this way the individual is connected with his own life history in a more intense manner, though not in its individuality and meaningful wholeness, but rather as a mere informational form (*Datenraster*), whose capacity to be communicated and employed in a universal manner derives precisely from its complete abstraction from the meaningful contexts and social relations in which the data first arose.... The individual can no longer determine how he is represented by others.[30]

These reflections on the discursive nature of the database prefigured many of the influential postmodernist arguments later made by Gilles Deleuze, Jean Baudrillard, Mark Poster, and the surveillance studies school.

The substitution of electronic linkages and remote, online access for contextualized human judgment compounded this deformation of content by removing information from the control of its original owners: "The person who procures the data ceases to exercise the personal control function of someone charged with protecting a secret, and his patronage is succeeded by a glimmering spectrum of interests, when it comes to the construction of databases. Data files then lead a certain independent existence."[31] However, as Dammann explained, "it is the principle, which is inherent in the concept of integrated data processing, of storing information in ways that are separated from the purposes for which it is to be used, which deprives the concerned individual of a substantial proportion of his control competence."[32] The entire privacy protection project represented an attempt to contain this danger.

Privacy as Role-Specific Disclosure and Strategic Nonknowledge

The question was how to achieve this goal. None of the early privacy advocates argued that the constitutional right to the free development of the personality implied the existence of an unlimited, subjective right to privacy. Rather, they maintained that the best way of balancing privacy and access rights was to ensure that the communicative partners had access to the information that was appropriate and necessary for specific forms of social interaction in specific contexts (i.e., for the performance of social roles), to limit disclosure obligations to the minimum required by such interaction, and to ensure that this information did not bleed over into other contexts. These principles of contextual appropriateness, informational economy or parsimony, and the prohibition of unauthorized secondary use were to become the cornerstones of German privacy protection law.

At the time, the definition of privacy in terms of context- or role-specific disclosure was set out most clearly by sociologist Paul J. Müller. Müller explained that, in view of the increasing use of the new information technologies to store, retrieve, and integrate information, the conception of privacy in terms of a retreat into a sphere of seclusion (a snail's shell conception of privacy, as he called it) was both an ideology that assumed the existence of conditions that hardly ever existed in industrial society and an ineffectual strategy for protecting the ability of the individual to act autonomously *in* the world. Speaking with regard to the informational relations between the individual and the state, Müller argued that the private sphere is guaranteed by ensuring that different institutions require different information to carry out their responsibilities, which means that, to the extent that administrative action is based on the distribution of information according to function or competence, these institutions are only aware, and only need to be aware, of segments of individual existence. It is the simultaneity of distinct representations of the individual that creates the autonomy for individual action.[33]

This formulation, however, begged—or perhaps posed—the questions of precisely what information was appropriate and necessary in any given context and who made this determination. Simitis, as we have seen, argued that the collection of information was always an instrumental or strategic process. This meant two things. First, the fact that the meaning of information always inhered in the specific context within which it was disclosed meant that information should not be used for purposes other than those for which it had originally been collected. This was the final purpose principle.[34] Second, it was impossible to even begin thinking about what information might be appropriate and necessary in any given context— and thereby balance privacy and access rights—until the purpose for collecting the information, the strategic interests that structured the informational relations of this context, the underlying power relations, and the potential benefits and harms had been identified. "No privacy regulation can therefore," Simitis explained, "do without a comprehensive inventory of data and the contexts in which they will be used. . . . Only those who have knowledge of both can investigate the potential for conflict contained in information and develop criteria for a regulation."[35]

If Müller's argument approximately restates Nissenbaum's conception of contextual integrity, then Simitis's comments point to the political and social conflicts that shape these contextual norms. Moreover, this shift from the assumption that, by their very nature, different kinds of information should enjoy different degrees of protection to the belief that the protection to be afforded depended on the context in which it was used marked the transition to a functional or informational conception of privacy.[36]

This point was made at the time by a number of early privacy advocates. Both Simitis and Otto Mallmann argued that privacy had no abstract, decontextualized essence and that its meaning could be determined only through the political and legal regulation of information flows in specific contexts based on the prior investigation of the conflicts that inhered in these contexts.[37] Müller insisted that privacy protection laws did much more than simply regulate the collection of personal information. Rather, he argued, such laws would govern what he called the "informational economy" of institutions and social systems. In so doing, they exerted substantial influence on the distribution of both personal information and social power. This led him to the conclusion that privacy protection law was a form of social policy to remedy the specific social problems of the information society.[38] The jurist Herbert Fiedler, who at the time was an influential commentator on privacy law, argued that any attempt to understand what was at stake in the privacy discussion could succeed only by rising to the level of a critical theory of that society.[39] Podlech provided the most general formulation of this problem when he argued that the task of privacy protection law was to determine how the new information technologies were altering the conditions for the legitimate exercise of political and economic power.[40]

All of these considerations shaped the definition of privacy protection, or *Datenschutz*, as strategic nondisclosure—or what Julie Cohen has called "semantic discontinuity."[41] Müller, for example, argued that

> the role-specific or selective dissemination of information means controlled nonknowledge of things that "do not belong to the matter at hand" in any given instance. Autonomy is preserved by evaluating them separately so that different interaction partners know different things. In this way, there is no general transparency of individual existence. . . . The structure of the private sphere in industrial societies is based on this simultaneity of different representations, not in a generalized nonknowledge.[42]

Similarly, Simitis argued that the private sphere could be said to exist only to the extent that "the controlled dissemination of information creates spaces of freedom. To this extent, it rests upon the legally [and therefore politically] managed selection and channeling of information." The task of privacy protection law was to establish the distinctions between the information to be disclosed in different contexts. Privacy itself was, he concluded, "nothing other than institutionalized provision for targeted informationlessness between the individual and his environment. . . . The core of all privacy protection legislation is, so to speak, calculated nonknowledge."[43]

All of this puts us in a position to understand the contemporary obsession with "profiles" and "dossiers."[44] Critics then and now have argued that the dangers associated with such profiles were exaggerated.[45] However, the literalism of such arguments overlooks the extent to which profiles provided a way of talking about the real, if difficult-to-examine, problems associated with more modest linkages within and between integrated information systems.

In 1974 Benda published an essay on the private sphere and personality profiles. In this piece he worried that integrated information systems were radically altering the inherited structures of the public administration, as well as the norms that governed its functioning, and thereby rendering obsolete those constitutional protections that were sustained by older administrative arrangements and practices. With regard to the privacy problem, the real danger of integrated information systems lay, he argued, in their ability to bring together from all corners of the bureaucratic universe discrete pieces of information that had heretofore been held by separate agencies and that had only occasionally and at great cost been linked to one another. Benda argued, in a formulation that would have an influential afterlife, that the real danger lay not so much in the role-specific disclosure of information to the agents of the welfare state, but rather in the fact that integrated information systems deprived the individual of "the disposition over . . . to whom and for what purposes information is communicated. It is not information itself [that is, it is not its context-appropriate disclosure], but rather its *dysfunctional dissemination*, over which the concerned individual has no control, that destroys the private sphere" (emphasis added).[46]

While the postwar development of the welfare state was vastly expanding the state's need for personal information, much of which had to be regarded as "private" or "intimate," the citizens who demanded and benefitted from such social services could not at the same time, Benda insisted, refuse to provide the information required to deliver these services. On the other hand, he warned that the uncompromising defense of a narrowly circumscribed sphere of absolute privacy was not a viable solution and that the constitutional obligations to provide *Amtshilfe* could not be ignored. In the end, Benda optimistically concluded that the conception of privacy as the role-specific disclosure of information, in conjunction with steps to ensure the greatest possible transparency in the new and mysterious technology of electronic data processing, would make it possible to steer a middle path between all of these conflicting demands.[47]

The Private Sphere and Beyond: Information and the Degradation of Dignity

Viewed from the perspective of later developments, the central achievement of the census decision was the articulation of the right to informational self-determination as a concretization of—or, more precisely, as the addition of a new strand or dimension to—the prevailing doctrine of personality rights. But seen from the beginning, rather than the end, the constitutional jurisprudence that led up to the census decision was a messy affair.

The first step involved the institutionalization of the doctrine of personality rights. While libel and copyright law, as well as legislation governing the use of one's image for commercial purposes, had provided a means through which the individual could seek compensation for material damage to name, reputation, and creative efforts, before 1945 German courts had refused to recognize the right to be protected from immaterial injury to one's dignity and sense of self. However, the postwar proclamation of human dignity and the free development of the personality as the cornerstones of the new constitutional order altered the trajectory of German jurisprudence in this area. In 1954 the Federal Court of Justice (the Bundesgerichtshof, the country's highest appellate court in civil and criminal matters) codified the doctrine in its 1954 Schacht or Letter to the Editor decision.[48] Although the administration introduced a law to protect personality and honor in civil matters in 1959, the Bundestag never approved it because of the concern that such right could never be embodied in clearly defined legal norms and the fear that such a law would impose excessively narrow limits on the press.[49]

Personality rights would not be systematically linked to information and privacy until the turn of the 1980s. In the 1950s and 1960s German thinking on privacy was dominated by the concept of the private sphere. Heinrich Hubmann's 1953 study of the topic was the most influential attempt to develop an exhaustive taxonomy of the private.[50] However, the most basic problem with the concept of the private sphere was what contemporaries called its relativity—that is, the fact that the intimacy, sensitivity, or privacy of various matters was judged differently by different persons in different contexts. Many attempts were made to square this circle by means of the Ptolemaic strategy of identifying additional spheres, or shifting the boundaries of existing ones, in the futile hope of making theory coincide with the infinite variety of human social life. The result was such theoretical disarray that by 1971 Steinmüller and his collaborators could conclude, as we have seen, that the concept was unusable as the basis for privacy protection legislation.[51]

The concept of the private sphere entered into constitutional jurisprudence in an uneven manner not only because of the its ambiguities and contradictions, but also because the decisions that established its constitutional relevance also relied in unreflected ways on arguments that had nothing to do with the private sphere, but that later became key building blocks of the right to informational self-determination. The 1969 microcensus decision, which grew out of a challenge to those questions that asked about the vacation habits of the individuals surveyed, was one of the main points of reference in the 1970s debates over the use of personal data by the state.[52] In rejecting the challenge, the Court relied on two arguments. The second argument contained the classic justification of the private sphere cited at the beginning of this chapter: the person must have an interior space into which he could retreat because such a protected space was the precondition for the autonomous development of the personality. From this perspective, it was easy for the Court to conclude that, even though the microcensus sought information about private life, it did not require the disclosure of matters pertaining to the absolutely protected intimate sphere.

The first argument unfolded at an entirely different level. It began with a restatement of the constitutional commitment to human dignity. However, the issue at stake here was not whether penalties failing to complete the survey infringed on the freedom to develop the personality through action in the external world. Rather, in a passage that would become the touchstone for subsequent debate, the Court ruled that this dignity would be violated if the state sought "to compulsorily register and catalog a human being in a comprehensive manner—even if this were done in the form of an anonymous statistical survey—and thereby treat him like an object, which can be inventoried from every possible perspective."[53] In this respect, the microcensus decision represented a warning that the construction of personality profiles—that is, the comprehensive "registration and cataloging" of personal data—might diminish the freedom of the individual to choose how he would represent himself in social communication to such an extent that it would render the free development of the personality impossible.

The second major decision that helped codify the concept of the private sphere was the January 1973 ruling on the admissibility of clandestine tape recordings as evidence in criminal proceedings.[54] This decision is important for two reasons. First, in previous decisions the concept of a "final, inviolable domain of human freedom" had served to identify the limits of legitimate state action.[55] Although this might have sustained a definition of privacy as a societal sphere separate from the state, in the tape recording decision the Court refigured this domain of human freedom that lay beyond the limits of legitimate state power as the absolutely protected "core" (*Kernbereich*) of the intimate life of the individual.

Second, since the tape recording in question had been secretly made by a business partner of the appellant, who had then made it available to the police, what was at stake here was not the intrusion of the state into the private sphere to obtain information, but rather the constitutional protections that were to be accorded to the informational content of personal data, regardless of whether this data was deemed private.[56] In its ruling, the Court argued that the individual was entitled to those protections necessary for the development of the personality and that, therefore, the right to one's image and spoken word also had to include the right to determine who was permitted to record such words and the circumstances under which they could be replayed. Arguing in terms that were virtually identical to those that would be applied to integrated information systems in the census decision, the Court explained that, recorded on a magnetic medium, voice and intonation took on an existence that was entirely independent of both the speaker and the original context in which the words had been spoken and that the integrity of the personality would be diminished in essential respects if others were free to replay these words in contexts of their choosing without the consent of the speaker.[57]

In the March 1972 medical records and the May 1977 drug addiction counseling center decisions, which both addressed issues arising out of the seizure of treatment records by the police, the Court ruled that, since the data contained in these records arose in the private sphere of the patient and the advice seeker, it shared in the protections accorded to that sphere.[58] However, these decisions also raised the possibility that the disclosure of information, which was not regarded as sensitive or intimate, might in certain contexts still be so injurious to the person's sense of self or so harmful to his interests that it would still be deserving of protection. This line of thought raised the question of how the protection of nonintimate information could be constitutionally legitimated. This question was addressed in a cluster of decisions stretching from 1970 to the early 1980s.

The Loss of Control and Its Constitutional Remedy: The Right to Informational Self-Determination

The Constitutional Court had already stumbled over these issues in its January 1970 divorce papers decision. That case grew out of the appeal against an administrative decision that permitted the use of papers relating to divorce proceedings in a disciplinary action against the defendant, who was employed as a civil servant. The Court ruled here that, although the matters described in the papers pertained to the private sphere, they did not enjoy the absolute protection accorded to matters relating to the inviolable core of private life—if only because they had to be disclosed in order to obtain a divorce. At this point, the door was open—as it would be with the tape recording decision—to investigate the benefits and harms that might result from the use of this information in contexts other than the court proceedings for which it had originally been gathered. However, the Court chose not to follow this path and ruled instead that the infringement on personality rights resulting from the decision to make the papers available for the disciplinary hearing was far out of proportion to the demonstrated need for them.[59]

The Saroya decision of February 1973 and the Lebach decision handed down in June of that year were the first to suggest how privacy could be constitutionally adjudicated without relying on the concept of the private sphere.[60] The Saroya decision grew out of a suit to recover damages from a newspaper for the publication of a fictitious interview with the former wife of the shah of Iran. The complainant in the second case had been convicted as an accessory in the January 1969 murder of four soldiers at an army base in the town of Lebach; by the fall of 1972 he had served half of his sentence and was expecting to soon be released on parole; and he went to court to prevent a television network from broadcasting his name and picture in a film being made about the affair. In both cases, the complainants argued that these unauthorized and undesired depictions of their lives hindered the free development of the personality, though without either defaming them or making false statements. In addition, neither case dealt with matters belonging to the private sphere: in the Saroya case, the story could not have invaded the private sphere because it was entirely fictitious, and the film at issue in the Lebach case only painted a broad picture of the life of the complainant. As with the tape recording case, these cases turned on the violation of one's sense of self resulting from the loss of control over the meaning assigned to this data by others. In both cases, the question for the Court was whether there was a constitutional basis for preventing other persons from representing persons in ways that they felt infringed upon the development of their personality, even if this information was not deemed private.

The answer in the Lebach decision was that the right to one's image and spoken word also had to encompass—as a corrective to this loss of control—a right to dispose over the way that one was publicly represented and interpreted by others. In the Court's words, "every person may in principle himself and independently of others determine whether and to what extent his life (*Lebensbild*) may be publicly represented by others, either in full or in part."[61] The Court supported this argument with an analysis of how the mass media, which elicited intense emotional reactions by huge audiences, and the documentary reliance on the reconstruction of events, conversations, and thought processes, which blurred the boundary between fiction and reality, posed specific dangers for the ability of the individual to convince others that he could actually be anything other than the way he was portrayed by the media. These problems were compounded by the fact that the use of the crime and its interpretation as the organizing principle for a television program that aspired to create the illusion of authenticity threatened to mislead the viewer into accepting a foreshortened representation, which highlighted the negative elements of the personality, as a faithful representation of the entire person.[62] This sociological account of the use and possible distortion of personal data under the conditions of mass media, so to speak, pointed beyond the parsing of the private sphere and provided a model for the Court's later analysis of the use of personal information "under the conditions of electronic data processing." However, although the codification of a right to determine how the self could be represented by others made sense as a corrective to the unpredictable and uncontrollable interpretive freedom of one's communicative partners, the nature and extent of this right remained undefined in the Lebach decision.

Privacy, Identity, and Social Communication

The last major constitutional case to be considered is the 1981 Eppler decision, which adjudicated a suit by Erhard Eppler (SPD), a former minister for economic cooperation and central figure in the peace movement in the 1980s, against a local CDU group demanding that the latter cease attributing to him views on economic and social policy that he claimed never to have espoused.[63] In Eppler, the Court immediately emancipated its thinking from the approaches employed in previous cases by declaring that any remedy for the matters raised by the appellant could not be found in either the theory of the private sphere or any of the existing strands of personality law, but only in the general principle of personality rights. What the Court did in this case was reaffirm the right of the individual to determine how he would be represented to others and thereby to make a claim to be recognized as such by his communicative partners. "It can only be a matter for the individual person himself to determine the way that he should be recognized by others. To this extent," the Court reasoned, "the content of the rights of the personality is essentially determined by the bearer of these rights."[64] However, although the Court also recognized that it could not avoid granting the same right to the Other, who was protected by *his own* personality rights against the imperious demands for social recognition emanating from the original actor, neither its arguments in Eppler nor—to look ahead—those it set out in the census decision ever went beyond the juxtaposition of two conflicting rights.[65]

Podlech provided a fuller account of this process than did the Constitutional Court itself. In a commentary on Article 2, Par. 1 of the Basic Law, which was in press when the census decision was handed down and which was submitted as an amicus brief in the case, Podlech deconstructed the account of the relationship between the individual and society, and between the private and the public, that had been codified in the Investment

Assistance decision. He argued that, notwithstanding its constant protestations regarding the social nature of human existence, the Constitutional Court did, in fact, regard privacy as something that belonged to the isolated, sovereign individual. Podlech, however, argued that one could arrive at a more satisfactory understanding of privacy if one assumed that, as part of the process whereby the young were socialized into society and developed their individual identities, the individual personality developed not in isolation from others, but rather through communication with them.[66] To the extent that the personality developed through social communication, he concluded, privacy could not be conceived "as something pertaining to the isolated individual, which is then lost through communication with others and through the acquisition of a social dimension.... It is a social quality of the person."[67]

The question, then, was what social conditions would have to be satisfied to ensure the free development of the personality and the formation of individual identity in the process of social communication. In an important passage that would be taken over almost verbatim in the census decision, Podlech argued that a social order and legal system in which "the citizen can no longer know who knows what about him at what point and in what context" would be incompatible with the free development of the personality because the individual had to possess a clear enough idea of what personal data his communicative partners possessed and what meaning they assigned to this information in specific contexts so that he could—with a reasonable probability of success—reflexively incorporate their anticipated reactions into his identity, his self-representation, and his demand for social recognition.[68] In other words, what had to be protected, Podlech argued, was "the at least partial self-determination by the person" of what personal information was to be disclosed to different segments of his social environment.[69]

If privacy was a social quality of the person or if it defined a social and informational relationship among persons, then one had to begin—as many of the early privacy theorists examined above had argued—with an examination of the social interests that determined how these informational relations were structured. As Podlech explained, such interests gave certain parties an incentive to make use of available means to gain information regarding the very matters that other parties sought to keep private precisely so that they could influence or control these persons. On the other hand, he argued that the balancing of privacy and access rights by the Court was done in such an abstract manner that it could not do justice to the political nature of the process or to the fact that "today's law is the result of yesterday's politics, that the limitations on the freedoms imposed by this law are the outcome of a political contest in which others sought to impose these limitations."[70] Since individuals were always embedded in social relationships that were themselves shaped by power differences, the constitutional protection of individual privacy was necessary, Podlech concluded, because citizens could only give their consent to a social order if its laws ensured a minimal degree of privacy—that is, if they ensured at least a minimal space for autonomy and self-determination.[71]

The Social Determination of Privacy and the Object of Information Law

To the extent that privacy rights were constitutionally grounded in the right to the free development of the personality, they always had a subjective dimension.[72] However, Simitis, Otto Mallmann, Podlech, and Benda all rejected an understanding of privacy modeled on property rights,[73] and the final major challenge facing the early theorists of informational privacy was to show how such a subjective conception of privacy could be transcended. They attempted to do so by showing—as Podlech had done in his essay—that the underlying theory also provided a viable account of the role of privacy in the communication among individuals *in* society.

One of the earliest attempts to show how a theory of role-specific self-representation could be transposed from the individual level to communicative processes taking place at the social or systemic level can be found in a 1965 essay by Niklas Luhmann. Here, Luhmann conceived of the free development of the personality not in terms of freedom of action, but rather in terms of a right to self-representation within a communicative process that first enabled the individual to become aware of himself as a self-conscious individual, and he argued that dignity and freedom should be understood as the outcome of this process, rather than as qualities inhering in the subject.[74] Luhmann's description in this essay, which was frequently glossed by early privacy theorists, of the reflexive, communicative structure of self-representation, recognition, and identity formation and his analysis of how disclosure and concealment influenced the correspondence (or lack thereof) between self-representation and social role reframed the jurisprudential debate over personality rights in ways that would shape the subsequent debate over the nature of privacy.

Following Luhmann, Otto Mallmann took up the challenge of showing how role theory and the definition of privacy in terms of nonknowledge and role-specific disclosure could be used to conceptualize the social, informational, and power relations between individuals in society. Since the reflexive distancing of the subject from ascribed social roles was only possible if the partners in social interaction were not exhaustively informed regarding one another, Mallmann regarded the protection of privacy, which he defined as "situationally distinct domains of noninformation pertaining to the person," as an integral element of any general theory of social action.[75] The basic problem was that dossiers gave rise to increasingly comprehensive and detailed behavioral expectations on the part of the partner who possessed this information. This, in turn, put pressure on the actor to modify his behavior in order to conform to the increasingly narrow and rigid norms that "preformed" the communicative process and thereby created new forms of power and dependence. Taken to the logical extreme, there was the danger that an exhaustive dossier would so diminish the freedom of self-representation that the person would be transformed from a morally autonomous actor into a "mere object" for manipulation by others, thereby limiting the free development of the individual personality, injuring his dignity, and diminishing his concrete life chances.[76]

In the end, Mallmann concluded that in two respects privacy was a social relationship. On the one hand, the reflexive nature of identity formation meant that the development of the individual personality was always already entangled in social, communicative relationships with others. On the other hand, the specific dynamics of disclosure and concealment at work in this process were always determined by the interests and power relations that structured these relationships.[77] Therefore, he concluded, privacy protection should not be understood in terms of the withdrawal into a sphere of seclusion, but rather as the "demarcation of the limits of informational control in the interest of preserving and improving the chances of individual development."[78]

Mallmann made one final point of particular importance: that privacy was the essential precondition not only for the development of the personality, but also for the formation of democratic subjects. "It is the limitation of the transparency of behavior," he argued, "that first makes possible free communication, personal initiative, and participation in social and political events. Privacy is an indispensable, even if not a sufficient, precondition for autonomous action, for self-representation, for graduated distancing and the formation of identity."[79] The same point was made by Simitis. Although he criticized individualist conceptions of privacy because he believed that a degree of mutual transparency was essential to communication and social life, he also argued that limitations on this transparency were essential because they alone enabled citizens to develop into reflexive individuals capable of autonomous action and political engagement. As he wrote in 1982, the individual, whose actions are increasingly "registered" (*verdatet*) tends to become incapable of communication. He loses the competence for reflection on both his own development and the surrounding environment. The greater the perfection of information systems, the greater the extent to which they anticipate what the individual can think (*dem einzelnen vordenken*) and deprive him of the possibility of a rational dialogue regarding the necessity and the shaping of the expectations imposed on or by him. . . . A democratically structured state and a democratically structured society are, therefore, incompatible with the uncontrolled proliferation of personal information.[80]

The task of privacy protection law was, therefore, to secure the bases for both individual development and the realization of the social vision codified in the Basic Law by ensuring that the socially or contextually appropriate disclosure of information was not distorted by social power. The precondition for effective measures in this direction, Mallmann concluded, was the sociological investigation of the concrete contexts for the collection and use of information and of the social and power relations that structured them: "This is the foundation that first makes possible the prestructuring of the informational relations between the individual and the information system [that is, the information system of society]."[81] This raised the question of the scope and function of information law and its relation to privacy protection legislation.

If, in the 1960s, information had become a matter of social policy, it did not become a concern for the law until the 1970s.[82] While the term information law was initially used as an umbrella term for all of the diverse problems raised by the new information and communications technologies, in their contribution to a 1976 volume of essays, which represented the first attempt to define the new field, Willi Egloff and Georg Werckmeister argued that the focus on specific technologies was misleading. Instead, they argued that the domain of information law was coextensive with that of society itself because "it is hard to imagine any social phenomenon, or any legal regulation" that did not involve, at least indirectly, the exchange and use of information.[83] This meant that social systems also had to be understood as information systems, whose critical analysis had to be the starting point for any attempt to regulate the use of personal information in that society. As Steinmüller explained, although the "information systems [of society] and their relation to the social systems in which they are embedded" were the object of information law, the structure of the latter could be determined only on the basis of what he called "the prior socioeconomic conceptualization of the empirical structures of action and information."[84] In other words, the debate over privacy protection would be transformed into a critical theory of society as the focus shifted from the personality and privacy rights of the individual to the social determinants of informational relationships.[85]

However, this shift to what Podlech called the systemic level[86] also meant that information law could not be equated with privacy protection law. Access rights were no less fundamental than privacy rights, and, in the end, information law, as a form of social policy governing the information system of society, would be shaped by political choices among conflicting interests based on the analysis of the elemental structures of the society, the informational relations that they sustained, and the power relations with which they were infused.[87]

The drafting of the Federal Privacy Protection Law, which will be the topic of the following chapter, represented the first attempt to do what the early privacy advocates had argued was necessary: to analyze the ways in which personal information was used by individuals, firms, and the state, the social interests and social power that structured information exchange in these contexts, and the specific kinds of power generated by bureaucratic population surveillance and the use of electronic and manual technologies, and then on this basis to (re)negotiate the parameters for socially appropriate information exchange.

Notes

1. BVerfGE 6, 32 (41).
2. BVerfGE 27, 1, (6). This formulation was borrowed from Josef Wintrich, *Die Problematik der Grundrechte* (Springer, 1957), 15. Wintrich was a former president of the Constitutional Court. The microcensus, which has been carried out since 1957, is a statistical survey of a representative sample of the German population to gather economic and social information to supplement and update the data gathered by the decennial census.
3. Wilhelm Steinmüller et al., *Grundfragen des Datenschutzes* (July 1971), Drs. 6/3826, 48.
4. Beate Rössler, *The Value of Privacy* (Polity, 2004); and Stanley Benn and Gerald Gaus, "The Liberal Conception of the Public and the Private," in *Public and Private in Social Life*, ed. Benn and Gaus (Croom Helm, 1983), 31–66.
5. For a comparison of German and American approaches to privacy, see Edward J. Eberle, "Human Dignity, Privacy, and Personality in German and American Constitutional Law," *Utah Law Review*, no. 4 (1997): 963–1056; Eberle, *Dignity and Liberty: Constitutional Visions in Germany and the United States* (Praeger, 2002); and James Q. Whitman, "The Two Western Cultures of Privacy: Dignity versus Liberty," *Yale Law Journal* 113 (2004): 1151–1221.
6. In the felicitous phrasing of Whitman, "The Two Western Cultures of Privacy," 1213; and Samuel Warren and Louis Brandeis, "The Right to Privacy," *Harvard Law Review* 4 (December 1890): 193–220.

7. Paul Schwartz and Karl-Nikolaus Peifer, "Prosser's *Privacy* and the German Right of Personality: Are Four Privacy Torts Better than One Unitary Concept?," *California Law Review* 98 (2010): 1925–87; and William Prosser, "Privacy," *California Law Review* 48 (1960): 383–423. Edward J. Bloustein, "Privacy as an Aspect of Human Dignity: An Answer to Dean Prosser," *NYU Law Review* 39 (1964): 962–1007, is the most important American attempt since Warren and Brandeis to reformulate privacy rights in terms of dignity and personality rights.
8. Sarah Igo, *The Known Citizen: A History of Privacy in Modern America* (Harvard University Press, 2018), 159, argues that this semantic recasting of privacy in *Griswold* and subsequent cases effectively "hijacked" the privacy discourse that had developed over the preceding decade.
9. *Whalen v. Roe*, 429 U.S. 589 (1977) at 605; Paul Schwartz, "The Computer in German and American Constitutional Law: Towards an American Right of Informational Self-Determination," *The American Journal of Comparative Law* 37, no. 4. (autumn, 1989): 675–701; and Igo, *The Known Citizen*, 262–63, who joins Schwartz, "The Computer in German and American Constitutional Law," and Schwartz and Peifer, "Prosser's Privacy and the German Right of Personality," in characterizing *Whalen* as a missed opportunity and a path not taken.
10. Daniel Solove, *Understanding Privacy* (Harvard University Press, 2008).
11. BVerfGE 4, 7 (15–16): "Das Menschenbild des Grundgesetzes ist nicht das eines isolierten souveränen Individuums; das Grundgesetz hat vielmehr die Spannung Individuum—Gemeinschaft im Sinne der Gemeinschaftsbezogenheit und Gemeinschaftsgebundenheit der Person entschieden, ohne dabei deren Eigenwert anzutasten." Wintrich was the most important channel through which these ideas shaped the thinking of the Constitutional Court in the 1950s. See Samuel Moyn, "Personalism, Community, and the Origins of Human Rights," in *Human Rights in the Twentieth Century*, ed. Stefan-Ludwig Hoffmann (Cambridge University Press, 2011), 85–106, especially 102–5; and Ulrich Becker, *Das "Menschenbild des Grundgesetzes" in der Rechtsprechung des Bundesverfassungsgerichts* (Duncker & Humblot, 1996).
12. Similarly, Igo, *The Known Citizen*, 11, 25, 162, argues that privacy has served as a catch-all for concerns about modern life and what she terms the increasing "organization" of society.
13. Robert G. Moeller, *Protecting Motherhood: Women and the Family in the Politics of Postwar West Germany* (University of California Press, 1996); Elaine Tyler May, *Homeward Bound: American Families in the Cold War Era* (Basic Books, 1988); Michael Rogin, "Kiss Me Deadly: Communism, Motherhood, and Cold War Movies," *Representations* 6 (Spring 1984), 1–36; Deborah Nelson, *Pursuing Privacy in Cold War America* (Columbia University Press, 2002); Paolo Scrivano, "Signs of Americanization in Italian Domestic Life: Italy's Postwar Conversion to Consumerism," *Journal of Contemporary History* 40, no. 2 (2005): 317–40; and Paul Nolte, "Öffentlichkeit und Privatheit: Deutschland im 20. Jahrhundert," *Merkur* 686 (June 2006): 499–512. Igo, *The Known Citizen*; Lawrence Cappello, *None of Your Damn Business: Privacy in the United States form the Gilded Age to the Digital Age* (University of Chicago Press, 2019); and Deborah Cohen, *Family Secrets: Shame & Privacy in Modern Britain* (Oxford University Press, 2013) offer broad histories of privacy in the twentieth century, but do not specifically focus on the questions of informational privacy that lie at the heart of the present study.
14. Carola Sachse, *Der Hausarbeitstag. Gerechtigkeit und Gleichberechtigung in Ost und West, 1939–1994* (Wallstein, 2002); and Alice Weinreb, *Modern Hungers: Food and Power in Twentieth-Century Germany* (Oxford University Press, 2017), 122–95. Joe Perry studies the impact of consumerism and the media on family life and its privacy in "Healthy for Family Life: Television, Masculinity, and Domestic Modernity during West Germany's Miracle Years," *German History* 25, no. 4 (2007): 560–95. The later feminist critique of the

role of the public-private distinction in upholding power and gender hierarchies within the domestic sphere played no role in the German privacy protection debates in the 1970s.

15. James Chappel, *Catholic Modern: The Challenge of Totalitarianism and the Remaking of the Church* (Harvard University Press, 2018); Marco Duranti, *The Conservative Human Rights Revolution: European Identity, Transnational Politics, and the Origins of the European Convention* (Oxford University Press, 2017); and Moyn, "Personalism, Community, and the Origins of Human Rights."

16. Otto Mallmann, *Zielfunktionen des Datenschutzes. Schutz der Privatsphäre—Korrekte Information* (Metzner Verlag, 1977), 16–33. On the catalytic impact of the new mass media on early twentieth-century privacy law, see Samantha Barbas, *Laws of Image: Privacy and Publicity in America* (Stanford University Press, 2015); Cappello, *None of Your Damn Business*, 29–70; and Frank Bösch, *Öffentliche Geheimnisse. Skandale, Politik und Medien in Deutschland und Großbritannien 1880–1914* (Oldenbourg, 2009).

17. Simitis, "Chancen und Gefahren der elektronischen Datenverarbeitung," *NJW* 24, no. 16 (20 April 1971): 673–82, citation 675.

18. Simitis, "Datenschutz—Notwendigkeit und Voraussetzungen einer gesetzlichen Regelung," *DVR* 2 (1973): 138–89, citation 144–45.

19. Simitis, "Chancen und Gefahren," 675.

20. Simitis, "Datenschutz—Notwendigkeit und Voraussetzungen," 147.

21. Lenk, "Datenschutz in der öffentlichen Verwaltung," in *Datenschutz. Juristische Grundsatzfragen beim Einsatz elektronischer Datenverarbeitungsanlagen in Wirtschaft und Verwaltung*, ed. Wolfgang Kilian, Klaus Lenk, and Wilhelm Steinmüller (Athenäum-Verlag, 1973), 15–50, citations 17, 20, 33–34.

22. Steinmüller et al., *Grundfragen des Datenschutzes*, 113; Christoph Mallmann, *Datenschutz in Verwaltungs-Informationssystemen* (Oldenbourg, 1976), 12ff.; and Paul J. Müller, "Informationsflüsse und Informationshaushalte," in *Informationsrecht und Informationspolitik*, ed. Wilhelm Steinmüller (Oldenbourg, 1976), 95–109, especially 104. Müller showed how much information each branch of the public administration received from, and provided to, other branches. He concluded that what was actually taking place was a leveling up of the amount of information available to each and a corresponding erosion of the established practice that each branch had access only to the information needed to carry out its specific responsibilities.

23. Adalbert Podlech, "Verfassungsrechtliche Probleme öffentlicher Informationssysteme," *DVR* 1 (1972/73): 149–69; and Ernst Benda, "Privatsphäre und 'Persönlichkeitsprofil.' Ein Beitrag zur Datenschutzdiskussion," in *Menschenwürde und freiheitliche Rechtsordnung. Festschrift für Willi Geiger zum 65. Geburtstag*, ed. Gerhard Leibholz et al. (Mohr, 1974), 23–44.

24. The most important contemporary study of the topic was Bernhard Schlink, *Die Amtshilfe. Ein Beitrag zu einer Lehre von der Gewaltenteilung in der Verwaltung* (Duncker & Humblot, 1982).

25. Mallmann, *Zielfunktionen des Datenschutzes*, 70ff.

26. Simitis, "Datenschutz—Notwendigkeit und Voraussetzungen," 151–52; and Mallmann, *Zielfunktionen*, 78.

27. Lisa Gitelman, ed., *"Raw Data" is an Oxymoron* (MIT Press, 2013).

28. Simitis, "Chancen und Gefahren," 675.

29. Simitis, "Datenschutz—Voraussetzung oder Ende der Kommunikation?," in *Europäisches Rechtsdenken in Geschichte und Gegenwart. Festschrift für Helmut Coing zum 70. Geburtstag*, ed. Norbert Horn (Beck, 1982), II:495–520.

30. Ulrich Dammann, "Strukturwandel der Information und Datenschutz," *DVR* 3 (1974): 267–301, citation 277. Maria Los, "Looking into the Future: Surveillance, Globalization and the Totalitarian Potential," in *Theorizing Surveillance: The Panopticon and Beyond*, ed.

David Lyon (Willan Publishing, 2006), 69–94, argues that such surveillance has dehumanizing and desocializing effects, which lead to the "biographical uprooting" of the data subject.
31. Ulrich Seidel, *Datenbanken und Persönlichkeitsrecht unter besonderer Berücksichtigung der amerikanischen Computer Privacy* (Otto Schmidt, 1972), 139.
32. Dammann, "Strukturwandel der Information und Datenschutz," 275.
33. Müller, "Funktionen des Datenschutzes aus soziologischer Sicht," *DVR* 4 (1975): 107–18, citation 109; and Müller, "Die Gefährdung der Privatsphäre durch Datenbanken," in *Datenbanken und Datenschutz*, ed. Ulrich Dammann et al. (Herder & Herder, 1974), 63–90.
34. Podlech argued that the correlate of these two fundamental limitations on state power was the prohibition of what he called the "pragmatic-free" collection of information — that is, the collection of information without the prior specification of the purpose of such collection — because, without such specification, it was impossible to adjudicate the appropriateness of the subsequent use of this information. Adalbert Podlech, "Gesellschaftstheoretische Grundlage des Datenschutzes," in *Datenschutz und Datensicherung*, ed. Rüdiger Dierstein et al. (J. P. Bachem, 1976), 311–25, especially 318; and Podlech, "Aufgaben und Problematik des Datenschutzes," *DVR* 5 (1976): 23–39, especially 31–32.
35. Simitis, "Datenschutz—Notwendigkeit und Voraussetzungen," 152–53. These ideas were restated by Serge Gutwirth, who wrote in *Privacy and the Information Age* (Rowman & Littlefield, 2002), 34, that "privacy . . . is defined by its context and only obtains its true meaning within social relationships. The parameters, which pinpoint privacy and its effects on a situation, are the juxtaposed interests and rights as well as the traits and positions of the people involved. In this sense, privacy is a strategic notion. Its boundaries and limits vary strongly depending on the circumstances and the specifics of each case."
36. Mallmann, *Zielfunktionen*, 24: "informationsbezogener Privatheitsbegriff."
37. Mallmann, *Zielfunktionen*, 30; and Simitis, "Datenschutz—Notwendigkeit und Voraussetzungen," 153.
38. Müller, "Funktionen des Datenschutzes," 110; a similar claim was made by Herbert Fiedler, "Datenschutz und Gesellschaft," in *Informationsrecht und Informationspolitik*, ed. Steinmüller, 179–95, especially 185.
39. Fiedler, "Datenschutz und Gesellschaft," citation 193.
40. Podlech, "Aufgaben und Problematik des Datenschutzes," 24–25; and Podlech, "Gesellschaftstheoretische Grundlage des Datenschutzes."
41. Cohen, *Configuring the Networked Self: Law, Code, and the Play of Everyday Practice* (Yale University Press, 2012), 239–41.
42. Müller, "Funktionen des Datenschutzes aus soziologischer Sicht," 108.
43. Simitis, "Datenschutz—Notwendigkeit und Voraussetzungen," 153–54. Otto Mallmann, *Zielfunktionen*, 30, defined privacy in the same terms.
44. For examples of such concern, see Podlech, "Verfassungsrechtliche Probleme öffentlicher Informationssysteme," 157; and Adalbert Podlech, "Das Recht auf Privatheit," in *Grundrechte als Fundament der Demokratie*, ed. Joachim Perels (Suhrkamp, 1979), 50–68, especially 56–57. Podlech, who was the only person to offer such a definition, defined a personality profile as "the systematic collection of information regarding a multiplicity of spheres of life of an individual through the computer-assisted exploitation of information sources, most often for the purpose of making the future behavior of the information subject predictable or, especially with regard to crime prevention, reconstructing past behavior." Adalbert Podlech, "Art. 2 Abs. 1," *Kommentar zum Grundgesetz für die Bundesrepublik Deutschland* (Luchterhand, 1984), 317–59, citation 355. Sarah Igo discusses both the potential harms of such (computerized) dossiers and the legislative means adopted in the United States to mitigate these harms (the anemic 1974 Privacy

Act and the Fair Credit Reporting, Freedom of Information, and Family Educational Rights and Privacy Acts) in her analysis of the "record prison" in *The Known Citizen*, 22–63.
45. See, for example, the damning assessment in Hans Peter Bull, *Sinn und Unsinn des Datenschutzes* (Mohr Siebeck, 2015), 32–34; as well as Karl-Heinz Ladeur, "Datenschutz—vom Abwehrrecht zur planerischen Optimierung von Wissensnetzwerken," *Datenschutz und Datensicherung* 24, no. 1 (2000): 12–19, who characterizes (13) the threat ostensibly posed by personality profiles as a "mystification"; and Hans-Heinrich Trute, "Verfassungsrechtliche Grundlagen," in *Handbuch Datenschutzrecht*, ed. Alexander Roßnagel (Beck, 2003), 156–87, especially 171.
46. Benda, "Privatsphäre und 'Persönlichkeitsprofil,'" 37.
47. Ibid., 39–44.
48. BGH 13, 334; Horst-Peter Götting et al., eds., *Handbuch des Persönlichkeitsrechts* (Beck, 2008), chapters 1–2; and Podlech, "Art. 2 Abs. 1."
49. Drs. 3/1237; Harry Krause, "The Right to Privacy in Germany: Pointers for American Legislation?" *Duke Law Journal* (1965): 481–530; Heinrich Hubmann, "Persönlichkeitsschutz ohne Grenzen? Betrachtungen zu einigen neueren Entscheidungen des BVerfG," *Archiv für Film-, Funk- und Theaterrecht* 70 (1974): 75–89; and Horst Ehmann, "Das Allgemeine Persönlichkeitsrecht. Zur Transformation unmoralischer in unerlaubte Handlungen," in *50 Jahre Bundesgerichtshof*, ed. Claus-Wilhelm Canaris (Beck, 2000), I:613–74. These reasons also underlay the opposition to privacy legislation in Great Britain in the 1960s. See Walter Pratt, *Privacy in Britain* (Bucknell University Press, 1979).
50. Hubmann, *Das Persönlichkeitsrecht*, 2. Aufl. (Böhlau, 1967 [original 1953]), 268ff., 320–32.
51. Drs. 6/3826, 51.
52. BVerfGE 27, 1.
53. BVerfGE 27, 1 (6).
54. BVerfGE 34, 238.
55. BVerfGE 6, 32 (41).
56. Marion Albers, *Informationelle Selbstbestimmung* (Nomos, 2005), 203.
57. This line of reasoning can be traced back to Kant's reflections on the impact of unauthorized republication on the identity and personality of the author. See Adrian Johns, *Piracy: The Intellectual Property Wars from Gutenberg to Gates* (University of Chicago Press, 2009), 54–55. However, the Court actually decided the case on entirely different grounds. Building on the concept of the private sphere set out earlier in its ruling, the Court maintained that, regardless of context, certain kinds of information were intrinsically more private or sensitive than others and that, therefore, the entire private life of the individual did not enjoy the same absolute protection as its core. Although the Court confessed its inability to describe this inviolable intimate sphere in the abstract, it had no doubt that the business dealings that were recorded on the tape did not fall within it. In the case at hand, it ruled that the infringement on the appellant's right to the spoken word, which was attributable to the surreptitious recording of potentially incriminating statements in the context of an ostensibly confidential conversation, outweighed the public interest in prosecuting the relatively minor offense for which the appellant was being investigated.
58. BVerfGE 32, 373 (379); and 44, 353 (372).
59. In its brief for the census decision, the interior ministry followed the reasoning on which the Court had relied in the divorce papers decision, while the Court followed the path that it had chosen not to take in the earlier decision. See Bundesminister des Innern to Präsident des Bundesverfassungsberichts, Betr.: Verfassungsbeschwerden (24 March 1983), 69–71, LAB B Rep. 004, no. 1108.
60. BVerfGE 34, 269; 35, 202.
61. BVerfGE 35, 202 (220).

62. BVerfGE 35, 202 (226–30).
63. BVerfGE 54, 148.
64. BVerfGE 54, 148 (155–56): "kann es nur Sache der einzelnen Person selbst sein, über das zu bestimmen, was ihren sozialen Geltungsanspruch ausmachen soll."
65. Albers, *Informationelle Selbstbestimmung*, 222–26.
66. Podlech, "Art. 2 Abs. 1," 337. The Court's understanding of privacy rights, Podlech argued, gave rise to a characteristic difference between German and American privacy law noted by Benda (and subsequently cited by many others). While sexual relations represented the core area of protection under American privacy law, the irony under German law was that "precisely the most intimate of human relationships presumes contact with the personality sphere of another person and to this respect gives the action a social dimension that precludes it from being ascribed to the more narrowly defined intimate sphere," thereby rendering them subject to public regulation. See Benda, "Privatsphäre und 'Persönlichkeitsprofil,'" 30; and Podlech, "Art. 2 Abs. 1," 337. Such reasoning had been the basis for the Court's 1957 decision (BVerfGE 6, 389) upholding the criminalization of male homosexuality: once this social dimension had been established, the door was open for the Court to conclude that homosexual activity was not entitled to the protection otherwise accorded to sexual life because it violated moral law.
67. Podlech, "Art. 2 Abs. 1," 337, 344. There are important parallels between Podlech's arguments here and the account of the social nature of privacy by Robert Post in "The Social Foundations of Privacy: Community and Self in the Common Law Tort," *California Law Review* 77 (1989): 957–1010. In this article, Post described the dialectical relationship between what he called the "social personality" and "civility rules" and then argued that, since the integrity of the individual personality depended on the observance of certain kinds of social norms, tort remedies for the violation of these rights reaffirmed the dignity and sacred aspects of individual identity, on the one hand, and both the social order and the social norms that enable an autonomous self to emerge, on the other. "This mysterious fusion of civility and autonomy," Post argues (974), "is at the heart of the intrusion tort." Post's reflections also enrich the concept of context by showing that, in determining whether a particular communicative act—that is, a particular disclosure—constitutes an invasion of privacy, all of the seemingly objective criteria that are often adduced to define contextual appropriateness must be evaluated in relation to these civility rules and the impact of the disclosure on the autonomous self.
68. Ibid., 340.
69. Ibid., 340–41.
70. Ibid., 344.
71. Ibid., 344–45. In "Individualdatenschutz—Systemdatenschutz," in *Beiträge zum Sozialrecht. Festgabe für H. Grüner*, ed. K. Brückner and G. Dalichau (R. S. Schulz, 1982), 451–62, Podlech had already argued (451–54) that individual privacy rights had to be supplemented by an analysis of the factors that determined the flow of information at the systemic level.
72. The 1971 memorandum by Steinmüller and his collaborators was the first widely read publication to employ the idea of a "right to informational self-determination" (Drs. 6/3826, 88, 93). Steinmüller, "Das informationelle Selbstbestimmungsrecht—Wie es entstand und was man daraus lernen kann," *RDV* 23 (2007): 158–61, later explained that he inserted the term at the very last minute to provide a handy formula for summarizing the conclusions reached by the group. Christoph Mallmann, who was the unnamed doctoral student referred to by Steinmüller in this essay, was one of the contributors to this memorandum. His 1974 Heidelberg dissertation, *Datenschutz in Verwaltungs-Informationssystemen*, contained (47–79) the first systematic exposition of the concept.

73. Mallmann, *Zielfunktionen*, 27; Podlech, "Aufgaben und Problematik des Datenschutzes," *DVR* 5 (1976): 23–39, especially 27–28; Benda, "Privatsphäre und 'Persönlichkeitsprofil,'" 34; and Simitis, "Datenschutz—Voraussetzung oder Ende der Kommunikation?" 512.
74. Luhmann, "Die Individualisierung der Selbstdarstellung: Würde und Freiheit," *Grundrechte als Institution. Ein Beitrag zur politischen Soziologie* (Duncker & Humblot, 1965), 53–83.
75. Mallmann, *Zielfunktionen*, 36–39, citation 39.
76. Ibid., 38–42. Mallmann noted that a number of people had suggested that the problems arising out of the process of selective, role-specific disclosure and concealment, and the resulting conflict between the public and the private person, could be avoided by abolishing privacy in the name of complete transparency. However, he argued that such suggestions ignored the fact that it was impossible to abstract from the communicative structures inherent in highly differentiated societies and that the underlying reasoning was deceptive because a fully transparent society "presumes not only a de-differentiated society, but one that has been freed of all conflict. It is only the abolition of all conflicts of interest that could make informational barriers superfluous" (42–43).
77. Mallmann, *Zielfunktionen*, 49–51, 54, 67–68.
78. Ibid., 54.
79. Ibid., 68.
80. Simitis, "Datenschutz—Voraussetzung oder Ende?" 513. Simitis restated this argument in "Reviewing Privacy in an Information Society," *University of Pennsylvania Law Review* 135 (1987): 707–46.
81. Mallmann, *Zielfunktionen*, 69.
82. Steinmüller, "Informationsrecht und Informationspolitik," in *Informationsrecht und Informationspolitik*, 1–20, citation 13. Other important early contributions to the field of information law include Georg Werckmeister, "Informationsrecht: Grundlagen und Anwendung," *DVR* 8, no. 8 (1978): 97–114; Jon Bing, "Information Law?," *Journal of Media Law and Practice* 2, no. 3 (1981): 219–39; Hans Peter Bull, "Die Grundprobleme des Informationsrechts," and "Was ist Informationsrecht?," both in *Datenschutz, Informationsrecht und Rechtspolitik*, ed. Bull (Duncker & Humblot, 2005), 17–37, and 38–50.
83. Willi Egloff and George Werckmeister, "Kritik und Vorüberlegungen zum Gegenstandsbereich von Informationsrecht," in *Informationsrecht und Informationspolitik*, ed. Steinmüller, 280–94, citation 283.
84. Steinmüller, "Informationsrecht und Informationspolitik," 15, 18.
85. Fiedler, "Datenschutz und Gesellschaft," 185.
86. Podlech, "Individualdatenschutz—Systemdatenschutz."
87. Ibid. This point was echoed by Steinmüller, "Informationsrecht und Informationspolitik," 19; Egloff and Werckmeister, "Kritik und Vorüberlegungen," 293; and Bull, "Was ist Informationsrecht?," especially 46–48.

Chapter 3

The Legislative Path to the Federal Privacy Protection Law, 1970–77

In this chapter, I will argue that the Federal Privacy Protection Law, which was approved at the turn of 1976/77, represented a novel and ambitious attempt to renegotiate the parameters for the socially adequate exchange of information in ways that would better correspond to the needs of the expanding welfare state and the emergent information society. However, the legislative path leading from the Federal Population Registration Law via the emergence of the new understanding of privacy documented in the previous chapter to the passage of a privacy law embodying these new norms was—by all measures and for a number of reasons—unusually long, complicated, and contentious.

First, in negotiating these norms, the legislature was faced with the challenge of balancing conflicting fundamental rights. The right to privacy and the right to information access—that is, the right of citizens, firms, and the state to collect, make use of, and disseminate the same personal information that data subjects wish to prevent—are mirror images of one another. Both rights, as well as the abiding conflict between them, are essential features of all liberal societies. Although the new theory of informational privacy was based on the principle that, depending on context, all personal information was potentially harmful and thus deserving of protection, its logic ran contrary to the right to information access, which, as codified in Article 5 of the Basic Law, guaranteed citizens the right to inform themselves "without hindrance from generally accessible sources." Moreover, not only did privacy and information access rights both rest on the same constitutional commitment to human dignity and the develop-

---

Notes for this chapter begin on page 127.

ment of the personality; the new privacy law also had to balance between individual privacy rights, on the one hand, and, on the other, freedoms of speech, action, and property, and the right of the state to acquire the information that it needed to carry out its diverse regulatory, welfare, and security responsibilities.

Many of the provisions of the law were designed to bring greater transparency to the processing of personal information. However, although these transparency tools enabled citizens to determine whether the specific provisions of the law were being adhered to, they could not themselves establish substantive norms governing the use of personal information, and the law did not include any provisions that spelled out either the normative status of privacy rights or their relationship to other constitutional rights.[1] Ultimately, the decision by the legislature to make generous use of elastic formulations to balance rights on important issues where legislators could not reach a consensus forced interpreters to make use of formal criteria to determine the substantive scope and meaning of the law. These issues did not come to the fore until the end of the decade, and they were resolved only—and, even then, only in part—by the 1983 census decision.

One of the great myths surrounding the Federal Privacy Protection Law was that it was a *privacy* law. However, as Genscher told the participants at the first public hearing that was held to permit organized interest groups to express their views on the proposed law, information access rights had to take precedence over privacy rights. "The starting point for all of our considerations," he declared "should be a commitment to the freedom of information, which should only be limited in the interest of the individual. I reject the opposite approach, which entails a blanket restriction on information and allows its use only in specifically authorized cases."[2] Despite this commitment to information access, Ministerialrat Herbert Auernhammer, who was responsible for drafting the law, insisted that, in view of the impossibility of delimiting the private sphere precisely enough to make it the object of legal protection, a privacy protection law could only be based on a theory of informational privacy.[3] Thus, from the very beginning the task of drafting the law was complicated by the challenge of balancing Genscher's liberal goal of protecting information access rights, the equally liberal goal of protecting individual privacy rights, and the consequences of the theory of informational self-determination, which was employed to mediate between these goals, but whose logic ran counter to both the freedom of information and a narrow circumscription of privacy interests and privacy harms.[4]

Second, the federal privacy law also represented a first step onto new legislative terrain. It went beyond existing codes of fair information practices and strove instead to codify—for both the public and the private sectors—substantive norms governing the kinds of information that could be collected and the purposes for which they could be used. While the drafting of the law depended on striking—for every sphere of social life where established communicative norms had been disrupted—an acceptable balance between the right to privacy and the right to information access, no law that was broad enough to cover all of the diverse uses of personal information was capable of balancing between the competing interests that were in play in each specific domain. However, the law was passed in the expectation that it would soon be supplemented by a series of domain-specific privacy laws, which—like the privacy provisions of the Population Registration Law—would balance the conflicting interests in individual domains and thereby transform the federal privacy law into a subsidiary statement of principles that applied directly only to those areas for which such legislation had not been adopted. In the end, the Federal Privacy Protection Law remained suspended between these two poles.

Third, the federal privacy law was drafted at a particular time, and the dangers against which it was intended to protect were still poorly understood. Legislators, officials, and academics made frequent use of analogies drawn from the industrial era to characterize the social problems attributed to the electronic processing of personal information. Information was apostrophized by Genscher as "the most important raw material of our time."[5] The anticipated impact of computers and telecommunications systems on social structures and economic processes was frequently likened to that of such revolutionary technologies as the steam engine, the railroad, the motor vehicle, and nuclear power. Steinmüller argued that the postwar advent of the new information technologies, their ability to produce new information through the processing of existing data, and the attendant mechanization of intellectual labor were the distinguishing features of a "second [or what more properly should have been called a third] industrial revolution."[6] Although these industrial analogies were often stretched, the one that was invoked most often was that between environmental and privacy protection.[7] Like the ecology, consumer protection, and peace movements, which were also reaching a critical mass at this time, the early privacy protection movement represented, as Giddens has argued, a reaction against the perfection of one of the four institutional clusterings of modernity—in this case, a reaction against the new forms of administrative power generated by the routine collection of personal information by large organizations and the use of computers to store, analyze, and disseminate this information.[8] In this respect, the present chapter should be read in part as a contribution to the history of consumer protection.

Regulatory Strategies and the Structure of the Privacy Protection Law

As we saw in chapter 1, in October 1970 Genscher had promised to bring in a privacy law in order to protect the private sphere from the possible injuries of electronic data processing, especially in conjunction with the Population Registration Law.[9] An initial draft of the federal privacy law was completed in October 1971, and a revised version was the subject of a November 1972 public hearing on the subject.[10] However, determining what dangers the law was supposed to protect against and how it was to achieve this goal involved a great deal of definitional and organizational labor.

Genscher's unbounded enthusiasm for electronic data processing carried over into his vision of the Federal Privacy Protection Law.[11] Although Genscher paid lip service to privacy rights, he valued them less as an end in themselves than as a means for ensuring that the efficiencies of integrated information systems could be captured for the general welfare, and privacy rights remained little more than a cipher for him.

Consent was, and remains, the cornerstone of privacy law in Germany and elsewhere.[12] However, in addition to the problems inherent in such permission, consent is not always forthcoming; it is impossible to rely upon it for mass data processing; and one of the purposes of the federal privacy law was to spell out the conditions under which information could be processed without individual consent.[13] The first section of the August 1972 draft, which was the basis for the November hearing, defined *Datenschutz* as all measures intended to prevent injury to what it obliquely referred to as "personal interests deserving of protection" (*schutzwürdige persönliche Belange*) as a result of the processing of personal information that was stored in formatted files (*Dateien*) — that is, in files that were organized according to predefined characteristics (database fields), that could be reordered and evaluated according to these characteristics, and that were intended for dissemination to others, regardless of whether this processing was done manually, electromechanically, or electronically. This definition of the scope of the law embodied that blanket prohibition on the processing of such information — subject to the exceptions enumerated in the law itself — that Genscher had opposed. In this way, it fueled the mistaken presumption that the purpose of the law was to establish the priority of privacy over access rights.[14]

Virtually every element of this dense formulation was controversial in one way or another. The term *Datenschutz* itself had always been a misnomer, or at least a slightly misleading abbreviation, because the federal law actually sought to protect "privacy" in the broad sense of the term, rather than data, and it regulated the processing of the latter as a means of achieving the former. In reality, the term was a holdover from the very first computer privacy regulations, whose primary goal had been to protect the confidentiality of electronic data, and it became increasingly inaccurate as the nature of the underlying privacy problem evolved in new directions.[15]

On the other hand, even though the term "formatted files" was closely related to the concepts used in other national laws, such as records, registries, and their electronic cousin, the database, it was more directly problematic. While all computer databases may have constituted formatted files in the sense of the law, not all formatted files were electronic. Nor were they all intended for dissemination. This imperfect overlap between formatting, intention to disseminate, and mode of processing raised important questions that shaped subsequent debate.

The concept of "personal interests deserving of protection" was no less problematic. Since all personal information was—depending on the context within which it was used—potentially harmful to the individual, it was impossible to enumerate a priori those uses that constituted a "misuse" of personal information, to quote the official title of the law, and the concept of "personal interests deserving of protection" served as a placeholder for harms that could only be determined from the specific context within which information was to be used. In the following I will translate *schutzwürdige persönliche Belange* as the "legitimate privacy interests of the individual"—even though the word privacy and its cognates were nowhere used in the body of the law to describe or legitimate the protections that it guaranteed.

The draft was based on the assumption that the storage and dissemination of formatted personal information by the public administration, by private firms processing personal information for their own use, and by firms engaged in the commercial processing and distribution of such information had to be regulated separately because each threatened personal privacy in specific ways. It sought to bring greater transparency to such processing through the casuistic regulation—for each of these different categories of data processors—of each of its stages: storage or registration, processing, dissemination, modification, and correction-blockage-deletion.

The second section of the law addressed the processing of personal information by the public administration. It permitted public offices and agencies to store personal information if the individual consented, if this were authorized by law, or if this were done in connection with the "lawful performance" of the responsibilities of the office. It also permitted the exchange of such information within the public administration if this information was to be used by the office receiving the information in connection with the lawful performance of its responsibilities. Both of these formulations were less restrictive than those found in the October 1971 draft, which had permitted the storage of personal information only if this information were "necessary" for the office to carry out its legal responsibilities.

Individuals were assumed to be the best guardians of their privacy rights. To ensure that the public would be in a position to watch over their rights, the draft required government offices and agencies to publish in their journals of record a description of the kinds of information that they held, and individuals were given the right to find out what personal information was held and to whom it had been communicated during the previous year, though the police and intelligence agencies were exempted from these requirements. Personal information held by the public administration was to be corrected if it was incorrect and clarified if it was unclear, and an explanation was to be appended if the accuracy of the information was contested, but could not be proven to be inaccurate. Information that had been stored improperly or that was no longer necessary to carry out the responsibilities of the data controller was to be deleted.

The third section regulated the processing of personal information by businesses for their own use. It permitted them to store personal information pertaining to those persons with whom they had either a contractual relationship or what the draft termed a "quasi-contractual relation of trust" (*vertragsähnliches Vertrauensverhältnis*) and to communicate this information to third parties if this were done for purposes consistent with these relationships. This provision applied to persons such as suppliers, customers, clients, patients, and employees. All of these authorizations were subject to the proviso that the storage and communication of such information did not conflict with the "predominant legitimate interests" (*überweigende berechtigte Interessen*) of the concerned individuals. In turn, these persons had the right to learn what personal information such companies held regarding them and what information they had communicated to others, though companies could refuse to provide this information if its disclosure would pose a serious threat to the continued operation of the firm (for example, if it revealed proprietary information). Companies were also required to appoint privacy officers with sufficient authority and independence to ensure compliance with the provisions of the law.

The fourth section regulated firms engaged in the collection and distribution of personal information in formatted files for commercial purposes. The draft sought to meet the needs of those branches of commerce that depended on the exchange of information regarding persons with whom they did not have a direct contractual relationship by specifying that a legitimate interest existed when such information was exchanged for advertising, consumer credit, insurance, and employment purposes. To compensate for this broad authority, these firms were subjected to stricter regulations. Commercial information firms were required to notify concerned individuals the first time that they disseminated their information to third parties. In addition, these companies were required to register with the supervisory authorities that were to be established by the states.

The fifth section detailed the penalties for the unauthorized dissemination of personal information.

Debating the Scope of the Law: Formatted Files and Personal Information

The November 1972 hearing gave those groups that would be most affected by the law the opportunity to present their views on the proposed legislation. In so doing, they exposed many of the ambiguities inherent in the assumptions underlying the law.

The decision to use the processing of personal information stored in formatted files to define and delimit the scope of the law skirted the all-important question of the precise nature of the dangers against which it was supposed to protect. At the time, this question was answered in three different ways. First, regardless of whether the information was processed manually, electromechanically, or electronically, formatting enhanced the addressability of the information contained in the files, and it rendered the individual more transparent to those who controlled this information. Second, formatting was the precondition for electronic storage and processing of information and thus for its integration and exchange, with all of the consequences for personal privacy that this entailed. Third, electronic data processing also facilitated the dissemination of information, which could then be used for secondary purposes in unanticipated and potentially harmful contexts. This was what officials had in mind when they defined formatted files as collections of information that were intended for dissemination; this concern was also embodied in the distinction between data processing by a company for its own use and its processing for commercial purposes.

These dangers overlapped in complex ways. If formatting was simply the precondition for the electronic processing of this information, then should the law not be explicitly limited to electronic data processing? On the other hand, if the potential harm were attributable primarily to the enhanced addressability resulting from the formatting of the data and if this harm was at least partly independent of the method used to process it, then it was only logical to extend the protections offered by the law to include card files and microfilm collections, as well as collections of paper files whose standardized layout permitted variable sorting and evaluation. Moreover, although the definition of a formatted file had been crafted precisely to include all collections of personal information that were not intended exclusively for internal use, files varied greatly in size, purpose, and the amount of information they contained, and in many cases it was impossible make a general determination as to whether information was, in fact, intended for dissemination to others.[16] The concrete meaning of the law depended on where emphasis was placed.

The administration was not the only body involved in the drafting of the privacy protection law. In December 1971, an interparliamentary committee composed of delegates from the major parties brought in its own draft. Like the administration draft, the version prepared by the interparliamentary committee focused on the regulation of "data processing" and databases, but specifically included those residual bodies of personal information that were still processed by "traditional" methods.[17] This approach was welcomed by both Genscher and Auernhammer, who argued that the public would not understand why the same information would be protected if it were held in electronic form, but denied such protection if it were recorded on paper.[18]

On the other hand, both Willi Birkelbach, the first Hessian privacy commissioner, and his successor Simitis maintained that the law should be limited to electronic data processing. Simitis argued that the advent of electronic data processing had "created that specific informational situation that has allowed the database to become an immediate danger to the individual." In contrast to Genscher and Auernhammer, they argued that it was not a question of treating the same information differently depending on the medium on which it was stored, but rather one of devising appropriate remedies for different dangers.[19]

There were also differences of opinion as to whether the collection of personal information should be regulated under the law. Although collection had been included in the very first draft of the law, it had been excluded from subsequent versions, in part because such a prohibition seemed incompatible with the right of individuals to observe and retain information on the world around them, in part because it was assumed that personal information would most often be recorded on paper before being formatted and transferred to a different medium for electronic processing, and in part because it was believed that such information could only become relevant for individual privacy rights once it was recorded on such a medium.[20] While Simitis argued that collection should be protected both because any information that had been collected could always be stored and later processed electronically and because it could be communicated to others even before it had been stored in a formatted file, justice ministry officials warned against regulating the collection information because such a provision would criminalize basic and socially necessary forms of communication: "In the commercial life of the future, one would have to be on guard against asking anyone anything about another person!"[21] The debate over the regulation of data collection would continue for the remainder of the decade, and the issue would only be definitively resolved by the 1983 census decision.

Discussion of the draft also set in motion a learning process with regard to the new concept of personal information. Determining precisely what information was to be considered "personal" in the sense of the law was a matter of particular concern for business. As the Association of German Mail Order Firms complained, on the basis of the broad definition of personal information contained in the law, "it cannot be clearly determined where the border between 'personal' and 'factual' (*sachbezogen*) data is to be drawn. *For data processing by business this conceptual distinction must be drawn much more narrowly* if it is to be meaningful and practicable for achieving the desired degree of privacy protection" (emphasis in original).[22] Similarly, the trade group representing the advertising industry complained that the draft law appeared to apply not only to information that was generally recognized as being sensitive and private, but also to data that pertained, instead, to what the group called the "commercial or economic sphere" (*geschäftlich-wirtschaftliche Sphäre*) — that is, to information pertaining to a "nonprivate domain oriented toward the external world."[23] Such arguments, however, could never entirely escape the gravitational pull of the claim that all such data might be used in ways that would restore its personal nature.[24]

Much of the debate pivoted around the role of personal information in determining both the scope of the law and how access and privacy rights — and the conflicting social interests with which they were aligned — would be balanced in specific contexts. From the very beginning, justice ministry officials had been critical of the new approach. They argued that the strategic decision to indirectly protect privacy rights by regulating the use of personal information pushed the real purpose of the law to the periphery and led to consequences that were both unintended and unacceptable: "The legislature cannot, for example, leave real secrets of the private sphere unprotected while protecting comparable facts — sometimes even through the use of criminal punishments — simply because they are 'personal information' without even requiring that this information be considered secret."[25] On the other hand, Simitis argued, as we saw in chapter 2, that business and government would never willingly do without any information that might enhance their planning capacity or make their work more efficient. Although he believed that the concept of the private sphere had become little more than a fictitious refuge in modern society, he nevertheless argued that the repeated reference to the concept reflected an awareness of the importance of establishing an "inviolable limit" to the collection and use of personal information. Where precisely this border should be drawn would have to depend on the detailed analysis of the conflicts inherent in concrete contexts. Therefore, even though the legislative decision to regulate the processing of personal information represented a better starting point for the law than the protection of the private sphere, Simitis argued that such an approach was not sufficient in itself. It simply named the problem to be solved, but did not and could not itself provide a solution because it was no more possible to define in the abstract what information was to be considered "personal" than it was to circumscribe the private sphere.[26]

Debate over the processing of personal information by the public administration focused on two main issues. First, the draft authorized the exchange of information within the public administration if the information was used in the course of the "lawful fulfillment" of the responsibilities of the office or agency providing the information or if the recipient had a "legitimate" interest in obtaining it. Critics pointed out that, in view of the open-ended planning and regulatory responsibilities of the welfare state, this language could be used to justify the collection of virtually any kind of information, and at the November 1972 hearing it was proposed that the storage of personal information again be restricted to that which was "necessary" (*erforderlich*) for the performance of the legal responsibilities of an office or agency.

Second, and more important, ministries and other federal agencies were large, complex organizations whose divisions and departments were responsible for many distinct tasks. The question was whether these various bodies were functionally related to such an extent that they should be entitled to unrestricted access to the information held by the others or whether their responsibilities were so distinct they would have to be considered third parties. This was the question of the informational unity of the state. In the summer of 1972, Podlech composed an alternative version of a privacy protection law. One of the central features of both his draft and that prepared by the interparliamentary committee was the insistence that narrow limits had to be imposed on the exchange of information within the public administration. "There is no general authorization to access, exchange, or make use of personal information at will," Podlech argued, "within an area of responsibility (*Geschäftsbereich*), between such areas, between ministries, or between semipublic organizations (for example, the social insurance funds). Each area of responsibility may . . . only access information that it itself stored."[27] Genscher, however, opposed this idea because it would have made it impossible to construct the kind of integrated database networks that were being planned at every level of government and by the private sector.[28]

Business groups, on the other hand, had an entirely different set of concerns. Not only did they argue that privacy legislation was superfluous because the kinds of information that were relevant for commercial intercourse belonged to the "commercial," rather than the private, sphere; they also insisted that such legislation was unnecessary because, unlike the public administration, businesses had no sovereign power to compel the disclosure of personal information. In contrast, they argued that the information they collected either came from generally accessible sources or was provided by individuals who had a choice as to whether to enter into contractual relations with the firm. In addition, they maintained that competition within the private sector precluded that concentration of power that was deemed to be a danger in the hands of the state.[29] On the other hand, there was a broad sense that it was more urgent to regulate the processing of personal information in the private sector than in the public. Not only, as Auernhammer argued, were the dangers posed by electronic data processing in the private sector greater than those in the public; private sector data processing was not subject to the same political and judicial oversight as the public administration.[30] In addition, Simitis argued that the existence of Schufa, the country's largest consumer credit reporting company, provided ample evidence that competition between firms did not preclude either collaboration or the concentration of informational power comparable to that found in the public sector. The only reason that Hessian law had not regulated electronic data processing in the private sector, he noted, was that the federal states lacked the authority to do so.[31]

One of the first signs of a nascent privacy consciousness among the general public was a willingness to question where those companies that filled their mailboxes with advertising material obtained their names and information on their personal lives and buying habits. While business groups argued that the freedom of information encompassed the right to gather the information they needed to identify and solicit potential customers, they also capitalized on complaints about unsolicited advertising to warn that if they not permitted to gather the information needed to carefully target potential customers, they would have to fall back on indiscriminate mass mailings, which would be both more costly and represent an even greater nuisance.[32]

Business groups also complained that the draft failed to give due weight to the legitimate interests of either commerce or the public itself.[33] As the representative of the National Association of Credit Agencies explained, their work benefitted not only business, but also consumers, because current mail order and credit sales practices would not be possible if such agencies were prohibited from collecting the information they needed. "Those who in the name of the public call for the imposition of even narrower limits [on the use of personal information]," the group insisted, "should bear in mind that the individual worker or consumer is not only interested in the comprehensive protection of his extremely abstract personality rights, but is also interested to a much greater degree in the most comprehensive and financially favorable participation in commercial life."[34] Instead of imposing more restrictive conditions on the exchange of personal information in the private sector, the Federation of German Industry argued that "the activity of such protective institutions [as Schufa and comparable information exchanges in the insurance industry] should rather be made easier for the purpose of preventing economic crime. There cannot be any valid ground for allowing privacy law to aid frauds or notoriously slow payers."[35] These groups felt that the best solution would be to simply exempt business from the law.

The proposed compliance mechanisms also provoked controversy. There was relatively little opposition—at least among legislators—to the plan to require companies to appoint privacy officers, at least as long as their authority did not infringe upon managerial prerogatives. However, ensuring compliance in the public administration was more controversial. Three possible approaches were considered: (1) self-regulation by ministries and federal agencies; (2) regulation by a federal agency, such as the Bundesrechnungshof (the equivalent of the American General Accountability Office); and (3) the commissioner model pioneered in Hessen. Since the Bundesrechnungshof was responsible for promoting the rationalization and efficiency of the federal administration, the second alternative would have been tantamount to appointing the fox to guard the informational chicken coop. While the 1972 draft would have made the ministries and federal agencies responsible for ensuring compliance within their respective spheres of authority, Birkelbach and Simitis argued that only an independent advocate would be able to effectively represent the interests of the public vis-à-vis the administration and act as both an ombudsman and as the institutionalized conscience of the public administration. However, many officials had reservations about the constitutionality of an independent commissioner, which looked to them suspiciously like a fourth branch of government.[36]

The law employed numerous elastic clauses to balance access and privacy rights and protect what the administration considered socially adequate forms of communication: the right of public offices and agencies to store personal information in conjunction with the "lawful performance" of their responsibilities, the "credible" claim by the public and the public administration that they had a "legitimate" interest in obtaining personal information from the office that had held it, the right to store such information if it were "consistent with the purpose" of contractual or quasi-contractual relationships in the private sector, and the "predominant legitimate interest" of the data subject in preventing the dissemination of this information, not to mention the "legitimate privacy interests of the individual." These provisions were so broad that in the abstract it was impossible to say what information could or could not be processed in any given instance. In some places, these interpretive problems were compounded by the concatenation of multiple conditions, some of which were phrased in negative terms. The end effect of such "cascades" of elastic clauses was, as Simitis complained, uncertainty and suspicion as to whether the purpose of the law was to limit or to authorize the use and exchange of personal information.[37]

Simitis pointed out that recourse to such elastic provisions was unavoidable as long as the law would apply to so many different kinds of information processing and that domain-specific laws were the only way to formulate access and privacy rights in a more precise manner.[38] Others, including Gabriele Erkelenz, the counsel of the League of German Consumer Associations, and the interparliamentary committee, argued that, intentionally or not, these elastic provisions privileged the rights of data processors over individual privacy rights.[39] Steinmüller went even further and argued that the real purpose of the law was simply to provide political cover for the construction of integrated information and planning systems and that it actually represented a set of legislative *violations* of the principles of privacy protection, rather than their systematic codification.[40]

The Privacy Law and the Population Registration System

Based on the input from the November hearing, interior ministry officials worked through the spring of 1973 to produce a revised draft, which was approved by the cabinet along with the draft population registration law in May and then submitted to the Bundestag in September of that year.[41] Cabinet approval of the draft privacy law cleared the way for parliamentary consideration of the Federal Population Registration Law, and both laws were given their first reading by the Bundestag on 29 November.[42] In

May 1974 the Bundestag domestic affairs committee held a hearing on the two laws.[43]

As the committee reviewed the law over the winter of 1975/76, it made a number of changes that cumulatively shifted the balance between privacy and access rights much further in favor of the former than had been the case with the administration draft. First, previous versions had protected formatted files that were intended for dissemination to third parties, but they had refused to extend the law to cover formatted files that were *suited*, but *not intended*, for dissemination. The domestic affairs committee, however, decided that the law should cover all formatted files, regardless of whether they were actually intended for dissemination. This would have entailed the costly extension of the law to internal data on customers, employees, and patients. Consistent with this reasoning, the committee also voted to abolish the exemption for paper files (*Akten*), collections of such files, and books, which would have otherwise fallen under the law to the extent that they were considered formatted files. Second, the committee decided to extend the law to cover the collection of information, though without making clear how this protection could be reconciled with individual freedom of information, and it correspondingly eliminated the exemption for data that was taken from generally accessible sources. Third, the processing of personal information in the public administration was to be subject to more restrictive regulations: state agencies were to be permitted to store and exchange personal information only if this were "necessary" to carry out their responsibilities; incorrect data was to be deleted if it could not be corrected; and data whose accuracy could not be verified or falsified was to be blocked, rather than simply marked as disputed. The committee also voted to create the new office of federal privacy commissioner to monitor compliance in the public administration. Fourth, while the 1972 draft had permitted businesses to store information within the framework of contractual or quasi-contractual relationships, the administration draft expanded the rights of businesses by permitting such storage as long as it was related to the goal or mission of the firm, a provision that would have authorized the collection and use of information for advertising and credit purposes. The domestic affairs committee voted to reverse this change and to impose more restrictive conditions on data processing for commercial purposes.[44]

The proposed restrictions set off alarm bells in the private sector, and business groups responded with an intense lobbying campaign, which was supported by the business wings of the liberal and conservative parties.[45] In response, the domestic affairs committee held another hearing in March 1976 to give business groups the opportunity to voice their concerns.[46] The hearing evidently convinced the committee of the merits of the administration draft, and, in the end, the domestic affairs committee reversed most of the changes that it had made over the previous winter.[47]

The decision by the domestic affairs committee to back away from the changes it had proposed only a few months earlier led many people to question whether the proper balance had been struck between the privacy and population registration laws. The flashpoint for these concerns was the national ID number, and, as we have seen, the ensuing conflict would have an unintended consequence of major importance for the population registration law.

At the 5 May 1976 meeting of the Bundestag legal affairs committee, CDU representative Benno Erhard pointed out that the privacy law did not contain any provision that would prevent the use of the ID number to bring together every piece of information held on the individual at every level of government; all that was necessary, he noted, was for some government office to declare that it had a "legitimate" interest in such information. He also worried that the ID number would, despite prohibitions, bleed over into the private sector and that the integration of the personal information held by private sector organizations, and its combination with that held by the public administration in a manner comparable to that detailed in the *Spiegel* article discussed in chapter 1, could lead to that complete registration of the individual personality. The best solution, he argued, was to prohibit the introduction of such a number, and the committee ultimately gave its blessing to the draft privacy law on the condition that no comprehensive population enumeration system be adopted.[48]

At the final readings of the law on 10 June 1976, the committee draft was approved by a sizeable majority.[49] However, many of the conservative suggestions that had been rejected by the Bundestag were reintroduced in the Bundesrat, and the mediation committee that was subsequently convened was able to reach a compromise only after two states unexpectedly reversed their positions. The amended version of the law was approved by the Bundestag on 10 November 1976 as the seventh legislative period was coming to an end; the law was promulgated on 27 January 1977; and most of its provisions were to take effect at the beginning of 1978.[50]

Professionalizing Privacy

The passage of the law led to a flurry of activity. Once the precise contours of the federal law had become clear, the states set about drafting their own privacy laws. Many states saw this as an opportunity to improve upon the federal law. For example, some of the state laws introduced the civil liability provisions that had been discussed, but not acted on, at the federal level, while others chose to regulate the use of personal information for medical and scientific research.[51] For a brief moment, there was a real concern that state legislation would lead to the Balkanization of privacy law.[52]

The passage of the federal and state privacy laws also accelerated growth of the privacy protection movement, the professionalization of privacy protection, and the development of the new field of privacy and information law. In December 1977, Hamburg law professor Hans Peter Bull was appointed as the first federal privacy commissioner.[53] All of the states—with the exception of Rheinland-Pfalz, which retained its commission model—appointed their own privacy commissioners. And it was estimated that the federal law would require the appointment of 6,000–9,000 corporate privacy officers.[54]

The privacy commissioners and the heads of the state regulatory authorities each formed a regular working group—the Conference of State and Federal Privacy Commissioners and the Düsseldorf Circle, respectively—to exchange experience and coordinate the enforcement of the new laws. The Society for Legal and Administrative Informatics (Gesellschaft für Rechts- und Verwaltungsinformatik) had already been established in 1974 as a forum for academic discussion. Both the German Association for Privacy Protection (Deutsche Vereinigung für Datenschutz), which served as a consumer protection organization to advise the public regarding their rights under the new law, and the Society for Privacy Protection and Data Security (Gesellschaft für Datenschutz und Datensicherung), which was an association of private-sector privacy professionals, were founded in 1977.[55] The first commentaries on the Federal Privacy Protection Law were also published that year.[56]

But what was the larger significance of the law? Despite all of the political sound and fury that had surrounded its passage, the law, which *Der Spiegel* described as a "collection of empty formulas and elastic clauses that has been spoiled by compromises,"[57] remained in the end what it had been in the beginning: an attempt to find an acceptable balance between access and privacy rights. Those who expected the law to give undisputed primacy to individual privacy rights were deeply disappointed, while those who feared that the law would prohibit established administrative and commercial practices were pleasantly surprised, even if they could not always recognize this or say so aloud.[58]

The law did, however, mark a sea change in social and legal sensibilities. If originally Genscher had hoped that the federal privacy law would quell nascent concerns about the impact of electronic data processing on individual privacy and thus clear the way for the broad adoption of the new technologies, his plan backfired. While the collection and use of personal information by the state had historically been regarded as an internal administrative process that had had no direct bearing upon the constitutional rights of the citizen, the law crystallized the principle that the collection and use of personal information by the state represented an "informational infringement" (*Informationseingriff*) upon the rights of the individual, which required explicit legislative authorization.[59]

Liberals, Social Democrats, and Competing Conceptions of Privacy Law

All of the parties recognized that the federal privacy law represented a first venture into uncharted legislative territory, that it was held together by carefully crafted compromises whose long-term viability was less than certain, and that it would soon have to be amended both to rectify these structural problems and incorporate the initial experience with its practical application. In fact, plans to amend the law were afoot even before it had been approved by the Bundestag.[60] However, the reform proposals advanced between 1980 and 1982 led to conflict within the governing coalition and forced the FDP and the SPD to more clearly articulate their divergent conceptions of the purpose and scope of privacy protection law.

The conservative parties presented their proposed revisions in January 1980; the Social Democratic-Liberal coalition presented its own plan the following month; the Bundestag held its first reading of both of these drafts in March; and in April the domestic affairs committee held a hearing on these proposals.[61] Initially, the main questions were as much strategic as substantive. On the one hand, legislators had to decide whether to push ahead with the reform of the law or to wait until after the domain-specific laws that were expected to be passed in the near future had been approved. On the other hand, while the brief coalition draft amendment, which simply bundled together changes on which there was already a consensus, could have been quickly adopted, this would have entailed the indefinite postponement of more substantive amendments. Although the legislative period ended before action could be taken, after the October 1980 election Helmut Schmidt promised that work on the amendment of the Federal Privacy Protection Law would continue under the new legislature.[62]

The list of the proposed amendments that were floated between 1980 and 1982 is as long as the law itself.[63] All of the parties supported the introduction, in one form or another, of civil liability for harms resulting from the misuse of personal information. Business, however, was skeptical of the proposal. Schufa, for example, claimed that the provision was superfluous. Even though it had been sued more than one hundred times, the company noted that none of the complainants had been able to prove that they had suffered any actual harm as a result of the misuse of personal information. Bull, on the other hand, argued that it was not appropriate for the risks inherent in the new information and communication technologies to be borne by the individual citizen, "who certainly benefits from this to a certain degree, but who in any given instance has very little control over the actual processing and who faces large, powerful organizations, which can make use of precisely this modern technology to advance their business or administrative aims."[64]

Conservative proposals to allow businesses to sell information gathered on the basis of contractual relationships for advertising purposes raised the question of whether unsolicited advertising actually constituted a meaningful infringement on individual privacy rights that required legislative remediation. Erkelenz objected to these proposals, noting that the bulk of the complaints that she received were directly related to such advertising, and Bull felt that these complaints were motivated by the fear that people were losing control over their information and their lives. On the other hand, advertisers insisted that unsolicited advertising fell well within the limits of socially acceptable interaction in a free society, even if some felt it to be a burden. They argued that the existing opt-out system (the so-called "Robinson lists") could satisfy the objections raised by that very tiny percentage of persons who actively objected to receiving direct mail without having to ban a practice that was tolerated, if not accepted, by the great majority and that was more efficient and less intrusive than available alternatives.[65] In addition, since 1976 the FDP had been pushing for a constitutional right to *Datenschutz*. The problem was that it was never clear whether the proposed right was supposed to take precedence over *Amtshilfe* or other constitutional rights. Neither the constitutional amendment adopted by North Rhineland-Westphalia in 1978 nor the corresponding plank in the platform adopted at the FDP's June 1979 national conference appeared to go beyond the balancing already undertaken by the Bundestag, and the FDP was never able to muster enough support to push through such an amendment.[66]

The most important contribution to the debate over the revision of the Federal Privacy Protection Law was an essay published in December 1981 by Rudolf Schomerus, who served as Ministerialrat in the interior ministry (and later in the office of the federal privacy commissioner) and who was a coauthor of one of the standard commentaries on the law.[67] Schomerus argued that the law suffered from what he called a "conceptual uncertainty" because the strategic decision to indirectly protect "personal interests deserving of protection" by regulating the processing of personal information forced interpreters to rely on a number of ersatz, largely formal criteria to determine whether information processing was permissible in specific instances. The problem, according to Schomerus, was that, without having at least a preliminary definition of what was ostensibly being infringed upon, it was impossible to determine whether an act actually constituted an infringement. There were only two ways to escape from this contradiction. The one, which was favored by Schomerus himself, was to return to what he considered a more authentically liberal conception of privacy law, which would permit access to and dissemination of personal information as a matter of principle and only prohibit those uses that had been specifically defined as *mis*uses. The only other logically consistent policy would be to move forward toward the comprehensive juridification of informational relations and the construction of what Schomerus disparagingly called a *Datenverkehrsordnung* or an information-processing regime.

When Schomerus launched this polemic, which was aimed at distinguishing between liberal and Social Democratic conceptions of privacy protection, he was an official in the office of the federal privacy commissioner, and his arguments were directed against his boss, the Social Democrat Bull. Nevertheless, the significance of Schomerus's arguments extended well beyond day-to-day politics. The conflict between the logic of the private sphere, which declared certain kinds of information to be worthy of protection but which left unprotected other types of information whose use could have been even more harmful depending on context, and the logic of informational self-determination, which declared all personal information to be potentially deserving of protection, but which on its own could provide no criteria for determining what information could be harmful to whom in specific contexts, was never resolved.[68]

Not surprisingly, Bull took issue with Schomerus. For Bull, the problem was not the existence of an informational regime, but rather the minimal degree of social protection that was offered by the existing regime, whose generous use of elastic clauses facilitated the "liberal" use of personal information and sanctioned a corresponding regime of social and informational power. Bull argued that information law should aspire to do precisely what Schomerus had said it should not attempt: "to protect against the socially undesirable effects of information technology," a formulation that was taken over into later Social Democratic proposals to amend the federal privacy law. These differences between Schomerus and his boss marked the point at which the two coalition parties parted ways with regard to information law.[69]

The contradictory views of the coalition parties were reflected in the preliminary draft completed in March 1982. Although the draft retained the more limited liberal goal of protecting against harm to the legitimate privacy interests of the individual, this limitation was hollowed out to a substantial degree by the other proposed changes, which expanded the scope of the law.[70]

The foundations of the coalition began to buckle in March 1982 as the FDP fared badly in several state elections, and, after Zimmermann replaced Baum when the new coalition took power in October of that year, he ordered a review of the draft reforms proposed by the social-liberal coalition.[71] The revised draft that was completed under the new government in June 1983 did not satisfy business groups, while the privacy commissioners complained that it offered fewer protections than the version that had been circulated in March of the previous year.[72] In any case, the legislative process was overtaken by census boycotts and then the Constitutional Court's final ruling on the legal challenges to the census.

Notes

1. On the distinctions between normative claims and transparency tools, and between privacy and data protection, see Paul de Hert and Serge Gutwirth, "Privacy, Data Protection and Law Enforcement: Opacity of the Individual and Transparency of Power," in *Privacy and the Criminal Law*, ed. Erik Claes et al. (Intersentia, 2006), 61–104.
2. Ministerium des Innern, ed., *Dokumentation einer Anhörung zum Referentenentwurf eines Bundes-Datenschutzgesetzes vom 7. bis 9. November 1972* (Bonn, 1973), 4.
3. Herbert Auernhammer, Vermerk Betr.: Vorbereitung eines Bundesgesetzes zum Schutz der Privatsphäre (7 January 1971), BAK B106/96305.
4. On the right to information processing, see Thomas Giesen, "Das Grundrecht auf Datenverarbeitung," *JZ* 62, no. 19 (2007): 918–27.
5. Hans-Dietrich Genscher, "Vorwort," *Das Informationsbankensystem. Vorschläge für die Planung und den Aufbau eines allgemeinen arbeitsteiligen Informationsbanken-System für die Bundesrepublik Deutschland* (Bonn, 1971), I:vii; and Auernhammer, Erklärung des Herrn Ministers bei der 1. Beratung des Initiativentwurfs . . . (18 January 1972), BAK B106/96306, Bd. 5.
6. Hans Peter Bull, "Datenschutz als Informationsrecht und Gefahrenabwehr," in *Datenschutz, Informationsrecht und Rechtspolitik* (Duncker & Humblot, 2005), 115–28; Herbert Fiedler, "Theorie und Praxis der Automation in der öffentlichen Verwaltung," *ÖVD*, 3/1971, 92–99, especially 92; Fiedler, "Rechenautomaten in Recht und Verwaltung," *JZ* 21, no. 21 (4 November 1966): 689–96, especially 689; Albert Osswald, *Der soziale Rechtsstaat als Herausforderung* (Stuttgart, 1974), 35; and Wilhelm Steinmüller, "Die Zweite industrielle Revolution hat eben begonnen. Über die Technisierung der geistigen Arbeit," *Kursbuch* 66 (December 1981): 152–88.
7. 1. Entwurf für die Einbringungsrede des Ministers bei der ersten Beratung . . . (no date, but 1973), BAK B106/96318, Bd. 34; "100445301111 — Das Schlimmste von King Kong," *Der Spiegel*, 26 November 1973, 66–87, citation 67; Jochen Bölsche, *Der Weg in den Überwachungsstaat* (Rowohlt, 1979), 13; and Frank Haenschke, *Modell Deutschland?*

Die Bundesrepublik in der technologischen Krise (Rowohlt, 1977). The hope was often expressed that the dangers of electronic data processing had been recognized earlier than those associated with environmental pollution and that they would, therefore, be more amenable to preventive measures.

8. Anthony Giddens, *The Nation-State and Violence* (University of California Press, 1987), 308–25. On the consumer protection movement, see Matthew Hilton, *Prosperity for All: Consumer Activism in an Era of Globalization* (Cornell University Press, 2009); Christian Kleinschmidt, "Konsumgesellschaft, Verbraucherschutz und Soziale Marktwirtschaft. Verbraucherpolitische Aspekte des 'Modell Deutschland' (1947–1975)," *Jahrbuch für Wirtschaftsgeschichte* 47, no. 1 (2006): 13–28; Frank Janning, "Die Spätgeburt eines Politikfeldes. Verbraucherschutzpolitik in Deutschland," *Zeitschrift für Politik* 51, no. 4 (December 2004): 401–33; and Kevin Rick, "Die Gründung der Stiftung Warentest als 'zweitbeste Lösung'? Verbraucherpolitik zwischen Verbraucherverbänden und Staat in den 1960er Jahren," *Historische Zeitschrift* 303, no. 2 (2016): 426–58. I have seen reference to only one privacy-oriented citizen's initiative from the early 1970s. There were, however, occasional television programs devoted to the topic. In September 1973, ZDF broadcast "Datenschutz—Bedürfnis einer bedrohten Gesellschaft. Computer dringen in die Privatsphäre ein." Sender Freies Berlin broadcast the two-part program by Gerd Hoffmann, "Der Jedermann-Steckbrief oder leben wir im Goldfischglas. Möglichkeiten und Gefahren der Datenbanken" (transcript in BAK B106/54307). "Der verdatete Bürger" was aired on WDR in January 1975, and two months later NDR broadcast "Der numerierte Mensch—Datenschutz und Menschenwürde." See BAK B141/60018 and B106/96322, Bde. 46–47.

9. Ministerialrat Schäfer, Vermerk betr. Entwurf eines Datenschutzgesetzes (14 June 1971), BAK B141/60007.

10. Entwurf eines Gesetzes zum Schutz vor Missbrauch von personenbezogenen Daten bei der Datenverarbeitung (Stand: 14. Oktober 1971), BAK B106/96305, Bd. 2.

11. Hans-Dietrich Genscher, "Elektronische Datenverarbeitung in Verwaltung und Wirtschaft," *Bulletin* (1971): 1597–600.

12. However, consent has always been a weak foundation, and it has become even more problematic with the advent of Big Data. See Daniel Solove, "Privacy Self-Management and the Consent Dilemma," *Harvard Law Review* 126 (2013): 1880–1903, as well as the literature on Big Data cited in the conclusion of this volume.

13. There was a strong family resemblance among the regulatory strategies adopted in West Germany and in both the other countries of Western Europe and North America. See Jon Bing, "A Comparative Outline of Privacy Legislation," *Comparative Law Yearbook* 2 (1978): 149–81; Frits Hondius, *Emerging Data Protection in Europe* (North-Holland Publishing Company, 1975); and Ulrich Dammann, Otto Mallmann, and Spiros Simitis, eds., *Data Protection Legislation: An International Documentation* (Alfred Metzner Verlag, 1977), which compiled most of the privacy laws that had been passed or that were under consideration at the time.

14. §1 of the draft defined *Datenschutz* as "alle Massnahmen, die geeignet sind, einer Beeinträchtigung schutzwürdiger persönlicher Belange bei der Datenverarbeitung personenbezogener Daten entgegenzuwirken, die in Dateien gespeichert sind," while §2 defined a formatted file (*Datei*) as "eine zur Auswertung und auch zur Weitergabe an Dritte bestimmte, nach festgelegten Merkmalen aufbereitete und geordnete Sammlung von Daten, ungeachtet der angewendeten Verfahren." Entwurf eines Gesetzes zum Schutz vor Missbrauch von personenbezogenen Daten . . . (Stand: 15. August 1972), BAK B106/96307, Bd. 7, which is reprinted as an appendix to Ministerium des Innern, *Dokumentation einer Anhörung*, 349ff.

15. In reviewing this draft before it was disseminated for comment, Minister for Labor and Social Affairs Walter Arendt warned (Bundesminister für Arbeit und Sozialordnung

to BMI [29 May 1972], BAK B141/60010) that this was the last opportunity to avoid institutionalizing the term *Datenschutz*. Drawing on Steinmüller, Arendt proposed the alternative term *Informationsschutz*.
16. Ministerium des Innern, *Dokumentation einer Anhörung*, 170–72; and Götting, Begriffsbestimmung "Datei" (2 March 1973), BAK B106/96331.
17. Drs. 6/2885, §§1, 4, 12.
18. Bayer. Staatsministerium des Innern to BMI (2 May 1973), BAK B106/69310, Bd. 17; and Ministerium des Innern, *Dokumentation einer Anhörung*, 6.
19. Ministerium des Innern, *Dokumentation einer Anhörung*, 17–18, 61; and *Datenschutz/ Meldegesetz. Sachverständigenanhörung, Gesetzestexte. Aus der öffentlichen Anhörung des Innenausschusses des Deutschen Bundestages vom 6. Mai 1974* (Presse- und Informationszentrum des Deutschen Bundestages, 1974), 55. These arguments were supported by the Justice Ministry. BMJ to BMI, Betr.: Entwurf eines Gesetzes . . . Stand: 9. März 1972 (5 June 1972), BAK B106/96307, Bd. 8.
20. See, for example, Ergebnisprotokoll der Ressortbesprechung am 26./27. April 1972 über den Entwurf eines Gesetzes zum Schutz vor Mißbrauch von Individualinformationen, BAK B106/96306, Bd. 6. Whatever validity the distinction between collection and storage may have had at the time disappeared with the advent of terminal-based workstations, which permitted the collection of information in native digital format, and the spread of the new media.
21. Ministerium des Innern, *Dokumentation einer Anhörung*, 21; and Göhler, Betr.: Entwurf eines Bundesdatenschutzgesetzes (14 April 1972), BAK B141/60009.
22. Bundesverband des deutschen Versandhandels, Stellungnahme . . . , BAK B106/96308, Bd. 11.
23. Ministerium des Innern, *Dokumentation einer Anhörung*, 83; Wirtschaftlichkeit und Datenschutz. Vorschläge des Ausschusses für wirtschaftliche Verwaltung (15 November 1975), BAK B106/96324, Bd. 52; and Rödl/Verband der Handelsauskunfteien to BMI (23 January 1973), in BAK B106/96308, Bd. 12.
24. Unions sought to selectively expand the scope of the law. Their primary goal was to impose tighter restrictions on the human resources management systems that were coming into use at the time, prevent employers from collecting any employee information beyond that which was absolutely necessary for the job that the individual was hired to do, and bring workplace privacy within the scope of collective bargaining agreements.
25. BMJ to BMI, Betr.: Entwurf eines Gesetzes . . . Stand: 9. März 1972 (5 June 1972), BAK B106/96307; and, with nearly identical wording, Göhler, Betr.: Entwurf eines Bundesdatenschutzgesetzes (14 April 1972), BAK B141/60009.
26. Ministerium des Innern, *Dokumentation einer Anhörung*, 16–17, 22–23; and Spiros Simitis, "Datenschutz—Notwendigkeit und Voraussetzung einer gesetzlichen Regelung," *DVR* 2 (1973): 138–89, especially 148–50.
27. Adalbert Podlech, *Datenschutz im Bereich der öffentlichen Verwaltung. Entwürfe eines Gesetzes zur Änderung des Grundgesetzes (Art. 75 GG) zur Einführung einer Rahmenkompetenz für Datenschutz und eines Bundesdatenschutz-Rahmengesetzes* (=DVR, Beiheft 1, J. Schweizer Verlag, 1973): 12; and Drs. 6/2885, §8.
28. Auernhammer, Erklärung des Herrn Ministers bei der 1. Beratung des Initiativentwurfs . . . (18 January 1972), BAK B106/96306, Bd. 5.
29. Bundesverband der Deutschen Industrie, Stellungnahme . . . (28 December 1972), BAK B106/96308, Bd. 11; Rödl/Verband der Handelsauskunfteien to BMI (23 January 1973), in BAK B106/96308, Bd. 12; and Göhler, Betr. Entwurf eines Bundesdatenschutzgesetzes (14 April 1972), BAK B141/60009.
30. Auernhammer, Vermerk, Betr.: Vorbereitung eines Bundesgesetzes zum Schutz der Privatsphäre (7 January 1971), BAK B106/96305; and Auernhammer, in *Dokumentation einer Anhörung*, ed. Ministerium des Innern, 136–37.

31. Stenographisches Protokoll über die öffentliche Informationssitzung des Innenausschusses (6 May 1974), BAK B106/96319, Bd. 39, 28–30.
32. Bundesverband der Deutschen Industrie, "Stellungnahme . . ." (28 December 1972), BAK B106/96308, Bd. 11.
33. Zentraler Kreditausschuß, Stellungnahme . . . , BAK B106/96308, Bd. 11.
34. Rödl/Verband der Handelsauskunfteien to BMI (23 January 1973), BAK B106/96308, Bd. 12; see also Deutscher Industrie- und Handelstag, Stellungnahme zu dem Entwurf . . . , BAK B106/96308, Bd. 11.
35. Bundesverband der Deutschen Industrie, Stellungnahme zu dem Entwurf . . . (28 December 1972), and Zentraler Kreditausschuß, Stellungnahme zu dem Entwurf . . . , both in BAK B106/96308, Bd. 11. These arguments were supported by the Federal Criminal Police. See Bundeskriminalamt/Herold to BMI (28 November 1972), BAK B106/96309, Bd. 14. One topic of constant concern was the lists of known or suspected swindlers maintained by the insurance industry.
36. Ergebnisniederschrift über die Besprechung am 15. Dezember über den Entwurf eines Gesetzes . . . (January 1972), BAK B106/96305, Bd. 2; Ministerium des Innern, *Dokumentation einer Anhörung*, 24–27, 137; and *Datenschutz/Meldegesetz*, 194–97. On the regulation and enforcement regimes adopted in other countries, see Bing, "A Comparative Outline of Privacy Legislation"; and David Flaherty, *Protecting Privacy in Surveillance Societies* (University of North Carolina Press, 1989).
37. Stenographisches Protokoll über die öffentliche Informationssitzung des Innenausschusses (6 May 1974), BAK B106/96319, Bd. 39, 62–63.
38. Ibid.
39. Ministerium des Innern, *Dokumentation einer Anhörung*, 58–59, 76–77.
40. Steinmüller, Stellungnahme zum Entwurf des Bundesdatenschutzgesetzes (12 July 1973), BAK B141/60018; Wilhelm Steinmüller, "Schutz vor Datenschutz? Informationskontrolle und planende Verwaltung," *IBM-Nachrichten* 23 (1973): 830–35; and Georg Werckmeister, "Informationsrecht: Grundlagen und Anwendung," *DVR* 8, no. 8 (1978): 97–114, who was unwilling to dismiss the possibility that the law simply served as a "political alibi" (101).
41. Drs. 7/1027. On the changes made in response to the hearing, see Referat V III 4, Betr.: Im Hearing zum Entwurf . . . vorgetragene Änderungs- und Ergänzungsvorschläge (November 1972), BAK B106/96310, Bd. 18; Auernhammer, Vermerk: Noch offene Probleme im Referentenentwurf eines BDSG (22 February 1973), BAK B106/96311; and Auernhammer, Zusammenstellung der Einwendungen gegen den Entwurf eines Bundes-Datenschutzgesetzes (May 1973), BAK B106/96312, Bd. 23.
42. Drs. 7/1027, 7/1059; and *Sten. Ber.*, 7. Wahlperiode, 67. Sitzung (29 November 1973), 4017–25.
43. *Datenschutz/Meldegesetz*. According to an August 1975 Infratest survey, 54 percent of respondents claimed that it was "very important" that their personal information be protected by law; 29 percent regarded this as "important," 12 percent as "less important," and 5 percent as "entirely unimportant." Surprisingly, these numbers remained virtually unchanged in 1984. See Hessische Landesregierung, ed., *Informationsgesellschaft oder Überwachungsstaat. Strategien zur Wahrung der Freiheitsrechte im Computerzeitalter* (Opladen, 1986), II:411.
44. Auernhammer, Kurzdarstellung der Änderungen des Entwurf eines BDSG durch den Innenausschuss (4 February 1976), BAK B106/96324, Bd. 52; and Werner Ruckriegel, Vermerk, Betr.: Beratungen im Bundestags-Innenausschuss (29 January 1976), BayHStA StK/13126.
45. Aktennotiz über das Gespräch mit Vertretern des Bankenverbandes, der Versicherungswirtschaft und des Versandhandels (27 January 1976), BAK B106/96325, Bd. 57;

the materials in B106/96326, Bd. 62; and Dr. Vaitl, Betr.: Bericht des Bayer. Staatsministers für Bundesangelegenheiten vom 20.2.1976, BayHStA StK/13126.
46. The transcripts of the hearing and the supporting memoranda can be found in Protokoll der 104. Sitzung des Innenausschusses . . . öffentliche Anhörung zu Fragen der Datenschutzgesetzgebung (31 March 1976), BAK B106/96324, Bd. 53 and BayHStA StK/13127.
47. Drs. 7/5277; Friedrich Schäfer to Wirtschaftsausschuss, Offene Fragen im Entwurf des Bundesdatenschutzgesetzes (8 April 1976), BAK B106/96324, Bd. 54; Gördel, Vermerk, Betr.: Koalitionsgespräch vom 6. April 1976 (7 April 1976), and Gördel to Parl. Staatssekretär Martin Grüner (14 April 1976), both in BAK B106/96327, Bd. 66; and Auernhammer, Stellungnahme zu den Vorschlägen des Innenministers NRW Dr. Hirsch (11 May 1976), BAK B106/96327, Bd. 66.
48. 97. Sitzung des Rechtsausschusses (5 May 1976), BAK B141/60025. See also FDP Thesen zur Fortentwicklung des Datenschutzes (3 May 1979) in both BAK B106/96336, Bd. 1 and 96338. The memorandum that was hastily drafted by the interior ministry to refute Erhard's constitutional arguments never penetrated to the heart of the matter. See BMI, Verfassungsrechtliche Stellungnahme zur Einführung eines Personenkennzeichens (13 May 1976), BAK B141/78783; and Kurzprotokoll. 111. Sitzung des Innenausschusses (19 May 1976), BAK B106/96325, Bd. 56.
49. *Sten. Ber.*, 7. Wahlperiode, 250. Sitzung (10 June 1976), 17741–45; and Drs. 7/5332.
50. Drs. 7/5497 and 7/5568; *Sten. Ber.*, 7. Wahlperiode, 258. Sitzung (20 November 1976); and Rudolf Schomerus, Kurzinformation für die Kabinettsitzung am 29. Juni 1976, BAK B106/96329, Bd. 71; and *BGBl.*, 1977, 201–14. Several significant changes were made at this committee stage. First, the final version of the law excluded those collections of personal information that were not intended for dissemination to third parties and that were not held in electronic form—i.e., the paper files, books, and Rolodexes whose status had been contested since the beginning. Second, the provision authorizing the public administration to provide "free data" to third parties was eliminated, though the Population Registration Framework Law still permitted (§21) the registries to provide basic information on specific individuals without requiring proof of legitimate interest, but not to do so in bulk form. The privacy law, on the other hand, permitted businesses to disseminate—both for their own use and for commercial purposes—in bulk and without further restrictions this basic information plus one other identifying characteristic on groups of individuals. Third, while the Bundestag draft had applied to the public administration at every level of government, the Bundesrat forced the Bundestag to limit the law to the federal administration and to permit the states to regulate the processing of personal information within their own domains.
51. Hirsch, Gegenüberstellung der Datenschutzgesetzentwürfe der Länder mit dem BDSG (November 1977), NRW NW 595/76; and Ruckriegel to Hirsch, Betr.: Änderung des Bundesdatenschutzgesetzes (9 February 1979), NRW NW 595/81.
52. The state privacy laws are reprinted in Hans-Joachim Ordemann and Rudolf Schomerus, *Bundesdatenschutzgesetz*, 3. Aufl. (C. H. Beck, 1982), 317ff. See also Innenminister NRW, Gegenüberstellung der Datenschutzentwürfe der Länder mit dem BDSG (June 1976), HHStA Abt. 502/12107a.
53. Hans Peter Bull, *Widerspruch zum Mainstream. Ein Rechtsprofessor in der Politik* (Berliner Wissenschafts-Verlag, 2012), 113ff.; and "Professor Spiros Simitis," *Der Spiegel*, 14 November 1977, 102. In his memoir, Bull references (116–17) the controversy over whether the office should be headed by a jurist or an information scientist. Simitis had turned down the position because he did not feel that the administration was willing to provide the new federal agency with adequate resources and influence. Simitis was a vigorous proponent of strict, but contextually defined, privacy rights, and he was not afraid to clash with the executive branch. The CSU—living down to its reputation—tried to paint

Simitis as a security risk because of the leftist politics of his brother, who later became prime minister of Greece.
54. ADL Verband für Informationsverarbeitung to Innenministerium Niedersachsen, Betr.: BDSG (10 February 1977), in NRW NW 595/76.
55. Thilo Weichert, "Deutsche Vereinigung für Datenschutz. DVD—30 Jahre sind nicht genug," *Datenschutz Nachrichten*, 2/2007, 56–61; and Kenneth Bamberger and Deirdre Mulligan, *Privacy on the Ground: Driving Corporate Behavior in the United States and Europe* (MIT Press, 2015), 204–6. There is no study of the work of corporate data protection officers in the 1970s and 1980s.
56. Ordemann and Schomerus, *Bundesdatenschutzgesetz*; Herbert Auernhammer, *Bundesdatenschutzgesetz* (Heymanns, 1977); and Simitis, Ulrich Dammann, Otto Mallmann, and Hans-Joachim Reh, *Kommentar zum Bundesdatenschutzgesetz* (Nomos-Verlag, 1977).
57. "Freier Markt," *Der Spiegel*, 26 December 1977, 56–57.
58. As Hans Peter Bull, "Neue Konzepte, neue Instrumente? Zur Datenschutz-Diskussion des Bremer Juristentages," ZRP 31, no. 8 (1998): 310–14, citation 311, later observed, neither the public administration nor the private sector was ever really forced to do without information that they deemed essential.
59. Eggert Schwan, "Datenschutz, Vorbehalt des Gesetzes und Freiheitsgrundrechte," *Verwaltungsarchiv* 66 (1975): 120–50; Spiros Simitis, "Bundesdatenschutzgesetz—Ende der Diskussion oder Neubeginn?" *NJW* 30, no. 17 (1977): 729–37, especially 731; and the discussion in Edda Weßlau, *Vorfeldermittlungen. Probleme der Legalisierung "vorbeugender Verbrechensbekämpfung" aus strafprozessrechtlicher Sicht* (Duncker & Humblot, 1989),160–203. The development of privacy protection law can be situated in relation to several trends in constitutional and administrative law described in Frieder Günther, *Denken vom Staat her. Die bundesdeutsche Staatsrechtslehre zwischen Dezision und Integration 1949–1970* (Oldenbourg, 2004), 298–309. In all of these respects, the Federal Privacy Protection Law represented an important supplement to the Code of Administrative Procedure.
60. Drs. 8/191 and 266; and Spiros Simitis et al., *Kommentar zum Bundesdatenschutzgesetz*, 2. Aufl. (Nomos, 1979), 48–49.
61. Drs. 8/3608 and 8/3703; Sten. Ber., 8. Wahlperiode, 205. Sitzung (6 March 1980), 16397–408; and Innenausschuss, Protokoll über die interne Anhörung zu den Gesetzentwürfen zur Änderung des Bundesdatenschutzgesetzes (21–22 April 1980), BAK B 106/96337, Bd. 5.
62. Sten. Ber., 9. Wahlperiode, 5. Sitzung (24 November 1980), 40.
63. Drs. 8/3608 and 8/3703; Diskussionspunkte zur Novellierung des BDSG (17 November 1980), BAK B106/96335; "Grundsätze für einen besseren Datenschutz," *Politik. Aktuelle Informationen der Sozialdemokratischen Partei Deutschlands*, July 1980; and Aufgabenschwerpunkte im Bereich des Datenschutzes für die Jahre 1979/1980, BAK B106/96336, Bde. 1–2.
64. Innenausschuss, Protokoll über die interne Anhörung, 41–44. All of the parties favored greater state protections than those offered under the information model that, according to Gunnar Trumbull, *Consumer Capitalism: Politics, Product Markets, and Firm Strategy in France and Germany* (Cornell University Press, 2006), otherwise shaped the West German consumer protection regime.
65. Innenausschuss, Protokoll über die interne Anhörung, 40–55. Through the 1970s and 1980s the Federal Court of Justice upheld the position of state regulators that targeted marketing was permitted within very broad limits—as long as marketers complied with opt-out requests—because, however burdensome direct mail advertising may have been, it did not rise to the level of an injury that was protected against by the law. But in a 1988 decision, the court ruled that citizens enjoyed a right—based in both property and personality rights—to protection against the delivery of unwanted advertising materials if such advertising reached a level of intensity or burdensomeness

where it could no longer be considered a minor inconvenience that all citizens had to tolerate as the price of living together with others. See Konrad Stollreiter, Betr.: Weitergabe von Meldeamtsdaten an Adressbuchverlage (29 January 1980), BayHStA LDSG no. 447; "Abwehransprüche gegenüber unerwünschter Briefkastenwerbung," *RDV* 5, no. 3 (1989): 124–25; and Jürgen Simon, "Direktmarketing: Optimierungsimpulse durch Rechtsschranken. Das Beispiel der Briefwerbung," *CuR* 2 (1986): 3–13.

66. "Thesen zur Fortentwicklung des Datenschutzes. Beschlüsse des 30. Bundesparteitages der FDP," in *Der Weg in den Überwachungsstaat*, ed. Bölsche, 189–93. The idea was taken up again at the national level in 1992–93 by the postreunification constitutional revision commission of the Bundestag. However, the commission reached no decision on the issue, in part because its members considered the right to already be part of the law of the land (Drs. 12/6000, 60–63). In 2008, the Greens proposed (Drs. 16/9607) the addition of a set of privacy rights to the Basic Law. On recent initiatives in this direction, see Michael Kloepfer und Florian Schärdel, "Grundrechte für die Informationsgesellschaft—Datenschutz und Informationszugangsfreiheit ins Grundgesetz?" *JZ* 64, no. 9 (2009): 453–62. In "Schützt den Datenkörper!," in *Technologischer Totalitarismus*, ed. Frank Schirrmacher (Suhrkamp, 2015), 29–37, Julie Zeh suggests (34) that a *digitales Grundrecht*, or a right to *Datenschutz*, which takes absolute priority over security, efficiency, and *Amtshilfe*, can best be likened to the constitutional rights to physical integrity and private property.

67. Rudolf Schomerus, "Datenschutz oder Datenverkehrsordnung?" *ZfR* 14, no. 12 (1981) 291–94.

68. As Schomerus asked, "Is the conclusion that every use of data that deviates from its original purpose amounts to an injury to the legitimate interests of the individual a correct one? Surely not! But lawmakers have not provided any criterion [by which to judge] when such a use is actually harmful . . . . Data processing is only harmful to the extent that it is suitable or intended to injure the legitimate privacy interests of the individual, whatever those may be." See Schomerus, "Datenschutz oder Informationsrecht?" and the accompanying letter to Ministerialdirektor Klaus Thomsen (15 May 1981), BAK B106/96338, Bd. 8.

69. Hans Peter Bull, "Datenschutz oder Datenverkehrsordnung?" *ZRP* 15, no. 2 (1982): 55–56; Bull, *Ziele und Mittel des Datenschutzes. Forderungen zur Novellierung des Bundesdatenschutzgesetzes* (Athenäum, 1981), citation 24–25; and Drs. 10/1180, 3. In "Datenschutz als Informationsrecht und Gefahrenabwehr," Bull identified four sets of dangers against which such legislation should protect: (1) the psychological discomfort from being made the object of curiosity and disclosure by others; (2) alienation resulting from the commercialization of personal information; (3) the occupational, economic, and other social disadvantages resulting from the dissemination of certain kinds of information; and (4) the illegitimate domination and social control resulting from the use of information technology.

70. Entwurf eines Gesetzes zur Änderung des Bundesdatenschutzgesetzes (Stand: 31. März 1982), BAK B106/96340; the resolution by the Konferenz der Datenschutzbeauftragten (31 March 1982); Drs. 9/2386, 110–15; the business criticisms of the more comprehensive juridification of information exchange in Ausschuß für wirtschaftliche Verwaltung in Wirtschaft und öffentlicher Hand (1 June 1982), and Bundesverband der Deutschen Industrie (11 June 1982), both BAK B106/96340; and Bundesministerium der Finanzen to BMI (18 June 1982), BAK B106/96341. The decision not to include provisions regulating the use of employee information was widely seen as a Social Democratic concession to one of the major constituencies of the FDP.

71. Anton Jaumann/Staatssekretär, Bayerisches Staatsministerium fur Wirtschaft und Verkehr to Zimmermann (14 December 1982), BAK B106/96344; and "Ziemlich mies," *Der Spiegel*, 12 September 1983, 23–26.

72. Erklärung der Konferenz der Datenschutzbeauftragten . . . (4 November 1983); Drs. 10/877, 67–68. According to Benjamin Michaels, "Wende? Jedenfalls nicht in Zimmermann's unteren Etagen," *Die Welt*, 23 August 1983, business complained that, under the guise of privacy protection, the draft was seeking to intervene "for social and economic policy purposes into the market economy."

Chapter 4

"Only Sheep Let Themselves Be Counted"
The 1983/87 Census Boycotts, the Census Decision, and the Question of Statistical Governance

The year 2021 is census time in Germany, and it appears that the new registry-based census will go off without any major disruptions. This stands in stark contrast to the situation in the 1980s, when opposition to the planned 1983 census brought about a wave of protests and a legal challenge that led the Constitutional Court to overturn central parts of the census law in codifying a new right to privacy.[1]

Although the law authorizing the census had been approved in March 1982 without controversy, in January and February 1983 a nationwide boycott movement sprang up out of nowhere. Initially, the Kohl administration, whose new coalition with the FDP was only confirmed by the March 1983 election, regarded the boycott more as a matter of concern for the police than for the political system and failed to realize that opposition to the census was not limited to a fringe of anarchists, *Autonome*, communists, and Greens. In fact, there was substantial opposition to the census among the supporters of all three of the established parties.[2]

Others turned to the courts for redress, and two weeks before the scheduled start of the census the Constitutional Court—in a move that dumbfounded the administration—issued a temporary injunction blocking the census. In its final ruling on the matter in December of that year, the Court concluded that parts of the census law violated the right to informational self-determination implicit in the country's constitutional commitment to human dignity and the free development of the person-

---

Notes for this chapter begin on page 169.

ality. The decision, however, did not mark the end of the matter. While the Kohl administration immediately set about drafting a new census law that would meet the conditions set out by the Court, it continued to disparage the privacy concerns that had motivated the protests and to insist on conducting a traditional *Totalerhebung*—that is, a door-to-door head count in which census takers are charged with seeking out and documenting every person residing within an assigned geographical area. This position limited the possibilities of constructive dialogue with a mistrustful public and ultimately led to a second boycott when a new census was scheduled for May 1987.[3]

One of the reasons for the historiographical neglect of the census is that it became the focal point for a set of related concerns that, until the 1970s debate on the surveillance state, had remained largely unarticulated.[4] In *The Nazi Census*, which was researched and written during the 1983 boycott, Götz Aly and Karl Heinz Roth sought to discredit the census by establishing continuities in personnel and policy between the population technocrats of the Third Reich and the statistical apparatus of the Federal Republic.[5] At the time, this slim volume exerted a pervasive influence on public thinking about the census. However, without denying the importance of such memory politics, I argue that the protests were a much more direct reaction to both the new information and communication technologies and the expanded use of information as a means of social planning and social control than to the Nazi past. The protesters were concerned above all else with the ways in which control over personal information and the new information technologies could be used to normalize and discipline the population, predetermine the available avenues for self-expression, transform the individual into a manipulable object deprived of agency and dignity, and forestall social protest and social change. The real purpose of the census, the protesters argued, was not so much to gather aggregate data for social planning (though that was bad enough for some of them) as to gather the individualized data needed for both all-encompassing social control of the population and for more targeted interventions against specific individuals.

It also is important to remember that, at the time of the census, "1984" lay just around the corner. If we look at the language of the protesters, we can see that they employed a rhetoric of mistrust, objectification, and instrumentalization. They saw the census (*Volkszählung*) as a forced interrogation of the people (*Zwangsbefragung*) or an inquisition into its soul (*Volksverhör*), as a painful measure being inflicted upon the nation (*Volksquälung*) by a state whose motives were neither clear nor trusted, as a kind of mass snooping program by the government (*Schnüffelnaktion*), and as an effort to ferret out the secret thoughts of the citizenry (*Aushorchung*). They feared that they would become "transparent citizens" (*gläserne Bürger*) standing naked and impotent before the gaze of the omniscient and perhaps malevolent state. Boycott groups offered a form of political pastoral care (*Zählsorge*) for those troubled by these prospects. The boycotts represented the zenith of a distinct privacy-based social movement, which was comparable in origins, aims, and significance to the environmental, peace, and women's movements. Although its influence has waxed and waned over the intervening years, it has never disappeared completely.

The census decision was a mixed blessing for the protesters: it legitimated their concerns, though without eliminating the underlying problem. The pause that followed in its wake created an opportunity for the Greens, who had emerged as the ambivalent leaders of a protest movement that they could neither control nor disavow nor provide with a coherent strategy capable of winning broad public support, to think systematically about the ways in which personal information was used to govern in modern society.

The 1987 boycott was a bitter, highly contentious affair that dragged on for a year as protesters struggled to get their message out and defend themselves against a state that regarded the boycott as a virtual terrorist challenge to its authority. It involved the protesters, and the Greens in particular, in two debates. On the one hand, the refusal by the Constitutional Court to hear legal challenges to the revised 1987 census law made it difficult for the protesters to find firm legal ground for continued opposition and gave rise to a debate over the relationship between representative democracy, extraparliamentary politics, and civil disobedience. On the other hand, the Court's demand that the administration determine whether the legitimate informational needs of the state could be met through less intrusive means than a full door-to-door count provided the Greens with an opportunity to criticize the use of statistics, and personal information in general, as a means of social governance. The struggle over these issues in the 1980s played an important, though heretofore overlooked, role in shaping the self-understanding of the Greens and was just as central to determining the political identity of the new party as its better-known environmental concerns.

The Census

The initial catalyst for the boycotts was the plan to use census data to update the population registers and meet the other informational needs of federal, state, and local government that could not be satisfied by anonymous or aggregate data.

The first call to boycott the 1983 West German census, which was issued in September 1982 by the West Berlin War Resisters' International, found only limited resonance. The members of this group were incensed by the fact that the government was spending hundreds of millions of marks on the census and deemed this data so essential that it permitted civil penalties to be levied on those who refused to provide the required information, while itself refusing to answer questions on such vital issues as the location of nuclear missiles. Asserting a right to such information, the initiative proclaimed—in a rhetorical flourish that would transcend divisions within the boycott movement—"if the government remains silent to protect nuclear missiles, then we will remain silent to protect peace! Politicians ask, but citizens do not answer!"[6]

But the boycott was really sparked by events in Hamburg. The Hamburg protests grew out of a meeting called to discuss the dangers of the human resources management systems that were coming into use at the time.[7] Although the census was unsuspectingly introduced into the discussion by a woman who had been summoned to work as a census taker, the participants quickly realized how explosive the issue was. The Hamburg protesters were initially upset by what they considered to be the "unsocial" effects of the census. Not only would the registry comparison, for example, have flagged people who claimed that they lived in West Berlin in order to avoid the draft, but who actually lived elsewhere; information on average rents in specific areas for apartments of a certain size would, they argued, also put landlords in a position to raise rents in the same way that knowledge of wage levels would enable employers to push wages down. If people did not defend themselves, they would be "digitized, cabled, planned, and sold out" (*verdatet, verkabelt, verplant und verkauft*).[8]

Although the pathos of these arguments clearly exceeded their analytical power, the protest movement quickly took on a life of its own, and commentators used phrases such as "snowball," "avalanche," and "prairie fire" to describe the speed at which it spread across the country. By the beginning of March, the Hamburg coordinating office counted four hundred boycott groups nationwide.[9]

Why did so many people find the 1983 census so dangerous? Not only did it not differ in any significant respect from previous postwar censuses; its scope had even been reduced in comparison to the 1970 census in order to save money, and many of the more intrusive questions had been eliminated. All of the controversial provisions were contained in §9 of the census law.[10]

As had been the case with previous postwar censuses, the 1983 law permitted local governments, which were directly responsible for carrying out the census, to use census data to update the population registries.

Although this comparison had aroused little controversy in the past, times had changed, and the emergence of a new privacy consciousness and the politicization of state surveillance gave the measure an unexpected resonance. The census count was important because it was the basis for determining representation in elected bodies at every level of government and calculating transfer payments among them. Since people often failed to notify authorities when they moved and were thus counted in more than one place, registry counts systematically overestimated the size of the population, but they did so in geographically unpredictable ways. Moreover, many people intentionally registered as residents in different places in order to take advantage of both differing approaches to the radicals decree and welfare policies that varied from state to state.[11]

The census, which had originally been planned for 1981, had been delayed by disagreements over the distribution of costs between the states and the federal government. State and local governments were unwilling to shoulder the costs that the federal government was asking them to bear unless local governments were allowed to use census data to update their population registries. When the census law was being debated by the Bundestag, both Bull and Simitis warned about mixing statistical and administrative data, and they later complained that the legislature had deemed the registry comparison more important than privacy concerns.[12] Bremen law professor Ulrich Mückenberger called this mixing of statistics and administration the "original sin" of the census law, and he even went so far as to argue that, "in contrast to initial appearances, the census law is not a statistical law with provisions for the occasional exchange of data. On the contrary: it is a data exchange law that makes use of statistical means to gather the information to be exchanged."[13]

The Bundestag had attempted to salvage the confidentiality of census data that it had traded away to secure the support of the states by stipulating that the information obtained through the registry comparison could not be used to the disadvantage of the respondent. However, it was not clear how officials could be expected to ignore their legal responsibilities simply because they had acquired certain pieces of information through the census. Moreover, the comparison itself could also be misused. The Munich government, for example, offered census takers a premium for uncovering people who were living in the city without having registered with local officials; this premium was doubled for unregistered foreigners. In both 1983 and 1987, younger neo-Nazis volunteered as census takers in order to ferret out undocumented aliens, as did some of their unreconstructed elders.[14]

The second paragraph of §9 permitted the federal and state statistical offices to provide individual census data—excluding name—to federal and state ministries if such information was necessary for the lawful performance of their responsibilities. The problem was that, in the computer age, the exclusion of the individual's name was no longer a guarantee of anonymity. This provision appeared to permit the interior ministry to make this partly anonymized census data available to the Federal Criminal Police, tax authorities, and the intelligence agencies, that is, to precisely those agencies that had both the supplemental, name-based data needed to de-anonymize census records and the incentive to do so. This was obviously not the intent of the Bundestag, but there was nothing in the wording of the law that specifically prohibited it.[15] This led the protesters to characterize the Federal Statistical Office as a potential "data supermarket," where the most diverse government agencies could freely help themselves to easily de-anonymized census data.[16] Coming as it did only a few years after the massive manhunt for the kidnappers of industrialist Hanns Martin Schleyer (chapter 8), protesters feared that internal security considerations might in some future crisis situation tempt the government to abrogate the protections traditionally accorded to census data just as American officials had done in interning people of Japanese descent during World War II.

The third paragraph of §9 had been the source of constant friction during the drafting of the law because the statistical needs of the federal government were very different from those of local government. Statistical data that had been aggregated across large geographical areas was of little use to local officials, who governed on a much smaller scale, and they had initially demanded that they be give detailed data down to the city block and building level.[17] However, the federal government was reluctant to allow local officials access to individual information with no strings attached because within such a small geographical area it was virtually impossible to preserve the anonymity of such data. The final version of the law permitted local governments to obtain name-based individual data for their own statistical analyses and to use individual data—without names—for social planning. Since local officials, who often wore more than one administrative hat, could easily put names to partially anonymized records, protesters could not resist the temptation to portray them as an electronic version of the Nazi block warden.[18]

To make matters even worse, the census forms themselves were designed in such a way as to positively encourage people to believe that their personal information would be misused. Since the questions began on the back side of the sheet identifying the head of household, it was impossible to anonymize the census data before the forms themselves were destroyed (something that had, in the case of the 1970 census, taken a full decade). People were also concerned about the eight-digit code printed on the form. Although the code was intended to be used only to monitor paper flow, it could also be used to link individual census data back to the specific individuals named on the paper form, and the absence of explicit regulations governing how these codes could be used and when the data had to be irrevocably anonymized encouraged people to think the worst about the government's respect for their privacy.

The Boycott, Round 1: Normalization, Discipline, and the Power of Information

In thinking about the census, the Third Reich was never far from the minds of the protesters. For example, as the Union of German Journalists wrote to the Hessian interior minister, "One does not need to have a guilty conscience or be a profound pessimist in order to see in a central computer storing more than 60 million citizens the utopia of the writer George Orwell dawning on the horizon a year before 1984. If this information falls into the wrong hands, then the political police of a dictatorship would receive a power that Hitler's Gestapo had only dreamed of."[19] Another letter writer, who characterized himself as disinclined toward the New Left, but who nevertheless preferred to remain anonymous for fear of retribution, pointed out that such collections of personal information were intrinsically dangerous. After all, the Nazis did not come to power carrying big signs announcing the crimes that they would later perpetrate. "It could be too late much faster than one thinks," the author warned.[20] Aly and Roth provided a scholarly foundation for such analogizing, which reached its high—or low—point in 1987, when the fundamentalist Green parliamentarian Jutta Ditfurth characterized the census as the "preliminary stage for mass extermination."[21]

People on both sides of the debate conceded that the census questions themselves were more banal than dangerous. However, this very banality created suspicions. It hardly seemed worth staging an entire census to learn whether someone drove or took the subway to work or how a person heated his or her house, especially since the personal information already held by the social insurance funds, the police, and other agencies was more sensitive than any of the questions asked by the census. On top of all of this, many people were skeptical of the value of census data for social planning because they did not see how, in the absence of the requisite insight and political will, census data would lead to more effective measures to combat the country's problems. In view of these manifest inconsistencies, the protesters could only conclude that the official contention that census data was necessary for better social planning (the slogan for the 1983 census was "Knowledge for the future" [*Wissen für die Zukunft*]) was nothing more than a transparent pretext for the registration of the population for security purposes.

The protesters, however, were less concerned about how this information might enhance the repressive power of the police than they were with the normalizing, disciplinary power to which it gave rise. This, I argue, is the key to understanding their thinking. As one anti-census pamphlet argued, the growing amount of information available, its concentration in public databases, and the ability to connect all of this data were giving rise to a surveillance state in which every action of each and every citizen—and not just a few anarchists—could be continuously monitored. According to this pamphlet,

> The great danger, which is rushing toward us, the danger of being registered by this security Moloch in a way that runs contrary to the democratic rule of law, lies in simply being different, in not corresponding to the norm. That means that man as an individual can *no longer move freely* and is, instead, to be pressed into conformity with normal behavior. *Every one of his steps should be determinable in advance.* (Emphases in original)[22]

These claims need to be understood as an extension of arguments made by privacy advocates at the time. Simitis, for example, argued with regard to the social insurance funds that reducing costs depended on the intensified surveillance of the individual recipient—that is, on both gaining access to additional information (beyond benefit history) in order to determine what circumstances that might have contributed to rendering the person eligible for these services in the first place and then on using this information to continuously monitor the behavior of the recipient. Similarly, planning for the optimal deployment of the labor force depended on knowledge not only of wage history, but also of training, work history, and other physical and psychological factors that might affect the performance of an individual worker in a specific position, as well as information about the physical demands and possible health dangers posed by the job itself. Simitis warned that access to this information would enable these bureaucracies to make individuals who deviated from accepted norms and expectations into the object of special surveillance and solicitude and give rise to measures to assist, correct, discipline, or discriminate against them. "The greater the degree to which the rationality of society is measured by the degree of adaptation to preformulated administrative expectations," he explained, "the greater the clarity of the manipulative function of data processing."[23]

When census protesters complained about the dangers of "*Verdatung*," they were not simply lashing out blindly against a new technology, but were instead echoing this academic discourse. The privileged object of their hostility was Horst Herold, and much of the rhetoric of the census protests must be understood as a response to Herold's claim that computers held the key to greater security against crime, terrorism, and social deviance. Herold's role in the computerization of policing and his conception of the preventive, normalizing role of police informatics will be examined in part III. However, the comments about the "security Moloch" cited above should be read as a direct response to a passage from a 1980 essay that was widely cited by the protesters. In the offending passage, Herold had written that

> the unlimited nature of information processing would make it possible to accompany the individual along the entire course of his life, to continuously compose snapshots, portraits, and profiles of his personality, to register, observe, and surveil expressions of his lifestyle, and to keep the data gathered in this way ready to hand without the grace of forgetting. The dangers of "Big Brother" are no longer simply products of imaginative literature. The current state of technology has made them into a reality.[24]

Of course, the protesters regarded the police surveillance system constructed by Herold as the very embodiment of those dangers against which he warned. But his vision of crime prevention and social control in modern society was the touchstone of the boycott in other ways as well. In a controversial, often-cited interview that he gave in 1980, Herold had laid out his conception of the relation between information, social deviance, policing, and prevention. He noted there that police files held extensive information on the childhood upbringing, education, family circumstances, and work history of criminals. Although this information represented a unique resource for understanding the causes of crime, Herold bemoaned the fact that its bulk, dispersal, and diverse formats, as well as resistance by both an uninformed public and traditionally minded police officials, all combined to prevent the police from fully exploiting the "epistemological privilege" bestowed on them by this material:

> First of all, we must be able to penetrate, disaggregate, and link in a multidimensional manner the huge amount of data that the police already possess. We can do this with current technology. This would be simple if there were no data neurosis. I would estimate that the German police possess around 15 million criminal files. These files contain data that has been piled up for years and years pertaining to why people do drugs, why they break into pharmacies in order to steal them, why people have had abortions, why they do this and that, how they ended up in a life of crime, and so on. All of this knowledge is simply lying around. Only we do not know what we really know. Only we cannot fully exploit this knowledge and combine it to create a portrait of society![25]

What distinguished Herold's position from more conservative views of the role of police information systems was his belief that these new technologies could make repression less necessary, not (simply) more effective: by mining the vast amounts of data available to the police, it would be possible to uncover the primary social causes of crime and deviance and then attack them at their origins before they could give rise to concrete dangers. This is what Herold called the social sanitary function of the police (chapter 9). As he explained in one of the most explosive passages in the interview, the ultimate goal of the police should be "to immerse themselves with an analytic eye into the massive amounts of accumulated facts relating *to all forms of abnormal, deviant behaviors in society* in order to provide society with rational insights, to correct its own legal system, and to devise instruments for preventing crime" (emphasis added).[26]

This passage was cited at every opportunity by the protesters. Many of them had had firsthand experience with investigations of their political attitudes in conjunction with applications for jobs in the public sector. Homosexuals felt themselves especially threatened by a computer-enabled war on deviance. As one pamphlet warned, "Let's imagine that the Nazi Gestapo had possessed a tool comparable to modern computer files, then terror against unwelcome contemporaries, including the later inmates of the pink triangle concentration camps, would have been even more perfect. Let's not make it so easy for the snoops . . . . We gays especially as a group, who have long been recorded in the 'pink lists,' should be especially critical here and join the boycott."[27]

One of the most striking images produced during the first round of the census boycott (figure 4.1) reflected a decidedly dystopian reading of the police and the census as vehicles for social normalization and disciplining. Here, the viewer looks through the legs of a towering soldier or riot policeman, who is identifiable by his fatigues and combat boots. Rather than simply crushing the population like an overweening Leviathan in a display of naked power, the policeman is carefully cultivating the population by using a wide-toothed garden rake (with unmistakable penile connotations) to weed out all of those individuals who deviated from prevailing social norms—represented by the long columns of uniform, anonymous persons with blank, unexpressive faces who are left behind.

The boycott movement was nothing if not diverse, and not all of the protesters were focused so closely on the new information technologies. Those on the more Marxist left linked the census directly to the problems of the capitalist state. For example, the Marburg Bunte Hilfe maintained that the primary function of the census was "to perfect economic planning in the sense of imperialism, to further secure the preventive, apparently continuous and omnipresent surveillance of the population, and make

Figure 4.1. The normalizing power of information technology. Source: The first appearance of this image was on the cover of *Volkszählungsboykott. Informationsmaterial* #1 (26 January 1983), in both AIfS SBe 444, VoBo-Büro Hamburg, Box 5, and AGG B.I.1, Nr. 243.[28]

possible targeted actions in the framework of counterinsurgency (measures to defend against covert struggle) and anti-riot planning (civil unrest) programs."[29] Despite the appeal of such claims to communist and anarchist groups, the primary object of concern for most of the protesters were the new information technologies, not the capitalist state.

Turning now to the actual events, while moderate members of the major parties turned to the courts, the boycotters, including the Greens, who first secured Bundestag representation in March of that year, took to the streets.[30] The problem was that calling on people to disobey the law was a misdemeanor, and both officials and the police pulled out all of the stops to block the protest: they closed down information stands and confiscated materials; cities refused to issue permits for protests or allow boycott groups to use public facilities for meetings; officials pressured banks to close the accounts of boycott groups; reports on boycott activities became part of the chancellor's daily security briefing; and, of course, people were prosecuted. While the boycotters were intent upon elbowing their way into the public sphere, the administration, the police, and the justice system were equally intent on denying them this symbolic victory. Only rarely did the courts side with the protesters on free speech grounds. In at least one case, even after the Constitutional Court had blocked the census, Berlin officials insisted on continuing to prosecute one particularly vocal protester, arguing that, at the time of his actions, the law was still in force.[31]

All adults between 18 and 65 were liable for service as census takers; selected individuals could be fined if they refused. Officials everywhere were worried about the number of people seeking to avoid the job, and, as the census date approached, many of those who had initially agreed to serve withdrew.[32] As a result, the cities were forced to rely to a much greater degree on civil servants, who were presumably more trustworthy and who could be disciplined for refusing to take on the job. This, however, created fresh problems since the public would presumably be less forthcoming to police, tax and justice officials, social workers, and any other civil servants, who might be in a position (and legally obligated) to act upon information that they became aware of as they collected the census forms and reviewed them for accuracy and completeness. Officials were also concerned with guarding against both fake and "Trojan" census takers, who might seek to undermine the census from within, ensuring the physical safety of real census takers, and taking down boycott signs and banners without arousing even more opposition. On the other side, protesters were busily setting up information stands, distributing fliers, holding meetings, and scribbling graffiti. They devoted a great deal of energy to devising ingenious ways of throwing sand into the gears of the census machine, such as explaining to the public that they could satisfy the letter of the law by providing all of the required information in a letter that was handwritten in miniscule Cyrillic script and by carefully warning that the census forms could not be read by computer if they had been soaked in the bathtub, though without, of course, suggesting that upstanding citizens should engage in such actions![33] Not all protest was nonviolent: the Braunschweig registry office was bombed on 11 April.[34]

There were also debates over the real motives for the boycott. Writing in the conservative *Frankfurter Allgemeine Zeitung*, criminal law expert Friedrich-Christian Schröder denied the legitimacy of the boycott, arguing that after the squatters movement and protests against the construction of the nuclear power plant in Brokdorf and the west runway at the Frankfurt airport, the census simply provided "a new stage on which the old enemies of our political system gather again."[35] This claim was echoed by Zimmermann, by State Secretary Horst Waffenschmidt (CDU), who repeatedly insisted that the protests had been stirred up by a small number of "enemies of the state," and by Manfred Rommel (CDU), the president of the German Association of Cities and Towns, who claimed that a call to disobey a properly passed law was nothing less than an attack on the rule of law.[36] But Hessian Minister President Holger Börner (SPD) defended those who protested out of concern for the confidentiality of census data against the conservative attempts to defame the boycott tout court.[37] At the other end of the spectrum, there were skirmishes over whether a boycott on privacy grounds was somehow more legitimate than decision to boycott in order to protest the government's refusal to be more forthcoming with information regarding the placement of nuclear missiles.[38] And a widely publicized public disputation between Günter Grass, who argued that there was more than ample reason to be mistrustful of the government, and Bull, who took a more moderate position on the issue, took place at the end of February.[39]

All of these differences of opinion were reproduced within the major political parties, and a number of politicians suggested postponing the census until the legal issues could be clarified.[40] However, administration officials were adamant that the census take place as scheduled.[41] The privacy commissioners were divided: while some became even more vocal in their criticisms of the census law, others maintained that census data could be adequately protected if the organizational and procedural measures they recommended were followed.[42] Although federal and state interior ministry officials agreed to most of these suggestions, this did not affect the substance of the registry comparison or the other key provisions, and no law whose concrete meaning depended on such an informal agreement could have been expected to survive review by the courts. Nevertheless, by early April officials at every level of government were literally sitting at their desks gleefully rubbing their hands together in the expectation that the Constitutional Court would quickly dispose of what they considered to be manifestly unfounded complaints so that they could send out fines en masse before the scheduled census date to ensure that these official admonitions would have the desired effect.

The Census Decision: From the Streets to the Courts

The first three months of 1983 witnessed a remarkable learning process, and by the end of March the privacy consciousness of the nation had been, as *Der Spiegel* noted, "fundamentally transformed."[43] This process also extended to the Constitutional Court itself.

The Court had received 102 formal complaints against the census and 1,121 less formal petitions.[44] On 23 March it agreed to hear the case and selected two complaints for oral argument on 12 April: the first was submitted by Maja Stadler-Euler (the daughter of one of the founders of the FDP and the former head of the FDP party caucus in the Hamburg legislature) and her law partner Gisela Wild; the other was submitted by Gunther von Mirbach, a law student and vice-chair of the Young Conservatives in Lüneburg, who was, in his own characterization, "certainly no enemy of the state."[45] Numerous amicus briefs were also filed in the case.

In her oral argument, Wild began by reassuring the justices that the census law was not opposed only by "anarchists and those who rejected the system," but also by upstanding citizens, who were concerned "that the state quest for omniscience was depriving the person of his private sphere. There are citizens who fear that one day they will be ruled as a number by machines and administered by anonymous powers because their data is linked in unfathomable channels."[46] Stadler-Euler and Wild set out a long list of reasons why the census was unconstitutional. They argued, among other things, that the census constituted precisely the compulsory registration and cataloging of the personality that the Court had declared unacceptable in the microcensus decision, that the individual questions penetrated into the inviolable core of the personality, and that the census was unconstitutional because the Bundestag had failed to take account of the impact of electronic data processing on the real uses of census data. More specifically, they claimed that the combination of technological advances, which permitted the networking of individual information systems, and the close organizational connections between state statistical offices and state information and planning systems meant that it was impossible to prevent the linkage of the information held in these different systems or eliminate the risk of the reidentification of statistical data. This was particularly insidious, as Wild explained, because, once one's personal data had disappeared into these "mysterious channels" (*unergründliche Kanäle*), it would be impossible to know how it was being used and whether the rights of the individual were being violated by these uses.[47]

These arguments were supported by other plaintiffs, including the German Association for Privacy Protection and Steinmüller (whose coplaintiffs included Podlech and the information scientist Klaus Brunnstein, head of the Hamburg FDP 1980–83, who demonstrated how easily census data could be reidentified). Although the Steinmüller complaint devoted a great deal of energy to analyzing the organizational, procedural, and technological weak spots in the organization of the census, it also hit the underbelly of much of the public debate, which had focused unproductively on the trustworthiness of public officials and the likelihood that census data would be "misused," by pointing out that the 1983 census took place in a "technical environment that had been completely transformed and that rendered previous security measures obsolete." As a result, Steinmüller argued, the privacy problem had to be reconceptualized not in terms of the misuse of statistical data, but rather in terms of its "normal use."[48]

Simitis argued that the registry comparison was unconstitutional because the nondisadvantagement clause made it impossible for the respondent to understand the consequences of his answers and act accordingly. He also claimed that computerization had raised novel constitutional issues, which had to be addressed before the census could be allowed to proceed. "Even census data that appears to be entirely innocuous," Simitis wrote in his brief, "can, when linked with other data, create dangers, which can no longer be adequately described using the categories of the microcensus decision." Integrated information systems, he explained, "can allow data that can itself not be considered sensitive to appear in a different light," and he insisted, citing Benda's 1974 essay, that it was this "dysfunctional dissemination" of information—that is, the loss of control over its secondary usage—that "destroyed the private sphere."[49]

The administration, on the other hand, considered the complaints to be manifestly unfounded and argued that the complainants had so little prospect of prevailing in a hearing on the merits of the case that the application for a temporary injunction should be thrown out. As a result, its brief was an intellectually anemic document that failed to engage at all with the arguments regarding the impact of the new information technologies.[50]

The views of the various parties regarding the most appropriate remedy if the Court were to rule against the administration can be arrayed along a continuum. Bull believed that the census could safely proceed as planned as long as the supplementary security measures devised by the privacy commissioners were observed. Simitis argued that the count itself was constitutional, but that, since the registry comparison would be conducted immediately afterwards (and thus before any future hearing on the merits of the case), only a temporary injunction could protect the population from the irreparable harms that they would suffer if the registry comparison and the other uses permitted under §9 of the census law were permitted to go ahead. Stadler-Euler and Wild, as well as Steinmüller and his coplaintiffs, argued that the count itself should be blocked because the mere electronic storage of the census data would have unforeseeable, uncontrollable, and irreparable consequences.[51]

The day following the oral arguments and two weeks before the census was scheduled to begin, the Court issued a temporary injunction blocking the count. The eight-member Court ruled unanimously that the various provisions contained in §9 raised so many serious questions that this part of the census would have to be suspended until the ultimate disposition of the case had been decided. The Court also ruled, though only by a 5–3 margin, that a partial stay of these additional uses of census data would not be sufficient because, until it was established whether the collection of this data "under the conditions of automatic data processing" violated the constitutional rights of the citizenry, the potential harm involved in letting the count itself go forward outweighed the cost of temporarily delaying it.[52]

Public reaction to the April injunction was mixed. There were predictable recriminations by the major parties, though all of them had voted for the law. While the Federal Association of Citizens' Initiatives for Environmental Protection interpreted the injunction as a victory for the extraparliamentary opposition, writing in the *Taz*, which served as the mouthpiece for the boycott movement, Vera Gaserow complained bitterly that the injunction had taken the wind out of the sails of a protest movement, which, if it had only continued for another month, would have led to the complete rejection of large-scale statistical surveys, rather than simply a temporary injunction against a few specific parts of the census. Even though the decision would never have happened without the pressure of the boycott, Gaserow concluded that "it is, nevertheless, the worst thing that could happen for the movement." On the other hand, writing in the CSU news magazine *Bayernkurier*, State Secretary Carl-Dieter Spranger (CSU) characterized the boycott as a "rehearsal for insurrection." The *Frankfurter Allgemeine Zeitung* described the decision as a "victory over the state" and scolded the Court for letting itself be misused by enemies of the state. The more liberal *Frankfurter Rundschau*, however, praised the protesters for teaching the nation to question the state, rather than to show unquestioning deference toward it. But it was Bull, writing in *Die Zeit*, who provided one of the best assessments of the protest:

> What has been said and written here at home over the past few weeks in the radio and the printed press, but also among neighbors and friends, within the family and among work colleagues, about the census scheduled for the end of April reveals more about our political situation than the statistics that one hoped would be generated by the great inquiry. The discussion reveals much about attitudes toward the state and the public administration, about anxieties and civil courage, about people's views on the effectiveness of law and its protections—but above all about how much the citizenry trusts and entrusts to its politicians and the civil service. There can hardly be a better example of the much-discussed legitimation crisis of the state.[53]

In temporarily setting aside the census, the Court explained that its ultimate ruling on the case would focus on the ways in which advances in statistics and electronic data processing since the 1969 microcensus decision were impacting the constitutional rights of the individual. Oral arguments on the merits of the case were to be held 18–19 October.[54]

The first issue that was addressed at the October hearing was the need for statistics. In her oral argument, Stadler-Euler characterized official statistics as "indispensable." Munich law professor Peter Badura, who represented the administration at the hearing, agreed, arguing that census data was an "existential condition" for the welfare state. And, as Zimmermann warned in frustration and incomprehension, "a state that is not even permitted to count its citizens, whose citizens can no longer be asked where they live and work, a state that cannot investigate the extent to which housing costs weigh upon its citizens, must abdicate politically, and especially in the domain of social policy."[55] On the other hand, Hamburg Justice Senator Eva Leithäuser (SPD) bluntly reminded the Court that the welfarist mandate of the state did not justify shoving aside the constitutional rights of the individual,[56] and Wild argued that the goal was not to deny the state information for specific purposes, but rather

> to stop the state from collecting data from its citizens without bounds and then using this data without limitation and control.... The person who loses control over his data, who no longer knows which of his data are being linked and processed in what context, feels himself to be hopelessly exposed to the power of the state apparatus. He is deprived of the possibility of making himself heard, of representing himself, of explaining himself, of exercising any active control. He cannot prevent his data shadows, and thus his personality, from being deformed by the apparatus.[57]

The debate over the constitutionality of the census pivoted more on the status of the final purpose principle than on any other issue. In his amicus brief, Simitis explained that the most basic prerequisite for effective privacy protection was the "narrowest possible formulation of the final purpose principle." Not only would this ensure the transparency of data processing; it would also insure its limitation because "as long as the conditions under which the processing of data are measured against the need for this data for a concrete, easily discernible and verifiable purpose, the scope of the data employed for this purpose will necessarily be limited." On the other hand, wherever such conditions were lacking, "the individual is threatened by the automatic processing of his personal information with the possibility of being transformed into an infinitely manipulable informational object."[58] Podlech distilled the consequences of this line of reasoning into even pithier terms, which would be taken over nearly verbatim by the Court in its final ruling, when he argued that a social order and legal system in which "the citizen can no longer know who knows what about him at what point and in what context" would be incompatible with the constitutional right to the free development of the personality.[59]

These arguments did not go unchallenged. In its brief, which was—in every sense of the word—a much weightier document than the one it had submitted in April, the interior ministry explained that the multifunctional use of census data grew out of its role as the cornerstone of the entire system of statistics that had been developed over the previous century; it insisted that the elimination of census data would severely diminish the value of the information collected by other surveys; and it argued that a door-to-door count with compulsory answers was necessary because sampling could not provide reliable information on small, geographically bounded populations. With regard to the status and scope of the final purpose principle, the ministry argued that not only did the Federal Privacy Protection Law permit the dissemination of personal data within the public administration if this were necessary for the lawful fulfillment of the responsibilities of the office receiving the data, but also that the Basic Law—in the principle of *Amtshilfe*—specifically required all federal and state agencies to provide each other all of the information needed to perform their constitutional duties (though it conceded that opinion was divided as to the scope of this authorization). Consequently, all of the actions authorized under §9 of the census law—including the use of statistical information for administrative purposes, which was the main point on which the constitutional complaint turned—were permissible because there was, the administration insisted, no constitutional basis for prohibiting "once and for all" the use for other purposes of information that had been collected for one specific purpose.[60]

The last major set of questions addressed the challenges posed by the proposed uses of census data to the Court's understanding of privacy rights. For Simitis, the starting point for reflection on this problem could no longer be either the intrusion into the private sphere or the ostensible sensitivity of certain kinds of data, but rather the analysis of the context in which data was to be used.[61] The counterpart to, or consequence of, this shift from the private sphere to context as the basic analytical category was the reconceptualization of privacy as a social relationship among individuals. As Simitis told the court, the goal was not to dissolve social bonds in favor of the "privatistic isolation" of the individual, but rather to preserve "that minimal degree of [social] distance, which every person needs in order to exercise his rights and thus to make a democratically structured state capable of sustaining its existence and functioning."[62] Or, as Podlech noted in the passage from his commentary on Article 2, Paragraph 1 that was cited in chapter 2, privacy could not be conceived "as something pertaining to the isolated individual, which is then lost through communication with others and through the acquisition of a social dimension .... It is a social quality of the person."[63]

The administration, on the other hand, held fast to both the concept of the private sphere and to the Court's arguments in the microcensus decision. In its brief, the administration argued that the inviolable core of the private sphere was far narrower than claimed by the complainants, that the census questions did not individually intrude upon the protected private sphere or collectively entail the registration of the personality, that the census did not ask for information that was not already known in one form or another to the public administration, that privacy rights ceased to be absolute as soon as one entered into relation with the external social world, that the right to anonymity had to be weighed against the needs of the state, and that, in balancing these needs, the Bundestag had made—with respect to the registry comparison and the availability of census data to other agencies— a legitimate decision that census data was to enjoy less anonymity than that otherwise accorded to federal statistical data.[64]

In its final ruling on the case in December of that year (which will be discussed in detail in chapter 5), the Court upheld the constitutionality of the census itself, though it did not do so without qualification. However, the Court overturned both the registry comparison and the provisions governing the additional use of census data by federal and local government.[65]

The census decision injected a distinctly liberal element into a German political tradition, which had traditionally viewed the sovereignty of the state and the unhindered functioning of the executive branch as the guarantee of the rights of its citizens. Even though most of those who had challenged the census law in court had sought to block both the census and the planned secondary uses of the information collected, they were nevertheless vindicated by the decision, and the Court's awareness of the ways in which electronic data processing was creating new dangers to personality rights that could not be theorized in the language of earlier privacy decisions was due in no small part due to the boycott movement.[66] It is, however, less clear whether the decision met the expectations of those protesters, who increasingly rejected the use of statistical data as a medium of social governance.

The Boycott, Round 2: "Im Mittelpunkt steht immer der Mensch"

The second round of the boycott was longer and more complicated than the first, which had been abruptly truncated by the temporary injunction, and I would like to begin by describing the boycott itself before turning to an analysis of the critique of statistical governance through which the Greens came to understand the significance of the protest.

Almost immediately after the Court decision, the administration set about drafting a new census law that would satisfy the conditions set out by the Court. For a moment, it appeared that the administration would again give in to the demands of the cities for access to individual information. However, since none of the parties was willing to take a chance on getting burned, the administration quickly retreated in the face of criticism from the privacy commissioners, and everyone felt that the law that was approved by the Bundestag in September 1985 could pass constitutional muster.[67] This was perhaps the chief reason why the 1987 boycott remained more confined to the left-alternative milieu than had been the case in 1983.

Since early 1986, many of the groups that had mobilized against the census in 1983 had focused their energies on the packet of security laws that had been introduced by the administration in January of that year (chapter 5).[68] Efforts to revive the slumbering boycott movement began with a December 1986 coordinating meeting, which was sponsored by several civil liberties groups, who hoped to halt the advance of the surveillance state and its "informational armament." By the end of April 1987 there would be approximately one thousand boycott groups nationwide.[69] The Greens caused a minor uproar when their delegates wore boycott buttons to the first session of the Bundestag in February 1987, and they caused a major uproar by posing with a boycott banner in front of the parliament building in Bonn. The first action earned them a sharp admonishment from the Bundestag office, and the second led to a fine of 8,400 marks from the Bonn police for demonstrating within the protected zone surrounding the Bundestag. Green parliamentarians and the authorities continued spar through the spring and summer. When at a press conference the Greens gave an official phone number as the contact address for people seeking information on the boycott, the number was blocked, and they were warned that the use of official facilities for such a purpose constituted an infraction of the Bundestag rules. A new office phone number was also blocked, only to be mysteriously unblocked several weeks later. The police also passed up no opportunity to search the offices of both the Green Bundestag delegation and those of the party's state organizations, in the former case demonstrably forcing the lock despite an offer to provide the key.

But the Greens were not the only targets of police repression, which was by all accounts equally sharp in states governed by conservatives and Social Democrats.[70] Across the country, information stands were banned, printed materials confiscated, and phones tapped. In Rhineland-Pfalz alone, there were at least 150 police raids on apartments, offices, and print shops. The Bremen government voted in May not to participate in the census, though the courts quickly forced the city to reverse its position. In Berlin, the state attorney sought to confiscate mail directed to twenty boycott organizations. The federal prosecutor even got involved in the prosecution of a protest-related misdemeanor, explaining that a 10,000 mark fine was not too high because of the possibility that the call for a boycott would encourage anarchist groups to engage in acts of terrorism.[71] Such a mentality equated a dispute over the role of the state with a terrorist attack upon it. Whether the fear that the boycotts would open the door to terrorism was real or just a pretext for intimidation, it came out later that the police were entering information on boycotters into the national criminal information system; they believed that this information would later be useful because those persons who committed major acts of political violence had always begun with smaller offenses.[72] However, the distance between snipping codes off a census form and putting up boycott posters, on the one hand, and acts of terrorism, on the other, was big enough to drive a truck through, and the repressive measures by the state represented an attempt—perhaps the first serious one since the banning of the Communist Party in the 1950s and the more recent Radicals Resolution—to criminalize unwelcome political speech and to use the concerted power of the state to intimidate political opponents.[73]

On the other side, once forced into a corner, protesters resorted to cat-and-mouse games with the police and the census apparatus. There were numerous cases where census takers had cardboard briefcases containing census papers taken away from them, including once at knifepoint and once at gunpoint, and officials decided as a precaution not to send census takers into the Hamburg Hafenstraße, choosing instead to rely on the postal service.[74] There were, however, instances of violence. The Leverkusen registry office was bombed, and an unsuccessful attempt was made to bomb the Oberhausen statistical office. The people who claimed responsibility for these actions portrayed their opposition to the census as part of a larger struggle against imperialism.[75] In addition, on 1 May a police raid on a boycott coordinating office in the Berlin district of Kreuzberg—the center of the city's alternative scene—set off two days of serious rioting, which was fueled by a host of underlying social factors. In this way the boycott quickly became an exercise in the art of not being governed, in part an effort—sometimes violent—to avoid being irrevocably incorporated into the informational infrastructure of the state, and in part an effort to stake out a physical and social space for an alternative culture within the interstices of this state by means of a carnivalesque inversion of its logic.[76]

Although the local groups were essentially autochthonous, as the group with the highest profile and the greatest resources, as well as the only one with a nationwide organization, it was inevitable that the Greens would take on a leading role in the boycott. But deciding on a strategy of their own and persuading the other groups to follow their erstwhile leaders was an entirely different story. The Greens had originally joined with a number of other groups in calling for a complete boycott, and, taking a lesson from 1983, they opted not to challenge the revised census law in the courts. The people, Hans Christian Ströbele argued, could only protect themselves by refusing to participate.[77] However, from the very beginning there were debates over just what this meant. Some people interpreted it as meaning that they should simply refuse to accept the census forms; this was the so-called "Bochum strategy." But the Greens also wanted to collect as many forms as quickly as possible in order to provide irrefutable evidence that the government had failed in its effort to force through the census and to thereby lower the threshold of resistance for others who may have supported the boycott in principle, but who feared retribution; this was the "Cologne strategy."[78]

The Bochum boycott group complained that the Greens were exploiting disagreements among the local groups in order to take over the leadership of the movement, and they argued that the Cologne strategy degraded local boycott groups into mere messengers whose role was exhausted in delivering over their census forms at the designated collection points. Such a strategy, they insisted, undermined the solidarity of the local groups and left their individual members to face official retribution on their own.[79] For their part, the communists seemed divided over whether to play off the local Green initiatives against the national party leadership, while claiming the former for themselves, or to condemn all of the Greens for diverting the protest into pseudo-radical channels.[80]

Despite their rhetorical commitment to the cause, the Greens remained reluctant to embrace the boycott wholeheartedly, and positions on the boycott reflected the division between the realist and the fundamentalist wings of the party. Even though he had been a strong supporter of the boycott in 1983, the more pragmatic Otto Schily, who later left the Greens for the SPD and eventually served as federal interior minister, opposed the 1987 boycott and criticized the party's tendency to claim moral superiority for its own position. In practice, many of the Greens advocated what came to be known as a soft boycott or *Schummellinie*, that is, a strategy of evasion, resistance, delay, disruption, and systematic falsification of census returns in ways that they hoped would escape the plausibility checks of the local census offices. This strategy was based on the assumption that throwing sand in the gears of the census machinery on such a massive scale would cause it to collapse while rendering the information collected of such doubtful accuracy as to be completely unusable. A classic example of such tactical resistance was a letter from Petra Kelly to the Bonn census office asking officials there to kindly answer 125 detailed questions so that she could make an informed decision about completing the form.[81] However, opponents of the *Schummellinie* argued that it was naive to believe that local officials would simply throw up their hands in resignation in the face of such resistance; they also pointed out that those who adopted such a strategy were willing, in principle, to give the state the information it asked for and that this strategy made it easy for census officials to pick off protesters one by one once they had them in their sights.[82]

Despite the unwillingness of many Greens to fully commit to the boycott, the party was criticized from all directions for its willingness to ignore the principle of majority rule.[83] While some Greens claimed—echoing the argument that had been made against the stationing of NATO nuclear weapons in Germany—that the census posed such an immediate existential danger as to justify resistance, the legal staff of the Green Bundestag delegation argued that the idea of civil disobedience could not compensate for the legitimation deficit of the boycott. Instead, they argued that the expansion of democracy and individual liberty had always been the result of political struggle and that, in reality, the boycott represented a constitutional rights movement on behalf of a right that had been formally recognized, but that had yet to be translated into substantive policy.[84]

However, the 1987 boycott never became a mass movement comparable to its 1983 predecessor. As Stephan Maria Tanneberger, the coordinator for the Greens in North Rhine-Westphalia, observed, even though many people had in the intervening years joined groups to protest the security laws and state technologies of surveillance and social control, the boycott had remained a single-issue movement because protesters had been unable to establish the connection between the census and broader social problems. But Tanneberger still harbored the hope that it would be possible to transform the boycott into a new social movement: "Why should it be a pipe dream to organize . . . a national network of initiatives concerned about the development of control and surveillance technologies comparable to those of the peace and anti-nuclear movements?"[85]

Once the actual counting began in late May, the boycott shifted into a different register. Mounds of census returns piled up in local offices, and it was clear that no one was going to know anything for certain until officials had had time to work through these papers. Moreover, no one knew how accurate the returns were. The revised census law permitted persons to return their forms by mail. While this protected census data from the prying eyes of census takers, who often lived in the neighborhoods where they were required to canvas, it deprived census takers of the opportunity to review individual returns for completeness and accuracy. As a result, it was estimated that anywhere between 20 percent and 60 percent of the returns submitted by mail either contained incorrect data or were not completely filled out.[86] One thing that was clear, however, was that all of the organizational precautions that the court had required census officials to take in order to protect the privacy of personal data during the census itself were widely, and intentionally, ignored.[87] For example, the Bavarian State Statistical Office reported with satisfaction in August that a substantial proportion of those persons who had called for a boycott had actually submitted their properly completed forms. However, as *Der Spiegel* noted, either this number had been made up or it had been obtained through the illegal use of the census returns.[88]

The Greens reported that by mid-summer over 800,000 forms had been turned into the central boycott coordinating office in Bonn; this represented a little more than 1 percent of the total population and perhaps as much as 3 percent of all heads of household. Census officials claimed that, nationwide, the participation rate and the quality of the data collected was quite high, but that in a number of the larger cities the accuracy of the data was impaired by low response rates, high error rates, and manifestly evasive answers.[89] Those who failed to return their forms could expect to receive warning letters from local officials, followed by successive rounds of fines and penalties. All in all, the administrative epilogue to the 1987 census is loathsome and depressing.[90]

By the early fall, these fines were beginning to take their toll on the movement, which was clearly running out of steam, and in early October the refusal of the Constitutional Court to review complaints against the census dealt the boycott a serious blow.[91] By this time, boycotters were coming to a more realistic, though not necessarily disillusioned, appraisal of the situation. Even before the Court decision, Roland Appel—the coordinator of the Green working group on law and society, the party's liaison to the boycott movement, delegate to the North Rhineland-Westphalia Landtag in the 1990s, and later a management consultant specializing in privacy and civil liberties—had argued that the success of the movement was to be measured not only by the number of blank forms collected, but also by the political discussion of the new technologies and the use of personal information that had been prompted by the boycott.[92] This point was echoed by the Bavarian Greens, who noted at the end of October that most people had put the boycott behind them in one way or another; they "had held out through fines and penalties, objections, petitions and complaints, but in the end they couldn't get out of filling out (one way or another) the census form." Nevertheless, neither they nor other groups considered the boycott a failure. As the Berlin political scientist and civil libertarian Wolf-Dieter Narr wrote in the name of the Committee for Constitutional Rights and Democracy, it was important that a sizeable minority had stood up for civil liberties and that a much larger number had filled out the forms only under duress. But, Narr emphasized, there was no reason for boycotters to hold out at any cost.[93] As one group calling itself the Data Pirates argued, collective political action was more important than ever before because the Constitutional Court's refusal to overturn the revised census law deprived the soft boycott of whatever political rationale that it might once have had: "The boycott movement is by no means a revolutionary movement, but it is more than an association of progressive attorneys. For those protesters for whom . . . the boycott movement is at an end, there must be a means of articulating [their beliefs]. These protesters make up the largest part of the movement and need to be mobilized . . . This potential for resistance is more impressive than a few hundred people willing to file legal motions!"[94]

Nevertheless, it was clear that the boycott, hard or soft, was not going to bring the administration to its knees. By the spring of 1988, most cities were reporting return rates in excess of 98 percent. As for the stragglers, the census law permitted officials to take information from the population registries as a last resort, so that, by the time Zimmermann presented the preliminary results of the census, he was technically correct to claim that nearly 100 percent of the population had participated. However, his claim that these results were due to the success of the administration in convincing people of the need for their information and the state's commitment to protecting their privacy was part delusion, part newspeak.[95]

Die Zeit was less overtly ideological, but no less critical, in its assessment of the boycott. The liberal paper argued that those who disputed the need for statistical data failed to understand that the welfare state had to do its best to manage the problems with which it was confronted and that, at a minimum, reliable data would increase the probability that the outcomes would be good. As proof, the paper noted that the actual census count for West Berlin had come in at 2,041,000. However, while a census count based solely on the regular updating of the population registries would have found a population decrease of 241,000 persons, the actual decline was only 108,000. The difference between the two figures was approximately 133,000 persons, "an entire additional big city for which schools, apartments, and public spaces must be planned."[96]

The census boycotts also gave the Greens an opportunity to think not only about privacy and surveillance, but also about the purpose of the census and the ways in which statistical information was used as a medium for social governance. The pamphlet *Only Sheep Let Themselves Be Counted* began by explaining why the compulsory collection of statistical data was incompatible with individual self-determination. Not only did such data pools lend themselves to misuse; the collection of statistics in this manner was also based, they argued, on an elitist, authoritarian conception of democracy.[97] One could, as *Die Zeit* had done, argue that better statistics make for better policy. However, compulsory answers to census questions whose phrasing reflected the interests of the organizations collecting and using the data inevitably degraded the individual into the object of technocratic rule, and the Greens maintained that statistics collected under such conditions could not lead to better policy if the ways in which the problem was defined ignored the real needs of the individual. Such an approach was characteristic of what they called an "authoritarian conception of the welfare state," in which the state "determines . . . the objective data, defines social problems, and informs citizens about what it has defined as their needs. Citizens are now and again called to the polls, but their desires in the areas of housing, work and transportation are merely subjective and, therefore, statistically and politically irrelevant. We reject such a conception of politics."[98]

The outcome of this process is captured in figure 4.2. Here, the individual has been emptied of all concrete needs and desires to such an extent that he can appear only as the passive product of the cold, rectangular logic of social planning and of the abstract statistical schemata through which he is represented. In this view of the world, the individual is not a real person, but a cipher devoid of all agency, individuality, and possibility of self-realization. He becomes simply one more element in the calculable structure of the planned society. Constructing a viable alternative to the rule of bureaucracy and technocracy would require, the Greens argued, the complete alteration of the institutions, processes, and principles of representative democracy because only such changes would make it possible for political decision-making "to orient oneself toward the true, actual needs of the population."[99]

Although the Court had upheld the idea of a full census, it had not done so without qualification. It had ruled that, based on the current state of statistical knowledge, it was not possible to disprove the administration's claim that only a door-to-door count with mandatory answers could fulfill the informational needs of the state, but that, before another such census were undertaken, the administration would have to determine whether these needs could be satisfied through less expensive and less intrusive methods.[100] These issues were addressed at a February 1985 hearing on the microcensus law, which had to be revised to ensure its constitutionality in advance of the survey scheduled for later that year.[101]

"Only Sheep Let Themselves Be Counted" 161

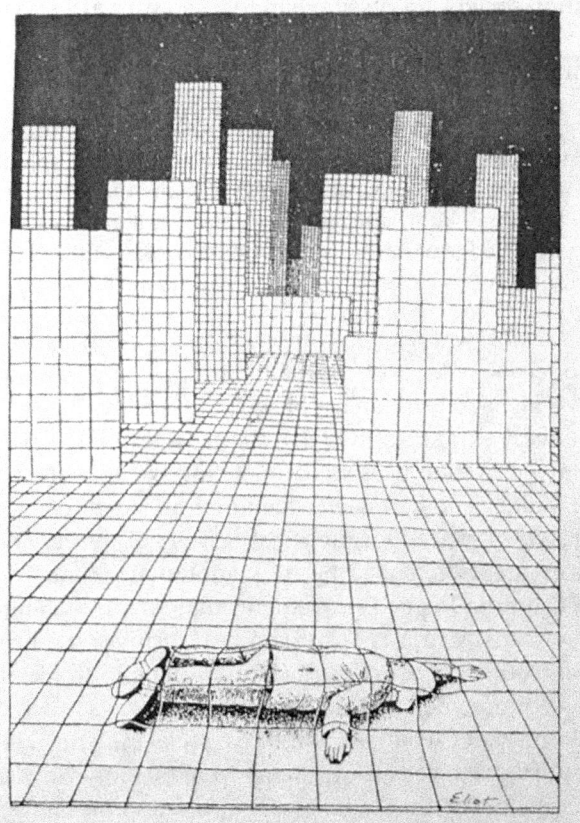

Figure 4.2. The reduction of the individual to an object of technocratic rule. Source: *Volkszählung. Die nächste kommt bestimmt!* (undated), AGG Bestand B.II.1, Nr. 2522(2).

In view of the Court's concerns, the administration rolled out all of the big statistical guns to buttress its claim that a door-to-door count represented the only way to collect the information needed to govern the welfare state. Since the end of the 1960s, state officials and social researchers had been working to develop a system of social indicators that they hoped could be used to plan social programs and then assess their success in producing "welfare" and enhancing "quality of life." One of the leading German figures in this field of empirical social research was the sociologist Wolfgang Zapf.[102] At the hearing, Zapf linked the need for census data to the advent of the information society. He noted that, although there had been much recent debate concerning the transition from an industrial to an information society, discussion had focused primarily on the ways that technology was altering productive and administrative processes, but not on information itself. However, he warned,

> a society that is not informed regarding the elementary processes of its life is not an "information society." ... A society with television programs, interactive terminals, video phones, and personal computers is not an information society if it does not know anything about itself, if it does not have empirically grounded knowledge of its structures and processes, of the objective and subjective condition of its citizens, of old and new inequalities.

For Zapf, statistical knowledge constituted the "informational infrastructure" of modern society, and census data represented an "informational tax" owed by all citizens as an act of social solidarity.[103]

Virtually every expert testified that the census and the microcensus had to be maintained in their present form. Tellingly confusing cause with effect, Egon Hölder, who had been appointed president of the Federal Statistical Office in May 1983, argued that it was not the resistance aroused by mandatory answers, but rather the emotionally charged political climate created by the boycott movement, that was threatening to impair the quality of census results. Zapf similarly blamed the privacy discussion of recent years for encouraging individuals to think of themselves as self-enclosed monads and thus to neglect the ways in which they were enmeshed in market exchanges and other social systems. He argued that mandatory answers to census questions were the only way to prevent the worrying gap between the rights of the individual to state social services and "the willingness of the citizen to make possible the rational organization of basic needs by providing [the necessary] knowledge" from growing too wide.[104]

There was more than a little irony—and hypocrisy—involved in these arguments. In 1981, when federal, state, and local governments were still wrangling over the cost of the census, federal officials had, in fact, proposed the combination of a simplified count to determine the actual size and geographical distribution of the population and a sample (5–10 percent of the total population) to gather more detailed information. However, this proposal was rejected because it would not have provided the detailed knowledge required by local government.[105] At the 1985 hearing, the only two establishment figures to express reservations regarding the need for a door-to-door count were the influential public opinion pollster Elisabeth Noelle-Neumann and the Berlin statistician Bernd Kolleck.[106]

From the perspective of the Greens, what such arguments overlooked was that statistical data always reflected the interests, the definitional power, and the logic of domination of those bureaucratic organizations that collected and controlled this information, and they linked the increasingly authoritarian informational policies of the state to an intensified concern for internal security and to the need to preventively manage the interrelated social, political, and economic problems that were threatening the stability of the capitalist welfare state.[107] As Ulrike Erb, one of the Green experts on the new information technologies, explained, the bureaucratic structures of the country's political and economic systems shared a common logic that enabled them to define what counted as statistical knowledge, to organize this information in ways that corresponded to their own interests, and then to impose these schemata upon the public via mandatory answers. The problem with a census organized in this manner, she argued, was not that it collected too much information, but rather that it did not collect enough information and that the information that it did collect was systematically distorted by the imposition of these alienating and disempowering schemata of social knowledge. The statistical categories used by the census, Erb argued in the language of *Betroffenheit*, which embodied that longing for authentic experience that lay at the core of the new social movements, "always distort the reality they represent because they filter selective aspects out of a complex system and neglect other essential factors . . . A survey of the entire population, which is organized to produce computer-compatible answers, can never serve the humane solution of individual, regional and social problems." In order for the census to really contribute to the solution of urgent social problems, it would, she maintained, have to inquire into the real "*needs* and *desires*" of the population (emphases in original). What Erb and others meant by this was that the census should not simply inquire into the education, income, and means of transportation used most often by the individual. Rather, the census should ask "what activity one would like to engage in, whether one's income is sufficient to live on, and where one would like to see public transportation expanded in order to be able to dispense more often with driving."[108]

It was precisely this issue that so many people had in mind when they argued that the mere collection of data—so long as it had been prestructured by those who wished to use it for planning purposes—created a near-irresistible pressure to adopt certain kinds of policy responses. As the Greens explained,

> The census asked about the means of transportation that citizens use (or had to use) on the way to work, but not about which means of transportation they wanted. Thus, whoever is forced to use their car will provide data that can then be later used to justify the building of new streets and the expansion of existing ones. In this and similar ways, anonymous housing ghettos, city centers dominated by banks, expressways, and mammoth schools were justified by planners in the past.

This created a perverse situation in which, according to a Green policy paper, "the state is no longer there for the citizen, but rather the citizen for the state"—that is, a situation where "the citizen . . . is not asked for his opinion, but only for his data, which is then used to dominate him." In this way, Erb explained, a politically incapacitated citizenry was "forc[ed] into a permanent-press data corset" and so maneuvered by the census questions as to create a situation "where they can no longer pose any inconvenient demands or express individual interests. . . . In order to govern people and communities, they are reduced to categorizable and calculable data."[109]

The visual culture of both the 1983 and the 1987 boycotts was dominated by a single, pervasive image: the bar code.[110] As noted above, the census forms carried an eight-digit code, which was used to monitor paper flow and which was also printed in bar code form so that the return could be read automatically. This captured the imagination of the moment. In some instances, the stripes symbolized real bars that held the individual digitally captive or that were to be broken or bent by the boycott to liberate the population from the grasp of the state and its statistical apparatus. In others, the bars were used to represent the *Verdatung* of the individual and his transformation from an individual person into a manipulable cipher. This use is distilled in the poster by the graphic artist Klaus Staeck (figure 4.3), whose caption reads "The individual always stands at the center," or, in a more figurative rendering, "Man [or the unalienated individual] is always the measure." The way in which the face (or the head—in either case, the seat of the person's individuality) is covered or replaced by a bar code symbolized the ways in which the fullness of individual experience was hollowed out and diminished by being forced into the statistical categories that reflected the logic of technocratic rule and that could be reorganized and combined to create a virtually infinite number of data doubles, none of which corresponded to the individual's sense of self.

Nevertheless, even though the Green critique of statistical governance did not depend on the apocalyptic environmentalism of the fundamentalist wing of the party, there was always the danger that such an emphasis on immediacy and authenticity would imprison its advocates within their own subjectivities and make it impossible to put Erb's alternative vision into practice for communities that were larger and more complex than the alternative milieu.

Green reflections on privacy protection from the 1980s were both fragmentary and programmatic. However, control over information and information technology was one of their defining concerns.[111] They drew freely on Jürgen Habermas's concept of the colonization of the life-world to challenge the dominant cultural codes on which social reproduction in

Figure 4.3. "Man is always the measure." Source: Klaus Staeck.

industrial society depended.[112] On the one hand, they rejected a worldview that was "only oriented toward technical progress, economic rationality, and an interest in profit and 'security' and which neglects important human values and rights to the protection of the individual and social sphere." In such a society, they maintained, digitized (*verdatet*) people "are calculable and manipulable by those who control the data."[113] On the other hand, they criticized the deleterious effects of both the progressive displacement of direct human communication by the technologically mediated exchange of signs and the expanding use of taxonomic schemata to classify, store, and retrieve the formalized knowledge generated by this process.[114] They claimed that these problems could be avoided by ensuring that only *sozialverträglich* technologies—that is, technologies that were consistent with, or which perhaps even promoted, authentic forms of social life—were employed; however, they were more than a little skeptical as to whether any of the new information technologies could be redeemed for such a society.[115]

Although the early Greens focused primarily upon the techno-logic of the nascent information society, this does not mean that they were uninterested in the details of privacy legislation. Erb argued, drawing on Steinmüller, that the "social pollution" (*Sozialverschmutzung*) caused by the new information technologies was just as great a problem as environmental pollution, and she insisted that this problem could be adequately theorized only by expanding the concept of *Datenschutz* and transforming it into what she called "social sphere protection" (*Sozialsphärenschutz*).[116] The cornerstone of this strategy was the use of the new right to informational self-determination as a lever to limit the use of personal information as a mechanism for bureaucratic rule. After the census decision, the Greens complained that the privacy bills sponsored by the major parties systematically violated this right in the name of *Amtshilfe*, the fulfillment of the lawful responsibilities of public offices, and other, ostensibly higher, interests. In contrast, the Greens argued that that the only way to protect privacy rights was to eliminate such elastic clauses and require informed consent for each and every act of information processing.[117] The Greens thought that this goal could be achieved through the combination of two mechanisms. The first was the "data account statement" that they wished to see provided to everyone each month by every data controller.[118] These data account statements were an important transparency tool that would provide the citizenry with the information that they needed in order to assert their right to informational self-determination. These statements were to be complemented by a freedom of information law, which, they argued, was the only way to ensure that the administration was transparent to the citizen, rather than the other way around, and that citizens would have the information they required in order to play an active role in shaping public policy.[119] These demands were the two pillars of the Green privacy platform for the 1990 elections.[120]

Conclusion: Sixty Million Peas

The immediate outcome of the boycott was neither the re-enchantment of the state envisioned by Zimmermann nor the carnivalesque inversion longed for by the protesters, but rather an intense sense of disenchant-

Figure 4.4. *60 Million Peas*. Source: Anselm Kiefer. Photo: Jens Ziehe. Hamburger Bahnhof—Museum für Gegenwart.

ment and disillusionment. Although the state may have saved itself from abdication, it did so at the cost of dissipating the loyalty of many of its citizens. This mood was captured by Anselm Kiefer, who was one of the boycotters, in a work titled "60 Millionen Erbsen," or "60 Million Peas." This oversized installation was composed of large metal storage shelves holding dozens of thick, leaden folio volumes with peas pressed between their covers to represent the objects of the census (figure 4.4). Contained within their bureaucratic pods, the peas, which were dried and uncounted, make a powerful statement about the ultimate (in)significance of the census, while the uneven volumes give the unmistakable impression that, despite the ostensible importance claimed of the census as a tool for the rational governance of society, this particular archive represented a repository of knowledge that was seldom consulted and, in fact, hardly deserving of the name. Kiefer's ironic distance from the census is symbolized by the Hampelmann—a child's puppet-toy manipulated by pulling a string and here standing for the machinations of a state intent on asserting its authority over its citizens—hanging upside down from one of the volumes. The surveillance cameras mounted in the corners of the room make clear the connection between this massive act of bureaucratic futility and the looming surveillance state, while the film hanging out of the cameras raises the question of the legitimacy and the capacity—both technical and political—of the surveillance state, as well as role of the boycott in blunting the intrusion of the state into the private sphere.

The 1991 census was called off due to reunification, which was probably fortunate since there could not have been much enthusiasm for conducting another count so soon after the events of 1987. However, the methodological and political debate over the best means of determining the size and characteristics of the population continued, and by the mid-1990s a tentative decision had been reached to abandon the traditional door-to-door count. The 2001 census, which simply drew together information from the population registries and the microcensus, was a product of this transitional moment. The 2011 census was based on an entirely different approach. The starting point was a postal census of buildings and apartments, including data on persons living in these properties. This data was then compared to and integrated with information provided by the local population registries, the Federal Employment Agency, and those offices that maintained data on public employees, who were not monitored by the employment agency. Household information was constructed from individual information on the basis of shared addresses and other data. The Bundestag described this registry-based census as a "more convenient" (*bürgerfreundlicher*) method, which had been made possible by advances in information technology since the 1970s, and as a way of satisfying the Court's demand that less intrusive methods be used wherever possible.[121]

As noted at the outset, in contrast to the 1980s, there was surprisingly little public protest against either the 2011 or the 2021 censuses, and the question is, in part, whether the absence of such protest represents the result of a sea change in German political and privacy culture since the mid-1980s.[122] This is undoubtedly true, at least in part. The popularization of personal computers across the 1980s and 1990s certainly helped give the technology a human face, while hackers showed that it was possible to have fun using computers in subversive ways. The new information technologies also played a pivotal role in resolving the structural crises that had plagued many branches of industry since the early 1970s; they underlay the revolution in financial services and media; and they eventually gave rise to informational or surveillance capitalism. In short, the dire consequences predicted by the protesters did not happen, or at least did not happen in the way that they had envisioned, and the "Angst vor dem Computer" as a digitized Big Brother began to dissipate as the new technology gained greater acceptance as part of the everyday landscape.[123]

This does not, however, mean that the concerns of the protesters, and of the new social movements more generally, became irrelevant with the advent of a new neoliberal economic and cultural paradigm. Although privacy may no longer move the public as it did in the 1980s, in this, as in so many other domains, the declining radicalism of the new social movements and the alternative milieu has gone hand in hand with the absorption of their ideas into mainstream culture and the institutionalization of their concerns. As should be evident from previous chapters, the concerns of the protesters were by no means entirely novel. However, their sensitivity to the problems associated with integrated information systems, their analyses of both the normalizing, disciplinary effects of the new information technologies and the problems of statistical governance, and—not least—their role in persuading the Constitutional Court that the census did, in fact, raise questions that required a judicial answer helped expand the domain of the political and for the first time made the politics of personal information and the impact of informational power on constitutional rights a matter of immediate political concern for the broader public.

Notes

1. The chapter title is taken from Die Grünen, *Nur Schafe werden gezählt* (1987), AGG B.II.1, no. 2522.
2. According to the survey undertaken for the interior ministry in October 1983 by ipos/Institut für praxisorientierte Sozialforschung, BAK B106/115173.
3. The boycotts and the census decision are mentioned at most only in passing in both the growing historical literature on the 1980s and the literature on new social movements, the Greens, and the alternative milieu, and little has been written on them until quite recently. See Matthew Hannah, *Dark Territory in the Information Age: Learning from the West German Census Controversies of the 1980s* (Ashgate, 2010); Jonathan Voges, "Die Angst vor der Datendiktatur. Die Volkszählung in den 1980er Jahren und ihre Gegner," in *Ausnahmezustände. Entgrenzungen und Regulierungen in Europa während des Kalten Krieges*, ed. Cornelia Rauh and Dirk Schumann (Wallstein, 2015), 177–92; and Andreas Wirsching, *Abschied vom Provisorium, 1982–1990* (Deutsche Verlags-Anstalt, 2006), 393–98.
4. See, for example, Freimut Duve, "Katalysator gegen den Orwell-Staat," in *Die Volkszählung*, ed. Jürgen Taeger (Rowohlt, 1983), 25–30; and Hessischer Landtag Drs. 11/473, 6.
5. Götz Aly and Karl Heinz Roth, *The Nazi Census: Identification and Control in the Third Reich* (Temple University Press, 2004). Wirsching, *Abschied vom Provisorium*, 398, notes that such parallels with the Third Reich were "occasionally plausible, but often unsatisfying."
6. According to Senatsrat Rolf-Peter Magen to Die für die Dienstaufsicht über die Statistischen Landesämter zuständigen obersten Landesbehörden, Betr.: Boykott der Volks-

zählung (11 February 1983), LAB B Rep. 004/1114, the group had begun calling for a boycott at the end of 1982, but its first public event—which may have been the first time that this slogan was used—did not take place until early February. See also "Politiker fragen—Bürger antworten nicht!," *Umweltmagazin* 6, no. 2 (April 1983): 19–24. Within days, the slogan had made its way into the mainstream media: Klaus Pokatzky, "Politiker fragen—Bürger antworten nicht," *Die Zeit*, 11 February 1983.
7. Verdatet, verkabelt, verkauft. Nein zu Personalinformationssystemen, AIfS SBe 444, Antirepressionsbewegung, box 5.
8. Grün-Alternative Liste (Hamburg), *Volkszählung 83. Die Schaffung des "gläsernen" Menschen* (undated, spring 1983), AIfS SBe 444, VoBo-Büro Hamburg, box 1; *Volkszählung?* (Reutlingen), AGG B.I.1, no. 243; and Eva Hubert, "Politiker fragen—Bürger antworten nicht!" in *Volkszählung*, ed. Taeger, 258–59.
9. Hubert, "Politiker fragen—Bürger antworten nicht!" 260; and "'Ohne Drohgebärde, ohne Angst,'" *Der Spiegel*, 18 April 1983, 17–23, especially 20.
10. *BGBl.* (1982): 369–72; and Drs. 9/1068.
11. When I was conducting research for this book, one German professor stated that, at the time, he was registered in five different cities in five different states for just these reasons. Communes (*Wohngemeinschaften*) and squats remained the last blank spaces on the state's map of its own interior, and, according to Hannah, *Dark Territory*, 16–23, 68–70, one of the goals of the census (and the house searches conducted by the police as part of their plan to map the radical milieu) was to render these dark territories light and legible.
12. Drs. 8/2460, 19–20; and Simitis to Staatssekretär Reinhart Bartholomäi (29 January 1979), HHStA Abt. 502/5570b.
13. Mückenberger, Rechtsprobleme der Volkszählung 1983. Anlage zur Verfassungsbeschwerde vom 15.3.1983, LAB B Rep. 004/1111.
14. "Hamburger Rechtsradikale bieten sich als Volkszähler an," *FR*, 9 May 1987. One elderly woman volunteered to again work as a census taker not because she valued the bounty being offered for uncovering illegal residents, but because doing so lay close to her heart. Lucie Hennig to Innenverwaltung (28 March 1983), LAB B Rep. 004/1117. The same issue resurfaced with regard to the 2011 census. See "Sachsen gegen NPD-Volkszähler," *Taz* online, 23 January 2011, http://www.taz.de/1/politik/deutschland/artikel/1/sachsen-gegen-npd-volkszaehler/.
15. Dr. Gisela Wild vor dem Bundesverfassungsgericht am 12.4.1983 in der mündlichen Verhandlung . . . , 4–5, in the Stadler-Euler/Wild papers.
16. "Jeder Hirte zählt seine Schafe," *Taz*, 28 January 1983; "Das Statistische Bundesamt als Daten-Supermarkt," *Taz*, 14 February 1983; "Volkszählung '83: Ausgeforscht und abgespeichert," a special supplement to the short-lived Hannover newspaper *NaNa* (no date), AGG B.I.1, no. 243.
17. Verband Deutscher Städtestatistiker, ed., *Statistik im Spannungsfeld der Gesellschaft* (Verband deutscher Städtestatistiker, 1984). The desiderata of local government are vividly set out in the correspondence in NRW RW 391/884. In fact, in seventy cities, local officials planned to supplement the national census with their own surveys. See, for example, Senator für Inneres, Senatsvorlage no. 1021/82 (10 August 1982), LAB B Rep. 004/1120.
18. "Der Blockwart läßt grüßen," in Die Grünen (Landesverband Hamburg), *Unsere Daten selbst schützen—Die Volkszählung boykottieren!* (1987), AIfS SBe 444, VoBo-Büro Hamburg, box 2; and Die Grünen im Bundestag, *Vertrauen zählt. Vernunft boykottiert. Dokumentation Hearing 12.5.87*, AGG B.II.1, no. 3129.
19. Deutsche Journalisten-Union to Hessischer Innenminister Herbert Günther (23 February 1983), HHStA 502/5573.

20. Anonymous letter to Hessian Ministerpräsident Holger Börner (29 March 1983), HHStA 502/5573.
21. "Heftiger Streit bei den Grünen über Kampagne gegen die Volkszählung," *SZ*, 27 May 1987. Zimmermann rejected any comparison with the Nazi census as "tasteless." Norbert F. Pötzl and Jörg R. Mettke, "'Wo ist denn die Intimität?' Interview mit Innenminister Friedrich Zimmermann," *Der Spiegel*, 28 March 1983, 45.
22. *Totale Überwachung. Die neue Welt von 1984—Info* (undated), AIfS SBe 444, VoBo-Büro Hamburg, box 5. Similar sentiments can be found in "Der Blockwart läßt grüßen," in Die Grünen (Landesverband Hamburg), *Unsere Daten selbst schützen—Die Volkszählung boykottieren!* (1987), AIfS SBe 444, VoBo-Büro Hamburg, box 2.
23. Spiros Simitis, "Reicht unser Datenschutzrecht angesichts der technischen Revolution?" in *Informationsgesellschaft oder Überwachungsstaat. Strategien zur Wahrung der Freiheitsrechte im Computerzeitalter*, ed. Hessische Landesregierung (Opladen, 1986), I:27–48, citation 42; and Simitis, "Datenschutz: Voraussetzung oder Ende der Kommunikation?" in *Europäisches Rechtsdenken in Geschichte und Gegenwart. Festschrift für Helmut Coing* (Beck, 1982), 495–520.
24. Horst Herold, "Polizeiliche Datenverarbeitung und Menschenrechte," *RuP* 16, no. 2 (1980): 79–86, citation 80–81.
25. "Herold gegen Alle. Gespräche mit dem Präsidenten des Bundeskriminalamtes," *Trans-Atlantik* 11 (1980): 29–40, citation 36.
26. "Herold gegen Alle," 36. For the *Taz*, such deviance, and the state use of information to control it, was the product of a specific moment of social crisis. See the analysis in Autonomie (Sabine), "Den Untergrund transparent machen. Volkszählung als Planungsinstrument," *Taz*, 12 April 1983, 3.
27. Schwule—Boykottiert die "Volkszählung"! (undated), AGG B.II.1, no. 3374. Investigations by the privacy commissioners concluded that neither the Federal Criminal Police nor any of the state police forces were maintaining records on homosexuals simply because of their sexual orientation. Helmut Bäumler (of the federal privacy commissioner staff) to Jutta Oesterle-Schwerin (14 January 1988), AGG B.II.1, no. 5497.
28. I would be remiss if I failed to note the similarities between this image and the famous Apple Macintosh "Big Brother" commercial that was broadcast in January 1984.
29. Bunte Hilfe (Marburg), *Volkszählung und Kriegsvorbereitung*, AIfS SBe 444, Antirepressionsbewegung, box 5. See also *Volkszählung?* (Reutlingen), AGG B.I.1, no. 243.
30. Die Grünen (Hessen), *Volkszählungsboykott!* and the Berlin Alternative Liste, *Volkszählung '83? Ohne mich!* AGG B.II.1, no. 3319.
31. See the correspondence in LAB B Rep. 004/1113.
32. "Immer mehr Volkszähler verweigern Mitarbeit," *FR*, 7 April 1983.
33. For one such example, see Bunte Hilfe—Startbahn West, *Rechtliche Informationen über die Auskunftspflicht bei der Volkszählung*, StAF S3/17.008.
34. "Schutz von Meldeämtern wird verstärkt," *FAZ*, 12 April 1983.
35. Friedrich-Christian Schröder, "Amnestie durch das Volkszählungsgesetz," *FAZ*, 11 April 1983.
36. Rede des parlamentarischen Staatssekretärs beim Bundesminister des Innern Dr. Horst Waffenschimdt im Bundesrat (18 March 1983), HHStA Abt. 502/5572a; and Rommel, "Boykott der Volkszählung–ein offener Rechtsbruch. Erklärung des Präsidenten des Deutschen Städtetags Manfred Rommel," *Kommunale Korrespondenz. Pressedienst des Deutsche Städtetags* (4 March 1983), HHStA Abt. 502/5572b. This charge was also made by some liberals. See Theo Sommer, "Freiheit, Freiraum und Fragebögen. Warum die Volkszählung verschoben werden sollte," *Die Zeit*, 25 March 1983.
37. Bundesrat, Plenarprotokoll, 520. Sitzung (18 March 1983), 64–67.
38. Michael Schroeren, "Betr.: Volkszählungsboykott," *Taz*, 21 February 1983.

39. Günter Grass and Hans Peter Bull, "Ein Streitgespräch," in *Volkszählung*, ed. Taeger, 42–57; and Hans Peter Bull, *Widerspruch zum Mainstream. Ein Rechtsprofessor in der Politik* (Berliner Wissenschafts-Verlag, 2012), 141–46. Bull, *Sinn und Unsinn des Datenschutzes* (Mohr Siebeck, 2015), 68, has recently spoken more harshly of the "virtually hysterical boycott movement against the harmless census."
40. Hannah, *Dark Territory*, 70–76.
41. *Sten. Ber.*, 10. Wahlperiode, 3. Sitzung (30 March 1983), 37–51.
42. Simitis, Zwischenbericht des Hessischen Datenschutzbeauftragten zur Volkszählung 1983 (14 March 1983), HHStA Abt. 502/5572b; Konferenz der Datenschutzbeauftragten zur Volkszählung, 83 (22 March 1983), HHStA Abt. 502/5573; and Ergebnisvermerk. Besprechung des BMI mit den obersten Landesbehörden über den Forderungskatalog der Datenschutzbeauftragten in ihrer Konferenz vom 22. März 1983, LAB B Rep. 004/1119.
43. "Volkszählung: 'Läßt 1000 Fragebogen glühen,'" *Der Spiegel*, 28 March 1983, 30.
44. "Heute Entscheidung über die Volkszählung," *FAZ*, 13 April 1983.
45. "Probieren, ob's legal geht," *Die Zeit*, 22 April 1983. While Stadler-Euler supported the boycott, Wild opposed it as long as there was a possibility of gaining redress through the courts.
46. Dr. Gisela Wild vor dem Bundesverfassungsgericht am 12.4.1983 in der mündlichen Verhandlung . . . , 2, in the Stadler-Euler/Wild papers.
47. Stadler-Euler and Wild, Verfassungsbeschwerde (5 March 1983), and Mirbach, Verfassungsbeschwerde (21 February 1983), both in LAB B Rep. 004/1110; and Dr. Gisela Wild vor dem Bundesverfassungsgericht am 12.4.1983 in der mündlichen Verhandlung . . . , 7. They presented other reasons as well, but these were the most important.
48. Deutsche Vereinigung für Datenschutz, Stellungnahme . . . , and Steinmüller, Verfassungsbeschwerde . . . (23 March 1983), 27, both in HHStA Abt. 502/5575a; and "Beten, daß die Sicherungen halten."
49. Simitis, Stellungnahme zu den Verfassungsbeschwerden . . . , 4–8, LAB B Rep. 004/1110; and Simitis, "Mündliche Stellungnahme vor dem Bundesverfassungsgericht zu den Verfassungsbeschwerden gegen die Volkszählung 1983" (12 April 1983), HHStA Abt. 502/5574.
50. Bundesminister des Innern to Präsident des Bundesverfassungsgerichts, Betr.: Verfassungsbeschwerden . . . (24 March 1983), LAB B Rep. 004/1110.
51. Bull/Bundesbeauftragter für den Datenschutz, Stellungnahme zu den Verfassungsbeschwerden . . . (24 March 1983), section 4, LAB B Rep. 004/1110; Simitis, Stellungnahme zu den Verfassungsbeschwerden, 8–11; Dr. Gisela Wild vor dem Bundesverfassungsgericht am 12.4.1983 in der mündlichen Verhandlung, 8–10; and Steinmüller, Verfassungsbeschwerde, 31.
52. Einstweilige Anordnung, LAB B Rep. 004/1110 and HHStA Abt. 502/5574; and "Aufgeschoben ist nicht aufgehoben," *SZ*, 14 April 1983.
53. "BBU wertet Entscheidung als 'Erfolg der Initiativen,'" *FR*, 14 April 1983; Vera Gaserow, "Widerstand geklaut," *Taz*, 14 April 1983; Friedrich Karl Fromme, "Ein Sieg über den Staat," *FAZ*, 14 April 1983; "Nicht nur aufgeschoben," *FAZ*, 15 April 1983,; Hans-Herbert Gaebel, "Niederlage von Untertanen," *FR*, 15 April 1983; Spranger, "Der geprobte Aufstand," *Bayernkurier*, 23 April 1983; and Hans Peter Bull, "Der Staat—nur ein datengieriger Riese?" *Die Zeit*, 15 April 1983, 56.
54. On the oral arguments, see "'Fast hätte es eine Schlägerei gegeben,'" *Die Zeit*, 21 October 1983, 2; and "Datenschutz-Beauftragte äußern sich fast durchweg kritisch," *FAZ*, 20 October 1983.
55. Stadler-Euler vor dem Bundesverfassungsgericht am 18.10.1983 in der mündlichen Verhandlung, Stadler-Euler/Wild papers; Badura, Entwurf des Plädoyers für die Bundesregierung (18 October 1983), LAB B Rep. 004/1109; and Erklärung von Dr. Friedrich Zimmermann (18 October 1983), LAB B Rep. 004/1111.

56. In her oral argument, LAB B Rep. 004/1111.
57. Wild, Vor dem Bundesverfassungsgericht am 18.10.1983 in der mündlichen Verhandlung.
58. Simitis, Stellungnahme des Hessischen Datenschutzbeauftragten in der mündlichen Verhandlung, 1–3.
59. Adalbert Podlech, "Art. 2 Abs. 1," *Kommentar zum Grundgesetz für die Bundesrepublik Deutschland* (Luchterhand, 1984), 317–59, citation 340.
60. Bundesminister des Innern to Präsident des Bundesverfassungsgerichts, Betr.: Verfassungsbeschwerden (28 June 1983), 66, LAB B Rep. 004/1108. These points were restated in Ministerpräsident des Landes Schleswig-Holstein to Bundesverfassungsgericht, Betr.: Verfassungsbeschwerden . . . (21 June 1983), 25–30, LAB B Rep. 004/1111.
61. Simitis, Stellungnahme des Hessischen Datenschutzbeauftragten in der mündlichen Verhandlung, 3.
62. Ibid., 2.
63. Podlech, "Art. 2 Abs. 1," 337, 344.
64. Bundesminister des Innern to Präsident des Bundesverfassungsgerichts, Betr.: Verfassungsbeschwerden; and Badura, Entwurf des Plädoyers für die Bundesregierung, 6; see also Finanzminister des Landes Baden-Württemberg to Präsident des Bundesverfassungsgerichts, Betr.: Verfassungsbeschwerden . . . (29 June 1983); and Friedrich Karl Fromme, "Was ist zweckmäßig, was braucht der Sozialstaat, wo liegen Grenzen der Verfassung bei der Volkszählung?" *FAZ*, 20 October 1983.
65. BVerfGE 65, 1 (64–70).
66. "'Ohne Drohgebärde, ohne Angst,'" 18; and the court's introductory statement, BVerfGE 65, 1 (2–3).
67. Referat O II 3/Einwag, Betr.: Koalitionsgespräch am 11. Oktober 1984 (3 October 1984), BAK B106/101952, Bd. 5; Drs. 10/2814 and 3843; Ruth Leuze to Axel Wernitz, Betr.: Entwurf eines Volkszählungsgesetzes (16 June 1985), and Simitis to Wernitz, Betr: Entwurf des Volkszählungsgesetzes 1986 (21 May 1985), both AGG B.II.1, no. 3190(2); and *BGBl.*, 1985, 2078.
68. Volkszählungsurteil auf den Kopf gestellt: Legal in den Überwachungsstaat. Aufruf der Humanistichen Union zu Widerstand gegen unbeschränkte Datenerfassung im "Sicherheitsbereich" (December 1985), and Ströbele in Unterarbeitsgruppe Innere Sicherheit, Protokoll vom Koordinationstreffen "Überwachungsgesetze" am 12.4.1986, both AGG B.II.1, no. 132.
69. AIfS SBe 444, VoBo-Büro Hamburg, box 5a; and "Neuer Aufruf zum Boykott," *Taz*, 9 December 1986.
70. For a sampling of such measures, see Repressalien im Zusammenhang mit der Volkszählung, AGG B.II.1, no. 5466.
71. "Zähler und Gezählte," *Die Zeit*, 12 June 1987.
72. Karsten Plog, "Boykotteuere landeten in Polizeidatei," *FR*, 12 January 1988; and "Mehr Zählungsgegner in Datei," *FR*, 14 January 1988. Federal Privacy Commissioner Alfred Einwag found that more than half of the 21,000 names in this file had been entered for cases of minor property damage (including snipping the numerical codes off the census forms), that another large group were related to insults, trespassing, or resisting arrest charges in conjunction with blockades and demonstrations, and that about 75 percent of the total number of names contained in the file were due to minor offenses that, in the absence of other evidence, did not satisfy the criteria for entry into the political criminality database. Einwag to BMI, Betr.: Datenschutzrechtliche Kontrolle bei der Abteilung Staatsschutz des BKA (7 December 1988), AGG B.II.1, no. 6009; and Ruth Leuze, Baden-Württemberg Landtag Drs. 9/5230, 51–53. On the prosecution of such cases, see Peter Quint, *Civil Disobedience and the German Courts* (Routledge, 2008).
73. Roland Appel, Über den Bogen hinausdenken—vom Volkszählungsboykott zur Bürgerrechtsbewegung, AGG B.II.1, no. 5466(2).

74. "Voll in die Hose," *Der Spiegel*, 25 May 1987, 129, 132.
75. Kommunikee: Die Bombe ist gezündet—der Widerstand auch, Solidarität mit den Gefangenen. Wir lassen uns nicht spalten, and Kampf der Volkszählung! Pressespiegel (Redaktionsschluß: 27.5.87), both in AIfS SBe 444, VoBo-Büro Hamburg, box 2.
76. For the carnivalesque aspects of the protest, see, for example, the film *Ach wie gut, daß niemand weiß*... (Vergisses Produktion, 1987), AIfS.
77. Koordinationsbüro Volkszählungsboykott, *Gegen den Überwachungsstaat* (11 December 1986), AGG B.II.1, no. 3196; "Resolution des Bundeshauptausschusses der Grünen vom 15. Februar 1987," *Blätter für deutsche und internationale Politik* 32 (May 1987): 631; and "Grüne wollen nicht in Karlsruhe klagen," *FAZ*, 5 March 1987.
78. Kurzbericht vom Initiativentreffen am 26.4. in Köln and Beschluß der Bundeskonferenz am 26.4.87, AGG B.II.1, no. 6017 (2).
79. VoBo-Gruppe Bochum-Langendreer, ed., *Rundbriefe zum Mikrozensus and Volkszählung*, no. 11 (June 1987), AIfS SBe 444, VoBo-Büro Hamburg, box 3.
80. "Kampf der Volkszählung!," special issue of Gegen die Strömung. Organ für den Aufbau der marxistisch-leninistischen Partei Westdeutschlands (April 1987), AIfS SBe 444, box 2.
81. Kelly to Erhebungsstelle Bonn (27 May 1987), AGG Kelly papers no. 227.
82. "Volkszählungs-Boykott 1987—Schaumgebremst?" VoBo-Gruppe Bochum-Langendreer, ed., *Rundbriefe zum Mikrozensus and Volkszählung*, no. 4 (October 1986), "Über das Schummel und halbherzige Vorschläge zur Durchführung des Boykotts," Ibid., no. 6 (December 1986), and the articles in *Rundbriefe*, no. 11 (June 1987), all in AIfS SBe 444, VoBo-Büro Hamburg, box 3.
83. Roderich Reifenrath, "Legalität—Legitimität," *FR*, 25 February 1987; and Schnoor to Vollmer (3 March 1987), AGG B.II.1, no. 3103.
84. "Schily empfiehlt Methode Schwejk," *Taz*, 25 February 1987; Oliver Tolmein, "Wir untergraben unsere Position," *Taz*, 26 February 1987; "Die Grünen und der Boykott," *FR*, 10 March 1987; and Fraktion Die Grünen im Bundestag/Justitiariat, Über den Unsinn einer Volkszählung, den Sinn eines Volkszählungsboykottes und dessen legitimatorische Probleme (undated), AGG B.II.1, no. 2522.
85. Die Grünen NRW, Info-Mappe, 3. Aussendung (4 June 1987), AIfS SBe 444, VoBo-Büro Hamburg, box 3. For organized protest against the ID card, see chapter 7.
86. "Fehlerquoten bis zu 60 Prozent bei 'Volkszählung per Post,'" *FR*, 4 July 1987.
87. "Den gläsernen Menschen wollen die Bürger auch jetzt nicht," *FR*, 22 January 1987; Leuze, Baden-Württemberg Landtag Drs. 9/5230, 17–59; and Claus Henning Schapper, Hamburg Bürgerschaft Drs. 13/1412, 48–66.
88. "Schwache Intelligenz," *Der Spiegel*, 3 August 1987, 67–68.
89. Ibid.
90. Hannah, *Dark Territory*, 157–92.
91. "Volkszählung: Massenwiderstand endgültig abgehakt?" *Taz*, 14 October 1987.
92. Appel, Bericht zur Klausurtagung 28./29.8, AGG B.II.1, no. 3103(2).
93. Winfried Eckardt, Die Grünen, Landesverband Bayern, Volkszählung 87—(Vorläufiges) Resümee einer Kampagne. Bericht an den Landesausschuss der Grünen am 31.10.87 in Regensburg, AGG Petra Kelly papers, no. 227; and Narr, Offener Brief an alle diejenigen, die sich nicht ohne weiteres "volkszählen" liessen, insbesondere aber an die Volkszählungs-Boykott-Initiativen (5 November 1987), AGG C NRW LaVo/LGSt 01/41.
94. Datenpiraten, Thesenpapier zur Perspektive der Vobo-Bewegung in Hamburg (undated but October 1987), AIfS SBe 444, VoBo-Büro Hamburg, box 3.
95. "Ergebnisse der Volkszählung 1987," *Bulletin*, 1 December 1988, 1488–89. See the criticism in "Die Predigt wurde nicht verstanden," *Die Zeit*, 22 November 1987.
96. Horst Bieber, "Neue Fakten übers Volk," *Die Zeit*, 16 December 1988; and Bieber, "Viele Fragen—und welche Antworten?" *Die Zeit*, 20 February 1987.

97. Die Grünen, Nur Schafe werden gezählt (1987), AGG Bestand B.II.1, no. 2522.
98. Fraktion Die Grünen im Bundestag/Justitiariat, Über den Unsinn einer Volkszählung..., AGG B.II.1, no. 2522.
99. Entschliessungsantrag der Abg. Dr. Vollmer, M. Such und der Fraktion Die Grünen/Bündnis 90 (23 October 1990), AGG Bestand A. Manfred Such, no. 84; Die Grünen, *Nur Schafe werden gezählt*; and Roland Appel, "Volkserfassung—Zweiter Versuch," in *Totalerfassung*. *"Sicherheitsgesetze," Volkszählung, Neuer Personalausweis, Möglichkeiten der Gegenwehr*, ed. Martin Kutscha and Norman Paech (Pahl-Rugenstein, 1986), 45–59, especially 56–58.
100. BVerfGE 65, 1 (55); and Simitis, Stellungnahme zu den Fragen des Bundesverfassungsgerichts..., 6–11.
101. Drs. 10/2600.
102. Wolfgang Zapf, "Soziale Indikatoren: Eine Zwischenbilanz," *Allgemeines Statistisches Archiv* 60 (1976): 1–16; Zapf, *Sozialberichterstattung: Möglichkeiten und Probleme* (Schwartz, 1976); Wolfgang Glatzer and Wolfgang Zapf, eds., *Lebensqualität in der Bundesrepublik* (Campus Verlag, 1984); and Zapf, "Social Reporting in the 1970s and in the 1990s," *Social Indicators Research* 51, no. 1 (2000): 1–15.
103. Zapf, Stellungnahme (11 February 1985), AGG B.II.1, no. 139.
104. See the memoranda by Hölder, Heinz Grohmann (president of the Deutsche Statistische Gesellschaft), the Deutsches Institut für Wirtschaftsforschung, and Zapf for the domestic affairs committee hearing on the microcensus law, AGG B.II.1, no. 139.
105. Niederschrift. 486. Sitzung des BR-Ausschusses für Innere Angelegenheiten (23 March 1981), LAB B Rep. 004/1123; Präsident des Statistischen Bundesamt to Leiter der Statistischen Landesämter, Betr.: Volkszählungsentwurf 1982, hier: Besprechung über mögliche Kürzungsvorschläge (21 August 1981), LAB B Rep. 004/1124; and Ergebnisniederschrift über die Besprechung mit den Dienstaufsichtsbehörden der Statistischen Landesämter... (16 April 1980), HHStA Abt. 502/5570b.
106. Institut für Demoskopie/Noelle-Neumann, Gutachten zur Frage einer Volkszählung als Totalerhebung... (14 October 1983), and Kolleck, Gutachterliche Stellungnahme zur geplanten Volkszählung (22 June 1983), both in the Stadler-Euler/Wild papers.
107. See Roland Appel, Sicherheitsstaat und formierte Gesellschaft als Strukturelemente konservativer Politik, AGG B.II.1, no. 5466; and Appel, "Vorsicht Volkszählung!" in *Vorsicht Volkszählung!*, ed. Roland Appel and Dieter Hummel (Kölner Volksblatt Verlag, 1987), 12–36. Appel's arguments here are similar to those advanced by Joachim Hirsch in *Der Sicherheitsstaat. Das "Modell Deutschland," seine Krise und die neuen Sozialen Bewegungen* (Europäische Verlags-Anstalt, 1980).
108. Ulrike Erb, "Volkszählung zwischen den Interessen von Volk und Staat," in *Vorsicht Volkszählung!*, ed. Appel and Hummel, 82–85; and Karl-Heinz Stamm, *Alternative Öffentlichkeit. Die Erfahrungsproduktion neuer sozialer Bewegungen* (Campus, 1988). Joachim Häberlen, *The Emotional Politics of the Alternative Left: West Germany, 1968–1984* (Cambridge University Press, 2018) argues (79) that the political project of the alternative left should be understood "as a struggle against a categorizing rationality that imposed limitations upon people's imaginations, dreams and desires."
109. Erb, "Volkszählung zwischen den Interessen von Volk und Staat"; BVG-Verhandlung zur Volkszählung (19 January 1984), AGG B.II.1, no. 3255; Die Grünen, *Nur Schafe werden gezählt*; and Götz Aly, "Volkszählung an sich," *Taz*, 11 April 1983.
110. One measure of the pervasiveness of this image was its appearance four times each in *Der Spiegel*, no. 13, 28 March 1983, and no. 21, 18 May 1987.
111. This point has been neglected in the existing literature. For example, there is no mention of privacy protection or information technology in Silke Mende's otherwise richly textured *"Nicht rechts, nicht links, sondern vorn": Eine Geschichte der Gründungsgrünen* (Oldenbourg, 2011). Andrei Markovits and Philip Gorski, *The German Left: Red, Green*

and Beyond (Oxford University Press, 1993), 153, are correct in maintaining that the real focus of Green politics was the defense of the reproductive sphere and of individual autonomy in relation to bureaucratic domination.

112. Alberto Melucci, "The New Social Movements: A Theoretical Approach," *Social Science Information* 19, no. 2 (1980): 199–226; and Melucci, "The Symbolic Challenge of Contemporary Movements," *Social Research* 52, no. 4 (Winter 1985): 789–816.

113. Lieber ständig übermüdet als ständig überwacht (unsigned, no date), AGG Bestand A—Manfred Such, no. 84.

114. Barbara Böttger, Thesen zur Schwerpunktsitzung der Fraktionen zu den Informations- und Kommunikationstechniken (30 May 1989), AGG B.II.1, no. 6008.

115. For example, Werner Rammert, "Gegen das Projekt einer 'Computer-Gesellschaft' — Überlegungen zu grün-alternativen Gegenstrategien," in *Die Zukunft der Informationsgesellschaft*, ed. Philipp Sonntag (Haag & Herche, 1983), 47–67. For a brief discussion of the concept of *Sozialverträglichkeit* and of the theoretical context within which it arose, see Gotthard Bechmann, "Risiko als Schlüsselkategorie der Gesellschaftstheorie," *KritV* 74, no. 3–4 (1991): 212–40, especially 232–35.

116. Erb, Ansätze für einen neu verstandenen "Datenschutz" bzw. für den Schutz der Sozialsphäre beim Einsatz von Informations- und Kommunikationstechnologien (August 1984), AGG Bestand A—Manfred Such, no. 84 (2).

117. Erb, Einschätzung des Entwurfs . . . der SPD (August 1988), AGG Bestand A—Manfred Such, no. 85(2), which was a critique of a proposed Social Democratic amendment (Drs. 11/3730) to the federal privacy law. The Bundestag rejected this proposal, Drs. 11/7235, 101.

118. Erb, Einschätzung des Entwurfs . . . der SPD.

119. Synopse zu Art. 1 des Entwurfes eines Gesetzes zur Fortentwicklung des Datenschutzes . . . , marginal comment to §17 (summer 1989), AGG B.II.1, no. 5491; Hartmut Gaßner, Arbeits- und Diskussionsskizze zum Entwurf eines Allgemeinen Akten- und Datenzugangsrechts für die Fraktion Die Grünen im Bundestag (18 February 1988), AGG B.II.1, no. 6009; and Karin Heuer, Einige "Thesen" und Forderungen—Grüne Ideen zu Datenschutz (probably 1984/85), AGG Bestand A—Manfred Such, no. 84.

120. Die Grünen, Das Programm zur 1. gesamtdeutschen Wahl 1990 (Die Grünen, 1990), 37.

121. Heinz Grohmann, "Von der Volkszählung zum Registerzensus: Paradigmenwechsel in der deutschen amtlichen Statistik," *Wirtschafts- und Sozialstatistisches Archiv* 3, no. 1 (June 2009): 3–23; Drs. 16/12219; and *BGBl.*, 2009, 1781. In the aftermath of the 1987 boycott, Horst Bieber, "Neue Fakten übers Volk," *Die Zeit*, 16 December 1988, still found the traditional *Totalerhebung*, with all its faults and limitations, preferable to a Scandinavian-style registry-based census.

122. One explanation is that, since only a small proportion of the total population were personally interviewed, not as many people felt directly affected by the census as was the case in 1987.

123. Hans Peter Bull, *Datenschutz, oder Die Angst vor dem Computer* (Piper, 1984); and Marcel Berlinghoff, "'Totalerfassung' im 'Computerstaat.' Computer und Privatheit in den 1970er und 1980er Jahren," in *Im Sog des Internets. Öffentlichkeit und Privatheit im digitalen Zeitalter*, ed. Ulrike Ackermann (Humanities Online, 2013), 93–110.

Chapter 5

Out of the Frying Pan and into the Fire
The Census Decision, Party Politics, and the Revision of the Federal Privacy Protection Law

The passage of the Federal Privacy Protection Law did not so much bring the development of information law in Germany to a successful conclusion as mark the transition to a new and more contentious phase, and within a few years the census decision both altered the rules of the legislative game and raised the stakes of its outcome. Although the decision of the Constitutional Court was praised at the time as the Magna Carta of privacy rights and its message likened to that of the Sermon on the Mount, since the turn of the century the Court's reasoning has been the object of increasingly intense criticism. For example, Marion Albers has argued that its construction of the right to informational self-determination represented a first, and in important respects "unsuccessful," attempt to resolve the constitutional issues surrounding the use of personal information, and Karl-Heinz Ladeur has criticized the right as a "defective juristic construct."[1]

Chapter 2 traced the development of constitutional jurisprudence relating to privacy and the private sphere up to the early 1980s; the account of the oral arguments before the Court in chapter 4 analyzed how the concept of privacy was being reconceptualized in response to the development of integrated data processing and the use of computers for population surveillance; and the current chapter will begin with a detailed examination of the Court's reasoning in the census decision. In this section I will argue that the Court's exposition of the right to informational self-determination facilitated its later misinterpretation in individualist, subjective terms, but

---

Notes for this chapter begin on page 200.

that, in fact, it represented a continuation of that larger inquiry into the preconditions for the development of the personality in social communication under specific social and historical conditions that was analyzed in chapter 2.

The relationship between privacy and internal security had been an important point of contention since the late 1970s, as we shall see in Part III. However, the debate did not really come to a head until the 1980s, when the census decision forced the administration to take on the controversial task of legislatively authorizing the informational activities of the security agencies and to do so at the very moment when the Conservatives were replacing the Social Democrats as the senior partner in the governing coalition. The legislative history of the privacy law and the law governing the Domestic Intelligence Agency will be the focus of the remainder of the chapter.

Although the conservative parties had vigorously defended privacy rights as long as they were in the opposition, once they came to power they subordinated privacy rights to the unhindered functioning of the security apparatus. Were it not for the census decision, Zimmermann would have left the reform of the Federal Privacy Protection Law to die on the vine. He supported the protection of personal information against "misuse," that is, against unauthorized access and use. However, he only supported privacy rights as long as they did not prevent the security agencies and the civilian administration from gaining access to the information that was necessary to satisfy his expansive interpretation of security. This is what he had in mind when he spoke of a "rational, balanced relation" of "privacy interests to the other legitimate interests of the citizen, including their interest in security."[2] Their belief that security was the "indispensable precondition for the freedom and development of the citizen"—to quote Paul Laufs (CDU)—left Conservatives tone deaf to the arguments of privacy advocates, whom they could only accuse of maliciously stirring up mistrust against the state, the police, and the intelligence agencies.[3]

The census decision made it necessary, as we noted in the Introduction, to revise every law governing the use of personal information in the public administration, and, from 1984 to the end of the decade, the amendment of the Federal Privacy Protection Law was directly linked to the revision of these other laws, especially those governing the intelligence agencies. The conservative parties were unwilling to approve a revised Federal Privacy Protection Law before they had secured approval of these laws in order to insure that the security agencies and the civilian administration would be given greater latitude to collect and exchange personal information than they would otherwise have had under an amended privacy law. However, the political pivot of the FDP from the Social Democrats to the conservatives was motivated primarily by differences over economic policy, and the party (or at least the leaders of its civil libertarian wing), whose thinking regarding privacy and security often had much more in common with the views of the privacy commissioners than with those of their new coalition partners, maintained that individual freedom depended on the careful delimitation of state power, rather than its expansion. These conflicts within the coalition, together with the intrinsic complexity of the material, led to legislative gridlock, and most of these laws were only approved on the eve of reunification. Liberal and conservative views on the relationship between privacy and security reflected their divergent conceptions of the state. Even though the FDP forced the conservative parties to make numerous concessions, the laws that were ultimately approved by the Bundestag reflected the priorities of the conservative parties to a greater extent than those of the FDP and the privacy commissioners, and they codified the established informational practices of the civilian administration and the security agencies, rather than limiting them in any substantive way.

The Census Decision: Trying to Bring It All Together

The final decision on the census case was handed down in December 1983. The literature is virtually unanimous in tracing all of the problems of both the decision and subsequent privacy law to the Court's apparent construction of the right to informational self-determination as an subjective, individual action right "to determine the conditions under which his personal information shall be disclosed and used."[4] However, it is far from clear that the Court actually understood the right in this way. I argue—paralleling Albers—that the Court only incorporated in a fragmentary manner the literature discussed in chapter 2, that in places its exposition of the right to informational self-determination was ambiguous, and that in other places it simply failed to address important issues. Most important, the formulation of the right did not take adequate account of those aspects of social communication that could not be reduced to the subjective intent of the actor. Even if they could not be articulated in the language of an individual right to informational self-determination, these considerations had figured prominently in the earlier privacy literature, and any attempt to chart a future for German privacy law will depend as much on recovering those dimensions of earlier privacy discourse that were neglected by the census decision as on going beyond it.

As we saw in chapter 2, the Court had articulated the idea of a right to informational self-determination in response to the loss of control over both personal information and the meaning attributed to this information by others. However, although neither this line of thought nor those provisions of the census law authorizing the use of census data for purposes unrelated to the actual count of the population depended in any way on the use of computers, the Court felt it necessary to revisit the line of reasoning developed in Eppler because the individual's control over how he was represented to others was being endangered in new ways by integrated data processing. On the one hand, the new information technologies had eroded the protections heretofore guaranteed by the dispersal of personal information among separate paper-based filing systems; as the Court noted, personal information can now, "technically speaking, be stored without limit and at any moment be called up in a matter of seconds without regard for physical distance." On the other hand, at the same time that these technologies were making it easier to construct a more comprehensive picture of the individual, the growing asymmetry in the informational relations between communicative partners attributable to integrated data processing was diminishing "in a previously unknown manner" the freedom of the individual to both know how he was viewed by others and to adjust his self-representation to this knowledge.[5]

In the census decision, the Court asserted that the personality rights and the dignity of the individual could be violated by excessive uncertainty regarding what was actually known about the individual by possible communicative partners. As the Court explained in terms that were taken near verbatim from Podlech,

> whoever cannot with sufficient certainty determine what personal information about him is known in specific domains of his social environment, and whoever cannot form a reasonable idea of the knowledge held by the people with whom he may enter into communication, may find his freedom to autonomously plan and make decisions to be constricted in essential ways. Any social order (as well as the legal order that makes it possible) in which the citizen can no longer know who knows what about him, when, and in what context would not be compatible with the right to informational self-determination.[6]

The grounds for this uncertainty were twofold. First, it was inherent in the functioning of integrated information systems that the data they contained could be accessed by users for purposes that were quite different from those for which the information had originally been collected. Second, the Court did not speak here of data, but rather of "information" and "knowledge," that is, of the meaning attributed to data by the persons with whom the individual entered into communication. Even though the Court spoke the language of communication and thus took account of the fact that the meaning attributed to personal data by one's communicative partners could never be controlled by the individual himself, it did not clarify how the right to dispose over one's personal data could be reconciled with the rights of others to determine the informational content or meaning of this data.[7] As a result, German privacy law has been plagued by the contradiction between what appeared to be a subjective right to control the use of personal data and an undertheorized communicative dimension, whose exploration would have been necessary to move beyond the abstract opposition of self and other.

The passage cited above continued with an account of how this growing informational asymmetry impeded identity formation, hollowed out the social self, and ultimately impaired the functioning of a democratic polity:

> Whoever is uncertain whether behavior that deviates from the norm may be registered at any time and permanently stored, used, or further disseminated as information will try to avoid attracting attention through such behavior. Whoever can anticipate, for example, that participation in a demonstration or a citizens' initiative will be registered by state officials and that this information might eventually cause him harm may choose not to exercise his corresponding constitutional rights (Basic Law Articles 8 and 9). Not only would this limit the opportunities for individual development. It would also have a negative impact on the common good because self-determination is an elemental condition for the functioning of a free, democratic polity, which is founded upon the capacity of its citizens to act and participate.[8]

This claim that a degree of privacy or social space was necessary for the formation of the reflexive, self-determining subject required for democratic social life implied that the right to informational self-determination had a value for the functioning of a democratic system that could not be reduced to the value that it held for the individual members of that community.

Regardless of the unresolved theoretical problems in this line of reasoning, these considerations led the Court to its central conclusion. Since "under the conditions of modern data processing" the free development of the personality depended on protecting the individual against the "unlimited" collection, storage, use and dissemination of personal data, the Court concluded that the personality rights contained in the Basic Law had to encompass the "right of the individual in principle to determine the conditions under which his personal information shall be disclosed and used."[9] Although the Court's language here could be interpreted to mean that this right only applied to personal information that was stored in formatted files and processed electronically, integrated data processing had always been understood simply as one—albeit increasingly important—way in which control over personal information could be lost, and, after a brief moment of uncertainty, it was soon accepted as established fact that the right to informational self-determination applied to all uses of personal information, not merely to information that was processed electronically.[10]

The Court immediately qualified this right by explaining that the individual did not enjoy absolute, unlimited control over "his" information. As we have seen, since the 1950s the Court had maintained that the Basic Law conceived of the person not as an isolated, sovereign individual, but rather as a social being, whose life was embedded in the community and whose actions were oriented towards its members, and in the census decision the Court explained that individual "is rather a personality, which develops within the social community and *is reliant upon communication*" (emphasis added). Although the Court maintained that, as a representation of social reality, "information" could never be reduced to the meaning ascribed to data by the actor (that is, that such a representation "cannot be assigned exclusively to the concerned individual"[11]), it made no effort to explore either the reflexive nature of this communicative process or to incorporate such reflections into its understanding of the nature and scope of privacy rights.[12] Instead, the Court simply fell back on its established position that, as a social being, the individual had to accept limitations on his rights if required by an overriding public interest.[13]

Once the Court had completed its exposition of what it regarded as the constitutional bases of the right to informational self-determination, it proceeded to describe the dangers associated with electronic data processing in order to lay the foundations for its ruling on the matter at hand: the census. The Court did not dismiss the notion that certain kinds of data were intrinsically sensitive or private. However, it argued that the protections to be afforded to the individual could not be based "exclusively" on such considerations, and its argument focused instead on the need to analyze the harms resulting from the potential use of information in specific contexts. To the extent that even the apparently most insignificant piece of data could acquire an entirely new significance if electronic data processing facilitated its use in new and unexpected contexts, the Court concluded that "under the conditions of automatic data processing there is no longer any such thing as an 'insignificant' piece of data."[14]

The meaning of this often-cited dictum depended on how one understood the right to informational self-determination. If one understood it as an individual, dispositional or property right, it could be taken to mean that the scope of individual control over personal data was virtually unlimited and that explicit legal authorization was required in every instance for the processing of personal data. At the time, this statement was widely understood in precisely this way.[15] However, such a reading does not give due weight to the argumentative context within which the claim was made. In fact, the decision did not declare that all personal data were, in fact, deserving of protection. Rather, the Court simply pointed to the possibility that, under the conditions of automated—that is, integrated—data processing, any piece of personal data could take on a new and potentially harmful meaning when linked in unpredictable ways to other such data, and the decision can with equal validity be read as arguing simply that the nature of these potential linkages and the possible harms to which they might give rise would have to be investigated before it could be determined whether such uses actually entailed such a serious infringement on the right to informational self-determination that they required explicit legislative authorization.

In the next section, the Court set out the conditions that would have to be met if the collection, use, and dissemination of personal data by the state were to be consistent with the right to informational self-determination. The heart of the Court's ruling here was the codification of a narrow version of the final purpose principle. The Court argued that the state could only compel individuals to disclose personal data if the legislature defined precisely and for each broad domain the specific purpose for which the data would be used.[16] This meant, on the one hand, that the state was not permitted to collect personal data in the hope that it would eventually be useful for some future purpose (*auf Vorrat*).[17] On the other hand, the Court's reasoning also meant that data could only be used for the purpose for which its collection had been authorized. The two greatest dangers—the one technological, the other constitutional—to any narrow construction of the final purpose principle in the public sector were integrated information systems and the doctrine of *Amtshilfe*. In another of its more controversial dicta, the Court insisted (mixing the two distinct arguments) that, in view of the specific dangers associated with electronic data processing, data collected by the state had to be so strictly protected that not even the constitutional principle of *Amtshilfe* could be invoked to justify the use of this data for other, secondary, purposes.[18]

The Court concluded the relevant section of the ruling by explaining that two sets of institutional mechanisms were necessary to insure that the right to informational self-determination was upheld in practice. First, the Court reaffirmed a set of individual transparency rights. Second, in his brief for the October hearing, the newly appointed Federal Privacy Commissioner Reinhold Baumann had explained that the enormous increase in power that had accrued to the state as a result of advances in information technology would be constitutionally questionable in the absence of special institutions—that is, the privacy commissioners—charged with continuously monitoring its informational activities, especially in those areas—primarily the work of the security agencies—that were not subject to the control of the concerned individual.[19] In its decision, the Court followed this lead, arguing that the expertise of politically independent commissioners was essential to protecting the constitutional rights of the individual for whom the functioning of automated data processing systems otherwise remained "opaque." This aspect of the decision greatly enhanced both the corporate self-consciousness of the privacy commissioners and their influence with the Bundestag.[20]

Ultimately, the Court upheld the constitutionality of the census itself. In laying the basis for this part of its ruling, the Court argued that the collection of statistical data was permitted, if not in fact required, because it was necessary for the state to fulfill its constitutional obligation to promote the general welfare. Citing Simitis's brief, the Court argued that two of the defining characteristics of statistical data—the failure to impose a narrowly defined final purpose and the corresponding use of the data for multiple purposes—favored precisely those tendencies that privacy protection law sought to constrain and that, therefore, census data by its very nature had the potential to lead to the total registration and cataloging of the individual.[21] Consequently, the Court insisted that such data could only be collected and used under certain conditions, that it had to be anonymized at the earliest possible point, that organizational precautions had to be taken to protect it at those stages of the census when it could still be connected to specific individuals, and that it had to be protected against de-anonymization. However, the Court also warned that the linkage—especially by means of a national ID number—of census data to the other personal data held by public administration would represent an unacceptable secondary use of that data.[22]

In the end, the Court ruled that the census itself—but not, as we saw in chapter 4, the other uses authorized under §9—satisfied all of these conditions with the exception of the requisite organizational and procedural precautions, which it expected the legislature to include in a revised census law.

Party Politicking in the Aftermath of the Census Decision: The Origins of the Omnibus Bill

The census decision initially led to a mood of doom and gloom in the administration, where officials warned that a maximalist reading would lead to "the paralysis of large parts of the administration and an incalculable growth in bureaucracy."[23] Nevertheless, it was not immediately clear which laws would have to be amended, or what specific changes would have to be made, to bring them into compliance with the decision, and it took two years for the coalition to bring in all of the necessary legislation—and another four years before all of these laws were approved.

Security policy was, along with social and legal policy, one of the areas in which there were important differences between the FDP and the Union parties, and from the very beginning the coalition was sharply divided over the planned amendment of all of the laws affected by the decision.[24] The top priority of the conservatives was to codify the real or presumed authority of the security agencies, preserve the current scope of information exchange among them, and do so without diminishing their efficiency and "suffocating" them in a flood of detailed regulations.[25] The FDP, on the other hand, refused to give a blanket endorsement to the authority that was claimed by the security agencies, but that always seemed to exceed the letter of the law, and the party frequently made common cause with the privacy commissioners. Together they sought to use key conditions set out in the census decision—explicit statutory authorization in a precise and domain-specific manner for the collection of specific kinds of information, transparency rights, and the review authority of the privacy commissioners—as levers with which to overturn the excessively broad demands of the conservatives.

Security officials desperately wanted to avoid an open political debate over the precise scope of the informational authority of the police and the intelligence agencies and the attendant possibility that they would then have their hands tied by whatever regulations emerged from the legislative process. Such a debate was certain to be protracted and contentious. Initially, the administration hoped that it might be possible to cram all of the necessary authorizations into the Federal Privacy Protection Law itself. However, not only did the federal privacy law not cover either the collection of information or its storage in the paper files that were still the primary medium used by the police to record their data. It was also impossible to do justice to the specific needs of the security agencies in a privacy law without overburdening it with too many exceptions and qualifications and, in effect, transforming a privacy *protection* law into its opposite: a law *authorizing* information collection and exchange by the security agencies.[26]

In the end, they concluded that the only option was to introduce domain-specific laws regulating both the collection and exchange of information that the police carried out on their own authority and the investigative work that they undertook on behalf of prosecutors,[27] while concerns about the legal bases for the exchange of information among the intelligence agencies and between these agencies and the police soon took on a life of their own in the form of a controversial draft "informational collaboration" law, which, in turn, overlapped in part with plans to regularize the work of the Military Counterintelligence Agency.[28]

There was, however, one additional problem. While the conservatives refused to approve a revised privacy law until the informational authority of the security agencies, which exceeded the rights that the public administration was expected to have under the anticipated amendment, had been secured, the FDP refused to move ahead with the ID card and passport laws or the new motor vehicle information system ZEVIS (chapter 7) until a comprehensive agreement had been reached limiting the collection and use of personal information in the security sector.[29] In October 1984, the leaders of the coalition parties reached an agreement whereby the new ID card law, which was the top concern of the conservatives, would not be brought in until work on the privacy and security laws had progressed to the point where they were ready for parliamentary consideration. The administration hoped to bring in all of the necessary legislation in spring 1985 and quickly secure its passage so that the ID card law could go into effect at the beginning of 1986.[30]

The FDP's reservations regarding the privacy provisions of the security laws weighed heavily on the coalition across most of 1985. Nevertheless, both parties were under pressure to prove that they were capable of putting this central plank of the coalition agreement into practice, and by the end of the year they had reached agreement on all of the laws with the exception of the informational collaboration law. The ID card law was approved by the Bundestag on February 28, 1986; two days later the administration brought in, as the embodiment of the linkages demanded by the FDP, an omnibus law that bundled together the major privacy and security laws; and in April the administration introduced, as promised, the informational collaboration law.[31]

Debating the Federal Privacy Protection Law

The census decision had set out a number of criteria that would have to be met in order to secure the right to informational self-determination. However, the precise manner in which they would have to be implemented in order to achieve this goal was a matter of interpretation, and the liberal FDP and the Union parties differed in characteristic ways on these issues.

First, since coming to power, the Conservatives had supported only a minimalist conception of privacy protection; they took umbrage with Bull's activism; their concern to reestablish the authority of the state led them to see every criticism as proof that the privacy commissioners were seeking to become "an independent control authority for the entire public administration, in addition to the administrative courts"; and one of their main goals was to limit the authority of the federal privacy commissioner.[32] These policies also lay behind the May 1983 appointment of Reinhold Baumann, a relatively unknown administrative jurist, to succeed Bull in the increasingly high-profile position of federal privacy commissioner.[33]

Although the census decision made the regulation of the collection of personal data by the public administration unavoidable, there was nothing that dictated that this be done within the scope of the Federal Privacy Protection Law or that it be subject to review by the privacy commissioner. The coalition draft sought to kill two birds with one omnibus bill by hiving off data collection and all information processing that did not involve formatted files and regulating these activities in a separate law, the Code of Administrative Procedure, which did not provide for review by the federal privacy commissioner. In contrast, the FDP wanted to expand the protections offered by the privacy law to include the very activities that the conservatives wished to exclude and to bring them within the purview of the federal privacy commissioner. For their part, the privacy commissioners argued that the conservative strategy was both incompatible with the letter of the census decision and politically ill-advised.[34]

These debates over the authority of the privacy commissioner also raised other issues whose importance derived largely from their implications for the security laws. The authority to review the collection of information and its subsequent storage in paper files meant that the privacy commissioner would have to be permitted to audit the work of the intelligence agencies. However, conservatives and security officials argued that giving the commissioner the authority to evaluate whether the collection of this information was necessary and appropriate for their work would be tantamount to permitting him to put his own professional judgment ahead of that of both the officials in charge of these agencies and, ultimately, the responsible ministers. The privacy commissioners rejected these claims, noting that they had reached workable agreements with the state intelligence agencies. Moreover, as Baumann argued, reviewing the need for specific information and its appropriateness for the work of any agency was "the most primordial" task of the commissioners. The conservatives, who were keen to protect the prerogatives of the security agencies, did not accept these claims, and a provision—which Simitis claimed would make the independent privacy commissioners entirely superfluous—stating that the review authority of the federal privacy commissioner should not be understood to prejudice the judgment and responsibility of the offices and agencies themselves was inserted into the coalition draft.[35]

The second important issue related to data collection in the private sector. This involved the collision of different strands of personality rights:

the right to privacy and the rights to information, property, and action. The group representing the banking industry argued that the regulation of data collection in the private sector would lead to the limitless expansion of the law and the creation of an oppressive information processing regime. It supported the administration decision to exclude both formatted paper files and internal electronic ones from the law.[36]

The third major issue that had to be resolved was just how "precisely and domain-specific" the provisions governing the collection (and subsequent exchange) of data had to be circumscribed. This was the most important question raised by the census decision. It was also the point at which opinions diverged most systematically.

Conservatives argued that the legislature had the latitude to define the "purposes" for which information was to be collected as widely as it deemed necessary. However, Benda and others warned that such purposes as "the common good" or "public security" were inconsistent with the right to informational self-determination because they were so broad that they would negate any meaningful version of the final purpose principle and render judicial review impossible. Moreover, simply stating the purpose or mission of a public office or agency, Benda insisted, did not authorize the employment of all available means to fulfill these responsibilities. The decision, he insisted, required both precise, domain-specific norms and the concrete specification of the (informational) means that could be employed to achieve these ends.[37] The coalition draft privacy law explicitly stated that the storage of personal data was only permitted for specific purposes. However, not only did the refusal to include a provision governing the collection of data deprive it of any standard by which to measure whether the use of the data was consistent with the purpose for which it had been collected. The draft also contained so many exceptions that it rendered the final purpose principle virtually meaningless.

The fourth set of issues raised by the census decision pertained to the measures that were necessary if the individual were to know who possessed what personal information pertaining to him in specific contexts. This principle pointed in different directions. On the one hand, privacy advocates argued that transparency would be best guaranteed if data were collected directly from the individual, rather than aggregated via transfers from other data holders. On the other hand, Bernd Lutterbeck, who had been one of the coauthors of the 1971 Steinmüller memorandum, and others argued that a freedom of information law was the precondition for the full realization of these transparency rights.[38] This was one of the origins of later German freedom of information legislation.

But the problem that gave this issue its political resonance at the time was the question of whether, and, if so, to what extent, the police and the intelligence agencies should be required to disclose the information that they held on specific individuals. While such transparency was the only way for concerned individuals to insure that their rights had not been violated, conservatives, who harbored an obsessive fear that such a right would be misused by foreign agents and left-wing radicals, insisted that there could be no transparency rights in the security sector, especially with regard to the intelligence agencies, who should not even be obligated to justify their refusal to disclose information. The FDP, and with them the privacy commissioners, argued that such a blanket exemption violated the right to informational self-determination. The conservatives were willing to compromise with the FDP with regard to the police, but not the intelligence agencies. The furthest that they would go with regard to the latter was to permit the federal privacy commissioner to review refusals by the intelligence agencies and allow him to report to the individual only whether or not his or her rights had been infringed upon.[39]

There was one last set of issues that was not directly related to the conditions set down in the census decision, but that wound its way through these debates: the impact of new technologies on the regulatory paradigm embodied in the Federal Privacy Protection Law. As we have seen, the first privacy protection laws had been based on the assumption that personal information would be processed by centralized information systems running a limited repertoire of programs on mainframe computers. However, by the turn of the 1980s this assumption was being undermined by the spread of personal computers, the transformation of office equipment into multifunctional terminals, and the dispersion of data processing within large corporations. These innovations permitted users with considerably less expertise and investment to process personal information decentrally and out of sight of regulators. Nor could the original privacy paradigm be easily applied to the new media: information was provided freely by the user; such systems did not depend on formatted files; and the analytical focus of the federal privacy law on the distinct phases of data processing was irrelevant to systems in which there was no meaningful distinction between collection, storage, transmission, and use. Bull and Simitis both questioned the continued viability of the original privacy protection paradigm and criticized the coalition draft for failing to respond to this challenge.[40]

The hearings that were held on the omnibus law in April 1986 confirmed the FDP belief that key elements of the draft privacy law did not satisfy the conditions set out in the census decision, while the party regarded other elements as unacceptable on political grounds. By June of that year, it had become clear to both of the coalition parties that differences over the privacy and security laws were still so great that they could not be passed before the Bundestag halted its deliberations in order to prepare for the upcoming January 1987 election.[41] A new, and even more problematic, draft would not be ready until November 1987.

The Domestic Intelligence Agency: Liberalism, Conservatism, and the Scope of State Power

Since the reform of the Federal Criminal Police and Border Police laws could not be undertaken until the outcome of state-level reforms had become clear, the most important federal security laws that were being amended in conjunction with the ID card and privacy laws were those regulating the Domestic Intelligence Agency and "informational collaboration" in the security sector. However, the task of balancing privacy, security, and freedom in this area raised a number of issues.

First, the precondition for judging both the data collection practices of any agency or office and its adherence to the final purpose principle was the "precise and domain-specific" definition of its mission and responsibilities. The privacy commissioners argued that the draft Domestic Intelligence Agency law failed to satisfy this requirement in virtually every respect.[42]

The second issue was the degree of concreteness or specificity of the purpose for which information was to be collected. The draft simply stated that the Domestic Intelligence Agency was authorized to collect the personal information that was "necessary to carry out its responsibilities" and to store and use this information "for the purposes of the agency." Simitis argued that, if the law were approved in this form, it would authorize precisely what the Court had tried to prevent in the census decision and result in "the use of his data in ways that [the concerned individual] cannot understand or control and whose consequences he cannot imagine." In addition, the draft made no effort to insure that the intrusiveness of the methods employed to collect information were proportional to the seriousness of the purpose for which it was to be collected.[43]

The third set of issues revolved around the strictness with which the final purpose principle was to be defined within the security sector. In its March 1985 privacy program, the FDP had had expressed the hope that a more explicit legislative definition of the responsibilities of the different security agencies would lead to a reduction in both the information collection by these agencies and the exchange of information among them.[44] In this they were at one with the privacy commissioners. However, the top priority for the conservatives was to preserve the exchange of information within the security sector in its current dimensions, and they freely admitted that the purpose of the amendments to the Domestic Intelligence Agency law was to provide a legal basis for the routine transgression of the final purpose principle.[45]

While the FDP was critical of the intelligence service law, the party characterized the informational collaboration law as an abomination, which "contradicts the liberal understanding of the protection of security and of civil liberties," and complained that the proposal "transforms into its opposite the Constitutional Court's demand for the creation of a legal basis in privacy law that will be comprehensible to the citizen and protect his rights."[46] The law required the Federal Criminal Police, the Border Police, the Customs Administration, state police forces, the federal and state domestic intelligence agencies, the Military Counterintelligence Agency, the Foreign Intelligence Agency (the Bundesnachrichtendienst), and prosecutors to inform each other—on their own initiative—whenever there were "indications" that information they obtained could be relevant for any of the other agencies. In return, the federal and state intelligence agencies could request information from all of the federal and state police forces if they deemed this necessary to carry out their responsibilities or if this information could only be procured in other ways through disproportionate effort or more intrusive measures. In a memorable image, Burkhard Hirsch (FDP)—Interior Minister of North Rhineland-Westphalia (1975–80) and Bundestag representative (1972–75 and 1980–98)—likened such promiscuous information exchanges among the police and the intelligence agencies to "informational group sex with the consent of the madame."[47]

There was a second dimension to this dispute over the final purpose principle that was even more controversial. In the run-up to the establishment of the Federal Republic, the Allies had sought in two ways to prevent the abusive concentration of police power. On the one hand, they devolved police power as far as possible to local government and permitted the federal government to play only a residual, coordinating role in policing. This was the origin of the Federal Criminal Police (chapter 6). On the other hand, although the Allies permitted the federal government to establish an intelligence agency to collect information for the purpose of "protecting the constitution," this nascent domestic intelligence agency was not permitted any police powers (i.e. the power to arrest persons, carry out searches, etc.), and it was to be organizationally separate from the police. By threatening this "separation rule," the security laws of the 1980s appeared to alter existing constitutional arrangements.

Since early 1984, the exchange of information between the police and the intelligence agencies had been a recurring point of concern and controversy, in particular whether the intelligence agencies could request that the police engage in information-collection activities—most often house searches—that the intelligence agencies themselves were not authorized to undertake and then to communicate to them any relevant information that had been gathered during such searches. The question was whether the organizational separation between the police and intelligence agencies and the different powers granted to them (the authority to use force or covert means) also meant that the information gathered by these different means had to be kept separate, or whether the broad identity of functions (the protection of internal security) was sufficient to justify the exchange of information across institutional boundaries? Since an affirmative answer to this latter question would render the organizational separation of the different agencies meaningless, this, in turn, raised the question of whether the separation rule was, in fact, an integral element of the written constitution or whether it had simply been an institutional convenience whose raison d'être had disappeared in the interim?

If the police and the intelligence agencies had different responsibilities or missions, then allowing the police to carry out searches for the intelligence agencies and communicate information they obtained in this way represented a gross violation of the final purpose principle, and initially some security officials had opposed such activity.[48] However, the Kohl administration increasingly challenged the constitutional status of the separation rule and employed the rhetoric of internal security to make the political claim that the shared responsibility for protecting public security permitted, if it did not require, the police and the intelligence agencies to cooperate with one another. Organizational separation, the administration insisted, could not be allowed to lead to informational compartmentalization, and its ultimate success in gaining acceptance for this position marked a major shift in both the meaning of internal security and the "security architecture" of the republic.[49] This and the other issues discussed in the preceding paragraphs gave the debate over the final purpose principle an unexpectedly broad political resonance, and this blurring of institutional boundaries and constitutional limitations was one of the leitmotifs of the surveillance state debate of the 1970s and 1980s.[50]

The debate over privacy and security did not really come to a head until after the census decision, and the question is what do these debates over the security laws tell us about the nature of liberalism and conservatism?

In the February 1986 Bundestag debate on the national ID card, Baum conceded that automation had brought greater efficiency to the workings of the state bureaucracy. However, he worried that the electronic quest for ever more perfect information was progressively circumscribing the scope of individual freedom. In contrast to the conservative argument for freedom through security, Baum insisted that the limitation of state surveillance was the price that had to be paid to preserve this freedom.

The state, Baum declared, "must be willing to accept the consequences of incomplete information and pursue its responsibilities in the awareness of the informational limits [that it faced]. The effectiveness of state action is certainly important. But in a state governed by the rule of law effectiveness must also be measured against the safeguarding of constitutional rights."[51] These ideas were reiterated in the privacy program adopted at the May 1986 FDP conference. "The state does not need to know everything," the program declared. "It must also have to courage to accept gaps" in its knowledge. The program also sought to distance the party from the conservatives by insisting that "the protection of personality rights is a responsibility of the state, not something it should regard as a security risk."[52]

The conservatives saw matters differently, and their proposals to amend the Federal Privacy Protection Law, the ID card law, and the various security laws followed a logic that was very different from that informing liberal policies. They gave priority to maximizing the effectiveness of the security agencies by eliminating all of the limitations that liberals saw as basis for individual freedom and security against an overweening state. They downplayed the import of the right to informational self-determination ("Privacy protection does not mean unlimited control over one's own data") and accentuated the baneful consequences of the privacy protection law ("The legal norming of all informational relations and an excessive exaggeration of the final purpose principle would lead to a flood of [unnecessary] regulations").[53]

However, these criticisms also reveal a fundamental difference between the liberals and the conservatives regarding the relation between privacy, security, and freedom. In a handwritten comment on the FDP program, a Bavarian official—most likely Heinz Honnacker, the head of the police law department in the state interior ministry, a well-known commentator on police law, and later justice on the Federal Administrative Court—argued that the liberals entangled themselves in contradictions by applying the privacy lever at the wrong place. According to Honnacker, their basic problem was that they wanted to retain the traditional responsibilities of the state while limiting the freedom of the administration to achieve these ends. However, he insisted, "the limits of the activity of the state must be defined in terms of the responsibilities assigned to the state, not by hindering the fulfillment of these responsibilities."[54]

One of the new motifs in the debate over police surveillance in the second half of the 1980s was the notion of a constitutional right to security. However, sovereignty is indivisible, and Honnacker's formulation is revealing because he would never have agreed that this quintessential state responsibility could have been limited without abandoning the Hobbesian conception of the sovereign state as an institution standing over and above civil society. Nor could he have accepted any form of privacy protection that would have entailed a substantive limitation on the scope of state activity in this domain. Precisely here lay the unbridgeable difference between the FDP and its coalition partners with regard to privacy in the security sector.

At Long Last: The 1990 Revision of the Federal Privacy Protection Law

The final stretch along the long road to the revision of the Federal Privacy Protection Law did not start in an auspicious manner. After the January 1987 Bundestag elections, Zimmermann ordered ministry officials to compose new drafts of the privacy and security laws. These drafts, which were completed in November of that year, dramatically altered the balance between privacy and security in favor of the latter.[55] *Die Zeit* warned that the information exchanges between the intelligence agencies, the police, and prosecutors envisioned by these "excessive and uncompromisingly formulated" laws would be a "concentration of information in the hands of the state of truly frightening proportions," and the FDP declared that there was no chance whatsoever that the informational collaboration law, which had been the—unstable—linchpin of the coalition compromise during the previous legislative period, would be approved in the proposed form.[56]

Hesse, Bremen, and North Rhineland-Westphalia had all amended their privacy protection laws in 1987/88. This put pressure on the Kohl administration to move ahead in order to forestall the further fragmentation of privacy law—and to do so in a more liberal spirit than the interior ministry supported. Despite this movement at the state level, things did not get much better at the federal level in 1988. At the beginning of the year, the state secretaries in the justice and interior ministries, Klaus Kinkel (FDP) and Hans Neusel (CDU), were charged with working out a compromise. However, the drafts that they submitted in October reflected the same shortcomings as the January 1986 omnibus bill. The most important change at this point was that the freestanding informational collaboration law was dropped—with the relevant provisions being distributed among the various intelligence service and police laws. But Otto Lambsdorff was less accommodating to the conservatives than Martin Bangemann, whom he had succeeded as party chair only a few weeks before, and he was unwilling to force this compromise through over the objections of Baum, Hirsch, and others in the civil liberties wing of the party. An intraparty compromise was reached whereby the FDP agreed to support the laws when the cabinet met in December, but at the same time to present a three-page list of "reservations" regarding the drafts for which the party had just voted. Some of these reservations detailed provisions that they found completely unacceptable; others identified issues that still required serious discussion and possible renegotiation.[57]

From this point onward, the legislative process began to move forward more rapidly. Although the states had reached a consensus on the federal privacy law by the beginning of 1989, the interior ministry rejected most of the changes to the administration draft that had been proposed by the Bundesrat.[58] However, in April Zimmermann was replaced as interior minister by Wolfgang Schäuble (CDU) as part of a cabinet reshuffling. His departure cleared the way for progress on the privacy and security laws; the domestic affairs committee held hearings on the privacy and security laws in June of that year; and by the turn of 1990 the coalition parties had reached an agreement on the final wording of the Federal Privacy Protection Law.[59] Debate on the security laws, on the other hand, dragged on through the spring of 1990.

Finally, at the end of May 1990, the domestic affairs committee reported the bill back. Although the committee version of the omnibus law was immediately approved by the Bundestag, the Bundesrat called for the formation of a conference committee to resolve the differences between the bills approved by the two bodies.[60] The conference committee report that was submitted in mid-September was quickly approved by both houses, thereby bringing to an end the long, bitter, complex, and in many ways disappointing efforts to revise the Federal Privacy Protection Law.[61]

The issues involved in this final round of politicking were not fundamentally different from those that had arisen in conjunction with the 1986 omnibus bill. Zimmermann's plan to limit the role of the federal privacy commissioner was such a blatantly political maneuver with such questionable consequences that his successor could not support it. Although the rejection of the Zimmermann plan meant that collection would now be included within the privacy law, there remained important differences. However, the balance of power in the Bundesrat shifted after the governing conservative-liberal coalition lost its majority in the June Landtag election in Lower Saxony and was succeeded by an SPD-Green government. With a Social Democratic majority, the Bundesrat favored both a broader law and more restrictive formulations on permissible data use than did the legislature.

The privacy commissioners also argued that it was important to extend to paper files the full protections offered to electronic data processing because advances in office technology, which made it possible both to find specific pieces of information in unformatted files and to automatically retrieve individual paper documents, were rendering "obsolete" the distinction between formatted electronic files and paper files.[62] However, the legislature, which was more sensitive to the potential financial impact of the law on German firms and their international competitiveness, wanted to exempt paper files in the private sector. In its final version, the law applied to all forms of information processing in the public administration, while in the private sector the law only applied to personal information that was held in formatted files.

The provisions governing the collection of personal information in the public sector were formulated to insure greater transparency. Although decision not to categorically exempt the police or the intelligence agencies from the obligation to disclose what information was held on a petitioner was an important symbolic victory for the FDP, this right was hedged in by generous qualifications and exemptions. This was the compromise that the FDP had to accept in order to bring the police and the intelligence agencies within the ambit of the law.

The Bundestag and the Bundesrat both rejected Zimmermann's attempt to neuter the federal privacy commissioner. However, at the time, fully half of all complaints and questions that came to the federal privacy commissioner from the general public related not to the electronic processing of data held in formatted files, but rather to more traditional forms of data processing.[63] While the Bundesrat did not want to restrict the commissioner's review authority in this area, the Bundestag followed older drafts in limiting such authority to cases where either the commissioner or the concerned individual already possessed evidence that his rights had been violated. In the end, the two houses split the difference: the authority of the commissioner was limited to cases where there was evidence that individual rights had been violated, but the commissioner was then permitted to investigate the underlying causes.

There still remained two important points of controversy. The first dealt with the use of personal information for marketing purposes. On this issue, the parties were able to reach a workable compromise: the law allowed businesses to use information in most of the ways proposed by the administration, but individuals were given an opt-out right.[64] Second, the law still did not include domain-specific regulations for the credit reporting, insurance, banking, and commercial telecommunications industries, or for human resources management systems. All of these were areas where the collection and use of personal information was growing exponentially, especially as a result of the electronic capture of transactional information, and where formal consent was often undermined by de facto inequalities in power.[65]

Regulating the Spooks

It is more difficult to assess the significance of the Domestic Intelligence Agency Law.

First, the privacy commissioners argued that the right to informational self-determination required a greater differentiation among the agency's tasks. Without a precise definition of the mission(s) of an organization, it would be impossible to determine what information was necessary to fulfill its responsibilities, establish what information-collection methods were appropriate and proportional for each purpose, or monitor compliance with the final purpose principle. In contrast, intelligence officials insisted that in practice it was impossible to draw such neat distinctions.[66] The Bundesrat and then the conference committee added detailed definitions of the dangers that the agency was to combat.[67] However, the privacy impact of this provision was blunted by the fact that the conference committee only required the compartmentalization of information with regard to security clearances, but not with regard to the primary responsibilities for defending against extremism, espionage, and terrorism. Moreover, since the anti-constitutional "activities" that the Domestic Intelligence Agency was authorized to monitor presumed a certain degree of organization, debate had often stumbled over whether it was possible to monitor organizations without collecting information on their individual members.[68] In hopes of eliminating these ambiguities, the law also defined both the terms under which individual actions could be said to constitute support for an organization and those under which these actions would be considered "activities" in the sense of the law, even if they were not undertaken in support of an organization.

Second, in contrast to the administration draft, which had skirted the issue entirely, the final version of the law included a provision, which predicated the collection of information on extremism, espionage, and terrorism on the existence of "factual indications" of involvement in these activities. This had been an important point for the FDP.

Third, the privacy commissioners called on the legislature to enumerate, or at least give typical examples of, the covert methods that could be employed to carry out the newly defined responsibilities of the agency. Although the Bundestag acceded to this demand, it is difficult to believe that it contributed in any notable way to protecting privacy. More important, while the administration draft had required the agency to regularly report on its covert activities to the parliamentary commission responsible for monitoring phone taps and postal surveillance (the so-called G-10 commission), the domestic affairs committee put some bite into this provision by imposing the same limitations on the use of the information collected via covert means as were imposed on information gathered by phone taps and postal surveillance.

Fourth, the law sought to resolve some of the outstanding questions regarding the relation between the intelligence agencies and the police by prohibiting the former from "requesting" that the police undertake actions that the agency was not authorized to undertake on its own. It further stated that, if the agency requested information from any other office, this office could only provide the information that it had already collected in the course of its own work. Although these provisions appeared to limit the erosion of the separation rule, the underlying problem remained: as long as the police were permitted or required to communicate potentially relevant information to the intelligence agencies, this prohibition remained a distinction whose substantive difference was difficult to fathom.

Fifth, as we have already noted, the law did not give the intelligence agency a blanket exemption from the obligation to disclose what information it held on specific individuals. However, it did include broad exceptions, and it exempted the agency from having to explain the reasons for refusing to disclose information.[69] Sixth, and most important, all of these restrictions, qualifications and distinctions notwithstanding, the law authorized, with no meaningful limits or prohibitions, all of the interagency exchanges of information whose codification had been Zimmermann's top priority since the census decision.

Inflation, Complexity, and the Limits of Privacy

This history raises the question of the ultimate impact or meaning of the Federal Privacy Protection Law.

At the April 1980 hearing on the reform of the Federal Privacy Protection Law, Herbert Fiedler predicted with uncanny prescience that the future course of privacy protection law would be defined by the principle *nullum datum sine lege*—no information without an authorizing law.[70] Although this juridification of informational relations in every domain of social life was irreversible, the census decision gave it an entirely new dynamic. As Bull has recently written, since the decision "legislators have been unceasingly occupied with regulating a process that had previously been regarded as legally permissible. The legislative machine has been running in high gear because we now have higher expectations for the exhaustive codification of legal norms for all spheres of social life—and because sufficient legal authorization is indispensable for countless state activities, especially for the security agencies."[71]

While the 1980s were anything but a decade of deregulation in the domain of privacy protection, the reliance on formal criteria as a substitute for substantive norms regarding the parameters of permissible informational activity in areas where there was no political consensus insured, as Schomerus and Honnacker predicted, that the emerging body of information law would be dense and opaque. As Wolfgang Hoffmann-Riem wrote shortly before he was appointed to the Constitutional Court, the juridification of privacy was leading to the defeat of privacy protection law at the very moment of its apparent triumph: "The picture is characterized by complicated rules for their application, nested references to other regulations, multiple special rules, and open-ended authorizations for the balancing of interests."[72] Privacy law had become too complex even for experts.

Conservatives were right to worry about this trend, but shortsighted and partisan in blaming the privacy commissioners and the other parties for a secular process to which everyone contributed and from which no one could escape. However, not all juridification was trivial or even undesirable. Even such innocuous practices as direct mail raised important questions of principle, and privacy law was becoming the primary domain in which and the chief means through which the new forms of social conflict characteristic of the information society were being fought out.

In a memorandum that he submitted in advance of the June 1989 domestic affairs committee hearing on the federal privacy law, Simitis explained that the real significance of the census decision lay in the fact that it had established the right to informational self-determination as the norm rather than the exception: "When it is a question of the processing of personal information, it is not the concerned individual who must justify himself [i.e. justify his privacy rights], but rather those who wish to use this data." To provide the comprehensive protection of the right to informational self-determination mandated by the Court, he continued, a revised privacy law would have to begin with the collection of data, apply to data processing in both the public and private sectors and without regard to the medium on which the data was stored, impose a narrow formulation of the final purpose principle, and provide for review by an independent privacy commissioner.[73] Constitutional norms could only be satisfied, Simitis insisted, when every act of data processing was authorized by law, "every single one."[74]

This was what I call the strong or maximalist reading of the decision. It was just such a reading that created the expectation that the census decision would lead to the limitation, if not the rollback, of population surveillance by both the state and the private sector. However, whatever the problems with the Court's reasoning, the census decision clearly authorized a balancing of interests, and to a far greater extent than many people expected (and desired) the Federal Privacy Protection Law simply codified the existing informational practices of business and the public administration. In this respect, at least, the strong interpretation of the census decision did not determine actual regulatory practice.

Podlech noted at the time that "a privacy protection law is only as good as the way it regulates the intelligence agencies."[75] Measured against this standard, Germany had an increasingly complex body of information law that had codified what the major parties, and presumably the voters who stood behind them, considered to be socially adequate forms of information collection, use and exchange by business and the state. Although the FDP forced the conservatives to modify the proposed security laws to insure that they complied more fully with the rule of law, neither they nor the privacy commissioners were able to fundamentally alter the Hobbesian logic that underpinned conservative policy in these domains. As a result, the substantive impact of the privacy protection law was felt primarily around the margins: surveillance by the Domestic Intelligence Agency was predicated on "factual indications," rather than on mere "indications;" information collected by the intelligence agency on children under sixteen could only be stored in paper files, not computers; and an opt-out provision was adopted to protect Germans against the violation of their personality rights by unwanted junk mail. As we shall see in later chapters, the Social Democrats eagerly supported the modernization of the police and the expansion of their surveillance capacity during their years in office. Although they certainly would have been pulled towards the center on one issue or another by the FDP, it is not clear whether, despite all of the partisan politicking of the 1980s, the outcome of the post-census decision reforms would have been fundamentally different if the SPD/FDP coalition had remained in office.

Notes

1. Marion Albers, *Informationelle Selbstbestimmung* (Nomos, 2005), 151; and Karl-Heinz Ladeur, "Das Recht auf informationelle Selbstbestimmung: Eine juristische Fehlkonstruktion," *DÖV* 62, no. 2 (January 2009): 45–55.
2. Ansprache vor dem Bundestags-Innenausschuss (8 June 1983), BAK B106/83849, Bd. 9.
3. Laufs, *Sten. Ber.*, 10. Wahlperiode, 202. Sitzung (28 February 1986), 15526; see also Bundesfachausschuss Innenpolitik, Thesenpapier "Innere Sicherheit und Datenschutz," and Thesen der CDU zum Datenschutz (22 October 1984), both in BAK B106/101408, Bd. 6.

4. BVerfGE 65, 1 (1): "die Befugnis des Einzelnen, grundsätzlich selbst über die Preisgabe und Verwendung seiner persönlichen Daten zu bestimmen."
5. BVerfGE 65, 1 (42). These passages simply restated Benda's 1972 warning regarding the uncontrolled, "dysfunctional dissemination" of personal data.
6. BVerfGE 65, 1 (43). Hans Peter Bull, *Informationelle Selbstbestimmung—Vision oder Illusion?* (Mohr Siebeck, 2009), 30–31, 45–48, argues that the complete transparency of *others* to the subject is just as much an obstacle to freedom as the complete transparency of the *subject* to others. Even if one could learn precisely what data others possessed regarding us and how they would interpret it, such knowledge would be self-defeating, he argues, because the elimination of all uncertainty and risk would eliminate the possibility of genuine freedom.
7. Ladeur, "Das Recht auf informationelle Selbstbestimmung," 48, argues that, to the extent that emphasis is placed on the dependence of one's own identity on the prior interpretation of personal data by the communicative partner, it is more proper to speak of "heteronomous determination" (*Fremdbestimmung*) than of self-determination.
8. BVerfGE 65, 1 (43). In contrast, the US Supreme Court ruled, in *Laird v. Tatum*, 408 U.S. 1, 13–14 (1972), that such a deterrent, "chilling" effect did not constitute grounds for challenging state surveillance; the Court restated this position in *Clapper v. Amnesty International* 133 S. Ct. 1138, 1152 (2013).
9. BVerfGE 65, 1 (43).
10. The Court explicitly affirmed this position in its 1988 legal incapacity decision, BVerfGE 78, 77 (84).
11. In "Das Volkszählungsurteil oder der lange Weg zur Informationsaskese," *KritV* 83, no. 3–4 (2000): 359–75, Spiros Simitis argued (368–69) that this passage marked the emancipation of informational self-determination from its origins in personality law. However, Podlech, "Art. 2 Abs. 1," has shown that personality law need not lead to an individualist understanding of the right to informational self-determination such as that criticized by Simitis.
12. One reason the ruling itself did not express these ideas with anything near the desired level of clarity was the tactical decision not to cite any scholarly literature. According to Steinmüller and Lutterbeck, they were considered to be so far to the left that, had the Court cited their 1971 memorandum, it would have been impossible to convince a majority of the justices to support the new right. On the other hand, Podlech was not politically suspect. But since it was impossible to cite Podlech's commentary on §2 Abs. 1 without also making reference the memorandum by Steinmüller and Lutterbeck, the justices decided not to cite any literature at all. The rapporteur on the case, Hermann Heußner, was the only justice versed in the new technology. According to Steinmüller, it was Heußner (supported by Benda) who slowly brought around the other justices. See the interviews with Lutterbeck and Steinmüller, https://www.datenschutzzentrum.de/interviews/.
13. BVerfGE 65, 1 (43–44): "ist vielmehr eine sich innerhalb der sozialen Gemeinschaft entfaltende, auf Kommunikation angewiesene Persönlichkeit."
14. BVerfGE 65, 1 (45).
15. For criticisms of such a reading, see Hans Peter Bull, "Neue Konzepte, neue Instrumente?" *ZRP* 31, no. 8 (1998): 310–14, especially 313; Ladeur, "Das Recht auf informationelle Selbstbestimmung," 47; and Karl-Heinz Ladeur, "Datenschutz—vom Abwehrrecht zur planerischen Optimierung von Wissensnetzwerken," *DuD* 24, no. 1 (2000): 12–19, which reformulates the concept of personality profiles—without using the term—in the language of Big Data.
16. BVerfGE 65, 1 (46).
17. Although the concept of *Vorratsdatenspeicherung* was initially introduced as a foil for the final purpose principle, it took on new importance with EU directive 2006/24 requiring

internet service providers to retain telecommunications metadata for later use by law enforcement agencies. It has since become the object of constitutional adjudication in Germany and elsewhere. In 2010, the Constitutional Court overturned the law implementing the EU rule, and in 2014 the European Court of Justice overturned the EU directive itself. Since then, the parties in the Bundestag have oscillated between efforts to craft a constitutionally acceptable law and attempts to ban the practice altogether.

18. BVerfGE 65, 1 (46). The ruling spoke of the need for an "amtshilfefester Schutz gegen Zweckentfremdung," a phrase that was borrowed from Simitis, Stellungnahme zu den Fragen des Bundesverfassungsgerichts..., 12, LAB B Rep. 004/1109.
19. Baumann, Stellungnahme des Bundesbeauftragten für den Datenschutz... zu den Verfassungsbeschwerden..., 10–11, LAB B Rep. 004/1110.
20. BVerfGE 65, 1 (46).
21. BVerfGE 65, 1 (48); and Simitis, Stellungnahme zu den Fragen des Bundesverfassungsgerichts, 5.
22. BVerfGE 65, 1 (48–53).
23. Interview Bull; and Abteilungsleiter V & O to State Secretaries Fröhlich and Kroppenstedt, Auswirkungen des Volkszählungs-Urteils... (11 January 1984), BAK B106/115601, Bd. 1, which also warned that a minimalist reading would not do justice to the importance that the Court placed on the decision.
24. Andreas Wirsching, *Abschied vom Provisorium, 1982–1990* (Deutsche Verlags-Anstalt, 2006), 107–16, 154–71, describes the conflicts within the coalition and the difficult FDP search for issues that would distinguish them from the conservatives.
25. IS 2/Eckart Werthebach to Zimmermann, Betr.: Bereichsspezifische Datenschutzregelungen im Sicherheitsbereich (1 June 1984), and untitled memorandum to Abteilungsleiter P (undated, but June 1984), both BAK B106/101408, Bd. 4; and IS 2 to P I 5, Betr.: Erarbeitung bereichsspezifischer Vorschriften... (11 September 1984), BAK B106/101408, Bd. 5.
26. Einwag to Staatssekretär Kroppenstedt (23 May 1984), BAK B106/96347, Bd. 25.
27. IS 2/Werthebach, Betr.: Auswirkungen des Bundesverfassungsgerichtsurteils..., hier: Erweiterung der BDSG-Novelle (31 March 1984), and P I 5/Kersten, Betr.: Auswirkungen des Urteils..., hier: Polizeiliche Informationsgewinnung und -verarbeitung (22 May 1984), both in BAK B106/101407, Bd. 2; IS 2/Werthebach to Minister, Betr.: Bereichsspezifische Datenschutzregelungen im Sicherheitsbereich (1 June 1984), BAK B106/101408, Bd. 4; and P I 5/Kersten, Vermerk, Betr.: Sitzung des Unterausschusses "Recht der Polizei" vom 14.–16. Mai 1984, BAK B106/115601, Bd. 2.
28. Kersten, Betr.: Auswirkungen des Urteils... (6 March 1984), BAK B106/101951, Bd. 2; Siegfried Fröhlich to Paul Laufs (19 June 1984), BAK B106/101951, Bd. 4; and MinDirig Alfred Einwag/Arbeitsgruppe "Volkszählungsurteil" to Staatssekretär Fröhlich, Betr.: Prüfung der Auswirkungen... (20 March 1984), BAK B106/101407, Bd. 3. An overview of conservative plans and the points of controversy with regard to all of these security laws can be found in Einwag/Stellv. Abteilungsleiter IS to Zimmermann, Betr.: Bereichsspezifische Datenschutzregelungen im Sicherheitsbereich, hier: Koalitionsgespräch am 15. Oktober 1984, BAK B106/101951, Bd. 5.
29. Einwag to Zimmermann, Betr.: Bereichsspezifische Datenschutzregelungen im Sicherheitsbereich, Einwag, Vorblatt zur Ausarbeitung Personalausweisgesetz (undated, but fall 1984), and the following untitled Ausarbeitung, Entwurf für ein Statement zu TOP 6 der Sitzung der Arbeitsgruppe Inneres, Umwelt und Sport der CDU/CSU-Fraktion am 6.11.1984, all in BAK B106/101408, Bd. 6; and Vorschlag FDP. Entwurf einer Entschliessung des deutschen Bundestages, BAK B106/101952, Bd. 5.
30. Staatssekretär, Vermerk, Betr.: Koalitionsgespräch (15 October 1984), BAK B106/122705, Bd. 9; Vorläufiger Zeitplan für die Erarbeitung bereichsspezifischer Vorschriften in den Fachgesetzen der Sicherheitsbehörden, and Karl Miltner (CDU) to Zimmermann (26 October 1984), both in BAK B106/101408, Bd. 6.

31. Drs. 10/4737 and 5344; "Weiterhin Streit in der Koalition um den Datenschutz und die innere Sicherheit," *FAZ*, 26 March 1985; "Die 'politischen Grenzen' in der Koalition," *FAZ*, 5 September 1985; and "Die Parteiführer der Koalition erklären den Streit um die innere Sicherheit für beendet," *FAZ*, 11 January 1986.
32. CDU/CSU-Fraktion. Arbeitsgruppe Inneres, Umwelt und Sport, Betr.: Klausurtagung... am 25./26. Mai 1984, BAK B106/101408, Bd. 4.
33. "Gewisse Affinität," *Der Spiegel*, 16 May 1983; and "Brav statt unbequem?" *Die Zeit*, 20 May 1983. In its report on the oral arguments on the census, "Ein Kinderspiel," *Der Spiegel*, 24 October 1983, 48–52, noted that after only a few months on the job Baumann had learned a lot and put a great deal of distance between himself and his former boss.
34. Abteilungsleiter O to G 1, Betr.: Zusammenstellung innenpolitischer Vorhaben für die Hausleitung... Novellierung des BDSG (9 May 1985), BAK B106/96353, Bd. 32; and the memoranda by Bull, Baumann, and Bernd Lutterbeck for the domestic affairs committee hearing on the omnibus bill in April 1986, BAK B106/96362.
35. Stenographisches Protokoll über die 72. Sitzung des Innenausschusses, Öffentliche Anhörung von Sachverständigen zu dem Entwurf eines Gesetzes zur Änderung des BDSG (Drs. 10/1180) (June 24, 1985), BAK B106/96362, 131-37 (as well as the memoranda submitted for the hearing in B106/96361); Simitis, Stellungnahme zum Entwurf eines Gesetzes zur Änderung des Bundesdatenschutzgesetzes... für die öffentliche Anhörung des Innenausschusses... am 28.4.1986, and Entschliessung der Konferenz der Datenschutzbeauftragten... vom 18. April 1986 zur Änderung des Bundesverfassungsschutzgesetzes, both in Berlin DSB, Goldene Ordner, Bd. 1.
36. See the memoranda from the Zentraler Kreditausschuß (5 June 1986), and Bull (1 April 1986), both in BAK B106/96361; and Simitis, Stellungnahme zum Entwurf eines Gesetzes.
37. Stenographisches Protokoll über die 72. Sitzung des Innenausschusses..., 20f., 102ff., 159–64; and Benda, "Das Recht des Bürgers auf informationelle Selbstbestimmung," 10, 13ff.
38. See the memoranda from Lutterbeck (1 April 1986), and the Zentraler Kreditausschuß, BAK B106/96361; the remarks by Fiedler in Stenographisches Protokoll über die 72. Sitzung des Innenausschusses..., and the comments made at the 1979 FDP privacy congress (15 December 1979), BAK B106/96336, Bd. 2.
39. Abteilungsleiter O to G 1, Betr.: Zusammenstellung innenpolitischer Vorhaben für die Hausleitung... Novellierung des BDSG (9 May 1985), BAK B106/96353, Bd. 32; and Baumann's memorandum for the April 1986 hearing.
40. See the memoranda by Bull and Baumann for the April 1986 hearing, and Simitis, "Reicht unser Datenschutzrecht angesichts der technischen Revolution?" in *Informationsgesellschaft oder Überwachungsstaat. Strategien zur Wahrung der Freiheitsrechte im Computerzeitalter*, ed. Hessische Landesregierung (Opladen, 1986), I:27–48, especially 38, 40; as well as Klaus Dette, *Zweiweg-Kabelfernsehen und Datenschutz* (Minerva, 1979); Reinhold Baumann, "Datenschutz angesichts neuer Technologien," *RDV* 4, no. 1 (1988): 9–13; and Jochen Schneider, "Datenschutz und neue Medien," *NJW* 37, no. 8 (1984): 390–98.
41. Arbeitsgruppe Innenpolitische Grundsatzfragen—Der Planungsbeauftragte, Betr.: Arbeitsplanung bis zum Ende der Legislaturperiode (26 June 1986), BAK B106/96360.
42. Simitis, Stellungnahme zum Entwurf eines Gesetzes..., and Entschliessung der Konferenz der Datenschutzbeauftragten... vom 18. April 1986 zur Änderung des Bundesverfassungsschutzgesetzes, both in Berlin DSB, Goldene Ordner, Bd. 1; "Redaktionelle Stellungnahme zum... Bundesverfassungsschutzgesetzes," *CILIP* 23 (1986): 56–66; and Stellungnahme by the Bundesamt für Verfassungsschutz (27 March 1986), BAK B106/96362.

43. Simitis, Stellungnahme zum Entwurf . . . Änderung des Bundesverfassungsschutzgesetzes (10 April 1986), Berlin DSB, Ordner: Goldene 7, Bd. II.
44. Beschluß des Bundesvorstandes der FDP vom 23.3.1985, BAK B106/122706, Bd. 10.
45. Neufassung des Bundesverfassungsschutzgesetzes, hier: Presseerklärung des BfD vom 23. Januar 1986, BAK B106/96357. The law also permitted the Domestic Intelligence Agency to communicate information to the Allied forces stationed in the country.
46. "FDP-Programm zum Datenschutz."
47. Cited in "Falsche Richtung," *Der Spiegel*, 25 January 1988, 18. Eggert Schwan struck a similarly alarmist tone ("Notfalls Knarre," *Der Spiegel*, 16 June 1986, 62–63), arguing that if the packet of security laws, including the informational collaboration law, were passed, then the country would find itself in the same situation as in 1933: "facing the creation of a Gestapo."
48. For example, Referat P I 5/Kersten to P II 1, Betr.: Änderung des Bundesverfassungsschutzgesetzes (28 February 1985), BAK B106/122705, Bd. 9.
49. See Bundesminister des Innern, Gesetzliche Regelung der informationellen Zusammenarbeit . . . (9 October 1984), included as an appendix to Einwag/Stellv. Abteilungsleiter IS to Minister Zimmermann, Betr.: Bereichsspezifische Datenschutzregelungen im Sicherheitsbereich, hier: Koalitionsgespräch am 15. Oktober 1984, BAK B106/101952, Bd. 5; and Überblick über die von der Union noch in dieser Legislaturperiode zu erreichende Ziele . . . (February 1985), BAK B106/122706, Bd. 10. Ernhard Denninger, "Die Trennung von Verfassungsschutz und Polizei und das Grundrecht auf informationelle Selbstbestimmung," *ZRP* 14, no. 10 (1981): 231–35, argued that the separation rule had to be considered as an element of the constitution, while Christoph Gusy, "Das verfassungsrechtliche Gebot der Trennung von Polizei und Nachrichtendiensten," *ZRP* 20, no. 2 (1987): 45–52, argued that it was of lesser rank and could be altered by a simple law; see also Marion Albers, *Die Determination polizeilicher Tätigkeit in den Bereichen der Straftatenverhütung und der Verfolgungsvorsorge* (Duncker & Humblot, 2001), 221–30.
50. There was also controversy over whether the national intelligence information system NADIS (Nachrichtendienstliches Informationssystem), which had originally contained only index data telling users where they could find investigative files relating to specific individuals, was to be transformed into a more robust system comparable to the criminal information system INPOL.
51. Baum, *Sten. Ber.*, 10. Wahlperiode, 202. Sitzung (28 February 1986), 15530–31.
52. "FDP-Programm zum Datenschutz," *DuD* 10, no. 6 (1986): 376–77, in BayHStA MInn 97094; and Beschluss des Bundesvorstandes der FDP vom 23.3.1985, BAK B106/122706.
53. Themen für Koalitionsgespräch: Datenschutz, BayHStA MInn 97094.
54. Marginal comments on FDP-Programm zum Datenschutz, BayHStA MInn 97094.
55. All of these drafts are reprinted in *CILIP* 29, no. 1 (1988); see also "Datenschutz und innere Sicherheit," *FAZ*, 21 January 1988. At this point, the informational collaboration law was renamed the "Intelligence Service Information Provision Law" (Verfassungsschutz-Mitteilungsgesetz). This reaction also took its toll on the privacy commissioners themselves. In Baden-Württemberg, Ruth Leuze, who had been involved in the drafting of police law in the mid-1970s, but who had emerged as a combative defender of privacy rights, was constantly attacked by conservative politicians. At the federal level, Reinhard Riegel, the highly respected head of the public security department in the office of the Federal Privacy Commissioner, was transferred—as punishment for his work there—to a department where he could do no harm to Zimmermann's political plans. And the 1988 appointment of Alfred Einwag, who had overseen the drafting of the security laws in the interior ministry, to succeed Baumann Federal as Privacy Commissioner was widely regarded as yet another attempt to diminish the importance of the office. See Hanno Kühnert, "Unbequem, also unerwünscht. Die CDU will die von ihr gewählte Datenschutzbeauftragte loswerden," *Die Zeit*, 15 May 1987; "Unheimlich

getrödelt," *Der Spiegel*, 1 June 1987; "Kontroverse um die Versetzung eines Datenschutz-Referenten," *FAZ*, 2 August 1986; and "Wichtig, aber nicht beliebt," *Die Zeit*, 3 June 1988.

56. Hans Schueler, "Neue Zumutung. Wieder Ärger über Zimmermanns Pläne," *Die Zeit*, 29 January 1988; and "Koalition abermals uneins über Datenschutz und innere Sicherheit," *FAZ*, 21 January 1988.

57. "FDP stimmt dem Gesetzentwurf zum Datenschutz unter Vorbehalten zu," *FAZ*, 29 November 1988; "Änderungswünsche beim Datenschutz," *FAZ*, 1 December 1988; and "Das Kabinett berät abschliessend über Sicherheitsgesetze," *FAZ*, 21 December 1988.

58. Bundesrat Drs. 611/88 (10 February 1988), and 597. Sitzung (10 February 1989), 25–33; and Bundestag Drs. 11/4306, and *Sten. Ber.*, 11. Wahlperiode, 141. Sitzung (28 April 1989), 10472–86.

59. The minutes and supporting memoranda for the June 1989 hearing are reprinted in Deutscher Bundestag, ed., *Fortentwicklung der Datenverarbeitung und des Datenschutzes* (Bundestag, 1990).

60. Drs. 11/7235; and *Sten. Ber.*, 11. Wahlperiode, 214. Sitzung (31 May 1990), 16776–800.

61. Drs. 11/7843; and Gesetz zur Fortentwicklung der Datenverarbeitung und des Datenschutzes, *BGBl.*, 1990, 2954–81.

62. Deutscher Bundestag, *Fortentwicklung*, 256, 258.

63. According to Einwag in Deutscher Bundestag, *Fortentwicklung*, 121. The office had historically investigated such petitions because it was responsible for monitoring compliance not only with the federal privacy law, but also with other federal privacy regulations.

64. For the position of the advertising industry, see the memorandum by Dr. Wronka/Zentralausschuß der Werbewirtschaft, in Deutscher Bundestag, *Fortentwicklung*, 168–83.

65. Deutscher Bundestag, *Fortentwicklung*, 63–73, 77–79, 204–14, 261, 264–65, 285–87, 347; and Deutsche Gewerkschaftsbund, Stellungnahme zum Entwurf eines Artikelgesetzes . . . (12 February 1988), Bestand A: Manfred Such, no. 85.

66. Deutscher Bundestag, *Fortentwicklung*, 417–18, 657, 850–52.

67. Simitis in Deutscher Bundestag, *Fortentwicklung*, 725, noted that reviews of intelligence agency files by the privacy commissioners had shown that the imprecise definition of the tasks of the agencies was one of the most important reasons why the agencies collected information that was not relevant for their responsibilities.

68. See, for example, the exchange between Einwag and Federal Criminal Police president Gerhard Boeden in Deutscher Bundestag, *Fortentwicklung*, 465–67, as well as the comment by Simitis, 480, who declared the dispute to be irrelevant.

69. Especially interesting on this point are the comments by Leuze, Bavarian Privacy Commissioner Sebastian Oberhauser, and Simitis in Deutscher Bundestag, *Fortentwicklung*, 433–37, 723–24. The difference between "indications" and "factual indications" is discussed on 352n37.

70. Bundestag Innenausschuss, Protokoll über die interne Anhörung zu den Gesetzentwürfen zur Änderung des Bundesdatenschutzgesetzes (21–22 April 1980), BayHStA StK/13129, 19ff.

71. Hans Peter Bull, "Konkreter Realismus statt abstrakter Polemik. Ist Datenschutz ein Grundrecht?" *Neue Gesellschaft/Frankfurter Hefte* 56, no. 12 (2009): 34–37, citation 35. On the concept of juridification, see Gunther Teubner, "Juridification: Concepts, Aspects, Limits, Solutions," in *Juridification of Social Spheres: A Comparative Analysis in the Areas of Labor, Corporate, Antitrust and Social Welfare Law*, ed. Gunther Teubner (De Gruyter, 1987), 3–48.

72. Wolfgang Hoffmann-Riem, "Informationelle Selbstbestimmung in der Informationsgesellschaft—Auf dem Wege zu einem neuen Konzept des Datenschutzes," *Archiv des öffentlichen Rechts* 123 (1998): 513–40, especially 515–17. See also Bull, *Informationelle Selbstbestimmung*, 58; and Bull, "Neue Konzepte, neue Instrumente?" Reinhard Kreissl

and Lars deliver an even more damning assessment in "Wer hat Angst vom Großen Bruder?," special issue, *Leviathan* 25 (2010): 281–98, especially 282–83.
73. Simitis in Deutscher Bundestag, *Fortentwicklung*, 253–61, citation 254.
74. Deutscher Bundestag, *Fortentwicklung*, 35–37. For a conservative counterstatement, see the memorandum by Peter Badura in Deutscher Bundestag, *Fortentwicklung*, 148ff.
75. Podlech, Stellungnahme zur Anhörung vor dem Innenausschuss . . . (24 March 1986), BAK B353/4603, where he concluded that the administration's draft security laws were, in detail and in their underlying conception, unconstitutional.

Part III

THE PRECAUTIONARY TURN

Security, Surveillance,
and the Changing Nature of the State

Chapter 6

Paper, Power, and Policing, 1948–72
The Federal Criminal Police on the Cusp of the Computer Age

"The exploitation of information is," Berlin Kriminaloberrat Hans Kaleth observed at an April 1967 meeting of state and federal police officials, "the alpha and omega of criminalistic labor,"[1] and, if we believe Horst Herold, the police were the largest information processing enterprise in the Federal Republic.[2] However, the organization of the police, their ability to bring this information to bear on populations and individuals, and the very ways in which they went about doing their work were all determined by the technologies and bureaucratic structures available to them to process this information. This chapter will use the history of the Federal Criminal Police to study both the limits imposed on the administrative power of the police by the reliance on manual, paper-based information processing systems and the rationale for the expanded use of electronic data processing by the Federal Criminal Police. But the use of these technologies for administrative purposes was still in its infancy, and, as we shall see below, from the mid-1960s through the turn of the 1970s, local, state, and federal police agencies were all working—in conjunction with each other, with the major computer manufacturers, and with their counterparts in other countries on both sides of the Atlantic—to show how computers could be used for criminalistic purposes.

The limited ability to centralize and integrate information held in paper form forced state and local police forces to maintain their own sets of criminal records, multiplied the amount of redundant record keeping, and diminished the value of the information held by each. An integrated data

---

Notes for this chapter begin on page 243.

processing system appeared to offer an ideal solution to all of these problems, and the decision to create an integrated national criminal information network was made in principle at the end of 1966. Nevertheless, the federalist organization of the security sector was an obstacle to the construction of such a network, and the project remained stalled until the end of 1971.

Since it worked primarily with information reported by the states, the Federal Criminal Police could not fully computerize its own information processing system without being integrated into a national criminal information network, which would link its system to the criminal information systems that were being planned by the states. However, the spring 1969 decision to construct an information system for the agency consumed many of its resources and diverted its attention away from the construction of such a network. These two projects diverged because the Federal Criminal Police were structurally incapable of taking the lead in the construction of a national criminal information system and lacking any institutional incentive to do so. Since the establishment of the Federal Criminal Police, the criminalistic energy and expertise of the agency been sapped by its subsidiary role, which had prevented it from becoming more than what one police official disparagingly called a "mere post office agency" (*reine Briefkastenbehörde*).[3] Although it made little sense to intensify and accelerate the information flowing through the Federal Criminal Police unless the agency were allowed to play a more active role in investigating offenses of national importance and engaging in operative work to track down suspects, the states jealously guarded their prerogatives in this domain.

This unsatisfactory arrangement was not altered until the early 1970s. While the decision that was taken in the winter of 1971/72 to construct the national criminal information system INPOL was due in no small part to Herold's appointment as head of the Federal Criminal Police, it was also part of a cluster of security measures implemented between 1971 and 1973 in response to the perceived threats posed by the New Left, political extremism, and the first acts of domestic terrorism. The SPD/FDP coalition initially understood crime as a social problem and sought to promote internal security through social reform. At the same time, however, the coalition regarded improved policing as the key to meeting the terrorist challenge without abandoning the rule of law, and the measures adopted in the early 1970s collectively created the precondition for the administrative and criminalistic modernization of the Federal Criminal Police and the expansion of its authority, especially in combatting terrorism and organized crime, across the 1970s.

The history of police informatics has historically been linked, both rightly and wrongly, to Herold personally. The account below will show that the West German police had been interested in the use of electronic data processing for criminalistic purposes since at least 1965/66. On the other hand, Herold himself was one of the leading figures in the field during this early period, and, before being chosen by Genscher to lead the Federal Criminal Police into the computer age, he had earned a national reputation for his innovative use of computers as head of the Nuremberg police. It was Herold who ultimately provided the vision for the construction of INPOL and the energy to ensure that this high-profile project was completed on time.

Most of those who supported the use of electronic data processing by the police did so because they believed that computers would increase the speed, accuracy, and efficiency with which the police carried out their traditional record-keeping and information exchange tasks. In contrast, Herold believed that computers would revolutionize the work of the police, and he regarded the systems that were being developed in the late 1960s and then built out in the first half of the 1970s as the precondition for the full exploitation of the new technology, not as the fulfillment of a limited vision of greater administrative efficiency. He believed that the use of the new information technologies to analyze the information held by the police would lead to the discovery of the social causes of crime, and he expected that in the foreseeable future these technologies would make it possible for the police to engage in the primary prevention of crime, rather than its post facto repression, that they would shift the day-to-day work of detectives from the collection of evidence at the crime scene to its analysis at the computer terminal, and that they would alter both the organization of the police and its position in the political system of the Federal Republic. Herold was deeply influenced by cybernetics, and he believed that many of these changes would follow in a quasi-automatic manner once the existing police information system had been freed from its bureaucratic fetters, computerized, and transformed into a mechanism for disseminating criminal information to the periphery, where investigations and operative measures would generate feedback that would lead to the continuous optimization of the work of the police. However, as we shall see in this and later chapters, Herold's imagination constantly exceeded both available technologies and the support of his political allies and made him into the most visible target for critics of the new police surveillance.

Militant Democracy and Internal Security

I would like to begin this chapter with an account of the history of internal security in West Germany from the founding of the country to the mid-1970s. The police are, together with the domestic intelligence agencies, the cornerstone of the internal security apparatus of any state, and an account of the organization of the police, the perceived nature of the threats to internal security, and the methods adopted to combat these threats will enable me to show how civil liberties and state power were balanced during these years. This will also provide the context needed to understand the developments to be recounted in this and the following chapters.

For the men and women who met in the summer and fall of 1948 to draft a constitution, the security and stability of the country depended on drawing the proper lessons from the demise of the Weimar Republic. They were divided along party lines as to whether granting extensive emergency powers to the executive would pose a greater danger to the new democracy than the internal unrest against which these powers were intended to protect. On the other hand, they were united in the belief that, unlike the Weimar Republic, the Federal Republic had to be a "militant democracy" capable of protecting itself against those who might misuse the fundamental rights guaranteed by the Basic Law to undermine the "free, democratic order."[4]

The Allies had originally viewed unregenerate Nazis as the greatest threat to the security of the new state and had taken steps to exclude those who had been directly implicated in the crimes of the regime from public life. However, de-Nazification was both contentious and ineffectual, and after 1949 the Adenauer administration was committed to the reintegration of those former Nazis who demonstrated their loyalty to the new democracy. A May 1951 law allowed all former civil servants who had not been classified as war criminals or as persons who otherwise bore personal responsibility for Nazi policies to return to public employment at their previous rank, and by the mid-1950s a substantial proportion of the leading positions in the security agencies and the relevant departments of the interior ministry were occupied by men who had played important roles in the Nazi security apparatus. Their wartime activities would not come back to haunt them until the 1960s.[5]

The authors of the Basic Law were equally concerned about communism, and, together, the reintegration of those right-wing critics of democracy, who were willing to pledge nominal allegiance to the new state, if not to its democratic ideals, and the deepening of the Cold War transformed the anti-subversion provisions of the Basic Law into a weapon that was directed almost exclusively against the Left. In September 1951, the cabinet adopted a resolution declaring membership in a number of communist organizations (as well as the neo-Nazi Socialist Reich Party) to be incompatible with the requirement that, in all aspects of their lives, civil servants had to demonstrate an active commitment to the democratic order.[6] In November 1951 an amendment to the Criminal Code opened the door to the prosecution of virtually any communist-related activity. And that same month the administration invoked a provision of the Basic Law, which allowed it—with the approval of the Constitutional Court—to restrict the rights of those engaged in anti-constitutional activities, and asked the Constitutional Court to ban the Communist Party, a request that was finally approved in April 1956. The problem with this approach is that it subordinated the substantive meaning of democracy and the rule of law to the security of the state and rendered politically invisible the resulting restrictions on individual rights.[7] This structural imbalance between civil liberties and the professed security needs of the state was the defining feature of the postwar internal security regime and an essential element of the settlement that Eckart Conze had in mind when he observed that what was sought in the 1950s was less a free political and social order than one that could offer security against the communist threat.[8]

For the victorious Allies, the concentration of police power in the hands of the SS was one of the most palpable symbols of Nazi totalitarianism, and in the American and British occupation zones the devolution of responsibility for policing to local government—with state officials possessing only attenuated supervisory authority, but no central control, over local police forces—was an important element of their plan to democratize German society.[9] In the assembly convened to draft the country's postwar constitution, the debate over the respective virtues of federalism and centralism spilled over into the domain of policing.[10] While most of the delegates opposed the communalization of the police and called instead for the re-creation of the state-level police agencies that had existed before 1933, opinion was divided over how best to coordinate the pursuit of those offenders who were active across state lines. Although a small number of Bavarian federalists argued that state police forces were capable of collaborating directly with one another without the need for a national police agency, both the SPD and most of the CDU wished to give more extensive police powers to the federal government. However, the Allied powers retained the last word in such matters, and the uncertainty that hovered over these issues was finally dispelled in April 1949, when, against the background of the deepening Cold War, the military governors of the three occupation zones issued a joint memorandum (the so-called *Polizeibrief*), which permitted the federal government to establish a police agency—the Federal Criminal Police, which will be one of the central institutional actors in part III—to collect and disseminate information on criminal offenders, gather statistics, and coordinate the investigation of offenses against federal laws, but which prohibited the agency from issuing orders to state and local police.[11] The Allied memorandum also permitted the establishment of an intelligence agency to collect information on subversive activities directed against the federal government. This was the origin of the Domestic Intelligence Agency and of the separation rule discussed in chapter 5.

By the mid-1950s, the states had largely succeeded in reasserting their control over the local police.[12] However, the criminal police were only one component of the internal security apparatus of the early Federal Republic. Politicians and security officials alike remained fixated on the communist threat, which was the hinge between internal and external security. They feared that communist infiltrators and agitators could instrumentalize political and industrial unrest to open the door to an incursion by the militarized police units (the Volkspolizei) that had been established by the East German government, and through the entire decade internal security would be conceptualized almost exclusively in relation to such states of exception, rather than the problems of ordinary crime.[13]

The outbreak of the Korean War drove these fears to new heights. Three days after the North Korean invasion of the South, the Allied High Commission permitted the states to create a 10,000-man riot police (*Bereitschaftspolizei*). However, officials maintained that the decentralization of the riot police at the state level and the debilitating fragmentation of the uniformed constabulary (the *Schutzpolizei*) at the communal level made it impossible to marshal the forces that would be required to put down any large-scale unrest that threatened either the federal government or those of the individual states. The danger was rendered more acute by the absence of both an army as a force of last resort and legislation that would permit the federal government to assert central control over the local police in case of national emergency.[14]

In March 1951, the Bundesrat approved the creation of a 10,000-man Federal Border Police (*Bundesgrenzschutz*) to at least partially fill this gap. The Border Police was superfluous for its nominal task because the border was already patrolled by the customs service, which reported to the finance ministry, and no more than a small fraction of its members were ever involved in policing the movement of people and vehicles across the border. In reality, the Border Police functioned as a military force that provided the federal government with an instrument for defending against armed civil conflicts and producing that violence that Adenauer and his security officials considered essential to the existence of a proper state. Into the second half of the 1960s, the role of the police continued to be understood primarily in terms of protecting against the threat of subversion from within in order to ensure that the country would be able to protect itself against communist aggression from without, and the Border Police remained a hybrid militarized police until the early 1970s.[15]

The formation of the Grand Coalition made it possible for the administration to secure the two-thirds majority in the Bundestag required to modify the Basic Law and add the emergency provisions that could not be agreed on by the Parliamentary Council in 1949. The passage of these laws persuaded the Allies to relinquish their rights to intervene in West German domestic affairs and opened the way to the demilitarization of both the Border Police and internal security policy more generally. The Emergency Laws were also a major catalyst for the formation of the country's extraparliamentary opposition, which arose in that space on the political left that had been left vacant when the SPD joined the Grand Coalition, and the parliamentary consideration of the Emergency Laws served as a rallying point for the movement between 1966 and 1968.[16]

But the focus of internal security and the attendant balancing of civil liberties and state authority also shifted in other, equally fundamental, ways during these years. The SPD and the social-liberal wing of the FDP viewed ordinary crime as a social problem, and they believed that the social policy measures included in their domestic reform program would enhance internal security in ways that were very different from both the anti-communism of the 1950s and the law and order rhetoric of the contemporary conservative opposition. In the later words of Hamburg Interior Senator Werner Staak (SPD), internal security involved more than combatting crime and protecting citizens and their property against diverse dangers. It was also a "social concept" that was "based on . . . the creation of domestic peace, which was to be achieved through the provision and guarantee of equality of opportunity and rights and through social security." However, this security was endangered by much more than rising crime rates and a growing number of motor vehicle accidents. "The refusal of social security, the diminution of the quality of life through environmental damage, and the misuse of economic power under the appearance of law," he noted, "undermine domestic peace. Only one who brings about equality of opportunity and equality before the law contributes to internal security."[17]

The problem is that this account of the welfarist reconfiguration of internal security articulates poorly with the actual development of the police and their surveillance capacity in the 1970s because at the very moment when criminal policy was making this preventive, social turn, internal security was being repoliticized in response to the New Left and, later, left-wing terrorism, which challenged both the authority of the state and the legitimacy of the social order.

This is not the place to explore the origins, history, and legacy of that sprawling, multidimensional social movement that is alternatively known as the New Left, the extraparliamentary opposition, the anti-authoritarian movement, the student movement, or simply "1968." However, the failure of the New Left to block the passage of the Emergency Laws led to the fragmentation of the movement. In the aftermath, those who retained their faith in social revolution gravitated toward the centralized, mostly Maoist communist parties—known collectively as the "K-Groups"—in their search for a revolutionary subject. A far larger number flooded into the reformist SPD and its youth organizations, thereby setting the stage for a decade-long struggle between an older party leadership, whose political worldview had been shaped by their conflicts with the communists both before 1933 and after 1945, and its younger, more radical members. Those who were more interested in seeking self-realization and community than in party-based social revolution pursued a broad spectrum of activities that were later known collectively as the "alternative" movement. And while the K-Groups generally shied away from political radicalism in favor of theoretical navel-gazing and fruitless attempts to convince the working classes of the merits of their particular brands of communism, a relatively small number—at most 1,000–2,000 persons, including active members and their supporters—turned to terrorism in hopes of effecting fundamental social and political change.[18] The most important of these groups, which in the early 1970s crystallized around Andreas Baader, Ulrike Meinhof, Gudrun Ensslin, and Horst Mahler, was the Red Army Faction (RAF). The three other main terrorist groups were the Socialist Patients Collective, the June 2 Movement, and the Revolutionary Cells.[19]

Although the social protest of the New Left was a global phenomenon, the peculiar intensity of the conflict in West Germany derived from the role of terrorism as a mechanism for mastering the country's Nazi past. As Jeremy Varon has argued, the escalation of the Vietnam War after 1964 had a complex radicalizing effect on the West German New Left, which came to see the struggle against American imperialism as a way of contesting what they regarded as the fascist tendencies of their own society and, at the same time, making good for the moral failings of the generation of their parents, whose continued support for the war was regarded an unrecognized extension of their own unexpiated complicity in the crimes of the Nazi regime. The media-fueled identification of the radical left with national liberation struggles in the periphery, their belief in the obligation to contest the structural violence of capitalism, the search for an Archimedean point from which to overturn the totalitarian one-dimensionality of the consumerism that anchored the fortunes of the First World to those of the Third, the faith that the redemption of the world from the imperialist plague depended on the intensity of the urban guerilla struggle in the metropole, and an increasingly abstract view of the world, which all too easily reduced real lives to ciphers in the abstract logic of history, drove left-wing terrorism, and the RAF in particular, toward a form of violence that was no less murderous than that from which they were trying to redeem the nation.[20]

But the psychic structures of politicians and security officials were also shaped by their experience of the Weimar Republic and the Third Reich,[21] and their commitment to militant democracy led them to maintain that terrorism represented such a threat to the stability and security of the Federal Republic that they were required to make use of all available means to combat this danger if they themselves were not to be guilty of the same democratic weaknesses as the parties of the Weimar Republic. The result was a spiral of violence and counterviolence, which again raised the question that had originally vexed the Parliamentary Council: could a democracy successfully turn back such an exceptional threat without turning its back on the central tenets of the democratic order?

The most important step taken in the early 1970s to protect the state—and through it, the democratic order—from the threat of political extremism was the Radicals Resolution, which was adopted by Brandt and the minister presidents of the federal states on 28 January 1972. In its substance, the decree did not go beyond the September 1951 loyalty decree approved under Adenauer. It represented an attempt to hinder the "long march through the institutions" of the Federal Republic that had been called for by Rudi Dutschke, the brilliant and charismatic leader of the Socialist German Students Association. The Radicals Resolution was controversial for a number of reasons: it asserted in a very public manner the authority of the state to abridge the constitutional rights of civil servants (most importantly, the rights to free expression and political engagement); the decision to inquire into the loyalty of every applicant for public employment led to the investigation of a substantial proportion of the younger generation—1.3 million persons by 1978—by the domestic intelligence agencies; and the resolution appeared to turn the rule of law on its head by promising individual scrutiny, while basing the review process on the prejudicial presumption that mere membership in supposedly anti-constitutional parties gave rise to sufficient doubt regarding the loyalty of the applicant to justify the rejection of the person's application. The program, which entangled those whom the intelligence agencies deemed potential threats in a review process that derived in equal parts from Orwell, Kafka, and Koestler, alienated the younger generation, discredited West German democracy in the eyes of the world public, and added fuel to the debate over the surveillance state. In 1978–79 the federal government and those states governed by the SDP-FDP coalition abandoned the 1972 resolution in favor of a more liberal policy, which called for investigations only in exceptional cases, affirmed the presumption of loyalty, and provided more extensive procedural safeguards for those whose loyalty was called into question.[22]

The history of left-wing terrorism in West Germany has been well told by others, and the goal of part III is, instead, to recount the less well-known story of state counterterrorism policies, the role of information and computerization in these measures, and the privacy conflicts that they raised. However, it is important to at least briefly review the history of terrorism because it provides the chronology and context for the argument to follow.

In retrospect, the first act of left-wing terrorism in West Germany was the firebombing of two Frankfurt department stores by Baader, Ensslin, Thorwald Proll, and Horst Söhnlein on the night of 2–3 April 1968.[23] The four were convicted in October of that year, but were released in June 1969 pending the outcome of their appeal, which was rejected in November. While Söhnlein reported to serve the remainder of his sentence, Baader, Ensslin, and Proll went underground and escaped to Paris. Although they were soon joined by Proll's sister Astrid, Proll himself left the group and later turned himself in to police. Baader was arrested in April 1970, but, during an outing to the Central Institute for Social Questions in the Dahlem district of Berlin, he was "liberated" from police custody on 14 May by a commando that included, among others, Ensslin and the radicalized journalist Ulrike Meinhof. The following month, the group published a declaration in the radical journal *Agit 883* calling on the proletariat to mobilize for class struggle and "build up the Red Army." Across 1971, the group staged a number of bank robberies to procure the money needed to finance their life on the run and engaged in shootouts with the growing number of policemen seeking to arrest them.[24] Although the RAF justified its existence with reference to Marx, Lenin, and Mao, the group made a virtue of its theoretical threadbareness by insisting on the "primacy of practice"—a doctrine that reflected their belief that acts of terrorism would bring a revolutionary situation into existence, rather than give expression to existing social contradictions. In April 1971, they distilled their tactical ideas in a sixteen-page paper titled "The Urban Guerilla Concept."[25]

Although the police had little trouble identifying the likely perpetrators of these actions, they were initially much less successful in tracking them down, and they were unable to prevent the RAF from carrying out a series of bombings—known as the "May Offensive"—in May 1972. On 31 May, the special investigatory commission that had been established within the Federal Criminal Police to investigate the offenses committed by the Baader-Meinhof group worked together with the regional investigative commissions established by the states in a coordinated nationwide action known as "Operation Wasserschlag," which mobilized all of the country's police under the direction of the Federal Criminal Police. Border Police helicopters were used to ferry officers to flying checkpoints; other officers established checkpoints along every major road and rail route and conducted raids of known haunts of RAF members; and approximately sixty suspicious "objects" were placed under surveillance. The action, which could never have been carried out on such a scale without centralized coordination, was surprisingly successful. The next morning Baader, Jan-Carl Raspe, who most likely constructed the bombs used in the May offensive, and Holger Meins, another of the original members of the group, were captured in Frankfurt as they sought to enter an apartment that was under police observation. Clues gathered there led to the capture of eight more RAF members over the following six weeks. These arrests weakened the group to the point that its continued existence seemed unlikely.[26]

The history of the RAF has been written in terms of three successive generations. The members of the first generation, along with a number of members of the Socialist Patients Collective, are shown in the famous wanted poster (figure 6.1) from the early 1970s. In addition to helping finance their lives on the run, RAF violence served to demonstrate the weakness of the state, hold its individual agents responsible for their "crimes," provoke the security agencies into revealing their hidden fascist proclivities, and, at least in theory, resolve the endless search for a revolutionary subject.

Although violence declined in 1973/74, this lull was actually a gestational period that by the end of 1974 had given birth to the second generation of the RAF, whose members had been radicalized by their involvement in the anti-torture and prisoners' rights committees founded to protest the conditions under which incarcerated RAF members were being held, by the passage of a packet of laws intended to prevent RAF members from disrupting their forthcoming trial (scheduled to begin in May 1975), and by the death of Meins on 9 November 1974 after a two-month hunger strike. Across the second half of the 1970s, the activities of the second generation increasingly focused on the all-consuming goal of freeing the incarcerated members of the founding generation.

The assassination of Berlin superior court judge Günter von Drenkmann by the June 2 Movement the day after the death of Meins was the first act in a new wave of political violence—one that would not crest until the fall of 1977. The first major action after the killing of Drenkmann came in February 1975, when the CDU Berlin mayoral candidate Peter Lorenz was kidnapped by members of the June 2 Movement. Lorenz was freed a week later in exchange for the release of five members of the group, who were permitted to fly to Yemen. However, even before six members of the RAF, calling themselves the Kommando Holger Meins, stormed the West

Figure 6.1. Wanted persons poster: "Violent anarchists—the Baader-Meinhof Band" (ca. 1970–72). Source: Bundesarchiv, Plak. 006-001-058.

German embassy in Stockholm on 24 April in a disastrous attempt to force the German government to release Baader, Meinhof, Ensslin, and twenty-three other RAF prisoners, the administration had resolved not to succumb to such pressure in the future. After two German officials had been killed by the group to demonstrate their resolve, the embassy siege ended abruptly in failure and confusion when an RAF member accidentally set off one of the bombs that they had planted.

In May 1976, Meinhof hanged herself in her cell in the modern, high-security prison in the Stammheim district of Stuttgart, where the leaders of the RAF were imprisoned during their trial, and, in April 1977, Baader, Ensslin, and Raspe were given life sentences on numerous charges. On 7 April, shortly before these sentences were handed down, attorney general Siegfried Buback was assassinated in Karlsruhe. These sentences ratcheted up the pressure on the remaining members of the RAF to free their comrades. On 30 July, Dresdener Bank chairman Jürgen Ponto was killed in an unsuccessful kidnapping attempt, and on 25 August a rocket attack on the attorney general's office in Karlsruhe went awry when the launcher failed to function properly. This chain of events culminated with the kidnapping of industrialist Hanns Martin Schleyer on 5 September.

The Schleyer kidnapping set in motion a six-week national trauma known as the "German Autumn." As both a former member of the SS and a living symbol of the capitalist order, Schleyer embodied for the Left all of the historical continuities and moral failings of the country's founding generation. Pressure on the West German government was increased even further on 13 October, when a group of Palestinian terrorists collaborating with the RAF hijacked a Lufthansa flight, which was ultimately flown to Mogadishu, the capital of Somalia. However, on the night of 17–18 October, all of the passengers and crew (with the exception of the pilot, who had been shot two days before) were rescued by the elite counterterrorism group GSG 9, which had been formed after the Palestinian attack on Israeli athletes at the 1972 Olympic games. That night, under the watchful eyes of Baden-Württemberg police and prison authorities, who must have known about both the weapons that had been smuggled into their cells and their plans, Baader, Ensslin, and Raspe took their own lives in an act of collective suicide that they hoped would be understood as an act of political murder by a vengeful state. Schleyer's body was found the next day in the trunk of a car in the French city of Mulhouse.

Despite the fierceness of the public debate over terrorism and state violence in West Germany, the recent literature has emphasized the unexceptionality of the country's counterterrorism policies in comparison with those of other West European countries.[27] There is a debate over whether government actions during the Schleyer kidnapping constituted a state of exception.²⁸ Although the rule of law may have been bent, Karrin Hanshew has argued that the modernization of the police, democratic political education, and the judicious use of force by the Social Democratic government finally made it possible to move beyond the concerns that had shaped internal security policy in the postwar era: conservatives came to see that a democratic state could protect itself without having to place excessive power in the hands of an unrestrained executive; the Social Democrats abandoned their previous reservations regarding state power; and the extraparliamentary left reconciled itself with the democratic system and began to explore the possibilities of nonviolent political and cultural engagement.²⁹ As we shall see in chapters 7–9, the extension of privacy protection law to the police and the intelligence services marked in yet another way the end of the postwar era of internal security.

The Federal Criminal Police and Its Files

The law establishing the Federal Criminal Police was approved in March 1951. In addition to Allied concerns about the abuse of power by a national police force and the insistence by the states on retaining control over their security forces, the basic criminalistic rationale for the federalist decentralization of policing was the belief that most crime was local, that the states would coordinate the prosecution of offenses committed within their own borders, and that therefore a national agency was needed only in a subsidiary capacity to coordinate the pursuit of a small residuum of mobile, habitual, and particularly dangerous offenders. Consequently, the law established a Federal Criminal Police *office* to provide this coordination, but not a federal criminal police *force*. This new agency was responsible for collecting and analyzing information relating to crimes whose significance extended beyond the borders of the state where they were committed, providing the states with intelligence relating to connections between crimes that would not have been visible to these agencies on their own, and maintaining fingerprint and mug shot files, as well as forensic laboratories. Although the subsidiary nature of the federal police was reinforced by the fact that the law reserved the prevention and the investigation of crime to the states, it did permit the Federal Criminal Police to investigate specific crimes if state officials asked the agency to take over the case or if the federal interior minister ordered it to do so for "important" reasons.³⁰

In this section I will argue that the history of two of the information systems on which the Federal Criminal Police relied to carry out these responsibilities—the file of crimes and criminals compiled from the National Crime Reporting System, on the one hand, and the wanted persons and stolen objects files, on the other—illustrate with particular clarity the ways in which available information technologies limited the administrative power of the agency.[31]

The National Crime Reporting System employed by the West German police had taken shape conceptually and administratively in the 1920s and 1930s.[32] It rested on two fundamental criminalistic doctrines, which were restated in the preamble to the Federal Criminal Police law. In contrast to the criminal of opportunity, who was tempted into criminal actions by external circumstances and whose activities remained limited to a narrow geographical region, the preamble defined the professional or habitual criminal (*Berufsverbrecher*), who was to be the proper object of concern of the federal police agency, as a person who

> is driven by his disposition [or psychological constitution; *Veranlagung*] to seek out the opportunity to commit a crime. He specializes in specific types of crime, and he commits them using a modus operandi that remains consistent in its details. He persists in these habits; this is the principle of perseverance. Freed from the chains of middle-class life, he lives out his impulses and is not bound to a single locale. He seeks out the metropolis in order to disappear and dispose of his ill-gotten goods. He is active translocally as a mobile offender.[33]

The National Crime Reporting System was designed primarily to combat the dangers believed to emanate from this criminal-biological construct.

On the one hand, the system was built around the concept of perseverance. It was based on the assumption that, through the commission of crimes, career criminals acquired certain kinds of knowledge and developed certain mental and physical skills, that—once perfected—the possession of this knowledge and skill set provided criminals with a powerful incentive to continue to commit the same offense (or at least similar ones) using a distinctive modus operandi, and that a well-designed and sufficiently discriminating classificatory schema would enable the police to identify the perseverant modus operandi that was unique to any given criminal.[34] The reporting system followed the Criminal Code in dividing the criminal universe into major classes (capital offenses, theft, fraud, etc.), which were in turn divided into groups and subgroups.

On the other hand, it was also conceived as a response to the peculiar impulsiveness of the habitual offender, which manifested itself in both the mobility of these persons and their propensity to commit more serious crimes than those committed by the criminal of opportunity. The Federal Criminal Police Law used specific characteristics of the habitual or professional criminal (geographical mobility across state lines and the national relevance of the more serious offenses characteristic of this group) to legitimate, and delimit, the authority of the agency. Nevertheless, by the beginning of the 1960s, the expansion of both the workload of the Federal Criminal Police and the size of its files had begun to reveal the conceptual and practical limitations of the National Crime Reporting System in the age of paper.[35]

Although the rigid taxonomy employed by the police predetermined what evidence could and could not be considered relevant, every strategy proposed to compensate for this limit multiplied the amount of information to be processed. In the analog world, it was impossible to record each and every characteristic that might later be used to identify a distinctive modus operandi, and the use of these classifications reduced both the amount of information that had to be collected and the number of past offenses to which new crimes had to be compared. However, every new subgroup that was created to more finely distinguish one modus operandi from another increased both the complexity of the system and the information processing burden on its users. For example, the Berlin police divided the category of con artists into forty-eight subcategories that were physically denoted through the use of metal tabs of differing shape and color placed in specific locations. Even though this mechanism required the user to remember the meaning of the specific location, color, and shape of each of the tabs, this number of subclassifications was still not large enough to capture all of the distinct modi operandi employed by such offenders. In addition, while the existence of fixed classifications made it difficult for detectives to think across classificatory borders if they were unable to match a crime to a known modus operandi within the category to which it was believed to belong, adding cross-references to other closely related categories multiplied the number of cards to be examined.[36]

The steady growth in both the absolute number of crimes being reported and the number of distinct ways in which this information needed to be combined, sorted, and compared exceeded the memory and mental capacities of even the most skilled detective. The early supporters of police informatics argued that these comparisons could be carried out efficiently, accurately, and without mental fatigue by punched cards or computers if the relevant information could be properly coded. Their mantra was that, in contrast to manual files, which could only be sorted and analyzed according to a single criterion, the value of electronic data processing lay in the fact that it could analyze large quantities of modus operandi data in different combinations in a single run.[37]

These issues had real world consequences for the Federal Criminal Police, whose effectiveness declined perceptibly between the mid-1950s and the mid-1960s.[38] The reasons for this decline were documented in an audit of the agency's organization and operations, which was conducted by the interior ministry in 1965. The audit, which was led by Ministerialrat Alfred Faude, attributed some of the agency's problems to the "lethargy" that crept in all too easily when detectives were bound to their desks and deprived of the opportunity to hone their skills through field investigations and crime scene work. The report also noted how the growing number of serious offenders was imposing burdens on the Federal Criminal Police that the agency was not equipped to meet.[39]

The audit found the division responsible for managing incoming crime reports to be in deplorable condition. The ballooning number of crimes that were deemed as being of national relevance had led to the creation of subclasses that were so bloated—some containing more than 3,000 cards—that they could not be analyzed systematically, even if the detectives had not been so occupied with the clerical maintenance of these files that they had little time to focus on their criminalistic responsibilities.

There were also backlogs in every area because the individual detectives responsible for maintaining the files relating to specific (sub)classifications were frequently absent due to sickness, vacation, or temporary reassignment to night or weekend duty—or even to guard duty at the agency's office. The problems of the department were also attributable in part to the reporting practices of the state criminal police agencies, which sometimes overburdened the federal police with indiscriminate reporting, while at other times failing to report crimes of obvious national importance. In turn, the limited intelligence provided by the federal police diminished the interest of the state agencies in ensuring the completeness and accuracy of the information that they did report. The result was a vicious circle in which the limited effectiveness of the Federal Criminal Police was both cause and consequence of the poor quality of the information available to it.[40]

The audit concluded that the methods currently employed to organize and analyze the information held in the agency's files would not in the long run result in a satisfactory clearance rate. The only proposed reform that the report found promising was the plan to supplement the existing crime reporting system, which was organized exclusively around the crime and the modus operandi employed in its commission, with information relating to the perpetrator. However, the auditors noted that such a reform, which would have required the collection and processing of even more information, could not be implemented on the basis of manual information technologies; only the introduction of automated data processing could "eliminate the dilemma currently faced by the National Crime Reporting System."[41]

The agency also maintained a central list of suspects, accused persons, convicted offenders, and missing persons. The serial numbers assigned to these cards were used as identifiers for the agency's fingerprint and investigatory files. The number of cards contained in this central persons file was also growing rapidly during these years. It increased from 990,000 in 1955 to 1,661,000 in 1960 to 2,115,000 in 1964. The maintenance of this file was so labor intensive, the audit noted, not simply because of the number of records, but also because the staff had to spend so much of its time determining whether a person was already listed in the agency's file and, if so, his or her file number. The department's workload, the audit estimated, could be reduced by 25 percent simply by requiring that this number be used in all correspondence.

The other major division of the Federal Criminal Police, whose information processing system is of relevance in the present context, was the one responsible for maintaining lists of wanted persons and stolen objects. The procedures for producing these lists was a model of redundancy, fragmentation, disorganization, bureaucratic ponderousness, and technological limitation. They were compiled on the basis of warrants issued by the state police agencies and submitted by post or teletype to the Federal Criminal Police headquarters in Wiesbaden. Part of the reason these lists was so long was that there was no mechanism for integrating the different lists or eliminating multiple entries submitted by different police agencies at different times for different purposes. Bulletins were published monthly, but the manual production process was so slow that by the time they reached local police the information they contained was four to six weeks out of date.[42]

The officers employed in this division were so overburdened by processing new warrants and renewing or deleting old ones that they had little time to provide the states with advice on where these persons might actually be found. In addition, the bulletins were so large that they were difficult to use. For example, the November 1967 wanted persons bulletin contained 75,000 names in 887 closely printed pages. In theory, the local population registries were to regularly compare the entire bulletin to their own files. However, this was such a tedious and time-consuming activity that it inevitably got pushed to the bottom of the stack. For obvious reasons, the wanted persons and stolen objects files were a high priority when the police began to automate their systems at the end of the decade.

The audit had been carried out to evaluate a request by the agency for more professional staff. Although the auditors concluded that the agency's work was indeed being hindered by the inability to fill a large number of positions, they also insisted that the agency did not need to hire additional detectives because many officers were employed in activities that could more properly be carried out by civilian civil servants or clerks. Most of the recommendations made by the auditors were met with a deaf ear by

Paul Dickopf. Dickopf, who embodied all of the problematic continuities between the Third Reich and the security agencies of the early Federal Republic, had played a pivotal role in the founding of the Federal Criminal Police; he had served as de facto vice-president since 1953; and he had been appointed president in January 1965.[43] In a 210-page response, Dickopf argued that virtually all of the proposed changes in the organizational structure of the agency and its internal information flows would cause more problems than they would solve and that, in any case, it would be impossible to put them into practice without first hiring more staff. He also warned against proposals to make use of new office technologies, including electronic data processing, because he suspected that they would "in all likelihood entail organizational repercussions that cannot yet be foreseen." Dickopf's counterproposal was the direct opposite of the strategy proposed by the auditors: instead of improving the work of the agency through organizational and administrative reform (including computerization), Dickopf argued that the best strategy was to "leave the existing organizational structures unchanged until the overall conditions have improved."[44]

By the second half of the decade, politicians, the public, and even the police themselves were coming to doubt whether the Federal Criminal Police was capable of performing its appointed tasks. Already in 1966, one newspaper had spoken of the "criminalistic bankruptcy" of the federal police, which it attributed to the reluctance of the agency and its president to embrace the new technologies.[45] Dickopf's skepticism regarding the possibility of automating the modus operandi system was not unfounded.[46] However, his predilection for traditional ways of doing things was well known, and Willi Weyer (FDP), the interior minister of North Rhineland-Westphalia, described him as a "brake shoe" slowing the modernization of the agency.[47] As Herold harshly judged from a later vantage point, the failure to modernize the agency's information processing technologies had brought it to the verge of operational paralysis: "The steadily growing information avalanche got caught and suffocated—incapable of being analyzed—in outdated manual card files and filing systems, in outdated wanted bulletins and files. Valuable equipment and confidential papers had to be stored in corridors and hallways [as shown in figure 6.2]. The shortage of usable space was of catastrophic proportions."[48]

Integrated Solutions and a National Network

Although the information management problems faced by the Federal Criminal Police may have been particularly acute, the state criminal police agencies and the police departments of a number of the nation's larger

Figure 6.2. Fingerprint files stored in the stairwell of the Federal Criminal Police (1970). Bundesarchiv, B131/Bild-01425-027.

cities were also keenly interested in using electronic data processing to rationalize their work and — to use the dominant metaphor of the period — "intensify" their crime-fighting efforts. This interest cannot be traced back to a single origin. However, by 1965–66 it had reached a critical mass, and the decision to construct an integrated criminal information system for the entire country was made by the end of the latter year.

In West Germany's federalist system, the central body for the coordination of domestic policy was the Conference of State and Federal Interior Ministers, whose resolutions, which were negotiated at the group's regular meetings, would either be implemented independently by the ministers in their respective states or, if necessary, become the object of coordinated consideration by the state legislatures. In matters pertaining to public security, the work of the Conference was supported by a committee known as Working Group II, which was made up of senior officials in the security departments of the state and federal interior ministries. Like the Conference, this group was a political body, whose reports and recommendations provided the basis for the deliberations of the interior ministers. Working Group II was itself supported by the Working Group Kripo (i.e., *Kriminalpolizei*), which was composed of the heads of the federal and state criminal police agencies. This group provided the policy makers in

Working Group II with expertise in the area of policing. All of these bodies will play important roles in this and the following chapters.

In the summer of 1965, the Conference of Interior Ministers charged Working Group II with developing proposals for making crime fighting more effective, and, in conjunction with this task, the following summer the group established a commission on electronic data processing, which was to develop a plan for the deployment of the new technologies by the criminal police. In the report that it submitted in December of that year, which drew on input from eight leading computer manufacturers, the commission argued in sweeping terms that the full potential of the new technologies could not be realized if electronic data processing were employed only to meet the information processing needs of geographically limited police districts, or even those of the individual federal states, or if it were used to build stand-alone systems to meet the discrete information processing needs of the police. Instead of such partial solutions, the commission argued that the goal should be a fully integrated system for all of the state and federal police forces. Such a system was necessary, the report continued, "because crime fighting can only be significantly intensified through the use of electronic data processing if *all* of the data on persons, objects and crimes that has heretofore been held in separate collections and card files of all different areas can be analyzed in *every* state and by the Federal Criminal Police." Not only would this integrated system have to link local police districts, state police forces, the Federal Criminal Police, and Interpol; it would also have to include those civilian offices, such as the population registration offices, motor vehicle registration offices, and the Central Aliens Registry, that held information the police needed to carry out their responsibilities. The computer systems maintained by all of these different agencies would have to be connected using the new communication technologies, rather than through the transfer of computer tapes, because this was the only way to establish real time access. The proposed system would also have to be interoperable, scalable, redundant, secure, and capable of timesharing.[49]

At the same time that the commission was preparing its report, many of the states were themselves establishing committees to determine how their own police agencies could make use of electronic data processing.[50] These committees immediately focused on the potential of, and the obstacles to, data integration. The Bavarians explained that one consequence of the decentralization of police authority was that

> Many local card files containing basically the same content must still be maintained. This is the only way to satisfy the informational needs of the individual police districts. With the exception of Munich, these are all manual card files,

which can only be retrieved and analyzed according to a single criterion. This means that it is necessary, even at the local level, to maintain numerous card files side-by-side containing the same information, but ordered according to different criteria.

Similarly, officials in North Rhineland-Westphalia noted that the main obstacle to the creation of an integrated criminal information system was the fact that the central persons files maintained by the various police forces were organized in forty or fifty different ways. Integrated data processing presupposed, they concluded, the adoption of uniform data record structures and collection procedures.[51]

In Bavaria, Herold convinced state officials that, before any work was begun on a state criminal information system, it was necessary to determine what such a system was supposed to achieve, how it was to function, and how it was to be integrated into the national criminal information system that had been proposed by the commission, and in December 1966 — at the very moment when the commission submitted its report — Herold presented a plan for such a system.[52] He began by arguing that, instead of developing electronic data processing systems that would enable existing organizations to function more efficiently, these organizations should themselves be reorganized to conform to the inner logic and functioning of the new machines. "This necessary reversal of the problems that have arisen," he followed, "will lead to novel insights and to the renunciation of previous work techniques and inherited thought processes. In many areas this makes it necessary to reorganize things from the bottom up." The implications of this line of thought could be summed up, he concluded (in a variation on Marx), in the idea that "electronic being determines the consciousness of the police" (*Das maschinelle Sein bestimmt das polizeiliche Bewusstsein*).

Since the beginning of the decade, the police had applied electronic data processing in four main areas: the maintenance of internal lists of such things as crimes, investigations, and traffic offenses; the administration of payroll and property; tracking wanted persons and stolen objects; and, lastly, the comparative labor involved in the analysis of crime reports. However, Herold regarded all of these efforts to automate routine administrative tasks as so much brush that would have to be cleared away before one could even begin to understand that the real importance of computers was to be found not in their role as administrative or efficiency tools, but rather in their ability to create information. In the past, Herold argued, criminology, like medicine, had tended to generalize — weakly and imprecisely — from individual cases. However, the more data that could be incorporated into such generalizations, the greater their power. Since electronic data processing was able "to link gigantic masses of data in every conceivable combination and produce up-to-date quantitative statements in a very short time," it would, Herold argued, bring about a revolutionary expansion of the information processing capacity of the police and put them, for the first time, in a position where they could "discover rational insights into the causes and driving forces of crime."

What was truly breathtaking about Herold's vision, and what was later profoundly troubling, was the scope of the information that would have to be collected and analyzed in order to attain these goals. Identifying the primary social causes of crime would, he explained, require the "comprehensive collection of all data pertaining to criminals and their crimes in the systematic, machine-compatible form of 'offender or offense records,' which reach from identifying information and information on family, living, legal, property and social conditions to criminal-biological and criminal-sociological data and include all of the information that is already being collected in paper and card files" (entire passage italicized in original). This information need not—indeed, could not—be gathered all at once. Rather, it would have to be accumulated gradually through the incorporation of the documents generated at every significant stage in the life of an individual, from birth certificates and childhood vaccinations to apprenticeship certificates and eventual criminal sentences.

Herold's comments on the internal organization of the system were largely limited to spelling out the criteria that would have to be satisfied by a systems analysis. On the other hand, the description—as a negative example—of how the information contained in criminal complaints had to be copied in whole or in part as many as eight times in order to complete the different forms, file cards, and diaries maintained by the police provided Herold with an opportunity to address one of his abiding concerns. This copying and recopying to forms whose language, categories, and check boxes did not always correspond to one another virtually invited the persons doing these transcriptions to leave out, add, or subjectively inflect this information, and Herold argued that it did no good to obtain access to all of the above information unless at the same time a "closed data channel leading from the crime scene to the machine" were established to ensure the "absolute purity" of the data. What this meant in practice was that all forms would have to employ a common formalized language that included all of the criteria or descriptors needed to exhaustively capture every criminalistically relevant aspect of the crime that they sought to describe. Tailoring all of the forms employed by the police "to collect information in a schematic, complete, clear and easily comprehensible manner that is focused exclusively on facts," would also, Herold hoped, "awaken in every person a need to think in 'computer compatible' terms." This is what he meant by the electronic determination of consciousness.

Even though most of the information needed by the police when they first encountered a suspect individual was generated locally, Herold argued that this data would have to be stored centrally because it was relevant beyond the local level. However, Herold's ideas concerning the respective roles of the state and federal police were shaped by the available technology. In view of the limited capacity of the computers available at the time, the centralized storage of all of the relevant criminal information was out of the question. Instead, Herold opted for a curious division of labor in which each of the state criminal police forces would assume nationwide responsibility for storing and processing information relating to a single task, such as wanted persons, the compilation of statistics, and so on. He assigned the Federal Criminal Police the privileged role of conducting—on the basis of the information held by the state data centers—basic research into the causes of crime. By overcoming the limits on the understanding of the "essence of crime" imposed in the past by the inability to process all of the available data, electronic data processing, Herold concluded, "will transform the basis for crime fighting from an intuitive into a rational one."

Herold's vision of an integrated national criminal information system was a fascinating intellectual document, which reached—as he certainly intended—far beyond the practical problems of the moment, and the intention was to feed a revised version of his proposal back to Working Group II as the basis for continued work on the integrated national criminal information system.[53]

A Stand-Alone Solution for the Federal Criminal Police

The members of the Working Group II commission on electronic data processing did not have the time or expertise required to design the system that they envisioned, and, in the same report in which they called for an integrated solution to the information processing needs of the police, they also called for the establishment within the Federal Criminal Police of a dedicated working group to carry out the task. This proposal was approved by the Conference of Interior Ministers in May 1967; the group was to begin work in September; and in January 1968 they were joined by seven detectives, who were seconded by the states. The first and most important task of the group was to conduct a systems analysis to determine the informational needs of the agency, the possible sources of this information, which functions were ready to be automated, the file structures that would be required for such a system, its architecture, how information was to be exchanged with state and local police, and what technologies (including mainframes, software, peripherals, and networks) would have to be employed in its construction.[54] However, from the very beginning there was a disjunction between the establishment of a working group to push ahead with the concrete planning for an integrated national criminal information system and the actual work of the group, which focused on the automation of the Federal Criminal Police but with no clear vision of how this might contribute to the construction of the proposed system.

Local, state, and federal police agencies worked diligently across the second half of the decade to adapt electronic data processing for their own purposes. However, this work was fragmented, experimental, and nowhere near being ready to be rolled out on a national scale.[55] Nevertheless, in January 1969 Dickopf asked Interior Minister Benda for permission move ahead with the construction of a "general criminal information system."[56] This marked a dramatic departure from the obstructionism that he had displayed regarding the 1965 Faude report. Dickopf argued that electronic data processing had the potential to greatly enhance the administrative efficiency and operational effectiveness of the police because the wanted persons and stolen objects files had already assumed such dimensions that they could no longer be analyzed by human means alone. Moreover, since the operation of these two major departments was so tightly integrated with the work of so many other departments, it made little sense to automate the former without at the same time automating the departments from which they received information or to which they provided it.

Dickopf was willing to take the plunge at this point for three reasons. The first was the political pressure to increase the efficiency of the agency and improve the poor profile that it cut in comparison to the state police agencies. Second, although systems analysts were in short supply and demanded handsome salaries in the private sector, in November 1968 the agency had succeeded in hiring mathematician Leo Rouette, who, as chief systems analyst and head of the working group, would be responsible for designing the system and supervising its construction. Third, Dickopf recognized that the construction of such a system required a long lead time. Not only could it only be built in stages because of the perennial shortage of programmers and analysts. It also made no sense to acquire an expensive computer if there were no data to populate its files, and Dickopf calculated that it would take two to three years, fifty to sixty clerks, an indeterminate number of detectives, and a substantial amount of resources to digitize the agency's files.

Ministry officials supported the plan because they, too, believed that the root of the agency's problems was the inability to exploit the information held in its files, and the proposal was included in Benda's Five-Year Plan to Increase the Effectiveness of the Federal Criminal Police, which was approved in the waning months of the Grand Coalition. This plan also included funds to double the agency's staff to 1,800 (with many of the new positions to go to a new electronic data processing department) and purchase a mainframe, which was to be installed by the end of 1971.[57]

The working group that had been created in 1967 initially focused on two projects. The first was the automation of the modus operandi system, a problem on which the electronics subcommission of the Working Group Kripo had been working since 1965.[58] Although this task had provided much of the initial impetus for the use of electronic data processing by the police, formalizing the tacit knowledge of detectives was a difficult undertaking, and in practice the process led to lists of descriptors that were—by orders of magnitude—too large for everyday use.[59] However, by the turn of 1968, the work of the federal police working group had progressed to the point where the agency was able to run a test comparison on two hundred known and sixty unknown offenders using a list containing 1,550 individual descriptors. Although the test showed that the programming problems could be solved, the discriminating power of the program was limited by both the quality of the data gathered in the field and the precision of the descriptors.[60] The length of these lists suggest that electronic data processing did not so much solve the problem of formalizing tacit knowledge as reveal its actual scope. Both these conceptual problems and other, more urgent, priorities led to the suspension of work on the modus operandi system at the beginning of 1969.[61] We will return to this project in chapter 7.

The other project that quickly came to dominate much of the attention of the working group, was the development of a wanted persons system, which Rouette and Dickopf envisioned as the core of the agency's integrated information system. As we saw above, the process for maintaining the wanted persons list and producing the wanted persons bulletins literally cried out for automation, and the catalyst for work on an automated system was provided by the November 1967 national wanted persons day (Bundesfahndungstag). Since the 1950s, the number of reported crimes had risen three times as fast as the population rate (with property crimes, such as auto theft and theft from both vehicles and the new self-service stores accounting for much of the increase). However, over the same period the percentage of crimes solved by the police had declined from more than 70 percent in the 1950s to a little more than 50 percent at the end of the 1960s. The police attributed this trend to a number of factors, including the cultural and moral decline associated with growing affluence, the liberalization of the Criminal Code and the Code of Criminal Procedure, the loosening or lax enforcement of population registration regulations, and the increasing (auto)mobility of the population, both at home and within the Common Market.[62]

In response, the state police agencies proposed in December 1966 that they collaborate with each other and with civilian officials across the nation in a concerted effort to locate the 116,000 persons who were sought by the police at the time. The original focus of the action were the local population registries, which in the traditional manner were to be compared card by card with the national wanted persons list. However, the action was soon expanded to include virtually every major civilian database of personal information, including those of the labor offices, the social insurance funds, aliens registries, motor vehicle registries, and registries of seamen and persons without a fixed residence. It ultimately involved, in addition to the criminal police, the uniformed constabulary, the railroad and border police, and the staff of the civilian offices whose files were searched. This systematic combing of the diverse sources of state population information was flanked by police raids on red light districts, bars, train stations, shelters, highway rest stops, and other places where offenders were known to congregate.[63] If there were any action that was redolent of the Nazi-era police state, it was the national wanted persons day.

One element of this effort to ferret out the nation's most wanted persons was a plan to electronically match the 5.5 million names contained in the municipal population registries that had already been automated against the national wanted persons list. This represented the first time that electronic data processing had been used in this way, and on such a scale, by the police.[64] In terms of the number of persons arrested, the operation seems to have been moderately successful.[65] However, in the present context, the national wanted persons day is important because it revealed both the potential of the new technology and the obstacles that would have to be overcome before it could be routinely employed. The different registries stored their information in different formats, and there was no way to check for variant spellings of common names. These issues made it clear that sweeping changes would have to be made in the way in which personal information was maintained within the public administration before the police could make routine use of electronic data processing. In response, in the summer of 1968 the Conference of Interior Ministers established a subcommittee to develop uniform national guidelines for the automation of the population registries—a project that fed back into the developments discussed in chapter 1.[66]

While the action generated new interest in electronic data processing on the part of the police, it also raised novel concerns that helped define the meaning of privacy in the security sector. Both the Federal Labor Administration and a number of sickness insurance funds initially refused to open their files to the police, claiming that a special relationship of trust with their clientele obliged them to protect the confidentiality of this information. Dickopf, on the other hand, argued that, as was already the case with the local population registries, the police should be permitted to regularly compare the national wanted persons list with the files of the social insurance funds and state statistical agencies, even if this required the modification of existing legal restrictions on the use of such information.[67]

Despite these problems, the development of an automated wanted persons system remained a top priority for the police. By the spring of 1969, the agency was able to provide copies of the wanted persons tape to the four state police agencies capable of using them.[68] The digitization of this information was also an important step toward the development of an online system. Dickopf hoped that automation would transform the paper chase for wanted persons into a "permanent, general *Fahndungstag*," and he believed that the rollout of such a system would constitute the "first great contribution of electronic data processing to the intensification of crime prevention."[69] Although work on the offline wanted persons system had been completed by the end of 1971, the real-time, decentralized entry of information by state police could not commence until the INPOL network had been built out, which would not take place until the middle of the decade.[70]

Like the wanted persons and stolen objects files, the fingerprint file maintained by the Federal Criminal Police was also a model of fragmentation, redundancy, and inefficiency.[71] In the 1960s, five different systems were used by the states to classify fingerprints. Whenever a person was fingerprinted, the prints had to be classified, compared with prints already held, and filed by the state police. The process was then repeated by the Federal Criminal Police, who received a copy of every set of prints collected by the states, using its own system. Studies showed that much of this labor was doubly redundant because 35 percent of these persons had already been fingerprinted at some point. The magnitude of the problem was further increased by the increasing number of fingerprints held by the Federal Criminal Police, which grew from 1,055,000 to 1,551,000 between 1960 and 1965. On top of all of this, the classification system itself was so rough that detectives still had to manually compare fingerprints submitted by the states with an average of 220 cards to determine whether an incoming set of prints matched any of those already held by the agency. As a result, it generally took the agency one to two weeks to process a set of prints, and only 3 to 5 percent of those cases where individual prints had been found at a crime scene were solved through searches of the agency's files.

In 1966, the Working Group Kripo established a committee to develop a new classification system that would make use of electronic data processing to eliminate these redundancies and speed up the search process. By 1970, the group had successfully tested a new system for coding fingerprints. The long-term plan was for the Federal Criminal Police to assume responsibility for classifying all fingerprints using the new system and simply send the resulting formulae back to the state police. Although the agency had already begun using the new system internally, it could not replace the older system until the infrastructure had been built to permit the states to electronically query the central file.

The new system offered several advantages. In contrast to the old system, which was limited to twenty-four characters to encode a ten-finger set of prints, the new computerized system used 1,000 characters. In addition, not only did the new system eliminate the redundant coding by state and federal police; the greater discrimination of the new system radically reduced the number of potential matches that had to be manually reviewed. It also permitted the comparison of crime-scene prints from individual fingers against the entire INPOL database. Herold expected that the new system would be able to conduct such searches in less than a minute and that the number of matches to crime scene prints would rise to as high as 55 percent.[72]

Although the electronic data processing commission of Working Group II had called for the creation of a national integrated criminal information system in December 1966, by early 1969 the states were beginning to voice their displeasure at the failure of the working group to take the lead in planning such a network. They complained that, under Rouette's leadership, the group was focusing exclusively on the needs of the federal police and that the resulting lack of coordination was leading the states to develop independent systems that could not be easily integrated into a common network.[73] For his part, Rouette argued that, even though he had to give top priority to the computerization of the Federal Criminal Police, work on both the wanted persons system and the basic data record represented important steps toward the ultimate goal of a national criminal information network. Nevertheless, he confessed that he had not given any thought to what such a network might look like, and he appeared to believe that work on the state systems had already progressed to the point that it was impossible to ensure their future compatibility.[74]

This conflict festered through the remainder of that year until the electronic data processing subcommission of Working Group II and the working group in the Federal Criminal Police both stumbled back onto a question that had determined some of the key features of the network proposed by Herold at the end of 1966. The working group within the Federal Criminal Police had been attempting to develop a standard data record for the wanted persons system, which could be returned in response to queries from state and local police agencies. Although the proposed record structure was deemed unsatisfactory, this question did shift the focus from the internal needs of the Federal Criminal Police back to the question of the networked exchange of information between state and federal police agencies. However, neither these groups nor the additional committees that were established in 1970 were able to craft a master vision of the proposed national network, and Helmut Karl, who had replaced Rouette as the chief systems analyst for the federal police, promised to submit his own network master plan by the end of May 1971.[75] These plans and promises were overtaken by the June announcement that Herold would succeed Dickopf as president of the Federal Criminal Police.

Terrorism and the Political Parameters of an Integrated National Criminal Information Network

By the turn of the 1970s, the changing understanding of internal security and the growing importance of those kinds of crime that could not be investigated by the states alone had made police officials and politicians more willing to consider expanding the investigatory role and the informational authority of the Federal Criminal Police. These debates also left their mark on the master plan for INPOL. However, the decision to approve this plan, which we will examine in the next section, was part of a cluster of measures adopted between 1971 and 1973 to alter and expand the role of the federal police.

At the beginning of 1969, all three of the major parties floated proposals to amend the 1951 law governing the Federal Criminal Police. However, they were well aware that the states would block any substantive expansion of its authority, and the amendment that was approved in July of that year was quite limited.[76] Within a few years, however, the legislature would agree to many of the changes that it had shied away from in 1969 and to the extension of the agency's informational authority in ways that were not even on the horizon at that time.

All of the measures discussed above to rationalize, modernize, and computerize the work of the Federal Criminal Police had flowed into Benda's 1969 proposal, and they were then folded into the October 1970 Action Plan for the Modernization and Intensification of Crime Prevention. The Action Plan promised more money, additional positions, and changes to civil service regulations in hopes of solving the agency's perpetual manpower crisis. In addition, in the past, whenever the federal police had assumed responsibility for investigating a specific crime, a special group or investigatory commission had to be assembled on an ad hoc basis. However, the absence of a dedicated investigative department had made itself felt more sharply over the previous year, in part because the interior minister had made greater use of his authority to have the Federal Criminal Police take over the investigation of specific crimes, especially white-collar crime and political violence. In November 1969, a special department was established within the agency's Protective Services Division (Sicherungsgruppe) to collect information on political violence and crimes committed by foreigners; this group carried out the investigations that were assigned to the agency; and the ministry planned to further expand the staff of the department and regularize its new responsibilities. This was the origin of the agency's counterterrorism division, which would acquire vastly expanded investigative authority across the middle of the 1970s.[77]

The decision to construct a national criminal information system cannot be understood apart from the changing position of the Federal Criminal Police in the federal structure of the security sector, and growing concern with political radicalism and terrorism played a pivotal role in justifying the expanded authority of the agency. On 27 January 1972, the Conference of Interior Ministers formally approved the master plan for the construction of INPOL. The following day, the heads of the federal and state governments approved the Radicals Resolution, and that same day Genscher ordered the Federal Criminal Police to take over responsibility for investigating the crimes committed by the RAF. Two months later, Genscher announced the administration's "targeted program" for internal security, which continued the massive infusion of financial resources into the federal security agencies that had begun in 1969–70.[78]

At the same time, the Conference of Interior Ministers was completing work on the "Program for the Internal Security of the Federal Republic of Germany," which had been in the making since the fall of 1970 and which was finally approved in June 1972. This document, which sought to redefine the relationship between the army, the Border Police, and the regular police agencies while promoting the reorganization and modernization of the latter, began with an oblique reference to the need not only to protect the individual against crime, but also to protect the state itself and the democratic order against the unnamed threats of radicalism and terrorism.[79] Three elements of this lengthy laundry list of administrative and legislative measures are relevant in the present context.

First, the program called for redefining the role of the Federal Criminal Police as the "central coordinating office" (*Zentralstelle*) for the West German police, and it proposed giving the agency primary responsibility for investigating certain kinds of crime and improving cooperation between federal and state police in the investigation of such cases. A law to amend the Federal Criminal Police Law in this sense was proposed in February 1973 and approved in June of that year.[80]

Second, as we saw above, the 1951 law establishing the agency had authorized it to collect and evaluate information on crimes whose significance was "not simply limited to the area of a single state." The Bundestag recognized that effectively combatting crime that operated on an increasingly broad geographical scale required a greater degree of informational centralization, and the 1973 amendment eliminated this subsidiary clause and belatedly designated the Federal Criminal Police and its information system INPOL, which had been approved eighteen months before, as the central coordinating office or hub through which the exchange of criminal information between the state and federal police was to take place.

The law also made a third important change. Although the primary responsibility of the agency was to support the state police forces, the Bundestag also argued that the Federal Criminal Police could no longer be limited to playing a "mere supporting role." There were categories of crime—international trade in weapons, explosives, and drugs, as well as counterfeiting—where investigations depended less on local knowledge than on specialized knowledge of international connections and the ability to investigate crimes across the borders of the federal states. The amendment gave the agency primary responsibility for investigating these crimes and the lesser offenses that were committed in connection with them, as well as politically motivated crimes against the constitutional officers of the Federal Republic. The Bundestag shied away from giving the agency the authority to investigate *all* crimes with such international connections because legislators feared that this would open the door to the transformation of the Federal Criminal Police into a national police force comparable to their *bête noire*, the FBI.[81]

The states saw these as limited, provisional concessions, not as the abandonment of their federalist prerogatives. However, in chapter 8, we will see how this centralism acquired a dynamic of its own as the Federal Criminal Police assumed more and more responsibility for combatting terrorism. In the next section, we will see how this conflict between centralism and federalism left its mark on the architecture of INPOL.

Centralism, Federalism, and the Architecture of INPOL

Although successive administrations adopted measure after measure from 1969 to 1973 to increase the effectiveness of the Federal Criminal Police, none of these reforms directly addressed the question of how to build the proposed national criminal information network, which was regarded as the precondition for achieving this larger goal. The solution to both this problem and that of the computerization of the Federal Criminal Police itself—issues that had gone their separate ways since the end of 1966—came with surprising rapidity after Herold took office in September 1971. However, the network that was approved at the turn of 1971/72 was ultimately shaped in important ways not only by the informational needs of the police, but also by the resistance of the states to the erosion of their prerogatives by the same informational centralization that the administration hoped would compensate for the inefficiencies inherent in the federalist structure of the security sector.

Herold's ideas concerning the reorganization of the police and the role of electronic data processing in this process were influenced by two studies that were being carried out at the time. In April 1970, Genscher had appointed a blue-ribbon commission to examine the organization of the Federal Criminal Police, work processes and information flows within the agency, and the scope of its authority. Herold assumed the leadership of this commission after his appointment to head the agency, and its recommendations, which were reported to the interior ministry as it proceeded with its investigations and deliberations, flowed into the measures described in the previous section.

A second study was being carried out at the same time by the management consulting firm Kienbaum. In its final report, the Kienbaum staff concluded that, at least at its lowest levels, the departmental structure and work processes of the agency—including the use of a large number of individual files—were appropriate for carrying out its legal responsibilities based on the use of conventional office technologies. However, its analysis of the operation of the agency as a whole diagnosed many of the same problems as the 1965 Faude report and attributed them to the same causes, including personnel, equipment, and facilities that had not kept pace with the growth and changing nature of crime and to the "insufficient use of new findings and technologies to master the administrative, managerial, and communication problems of a large bureaucracy, which is responsible for both large-scale, routinized and individualized tasks and which in addition requires the close and very intensive exchange of information with external offices at home and abroad."[82] The consulting firm also concluded that the agency's informational needs could not be met through the use of conventional means, even with more staff, and its proposals were based on the assumption that the agency would be reorganized in conjunction with the comprehensive adoption of electronic data processing.[83]

Almost immediately after taking office, Herold had been asked by Genscher to prepare a master plan for an integrated national criminal information network and a plan for the reorganization of the agency itself.[84] In the fall of 1971, the Kienbaum consultants worked with Herold and his staff to develop an initial version of a master plan for the computerization of the police.[85] However, the plan that Herold actually proposed altered in significant ways the ideas that he had developed in collaboration with the Kienbaum consultants.[86]

Like the plan that he had drafted for the Bavarian police in 1966, the system that Herold proposed in November 1971 was organized around the distinction between information that was needed by police officers when they first encountered suspect persons and information that was collected in the course of subsequent investigations. Although the former included only basic identifying information, this information had to be as complete, accurate, and up to date as possible. To meet these demands, Herold argued, the relevant information would have to be stored directly on a central computer maintained by the Federal Criminal Police because, he implied, intermediate storage—in state systems—would diminish its currency to an unacceptable degree, and it would have to be entered, and be available for access, by local police agencies in real time. Other information, especially investigatory files and the more extensive information on crimes and their perpetrators collected through the National Crime Reporting System, was to be stored by the state police agencies, and only basic index data would be sent on to the national computer.

Herold estimated that the network would require ten in- and output stations for the agency itself and another 130 such stations for all of the nation's criminal-geographical regions plus an additional 300 output-only terminals for border crossings and ten for foreign offices, such as Interpol.[87] One of the many benefits of such a system was that it would also include local arrest warrants, which had not previously been included in the national wanted persons system, but which accounted for 60 percent of the total number of persons sought. Herold expected the wanted persons, stolen vehicles, and fingerprint systems to go online in July 1973, and all of the planned in- and output stations, as well as the Crime/Criminal Database and the criminal record index system, were to be operational by the middle of the following year.

However, instead of networking independent state systems, what Herold proposed was a federally operated network, which would reach from Wiesbaden all the way down to the local police districts, effectively bypassing the state information systems that were being planned at the time. Herold hoped to render this infringement on state prerogatives more palatable by letting the states make use of the agency's mainframe "as if it were their own" and by extending the network so deeply into the territory of the states that there would be compelling practical and financial advantages for the states to accept the proposal.

Herold believed that the (re)organization plan proposed by Kienbaum "correspond[ed] to the functional needs of the agency in a phase of accelerated transition to the introduction of electronic data processing," and he put the plan into effect in January 1972.[88] The states, however, were dead set against Herold's plan for a federal network because they feared that it would hollow out their competence in the security domain.[89] However, in mid-January a compromise was worked out to secure the centralized storage of the data needed by frontline police officers without diminishing the role of the states. This compromise forced Herold to abandon the more pronouncedly centralist features of the plan that he had proposed in the fall. It stipulated that, once the network had been completed, the local police would enter data into the central federal files through their respective state systems. But rather than serving as the primary repository for information on wanted persons and stolen objects, the federal system was to function only as a clearinghouse: the files that were to be consolidated at the federal level were then to be mirrored in the state criminal information systems, and the Federal Criminal Police were to be responsible simply for ensuring that the updated information they received from across the country was immediately reflected in these mirror files. This compromise, which might be characterized as an electronic form of collaborative federalism, was then approved by the Conference of Interior Ministers on 27 January, though only at a technical price that will be discussed in chapter 7.[90]

With the approval of a workable master plan for an integrated criminal information network, the West German police had taken the decisive step from the age of paper to the computer age.[91] The increases in administrative efficiency and operational effectiveness that the computer was expected to bring promised to increase the administrative power of the police, make it at once more routinized, continuous, intensive, extensive, and individualized, and transform the country into a more integrated, and more secure, criminalistic space. This process will be examined in more detail in chapter 7.

Notes

1. 48. Tagung der Arbeitsgemeinschaft der Leiter der LKÄ mit dem BKA (5–6 April 1967), BayHStA MInn Aktenzeichen IC1-490-1, Bd. 1.
2. PA-DBT 3114, 8. Wahlperiode, Anlage zum Kurzprotokoll Nr. 40 der Innenausschusssitzung vom 8. März 1978 (21 March 1978), 135.
3. "Rund um die Uhr," *Der Spiegel*, 2 June 1969, 88.

4. Karrin Hanshew, *Terror and Democracy in West Germany* (Cambridge University Press, 2012), 34–67; and Martin Diebel, "Planen für den Ausnahmezustand. Zivilverteidigung und Notstandsrecht," in *Hüter der Ordnung. Die Innenministerien in Bonn und Ost-Berlin nach dem Nationalsozialismus*, ed. Frank Bösch and Andreas Wirsching (Wallstein, 2018), 498–535, especially 516ff.
5. On the role of Nazi-era security officials in the Federal Criminal Police, see Imanuel Baumann et al., *Schatten der Vergangenheit. Das Bundeskriminalamt und seine Gründungsgeneration in der frühen Bundesrepublik* (Luchterhand, 2011).
6. In contrast to virtually all of the literature, which has argued that the concept of internal security acquired its broad resonance in relation to terrorism and left-wing radicalism only in the 1970s, Dominik Rigoll, *Staatsschutz in Westdeutschland. Von der Entnazifizierung zur Extremistenabwehr* (Wallstein, 2013), 485ff., argues that it had played a central role in West German politics since the founding of the country.
7. Rigoll, *Staatsschutz in Westdeutschland*, 33–140; Dominik Rigoll, "Kampf um die innere Sicherheit: Schutz des Staates oder der Demokratie?" in *Hüter der Ordnung*, ed. Bösch and Wirsching, 454–97; and Sarah Schulz, *Die freiheitliche demokratische Grundordnung. Ergebnis und Folgen eines historisch-politischen Prozesses* (Velbrück, 2019).
8. Eckart Conze, "Sicherheit als Kultur. Überlegungen zu einer 'modernen Politikgeschichte' der Bundesrepublik Deutschland," *VfZ* 53, no. 3 (2005): 357–80, especially 368–69; a similar point is made by Josef Foschepoth, *Überwachtes Deutschland. Post- und Telefonüberwachung in der alten Bundesrepublik* (Vandenhoeck & Ruprecht, 2012), 155.
9. Daniell Bastian, *Westdeutsches Polizeirecht unter alliierter Besatzung (1945–1955)* (Mohr Siebeck, 2010), 9–77; and Falco Werkentin, *Die Restauration der deutschen Polizei. Innere Rüstung von 1945 bis zur Notstandsgesetzgebung* (Campus Verlag, 1984), 23–55. In the French zone, policing remained the responsibility of the state government. On the postwar history of the West German police, see Klaus Weinhauer, *Die Schutzpolizei in der Bundesrepublik zwischen Bürgerkrieg und innerer Sicherheit. Die turbulenten sechziger Jahre* (Schöningh, 2003); Stefan Noethen, *Alte Kameraden und neue Kollegen. Polizei in Nordrhein-Westfalen 1945–1953* (Klartext, 2003); and Jose Raymund Canoy, *The Discreet Charm of the Police State: The Landpolizei and the Transformation of Bavaria, 1945–1965* (Brill, 2004).
10. Hanshew, *Terror and Democracy*, 36–43.
11. Bastian, *Westdeutsches Polizeirecht*, 139–58.
12. Werkentin, *Restauration*, 117–26.
13. Albrecht Funk and Falco Werkentin, "Die siebziger Jahre: Das Jahrzehnt innerer Sicherheit?" in *Wir Bürger als Sicherheitsrisiko*, ed. Wolf-Dieter Narr (Rororo, 1977), 189–210.
14. Werkentin, *Restauration*, 77–86.
15. Ibid., 86–97; and David Michael Livingstone, "The Bundesgrenzschutz: Re-civilizing Security in Postwar West Germany, 1950–1977," dissertation, University of California, San Diego, 2018.
16. Martin Diebel, *"Die Stunde der Exekutive": Das Bundesinnenministerium und die Notstandsgesetze 1949–1968* (Wallstein, 2019). Since the early 1950s, another area where civil liberties had been subordinated to the ostensible needs of the state in its struggle against communism was the surveillance of post and telecommunications by the Foreign Intelligence Service. As Foschepoth, *Überwachtes Deutschland*, 174–86, notes, the Emergency Laws legalized such surveillance without limiting it to an eventual state of emergency.
17. Staak, Problemfeld der inneren Sicherheit (15 February 1977; Vorlage für Klausurtagung 21./23.1977), StAH 136-1/2432. David Garland, *The Culture of Control: Crime and Social Order in Contemporary Society* (University of Chicago Press, 2001), charts the collapse since the 1980s of the rehabilitative ideal, which was the complement to the social understanding of deviance that underlay this Social Democratic approach to internal security.

18. This estimate of the number of terrorists and supporters is taken from Sven Reichardt, *Authentizität und Gemeinschaft. Linksalternatives Leben in den siebziger und frühen achtziger Jahren* (Suhrkamp, 2014), 12.
19. While the Revolutionary Cells maintained a relatively distinct identity, many members of the other two groups ultimately joined the RAF. The standard account of the RAF is Stefan Aust, *Der Baader Meinhof Komplex*, 2nd expanded edition (Hoffmann und Campe, 2007). Wolfgang Kraushaar, ed., *Die RAF und der linke Terrorismus*, 2 vols. (HIS Verlag, 2006), brings together the most important scholarship on the topic.
20. Varon, *Bringing the War Home: The Weather Underground, the Red Army Faction, and Revolutionary Violence in the Sixties and Seventies* (University of California Press, 2004); Gerd Koenen, *Das rote Jahrzehnt. Unsere kleine deutsche Kulturrevolution, 1967–1977* (Kiepenheuer & Witsch, 2001); and Donatella Della Porta, "Politische Gewalt und Terrorismus. Eine vergleichende und soziologische Perspektive," in *Terrorismus in der Bundesrepublik. Medien, Staat und Subkulturen in den 1970er Jahren*, ed. Klaus Weinhauer, Jörg Requate, and Heinz-Gerhard Haupt (Campus Verlag, 2006), 33–58, especially 55.
21. This is a central theme of Stephan Scheiper, *Innere Sicherheit. Politische Anti-Terror-Konzepte in der Bundesrepublik Deutschland während der 1970er Jahre* (Schöningh, 2010).
22. Rigoll, *Staatsschutz in Westdeutschland*, 335–456; Alexandra Jaeger, *Auf der Suche nach "Verfassungsfeinden": Der Radikalenbeschluss in Hamburg 1971–1987* (Wallstein, 2019), who argues (21–22) that the most important feature of the decree was not the decision to investigate every applicant for public employment (the *Regelanfrage*), but rather the politically motivated shift in legal reasoning that legitimated the abridgment of the constitutional rights of these persons; and Gerard Braunthal, *Political Loyalty and Public Service in West Germany: The 1972 Decree against Radicals and Its Consequences* (University of Massachusetts Press, 1990). Jaeger argues (11) that the decision is more properly denominated as a "resolution" (*Beschluss*) in order to emphasize that it represented a statement of political intention rather than a formal administrative decree (*Erlass*). The balance between constitutional rights and state authority was also at issue in the slightly earlier conflict over laws governing public assembly and freedom of speech. See Jörg Requate, *Der Kampf um die Demokratisierung der Justiz* (Campus, 2008), 174ff.
23. This statement is, of course, a calculated exaggeration. Although there were many other acts of political violence in the late 1960s, to the extent that the department store bombings set in motion a string of events that led to the founding of the RAF, this foreshortening is justified for the purposes of the following narrative.
24. For a chronology of the group's actions from 1968 through mid-1972, see *Der Baader-Meinhof-Report. Dokumente—Analysen—Zusammenhänge* (Hase & Koehler Verlag, 1972), 135–42.
25. "The Urban Guerilla Concept," in *The Red Army Faction: A Documentary History*, ed. J. Smith and André Moncourt (Kersplebedeb, 2009), I:83–105.
26. Aust, *Der Baader Meinhof Komplex*, 325.
27. Hanshew, "Beyond Friend or Foe? Terrorism, Counterterrorism and a (Transnational) Gesellschaftsgeschichte of the 1970s," *GuG* 42 (2016): 377–403, citation 380; Markus Lammert, *Der neue Terrorismus. Terrorismusbekämpfung in Frankreich in den 1980er Jahren* (De Gruyter, 2017); Tobias Hof, *Staat und Terrorismus in Italien 1969–1982* (Oldenbourg, 2011); Johannes Hürter, ed., *Terrorismusbekämpfung in Westeuropa. Demokratie und Sicherheit in den 1970er und 1980er Jahren* (De Gruyter, 2015); and Hürter, "Anti-Terrorismus-Politik. Ein deutsch-italienischer Vergleich, 1969–1982," *VfZ* 57, no. 3 (2009): 329–48.
28. Wolfgang Kraushaar, "Der nicht erklärte Ausnahmezustand. Staatliches Handeln während des sogenannten Deutschen Herbstes," in *Die RAF und der linke Terrorismus*, ed. Kraushaar, II:1011–25; and Petra Terhoeven, "Im Ausnahmezustand. Die Bundesrepublik während des 'roten Jahrzehnts' (1967–1977)," in *Ausnahmezustände. Entgrenzungen*

und Regulierungen in Europa während des Kalten Krieges, ed. Cornelia Rauh and Dirk Schumann (Wallstein, 2015), 67–91.

29. Hanshew, Terror and Democracy, especially 260; Dirk Moses, German Intellectuals and the Nazi Past (Cambridge University Press, 2007), who argues (48–50, 218, 280ff.) that the "Weimar syndrome" was finally overcome after 1989 as generational change finally made possible the development of a "basic trust" toward the country's history and its political institutions; and Michael März, Linker Protest nach dem Deutschen Herbst (Transkript Verlag, 2012).
30. Drs. 1/1273; and BGBl., 1951, 165.
31. Neither the information processing challenges faced by the state and federal police in West Germany nor the solutions they proposed are by any means unique. See James Rule, Private Lives and Public Surveillance: Social Control in the Computer Age (Schocken, 1974), 47–174, on the computerization of policing, motor vehicle registration, and national insurance in Britain; and Keith Breckenridge, Biometric State: The Global Politics of Identification and. Surveillance in South Africa, 1850 to the Present (Cambridge University Press, 2014).
32. Patrick Wagner, Volksgemeinschaft ohne Verbrecher (Christians, 1996), 79–107; Imanuel Baumann, Dem Verbrechen auf der Spur. Eine Geschichte der Kriminologie und Kriminalpolitik in Deutschland 1880 bis 1980 (Wallstein, 2006); Richard Wetzell, Inventing the Criminal: A History of Criminology, 1880–1945 (University of North Carolina Press, 2001); and Peter Becker, Verderbnis und Entartung. Eine Geschichte der Kriminologie des 19. Jahrhunderts als Diskurs und Praxis (Vandenhoeck & Ruprecht, 2002).
33. Drs. 1/1273, 5.
34. Richtlinien für den kriminalpolizeilichen Meldedienst, BAK B131/1321; and Hannes Mangold, Fahndung nach dem Raster. Informationsverarbeitung bei der bundesdeutschen Kriminalpolizei, 1965–1984 (Chronos, 2017).
35. Kaleth, Die elektronische Datenverarbeitung. Ein Beitrag zur Automatisierung der kriminalpolizeilichen Karteiarbeit (Bundeskriminalamt, 1961).
36. Kaleth, Die elektronische Datenverarbeitung, 11–30.
37. For example, Polizeipräsidium, Betr.: Einsatz elektronischer Datenverarbeitungsanlagen für integrierte Informationsverarbeitung bei den Polizeien in Bayern (20 October 1966), BayHStA MInn IA7-490-6.
38. Bericht über eine Organisations- und Geschäftsprüfung beim Bundeskriminalamt (26 July 1965), NA 9, BAK B131/1318. This document consisted of an overview and separate parts discussing the work of the different departments of the agency. These parts were numbered according to the department abbreviation (in this instance, NA, for Nachrichtensammlung) and page number.
39. Bericht über eine Organisations- und Geschäftsprüfung, 3–8.
40. Bericht über eine Organisations- und Geschäftsprüfung, 8–9, NA 5–12.
41. Bericht über eine Organisations- und Geschäftsprüfung, NA 13–15, citation NA 15.
42. Bericht über eine Organisations- und Geschäftsprüfung, ZF 1ff.; the gloss on these comments in Horst Albrecht, Im Dienst der Inneren Sicherheit. Die Geschichte des Bundeskriminalamts (Bundeskriminalamt, 1988), 139–40, 149–53, 241–42; Kurt Lach, "Bundeskriminalamt im Rahmen der Fahndung," Kriminalistik 24, no. 5 (May 1970): 228–34; and "Zu laut, zu langsam," Der Spiegel, 7 April 1969, 40–49, 52, 54, 57–58.
43. Baumann et al., Schatten der Vergangenheit.
44. Stellungnahme des Bundeskriminalamts zum Bericht über eine Organisations- und Geschäftsprüfung beim Bundeskriminalamt in Wiesbaden vom 27.7.1965, BAK B131/1319. Dickopf had been singing the same woeful tune for years. See Memorandum: Aufgabe und Entwicklung, Lage, Zukünftige Gestaltung (31 January 1955), BAK B131/1321.
45. "Vor der kriminalistischen Pleite? Bundeskriminalamt hält noch nicht viel vom Einsatz von Computern," Bonner Rundschau, 28 June 1966, BAK B106/91144.

46. 51. Tagung der AG der Leiter der LKÄ mit dem BKA am 23./24.10.1968: Bericht über den Stand der EDV in der bayerischen Polizei, BayHStA MInn IC1-490-1, Bd. 2; and Dickopf to Bundesminister des Innern (19 July 1966), BAK B106/91144.
47. "Zu laut, zu langsam," 54. See also the comments in Dieter Schenk, *Der Chef. Horst Herold und das BKA* (Spiegel-Verlag, 1998), 54, 70–71.
48. Cited in Albrecht, *Im Dienst*, 156. For other appraisals of the state of the Federal Criminal Police, see "Die Aufgaben des Bundeskriminalamts," BAK B106/91145, Bd. 4; "Zu laut, zu langsam"; and "Rund um die Uhr."
49. Bericht der Kommission "Elektronik" des Arbeitskreises II, BAK B106/91144; and Innenministerium NRW/Ruwe to Innenministern/-senatoren, Betr.: Bericht der Kommission "Elektronische Datenverarbeitung" des AK II (6 December 1966), BayHStA MInn IA7-490-12, much of which was reprinted in Heinz Ruwe, "Stand und Entwicklung der elektronischen Datenverarbeitung in der Polizei," in *Die elektronische Datenverarbeitung. Möglichkeiten ihres Einsatzes für die Kriminalstatistik, bei der Gefahrenabwehr und der Erforschung des Sachverhalts*, ed. Polizei-Institut Hiltrup (Hiltrup Polizei-Institut, 1968), 41–63.
50. For example, I C 1, Betreff: Einsetzen einer Kommission für the Datenverarbeitung bei der Kriminalpolizei (13 September 1966), BayHStA MInn IA7-490-6; and IV A 4 to Direktor des Landeskriminalamts NRW, Betr.: Aufbau eines Sondersachgebietes "Elektronische Datenverarbeitung" beim LKA (31 December 1965), NRW NW 324/2.
51. Polizeipräsidium, Betr.: Einsatz elektronischer Datenverarbeitungsanlagen für integrierte Informationsverarbeitung bei den Polizeien in Bayern (20 October 1966), BayHStA MInn IA7-490-96; Landeskriminalamt to Innenminister, Betr.: Elektronische Datenverarbeitung (14 October 1966), NRW NW 324/2; Landeskriminalamt to Innenminister, Betr.: Einsatz von elektronischen Datenverarbeitungsanlagen zur Verbrechensbekämpfung (10 January and 11 April 1967), and Landeskriminalamt NRW, Abschliessender Erfahrungsbericht über den Einsatz elektronischer Datenverarbeitungsanlagen ... (26 January 1968), all in NRW NW 324/3.
52. I C 1, Betreff: Vorbereitung der Einführung elektronischer Datenverarbeitungsanlagen für die Polizei (29 November 1966), and Herold, Organisatorische Grundzüge der Elektronischen Datenverarbeitung im Bereich der Polizei (Rohentwurf) (3 December 1966), both BayHStA MInn IA7-490-6. All of the quotations in the following paragraphs are from this latter document.
53. According to I C 1, Betreff: Sitzung des Ausschusses "Elektronische Datenverarbeitung" am 6.12.1966 (9 December 1966), BayHStA MInn IA7-490-6, Herold's proposal was to be revised on the basis of input from the state criminal police and then submitted to Working Group II. Although long stretches of Vorschlag des Bayer. Staatsministeriums des Innern für eine Konzeption der Organisation der elektronischen Datenverarbeitung im Bereich der Polizei (undated), BayHStA MInn IA7-490-6, closely follow Herold, I have not seen any evidence that this proposal was ever discussed by Working Group II.
54. Arbeitsgruppe Elektronische Datenverarbeitung/Bundeskriminalamt to MinDirig Ruwe, Betr.: Tätigkeit der Arbeitsgruppe "Elektronik" der LKÄ/BKA (24 May 1968), BayHStA MInn IA7-490-12, Bd. 1; Kurzprotokoll über die Sitzung der Kommission "Elektronische Datenverarbeitung" des AK II (8 July [and the appended Zeitplan] and 11 December 1967), BAK B106/45869, Bd. 1. At the end of 1968 it was expected that this initial systems analysis would be completed in early 1969.
55. For snapshots of the work underway at the time, see Bundeskriminalamt to Leiter der Landeskriminalämter, Betr.: Einführung der automatischen Datenverarbeitung bei der Kriminalpolizei (June 1969), BayHStA MInn IC1-490-1, Bd. 2; 48. Tagung der Arbeitsgemeinschaft der Leiter der LKÄ mit der BKA (5–6 April 1967), BayHStA MInn IC1-490-1, Bd. 1; and I C/MinDirg Stoll, Elektronische Datenverarbeitung in der Polizei (29 November 1971), BayHStA MInn IA8-490-2, Bd. 1.

56. Dickopf to BMI/Benda (7 January 1969), BAK B106/91145, Bd. 4; and the memorandum by Rouette (24 February 1969), BAK B106/45869, Bd. 2.
57. Bundesminister des Innern to Bundeskriminalamt, Betr.: Einführung der elektronischen Datenverarbeitung beim Bundeskriminalamt (5 August 1969), BAK B131/1321 and B106/45869, Bd. 2; Ministerialrat Lenhard/BMI, Vermerk (May 1969), and Bundesminister des Innern to Chef des Bundeskanzleramtes, Betr.: Bundeskriminalamt (20 June 1969), both in BAK B106/91145, Bd. 4; "Bundeskriminalamt soll schlagkräftige Zentrale werden," *Die Welt*, 27 May 1969; and "Informationen in Sekundenschnelle," *FR*, 30 May 1969.
58. Kurzprotokoll über die Sitzung der Kommission "Elektronische Datenverarbeitung" des AK II am 11.12.1967, StAH 136-1/1084.
59. Bundesministerium für wissenschaftliche Forschung, Ergebnisniederschrift. Besprechung über das Demonstrations-DV-Projekt "Kriminal-Datenverarbeitung" (4 November 1968), BayHStA MInn IC1-490-1, Bd. 2; and 48. Tagung der Arbeitsgemeinschaft der Leiter der LKÄ mit dem BKA (5–6 April 1967), BayHStA IC1-MInn 490-1, Bd. 1.
60. Dickopf to Bundesminister des Innern, Berichterstattung über das Bundeskriminalamt an den Deutschen Bundestag (11 December 1967), BAK B106/91145, Bd. 3. See the materials on this pilot project in BAK B106/45869, Bd. 1.
61. I C 6, Betreff: Sitzung der Kommission Elektronik des AK II am 14.1.1969, BayHStA MInn IA7-490-12, Bd. 1.
62. Auszug aus der Niederschrift über die Sitzung der ständigen Konferenz der Innenminister der Länder (3–4 June 1965), and Auszug aus dem Protokoll über die Sitzung des Arbeitskreises II "Öffentliche Sicherheit und Ordnung" der Arbeitsgemeinschaft der Innenministerien der Bundesländer (24–25 May 1966), both in BAK B106/91144; and Canoy, *The Discreet Charm of the Police State*, 231–61.
63. Vorschlag für die Durchführung eines allgemeinen Fahndungstages (undated), and Mitwirkung der Einwohnermelde- und Ausländerämter beim allgemeinen Fahndungstag 1967 (undated), both NRW NW 59/108.
64. Kurzprotokoll über die Sitzung der Kommission "Elektronische Datenverarbeitung" des AK II am 11. December 1967, StAH 136-1/1084; and press release, Elektronische Datenverarbeitung am Bundesfahndungstag (undated), BAK B136/15686.
65. In Nuremberg, for example, a Siemens computer took only eight minutes to match the nearly 481,000 names contained in the city's population registry against the wanted persons list of the Federal Criminal Police, while a manual review would have taken five hundred officials three weeks to complete. The process ultimately led to the identification of sixty-four persons sought by the police. Of these, twelve were quickly arrested; forty-seven had moved in the interim; and the police expected to arrest the remaining five persons. See "7. November 1967: Elektronik als Falle," https://www.nordbayern.de/region/nuernberg/7-november-1967-elektronik-als-falle-1.6829490.
66. Ruwe, "Stand und Entwicklung," 57–58.
67. Bundesminister des Innern to Bundesminister für Arbeit und Sozialordnung, Betr.: Durchführung eines allgemeinen Fahndungstages (26 September 1967), NRW NW 59/108; Interior Minister NRW to Regierungspräsidenten, Betr.: Bekämpfung der Kriminalität, NRW NW 324/122; Dickopf, Bestandsaufnahme zur gegenwärtigen Situation in der Kriminalpolizei in der Bundesrepublik Deutschland aus der Sicht des Bundeskriminalamtes (7 June 1970), B131/598, 22; and "Alles möglich," *Der Spiegel*, 26 February 1968, 60–61.
68. Arbeitsgruppe Elektronische Datenverarbeitung/Bundeskriminalamt to MinDirig Ruwe, Betr.: Tätigkeit der Arbeitsgruppe "Elektronik" der LKÄ/BKA (24 May 1968), BayHStA MInn IA7-490-12; and AG DV, Zu den Fragen des Bundesrechnungshofes (10 January 1972), BAK B106/45865.
69. Dickopf to Bundesminister des Innern (7 January 1969), BAK B106/91145, Bd. 4.

70. Albrecht, *Im Dienst*, 299–300.
71. Dickopf to Bundesminister des Innern, Berichterstattung über das Bundeskriminalamt an den Deutschen Bundestag (13 February 1968), BAK B106/91145, Bd. 3; Albrecht, *Im Dienst*, 306–9; and Horst Herold, "Rationalisierung und Automation in der Verbrechensbekämpfung," *Universitas* 31 (1976): 63–74, especially 69–70.
72. Herold, Elektronische Datenverarbeitung im Dienste der Polizei (9 September 1980), BAK B106/101309, Bd. 16.
73. I C 6/Joachim Schweinoch, Betreff: Sitzung der Kommission Elektronik des AK II am 14.1.1969, Schweinoch to Alfred Jaursch/Niedersächsisches Innenministerium (16 January 1969), and I C 6/Schweinoch, Betreff: Sitzung der Kommission "Elektronische Datenverarbeitung des AK II" am 22.7.1969, all in BayHStA MInn IA7-490-12, Bd. 1.
74. Kurzprotokoll über die Sitzung der Kommission "Elektronische Datenverarbeitung" des AK II am 7. April 1970, and Schweinoch, Betreff: Sitzung der Kommission EDV des AK II am 15.6.1970, both in BayHStA MInn IA7-490-12, Bd. 1; and Ergebnisprotokoll über die Besprechung am 13.4.1970, BAK B106/45869, Bd. 3. Rouette's most extensive reflections concerning the shape of a future network are found in his 24 February 1969 memorandum, BAK B106/45869, Bd. 2, and in Leo Rouette, "Probleme der automatischen Datenverarbeitung im Bereich des Bundeskriminalamtes," in *Grundlagenforschung und Kriminalpolizei* (Bundeskriminalamt, 1969), 119–27, where he argued (123) that it would be meaningful to think about constructing a network only once the individual systems were operational.
75. I C 5, Betreff: Sitzung der Kommission Elektronische Datenverarbeitung des AK II vom 3.5.1971 (11 May 1971), BayHStA MInn IA7-490-12, Bd. 1.
76. *BGBl.*, 1969, 1717–18; Drs. 5/4530; ÖS I 5 to ÖS II 1, Betr.: Weiterentwicklung des föderativen Systems (15 August 1968), and the reform proposal circulated by the justice ministry, both BAK B131/1508; and Anicee Abbühl, *Der Aufgabenwandel des Bundeskriminalamtes. Von der Zentralstelle zur multifunktionalen Intelligence-Behörde des Bundes* (Boorberg, 2010), 127–29.
77. Plan zur Erhöhung der Effektivität des Bundeskriminalamtes (July 1969), BAK B106/91145, Bd. 4; and Sofortprogramm zur Modernisierung und Intensivierung der Verbrechensbekämpfung, Drs. 6/1334.
78. "Schwerpunktprogramm 'Innere Sicherheit,'" *Bulletin*, 28 March 1972, 46–48. According to this plan, the staff of the Federal Criminal Police would have risen from 1,211 in 1970 to 2,062 in 1973, and the agency's budget would have grown from DM38.9 million to DM122 million during the same period. The Domestic Intelligence Agency and the Border Police were slated for proportional increases.
79. "Programm für die Innere Sicherheit der Bundesrepublik Deutschland—Teil 1," supplement, *Gemeinsames Ministerialblatt*, no. 31 (1972), 5, 8–9.
80. *BGBl.*, 1973, 701–3; Drs. 7/587; Abbühl, *Aufgabenwandel*, 129–37; and Karlheinz Gemmer, "Das Bundeskriminalamt—Zentralstelle polizeilicher Verbrechensbekämpfung?" *Kriminalistik* 30, no. 8 (August 1973): 337–42.
81. Drs. 7/587, 2–3.
82. Kienbaum Unternehmensberatung, Bericht über die Organisationsuntersuchung zur Verbesserung der Arbeitsabwicklung des Bundeskriminalamtes (25 February 1972), 119, BAK B131/588.
83. Kienbaum Unternehmensberatung, Bericht, 131.
84. Herold, Vortragspunkte für das Gespräch mit Herrn Bundesinnenminister am 15.12.1971, BAK B106/91142 und 45871, Bd. 7.
85. Kienbaum Unternehmensberatung, Bericht, 130ff.
86. Herold, Konzept für die elektronische Datenverarbeitung zu kriminalpolizeilichen Zwecken (undated), and BMI to Innenministerkonferenz, Betr.: Sitzung . . . (8 December 1971), both in BAK B106/45871, Bd. 7; Auszug aus der Niederschrift über die Sit-

zung des AK II . . . am 25./26. Oktober 1971, BayHStA MInn IA8-490-2, Bd. 2; I C 5/ Schweinoch, Sitzung der IMK am 16.12.1971 (13 December 1971), BayHStA MInn IA8-490-2, Bd. 1; and Vorlage des BKA—Bundeseigenes Datennetz (9 November 1971), BAK B106/85201, Bd. 2.

87. This number assumed that these regions would have an average population of 500,000. However, the estimated number of terminals envisioned was raised in January as the planned size of such regions was reduced to 300,000.
88. Herold to Bundesminister des Innern (10 December 1971), BAK B106/91142.
89. I C 5/Schweinoch, Sitzung der IMK am 16.12.1971 (13 December 1971), BayHStA MInn IA8-490-2, Bd. 1; and Schweinoch, Sitzung des AK II der AGdI am 24. Mai 1973, BayHStA MInn IA8-490-2, Bd. 2.
90. UAL V III/Hölder to Minister, Betr.: Arbeitsstand EDV-Vorhaben BKA (24 January 1972), BAK B106/85201, Bd. 3; EDV-Kommission des AK II to IMK, Betr.: Konzept für die elektronische Datenverarbeitung zu kriminalpolizeilichen Zwecken (21 January 1972), and Auszug aus der Niederschrift über die Sitzung der IMK am 27. Januar 1972: Die EDV-Kommission des AK II, both in BayHStA MInn IA8-490-2, Bd. 2.
91. On the status of the state criminal information systems, see I C/MinDirg Stoll, Elektronische Datenverarbeitung in der Polizei (29 November 1971), BayHStA MInn IA8-490-2, Bd. 1.

Chapter 7

The Quest for Security and the Meaning of Privacy
Computers, Networks, and the Securitization of Space, Place, Movement, and Identity

Security can be defined abstractly in terms of the quest to transcend the finitude and contingency inherent in the human condition.[1] To bring security to a state involves, among other things, determining the risks posed by specific individuals and groups and then taking steps to manage these risks by establishing control over the country's borders, places within this territory, movement among these places, and the identities of the population that inhabits them. This chapter will argue that the build-out of INPOL across the mid-1970s, in conjunction with the ongoing computerization of the civilian administration, greatly enhanced the ability of the West German police to secure their territory by making it possible to instantly query INPOL and the other databases that collectively defined the administrative identity of the person.[2]

As we saw in chapter 6, INPOL was originally conceived not only as a criminal information system for the police, but also as part of a broader network that would allow the police direct, real-time access to all of the information held in a number of civilian information systems.[3] The most important of these were the Central Vehicle Information System ZEVIS (Zentrales Verkehrsinformationssystem), which was operated by the Federal Motor Vehicle Bureau, the Central Aliens Registry (Ausländerzentralregister), and the Federal Central Crime Register (Bundeszentralregister), which held information on persons convicted for serious offenses, as well

---

Notes for this chapter begin on page 274.

as the local population registries and the registries containing the information pertaining to the new national ID cards, which—as we shall see below—were to be issued in the 1980s. All of these agencies were suffering from the same problems that had provided the impetus for the computerization of the police, and in the second half of the 1970s the computerization of these agencies at both the national and local levels was accelerated in response to police pressure. Rüdiger Bergien has described this as a process of "co-digitization."[4] However, although the police could hardly be denied access to the information held in these civilian information systems, computerization raised important questions regarding the permissible scope of data integration and the terms of automated access, and the ensuing controversies went a long way toward determining the meaning of the Federal Privacy Protection Law in the security sector.[5]

In addition, despite its real successes, INPOL was not all that it was cracked up to be in the popular imagination. In early 1977, Horst Herold proposed, as we shall see in the final section of this chapter, a new version of INPOL, which would have remedied, at least in principle, the problems of the current system and taken a big step toward the realization of his vision of the police as a cybernetic system. However, not only did this plan encounter resistance by the states and by those who were less confident than Herold of the revolutionary potential of the computer; two of its key component systems also raised important privacy concerns, which ultimately prevented them from playing their intended roles in the system envisioned by Herold.

Building Out INPOL

When the Conference of Interior Ministers approved the master plan for INPOL in January 1972, their approval did not extend to all of the component or subsystems that they eventually hoped to build, but only to the wanted persons and stolen items systems. These were rolled out surprisingly quickly. The wanted persons system was successfully tested in October 1972, and in November Genscher traveled to the Frankfurt airport to present the system to the press, who remained unaware that the system had crashed only two hours before. At the time, passports could not be read automatically (i.e., either optically or magnetically). Instead, cameras that projected pictures of the passports presented to immigration officials onto four screens in a back office, where other officers typed the information into INPOL terminals, were installed at fifteen windows in the international arrivals hall. The system formally began operation later that month.[6]

It initially ran on a Siemens 4004 located in the firm's Frankfurt data center, and it could be accessed through terminals located in the Koblenz headquarters of the Border Police, at fifteen important border crossings, and in the Protective Services Division of the Federal Criminal Police.[7] In February 1973, the system was migrated to the mainframe installed in the newly constructed computer center of the Federal Criminal Police in Wiesbaden, and in May of that year installation was completed on a second machine, which handled tasks that did not need to be carried out in real time.[8]

The systems for tracking stolen vehicles and missing objects with alphanumeric identifiers (weapons, currency, and blank ID cards and passports) were to begin operation in May and June 1973. In July 1973, the wanted persons system was to be expanded to include persons who were not formally sought by the police, but whose movement was to be monitored because they were regarded as persons of interest. This was the origin of what came to be known as *beobachtende Fahndung*, or passive tracking, which will be discussed in chapter 8. In April 1974, the interior ministers voted to move ahead with the automated fingerprint system, which finally went into operation in 1976–77. In September 1974, they approved the construction of a modus operandi system, whose fortunes will be discussed below.[9] At the same time that these federal systems were being built out, the states were busily constructing their own criminal information systems, most of which went into operation and were connected to INPOL between the end of 1973 and the end of 1975.[10] In December 1975, the interior ministers voted to move forward with the plan to connect INPOL to the most important information systems maintained by the civilian administration and to build out a second wave of INPOL applications, including a new system known as PIOS, which—as we shall see in chapter 8— became the core of the counterterrorism efforts of the federal police.

Securitizing Automobility

The development of a direct connection between the police and the Federal Motor Vehicle Bureau had been a top priority since the early 1970s; the integration of INPOL and ZEVIS was more advanced than the connections to other civilian information systems; and the privacy problems raised by greater police access to the data held by the office were correspondingly more complex.

The ownership of private automobiles had doubled during the 1960s, and both automobile theft and the use of automobiles in the commission of crimes had increased in step with the number of vehicles on the road.

Already in 1972, police claimed that vehicles were involved in the commission of 90 percent of all crimes. The task, they argued, was to ensure in both law and practice that license plates functioned as secure unique identifiers for the vehicles for which they had been issued.[11]

Since the early 1970s, terrorists had made wide use of vehicle identification papers that had been forged using blank forms stolen from motor vehicle offices. However, as police began entering the serial numbers of these stolen forms into INPOL, terrorists shifted to using counterfeited, stolen, or borrowed ID cards to rent vehicles. This led both to calls for legislation requiring people to report lost or stolen identification documents so that they could be tracked by the police and to efforts by the police to involve car rental companies in the surveillance of their customers. The Federal Criminal Police developed a *Raster* or pattern of distinguishing behaviors and characteristics that rental agents could use to identify suspicious customers. They also wanted the companies to verify the identity of customers who met specific criteria, retain identification documents during the rental period, and record this data for possible future use by the police. All of these proposals became central elements of Herold's master plan for combatting terrorism (chapter 8 and figure 8.1 ["Identification documents" and "Mobility"]). However, while the auto rental companies could not provide the desired information in electronic form, the police were ambivalent about investing the time and effort required to digitize it themselves. The rhetoric of the surveillance state notwithstanding, such technological limitations and conflicts of interest indicate the real limits on computerized surveillance at the time. Moreover, these policies could not have served as a permanent fix because terrorists were aware of the greater scrutiny being given to car rentals, and the members of the RAF increasingly chose to buy or steal, rather than rent, the vehicles they needed.[12] However, such theft created new problems, which became the focus of efforts to securitize vehicle identity.

In November 1977, Wolfgang Steinke, head of the forensic technology department of the Federal Criminal Police and later head of its counterterrorism division, confidently told the Bundestag domestic affairs committee that, by making it possible to distinguish individual vehicles from among identical, mass-produced objects, the "unalterable individualization" guaranteed by tamper-proof license plates would facilitate the electronic surveillance of traffic, make it impossible to sell stolen vehicles at a profit, make the use of motor vehicles for illicit purposes prohibitively risky, and thus deal a decisive blow to both mobile criminals and crime in general. The police were particularly concerned with doublets—that is, with cases where criminals would steal a vehicle and then outfit it with forged papers and license plates for another vehicle of the exact same make and model that was still in the possession of its rightful owner. The investigation of the 1977 assassination of Attorney General Siegfried Buback turned up evidence of twenty-five such doublets, and all eight vehicles used in the Schleyer kidnapping were camouflaged in this way. Electronic efforts to identify vehicles used by terrorists and criminals would not detect this ruse unless the chassis number were checked against the license plate. Ultimately, Steinke wanted a license plate that would be permanently attached to the vehicle. In addition, he hoped to set up a system of cameras — similar to those already in use on toll roads — to automatically check the license plate numbers of all vehicles passing by designated checkpoints. These infrared cameras, he noted, "can be installed at every conceivable location with favorable traffic conditions." However, these vehicular surveillance fantasies depended on the prior automation of the local population and vehicle registration offices and the creation of a comprehensive national motor vehicle information system that could be queried in real time.[13]

For security officials, the system that was in use at the time for registering vehicles and attaching identification tokens was the worst of all possible worlds: license plates were relatively easy to forge; they could be obtained without having to show proof of identity; and they could be easily attached to, and removed from, vehicles. Everyone agreed that the introduction of new plates and decals without close control over their issuance would not result in any increase in security. Moreover, as the police repeatedly pointed out, tamper-resistant license plates could not be considered apart from another key mechanism for securitizing the identity of vehicle owners and occupants: a counterfeit-proof ID card. In late 1981, the domestic affairs committee voted to allow the transportation ministry to move forward with the issuance of the new regulations, and the hope was that the secure license plate could be introduced by the fall of 1983.[14]

Although the choice among available securitization technologies may have been difficult, the plan to securitize motor vehicle identity was not controversial. The same cannot be said for the computerization of the Federal Motor Vehicle Bureau and the question of access to the data held in ZEVIS. The Federal Motor Vehicle Bureau began piloting the various components of the system in 1979–80; the pilot phase was completed in the fall of 1982; and the system was scheduled to be fully operational by 1984.[15]

Bull audited the Federal Motor Vehicle Bureau in August 1979, just as the first tests of ZEVIS were getting underway, and he was quite critical of the planned system. ZEVIS could be queried in a number of ways. The most controversial was the proposed "P(erson)-query," which would provide the address of the individual as well as information pertaining to all vehicles registered in the person's name. As we saw in chapter 1, the Bundestag had rejected the idea of a national population registry.

However, while the population (and ID card) registries were decentralized, the Federal Motor Vehicle Bureau possessed a central, digital collection of personal information on the owners of the thirty-two million vehicles registered in the country. Bull warned that the unrestricted use of the P-query was unacceptable because it could make ZEVIS into what one critic called "Big Brother's address book." In contrast to Bureau president Heinz Hadeler, who argued that the data collected by the agency had always been gathered for the purpose of making it available to other offices, Bull claimed that the exchange of information authorized by earlier vehicle registration laws had been intended to apply only to the local exchange of specific pieces of information and that the computerization of such exchanges gave the process a new quality that could not have been conceived by legislators at the time, but that made it necessary for the legislature to consider whether and, if so, to what extent information collected for vehicle registration purposes should be made available for other, unrelated, uses.[16]

This conflict was a classic example of how technological change, which made it possible to routinely do things on a mass scale that had simply not been possible before, was forcing the legislature to explicitly renegotiate the parameters of socially acceptable information exchange. After the census decision, the legislature asked the administration to refrain from building out ZEVIS any further until a firmer legal basis had been established, and at the time it declared that it could not countenance the introduction of the P-query even on a test basis.[17]

The amendment to the Motor Vehicle Code authorizing ZEVIS was one component of the omnibus law introduced by the conservative-liberal coalition in January 1986, though it was later considered separately.[18] This detailed law was a typical product of the post-census decision conjuncture. It authorized the maintenance at the local and federal levels of databases of registered vehicles; it spelled out the purposes for which registry information could be used, the specific information to be collected, how it was to be collected, and to whom it could be made available; and it authorized direct computer connections to the registries and enumerated the conditions under which information could be accessed online. With regard to the purposes of the registries, the law was both clear and opaque. On the one hand, it specified that the bureau's registries were to serve a number of vehicle-related purposes, including registration, the enforcement of traffic and insurance regulations, and taxation. On the other hand, it also stipulated that the registries could "provide information" regarding the owner of a vehicle, the vehicles owned by an individual, and the vehicle itself. The draft permitted the police and intelligence agencies to access registry data on a case-by-case basis, and it authorized the P-query, but only permitted its use for individual queries.[19] It also authorized a direct connection between ZEVIS and INPOL and allowed the bureau to routinely match vehicle-owner data against the national wanted persons list.

Federal Privacy Commissioner Baumann was highly critical of the draft, which, with the exception of the limitations on the P-query, codified virtually every conceivable use of bureau information by the civilian administration and the security agencies. Both he and justice ministry officials argued that a narrow construction of the final purpose principle should be imposed on registry data by prohibiting their use for purposes other than vehicle registration and the enforcement of traffic law—except under exceptional circumstances and narrowly defined conditions.[20] The FDP echoed these arguments.[21]

This difference between the position of the administration and that of the privacy commissioners and the FDP was the basic fault line running through the entire debate over the permissible uses of the information held in the population registries, the ID card registries, labor administration files, and the files of the social insurance funds. It was through measures such as this that the concrete meaning of the Federal Privacy Protection Law was ultimately defined. The outcome was equally typical: the draft law, which sanctioned current practice to a far greater extent than it limited these activities, was approved by the Bundestag in December 1986 with only minor changes, and it went into force in February of the following year.[22]

Securitizing Borders, Space, and Place

As we saw in chapter 6, the wanted persons bulletins were weeks out of date before they reached their intended users, and it was impossible to consolidate the many card files maintained by the police at every level of government or keep the individual files up to date. The build-out of INPOL effectively abolished these limits of time and space, as well as the problems involved in addressing individual documents held in large collections of paper files. The system thus made it possible to govern the state's borders, its domestic space, and specific places at a distance from the unlikely metropolitan center of Wiesbaden.

The number of INPOL-connected terminals increased at an accelerating pace across the 1970s and 1980s: from double digits, when the system first went into operation in late 1972, to 500 in 1974, 700 in 1976, 2,300 in 1980, 2,700 in 1986, and 4,900 in 1989. However, even this latter number fell short of the 8,000–10,000 that Herold ultimately envisioned.[23]

INPOL made an immediate impact on the policing of borders. Since verifying the identity of foreigners and their right to enter the country was a time-consuming task, only one in ninety vehicles crossing the border had historically been stopped for closer examination. The Border Police calculated that a direct connection to the Central Aliens Registry would reduce the time required to conduct identity checks at the border from more than twenty minutes to no more than three or four, while eliminating the need for both the police and immigration officials to maintain separate files. The long-term goal was to stop one vehicle in ten.[24]

By 1974, the Border Police had begun experimenting with the use of mobile terminals in both moving trains and train stations and to monitor the space between border crossings.[25] Although such devices were expensive, the interior ministry insisted that "regardless of his location at any given time, every officer involved in policing the border or checking passports [had to be able to] access the data contained in the INPOL wanted persons and objects databases at any time."[26]

By the late 1970s, borders and their surveillance had become even more important as German—and Italian—terrorists shifted their logistical centers to Belgium and France, as well as such neutral countries as Switzerland and Austria. One of the main problems faced by the Border Police was that official points of entry were fixed, and the easiest way to enter the country illicitly was simply to cross over the "green border." As Maihofer explained in 1978, the cardinal problem was that "today borders are borders for the police, but not for terrorists. The task is to reverse both parts of this equation and make the borders into greater risks for terrorists while, on the other hand, ensuring that they pose no meaningful obstacle to the collaboration of the police on both sides." His goal was to draw even tighter the mesh of border stations where individuals would be required to verify their identities, in part by increasing the number of officers patrolling unsecured borders: "We have to make the green border into a risk for terrorists."[27]

Since the attack on the 1972 Munich Olympics, West German security officials had become increasingly focused upon the international dimension of domestic terrorism. These concerns led to the founding in 1976 of the European Conference for Domestic Security (the so-called TREVI Conference) and to the internationalization of security policy. However, there were numerous obstacles to regional collaboration with regard to policing, and it was not until the 1995 Schengen Agreement (and the 2005 Prüm Treaty) that an institutional basis was created for the international exchange of information for crime and immigration control purposes.[28]

INPOL also made it possible to intensify policing within the domestic space of the state, and officials estimated that approximately 40 percent of the matches made there were directly attributable to the use of electronic data processing, especially the greater currency of the data.[29] In August 1977, the Conference of Interior Ministers decided that it was necessary to apply to the interior space of the state the same electronic surveillance methods that had so far only been used along the borders. They approved a new policy (which was not made public at the time) that required the police to conduct an identity check on every single person with whom they interacted, including not only accused persons and suspects, but also witnesses, people stopped for traffic controls, people involved in traffic accidents, and so on. But the implementation of this policy required the further expansion of the informational infrastructure of the police, and the interior ministers set a goal of increasing the density of INPOL terminals to one for every two hundred police officers by 1978.[30]

The police also sought to normalize space itself. For example, the RAF had initially preferred to establish safe houses, or what the police called "conspiratorial residences," in metropolitan districts populated by guest workers because they felt they would be protected by the anonymity of such areas. However, once the police caught on to this strategy, the RAF altered its tactics and sought either to hide in broad daylight by renting apartments in middle-class neighborhoods or to evade such surveillance by renting farmhouses, garages, workshops, or other commercial spaces.[31]

The police responded to this tactical shift with a campaign to encourage the public to be aware of spaces that were not being used in a manner consistent with their normal function. For example, the 1977 program Anonymous Hiding Places in Rural Areas urged the public to be aware of people who rented or purchased homes or farms but who then did not occupy the premises themselves, who added additional security features, whose own vehicles (or those of visitors) bore license plates from outside the area, who did not engage in agricultural activities, who isolated themselves from the local community, and so on. Similarly, the police warned the public to be aware of people who rented middle-class apartments, but who failed to furnish them with the accoutrements that would normally be expected of such residences, or who had people coming and going at unusual hours (figure 8.1 ["Apartments/Support bases"]).[32]

By early 1977, RAF members had altered their tactics yet again and begun to reside in hotels, both in West Germany and abroad. This points back to one last policy that was used to securitize space and movement through it: the hotel registration requirement. Many security officials continued to view this classical measure to securitize lodging as an effective means for combatting crime, and they argued that INPOL would enable them to exploit this potential source of evidence in a much more intensive manner. Others noted that the police would have to create a gigantic bureaucracy to evaluate overnight the fifty million hotel registration slips that would be filled out each year. Although few legislators believed that the hotel registration requirement would be a magic bullet, they ultimately decided to mandate the registration requirement (though not the identity check).[33] The new hotel registration requirement was appended to an amendment to the National ID Card Law in November 1978, and two years later it was integrated into the Population Registration Framework Law.[34]

The Admission Ticket to the Surveillance State: The National ID Card and the Securitization of Personal Identity

Neither the securitization of automobility nor that of hotel residency would have made any sense without the correlate securitization of personal identity, and the creation of a more secure ID card became a top priority in the second half of the decade. The cornerstone of this effort was the proposed counterfeit-proof, machine-readable ID card.

One of the reasons why the original members of the RAF were initially able to elude capture for so long was that they had broken into city halls and population registry offices and stolen blank ID cards and passports, along with the seals used to authenticate these documents. They were so successful that Baader later bragged that the RAF had its own population registration office.[35] The RAF also made use of genuine documents that had either been stolen from their owners or lent or "lost" by their bearers.[36]

The police were particularly concerned about these so-called *Ausweisverlierer*. This practice played a crucial role in the Schleyer abduction. The apartment where Schleyer was first held had been rented by RAF member Monika Helbing using the ID card of Annerose Lottmann-Bückler.[37] In response to a public appeal to report suspicious rentals, the building superintendent had notified the local police of the apartment where Schleyer was actually being held. Between 1970 and 1977, Lottmann-Bückler had "lost" her ID card four times, and her passport twice. She was also a member of the radical group Schwarze Hilfe and a contact person for people in the RAF milieu and for two persons who were the object of passive tracking.[38] Although the form on which this lead was recorded was misplaced, if the police had followed up on it and checked Lottmann-Bückler's identity in INPOL, these facts would certainly have raised a red flag and brought about closer scrutiny of the apartment rented in her name. Security officials felt that lost identification documents were such a potentially rich source of intelligence, especially regarding possible conspiratorial residences, that in the aftermath of the Schleyer kidnapping the intelligence agencies began to systematically monitor these *Ausweisverlierer*.[39]

The *Kennkarte* that had been introduced in the late 1930s had never become the exclusive means of authenticating personal identity, and the ID cards used in the postwar years, which lacked fingerprints and the multiple administrative checks that had been instituted by the Nazis, were less secure than their predecessors. Since the early 1960s, the interior ministry had been planning to amend the 1950 ID card law to bring it into alignment with the passport law and Common Market regulations, which allowed citizens to use ID cards, rather than passports, to travel between, and to establish their identity while residing within, member states.[40] But the card was also seen as a mechanism for enhancing the security of commercial intercourse in an increasingly anonymous, mass society, where contracting parties might have little personal knowledge of one another. In addition, the idea of making the ID card into a "universal card" that would replace a wide variety of documents (such as drivers licenses and vaccination records) was briefly mooted, but quickly abandoned because of differences in the regulations governing the format and content of these documents and the problems involved in keeping so much disparate information up to date.[41] Besides, officials were still having problems convincing people of the importance of possessing an ID card in the first place.[42]

Although counterfeit-proof ID cards and passports had been on the legislative agenda since at least the middle of the decade, the Germans had not been willing to move ahead on their own because they felt that the benefits of the new card would be minimal unless neighboring states also introduced comparable documents.[43] This reluctance to go it alone did not change until after the Schleyer kidnapping, and a corresponding law, which the Germans hoped would become a model for other countries, was introduced in August 1979.[44]

Although the text of the law focused exclusively on the security of the card, the preamble mentioned that it should be machine readable. However, this functionality was not included in the text itself, and the preamble did not present machine readability as something novel or otherwise deserving of comment. But the only conceivable purpose for such a functionality was to make it easier to electronically access information regarding the bearer by the intended primary users, the police. In view of the recent passage of the Federal Privacy Protection Law, the failure to explicitly authorize this functionality in the text or explain its purpose remains something of a mystery.

The version of the ID card law that came out of the Bundestag domestic affairs committee at the end of 1979 clearly reflected the influence of the privacy commissioners.[45] Initially, their main goal was to ensure that the serial number of the card did not serve as an ersatz national ID number that would permit the card to be used as a back door to all of the information contained in the population registries. They argued that these dangers could be contained only if the law authorized the collection of personal information solely for the narrow purpose of determining the identity and location of the bearer. The draft contained a provision intended to ensure that the process of issuing the cards would not be used to establish the kind of state-level registries of personal information that had been proposed by Maihofer in November 1977; it exhaustively enumerated the information that could be contained on the card; and it forbade the establishment of a national database of ID card numbers. To reinforce the fact that it was the cards themselves, rather than their bearers, that were being enumerated, the committee draft also stipulated that, when a card expired, its replacement would be assigned a different number. Although the draft prohibited the civilian administration from using the serial number to automatically access databases, it permitted the police to use the number for this purpose.

The committee draft was approved by the Bundestag in January 1980, and it was originally scheduled to go into effect in October 1981. However, delays in preparatory measures and disputes with the states over financing led the Bundestag to indefinitely suspend the effective date of the law in August 1981. The cost issue was eventually resolved, and the law was approved in February 1983. It was to go into effect in November of the following year. These plans were soon overtaken by the census decision, and in October 1984 the Bundestag indefinitely suspended the introduction of the card.[46]

The census boycotts and the Court decision together spawned a social movement directed against the ID card. What most worried these protesters was the fact that the card could be read automatically: all that a policeman or border guard had to do was to swipe the card through a reader in order to instantly verify the identity of the person. However, every time the card was swiped, it left behind electronic traces, or "data shadows," documenting the circumstances of the inquiry. These data shadows were themselves sensitive pieces of information. However, the individual had no knowledge of what information might be recorded in such instances and no control over how it might be used. These concerns are reflected in figure 7.1, which shows Zimmermann holding up the new ID card. Although he proclaims to what looks to be a dubious journalist that the new ID card hardly has any drawbacks (literally "shadow sides"), the card casts on the brick wall behind him a shadow that is far larger than the laws of perspective would lead the viewer to expect. This picture perfectly captures fear that the card would become yet another stone in the rising edifice of the surveillance state.

Figure 7.1. "The new ID card hardly has any drawbacks." Source: This drawing originally appeared in the *Hamburger Abendblatt*, 5 August 1983, 13; it was reprinted in *Entschuldigung, aber was ich beantworte, überlassen Sie freundlicherweise mir* (March 1987), AGG C NRW LaVo/LGSt 01/38. Reprinted with the permission of Karl-Heinz Schoenfeld.[47]

In October 1983, a congress of alternative groups met in Cologne to ponder the dangers posed by the new ID card and plot a campaign against it. The representatives of the sixty-odd groups who attended the gathering, which had been organized by the Green-Alternative List, the Communist League, and the Committee for Freedom of Thought (which itself was an offshoot of a number of boycott initiatives), warned in apocalyptic language that the "cabylon" of new information systems, which provided the infrastructure for state social control, was making it possible to instantaneously construct a total profile of each and every member of the population. The "brave new world" that this group saw looming on the horizon was not simply a "surveillance state," but rather "*a new social system*, a life- and machine world in whose center no longer stands the living person, but rather only combinations of signs. The citizen, who has been reduced to his instrumentalizable qualities, which can be interchanged with others, which can be constantly manipulated, made available for production and the office, controllable for leisure and procreation" (emphasis in original).[48] In other words, not only did those bureaucratic institutions that collected information impose their own logic and categories upon it, thereby alienating the individual from his information and limiting the way that he could present himself to others; this information could also—like an electronic Frankenstein—be reassembled in multiple ways to form data doubles in which the individual could not always see himself reflected.

They chose 1 April 1984 as a nationwide "wash day," when everyone was to be encouraged to "accidentally" run their paper identification documents through the laundry. This was to be followed the next day by the "Action Queue Up," when those persons whose ID cards had been ruined in the wash were to apply en masse for new cards. This would give the participants documents that would not have to be reissued in the machine-readable format until they expired while (hopefully) overburdening local officials and demonstrating the scope of popular opposition to the card. These two protests were then to be followed by a mass campaign to file requests with the public offices and private organizations that held the largest collections of personal information to disclose the information they held on the petitioners.[49] Although the ID cards presented an opportunity to protest against the "informationalization of society" and the "registration, influencing, and control of the citizen by the state," the protest ultimately gained broad support only to the extent to which it was harnessed to the census boycotts.[50]

In its 8 August 1983 issue, which appeared under the title "Total Surveillance," *Der Spiegel* also voiced its concern that the card might become the last element of a comprehensive system of social control that was threatening to transform a state based on the rule of law (*Rechtsstaat*) into one based on the rule of police law (*Polizeirechtsstaat*), "if not into an entirely different republic." The story itself focused on the possibility that, in the hands of an administration that valued security over freedom, the new identification document could become the "admission ticket to the surveillance state."[51] Hans Peter Bull also became increasingly critical of the card, which he claimed was "substantially more dangerous to civil liberties than the census,"[52] and Jürgen Seifert, the chair of the civil liberties organization Humanistische Union, argued that the ID card would have greater impact on individual freedom than many of the amendments to the country's constitution.[53] Zimmermann, however, lashed back at all such criticisms. He maintained that the card was to be used solely for tracking down criminals, not for controlling the population, and he insisted that any claims to the contrary were nothing other than attempts to defame the state and undermine public respect for it.[54]

The debate over the ID card law shifted into a new gear once the Constitutional Court issued its final ruling in the census case. Interior ministry officials initially denied that the census decision required any changes to the law, though they were willing to consider cosmetic alterations to make the law appear more "privacy friendly" and avoid what they termed "misunderstandings" and "mistrust."[55] Even though a number of interior ministry committees delved into the implications of the census decision, they could not definitively determine whether the census decision required the systematic revision of the ID card law or whether such changes were simply politically desirable.[56] This was another of those moments where it was less a matter of jurisprudential reasoning than of technological change overtaking established practices.

In April 1984, the interior ministry circulated a preliminary draft of a revised ID card law. This draft explicitly permitted the card to be read by machine; it permitted the comparison of the ID card and population registries; it regulated the processing of this information by the ID card office; and it specified that the serial number could not be used as a unique identifier for a database and that the card itself could not be used—except by the security agencies—to access such files.[57]

Baumann regarded the card as the capstone of a new informational infrastructure whose implications for individual privacy rights could not be clearly discerned, and he ultimately felt that the risks to individual rights outweighed the potential security gains associated with the card.[58] The FDP was even more strident in its opposition, and it saw the debate as an opportunity to profile its own position vis-à-vis its coalition partners. Like the privacy commissioners, the FDP wanted to maintain a strict functional separation between the ID card registries and the other responsibilities of the civilian administration and in this way to use the final purpose principle to create a separation of informational powers within the public administration. Most important, the FDP understood that all of these restrictions on the exchange of registry information or the use of the card to electronically access or link databases were worthless unless they could ensure that these protections would not be undermined by other laws granting the police and intelligence agencies access to this information. To forestall this danger, the FDP refused, as we saw in chapter 5, to sign off on the ID card law until agreement had been reached on the amendment of the security laws that were also being revised in the wake of the census decision.

Since the beginning, the administration had sought to portray the card as a way of making government more efficient and convenient for the citizen-consumer, especially by reducing the amount of time consumed by border controls. However, opponents of the law had always assumed that such claims were little more than transparent attempts to disguise its security function.[59] In the summer of 1983, a leaked 1978 interior ministry memorandum, which stated that "the introduction of the new ID card system creates the possibility of establishing—depending on the security situation—identity controls, whose intensity and purpose can extend all the way to total control in crisis situations," provided evidence to support these suspicions.[60]

The domestic affairs committee reported out the ID card law on 26 February 1986, and it was approved by the Bundestag two days later.[61] In the Bundestag, Paul Laufs (CDU) reaffirmed the administration's position, saying,

> This technical quality has clear benefits for the citizen. Automatic reading is convenient (*bürgerfreundlich*) and practical, and it corresponds to the state of technology with which we are already familiar in the form of bank check cards or the ID cards used by businesses. The inconvenient and labor-intensive process that is employed today for verifying identity will go faster and be error free without there being even the slightest change in the check itself or the attendant processing of information.[62]

Conservatives also insisted that privacy concerns could not be invoked to shield wrongdoers. Joachim Clemens (CDU) declared that "citizens who have nothing to hide have no need to fear the introduction of the new ID cards and passports," and that, at the same time, wrongdoers had no right to be protected from the consequences of their actions: "Privacy protection must not be allowed to become a shield for criminals" (*Datenschutz darf eben nicht zum Täterschutz werden*).[63]

It was in this context that former Interior Minister Baum argued that the state had to be willing to accept the incompleteness of its information as the price for preserving individual privacy and freedom.[64] Both the Social Democrats[65] and the Greens opposed the card. Ludger Volmer (Greens) argued that, in conjunction with other administration policies, the ID card was leading to the creation of a new Gestapo. "An ideal form of normal behavior, one to which everyone is expected to conform, is prescribed from above," he continued, and "friction, opposition, and criticism are to be abolished."[66] Hans-Christian Ströbele (Greens) conjured up the vision of a dystopian world in which the card could be used as a technology of social sorting to determine whether an individual would have access, for example, to a bank, the Bundestag itself, a soccer stadium, or even to a tennis match![67]

The final version of the law exhaustively enumerated the information to be collected by the ID card registries and specified that, after a transition period, the serial numbers of the ID card were not to be stored in the population registries. However, the FDP did not succeed in imposing a functional separation between the ID card registries and the other parts of the public administration, and the law permitted the registries to make their information available to other agencies if they were authorized by law to receive it or if they could not carry out their responsibilities without it. For the security agencies, this authorization was contained in the omnibus bill being considered by the Bundestag at the time. In the end, a card that was both itself more secure and that made it easier to determine at a distance whether the bearer fell into any suspect category contributed in multiple ways to the securitization of the state and its space.

INPOL-New and the Cybernetic System of the Police

In an address that he delivered when Interior Minister Werner Maihofer visited the Federal Criminal Police in July 1974, Herold noted that the agency was just about to bring to a close a "stormy initial phase" in which INPOL had literally been created out of nothing, and he expressed his hope that Maihofer would provide the support needed to complete his grand design.[68] However, at the time INPOL remained an unfinished torso—and an imperfectly functioning one at that. With the partial exception of PIOS, INPOL remained a tracking and tracing system. Work on the Crime/Criminal Database, which Herold regarded as the analytical engine that would bring the modus operandi system into the electronic world, remained suspended. The database of persons serving time had not been built, and INPOL was not connected in an integral way to the Central Aliens Registry, the population registries, or the motor vehicle offices. In addition, Herold considered the parallel storage of INPOL information in both the federal and state systems and its hierarchical architecture, which required all data to pass through state criminal information systems and then the Federal Criminal Police before being disseminated via different state systems down to the local level, to be technological abominations.

In addition, the technical consequences of this architecture were manifesting themselves at an exponentially increasing rate. The situation was further complicated by the fact that the eighteen mainframes employed by these agencies included six different models built by two different firms (Siemens and IBM) running four different operating systems and five different database systems, not to mention a variety of preprocessors and peripherals. This multiplied the amount of programming required to make the various systems interoperable, delayed the implementation of changes and upgrades, which were limited to the lowest common denominator, and endangered the stability of the network. In addition, a number of key INPOL subsystems ran on the computer of the Federal Criminal Police and could be accessed only from terminals that were directly connected to this central mainframe, but not from those that accessed INPOL through state criminal information systems.[69]

Herold presented the first version of his master plan for what became known as INPOL-new at the end of 1977.[70] His mantra was that detectives should be able to use the same procedures to access every INPOL application from every terminal and receive the same information displayed in the same format. In contrast to the original version of INPOL, in which separate databases were maintained for each main system, the new version would rely on a single information pool that could be accessed by all of the major INPOL systems, including the Central Persons Index (to which we shall shortly return), the wanted persons and objects systems, the planned registry of persons serving criminal sentences, the fingerprint database, and PIOS, all of which would be maintained centrally.[71] The state criminal police agencies would be required to either use mainframes that would be purchased by the federal government or purchase machines that complied with specifications established by the Federal Criminal Police.[72] The core of the new network would be a digital network called DISPOL (Digitales Sondernetz der Polizei), which would replace the separate networks currently being used to transmit data, sound, and images. Like ARPANET, it would use "smart nodes," which would permit every INPOL-enabled device to directly communicate with every other such terminal. This new network would also eliminate the time lag (sometimes as much as several hours) between the entry of data at the local level and its mirroring in the other state systems and thereby permit the new system to function end to end in real time.[73]

This digital network had a value for Herold that was far greater than its nominal role in overcoming the technical problems that plagued the original INPOL system, and he expected that it would mark a decisive step toward the transformation of the police themselves into a cybernetic system. Since the late 1960s, Herold had argued that the police would function most efficiently if they were organized as a cybernetic system—that is, as system that learned and optimized its performance on the basis of feedback generated by its interaction with its environment—and he believed that the mutual tactical adaptations by police and criminals would give rise to a feedback loop in which "crime automatically produces the organizational and operational forms needed to prevent more crime."[74] Or, as he elsewhere explained, "in this way crime, so to speak, determines (*steuert*) the means employed to combat itself."[75] The ultimate hope was that the police would be at the crime scene before the criminal.[76]

During his years as the head of the Nuremberg police, Herold had pioneered the new discipline of criminal geography.[77] While the analysis of the geographic distribution of crime promised to ensure the more rational deployment of available manpower, Herold also claimed that the new discipline would make it possible to understand how the specific characteristics of spaces and places gave rise to specific forms of crime and to use this knowledge for preventive purposes. In addition, Herold maintained it was possible to identify self-contained criminal-geographic regions, which were the proper geographical basis for the organization of the police because their borders corresponded "to the meter" with those of the socioeconomic regions identified by urban and regional planners.[78] The problem was that such a decentralized organization meant that no district would be in a position to benefit from the information held by other districts and that they might therefore develop into so many "islands, which are not only organizationally limited, but also informationally self-contained and isolated . . . [and] which exist only as a mere sum of units, which neither relate to nor communicate with one another, and which cannot be united to form a system."[79]

Cybernetics and the new information technologies held the key to turning this potential disadvantage into a strength. Herold contrasted cybernetic systems with traditional, bureaucratic forms of command and control, which were designed to report information up the hierarchy and toward the center and communicate commands in the opposite direction. The problem was, Herold argued, that such bureaucracies were structurally incapable of making optimal use of the information available to them. On the one hand, the interests and the understanding of the goals of the organization held by the local agencies never corresponded fully with those of the offices to whom they were reporting, so that the latter made decisions on the basis of information that was partial, distorted, or falsified. On the other hand, the increasing scale, scope, and complexity of modern societies made it impossible to govern them from a single central point. To escape from these structural distortions, Herold argued that governmental power had to be displaced downward and outward until the point had been reached where the available information was sufficient to govern a geographically delimited subsystem—that is, down to the level of the criminal geographic region, where the identity of the provider of information and its user would ensure that information was complete and current and that it had not been manipulated or preinterpreted.[80]

The next step, Herold argued, was to allow these elementary cybernetic systems to interact with one another in a process that would culminate in the reconstruction from the bottom up of a new, higher-level system of communication, feedback, and control. The result would be a "living organism with an electronic nervous system."[81] What he ultimately envisioned was a national information system "that would be controlled exclusively by criminal data, that would automatically [or spontaneously; *im Selbstlauf*] optimize itself without external intervention or political control, and that would, at the same time, abolish the previous hierarchy of central criminal agencies at the state and federal levels."[82]

Together, the flat, decentralized architecture of the proposed new INPOL system and the new digital network, which would subvert existing communication hierarchies, appeared to bring this vision of the police as a cybernetic organization, which had obsessed Herold since the mid-1960s, within reach. Herold envisioned a system of 8,000 terminals, which would give every police officer immediate access to "the entire knowledge of the police" and allow every officer "to have all information made available to him as if out of a single head or a single police brain."[83] Such a system would abolish the informational hierarchies found in every bureaucracy: "By eliminating every form of information that has previously been reserved to the privileged, to organizational centers, or to those who rule, in the future every person will literally know everything, a fact that will have a significance—a significance that cannot be overlooked, but that cannot yet be estimated—for the inner structure of the police, which are thereby approaching a technically induced fundamental democratization of the greatest dimensions."[84] In addition, by abolishing the distinction between intellectual and manual labor, it would give rise to a "fundamental reordering of the ways in which the police carry out their work."[85] The Conference of Interior Ministers approved Herold's plan for INPOL-new in August 1978 in a context that will be examined in chapter 8.[86]

Two of the proposed new INPOL systems provoked particular controversy. The one was the Crime/Criminal Database. After having been suspended in 1969, work on the modus operandi system was taken up anew in 1973, and in May 1974 the subcommittee charged with the task submitted its final report.[87] The problems involved in the project oozed out of the seams of this document. On the one hand, it glossed over the difficulties involved in determining what information was to be considered "objectively" relevant and ensuring that this information could be entered into the crime reporting system without distortion, the addition of superfluous detail, or the loss of essential information, while the decision to leave space for "special comments" represented at least an unconscious recognition of the limits of any formalized system of descriptors. On the other hand, it downplayed the problems involved in balancing the desire for total information and the effort involved in collecting it. Nevertheless, the committee was confident that, with the Crime/Criminal Database, research would

> for the first time obtain factual access to objectively recorded data on crime, whose volume and framing will open up a host of analytical perspectives. The intensive exploitation of the investigative possibilities created through the computer-compatible preparation of basic crime data will give criminalistic and criminological research a unique opportunity to obtain verified knowledge of crime and, through the scientific analysis of gigantic amounts of material, to enrich practice and theory, in particular, by providing empirical data for use in formulating strategy for criminal policy and determining criminalistic tactics.[88]

In September 1974, the Conference of Interior Ministers voted to move ahead with the development of the Crime/Criminal Database, and between 1975 and 1979 it was piloted on a nationwide basis for a select number of serious crimes and in the Saarland for all offenses.[89] Echoing Herold, Maihofer assured the Bundestag that this system would have "decisive effects not only on police prevention, but also on future legislative labor."[90]

This optimism soon proved to be misplaced. There was a huge disproportion between the amount of labor involved in coding the information and the resulting gains in crime-fighting efficiency, especially with regard to minor offenses, which made up the overwhelming majority of crimes, but whose information, which was itself often of poor quality, was only used infrequently. In addition, the prospect of such a vast, centralized database of criminal information raised privacy concerns. In April 1979, the Conference of Interior Ministers decided to abandon the project.[91]

The second set of problems was associated with the planned Central Persons Index (Zentraler Personenindex), which was to be a database of all of the individuals on whom criminal records were held by the federal and state police agencies. The Central Persons Index, which had originally been conceived as part of the Crime/Criminal Database, but which had been uncoupled from it after 1975, was to include basic identifying information, information on whether the person was wanted by the police, whether the person had served time, summaries of the crimes for which the person had been convicted, fingerprints, mug shots, and other descriptive information, as well as references to the files held on the individual by the different police agencies.[92]

The degree of redundancy among the estimated 12–15 million criminal files held by the police was unknown, though officials often cited a Hessian study that had shown that two-thirds of all offenders had criminal records in other districts. The purpose of the Central Persons Index was to bring greater transparency to this opaque mass of data by integrating all of the disparate records pertaining to specific individuals. The police believed that it would enable them to better combat serious crime and make investigations faster and more efficient by eliminating the need to regularly send circulars to all of the other state police forces asking if they held records pertaining to a specific individual. It was also necessary to enforce privacy law. As we shall see in chapter 8, the 1979 guidelines governing criminal records required the police to review these files after a specified period of time and to cull those that did not meet the criteria for further retention. The problem was that the retention period established by these guidelines was measured from the time of the person's most recent encounter with the police, and this could not be determined in the absence of an integrated national criminal records system.

But privacy considerations also mitigated against the project. The Central Records Index did not distinguish between crimes of national relevance and those of merely regional importance, and the privacy commissioners argued that the central registration of offenders of only regional importance was unnecessary and disproportional.[93] The police countered these objections by pointing out that the 1973 reform of the Federal Criminal Police Law had eliminated the provision restricting the activity of the federal police to information on crimes whose significance was not limited to a single state and that the legislature had justified the expansion of the agency's authority by noting that in many instances the importance of a crime could only be established by determining whether the offender had committed offenses in other regions.[94]

Although the Central Persons Index was supposed to be introduced by mid-1980 in the context of an INPOL upgrade, it made no sense to undertake all of the necessary work if the database was going to be fundamentally modified in the transition to INPOL-new. Consequently, in early 1980 the decision was made to replace the Central Persons Index with a new system known as the Criminal Records Index (Kriminalaktennachweis, or KAN).[95] This decision displaced, though without resolving, the problems that had arisen in relation to the Central Persons Index.

The name Criminal Records Index was a misnomer because its initial version had also included (as a vestige of its origins in the Crime/Criminal Database) information that went far beyond what was needed for a criminal records system. Moreover, by bringing together details on different offenses that could previously not have been seen in their totality, KAN actually functioned, the privacy commissioners argued, as a means of generating suspicion, while the inclusion of cases where the person had been acquitted or the charges dropped was inherently prejudicial. In such cases, KAN contained enough information to cast aspersions, but not enough to dispel them. "If the original files are not reviewed," Bull warned, "this can lead to a serious disadvantage for the concerned individual." In addition, the law governing the Central Crime Registry contained detailed regulations governing who could access registry data, and it imposed limits on the length of time in which convictions for specific offenses could be held against a person. By siphoning judicial records out of the Central Crime Registry and mirroring them in KAN, the proposed system was, they claimed, subverting these limitations. The system, they insisted, had to be limited to its original index function.[96]

In its final version, which was approved in January 1981, KAN only included references to files of national significance. Such determinations were to be made manually by the detectives or clerks who entered the information (rather than by the computer, as had been suggested), and the Federal Criminal Police were not to have access to regional KAN files. The time period for determining when a file was to be culled was to be determined based on the most recent entry into the central, rather than the regional, file. Lastly, KAN was only to contain—in addition to identifying information and reference data on where to find criminal files pertaining to the person—notations indicating whether the individual was armed, violent, or a user of intravenous drugs.[97]

While the privacy commissioners regarded this as a substantial improvement over earlier versions and as an important victory, the police were positively livid. They argued that the decision squandered the potential efficiency gains of the system, and they regarded it as a classic example of the mischievous influence of the privacy commissioners—all to no real end since it was still possible for the police to obtain the information they needed by means of that relic of the pre-electronic age: the circular.[98]

After he left office, Herold took the administration to task both for this decision and for the decision to abandon the Crime/Criminal Database. The latter decision, he bemoaned, had destroyed the basis for scientific research into the primary causes of crime before the Working Group Kripo could develop the capacity to analyze crime data using natural language to compensate for the manifest problems resulting from the use of lengthy lists of descriptors. The resumption of the project, he concluded, "hardly seems possible." The decision to reduce the Criminal Records Index to a mere shadow of its original self was no less regrettable. Not only did the minimal data set diminish the value of the database as a crime fighting tool; the failure to bring greater transparency to the criminal records held throughout the country diminished both police efficiency and personal privacy: "Today neither the police nor anyone interested in protecting privacy has any idea which police files contain what kinds of data on which citizens."[99]

In addition to these issues and those that arose with regard to ZEVIS, the states continued to harbor lingering federalist resentments regarding the assumption of so much police power by the federal government. Herold's successor, Heinrich Boge (SPD), did not share his faith in the revolutionary potential of the computer, and his vision of INPOL as a cybernetic system was quietly abandoned. Shortly after Herold was forced from office at the turn of 1980/81 (chapter 8), the interior ministers approved a new master plan that returned to the original idea of separate state and federal systems and made no mention of the Crime/Criminal Database.[100]

By the end of the 1970s, West Germany was a much more fully integrated security space within which criminal information flowed more intensively, more rapidly, and with greater penetration to the periphery than ever before. Much more information was being captured in native digital form, and detectives were reaching with increasing frequency for the keyboard rather than the card file or the folder. These processes were not by any means uncontested, and their outcome depended on individual personalities and the balance of political power at specific times. While the rejection of both the original version of the Criminal Records Index and the Crime/Criminal Database was part of the reaction by the FDP and those further to the left against the perceived excesses of police surveillance that followed in the wake of the German Autumn, securing broad access by the security agencies to the information contained in ZEVIS and the ID card registries was one of the top priorities of the conservative parties in the 1980s. Regardless of the specific outcomes, all of the databases, systems, and networks discussed in the preceding pages made it possible to collect, analyze, and exchange personal information in ways that could not have been conceived or carried out routinely and on such a scale before the advent of the computer, and the resulting conflicts over the use of the new information and communication technologies to securitize space, place, movement, and identity were instrumental in developing a new language of privacy and determining the concrete meaning of the Federal Privacy Protection Law for the security sector.

Notes

1. John T. Hamilton, *Security: Politics, Humanity, and the Philology of Care* (Princeton University Press, 2013).
2. The claim by Charles Maier, "Consigning the Twentieth Century to History: Alternative Narratives for the Modern Era," *AHR* 105, no. 3 (June 2000): 807–31, that the new information and communication technologies marked the close of the era of territoriality that had begun with the consolidation of territorial nation-states a century before is premature, at least in this respect.
3. Vorlage des BKA – Bundeseigenes Datennetz (9 November 1971), BAK B106/85201, Bd. 2; Bundeskriminalamt, Konzept für die elektronische Datenverarbeitung zu kriminalpolizeilichen Zwecken (21 January 1972), BayHStA MInn MInn 490–12, Bd. 2; and Staatssekretär Wolfgang Rutschke, "Eröffnungsansprache," *Datenverarbeitung. Arbeitstagung des Bundeskriminalamts Wiesbaden vom 13. März bis 17. März 1972* (Bundeskriminalamt, 1972), 9.
4. Rüdiger Bergien, "Südfrüchte im Stahlnetz. Der polizeiliche Zugriff auf nicht-polizeiliche Datenspeicher in der Bundesrepublik, 1967–1989," in *Wege in die digitale Gesellschaft. Computernutzung in der Bundesrepublik, 1955–1990*, ed. Frank Bösch (Wallstein, 2018), 39–63.
5. The networking of these systems was also a central element in Herold's master plan for combatting terrorism (chapter 8, and Figure 8.1 ["Persons" and "Legislation, Politics, Administration"]). Although the Federal Central Crime Register is only of second-

ary importance to the arguments being made here, the computerization of the Central Aliens Registry and its integration with INPOL is much more central. However, space limits make it impossible to pursue this in the necessary detail.

6. "Aufnahme des elektronischen Datenverbundes," *Kriminalistik* 27, no. 1 (1973): 26–28.
7. ÖS 6 to Minister, Betr.: Demonstration der Personenfahndung mit Hilfe der EDV (20 October 1972), BAK B106/85202, Bd. 4. Virtually everyone in the interior ministry and the Federal Criminal Police had argued in favor of acquiring an IBM 370 because of its superior performance, relatively low cost, and proven operating system. However, these factors had to be balanced against the anticipated impact of the decision on the domestic computer industry. Among the final contenders, AEG/Telefunken was the only firm that marketed a native German product (the TR 440, which had been developed with substantial subsidies from the German government), while the Siemens 4004/150 was based on an RCA design and would at most be assembled in Germany. However, both the AEG/Telefunken and Siemens operating systems were regarded as unproven. On the other hand, a number of the states had already acquired Siemens computers to run their criminal information systems. Genscher ultimately decided in favor of Siemens, though there is no document explaining the reasoning behind this decision. See the correspondence in BAK B106/45870, Bde. 5–6, 45871, Bd. 7. Siemens had already sold several comparable machines to the East German Ministry of State Security. See Rüdiger Bergien, "Programmieren mit dem Klassenfeind. Die Stasi, Siemens und der Transfer von EDV-Wissen im Kalten Krieg," *VfZ* 67, no. 1 (2019): 1–30.
8. Betr.: EDV-Vorhaben BKA (6 March 1972), BAK B106/85201.
9. Aufstellung eines Gesamtprogramms für den Ausbau des BKA-Informationssystems während der VII. Legislaturperiode (5 March 1973), BAK B106/85202, Bd. 5.
10. Horst Albrecht, *Im Dienst der Inneren Sicherheit. Die Geschichte des Bundeskriminalamtes* (Bundeskriminalamt, 1988), 305; Bundeskriminalamt/Herold to Arbeitsgemeinschaft der Innenminister/Leuze, Betr.: Fortschreibung des Gesamtkonzepts für das polizeiliche Informationssystem (INPOL), hier: Stand des Ausbaus des Verbundes (29 October 1974), BayHStA MInn 490-12, Bd. 3; and Helmut Karl, Vermerk, Betr.: Protokoll der Sitzung der Arbeitsgruppe EDV-Vorhaben BKA (19 June 1972), BAK B106/85201, Bd. 3. Schleswig-Holstein and Lower Saxony were among the early movers, while the Saarland avoided the problems involved in constructing its own system by availing itself of the option to store its criminal information on the computer operated by the Federal Criminal Police.
11. Herold in Schweinoch, Sitzung der "Kommission EDV" des AK II am 20./21. Januar 1972 (21 February 1972), BayHStA MInn 490-12, Bd. 2; and Bundeskriminalamt, Abschlussbericht über die Beratungen der Arbeitsgruppe "Bankenschutz" (6 June 1972), BayHStA MInn 89941.
12. This discussion is based on the materials in NRW NW 474/150. In mid-1978, some states were regularly reporting data on car renters, some irregularly, and some not at all. Approximately 0.6 percent of all checks of the identity of renters and the authenticity of the documents they presented returned positive results, though these did not necessarily relate to terrorism. Bundeskriminalamt/DV 11, Kurzfassung des Berichts "Zentralstelle des Verbundes" (5 May 1978), BAK B106/101305, Bd. 7.
13. Innenausschuss, PA-DBT 3114, 8. Wahlperiode, Protokoll Nr. 32 (9 November 1977), 6, 14–15; Wolfgang Steinke, "Technik als Unterstützung von Kraftfahrzeugfahndung— und Vorbeugung," *Kriminalistik* 32, no. 2 (1978): 54–56, which also spoke of an additional, "secret" use for the new technology; and Bergien, "Südfrüchte im Stahlnetz."
14. P II 5 to Minister/Baum, Betr.: Sitzung des Innenausschusses am 3. Februar 1982 (29 January 1982), BAK B106/83848, Bd. 5.
15. ZEVIS Zeitplan Stand: 15.09.1981, BAK B108/74383, Bd. 3. When work on ZEVIS began, the bureau held 72 million records, and each day it processed 60,000 changes and

answered 35,000 requests for information. Z 14 to Herrn Staatssekretär, Betr.: Dateien-Verbund-System des KBA (7 December 1977), BAK B108/74383, Bd. 1. The bureau had begun computerizing its punched card files in the mid-1960s and continued to rely on magnetic tape as the primary storage medium; where possible, police inquiries were processed each night as the tapes were being updated. Heinz Hadeler, "EDV im Kraftfahrt-Bundesamt — auch für die Polizei," in *Datenverarbeitung. Arbeitstagung des Bundeskriminalamtes*, 113–18.

16. Stephan Maria Tanneberger, "ZEVIS – Das Adreßbuch des großen Brüders," in *Vorsicht Volkszählung!*, ed. Roland Appel (Kölner Volksblatt Verlag, 1987), 96–108; Drs. 9/2386, 42–43; and Kraftfahrt-Bundesamt, Vermerk, Betr.: Einrichtung ZEVIS (16 January 1978), BAK B108/74383, Bd. 1. A national address book and telephone directory was later established by the 1996 Telecommunications Act (*BGBl.*, 1996, 1120–50), which obligated providers to collect this information and make it available for direct, electronic inquiry by the security agencies. The Bundesnetzagentur serves as the clearinghouse for this process. However, in May 2020, the Constitutional Court ruled (1 BvR 1873/13, 1 BvR 2618/13) that the law violated the right to informational self-determination because it failed both to adequately delimit the specific conditions under which this information could be accessed and used and to ensure that such infringements were proportional to the danger to be combatted. The Court also ruled that the law violated the constitutional protection of the privacy of mail and telecommunications.
17. Drs. 10/1719, 5, 38; and *Sten. Ber.*, 10. Wahlperiode, 85. Sitzung (20 September 1984), 6201.
18. Drs. 10/4737, 24–31, 57–76; and Drs. 10/6816, 5.
19. Einwag/Stellvertretender Abteilungsleiter IS to Bundesminister des Innern, Betr.: Bereichsspezifische Datenschutzregelungen im Sicherheitsbereich, hier: Koalitionsgespräch am 15. Oktober 1984, BAK B106/101952, Bd. 5.
20. Bundesbeauftragter für den Datenschutz, Presseerklärung zu den Sicherheitsgesetzen (23 January 1986) BAK B106/96357, Bd. 8; and P I 5/Ulrich Kersten, Vermerk, Betr.: Koalitionsberatungen . . . , hier: Zentrales Verkehrsinformationssystem (8 May 1985), BAK B106/122706, Bd. 10; Entwurf. Stellungnahme der Datenschutzbeauftragter zum Fahrzeugregistergesetz (ZEVIS) (25 February 1986), and Leuze, Stellungnahme. Entwurf eines Gesetzes zur Änderung des BDSG . . . und des Strassenverkehrsgesetzes (10 April 1986), both in Berlin DSB, Ordner: Goldene 7, Bd. II. For the administration perspective, see Einwag to Bundesminister des Innern, Betr.: Bereichsspezifische Datenschutzregelungen im Sicherheitsbereich, hier: Koalitionsgespräch am 15. Oktober 1984, BAK B106/101952, Bd. 5.
21. 37. Ordentlicher Bundesparteitag der FDP (23.–25. Mai 1986), Betr.: Liberale Position zur Innen- und Rechtspolitik im Wahlkampf für 1987, 7, BAK B106/96360, Bd. 4.
22. Drs. 10/6613; *Sten. Ber.*, 10. Wahlperiode, 254. Sitzung (5 December 1986), 19808; *BGBl.*, 1986, 486–93; Drs. 10/6816, 35–36; and Gerhard Fuckner, "Das Zentrale Verkehrsinformationssystem ZEVIS – ein Bundesmelderegister für die Polizei?" *CR* 4, no. 5 (1988): 411–16.
23. Herold to Arbeitsgemeinschaft der Innenminister/Leuze, Betr.: Fortschreibung des Gesamtkonzepts für das polizeiliche Informationssystem (INPOL), hier: Stand des Ausbaus des Verbundes (29 October 1974), BayHStA MInn 490–12, Bd. 3 (500 by the end of 1974); Horst Herold, "Rationalisierung und Automation in der Verbrechensbekämpfung," *Universitas* 31 (1976): 63–74, citation 64 (700 of an eventual 10,000); Vorschlag des Bundesministers des Innern für eine Neukonzeption des Informations- und Auskunftssystem der Polizei INPOL (20 April 1978), BAK B106/101305, Bd. 7 (1,300); Horst Herold, "Elektronische Datenverarbeitung im Dienste der Polizei," *Innere Sicherheit in den 80er Jahren. Symposium am 5. u 6. Mai 1980*, Hrsg. Rheinland-Pfalz Ministerium des Innern (Mainz, 1980), 39–61, citation 39 (2,300); *Der Spiegel*, no. 37, 1986, 55 (2,700); BMI to Vorsitzenden des Innenausschusses, Betr.: Beschlussempfehlung . . . (10 August 1989), AGG

Bestand A – Manfred Such, Nr. 99 (4,900 – including terminals, personal computers, mobile devices, and telex machines, though only 2,000 of these could access databases that ran on the mainframe of the Federal Criminal Police); and Herold, Elektronische Datenverarbeitung im Dienste der Polizei (9 September 1980), BAK B106/101309, Bd. 16 (20,000 connected devices planned in conjunction with INPOL-new).

24. Grenzschutzdirektion to BMI (12 October 1973), BMI, Vermerk, Betrifft: Anschluss der Grenzdienststellen an das polizeiliche Informationssystem (13 June 1975), and Ministerialrat Lenhard to Chef des Bundeskanzleramts (10 November 1975), all in BAK B106/85202, Bd. 6; and BGS I 4 to Z I 6, Betr.: Beschaffung der EDV-Anlage für das BKA (24 November 1971), BAK B106/85201, Bd. 2.
25. Wischnewski, Vermerk: Ergebnis der Sitzung der Projektgruppe "EDV-Vorhaben BKA" (16 January 1974), BAK B106/85202, Bd. 2; Pilotvorhaben "Bewegliche Terminals im INPOL-System" (Funkterminals) (30 March 1976), BAK B106/85202, Bd. 7; and "Mobilterminals für Direktzugriff zum Computer," *Die Polizei* 67, no. 7 (1976): 269.
26. BMI to BMF (20 May 1976), BAK B106/85202, Bd. 7.
27. Bericht des Bundesministers des Innern über den Stand der Terrorismusbekämpfung (10 May 1978), PA-DBT 3114, 8. Wahlperiode, 44. Sitzung, 50–53, and BAK BA106/83847, Bd. 4.
28. Eva Oberloskamp, *Codename TREVI. Terrorismusbekämpfung und die Anfänge einer europäischen Innenpolitik in den 1970er Jahren* (De Gruyter, 2017); Matthias Dahlke, *Demokratischer Staat und transnationaler Terrorismus: Drei Wege zur Unnachgiebigkeit in Westeuropa, 1972–1975* (Oldenbourg, 2011); and Ruben Zaiotti, *Cultures of Border Control: Schengen and the Evolution of European Frontiers* (University of Chicago Press, 2011).
29. Arbeitsgruppe "Ausbau Sicherheitsbereich," Ergebnisniederschrift der 5. Sitzung am 22. September 1975, BAK B106/102168, Bd. 5; and Unterabteilungsleiter O/Wischnewski, Vermerk, Betr.: Ergebnis der Sitzung der Projektgruppe "EDV-Vorhaben BKA" am 14. Dezember 1973, BAK B106/85202, Bd. 5.
30. Dr. Bochmann, Beratungsunterlagen für Kabinettsitzung (29 August 1977), BAK B106/83846, 25; Anlage zum Schreiben des BMI vom 27. Mai 1977, StAH 136-1/2432; Bayer. Staatsministerium des Innern to Präsidenten der Bayer. Landespolizei, Massnahmen zur Bekämpfung terroristischer Gewaltkriminalität (23 August 1977), BAK B131/1305; the materials in BAK B131/1580; and Maihofer's comments in 21. Sitzung des Innenausschuses (1 September 1977), 41–42.
31. Reinhard Rupprecht, Bericht zur gegenwärtigen Lage des Terrorismus in der Bundesrepublik. Prognose und Bekämpfungsstrategien (10 May 1977), BAK B106/83846, Bd. 1; and Innenministerium Baden-Württemberg to other interior ministries (29 July 1975), Anlage 1: Durchführung des kriminalpolizeilichen Vorbeugungsprogramms 1975, BAK B106/107117.
32. Raster "Anonymunterkünfte auf dem Lande," BAK B106/107117; and Bericht des Bundesministers des Innern über den Stand der Terrorismusbekämpfung (10 May 1978), BAK BA106/83847.
33. Drs. 8/1845, 13.
34. BGBl., 1978, 1712, and 1980, 1429–36 (§16, Abs. 2).
35. Cited in Dorothea Hauser, *Baader und Herold* (Hamburg, 1997), 172; *Der Baader-Meinhof-Report. Dokumente – Analysen – Zusammenhänge* (Hase & Koehler Verlag, 1972), 60–62; and "Dolde oder Bolde," *Der Spiegel*, 3 September 1979, 84–92. As of August 1977, 14,357 ID cards, 6,227 passports, and 427 blank driver's license and registration forms were listed in INPOL as stolen, and the police were forced to issue detailed regulations governing their storage in order to insure against further theft. Beratungsunterlagen für Kabinettsitzung am 31. August 1977, BAK B106/83846, Bd. 1.
36. Rupprecht, Bericht zur gegenwärtigen Lage des Terrorismus in der Bundesrepublik. Prognose und Bekämpfungsstrategien (10 May 1977), BAK B106/83846.

37. Tobias Wunschik, *Baader-Meinhofs Kinder. Die zweite Generation der RAF* (Westdeutscher Verlag, 1997), 203–5.
38. Dieter Schenk, *Der Chef. Horst Herold und das BKA* (Spiegel-Buchverlag, 1998), 295.
39. Such surveillance, however, was not a magic bullet. For example, in March 1976 the police checked the identity of nearly 350 persons who traveled through Tegel airport claiming to be the real owner of identification documents that had been reported lost, but determined that none of those persons were making fraudulent use of the documents in their possession. Schlussbericht über die erste Grenzbereisung durch Beamte des BKA (25 June 1976), BAK B106/85202, Bd. 7.
40. See the correspondence in BAK B141/73035.
41. *Sten. Ber.*, 7. Wahlperiode, 29. Sitzung (9 May 1973), 1497; the supporting materials in BAK B106 Nr. 45549, Bd. 5; Polizeiverkehrsamt to A2, Betr.: Entwurf einer Neufassung des Personalausweisgesetzes (23 February 1968), StAH 136-1/687; and Bayer. Staatsministerium des Innern to BMI, Betr.: Entwurf einer Neufassung des Personalausweisgesetzes (21 February 1968), StAH 136-1/688.
42. BMI to Innenminister, Betr.: Neufassung des Gesetzes über Personalausweise (14 December 1965), and Behörde für Inneres to Bundesminister des Innern, Betr.: Neufassung des Gesetzes über Personalausweise (19 August 1965), both StAH 136-1/687.
43. See Drs. 8/1667.
44. Drs. 8/3129, 5.
45. Drs. 8/3498 and 8/3570, 11–13.
46. *Sten. Ber.*, 8. Wahlperiode, 196. Sitzung (17 January 1980), 15661–66; and *BGBl.*, 1980, 270, 1981, 806, 1983, 194–195, and 1984, 1305.
47. This should be compared with the later photo (BAK B145 Bild-00088121) of a complacent Zimmermann holding up his own new ID card.
48. Vor den Ufern von Kabylon. Aufruf zum Ratschlag gegen die "Schöne Neue Welt" (June 1983), AIfS SBe 444, VoBo-Büro Hamburg, box 1.
49. "Kampagne gegen die Einführung der computerlesbaren Personalkarte," in *Der neue Personalausweis*, ed. Jürgen Taeger (Rowohlt, 1984), 151–54; and (Noch inoffizieller) Fahrplan für die Kampagne gegen die Einführung der computerlesbaren Personalkarte (undated), AGG B II 1/3087, Bd. 2.
50. Christa Reetz to Eberhard Walde/Bundesvorstand der Grünen (14 December 1983), AGG B.II.1/3087. The Greens spent the substantial sum of 15,000 Marks to fund a study of the ID card and the new information and communication technologies employed by the population registry system, the labor administration, and the police. See Studie zur Verwaltungsautomation und der Rolle eines maschinenlesbaren Personalausweises in der öffentlichen Verwaltung, erstellt von der Forschungs- und Beratungsstelle für Informationstechnologien (FORBIT) (Hamburg, Mai 1985), AGG B.II.1/5027. Pierre Piazza, *Histoire de la carte nationale d'identité* (Odile Jacob, 2004), explains (326ff.) why French opposition to a similar card gained only limited traction.
51. "Eintrittskarte für den Überwachungsstaat," *Der Spiegel*, 8 August 1983, 17–22.
52. Hans Peter Bull, "Perfekte Kontrolle," *Die Zeit*, 29 July 1983; and more pointedly in Bull, "Die 'Sicherheitsgesetze' im Kontext von Polizei- und Sicherheitspolitik," in *Sicherheit durch Gesetze?*, ed. Bull (Nomos, 1987), 15–43, especially 38–39.
53. Jürgen Seifert, "Der Bürger unter Aufsicht," in *Der neue Personalausweis*, ed. Taeger, 172–81, citation 173.
54. Kurzprotokoll. 2. Sitzung des Innenausschusses (8 June 1983), BAK B106/83849, Bd. 9.
55. Fröhlich, Mitzeichnungsvermerk zur Vorlage . . . (6 February 1984), BAK B106/104922.
56. Arbeitsgruppe "Volkszählungsurteil" to Staatssekretär Dr. Fröhlich, Betr.: Prüfung der Auswirkungen des Volkszählungsurteils des Bundesverfassungsgerichts auf den Sicherheitsbereich (20 March 1984), BAK B106/101407, Bd. 3.

57. Vorentwurf eines Fünften Gesetzes zur Änderung des Gesetzes über Personalausweise, BAK B106/101407, Bd. 3.
58. Baumann, Stellungnahme zu den Auswirkungen des Urteils . . . vorgelegt dem Innenausschuß des Deutschen Bundestages am 25. April 1984, BAK B106/101951, Bd. 3; Auswirkungen des Volkszählungsurteils – Entschliessung der Konferenz der Datenschutzbeauftragten des Bundes und der Länder (9 April 1984), BAK B106/96126, Bd. 5; and "Beschluß der Konferenz der Datenschutzbeauftragten in Bund und Ländern" (13 September 1983), in *Der neue Personalausweis*, ed. Taeger, 138–42.
59. See, for example, Ulrike Erb and Ulrike Riedel, Zum Personalausweisgesetzentwurf (13 April 1984), AGG Bestand A – Petra Kelly/243.
60. Referat ÖS 5, Einführung eines neuen Personalausweissystems – Problemanalyse/Systembeschreibung (Stand: 20. Januar 1978), AGG B.II.1/3087.
61. Drs. 10/5060, 10/5129; and *BGBl.*, 1986, 545, 548.
62. *Sten. Ber.* 10. Wahlperiode, 202. Sitzung (28 February 1986), 15525.
63. Ibid., 15514–15.
64. Ibid., 15530–31.
65. See the comments by Günther Tietjen, ibid., 15516–17.
66. Ibid., 15509–10. This charge earned Volmer a sharp rebuke from Konrad Porzner (SPD), whose grandfather had, in fact, been arrested by the Gestapo and sent to Dachau (15511).
67. Ströbele, ibid., 15521–22. As an alternative, the Greens proposed (Drs. 10/5129, 2) the introduction of a voluntary identification document containing only a minimal amount of personal information.
68. Horst Herold, "Moderne Methoden der Verbrechensbekämpfung," *Bulletin*, 17 July 1974, 863.
69. PA-DBT 3114, 8. Wahlperiode, Protokoll Nr. 36 (14 December 1977), Anlage 4.
70. Bundeskriminalamt, Neukonzeption des polizeilichen Informations- und Auskunftssystems INPOL (20 December 1977), BAK B106/101304, Bd. 5; and PA-DBT 3114, 8. Wahlperiode, Protokoll Nr. 36 (14 December 1977), Anlage 4.
71. This master INPOL database would be divided into five "pillars": (1) persons, (2) cases (*Fälle*), (3) institutions, (4) objects, and (5) things. The similarity between the "PFIOS" acronym used to describe this architecture and the PIOS system, which will be discussed in the next chapter, was not coincidental. See Herold, Elektronische Datenverarbeitung im Dienste der Polizei (9 September 1980), BAK B106/101309, Bd. 16; and Bundeskriminalamt, Erläuterungen zum Beschluss der AG Kripo . . . am 29./30. August 1979, BAK B106/101308.
72. PA-DBT 3114, 8. Wahlperiode, Protokoll Nr. 36 (14 December 1977), 8–10; and Maihofer in PA-DBT 3114, 8. Wahlperiode, 30. Sitzung des Innenaussschusses (26 October 1977), 14–15.
73. Vorschlag BMI für AK II am 27.4.78, BAK B106/101305, Bd. 7; and PA-DBT 3114, 8. Wahlperiode, 36. Sitzung (14 December 1977), and the attached appendices.
74. Horst Herold, "Kybernetik und Polizei-Organisation," *Die Polizei* 61, no. 2 (1970): 33–37, citation 36.
75. Horst Herold, "Neue Wege kriminalpolizeilicher Verbrechensbekämpfung," in *Kriminologische Gegenwartsfragen*, Heft 9: *Vorträge bei der XV. Tagung der Gesellschaft für die gesamte Kriminologie*, ed. Hans Göppinger and Hermann Witter (Ferdinand Enke, 1970), 208–34, citations 221–22.
76. Schenk, *Der Chef*, 129.
77. Horst Herold, "Kriminalgeographie – Ermittlung und Untersuchung der Beziehungen zwischen Raum und Kriminalität," in *Grundlagen der Kriminalistik. Eine Taschenbuchreihe*, Bd. 4, ed. Herbert Schäfer (Steintor-Verlag, 1968), 201–44; and Herold, "Die Bedeu-

tung der Kriminalgeographie für die polizeiliche Praxis," *Kriminalistik* 31, no. 7 (1977): 289–96.
78. Herold, "Intensivierung der Verbrechensbekämpfung," 160–71; "Neue Wege," 223–29; and "Künftige Einsatzformen der EDV und ihre Auswirkungen im Bereich der Polizei," *Kriminalistik* 28, no. 9 (1974): 385–92, especially 386.
79. Herold, "Künftige Einsatzformen," 386.
80. Herold, "Kybernetik und Polizei-Organisation."
81. Ibid., 33–34.
82. Horst Herold, "Die Polizei als gesellschaftliches Diagnoseinstrument," in *Die neue Sicherheit. Vom Notstand zur Sozialen Kontrolle*, ed. Roland Appel et al. (Kölner Volksblatt, 1988), 65–92, citation 67.
83. Herold, "Künftige Einsatzformen," 385; and Horst Herold, "Intensivierung der Verbrechensbekämpfung durch Einsatz elektronischer Datenverarbeitung – dargestellt am Beispiel eines Ballungsraumes," *Verbrechensbekämpfung heute und morgen. Arbeitstagung der bayerischen Kriminalpolizei* (1969), 130–75, citation 172.
84. Herold, "Künftige Einsatzformen," 385.
85. Ibid., 390; and Perspektiven der Kommunikation und Information für die Polizeien des Bundes und der Länder (27 April 1977), BAK B106/101305, Bd. 7.
86. Niederschrift über die Sondersitzung des Arbeitskreises II . . . am 6./7. Juli 1978, BAK B106/101305, Bd. 7; Beschlussniederschrift über die Sitzung der Innenministerkonferenz am 29. August 1978, BAK B106/101305, Bd. 8; and Baum to Chancellor Schmidt (5 September 1978), BAK B131/2049. For descriptions of the structure of INPOL as of their respective dates of publication, see Georg Wiesel and Helmut Gerster, *Das Informationssystem der Polizei INPOL. Konzept und Sachstand*, Bd. 46 (BKA-Schriftenreihe, 1978); Dieter Küster, "Das INPOL-System: Zielsetzung, Ausbaustand 1982," *Polizeiliche Datenverarbeitung* (Bundeskriminalamt-Vortragsreihe 28, 1983), 57–72; and Gerster, "Informationssystem der Polizei (INPOL)," *DVR* 12, no. 1–2 (1983): 19–71.
87. Betr.: Aufstellung eines Gesamtprogramms fur den Ausbau des BKA-Informationssystems während der VII. Legislaturperiode (5 March 1973), BAK B106/85202, Bd. 5; and Abschlussbericht der AG Straftaten-/Straftäterdatei (1 May 1974), StAH 136-1/1091.
88. Abschlussbericht der AG Straftaten-/Straftäterdatei (1 May 1974), and Hessisches Landeskriminalamt to Bundeskriminalamt, Betr: Stellungnahme zum Arbeitsergebnis der Fachkommission "Straftäter/-Straftaten-Datei" (27 December 1973), both in StAH 136-1/1091.
89. Küster, "Die Erprobung de Straftaten-/Straftäterdatei – ein erster Schritt zur allgemeinen Einführung," *Kriminalistik*, 29, no. 10 (1975): 433–37.
90. *Sten. Ber.*, 7. Wahlperiode, 155. Sitzung (13 March 1978), 10748.
91. Albrecht, *Im Dienst*, 306–7.
92. Küster, Bund und Länder errichten 1980 den ZPI. Kurzdarstellung aufgrund des INPOL-Manual 3/4 (Winter 1979/80), BAK B106/101308, Bd. 14.
93. Bull to Baum (12 November 1979), BAK B106/101320, Bd. 1.
94. Kriminalpolizeiamt des Saarlandes, Betr.: Neukonzeption des INPOL-Systems (7 December 1979), BAK B106/101320, Bd. 2.
95. Herold to MinDirig Krampol, Betr.: Fortentwicklung des polizeilichen Informationssystems INPOL (22 November 1979), BAK B106/101320, Bd. 1; and Herold to Ministerialrat Fritz/BMI (21 April 1980), BAK B106/101309, Bd. 15.
96. Bundesdatenschutzbeauftragter to Datenschutzbeauftragter der Länder, Betr.: INPOL – Neukonzeption, hier: Konzept für Aufbau und Führung des Kriminalakten-Nachweises (29 July 1980), BayHStA Landesdatenschutzbeauftragter, Nr. 414; and the correspondence in BAK B106/101321, Bd. 4.

97. P I 5/Kersten, Informationsvermerk, betr.: Konzept für Aufbau und Führung des Kriminalaktennachweises (6 January 1981), BAK B106/101322, Bd. 5; and Konzept für Aufbau und Führung des Kriminalaktennachweises (Stand: 13.5.81), B108/74383, Bd. 3.
98. See the juxtaposition of the views of the AG Kripo, the state interior ministries, and the federal interior ministry, BAK B106/101322, Bd.7; Drs. 8/3570, 47; and Ernst-Heinrich Ahlf, *Das Bundeskriminalamt als Zentralstelle* (Sonderband der BKA-Forschungsreihe, 1980), 345–48.
99. Herold, "Die Polizei als gesellschaftliches Diagnoseinstrument," citations 67, 86.
100. Beschlussniederschrift über die Sitzung der Ständigen Konferenz der Innenminister/-senatoren der Länder am 12. Juni 1981, BAK B108/74383, Bd. 3; Albrecht, *Im Dienste*, 314–15, 320–22; and the forum on the new master plan in *Die Polizei* 75, no. 10 (October 1984): 289–303.

Chapter 8

Mapping the Radical Milieu
Terrorism, Counterterrorism, and
the New Police Surveillance

The surveillance capacity of the West German police expanded immensely across the 1970s as they struggled to gain the upper hand over the new phenomenon of domestic terrorism. The RAF, which was responsible not only for the largest number of terror attacks during the 1970s, but also for those that garnered the most attention from the media, took over the New Left's understanding of the Federal Republic as an intrinsically repressive, latently fascist polity, and the group regarded their actions as provocations that, by forcing the state to reveal its true nature, would reenergize a fragmented and demoralized antiauthoritarian movement and open the door to a realm of revolutionary possibilities. Although the debate over political violence and democracy underwent endless permutations before collapsing of exhaustion in the aftermath of the German Autumn, the end effect of the RAF's efforts to spark an urban guerilla war was—as many critics had warned along the way—to strengthen the repressive apparatus of the state, not to shatter it.

The police distinguished between a "hard core" of active members; supporters, who engaged in some form of conspiratorial activity; and sympathizers, who were only of indirect concern to the security agencies because they limited themselves to mere verbal proclamations of solidarity, but who were the pivot of public debate over where to draw the line separating legitimate dissent from the advocacy of violence. These supporters and sympathizers constituted the radical milieu or "scene," and the former provided the vital logistical support without which the active

---

Notes for this chapter begin on page 315.

members of the RAF would not have been able to either satisfy their daily needs or carry out their actions.[1] Herold calculated, for example, that approximately forty people—including both active participants and those who served as lookouts and delivered vehicles to designated locations—must have been involved in the July 1977 assassination of Jürgen Ponto.[2] This radical milieu was also the most important channel through which young people were radicalized and transformed from peripheral sympathizers into active terrorists. As Herold noted in 1980, "In the Federal Republic between 600 and 700 persons are suspected of belonging to this circle. On their path to their terrorist careers, *all* terrorists have successively passed from the circle of sympathizers to supporters, and from there they were directly promoted to the hard core in waves of recruitment."[3]

As we saw in chapter 6, the concept of the habitual offender had provided the organizing principle for the National Crime Reporting System. In contrast, terrorists were figured by security officials as the antithesis of these offenders. As such, they embodied the limits of inherited forms of criminalistic knowledge, investigatory practice, and information processing.[4] As Gerhard Boeden (CDU), the first head of the counterterrorism division of the Federal Criminal Police (1975–78) and later vice-president of the agency (1983–87), noted laconically in 1977, "in this respect the modus operandi [of the RAF] no longer has clear contours."[5] However, the reliance by terrorists, and later organized crime, on strategies and tactics that could not be defeated using the methods developed to combat "ordinary" crime forced the police to develop an array of new surveillance practices. The goal of these surveillance practices, which will be the focus of this chapter, was to map the social topography of the radical milieu—that is, to identify the individual members of the scene and uncover the connections among them in order to peel back the successive layers of protection that surrounded the hard terrorist core like so many layers of an onion, disrupt the logistical support networks on which these terrorists depended, progressively restrict their room to maneuver, and, ultimately, locate, arrest, and prosecute them. If Mao had likened the peasantry to the water in which his guerillas could move about like fish, the strategy of the West German police was to "drain off" this water to leave the country's terrorists stranded high, dry, and vulnerable.[6] However, this strategy created its own legal and political problems.

For more than a century, the existence of a concrete danger or the well-founded suspicion that a specific individual had committed a crime had been the precondition for the use of force and the collection of personal information by the police, and this anchoring in narrowly delimited past events had been one of the most important means of limiting their power. However, the distinguishing characteristic of the new surveillance practices was that they sought either to uncover potential dangers before they had coalesced into concrete threats, rather than simply to protect against the latter, or to generate the initial suspicion whose existence had heretofore been the precondition for the collection of information—as part of a formal investigation by prosecutors and the police—regarding a specific individual. They displaced police surveillance into the *Vorfeld*, that is, into a domain of anteriority and conditionality, where the causal connections between the existing state of affairs and eventual harms were more mediated than permitted by current law. Although many of these surveillance practices made use of the new information technologies, their distinguishing feature was not the use of computers per se, but rather the systematic collection—in ways that were often made possible by the computer—of information on persons who did not meet the traditional criteria for police surveillance. These new surveillance practices collectively constituted the building blocks of a new form of postliberal precautionary surveillance, and, as such, they posed a direct challenge to liberal police law.

The pages that follow will provide a detailed account of the criminalistic rationale informing these practices and of the way they functioned as a regime of visibility to uncover forms of criminal behavior that would have remained invisible to traditional investigatory methods. However, the Federal Privacy Protection Law was being debated at the very moment that these new surveillance practices were being implemented, and the debates surrounding them played a central role in determining the concrete meaning of both privacy and its mirror image, internal security.

There is a second dimension to the history of police surveillance in the 1970s. The state interior ministers jealously guarded their prerogatives in the security domain, and they constantly struggled to balance the relative advantages of local knowledge and centralized coordination. However, across the middle of the decade many politicians and security officials became convinced that the successful prosecution of terrorism required central coordination at the national level. Terrorist actions, they noted, regularly crossed the borders of both the federal states and the country. Not only did the investigation of these offenses often require the expertise of the federal police. In addition the information gathered through the new surveillance practices was only of limited value unless it could be integrated, analyzed, and then used in a coordinated manner to direct further investigative and operational measures. As a result, the development of the new surveillance practices was complemented, and the associated political problems compounded, by the grudging, limited, and provisional acquiescence of the states to the centralization of counterterrorism authority in the hands of the Federal Criminal Police between 1975 and 1977. These two major threads in the history of police surveillance were brought together in the program for the eradication of terrorism that Herold crafted during these years.

This marriage of convenience between the federal government and the states was upset by the 5 September 1977 kidnapping of industrialist Hanns Martin Schleyer and the events that followed in its wake. The symbolic importance of the Schleyer kidnapping, which followed closely upon several other terrorist attacks, led to the temporary concentration of virtually all counterterrorism authority in the hands of the Federal Criminal Police and to an unprecedented—and politically unsustainable—intensification of police surveillance of the radical milieu. However, the failure to rescue Schleyer and, perhaps more important, the failure of the modernized, computerized security apparatus to prevent his kidnapping in the first place irreparably tarnished the aura surrounding the Federal Criminal Police and precipitated a Thermidorian reaction against the surveillance regime that had taken shape since 1975. Although this reaction was fueled in part by federalist disenchantment with the centralization of police power, the central concept of the broader public debate was the "surveillance state" (Überwachungsstaat), which was employed, I argue, to theorize the ways in which the new precautionary surveillance practices were eroding the principles of liberal police law. However, as we saw in the debate over the Domestic Intelligence Agency in chapter 5, and as we shall see in greater detail below, privacy rights were a central concern for left-liberal Interior Minister Gerhart Baum, and the institutionalization of privacy rights and civil liberties within the security sector (together with the retreat from the rigorous application of the Radicals Resolution at the federal level and in the states governed by the SPD-FDP coalition) marked the end of the postwar internal security regime.[7]

Investigation, Information, and the Expanding Remit of the Federal Criminal Police

The direct involvement of the Federal Criminal Police in the investigation of left-wing terrorism dates from January 1971. Since April 1968, state and local police—especially in Berlin—had shouldered primary responsibility for investigating the many offenses committed by the RAF. However, in January 1971 Genscher ordered the Federal Criminal Police to take over the investigation of the complex of crimes committed by the "Baader-Mahler-Meinhof band."[8] To carry out this task, a special investigatory commission (Sonderkommission, or SoKo) Baader-Meinhof, which was originally made up of eight detectives under the command of two senior officers, was established within the agency's Protective Services Division.

At the same time, the interior ministers agreed to Herold's proposal to establish regional special commissions to work with the SoKo Baader-Meinhof. The commission was responsible for collating the results of its own investigations and those of the regional special commissions, analyzing this information, providing the regional commissions with intelligence to assist in their investigations, supporting their work by seconding its own officers to work with them, and providing forensic expertise. In January 1972, Herold claimed—citing a list of RAF-related crimes that stretched from Berlin to Cologne, Kaiserslautern, Stuttgart, and Ulm— that the investigation would have broken down completely if the interior ministers had not supported the centralized coordination of decentralized investigations and operational measures.[9] In response to the RAF's May Offensive, the interior ministers moved to ensure even closer coordination between the state and federal police by giving the Federal Criminal Police the unprecedented and decidedly unfederalist authority to issue directives to the regional special commissions.[10] They also authorized a number of new surveillance practices, which will be discussed below.[11]

Although the coordinated measures that led to the capture of Baader, Raspe, and Meins at the end of May marked the beginning of the agency's involvement in counterterrorism, the centralization of police counterterrorism authority was neither linear nor foreordained, and at this point neither the interior ministers nor the Bundestag showed any interest in institutionalizing the agency's coordinating role.[12] With the specter of terrorism apparently banished, the regional special commissions were dissolved, and the authority that had been given to the Federal Criminal Police in May 1972 was revoked at the end of that year.

In the early 1970s, the administration had continued to maintain that terrorism was, at bottom, simply an extreme form of social deviance that should be combatted using the same means applied to other kinds of crime. The kidnapping of Lorenz and the attack on the Stockholm embassy in spring 1975, however, brought about a perceptible shift in the administration's thinking. The day after the embassy siege, Chancellor Schmidt told the Bundestag that "whoever wishes to reliably protect the rule of law must also be inwardly ready to make use of every measure that is permitted and required by the rule of law."[13] He had already explained what this meant after the Lorenz kidnapping. Since deterrence and the prospect of resocialization had no effect on "terrorists, who have consciously decided to rise up against our legal order and the rule of law, and in so doing to risk their own lives," all that was left, Schmidt concluded, was to use the repressive apparatus of the state to protect society from the dangers they posed.[14]

Even before the Lorenz kidnapping, Herold had been reflecting on what the police would have to do in order to meet the challenge of terrorism, and in February 1975 he had called on the heads of the state criminal police forces to approve a plan for the "total mobilization" of the police for the war on terrorism. At this meeting he warned the participants that "over the next years of our common professional life we will often sit together here with ever greater and more serious ramifications unless we succeed—through the common, almost revolutionary action of all involved agencies—in historically liquidating this phenomenon."[15] This proposal might be said to mark the point at which the progressive Social Democrat, who had originally hoped to use the new information technologies to identify the social causes of deviant behavior and make them the object of primary prevention, was consumed by his alter ego, the country's chief law enforcement official, who gradually lost sight of the preventive and rehabilitative dimensions of criminal policy and instead used the new surveillance practices in an increasingly narrow manner for repressive purposes.[16]

The counterterrorism program, which Herold proposed in early 1975 and which we shall examine in the next section, was not entirely novel. Rather, it built on surveillance practices that had been developed over the preceding years.[17] The measures adopted in 1972 were folded into the Guidelines for the Pursuit of Politically Motivated Violent Offenders, which was approved by the Conference of Interior Ministers on 15 February 1974.[18] These guidelines laid out a strategy to map, infiltrate, and unsettle the radical milieu, including the use of covert measures, which were to be carried out in close cooperation with the intelligence agencies, and systematic raids on communes. But they also revealed how fragmented and uncoordinated such surveillance could be after the coordinating authority of the federal police had been revoked at the end of 1972, and even as late as the end of 1974 police and prosecutors still knew relatively little about either the structures of the RAF or how support for the group within the radical scene was actually organized.[19]

All of this changed after 11 April 1975, when the Conference of Interior Ministers approved the new Principles for the Collaboration of Federal and State Police in Combatting Politically Motivated Violent Crime.[20] These principles, which were adopted six weeks after the Lorenz kidnapping, were the most important step in the 1970s toward the centralization of police authority in the hands of the Federal Criminal Police, at least in the domain of counterterrorism. The April 1975 agreement was based on the assumption that centralized coordination was necessary because counterterrorism investigations dealt with criminal complexes that could not be disaggregated into clearly demarcated individual offenses. It gave the Federal Criminal Police responsibility for collecting and analyzing information pertaining to all acts of political violence and for coordinating operative measures in the area. In practice, this meant that the state police agencies were required to provide the Federal Criminal Police information relating to some two thousand ongoing terrorism investigations. It also led to the establishment of centralized reporting systems to collect information generated by covert and targeted investigations, passive tracking, the surveillance of incarcerated terrorists, their visitors and their correspondents, and alibi controls. In return, the Federal Criminal Police were to keep the interior ministries abreast of their work through daily situation reports, which fill up thick volumes in the Federal Archive. All of the information flowing in through these reporting systems was stored in the new information system PIOS, which, along with these reporting systems, will be analyzed in the following sections.

At the beginning of 1974, the section of the Protective Services Division responsible for investigating subversive activities had been hived off to create a separate department, which absorbed the SoKo Baader-Meinhof later that year, and in May 1975 the Federal Criminal Police created an independent counterterrorism division to manage the new responsibilities delegated to the agency by the April agreement. This division, which had an initial staff of 145, was headed by Boeden.[21]

The creation, even if only temporarily and on a voluntary basis, of something akin to a German version of the FBI was a sign of the seriousness with which the interior ministers regarded the security situation. It was also a measure to which they only grudgingly agreed.[22] Nevertheless, Interior Minister Werner Maihofer announced at the time that the administration was planning to introduce a law that would institutionalize (and further expand) the authority of the Federal Criminal Police, including authorizing the agency to engage in preventive policing, a responsibility that had heretofore been reserved to the states.[23]

In August 1977, the Conference of Interior Ministers authorized the wider and more systematic involvement of the domestic intelligence agencies in support of the police, especially in monitoring those anti-torture and prisoner's rights groups that the police regarded as a prime recruiting ground for new terrorists. The interior ministry was also planning to request funding for an additional five thousand positions for the federal security agencies.[24] Lastly, several anti-terrorist laws expanded the tools available to the police to map the radical milieu.[25] These laws effectively authorized the extension of police surveillance far into both the *Vorfeld* of potential dangers and the social *Umfeld* of potential offenders,[26] and the police made ample use of these laws to stage raids on alternative bookstores and the left-wing press, which constituted the institutional core of the alternative public sphere.[27] The experience of being on the receiving end of such surveillance played a catalytic role in the consolidation of the privacy-based social movement that took shape at the end of the decade.[28]

Penetrating the Anonymity of the Milieu: Inmate Surveillance and Passive Tracking

Although the heads of the state police forces did not approve Herold's grand plan for the total mobilization of state and society for the liquidation of political violence in February 1975, most of the individual measures were approved by the interior ministers over the next three years. In their systematic integration, these measures represented, in the words of Dieter Schenk, Herold's biographer and former head of the Interpol office of the Federal Criminal Police, "a successful instrument for combatting terrorism, which is unequaled in the world."[29] The four most important, and most controversial, elements of this plan were the surveillance of prisoners, their visitors, and their correspondents; passive tracking; the new information system PIOS; and another innovation that only came into use at the very end of the decade, *Rasterfahndung* (computer matching). This and the following sections will analyze these practices and the privacy issues that they raised.

Terrorists may have acted in a conspiratorial manner, but they could not do so free from all constraints, and Herold made the logistical imperatives of life in the underground into the thread with which the police would eventually weave their map of the radical milieu. Not only did apartments have to be rented and groceries have to be bought; vehicles also had to be procured and then provided with registration papers. However, as Herold noted, "new needs arise with each extension of their logistics. The need for money to pay for food, apartments, automobiles, communications, and weapons continuously increased." These financial needs could be met only by bank robberies, whose planning and execution placed even greater logistical demands on the group and their supporters and thus set in motion an "incessantly escalating, constantly expanding spiral of needs," which consumed much of their energy and constantly exposed them to new risks. "Every action," Herold concluded, "reveals new information about their tactics and their logistical nerve centers."[30]

The presentation that Herold made to the Bundestag domestic affairs committee on 11 May 1977 recapitulated the one that he had made to the heads of the state criminal police forces in February 1975.[31] As can be seen from figure 8.1, at that point 183 persons were in custody on terrorism-related charges; arrest warrants had been issued for 30 additional named individuals; investigations were underway regarding 240 other persons; 400 persons were suspected of engaging in illegal actions, but had not yet been indicted; there were 800 persons whom the police thought likely to commit such actions in the future; and, lastly, there were an additional 5,005 supporters who had engaged in some form of conspiratorial activity that did not constitute an indictable offense. In Herold's exhibit, the two columns to the right of the graphic detail the surveillance methods that were being used to monitor these persons and the additional measures that the police wished to see implemented by the legislature or the civilian administration. However, most of the exhibit is devoted to detailing the logistical imperatives that the terrorists had to obey, the investigatory or operational measures required to choke off these activities, and the legislative and administrative measures required to authorize or support these measures.[32]

The inmate surveillance program had been authorized by the Conference of Interior Ministers in May 1972, but it was not transformed into a centralized electronic monitoring system until the summer of 1975. The central database of all RAF prisoners held in the different states and information on their visitors and their postal correspondents had been established because the police believed that visitors and attorneys were acting as intermediaries who enabled the incarcerated RAF members to communicate among themselves and direct the actions of their supporters on the outside.

It proved to be immensely useful in breaking through the anonymity of the radical milieu, and it became the anchor of the network of police surveillance practices built up from 1975 onward. "By means of prisoner surveillance," Schenk notes, "the Federal Criminal Police were able in a relatively short time to identify a substantial proportion of the RAF supporters and the successor generation. When supplemented with passive tracking and PIOS, this led to an almost complete overview [of the milieu]."[33] The forms that visitors were required to fill out provided the police with handwriting samples that could be matched against evidence collected in other investigations. The problem was that it was not clear whether the Federal Criminal Police had the authority to collect this information. Since it was not necessary for the orderly operation of prisons, it could only be used for preventive purposes, which were reserved to the states. In addition, the passage of the Federal Privacy Protection Law raised the question of whether, in the absence of explicit legislative authorization, the states themselves had the authority to collect this information.[34]

The second pillar of the computerized counterterrorism surveillance system, which was set up in the mid-1970s, was passive tracking (*beobach-*

tende Fahndung). This system had been on the drawing board since 1972, and it was approved by Working Group II in October 1973. Passive tracking allowed the police to construct profiles of the movement and social connections of persons suspected of eight categories of serious crimes. In September 1974, 9,697 persons were the object of such surveillance; approximately one-third of these were under observation for suspected involvement in drug trafficking, and another third were being monitored because of their presumed connections to left-wing political violence.

Figure 8.1. Herold's master plan for combatting terrorism. Source: PA-DBT 3114, 8. Wahlperiode, 15. Sitzung (11 May 1977); several entries whose meaning is not clear have been excluded.

Organizational levels	Police	Legislation, Politics, Administration
Persons		
Organizational Levels (Number of Persons) In custody 183 Arrest warrants issued 30 Ongoing investigations 240 Suspected of illegal activity 400 "Dangerous" (i.e., deemed likely to engage in illegal activity) 800 Supporters 5,005 (with 2,357 vehicles)	Inmate surveillance Central prisoner file (172) Central visitor file (12,664) Central contact file (59,826) Targeted tracking Fake identities Central identification department Covert tracking Observation (70, sporadically) §400a Criminal Code (2) Passive tracking (1,200) Alibi verification Verification of identity in cases of lost ID documents (suspicion of misuse)	Review of prison personnel and incarceration conditions (no isolation!) Harmonization of state police laws Preventive authority for Federal Criminal Police (amendment of §5, Par. 1 of the federal law) Executive authority for federal police working in the states Hotel registration and identification requirements Authority to compare computer files Authority to investigate in advance of concrete dangers Authority to use covert means Obligation of landlords to register empty apartments Organizational consolidation of Federal Criminal Police and Border Police Networking of INPOL, ZEVIS, Aliens Registry, and Central Federal Crime Registry Direct communications among police forces Increased security for secret documents Preventive detention for suspects under §129a Appointment of "plenipotentiaries" for federal and state governments Internationalization of passive tracking

Organizational levels	Police	Legislation, Politics, Administration
Logistics (Things)		

Weapons
  Purchase (domestic & foreign)
  Theft
Explosives
  Laboratories (manufacture)
  Theft and other means of procurement
	Central weapons identification department
	Central explosives identification department
	Public information campaign
	International exchange of information on weapons and explosives
		Amendment of military weapons law
		International harmonization of weapons law
		Mutual assistance between police forces
		Monitoring of legal weapons sales
		Increased security for depots
		Increased penalties for weapons theft
		Obligation of firms to maintain records on sales of surplus explosive components

Identification documents Stolen/lost	Central document identification department Search for lost and stolen documents Verification of authenticity of documents at border crossings, airports, etc.	Measures to insure that blank forms are securely stored and properly issued Use of tamper-proof paper Require car rental agencies to retain customer identification documents Requirement that identification be produced when registering residence, renting apartments, checking into hotels, and booking plane flights

Mobility
  Train
  Plane
  Vehicle
  Theft
  Rental
	INPOL identity verification at *all* border crossings and airports
	Establishment of checkpoints on highways and streets
	Guidelines for gas stations and car rental agencies
	INPOL vehicle tracking
	Monitoring of garages, workshops, and license plate producers
		Free train travel for detectives
		Police authorization to establish control points
		Procurement of terminals and radios
		Secure storage of license plates and registration papers
		Record-keeping requirements for businesses producing license plates and car rental agencies, including right of police to review these records

Means of communication
  Radio
  Phone
  Handwritten
	Central departments for identification of handwriting and typewritten material	Require proof that persons requesting new telephone connections are registered with population registration offices
		Prohibition on the manufacture of listening devices, securing police radio frequencies, radio monitoring

Organizational levels	Police	Legislation, Politics, Administration
Apartments/support bases	Central registry of suspect locations Campaigns to make the public aware of characteristics of terrorist safe houses and workshops	Support by telephone and utility companies
Money Donations Bank robberies	Monitoring for circulation of stolen bank notes (INPOL) Advice sheets for banks, businesses, and foreign institutions	Monitoring of legal flows of money Implementation of resolutions of bank protection commission on security measures
Workshops Printing, forgery, weapons, explosives, vehicles	Central departments for identification of papers and forgeries Public awareness campaign Measures listed above regarding weapons, explosives, and identification documents	
Propaganda Red and White aid groups, prisoners' rights groups, committees, publishers, bookstores, printers, media, churches		Extension of §86 of the Criminal Code to terrorist groups Public information campaigns Full use of existing possibilities: criminal prosecution, right to reply in public media, retractions, association law, demand for reimbursement for cost of police actions, §§88a and 90a of the Criminal Code
Abroad	Strengthening of border controls	Mutual assistance among national police forces
	Bundling of all information in PIOS	

Passive tracking did not involve the continuous, active observation of such persons, and the designation of persons as the object of such surveillance did not give the police the right to detain, search, or question them. Rather, it piggybacked on other laws: whenever police interacted with objects of passive tracking, they were to report relevant information gathered through observation and routine, unobtrusive questioning. Approximately 90 percent of all such encounters took place at border crossings, where the police had the right to question travelers about their destination and purpose, search their vehicles, and determine the identity of all persons traveling in the vehicle. This information was then to be entered into INPOL—hopefully, though not always successfully—without alerting these persons that they were the object of surveillance. Initially, once the state or federal police had decided that a person should be the object of passive tracking, the person was to remain in the system for three years on the assumption that this period would suffice to either collect the evidence needed to open a formal investigation or demonstrate that the initial suspicion was unfounded.[35] According to Herold, the "unique and outstanding significance of the permanent, routine, dragnet-like [and computerized] observation" of the radical milieu by means of passive tracking lay in the way that it helped link together the discrete pieces of information pertaining to the objects of such surveillance: "Every fact, every telephone number, every conspiratorial residence, and every vehicle must be stored in order to connect all of this data to form a great mosaic."[36]

Initially, there was little controversy regarding the legality of the program. However, by early 1976 the debate over the Federal Privacy Protection Law forced the administration to revisit the issue. If passive tracking were deemed an infringement on individual rights, then the task was to determine whether it was a preventive or a repressive measure and whether it was properly authorized.

The debate over the first question represented nothing less than an initial conflict over the meaning of the Federal Privacy Protection Law in the security sector. Critics argued that the practice involved precisely the kinds of information processing that the privacy law was intended to regulate, and they claimed that the systematic character of the observation and the computer-aided integration of the information gleaned from such encounters gave passive tracking a new and more invasive quality in comparison to the isolated, casual observations made by individual officers in earlier times. Others, however, argued that the picture of the movement of the person constructed through passive tracking was so fragmentary that it was questionable whether the practice could be said to entail such an infringement. Herold combined this reasoning with a restatement of older jurisprudence to argue that, since the information gathered through passive tracking was only used internally by the police, since it did not provide the basis for the use of force, and since it was not disclosed to third parties in a way that might harm the person's reputation, the practice did not infringe upon privacy rights.[37] At the time, though, sensibilities were changing, and most of those involved in this debate concluded that the practice did infringe on the privacy rights of the objects of such surveillance.[38]

As for the second question, while an interior ministry report claimed that passive tracking was primarily a preventive measure that was authorized by the general charge to protect against dangers, others argued that it had to be understood as a repressive measure since there was no instance in which passive tracking had contributed to preventing a terrorism-related crime. However, both positions had their own problems: if it were considered a preventive measure, this did not help the Federal Criminal Police, who were only authorized to investigate crimes, not to prevent them; if it were a repressive measure, opinion was divided over whether it was authorized under the Code of Criminal Procedure.[39] And, in any case, the police resisted such a classification because it would have limited their freedom to employ the practice. Moreover, although a 1974 interior ministry memorandum had affirmed the legality of passive tracking if there were "factual indications" (*tatsächliche Anhaltspunkte*) that the person would commit a serious crime in the near future, the author of the document questioned whether this condition was met by many of the people subject to such monitoring. As we shall see, much of the debate over precautionary surveillance pivoted on the degree of certainty of the prognosis that the person would commit a serious crime, and passive tracking and the other new surveillance practices functioned in the space created by such jurisprudential and criminalistic reasoning.[40]

Bull argued that passive tracking could not be based on either the general charge to protect against dangers—"unless one were willing to stretch the concept of 'a specific, imminent danger' to such an extent that it contradicted all previous tendencies to concretize and delimit the concept"— or the Code of Criminal Procedure, since the presumed involvement of the person in certain kinds of criminal activity did not meet the standard of well-founded individual suspicion. He warned that such surveillance "is experienced as a registration of one's everyday life, as something that leads in the direction of—and here I find myself forced to use the word—a surveillance state. It is not that such a state already exists—that is not what I am saying, and I have always disputed that idea. But it is experienced as a step in this direction, and that creates a real problem."[41]

In his May 1977 presentation to the domestic affairs committee, Herold insisted that such surveillance—and possibly even some form of preventive detention—was justified because the persons against whom it was directed had, in fact, been shown to constitute a concrete danger.[42] Herold claimed that information gleaned through passive tracking had enabled the police to identify those involved in the attack on the German embassy in Stockholm; that it had led to the identification of Hans-Joachim Klein, one of the leaders of the Revolutionary Cells, as one of those involved in the December 1975 attack on an OPEC meeting in Vienna; and that passive tracking alone had made it possible to identify the key members of the group around Siegfried Haag, one of the central figures in the second generation of the RAF. Not only did the movement of a cluster of persons under passive tracking enable the police to foresee that a major action was planned.[43] Herold also claimed that, when taken together with the papers carried by Haag, it was entirely predictable that the group was planning an action on the scale of the eventual assassination of Buback, even though it was not possible to determine in advance the precise time and target of the action. Nevertheless, the knowledge that an identifiable group was planning some action showed that passive observation had developed to the point where it was possible to "preventively meet these imminent crimes."[44]

These arguments were buttressed by the second exhibit, which showed the coalescence of the second-generation of the RAF around Haag and the connections of this core group to the Stockholm attackers, the terrorists freed in exchange for Lorenz, and the office of Klaus Croissant (the attorney who defended Baader at the Stammheim trial and who was himself convicted in 1977 of supporting terrorist activity), as well as the involvement of this group in a number of major and minor actions in 1976 and early 1977. The fact that many of these connections had been made through passive tracking reaffirmed Herold's belief that the expansion and refinement of the practice would transform it into an instrument for "genuine prevention." He insisted with reference to this exhibit that "those who will commit the next crimes are already known."[45]

Although the police called for the expansion of passive tracking, which was renamed "police observation" (*polizeiliche Beobachtung*) in the fall of 1977, the guidelines that were actually approved in January 1980 were substantially more restrictive. They permitted passive tracking only for repressive purposes, but not to protect against either concrete or abstract dangers, and only if there were "sufficient factual indications" (*zureichende tatsächliche Anhaltspunkte*) — the same concreteness of suspicion required to open a formal investigation — that the measure could lead to the solution of a serious crime or the apprehension of an offender. The limitation of such surveillance to three months (plus the possibility of renewal) and the requirement that the measure be approved by a prosecuting attorney, rather than by the police themselves, represented tangible restrictions compared to previous practice.[46]

The census decision forced a more explicit consideration of the issue, and we will take up the debate over passive observation and precautionary surveillance more generally in chapter 9. However, the information it generated revealed its full significance only when it was linked to the information generated by police investigations and other reporting systems. PIOS was the mechanism through which this was accomplished.

PIOS: The Logic and Practice of Precautionary Surveillance

The core of the counterterrorism surveillance apparatus constructed in the mid-1970s was a new system known as PIOS, which was an acronym for *P*ersons, *I*nstitutions (such as organizations or groups), numerical *O*bjects (such as addresses, serial numbers, and phone numbers), and *T*hings (in German, *Sachen*, such as vehicles, weapons, or other tools). PIOS was originally conceived as a tool to aid the prosecution at the Stammheim trial of the Baader-Meinhof group by indexing and cross-referencing all of the evidence that had been collected by the police in the course of their investigation of the complex of crimes linked to the group. However, PIOS was approved in the expectation that it would be developed into a larger and more powerful system that would make visible the "complexity" of criminal complexes by establishing connections—and possible criminal suspicion—that might have otherwise gone unnoticed in the investigation of a series of discrete offenses. After the centralization of information and investigational authority in the hands of the Federal Criminal Police in April 1975, PIOS became the central repository for the information flowing in through the prisoner surveillance, passive tracking, and covert and targeted tracking reporting systems. From this point onward, one could say with Schenk that, "like a vast [electronic] canopy PIOS embraces the concentrated knowledge of the police in the terrorism domain; it is comparable to a note pad in which everything from Flensburg [on the Danish border to the north] to Konstanz [on the Swiss border to the south] is to be found."[47]

By May 1977, the names of 78,584 persons, 2,400 institutions, 76,396 objects, and 33,134 things were stored in PIOS, and it was possible to query this data using basic operators ("and," "not," "equals," etc.). However, each of the state criminal police agencies initially had only one dedicated terminal through which to connect to PIOS, and access was restricted to officers assigned to the anti-subversion departments.[48] PIOS was so important, and controversial, because it enabled the police to bring together information on persons who may have been of only peripheral importance in any specific investigation, but whose appearance in multiple contexts might give rise to that degree of suspicion needed to open a formal investigation, and it was the technical means through which the information collected through these new surveillance practices accreted to individuals across time and space. The end effect was to indefinitely suspend the presumption of innocence for those caught in the electronic dragnet created to troll the radical milieu. This use of police surveillance to generate initial suspicion, rather than to confirm existing suspicion, also became one of the key motifs in the surveillance state debate.[49]

The privacy problems associated with PIOS were, as the justice ministry noted, "unique."[50] The criminalistic rationale for such surveillance is clear, even if its precise limits were a legitimate matter of dispute. The 1979 KpS Guidelines governing the collection of information by the police (to be discussed below) permitted the collection of information on "other persons." Although this group was supposed to comprise a small residuum of persons who could not be clearly assigned to other categories, it quickly threatened to become the largest category. Conservative politicians and the police argued that, since terrorists had begun as minor offenders, it was entirely legitimate to enter into PIOS information on anyone suspected of an offense relating to political protest or political violence.[51] The problem was that such reasoning effectively abolished the requirement that the police be able to demonstrate a concrete connection between these persons and the political potential violence that such surveillance was intended to prevent. The scope of such surveillance was made clear by a 1981 audit of the subversion department of the Federal Criminal Police by the Federal Privacy Commissioner. The report concluded that the police were entering into PIOS information on many persons who had no discernible connection to terrorism and that approximately two-thirds of the names stored in PIOS should be deleted.[52]

The second set of privacy problems related to the kinds of information held in PIOS and the conditions of its access and use. Herold once described the system as a "raw, unabridged version of investigatory files."[53] This was simply another way of saying that PIOS contained, in addition to the facts collected by the police in the course of their investigations, unverified information, suspicions, and allegations that could not be used in court. This raised obvious questions about how long such information should be retained and who should have access to it. But the issue went further than this, and it led to a revealing turf war between the police and the Domestic Intelligence Agency.

Both the police and the intelligence agencies were involved in the surveillance of the radical scene. However, the planned PIOS system appeared to encroach upon the domain of the Domestic Intelligence Agency, which claimed a monopoly on the systematic collection of information in the *Vorfeld* of political crime.[54] Police authority was in principle limited to the investigation of specific crimes that had already been committed. However, Herold insisted that the police had to be allowed to collect such *Vorfeld* information because acts of terrorism or subversion were simply the surface manifestations of networks that extended far beyond any individual crime, that, in order to uncover these connections, the police had to be permitted to retain and make use of information that was not directly related to the offender alone, and that they could not rely upon information collected by the intelligence agencies because they had to be able to identify the provenance of their information and explain its probative value in court. In the end, the interior ministry concluded that there was a certain overlap in the obligations of the two agencies and that a certain degree of duplication was necessary in order to ensure the integrity of the information collected by each.[55] This marked an important step in the institutionalization of precautionary surveillance by the police.

In the discussion of PIOS in the Bundestag domestic affairs committee, the worldviews of the privacy commissioners and the police directly clashed over PIOS. Bull argued that the reasoning of the police—that information on contact and other persons had to be collected because it could only later be determined whether they should be regarded as suspects—amounted to a confession that the objects of such surveillance did not meet the standards of well-founded suspicion and that, therefore, such surveillance was constitutionally questionable. Günter Ermisch (CDU), who both before and after his tenure as vice-president of the Federal Criminal Police (1978–81) served in high positions in the interior ministry, retorted—drawing on Herold's account of the fluid relationship between supporters and active terrorists—"But there *is* a kind of suspicion!"[56] But what Bull found most disconcerting was that the exceptional surveillance methods that had been pioneered in the war on terrorism were gradually being extended to other, less exceptional, forms of crime. "In this way, the storage of 'other persons,'" he noted with concern, "thus becomes a typical method for computer-aided crime prevention. The privacy problems associated with this activity will take up part of our attention in the coming years."[57]

Computer Matching: Rethinking the Parameters of Proportionality

The last of the new, computer-aided police surveillance practices developed during the 1970s was *Rasterfahndung*, or computer matching for criminalistic purposes. Like passive tracking, computer matching quickly became part of the criminalistic *sensus communis*. It was controversial less because of the quantity of information that could be processed electronically than because it drew large numbers of persons into the matching process without any prior establishment of probable cause.[58] The key question was whether the security gains promised by computer matching were proportional to the severity of the infringement on the informational rights of the individual entailed by the practice.[59]

There were two forms of computer matching. Positive matching involved the comparison of police data with other databases in order to locate known individuals. This was not an entirely novel practice. Even before INPOL was up and running, the police had matched the national wanted persons list against the local population registries wherever the latter had been computerized. However, positive matching was also used in other ways. In 1975, for example, the police in North Rhineland-Westphalia had matched their files against a sample of 10,000 students receiving financial support under the Federal Educational Assistance Law. There were arrest warrants for 235 of these students, while the police were trying to determine the whereabouts of 276 others. A similar comparison of INPOL data with the information on the 4.5 million persons held by the state's social insurance funds produced 42,000 hits.[60]

Negative matching, on the other hand, involved the comparison of police files with other databases in order to identify that small, residual population who because of their criminal or underground way of life could not exhibit the expected characteristics of the general or normal population. The first two well-known instances of negative matching took place in 1979–80. They followed a similar pattern intended to identify those persons whose underground existence did not permit them to pay their electricity bills under their own names. The one led to the capture of RAF member Rolf Heißler in Frankfurt in June 1979 (and to the incidental arrest of a major drug dealer). This action, which entailed the initial review of 18,000 utility customers, remains the most documented success of negative matching. The other took place as part of an ultimately unsuccessful attempt to locate what investigators believed to be a safe house used by Rolf-Clemens Wagner — a member of the second generation of the RAF, who was suspected of complicity in the Schleyer kidnapping — in Hamburg.[61] Although the fact that one paid one's utility bill in cash rather than by bank transfer might appear to be an utterly innocuous piece of information, computer matching showed that, in the proper context, it could be very revealing. There were few better illustrations of the Constitutional Court's dictum that, in the age of electronic data processing, there was no longer any such thing as "harmless" data.

The strongest defense of such matching came from Ermisch.[62] At the beginning of the decade, Baader had dandied about the scene in flashy clothes and stolen cars, so that BMWs were known colloquially as "Baader-Meinhof-Wagons." By the middle of the decade, the second generation of the RAF had adopted entirely different tactics. They had cut themselves off completely from their previous lives; they blended into their social environment under fake identities; and they had perfected counter-counterterrorism tactics. These developments substantially diminished the effectiveness of classical criminalistic methods, and the success of the Heißler investigation was proof, Ermisch claimed, of the appropriateness of computer matching as a means for identifying such persons. Moreover, even though matching made new informational demands on persons who would soon be shown to be nonsuspects, the practice met the constitutional standard of proportionality, he explained, because there was no less intrusive means of identifying these persons. Proponents argued that the potential harms of computer matching were further minimized by the restriction of the practice to serious crimes and by the fact that—in the case of negative matching—the police never even learned the names of the persons whose information was electronically reviewed and who were excluded as nonsuspects. Herold characterized the practice as "almost clinically sterile."[63]

None of Ermisch's arguments could be dismissed out of hand, and in 1980 federal and state privacy commissioners found no reason to object to those computer matching programs that had been undertaken to date.[64] However, Bull argued that the large-scale use of information without probable cause made legislative action unavoidable; much of the literature focused on defining more precisely the procedural protections required in order to ensure the proportionality of the measure; and, as we shall see in chapter 9, the issue was addressed again in the 1980s debate over the reform of police law.[65]

The Schleyer Kidnapping and the Disenchantment of the German FBI

On the afternoon of 5 September 1977, Hanns Martin Schleyer, the president of the National League of Employer's Associations and the National Association of German Industry, was kidnapped as he was being driven from work to his apartment in a Cologne suburb; his driver and the three policemen following in a chase car were killed.[66] Not only was the Schleyer kidnapping the most important political trauma in the history of the Federal Republic; it also precipitated a political reaction against, and a theoretical critique of, the surveillance apparatus that had been constructed over the preceding years, and the new concern for personal privacy to which this reaction gave rise marked the end of that peculiar balancing of civil liberties and state power that had been the defining feature of the postwar internal security regime.

During the hunt for Schleyer, political decisions were made by a crisis staff that included leaders of the major parties, the Bundestag leadership, and other members of the cabinet. Maihofer immediately placed the Federal Criminal Police in charge of the investigation; Herold assumed direct control over operational measures; and the central operational command was supported by a special commission and by a "coordinating staff" that served as the relay between the federal agency and the state police of North Rhineland-Westphalia, who had the necessary local knowledge and who could mobilize the requisite manpower in the region.

Immediately after the kidnapping, thousands of policemen fanned out across the country in search of Schleyer. They set up roadblocks on major traffic arteries; patrols were intensified to keep the kidnappers from escaping across the Rhine; trains were stopped in the middle of nowhere so that policemen could conduct identity checks; every available helicopter was pressed into service to erect flying roadblocks on the nation's highways; apartments belonging to any- and everybody in the radical milieu were searched; and the security agencies set about determining the whereabouts of all objects of passive tracking and their contact persons.[67]

This unprecedented centralization of police authority in the hands of the Federal Criminal Police was an ad hoc measure that ultimately created as many problems as it solved. Nevertheless, it quickly became the point around which the many discrete developments described in the previous pages coalesced to form a picture of the West German police that many people found worrisome, and a palpable sense of disenchantment with the modernized, centralized, computerized police surveillance apparatus constructed since 1975 made itself felt almost immediately. The doubled perception of the police as both omnipotent and ineffectual, the passage of the Federal Privacy Protection Law, and the growing strength of a privacy-based social movement directed against the perceived excesses of the "surveillance state" led to a reaction against the counterterrorism strategy that had been pursued under Genscher and Maihofer.

In their hunt for Schleyer, the police continued to develop new surveillance and tracking methods. Some of these, such as Action Red Light, turned into unintentional parodies of themselves.[68] Others were more promising. For example, many of the letters from the Schleyer kidnappers had been posted around 6:30 a.m. from the Paris Gare du Nord. In hopes of identifying the courier, the police collected the names of everyone between the ages of twenty-five and thirty-five traveling on the night train from Cologne, which arrived shortly before 6:30. Approximately 3,000 names were then matched against INPOL, and RAF member Werner Lotze was identified as the probable courier.[69]

Herold immediately concluded that Schleyer's kidnappers had to be holding him in a place that met certain criteria (easy access to highways, a garage and elevator that would permit them to enter and exit the building unseen, etc.), though this insight, like that into the logistical imperatives of life in the underground, owed little to the new information technologies.[70] As we have seen, the apartment where Schleyer was actually being held was quickly identified as a possible hideout by the local police.[71] However, the form on which the lead was recorded was lost somewhere between the special commission and the coordinating staff, and the local police did not have the authority to act on their own. Ultimately, the failure to act on this lead cost the police their best chance to rescue Schleyer before he was spirited off to The Hague a week later.[72]

Only days after the Schleyer kidnapping, *Der Spiegel* published a story in which it essentially declared all of the recent innovations in police surveillance to be irrelevant. The hermetic isolation of conspiratorial groups, the tactical shift to living inconspicuously among the middle classes, and the use of doctored rather than counterfeit identification documents meant that it was much more difficult to distinguish terrorists from the general population. As one police official concluded on a note of exasperation, "These days we have to treat everyone as a suspect." The computer systems of the police and intelligence agencies, the magazine argued, were incapable of answering questions of strategy; the Schleyer kidnapping had proven that neither INPOL nor PIOS could predict or prevent crime; the police had been unable to infiltrate terrorist groups; and the planned institution of a hotel identification requirement would, the magazine insisted, lead to the capture not of terrorists schooled in countertactics, but of petty criminals who were too stupid to ply their trade. The article implied, and Maihofer conceded, that there were intrinsic limitations on the ability of democratic societies to prevent terrorism.[73]

This new sensitivity to the limits of police surveillance went hand in hand with a greater willingness to recognize the importance of chance.[74] It also raised the question of the role of the public—and of the role of democratic political education, which was one of the centerpieces of Social Democratic policies toward political radicalism.[75] There are many instances where important leads were provided by building managers, shop owners, and that redoubtable German institution, the concierge or *Hausmeister*.[76] While some regarded these leads as proof of the ineffectualness of the police and the intelligence agencies, Baum argued that the cooperation of the public was an "elementary component" of police work and that police pressure had forced terrorists living underground to make mistakes, which were then capitalized upon by a watchful and supportive public.[77]

Nevertheless, it was impossible to avoid recognizing the slippage between the perfection of the surveillance apparatus and the inability to arrest those who were most intensively sought by the police. Many police officials blamed this on flawed strategy. In early November, *Der Spiegel* cited an anonymous memorandum on "federal-state relations in the security field" that had been circulating through the state police offices. This

Figure 8.2. Police officers rushing a mainframe computer to a crime scene. © Luis Murschetz, Munich.

document charged that, in the terrorism field, the Federal Criminal Police had added nothing of value to the work of the state police agencies. "To date, there has been no important case where the capture of a wanted person can be attributed to the investigations of the Federal Criminal Police," the memorandum concluded. "All notable terrorists," it continued, "were taken into custody by the state police forces without any concrete clues provided by the Federal Criminal Police." To drive home the point, the story was accompanied by a cartoon (figure 8.2) showing a team of police officers rushing a mainframe computer—in an oversized sedan chair—to a crime scene. Herold, however, still held fast to the belief that the centralized analysis of criminal information would reveal connections that could never be grasped by even the most experienced state detective.[78] Although the path that would ultimately be taken remained undecided in November 1977, by the next spring the political winds had clearly turned against Maihofer and Herold.

In the midst of the hunt for Schleyer, both Herold and the interior ministry circulated drafts for a new Federal Criminal Police Law. The amendments would have institutionalized the responsibility of the federal police for investigating terrorism, permitted the agency to issue instructions to the state police forces in such instances, and given it the preventive authority that Herold so keenly sought.[79] Herold and Maihofer also used the Schleyer kidnapping to argue that the Federal Criminal Police could fulfill its role as the hub of the national criminal information system only if the fragmented federalist architecture of INPOL were replaced by a more unified system, such as INPOL-new.[80]

In March 1978, Chancellor Schmidt asked former Interior Minister Hermann Höcherl (CSU) to investigate the loss of the lead to the apartment where Schleyer had been held and make recommendations for improving state counterterrorism measures. Although the report that Höcherl submitted in May of that year did not directly blame the Federal Criminal Police for the loss of the crucial lead, its recommendations amounted to a repudiation of the centralizing strategy pursued by Maihofer and Herold. The report argued that the current practice of charging the Federal Criminal Police with extensive investigatory responsibilities was overextending the agency's manpower while depriving investigators of the local knowledge that could only be provided by the state police. It proposed that as much investigatory authority as possible be returned to the states and that the Federal Criminal Police again concentrate on using their forensic and informatic expertise to support the investigative work of the state police forces. As the counterpart to the proposed circumscription of the investigative activity of the federal police, the report endorsed Herold's conception of INPOL-new.[81]

Höcherl's proposals were welcomed by the Conference of Interior Ministers, who in August 1978 revoked the expanded counterterrorism authority that they had given to the federal police in the spring of 1975. In his report, Höcherl had argued—echoing Herold—that the new information and communication technologies made it possible to combine organizational decentralization with informational centralization, and, at the same meeting where they rolled back the investigative and coordinating roles of the Federal Criminal Police, the interior ministers approved Herold's plan for INPOL-new. Since all of these measures could be implemented without amending the Federal Criminal Police Law, the ministers decided to defer further consideration of this issue. The census decision and the complications involved in the juridification of the new surveillance practices ultimately delayed the amendment of the law until 1997.[82]

In his report on this September 1978 meeting of the Conference of Interior Ministers, Staak noted that Baum was working intensively to dissipate the aura that had heretofore surrounded the Federal Criminal Police and the centralized, computerized surveillance apparatus constructed since the beginning of the decade.[83] This decision by the interior ministers, the *Hessische Polizeirundschau* observed, marked the end of an era in which politicians and the public alike had been mesmerized by the idea that terrorism and organized crime could be successfully combatted only by a centralized federal police. However, the publication observed, recent events had revealed this faith to be an illusion: "Above all, the failures of the past two years have created a space in which the doctrine of the centralized combatting of terrorism, which had been all-too-quickly canonized as doctrine of salvation, can be reexamined—this time in a more thorough manner." The interior ministers had at long last drawn the consequences of this reconsideration.[84]

Imposing Privacy Law on the Police

Maihofer's appointment as Interior Minister to succeed Genscher had reflected the influence of the social-liberal wing of the party. However, the shifting balance between the social and free market wings of the party, the personal disaffinities between Maihofer and both Schmidt and Genscher, and the resentment of the party left toward his anti-terror policies progressively undermined his support, and Maihofer resigned in June 1978, in part to take responsibility for both mistakes in the hunt for Schleyer and several surveillance scandals that had come to light during his tenure.[85] He was succeeded by Baum. As we saw in chapter 5, Baum's understanding of internal security balanced civil liberties and state power in a very different way than both his FDP predecessors as interior minister and the conservative parties, and privacy rights were the mechanism that he employed to impose new limits on police surveillance.

One of Baum's first actions on taking office was to establish, at the request of the domestic affairs committee, a commission to review INPOL and the other collections of personal information held by the Federal Criminal Police to determine whether they complied with the federal privacy law that had gone into effect at the beginning of the year.[86] The preface to the commission report, which was not completed until the following April, noted that privacy law was a test case for the willingness to impose legal limits on the use of technology and thus to distinguish what was legally permissible from what was technologically possible.[87]

The report, which reviewed thirty-eight separate paper and electronic information systems, concluded that virtually all of the files maintained by the Federal Criminal Police did, in fact, comply with the federal pri-

Figure 8.3. Herold (right) explaining his criminalistic philosophy to Privacy Commissioner Bull (left). Courtesy of Hans Peter Bull. Previously published in Hans Peter Bull, *Widerspruch zum Mainstream. Ein Rechtsprofessor in der Politik* (Berliner Wissenschafts-Verlag, 2012), 149.

vacy law.[88] Although Herold rightly noted that each of the databases maintained by the Federal Criminal Police had been authorized by the Conference of Interior Ministers, the passage of the Federal Privacy Protection Law meant that such measures now required formal legislative authorization. Bull's hasty comments concerning the illegality of some of the files poisoned his relationship with Herold, who took such charges as an attack on his own honor and that of the police as a whole. Eventually Bull and Herold were able to narrow, though never fully eliminate, the polemical distance that had originally separated them.[89]

Although there had been occasional inquiries as to whether INPOL complied with the privacy law being drafted, at the time no one had voiced any serious concerns in this regard.[90] However, much like the recent revelations concerning the American National Security Agency, the sheer scope of the information detailed in this report astonished the public and confirmed its worst fears. The liberal newspaper *Die Zeit* complained that politicians were failing to protect individual freedom, "which has always been based on the nonknowledge of the authorities," from the novel threats posed by the "total information network" that was being constructed in the security sector. If total security could be achieved only at the cost of total surveillance and total unfreedom, then the limitation of the information available to the police was a small price to pay, the newspaper reasoned, to preserve individual freedom.[91] These concerns reached a new level with the 1978 publication in *Stern* of a series of articles on security, order, and state violence, and with a weightier series of investigative articles that appeared the following year in *Der Spiegel* under the title "The Steel Net Is Being Drawn over Us."[92] The privacy audit and these publications were the catalyst for much of the discussion of the legality of passive tracking and PIOS cited in the preceding sections.

At the same time that this review was underway, the federal and state criminal police agencies were drafting guidelines for the creation and retention of criminal records. These regulations, which were known as the KpS Guidelines (Kriminalpolizeiliche personenbezogene Sammlungen), were approved by the Conference of Interior Ministers in March 1979. They represented an initial attempt to craft privacy regulations for the police, and the experience gained through the application of these guidelines was to eventually become the basis for future domain-specific legislation.[93]

The adoption of the KpS Guidelines led to a systematic review of the information held by the federal and state police agencies. Many of the problems identified by these audits related to information that had been entered into INPOL and PIOS when these systems first went into operation. However, by the early 1980s, Bull painted a more positive picture of the way that personal information was being handled by the police.[94] A large number of criminal records were culled during the following years.[95] In 1988, an audit by the federal privacy commissioner found that the number of individual names contained in the integrated internal security database APIS had been reduced by half in comparison with 1982; the audit found it particularly noteworthy that all of the individual criminal files had been reviewed for retention or destruction in accordance with the KpS Guidelines.[96] Similar processes were also underway at the state level.[97]

Many of the files that were deleted at the beginning of the 1980s were undoubtedly superannuated, and the extent to which this culling of low-hanging fruit enhanced either individual privacy or the efficiency of the police remains an open question. However, it still led to conflict between the privacy commissioners and the police. The most important of these conflicts, which was already discussed in chapter 5, went to the heart of the federal privacy law. Determining whether the police were adhering to privacy law and regulations required that they make at least a provisional determination regarding the need for specific pieces of information. The police disputed the competence of the privacy commissioners in this domain. As Alfred Stümper, a senior security official in Baden-Württemberg whose work will be examined in greater detail in chapter 9, argued, such decisions "must be reserved to the individual ministries and agencies because it is a determination that can only be made on the basis of the comprehensive, specialized knowledge that only they possess. The privacy commissioners have no understanding of these issues, and their competence does not entitle them to pass judgment on all of these questions."[98] While Bull was willing to defer to the judgment of the police to a substantial degree, he insisted that the privacy commissioners had to be free to determine whether basic conditions for collection of information had been met if the privacy protection law were not to be entirely eviscerated.[99]

Conflicts over privacy and the role of the Federal Criminal Police led to the steady deterioration of relations between Herold and Baum, and, after the October 1980 Bundestag election had strengthened the position of the coalition and solidified Baum's position, Herold concluded that there was little room left for him.[100] The lack of support from both conservatives, who could not tolerate either Herold's centralism or the progressive ideas that periodically flowed from his portable typewriter, and many members of his own coalition, who regarded him as the progenitor of the new surveillance, rendered his position more precarious, as did his supreme confidence that he alone was capable of managing the computerized apparatus that he had constructed and safely steering the ship of state past the dangers of domestic terrorism.[101] Herold's health problems, which were the consequence of wartime injuries, rendered him—in theory—unfit for police duty, and they provided the pretext to force him from office. His tenure officially ended on 31 March 1981.

His more practical-minded successor Heinrich Boge (SPD), who had previously served as head of the Hannover police and as Ministerialdirektor in the interior ministry, showed far less interest in the informationalization of policing, which had been the alpha and omega of Herold's work since the 1960s.[102] This was only one of many possible endings. It was not, however, an inevitable one, and it should not be forgotten that both the Schleyer investigation and the subsequent history of the West German police might have turned out very differently had the sheet of paper containing the lead pointing to the apartment in the Cologne suburb of Erftstadt, where Schleyer was being held, not been lost in the shuffle.

Theorizing the Surveillance State

The federalist critique of the centralization of power in the hands of the Federal Criminal Police was not the only discourse of disenchantment employed at the time to theorize the problems associated with the development of police surveillance. They were theorized from a different direction by a second discourse, whose central concept was the "surveillance state."[103] This discourse on the surveillance state was primarily a discourse of the civil libertarian left, and it was employed most often by critical intellectuals, who—unlike Genscher, Maihofer, Herold, and other officials—had the good fortune to not be personally responsible for enforcing the nation's laws and protecting public security.

At the time, Podlech defined the surveillance state as a polity in which "the state, as a centrally organized bureaucracy without any internal informational differentiation, . . . substitutes the exploitation of informational asymmetries and informational monopolies for the use of physical force and comprehensively controls the behavior of its citizens." This definition, which may have been the only one that was advanced at the time, captured important elements of this discourse: the role of information and its bureaucratic processing as the basis of state power, the unrestricted secondary use of personal information by the security agencies, and the shift in analytical focus from fascism, capitalism, and naked repression to the use of information for preventive or precautionary social control.[104]

A number of other, often overlapping, tropes were also woven into this discourse. The implementation of the Radicals Resolution, which inverted the presumption of loyalty and innocence and entailed the kind of snooping into individual beliefs and convictions that had long been regarded as the essence of the invasion of privacy, gave rise to a palpable sense that the security agencies were unable to distinguish between dissent and subversion. As we saw in chapter 5, the separation rule had been imposed to prevent the reestablishment of a secret police that possessed executive or coercive powers and employed covert methods. However, the increasingly widespread use of covert methods by the police, which will be discussed in greater detail in chapter 9, the expansion of precautionary surveillance in the *Vorfeld* of well-founded individual suspicion, and the use of such authority to generate suspicion, rather than to further investigate in cases where well-founded suspicion had already been established, were also important tropes in the discourse on the surveillance state.[105] Moreover, the use of information for social control was only possible so long as the agencies through which this power was exercised were not themselves accessible to democratic control. In an often-cited essay, Steinmüller described the problematic expansion of the arcane domain of the security agencies, and he regarded their immunity to outside control and the growing size and reach of their information systems as one of the factors behind the transformation of the Federal Republic into an illiberal "security state" (*Sicherheitsstaat*). In addition, the absence of democratic control over the security agencies meant that it was virtually impossible to escape their continued scrutiny once one had become the object of such surveillance. All of this gave rise to a Kafkaesque sense of helplessness resulting from the loss of control over one's personal information, one's identity, and one's freedom to anonymous bureaucracies.[106]

Information systems are useless without data to populate them. In a cover story on "The New World of 1984," which was published in January 1983, *Der Spiegel* spoke—misleadingly—of the transparency of nine million citizens whose data was stored in "secret" databases. As evidence, the magazine cited the databases maintained by a variety of organizations, from the social insurance funds and vehicle registration offices to book clubs and banks, as well as the fifteen million criminal records maintained by the police. What really concerned the magazine was the possibility that "a total electronic bureaucracy"—whatever that might have meant—could construct profiles or dossiers on every individual, their property, their business partners, and their lovers.[107]

The dangers associated with all of these political and legal trends were amplified by the new technologies. Drawing parallels with Orwell's *1984*, *Der Spiegel* rattled off a list of the new observational technologies (cameras, microphones, and bugs) and described the ways that they were being used to monitor individuals in their homes and in the wider world.[108] The magazine was equally concerned about the use of electronic data processing for organized surveillance of the population, and it ultimately concluded that the use of computers in these ways was opening the door to a more modern incarnation of the Orwellian surveillance state: "Big Brother has gone electronic. We do not yet live in a totalitarian surveillance state, but there are things that point in this direction."[109]

The central tropes of this rancorous discourse on the surveillance state all represented attempts to conceptualize one dimension or another of the erosion of the limits of liberal police law—either the legal, institutional, and political preconditions of this shift or its operational implementation. The underlying reasoning had been unintentionally spelled out by Maihofer at a November 1975 conference on police and prevention, where he warned that "just as efforts to combat crime can be carried ad absurdum by plans to achieve total repression, so we must not allow the precautionary principle—as a consequence of anticipated mistrust of each and every citizen—to lead to total correction and control by the state."[110] Much of this discourse focused on the consequences of these logics of total prevention and total repression, the ways in which they were displacing the traditional limits on police authority,[111] and their role in the governance of the welfare state.

For example, in 1979, the critic Hans Magnus Enzensberger undertook to explain the peculiar state of West German democracy to an American audience. In his talk, he described two overlapping regimes of repression and surveillance. The one, he argued, was characteristic of the authoritarian state as it had existed from the early 1800s to 1945 and beyond. The other, which had only recently emerged, was based on the political integration of the working classes by means of consumerism and social services. Societies of this latter type were governed, Enzensberger argued in terms that paralleled Foucault's contemporary lectures on liberal governmentality, not by repressing individual interests, but rather by normalizing social deviance. This was the project of total prevention, and Enzensberger presciently identified Herold as the master thinker of this governmental logic (which was, as we have seen, the focus of the census protests and which will be discussed in greater detail in chapter 9). For Enzensberger, Herold's conception of security depended not on the swiftness, sureness, and severity of repression, but rather on being able to "foresee and eliminate every imaginable malfunction [of the social mechanism], no matter what causes it or what its motivation may be," before it could manifest itself as a concrete social problem.[112] What Herold envisioned, according to Enzensberger, was "the preventive planning of a cybernetically controlled society without breakdowns"[113] — that is, one in which all potential disruptions were anticipated and forestalled — and he likened this vision of total prevention, which was ultimately predicated on total information and the total transparency of the individual, to a "New Atlantis of Internal Security" or a "Social Democratic City of the Sun."[114]

Another strand of the surveillance state literature focused on both the information required to democratically govern the welfare state[115] and on the limits and failures of such governance. This latter literature argued that state surveillance was the mechanism through which the logic of total repression functioned to contain those social conflicts that could neither be prevented in the manner described by Herold nor resolved in a democratic manner. In such accounts, surveillance served as an essential means of governance in a new sociopolitical formation: the authoritarian "security state" (*Sicherheitsstaat*).[116]

By 1986, the Greens and the diverse groups associated with the new party had begun to mobilize against both the packet of security laws discussed in chapter 5 and the proposed reforms of state police law, which we will discuss in chapter 9.[117] Their arguments focused on the dangers of total repression. For example, the National Working Group of Critical Police Officers, a civil liberties group closely associated with the Greens, warned that "in a state governed by the rule of law not everything that increases the efficiency of the police must be allowed. The means employed by the security agencies must be proportional to the intended goal, namely the preservation of a safe space for constitutional rights in a democratic society. Total security — even assuming that such a thing is actually possible in human society—would mean total unfreedom."[118] In North Rhineland-Westphalia, the Greens later turned with a vengeance against the liberal civil libertarian Burkhard Hirsch, claiming that the March 1990 state police law, which included the precautionary mandate that will be discussed in chapter 9, turned the census decision on its head in pursuit of the "illusionary hope that the expansion of police authority and the methods available to them will protect society against every danger and every form of crime."[119] And the National Working Group of Critical Police Officers bemoaned the death of the liberal state and ironically celebrated the advent of its successor: "Long live the preventive surveillance state!"[120]

Not everyone agreed with these accounts. But even those persons who recognized the dangers of the new surveillance were not necessarily willing to agree that the country had been transformed into a surveillance state. For example, Jochen Bölsche, the editor of the *Spiegel* series, warned against exaggerating the current state of affairs: "Whoever depicts the Federal Republic in 1979 as a perfected surveillance state conjures up that against which he warns."[121] In his second annual report, Bull reiterated his belief that the Federal Republic was not a surveillance state.[122] He also downplayed the idea that the security agencies were tightening their grip on the country: "The oft-feared integration of all of the information systems of the security agencies does not exist," he insisted.[123] As he later explained, "The Federal Republic was never a surveillance state, and it was never on its way to becoming one. There were failings, and there were also serious mistakes, by both the Federal Criminal Police and the Domestic Intelligence Agency. But this was not intentional, and it was not a structural feature of the system. In a number of individual cases, this led to harms. However, this was not the result of systematic surveillance or repression."[124]

The business magazine *Wirtschaftswoche* also refused to paint a uniformly bleak picture. The magazine was optimistic about the commercial potential of the new technologies (especially the interactive video terminal system under construction at the time by the Bundespost). Although it was also concerned about the impact of the machine-readable ID card, in the end the magazine concluded that "in the novel [1984] it was not machines, but man who ruled over man."[125] Although *Der Spiegel* had spoken of Big Brother having gone digital, the magazine also noted that the trends it had described were just that, trends, and it qualified the underlying technological pessimism by noting that these technologies could lead to the creation of a "total state" only if they were appropriated by an authoritarian regime. However, the magazine saw just such a constellation taking shape as a result of Zimmermann's appointment as interior minister.[126]

Writing from the civil libertarian left, the authors of the most important study of the West German police during these years criticized what they regarded as simplistic accounts of an omniscient, omnipotent surveillance state. Such accounts, they argued, generalized too quickly from such scandals as the Traube affair and took at face value both the normative, aspirational pronouncements by police officials and contemporary analyses of the techno-logic of the new police information systems. As a result, they failed to recognize the many systematic limitations on police surveillance. In contrast, they argued, the police were structurally incapable of generating the knowledge required to anticipate and preventively quash social conflict and political dissent. In fact, they claimed that the new surveillance reflected not so much the new power of the security agencies as an attempt to compensate for their fundamental insecurity and disorientation: "Criminologically and criminalistically society appears to have come out of joint . . . . If one reads the critical reflections on society and culture that are found in articles written about police strategy, it is impossible to avoid the impression that society has come off the rails and that it is losing its moral and cultural center."[127]

The census decision moved the surveillance state debate into the political mainstream. In September 1984, the Hessian government sponsored a symposium, which was attended by some four hundred politicians, security officials, privacy advocates, and journalists, on the topic "information society or surveillance state."[128] In November of that year, the Police Leadership Academy in Hiltrup sponsored a conference in hopes of deflating the overheated rhetoric of the surveillance state.[129] At this conference, Boge argued that privacy legislation was hindering the work of the police; he insisted that critics had conjured up a general crisis of trust in the police, whose surveillance was directed not at the general population but only at those suspected of breaking the law; and he appealed to the privacy commissioners to calm the waves thrown up by the new "privacy hysteria."[130] The same point had been made at the Hessian symposium by Heribert Hellenbroich (CDU), the president of the Domestic Intelligence Agency, who declared that he was more afraid of a rigid privacy regime, or what he called a "computer privacy surveillance state" (*Datenschutz-Überwachungsstaat*), in which individual privacy took priority over measures to promote the common good.[131]

The surveillance state debate tailed off after 1986–87 as its central concerns were refocused on the security laws discussed in chapter 5.[132] There was one final variant of the surveillance state discourse. While those on the left argued that the new surveillance practices were undermining liberty, privacy, and security, the police themselves articulated a positive version of the logic of total repression. In chapter 9, I will use this line of thought to analyze the debate over precautionary surveillance and the revision of liberal police law.

Notes

1. Horst Herold, "Taktische Wandlungen des deutschen Terrorismus," *Die Polizei* 67, no. 12 (1976): 401–5, especially 404; and Herold, "Perspektiven der internationalen Fahndung nach Terroristen. Möglichkeiten und Grenzen," *Kriminalistik* 34, no. 4 (1980): 165–71, especially 169.
2. PA-DBT 3114, 8. Wahlperiode, 21. Sitzung (1 September 1977), 34.
3. Herold, "Perspektiven der international Fahndung nach Terroristen," 169. The article "'Eigentlich müßte jeder verdächtig sein': Das Dilemma der Terroristen-Fahndung: Untergrund im Bürgermaske," *Der Spiegel*, 12 September 1977, 22–33, mapped out (30) a similarly direct path from the organizations solidarizing with imprisoned RAF members into the underground.
4. Hannes Mangold, *Fahndung nach dem Raster. Informationsverarbeitung bei der bundesdeutschen Kriminalpolizei, 1965–1984* (Chronos, 2017).
5. Boeden/Bundeskriminalamt, Betr.: Bekämpfung terroristischer Gewaltkriminalität (10 May 1977), BAK B106/83846, Bd. 1.
6. This topos was employed by Genscher, *Sten. Ber.*, 6. Wahlperiode, 188. Sitzung (7 June 1972), 10980; Herold, Vortrag bei der Evangelischen Akademie in Tutzing (6 December 1977), BAK B136/15687, Bd. 4; and Maihofer, PA-DBT 3114, 8. Wahlperiode, 11. Sitzung (14 April 1977), 36.
7. Both Petra Terhoeven, *Die Rote Armee Fraktion* (C. H. Beck, 2017), 91–92; and Dominik Rigoll, "Kampf um die innere Sicherheit: Schutz des Staates oder der Demokratie?" in *Hüter der Ordnung. Die Innenministerien in Bonn und Ost-Berlin nach dem Nationalsozialismus*, ed. Frank Bösch and Andreas Wirsching (Wallstein, 2018), 454–97, especially 497, argue that Baum's tenure as Interior Minister marked the end of the postwar internal security regime, though neither of them makes specific reference to the role of privacy law in this process.
8. *Sten. Ber.*, 6. Wahlperiode, 188. Sitzung (7 June 1972), 10979.
9. Minutes of the 27 January 1972 Conference of Interior Ministers in *Der Baader-Meinhof-Report*, 209–18, citation 210; and the supporting materials in BAK B131/1334.
10. Zusammenfassung der Grundlagen für die Zusammenarbeit zwischen Bund und Ländern bei der Bekämpfung politisch motivierter Gewalttäter (undated, but after April 1975), BAK B136/5055; resolution of the Innenministerkonferenz (22 May 1972) in *Der Baader-Meinhof-Report*, 219–20; and Dieter Schenk, *Der Chef. Horst Herold und das BKA* (Spiegel-Buchverlag, 1998), 106–11.
11. See the memorandum from the Ständiger Konferenz der Innenminister (22 May 1972), HHStA Abt. 544/866.
12. For an example of the obstacles to such coordination, see BMI/Ministerialrat Kurt Fritz to Herold, Betr.: Iststandfeststellungen und Sollvorstellungen für polizeiliche Aufgabengebiete (October 1973), BAK B131/1361.
13. *Sten. Ber.* 7. Wahlperiode, 168. Sitzung (25 April 1975), 11784.
14. *Sten. Ber.* 7. Wahlperiode, 155. Sitzung (13 March 1975), 10735.
15. Cited in Schenk, *Der Chef*, 199–200.
16. This did not, however, mean that Herold abandoned his earlier understanding of crime as a social problem. See Horst Herold, "Die Polizei als gesellschaftliches Diagnoseinstrument," in *Die neue Sicherheit. Vom Notstand zur Sozialen Kontrolle*, ed. Roland Appel, Dieter Hummel, and Wolfgang Hipped (Kölner Volksblatt Verlag, 1988), 65–92, especially 80.
17. Schenk, *Der Chef*, 109.
18. Grundsätze für die polizeiliche Fahndung nach politisch motivierter Gewalttätern, BAK B131/1579 und StAH 136-1/2455.
19. See the comments by former federal attorney Joachim Lampe, who prosecuted the government case against Siegfried Haag, in Eckhard Stasch, "Die Aktion 'Winterreise'

gegen die RAF. Die RAF-Prozesse - Ehemalige Bundesanwälte erinnern sich," video, Bundeszentrale für politische Bildung, 2008, http://www.bpb.de/mediathek/190754/die-aktion-winterreise-gegen-die-raf.
20. Sondersitzung des AK II am 2. April 1975: Bekämpfung der politisch motivierten Gewaltkriminalität, BAK B106/83836, Bd. 1; Zusammenfassung der Grundlagen für die Zusammenarbeit zwischen Bund und Ländern bei der Bekämpfung politisch motivierter Gewalttäter (undated), BAK B136/5055; and Regelung über die Zusammenarbeit von Bund und Ländern im Ermittlungs- und Informationsbereich zur Bekämpfung der politisch motivierten Gewaltkriminalität, NRW NW 408/2, Bd. 2.
21. Werner Maihofer, "25 Jahre Bundeskriminalamt," *Bulletin*, 26 March 1976, 319–22, claimed that this new division, whose staff had risen in the interim to 233, had played a major role in the capture of no fewer than 138 terrorists.
22. Beyer to BMI (12 May 1975), BAK B106/91142, noted that Schmidt's public speculations on the need for a kind of German FBI had been the signal for a temporary shift in the balance of federalist power. See "Ein deutsches FBI?" *Die Welt*, 1 September 1977.
23. See the record of Maihofer's press conference (7 May 1975), BAK B136/15687, Bd. 3.
24. PA-DBT 3114, 8. Wahlperiode, 21. Sitzung (1 September 1977), 41–42,44, and 79–83. Sitzung (26 April 1978), 49–51; ÖS 9 to Z I 5, Betr.: Massnahmen zur Bekämpfung des Terrorismus (31 August 1977), BAK B106/83846; and the appendices to the letter from the BMI (27 May 1977), StAH 136-1/2432. This latter measure would have increased the staff of the Federal Criminal Police from 2,545 to 3,867, the Federal Intelligence Agency from 1,758 to 2,723, and the Border Police from 25,653 to 28,336, while another thirty-two officials were to be hired by the public security section of the federal interior ministry.
25. Uwe Berlit and Horst Dreier, "Die legislative Auseinandersetzung mit dem Terrorismus," in *Protest und Reaktion. Analysen Zum Terrorismus*, ed. Fritz Sack and Heinz Steinert (Westdeutscher Verlag, 1984), 228–318; and Philipp H. Schulte, *Terrorismus und Anti-Terrorismus-Gesetzgebung: Eine rechtssoziologische Analyse* (Waxmann, 2008), 119ff.
26. Stefan Middel, *Innere Sicherheit und preventive Terrorismusbekämpfung* (Nomos, 2007), 219.
27. Uwe Sonnenberg, *Von Marx zum Maulwurf. Linker Buchhandel in Westdeutschland in den 1970er Jahren* (Wallstein, 2016); and Sven Reichardt, *Authentizität und Gemeinschaft. Linksalternatives Leben in den siebziger und frühen achtziger Jahren* (Suhrkamp, 2014), 297–301.
28. Klaus Weinhauer, "Staatsmacht ohne Grenzen? Innere Sicherheit, 'Terrorismus'-Bekämpfung und die bundesdeutsche Gesellschaft der 1970er Jahre," in *Rationalitäten der Gewalt. Staatliche Neuordnungen vom 19. bis zum 21. Jahrhundert*, ed. Susanne Krasmann and Jürgen Martschukat (Transkript, 2015), 215–38, especially 227; Reichardt, *Authentizität und Gemeinschaft*, 121–22, 135–40, 195–96, 207–8, 543–45, 566–68; and Michael März, *Linker Protest nach dem Deutschen Herbst* (Transkript Verlag, 2012).
29. Schenk, *Der Chef*, 201.
30. Herold, "Taktische Wandlungen des deutschen Terrorismus," especially 402–3.
31. PA-DBT 3114, 8. Wahlperiode, 15. Sitzung (11 May 1977). I have not been able to locate documents regarding the February 1975 meeting to which Schenk refers, but at this May 1977 meeting Herold stated (80) that his presentation corresponded in its essentials to the proposals made at that earlier meeting.
32. The Interior Ministry's anti-terrorism plan also included a number of legislative measures. See Interior Minister Maihofer to Justice Minister Hans-Jochen Vogel, Vorschläge zur Bekämpfung des Terrorismus (25 September 1977), BAK B141/64952.
33. Schenk, *Der Chef*, 206, 202.
34. ÖS 6/Bochmann to Minister, Betr.: Personenbezogene Informationssammlung des BKA . . . (8 December 1975), BAK B106/102168, Bd. 5, sets out the legal basis for all of the reporting services established in April of that year.
35. 61. Tagung der AG der Leiter der LKÄ mit dem BKA am 13./14.12.1972: Bericht der Projektleitung Datenverarbeitung, BayHStA MInn IA8-490-2; and Innenminister NRW to

Arbeitsgemeinschaft der Innenministerien der Länder, Betr.: Sitzung des Arbeitskreises II (15 October 1976), BAK B106/106668, Bd. 1.
36. PA-DBT 3114, 8. Wahlperiode, 21. Sitzung (1 September 1977).
37. Referat ÖS 9/Bochmann and Schöneich, Stellungnahme zum Entwurf eines Rechtsgutachtens . . . (30 November 1976), and Bundeskriminalamt/Herold (28 September 1976), both in BAK B106/106668.
38. Ministerialrat Kurt Fritz, Vermerk, Betr.: Rechtliche Zulässigkeit der beobachtenden Fahndung (14 March 1977), and Rechtsgutachten zur Zulässigkeit der beobachtenden Fahndung und der Verfügbarkeit polizeilicher Erkenntnisse im elektronischen Datensystem (undated, but April 1976), both in BAK B106/106668, Bd. 6.
39. ÖS 5/Regierungsrat Wlustel to ÖS 2 (13 August 1976), and Entwurf eines Rechtsgutachtens zur Zulässigkeit der beobachtenden Fahndung . . . , both in BAK B106/102168, Bd. 6.
40. Innenminister NRW to Arbeitsgemeinschaft der Innenministerien der Länder, Betr.: Sitzung des Arbeitskreises II (15 October 1976), BAK B106/106668, Bd. 1.
41. *Möglichkeiten und Grenzen der Fahndung* (BKA Vortragsreihe, Bd. 25, 1980), 60, 75, 73.
42. PA-DBT 3114, 8. Wahlperiode, 15. Sitzung (11 May 1977), 33–39, 80–84.
43. Herold claimed in a letter to Baum (29 November 1978), BAK B106/106668, Bd. 2, that almost all political violence could be prevented by means of an international passive tracking system (figure 8.1 ["Persons" and "Legislation, Politics, Administration"]). For an example of the kind of information on which such claims were based, see Bundeskriminalamt to BMI, Lagebericht Terrorismus (14 March 1978), 5–8, BAK B106/83847, Bd. 3.
44. See also Karl-Heinz Krumm, "Ohne BEFA würden wir nur wenige Terroristen kennen . . . ," *FR* (4 August 1978), 10–11. This was the rationale behind the demand (figure 8.1 ["Persons" and "Legislation, Politics, Administration"]) for the preventive detention of persons accused under §129a.
45. Herold's assessment was right on the money. At least two of the persons (Willy Peter Stoll and Monika Selbing) who had taken part in the occupation of the Amnesty International office, but who had not yet participated in a major terrorist action, would be involved in the kidnapping of Schleyer that September.
46. BMI/Ministerialrat Fritz to Bundesministerium der Justiz, Betr.: PDV 384.2 (7 January 1980), BAK B106/371229, Bd. 1. As soon as the new regulations went into effect, the number of persons who were the object of passive tracking decreased by half. Bundeskriminalamt to Länderinnenminster (30 December 1982), BAK B106/371229, Bd. 2.
47. Schenk, *Der Chef*, 212.
48. PA-DBT 3114, 8. Wahlperiode, 15. Sitzung (11 May 1977), 49–52. According to Referat V, Anlage 2 zum Schreiben vom 19. November 1981 (13 November 1981), BAK B347/209, these numbers had grown substantially by October 1981. The goals of PIOS were similar to the HYDRA database, which was constructed by the CIA in 1967 to make visible the presumed connections between both the New Left and civil rights groups and foreign communist governments. See Jens Wegener, "Order and Chaos: The CIA's HYDRA Database and the Dawn of the Information Age," *Journal of Intelligence History* 19, no. 1 (2020): 77–91. However, Wegener also notes that the analytical capacity of this system did not exceed those of index card and punched card systems, and PIOS was more advanced with regard to the use of basic operators to analyze structured data.
49. PIOS represented the electronic equivalent of the tracking system reportedly used by the tsarist political police. See Hannah Arendt, *The Origins of Totalitarianism* (Harcourt Brace Jovanovich, 1973), 433.
50. IV A 5, Betr.: Datenschutz bei polizeilichen Datensammlungen, insbesondere PIOS (21 April 1978), BAK B141/78798.

51. Roland Appel and Dieter Hummel, "Auch Terroristen haben mit Kleinigkeiten angefangen," *Vorgänge* 91, no. 1 (1988): 21–23.
52. Referat V, Anlage 2 zum Schreiben vom 19. November 1981 (13 November 1981), BAK B347/209. This elastic interpretation of "other persons" was still one of the main points of criticism when the department was audited for a second time in 1988, when auditors found that more than half of the "other persons," who made up approximately 80 percent of all the names registered in a consolidated PIOS internal security database (APIS), had only been charged with damaging or defacing public property—such as the census forms—in conjunction with the census protests. Einwag to BMI, Betr.: Datenschutzrechtliche Kontrolle bei der Abteilung Staatsschutz des BKA (7 December 1988), AGG B.II.1/6009.
53. IV A 5, Betr.: Datenschutz bei polizeilichen Datensammlugnen, insbesondere PIOS (21 April 1978), BAK B141/78798.
54. Innenminister Schleswig-Holstein/Verfassungsschutzabteilung to Bundesamt für Verfassungsschutz, Betr.: Zusammenarbeit zwischen Bund und Ländern . . . im Ermittlungs- und Informationsbereich (23 October 1975), BAK B106/102168, Bd. 5; Bundesamt für Verfassungsschutz to BMI/Merk, Betr.: Zusammenarbeit der Staatsschutzdienststellen der Bundesrepublik Deutschland auf dem Gebiet der automatischen Informationsbeziehungen (24 May 1974), BAK B106/102168, Bd. 2; and Bundesamt für Verfassungsschutz to BMI/Merk, Betr.: Abgrenzung INPOL/NADIS, hier: Das vom BKA geplante Anwendungssystem PIOS (30 June 1975), BAK B106/102168, Bd. 4.
55. Bundeskriminalamt/Herold to BMI, Betr.: Zusammenarbeit mit dem NADIS (6 May 1975), BAK B106/102168, Bd. 4.
56. PA-DBT 3114, 8. Wahlperiode, 75. Sitzung (21 June 1979): Fortsetzung der Beratung des Berichts des Bundesbeauftragter vom 14. Mai 1979 zum Dateienbericht des BMI.
57. Drs. 9/2386, 85–86.
58. Reinhard Riegel, "Rechtsprobleme der Rasterfahndung," *ZRP* 13, no. 11 (1980): 300–6.
59. Jürgen Simon, Gundel Simon-Ern, and Jürgen Taeger, "Wer sich umdreht oder lacht . . . Rasterfahndung: Ein Beitrag zur Gewährung der Inneren Sicherheit," *Kursbuch* 66 (December 1981), 20–25; Simon and Taeger, *Rasterfahndung* (Nomos, 1981); and Simon and Taeger, "Grenzen kriminalpolizeilicher Rasterfahndung," *JZ* 37 (1982): 140–45.
60. Vermerk, Betr.: Überprüfungen bei Leihwagenfirmen (3 June 1975), NRW NW 474/150; and Günter Ermisch, "Fahndung und Datenschutz—aus der Sicht der Polizei," *Möglichkeiten und Grenzen der Fahndung*, 63–77.
61. "'Die Position der RAF hat sich verbessert'"; and Hans Peter Bull, *Datenschutz, oder Die Angst vor dem Computer* (Piper, 1984), 239–45. BMJ, Problempapier zu den rechtlichen Grundlagen für Fahndungsmassnahmen . . . im Strafverfahren (15 May 1985), 5–6, BAK B106/111085, Bd. 1, describes a number of other matching programs that received no public attention at the time.
62. Ermisch, "Fahndung und Datenschutz—aus der Sicht der Polizei." See also Horst Herold, "'Rasterfahndung' – eine computerunterstützte Fahndungsform der Polizei. Begriff, Formen, Abläufe," *RuP* 21, no. 2 (1985): 84–97.
63. Horst Herold, "Polizeiliche Datenverarbeitung und Menschenrechte," *RuP* 16, no. 2 (1980): 79–86, citation 83.
64. Drs. 9/93, 51.
65. Bull, *Datenschutz, oder Die Angst vor dem Computer*, 242–43; Riegel, "Rechtsprobleme der Rasterfahndung"; and the comments by State Secretary Andreas von Schoeler in PA-DBT 3114, 8. Wahlperiode, 92. Sitzung (13 February 1980): Bericht des BMI über Folgerungen aus den Veröffentlichungen über die Rasterfahndung des BKA, 16–34.
66. Aust, *Der Baader Meinhof Komplex*, 483ff.; and Schenk, *Der Chef*, 273ff.
67. Hans Werner Hamacher, Vermerk, Betr.: Attentat auf Dr. Schleyer (7 September 1977), NRW NW 408/2, Bd. 1; Betr.: Fahndungsmassnahmen nach dem Tod von Hanns-Martin

Schleyer (20 October 1977), BAK B106/83846; and "'Wen suchen wir denn eigentlich?'" *Der Spiegel*, 7 November 1977, 26–33.

68. SoKo zur Bekämpfung des Terrorismus, Betr.: Probemassnahmen zur "Aktion Rotlicht" der Stadt Frankfurt zur wirksameren Bekämpfung des Terrorismus (17 October 1977), BAK B106/46506; and "Ran an die Kästen," *Der Spiegel*, 10 October 1977, 24–26.
69. "Die Position der 'RAF hat sich verbessert,'" 49.
70. Schenk, *Der Chef*, 293ff.
71. Herold's investment in forensic technology also paid off. Police analysts were able to determine from the soundtrack of the video sent by the kidnappers that Schleyer was being held in a location close to where a pneumatic crane was in operation. Current law permitted the police to search the homes of nonsuspects only if there were concrete indications that the person who was actually being sought could be found in the area. The April 1978 amendment to the Code of Criminal Procedure (StPO §111) permitted the establishment of checkpoints in public spaces to facilitate the capture of such persons and the seizure of evidence. *BGBl.*, 1978, 497–99.
72. Aust, *Der Baader-Meinhof-Komplex*, 508–10, 515–17, 520–21, 528–32.
73. "'Eigentlich müßte jeder verdächtig sein,'" *Der Spiegel*, 12 September 1977, 22–33. Herfried Münkler, "Sicherheit und Freiheit," in *Handeln unter Risiko*, ed. Münkler et al. (Transcript, 2010), 13–32, argues (23–24) that the use of the private sphere as a resource for attacks on public security, which is characteristic of asymmetric warfare, has led both to the expansion of state surveillance of public life and its intensified penetration into the private sphere.
74. "Auch die ausgefeilteste Kriminaltechnik braucht den Zufall," *FAZ*, 8 September 1977; and Hans Schüler, "Ratlose Fahnder hoffen auf den Zufall," *Die Zeit*, 16 September 1977.
75. Karrin Hanshew, *Terror and Democracy in West Germany* (Cambridge University Press, 2010), 124–33.
76. For example, BMI, Lagebericht Terrorismus (14 March 1978), and P I 2, Lagebericht Terrorismus (17 October 1978), BAK B106/83847, Bde. 3 and 4, respectively.
77. PA-DBT 3114, 8. Wahlperiode, 55. Sitzung (18 October 1978), 7–8.
78. "'Wen suchen wir denn eigentlich?'" To be fair, the magazine whistled a very different tune a few months later, when four German terrorists were captured in Yugoslavia. "'De lange arm van het Bundeskriminalamt,'" *Der Spiegel*, 5 June 1978, 26–31.
79. Both drafts can be found in BAK B131/1491. See also figure 8.1 ("Persons" and "Legislation, Politics, Administration"); and Referat 133, Vermerk für das Koalitionsgespräch am . . . 13.3.1978, and the juxtaposition of the interior ministry draft and version proposed by AK II, both in BAK B136/15687, Bd. 4.
80. PA-DBT 3114, 8. Wahlperiode, 33. Sitzung (10 November 1977), 5–9.
81. Drs. 8/1881 and 2889. Herold's assessment of the politics of the Höcherl report can be found in the draft letter (14 June 1978), BAK B131/2049.
82. Baum to Chancellor Schmidt (5 September 1978), BAK B131/2049.
83. Bericht von IMK (28 September 1978), StAH 136-1/2432: Baum "betreibt die 'Entzauberung' des BKA mit großer Intensität."
84. "Sinnvolle Lösungen," *Hessische Polizeirundschau* 5, no. 10 (1978): 3–8, citation 5.
85. Frauke Schulz, *"Im Zweifel für die Freiheit": Aufstieg und Fall des Seiteneinsteigers Werner Maihofer in der FDP* (Ibidem, 2011). One affair, which came to light in February 1977, involved the bugging of the home of nuclear scientist Klaus Traube by the Domestic and Overseas Intelligence Services. The others involved programs under which the Border Police were passing on information to the Domestic Intelligence Agency and the covert monitoring of communications between incarcerated RAF members and their attorneys.
86. Baum also followed through on the FDP's 1977 promise to investigate the social causes of political violence by commissioning a study that became the four-volume *Analysen zum Terrorismus* (Opladen, 1981–84).

87. Vorwort zum Ersten Bericht der Abteilung P des Bundesministeriums des Innern über Dateien/Karteien im Bereich des Bundeskriminalamtes (15 April 1979), BAK B141/78798. At the same time, Baum ordered a review—and the eventual limitation—of electronic data exchange between the Federal Criminal Police and the Domestic Intelligence Agency. This decision is documented in BAK B136/15688.
88. Erster Bericht der Abteilung P . . . (25 April 1979), BAK B141/78798; and "Bundesminister des Inneren: Erster Dateienbericht des Bundesinnenministeriums über die Daten und Karteien des Bundeskriminalamtes," *FR*, 28 and 30 April 1979. Only two files were deleted as a result of the review: the one containing the list of communes and their residents, the other the names of refugees from East Germany. The commune database, which had been set up in 1971, was blocked in 1976 after it had been determined that there was no relationship between communal living and terrorism, and then destroyed in 1979. See the fragmentary documentation for the "Dateienbericht" in BAK B106/101308, Bd. 13. Most of the files held by the Federal Criminal Police were still held in paper form. The balance between electronic and manual files was similar in Hamburg, where the state police maintained twenty-seven distinct collections of personal information. Only six of these (the various INPOL and PIOS systems and the state police information system POLAS) were electronic—in part because the police did not think it efficient to computerize records of persons convicted or suspected of various kinds of minor, local offenses. Rickert, Vermerk, Betr.: Realisierung des KAN (24 September 1982), StAH 241-4/128. The privacy commissioners sometimes praised the decision to maintain paper files because this limited the potential dissemination of information that—they argued—was not relevant to police in other states.
89. Bull retracted his sharper formulation in Datenschutz im Bereich des BKA, hier: ergänzende Stellungnahme für die Sitzung des Innenausschusses . . . am 13.6.1979, BAK B347/204.
90. Udo Kauß, *Der suspendierte Datenschutz bei Polizei und Geheimdiensten* (Campus Verlag, 1989), 87–106, argues that between 1970 and 1977–78 the Hessian privacy commissioner and the Rheinland-Pfalz Privacy Commission displayed only a limited awareness of the privacy problem in relation to the security agencies. The situation changed, he argues, with the first annual report (January 1979) of the Federal Privacy Commissioner.
91. Horst Bieber, "Wo Daten zur Drohung werden. Die Karteien des Bundeskriminalamtes offenbaren gefährlichen Übereifer," *Die Zeit*, 27 April 1979, 7.
92. The *Stern* pieces were reprinted as Peter Koch and Reimar Oltmanns, *SOS—Sicherheit, Ordnung, Staatsgewalt. Freiheit in Deutschland* (Gruner & Jahr, 1978); the *Spiegel* articles were collected with additional materials in Jochen Bölsche, *Der Weg in den Überwachungsstaat* (Rowohlt, 1979).
93. "Einführungserlaß der Richtlinien für die Errichtung und Führung von Dateien über personenbezogene Daten beim Bundeskriminalamt," *Gemeinsames Ministerialblatt* 32, no. 1 (5 January 1981): 114–19; and "Einführungserlaß der Richtlinien für die Führung kriminalpolizeilicher personenbezogener Sammlungen," *Gemeinsames Ministerialblatt* 32, no. 1 (5 January 1981), 119–23.
94. Referat V, Datenschutzrechtliche Prüfung bei der Abteilung Staatsschutz vom 7.9 bis 7.10.1982 (19 October 1982), BAK B 347/208.
95. Kurzprotokoll. 51. Sitzung des Innenausschusses (2 December 1982), BAK B106/83849, Bd. 8, 20–21; Reinhard Riegel, "Aktuelle Grundfragen beim Vollzug des Datenschutzes im Sicherheitsbereich," *Die Polizei* 74, no. 4 (1983): 101–6; and PA-DBT 3114, 9. Wahlperiode, 36. Sitzung (12 May 1982). Bundesminister des Innern, Zweiter Bericht über Dateien im Bereich des Bundeskriminalamts (19 March 1980), 27f., BAK B106/96335, Bd. 3, reported that thirty thousand files collected in conjunction with the major terrorist attacks of 1977 had been deleted.

96. Alfred Einwag to BMI, Betr.: Datenschutzrechtliche Kontrolle bei der Abteilung Staatsschutz des BKA (7 December 1988), AGG B.II.1/6009.
97. In 1982, the Hamburg police reported that the guidelines had led to the culling of 167,575 individual files, or 43 percent of the original number. Rickert, Vermerk, Betr.: Realisierung des KAN (24 September and 5 October 1982), StAH 241-4/128.
98. Alfred Stümper, "Wie soll es denn weitergehen?" *Die Polizei* 77, no. 6 (1986): 159–63, citations 159–60.
99. Referat V, Datenschutzrechtliche Prüfung bei der Abteilung Staatsschutz vom 7.9 bis 7.10.1982 (19 October 1982), the response by the interior ministry, Sachbestandsbericht zur Aussonderungsprüfung bei der Abteilung ST (June 1983), which contested many of the conclusions of the privacy commissioner, and Baumann to BMI, Betr.: Datenschutzrechtliche Prüfung bei der Abteilung Staatsschutz (5 December 1983), all in BAK B 347/208.
100. "'Der umstrittenste Mann der Regierung,'" *Der Spiegel*, 8 September 1980, 22–27.
101. Schenk, *Der Chef*, 433–44.
102. "'Die Position der RAF hat sich verbessert,'" 55.
103. A Google N-gram shows the usage of the term rising from near zero in 1975 to a peak in 1986–87.
104. Podlech, "Die Begrenzung staatlicher Informationsverarbeitung durch die Verfassung angesichts der Möglichkeit unbegrenzter Informationsverarbeitung mittels der Technik," *Leviathan* 12, no. 1 (1984): 85–98, citation 89. Hanshew, *Terror and Democracy*, 157, also notes a shift in the way the New Left understood state violence, with "cold technological perfection" and the specter of an Orwellian surveillance state gradually replacing Nazi racism as the basis of domination.
105. See the discussion in Edda Weßlau, *Vorfeldermittlungen. Probleme der Legalisierung "vorbeugender Verbrechensbekämpfung" aus strafprozeßrechtlicher Sicht* (Duncker & Humblot, 1989), 221–37.
106. Wilhelm Steinmüller, "Der aufhaltsame Aufstieg des Geheimbereichs," *Kursbuch* 56 (1979), 169–98; and Peter Brückner, Diethelm Damm, and Jürgen Seifert, *1984 schon heute oder wer hat Angst vorm Verfassungsschutz?*, 2nd expanded ed. (Neue Kritik, 1977). Collectively, these tropes closely correspond to the recent (2013) definition of the surveillance state by Privacy International in "Defining the Surveillance State," privacyinternational.org, 31 October 2013, https://privacyinternational.org/blog/1513/defining-surveillance-state.
107. "Die neue Welt von 1984," *Der Spiegel*, 3 January 1983, 19–30, citations 22–23.
108. These observational technologies were the focus of "Auf dem Weg zum Überwachungsstaat," *Der Spiegel*, 10 January 1983, 46–67.
109. "Die neue Welt von 1984," 22, 30.
110. Maihofer, "Eröffnungsansprache," *Polizei und Prävention. Arbeitstagung des Bundeskriminalamtes Wiesbaden* (Bundeskriminalamt, 1975), 7–9, citation 9.
111. Eggert Schwan, "Droht der Überwachungsstaat?" *Leviathan* 12, no. 4 (1984): 560–77, made the same point.
112. Hans-Magnus Enzensberger, "A Determined Effort to Explain to a New York Audience the Secrets of German Democracy," *New Left Review* 118 (November/December 1979): 3–14, citation 10. This essay was also published as "Unentwegter Versuch, einem New Yorker Publikum die Geheimnisse der deutschen Demokratie zu erklären," *Kursbuch* 56 (1979), 1–14, and, in abridged form, as "'Der Sonnenstaat des Doktor Herold': Hans Magnus Enzensberger über Privatsphäre, Demokratie und Polizeicomputer," *Der Spiegel*, 18 June 1979, 68–78.
113. Enzensberger, "A Determined Effort," 12.
114. Ibid., 14; and Enzensberger, "'Der Sonnenstaat des Doktor Herold.'"

115. Karl Markus Michel, "Über den Dataismus," *Kursbuch* 66 (December 1981), 63–81.
116. The most influential examples of this line of interpretation were Joachim Hirsch, *Der Sicherheitsstaat. Das "Modell Deutschland," seine Krise und die neuen sozialen Bewegungen* (Europäische Verlangsanstalt, 1980), 111–19; and Robert Jungk, *Der Atomstaat. Vom Fortschritt in die Unmenschlichkeit* (Rororo, 1977), 134–46.
117. Niedersächsisches Bündnis gegen den Überwachungsstaat, Protokoll des 1. Treffens vom 23.3.1986, Aufruf zur Bildung einer Hamburger Initiative gegen den Überwachungsstaat (undated), Berliner Koordinationstreffen gegen Überwachung (undated), Roland Appel, Bericht vom Kongress "Kein Staat mit diesem Staat?" in Bielefeld . . . (23 June 1986), Kabylon. Ein Gespräch mit dem AK Rationalisierung über Sicherheitsgesetze . . . (5 July 1986), all in AGG G.01 FU-Berlin, Spezialarchiv "Die Grünen," Nr. 115; Göttinger Initiativ gegen Computernetz (undated), and Erklärung des Kongresses "Freiheit stirbt mit Sicherheit" (December 1988), both in AGG B.II.1/6020.
118. Bundesarbeitsgemeinschaft Kritischer Polizistinnen und Polizisten, Landesgruppe NRW (23 November 1989), AGG A-Manfred Such/151.
119. Die Grünen NRW, Pressemitteilung (8 June 1989), AGG A-Manfred Such/151.
120. Bundesarbeitsgemeinschaft Kritischer Polizistinnen und Polizisten, Kritikforum Polizeirecht (23 April 1991), AGG B.II.2/644 (2).
121. Bölsche, *Der Weg in den Überwachungsstaat*, 9.
122. Drs. 8/3570, 4–5.
123. Drs. 8/3570, 42–43.
124. Cited in Schenk, *Der Chef*, 389.
125. "Angst vor Orwells Staat," *Wirtschaftswoche*, June 1984, 28ff., citation 33.
126. "Eintrittskarte für den Überwachungsstaat," *Der Spiegel*, 9 August 1983, 17–22.
127. Heiner Busch et. al., *Die Polizei in der Bundesrepublik* (Campus Verlag, 1985), 428–36, citations 428, 430–31. Stümper's writings provide many examples of this sense of cultural crisis. For example, see Alfred Stümper, "Die Polizei auf dem Weg in das Jahre 2000," *Kriminalistik* 33, no. 6 (1979): 254–58, especially 255; and Stümper, *Systematisierung der Verbrechensbekämpfung* (Boorberg Verlag, 1981).
128. Hessische Landesregierung, ed., *Informationsgesellschaft oder Überwachungsstaat. Strategien zur Wahrung der Freiheitsrechte im Computerzeitalter*, 2 Bde. (Opladen, 1986).
129. "Datentechnik = Überwachungstechnik? Alptraum oder Hoffnung?" *Die Polizei* 76, no. 4 (1985): 97–110.
130. Boge, "Datenschutz: Hoffnung oder Hemmnis?" *Die Polizei* 76, no. 4 (1985), 108–10, citation 110.
131. Hessische Landesregierung, ed., *Informationsgesellschaft oder Überwachungsstaat*, II:62.
132. Martin Kutscha and Norman Paech, *Totalerfassung. "Sicherheitsgesetze," Volkszählung, Neuer Personalausweis, Möglichkeiten der Gegenwehr* (Pahl-Rugenstein, 1986).

Chapter 9

The Reform of Police Law
Datenschutz, the Defense of Law,
and the Debate over Precautionary Surveillance

At the end of the 1970s, politicians and police officials were faced with growing uncertainty regarding the legal status of the new surveillance practices. Inmate surveillance, passive tracking, computer matching, and PIOS, as well as covert observation and the expanded use of informers, undercover agents, and new observational technologies, all pushed beyond the limits of liberal police law. The uncertainties surrounding these practices had been crystallized by the passage of the Federal Privacy Protection Law, which codified the principle that the collection of personal information by the state entailed an infringement on the constitutional rights of the citizen and raised the question of whether the original authorization by the Conference of Interior Ministers provided an adequate basis for such surveillance.

Although these problems could initially be finessed by taking recourse to the general charge to protect against dangers to public security, which stood in one form or another at the head of every state police law, the census decision made the legislative codification of the informational activities of the police unavoidable. The ensuing debate over the reform of police law pivoted around the questions of whether concrete dangers and well-founded individual suspicion represented an inviolable constitutional minimum or whether the police should be permitted to act under less restrictive conditions (and, if so, how such authorization would have to be formulated in order to remain consistent with the rule of law). These questions would dominate public attention through the remainder of the decade and beyond.

Notes for this chapter begin on page 349.

The framework for this debate had been established at the beginning of the 1970s, when the Conference of Interior Ministers had called for—as one element of the internal security plan adopted in June 1972—the harmonization of state police laws.[1] This goal was to be achieved through a Model Draft for a Uniform Police Law for Federal and State Government, which was to provide a template for the revision of these state laws and, in modified form, the laws governing the federal police agencies. Although the authors of the Model Draft claimed that it simply codified the existing authority of the police, in reality it expanded this authority in important ways, though it did so using language and reasoning that obscured, rather than justified, these changes. Moreover, the Model Draft did not address the informational activity of the police, and, following the census decision, the Conference of Interior Ministers commissioned the drafting of model provisions to regulate this dimension of their work. The resulting document was known in clumsy bureaucratic language as the Preliminary Draft for the Amendment of the Model Draft for a Uniform Police Law. Both the Preliminary Draft and the state police laws that were amended on the basis of this model included extensive provisions regulating the collection, use, and exchange of personal information. The cumulative effect of this process of juridification was to transform police laws from laws regulating the use of force into domain-specific information access and privacy laws.[2]

The Preliminary Draft, which will be the main focus of this chapter, explicitly authorized the precautionary collection of information in the *Vorfeld* of both concrete dangers and well-founded individual suspicion. This precautionary mandate was grounded in a new conception of internal security that focused less on communism than on the dangers posed by terrorism and organized crime. Drawing on Foucault, I argue that these new surveillance practices represented a form of illiberal governmentality that obeyed the logic of total repression described by Maihofer.[3] However, the precautionary surveillance through which this form of governmentality operated could never be subjected to legal norms, and after the census decision privacy protection law became the primary theoretical tool for defending the idea of law and the liberal logic of informational parsimony against the transgressive logic of precautionary surveillance and the imperious claims of the new understanding of internal security.

Precautionary Surveillance and the Illiberal Governance of an Ungovernable Future

Almost without exception, the security officials responsible for crafting the new police laws of the period were men of practical concerns with few theoretical ambitions. However, Foucault can help us understand the governmental rationality that implicitly informed this legislation.

In the lectures that he delivered at the Collège de France between 1975 and 1979, Foucault sketched out the logic of what he called liberal governmentality, which functioned by altering the incentives that were embedded in the milieu in such a way that the free pursuit by the individual of his or her interests and dispositions would ensure the proper functioning of the natural laws of the population.[4] However, it was the encounter with the limits of liberal governmentality that gave rise to illiberal governmentality, whose distinguishing feature was the rearticulation from within the social domain of sovereign power and its use to repress the disorder and deviance attributable to those incorrigible delinquents who resisted the allure of government through freedom. But this rearticulation of sovereign power from within the social domain does not simply involve the application of the law, but rather its transcendence and repositing, while the generalization of this state of exception involves — at the logical extreme — the hollowing out and destruction of law through state violence.[5] This mode of governmentality provides the key to understanding the rationality, transgressive nature, and temporal structure of precautionary surveillance.

To the extent that the future grows in a regular, predictable manner out of the past, the individual can be governed through laws and prohibitions. This principle is mirrored in the temporal structure of liberal police laws, whose orientation toward specific past events limits the authority of the police. But, as we shall see in greater detail below, security officials argued that the methods employed by terrorists and organized crime rendered their actions radically unpredictable in comparison with perseverant modus operandi employed by the professional or habitual criminals described in chapter 6, and this in turn raised the question of how the future was to be governed when the connection between past experience, present conditions, and future events was so uncertain that threats could be identified only on a post facto basis.

Claudia Aradau and Rens van Munster argue that such radically discontinuous futures are constructed through an untheorized discourse of exceptionality, which generates specific forms of security knowledge and corresponding security practices.[6] In the following I argue that the proposed amendments to the state police laws in the 1980s and 1990s were, in fact, informed by such a discourse and that, in contrast to those methods employed to "prevent" dangers that grow organically out of the past, the new police law relied on the idea of *Vorsorge* — or what I will call "precautionary" surveillance and intervention — to legitimate the use of exceptional power to anticipatorily govern a future that was figured as uncertain, unknowable, and potentially catastrophic.[7] These exceptional powers enabled the police to act in instances where the connection between the current state of affairs and a future concrete danger was more mediated and conditional than permitted by liberal police law and to collect information regarding that domain of unforeseeable dangers known as the *Vorfeld*—and then take actions that they hoped would succeed in forestalling the occurrence of these dangers. The problem, as Erhard Denninger has noted, is that, once we move beyond the limits imposed by concrete dangers and well-founded individual suspicion, there are no intrinsic criteria by which such dangers can be delimited, "either with respect to the determination of the sphere of risky persons, the means that can be employed to learn about and defend against these risks, or the goals of those measures to be taken in the interest of security."[8] Consequently, the proponents of precautionary surveillance insisted that, in order to preempt unknown unknowns, police surveillance authority would have to be as broad as the indeterminate, and indeterminable, field of potential dangers. By definition, such spaces of exceptionality transcend every attempt to impose legal norms upon police surveillance without, however, being able to guarantee the success of such activity, and such a strategy entails a wager that the blank check written to security agencies will—at some point in a permanently deferred future—be repaid proportionally in the currency of freedom.

These ideas can be used to make sense of both the diverse security practices codified by the Preliminary Draft, which all sought to redeem this promise to protect against unforeseeable dangers and facilitate the prosecution of future crimes, and the work of the two leading theorists of precautionary surveillance: Horst Herold and Alfred Stümper, who was *Landespolizeipräsident* in Baden-Württemberg from 1970 to 1990 and head of the public security division in the state interior ministry.[9]

Already in his first major publication, Herold had argued that all of those who believed that the real significance of computers lay in their ability to make "searching and finding" (*fahnden und finden*)—that is, to make the tracking and tracing of people and objects—faster, more efficient, and more accurate failed to understand the radical novelty and disruptive potential of computers. He claimed, instead, that the new information technologies would lead the police beyond mere "searching and finding" and into the new domain of "searching and researching" (*fahnden und forschen*)—and that they would do so in a way that would alter the nature of social governance and police work, the organization of the police, and their position in the political system of the Federal Republic.[10]

Although Herold claimed that he had been deeply influenced by Marx, his work was characterized by a positivist conception of social knowledge and a persistent antipathy to psychologizing explanations of human behavior, both of which perhaps had as much in common with Quetelet as with Marx. As he later confessed, "I am an objectivist. I mean that all phenomena have their objective causes and exhibit an objective lawfulness."[11] Consequently, he frequently made reference to the "essence" of crime, its "objective laws," and its "causes,"[12] all of which were to be revealed through the analysis of social data. Herold argued that the police possessed an "epistemological privilege" (*Erkenntnisprivileg*) arising out of their direct confrontation with the full spectrum of deviant behavior,[13] but that their ability to exploit this knowledge in order to uncover "usable facts" on which to base criminal policy had historically been limited by the technologies available to process this information.[14] However, he believed that computers had solved these problems "in a universal manner" and thus made it possible for the police "to penetrate the mass of their data in a systematic, analytic manner guided by the practical intent of making prognoses." The knowledge generated through this analysis would, Herold insisted, transform criminology from a "tentative undertaking into a genuinely positive science."[15]

As we saw in chapter 4, Herold's confidence that the electronic analysis of the information contained in criminal files would enable the police to understand, and to forestall, all forms of abnormal or deviant behavior made him the focus for much of the ire of the census protesters. He believed that knowledge of the chains of social causality would make it possible to foresee how a particular concatenation of conditions would lead to certain kinds of behavior and enable the legislature to organize the milieu and deploy (dis)incentives in ways that would alter the strategic calculations that led these persons to deviate from social norms. With the help of sociology, cybernetics, behavioral research, and computers, Herold claimed, the analysis of the information held by the police could reveal "the relations to disposition, environment, society and to the proximate causes [of crime]" and thus contribute "rational insights to the legislative process with the goal of formulating practicable norms that correspond to reality."[16] In turn, this would make possible the "targeted influencing—by means of a criminal policy based on these rational insights—of presumptive offenders, offender groups, and the causes of their actions through the diverse means of the sciences, of politics, and legislation."[17] In constantly changing formulations, Herold characterized this strategy of governing through the carefully calibrated tactical disposition of the milieu on the basis of the knowledge of the laws of social causality as the "social sanitary" (*gesellschaftssanitär*) function of the police.[18] His ultimate goal was to use this positive knowledge "to prevent problems *before* they manifest themselves, and most certainly before they become threatening."[19]

There is a clear parallel between Herold's desire to prevent crime at its origin through the reflexive application of the natural laws of deviant behavior and the rationality of liberal governmentality, and his vision of primary prevention amounts to nothing other than the belief that the milieu could be shaped in such a creative, comprehensive manner as to anticipate all possible forms of deviance and establish the incentives needed to guide incipiently deviant behavior back into the natural channels of "normal" behavior.

The picture is very different when we look at Stümper, whose strategy for governing the future is the illiberal mirror image of Herold's early theorizing, if not of his actual professional work. From the beginning, Stümper envisioned the transcendence of law as an opening for the use of exceptional power for repressive purposes. While Stümper argued that the distinction between preventive police and repressive prosecutorial labor was antiquated, his suggestion that the two should be subsumed under what he called "operative" work[20] was a conceptual Trojan horse that enabled him to shift the focus of police work from concrete dangers and individual suspects—with all of the constraints this entailed—to unforeseeable dangers and the systematic collection of information in the *Vorfeld* of potential crime.[21]

Stümper argued that the goal of operative work was to eliminate crime "at its roots" (*schlechthin*), rather than to investigate and prosecute individual offense in a reactive and "petty bourgeois" manner.[22] In its scope and its technocratic faith in the ability to make society into the object of conscious human control, Stümper's notion of operative work is comparable to the social sanitary mission that Herold envisioned for the police. However, it differs in both its illiberal nature and exclusionist thrust. His writings are focused almost exclusively on the use of operative work to disrupt criminal organizations and their logistics, and there is virtually no mention of either primary prevention or the rehabilitation of offenders. As Stümper explained, the ultimate goal of operative work was to "ferret out the basis and logistics of organized crime and either immediately destroy it at its point of origin or, in those cases where it had already progressed to the point where it is broadly and deeply rooted, to first carefully gather intelligence on all of its interconnections and relations and then radically attack it at its very roots."[23]

The claims for such exceptional power were authorized by the way in which the concept of "organized crime" figured the dangers that were to be combatted. According to Stümper, organized crime was crime that was "systematically planned, carried out by organized groups, covert in origin and largely conspiratorial," that made use of the latest technologies and modern infrastructures, that employed highly sophisticated tactical methods, and that typically operated in fields such as counterfeiting and the smuggling of drugs, weapons, and stolen vehicles, which spanned international borders.[24] These characteristics, he argued, rendered it immune to police practices that were tailored to combatting ordinary crime.[25] One could well question Stümper's assumption that, in simpler times past, crime had not been planned, that it had not been carried out by organized groups, and that it had not entailed the use of conspiratorial methods, as well as his attempt to bring so many disparate forms of crime together under a single concept. Nevertheless, the main point here is that all of these arguments work together to figure organized crime as a danger that could be successfully combatted only through precautionary surveillance and operative work.[26]

Much of the recent literature on security has noted the expansion of the concept since the 1970s, and Stümper's work represents an early, yet ideal-typical, example of this trend.[27] Security, Stümper argued, was as totalizing, as complex, and as precarious as modern society itself and as indivisible as sovereignty.[28] Security had to encompass not only domestic and foreign policy, but also psychological, social, economic, energy, and overall political factors.[29] His insistence that security was an element that "pervaded the totality of human, social, economic and political life" echoes the indefinite scope and empirical, situational practice of early modern *Polizei*.[30] The problem was that, since responsibility for the government of each of these domains lay in different hands, no single agency possessed the knowledge needed to understand the problem in all its scope and complexity and to formulate appropriate policies. The solution lay in the creation of an all-encompassing department of homeland security, or what Stümper called a "general direction for internal security," which would function as a central research, planning, and operational agency for the comprehensive security policy described above—and which would coordinate the work of all branches of the public administration to achieve these security goals.[31]

The concepts of total prevention and total repression to which Maihofer referred in his 1975 talk precisely describe the projects set out by Herold and Stümper, respectively. Their shared desire to eliminate crime at its origin—that is, before it could manifest itself in concrete forms of deviant behavior—put wind in the sails of those who complained that the Federal Republic was on its way to becoming an authoritarian surveillance state. In retrospect, Maihofer's statement can be read as a warning against the problematic consequences of both liberal and illiberal attempts to secure the present against an uncertain future.[32]

The Reform of Police Law before the Census Decision

The 1882 Kreuzberg decision of the Prussian Superior Administrative Court had codified the principle that the police were responsible only for protecting against concrete dangers to public security, not for promoting public welfare in the manner of early modern *Polizei*. Although the 1931 Prussian Police Administration Law, which established the model for subsequent police law, especially in the north German states, was the first law to define the general charge to the police in these terms, twentieth-century police law was characterized by a tension between the principle that the police—like that of every other branch of the public administration—could act only under specifically defined conditions and the need for a subsidiary general clause, which would give them the leeway to respond to specific dangers that had not been anticipated by the legislature.[33] While the general charge of the Prussian police law had assumed totalitarian dimensions during the Third Reich, the principles of the country's postwar constitution required that the specific duties of the police, as well as the specific means that they were authorized to employ to fulfill these obligations, be spelled out as fully as possible. The Model Draft drew the logical consequences of this trend by comprehensively regulating the "standard measures" regarding the use of force by the police while minimizing the residual scope of the general charge and harmonizing the different state laws with one another.[34]

The final version of the Model Draft was approved by the interior ministers in November 1977.[35] While the officials who crafted the document proposed that the police be charged with "upholding" public security and order, the interior ministers opted for the more narrowly—and negatively—defined task of "protecting against dangers to public security and order."[36] But most of the debate focused on two articles that expanded police authority in ways that were not reflected in this relatively traditional formulation of the general charge.

The first article permitted the police to stop and conduct identity checks on persons encountered at (1) "dangerous places," which were defined as places where, on the basis of "factual indications and experience" (*tatsächliche Anhaltspunkte erfahrungsgemäß*),[37] crimes were planned, prepared, or perpetrated, where persons without residence permits (i.e., illegal immigrants and criminals) congregated, where criminals sought refuge, and where prostitution was practiced; (2) "endangered places," such as public office buildings, utilities, and transportation systems, if there were indications that these might be the object of an attack; and (3) at checkpoints established on the basis of the dragnet paragraph of the Code of Criminal Procedure.[38]

This marked the first time that the police had been authorized to use force—to detain individuals, verify their identity, and search their belongings—in the absence of evidence that these persons represented a concrete danger. Commentators pointed out that this authority would permit continuous raids on any number of semipublic locations, such as airports, train stations, department stores, and bars, where petty crimes were committed on a regular basis, as well as on immigrant neighborhoods.[39] Future Constitutional Court justice Wolfgang Hoffmann-Riem characterized the new stop-and-search authority at dangerous places as "an absolute novum." He judged that it would "just barely" be legal if it were limited to serious crimes, but that in its present form it was unacceptable.[40]

The second controversial article, which was the logical pendant to this new stop-and-search authority, permitted the police to take fingerprints and mug shots if this were necessary for what the Model Draft called—without explanation or elaboration—the "preventive combatting of crimes" (*die vorbeugende Bekämpfung von Straftaten*) because the concerned individual was suspected of having committed a serious crime and because the way in which this crime had been committed indicated that there was a danger that the person would commit additional serious offenses in the future. This went beyond the recognized authority of the police to collect such information to protect against concrete dangers; it appeared to be yet another method for collecting information in advance of anticipated crimes; and it raised the questions of precisely what was entailed by the preventive combatting of crimes, whether such activity was legitimate and constitutionally permissible, and, if so, whether it was more properly regulated under police law or the Code of Criminal Procedure. While the official commentary asserted that the preventive combatting of crimes was subsumed under the general charge to protect against dangers to public security and order, this claim rested on the problematic inverse conclusion that any police activity that did not involve the investigation of a specific crime was necessarily authorized by the general charge to the police.[41]

In an influential early commentary on the Model Draft, Hannover prosecutor Fritz Sydow noted that, functionally, police measures directed against persons encountered in dangerous places were more closely related to the investigative work that the police carried out on behalf of prosecutors than to protecting against concrete dangers because their real purpose was to collect information for possible future use. Sydow suggested that the preventive combatting of crime actually represented a new charge to the police, but that it could be subsumed under the existing charge only if the task of protecting against dangers was understood in such a broad sense that it also encompassed the deterrent effect of criminal prosecution resulting from the collection of this information. The problem was that such a broad reading of the general charge to the police would have effectively annexed the investigatory authority that the Code of Criminal Procedure reserved for the justice system and undercut the procedural protections it offered.[42]

When the Model Draft was being drafted, justice ministry officials repeatedly suggested that the dangers against which the police were supposed to protect should be defined more narrowly and concretely and that the law should codify those informational practices, such as the covert recording of sound and images, which were already being employed by the police on the basis of the general charge, but whose explicit authorization was certain to provoke further controversy.[43] However, the Federal Privacy Protection Law was entering the final stages of the legislative process at the same time that the Model Draft was being finalized, and the group drafting the law excluded—on orders from above—both the new surveillance practices and the broader question of the informational activity of the police.[44]

In staking out a path for the legislative approval of these new powers and putting pressure on the state legislatures to act, the Model Draft fulfilled its raison d'être. But the proposals contained in the Model Draft did not go unchallenged, and in 1979 a group of liberal academics, including Denninger, Podlech, and Hoffmann-Riem, who were characterized by one member of the group as the extraparliamentary opposition of the legal guild, published an Alternative Draft for a Uniform Police Law for Federal and State Government.[45]

The Alternative Draft grappled more explicitly than the Model Draft with the problems resulting from the expansion of police authority into the *Vorfeld*. In the past, the authors argued, the police had been authorized to protect against concrete dangers by using force only against those specific persons who were judged to be responsible for these dangers. The Model Draft threatened to eliminate these limitations, and the authors of the Alternative Draft argued that, if it were to be approved in its present form, "one of the foundations of police law, which had been inherited from the rule of law, would be torn down and a platform erected for invasive police measures in the *Vorfeld* of protection against [concrete] dangers."[46]

The authors of the Alternative Draft were not insensitive to the potential benefits of precautionary policing, and they noted that, "in view of the vulnerability of many domains of social life and technical facilities, the prevention of dangers (including the preventive combatting of crime), that is, combatting dangers before they have coalesced into concrete dangers in the sense of police law, is an undeniable need of modern polities."[47] Recognizing that such precautionary action was essentially informational in nature and that it involved a type of activity that could not be subsumed under the general charge to protect against (concrete) dangers, the Alternative Draft explicitly authorized the collection of personal information for the preventive combatting of crime while limiting the overall impact of this exceptional activity on civil liberties by predicating it on factual indications that the concerned individual intended to commit one of the particularly serious offenses that were enumerated in the draft.[48]

The authors of the Alternative Draft considered information processing to be "the most general, comprehensive, and—in highly industrialized and differentiated societies—one of the most effective means of exercising state power," and they viewed passive tracking and the other new surveillance practices, which were being employed for precautionary purposes far beyond the field of counterterrorism, as examples of the worrisome tendency "to use electronic data processing to systematically monitor entire domains of social life."[49] These concerns led them to include extensive provisions governing the storage, processing, and exchange of personal information by the police. These provisions mimicked the language of the Federal Privacy Protection Law while extending these protections to information held in paper files. At the time, the KpS Guidelines (chapter 8) had not yet been adopted, and this section of the Alternative Draft represented the first attempt to draft guidelines for the processing of personal information in the security sector.[50]

By the turn of 1979, almost all of the states had either reformed their police laws or were in the process of doing so, though many of these legislative initiatives soon stalled. Although all of these state reforms had taken the Model Draft as a starting point, they deviated from it on a number of important points as state legislators struggled with the same problems as the authors of the Model Draft. However, all of the reformed laws did take over the controversial regulations on identity checks and fingerprinting.[51] The Alternative Draft was intended as an intervention into this fluid legislative context. Its direct influence, however, was limited. At the time, Bremen was the only state to incorporate provisions regulating the collection and processing of personal information into its police law.[52]

Part of the reason politicians and police officials were so reluctant to include informational provisions in the state police laws is that they were vexed by the difficulty in articulating legal norms to govern precautionary surveillance, and they feared the consequences of further efforts in this direction. For example, Egbert Möcklinghoff (CDU), interior minister of Lower Saxony, warned his colleagues that the new methods used to collect information for preventive purposes—such as passive tracking and targeted observation—entailed infringements upon individual rights that went beyond what was authorized by the Model Draft, and he wondered if this problem could be solved by including appropriate provisions in the state police law. In contrast, Karl Krampol, a senior police official in the Bavarian interior ministry, reminded his colleagues that, when the Model Draft was being drafted, they had broken off the debate because this domain of police activity was "not accessible to normative regulation." He thought that the group was unlikely to enjoy greater success with a second attempt, and he called on his colleagues to do everything in their power to stem the trend to regard the informational activity of the police as an infringement upon individual rights requiring legal authorization.[53] In the end, though, the census decision forced the states to revisit their police laws and directly address issues that they had heretofore tried to avoid. As we shall see in the following, their efforts to norm the unnormable transformed police laws that had heretofore governed the use of force into information laws and accelerated the inflationary juridification of police informational activity against which Krampol had warned.

The Conservative Response to the Census Decision

The drafting of new information access and privacy provisions to supplement the Model Draft proceeded in parallel with federal legislation discussed in chapter 5. An initial version of the Preliminary Draft was completed in October 1984. However, this draft was received coolly by the administration and police officials because it was based on an excessively "privacy friendly" reading of the census decision and did not authorize the precautionary collection of information.[54] A second version was completed in February 1985.[55] Although this second version was approved by the Conference of Interior Ministers in April as the basis for further consideration, it was harshly criticized by everyone outside the security community. In October 1985, the interior ministers asked that the February draft be revised to take account of the criticisms by the justice ministry and the privacy commissioners.[56]

As security officials began to seek a more satisfactory formulation of the precautionary charge, they set out more explicit justifications for this activity. As Stümper wrote to Burkhard Hirsch, it was important to emphasize the positive rationale for precautionary information collection because the legitimate aims of privacy law "are increasingly being grounded in constitutional rights, individualized to an ever-greater extent, and extended into trivial areas, and [are] thus threatening to impact the operational functioning of the administration." In contrast, he insisted, "we must not allow there to be any doubt that the use of electronic data processing by the police is in principle not directed against citizens and their freedom, but in contrast serves in important ways to protect their constitutional rights."[57]

The interior ministers supported these claims with references to Josef Isensee, whose essay on *The Constitutional Right to Security* had argued that the state's security mandate trumped all other rights, and to a more recent publication by the jurists Rupert Scholz (CDU), who later served briefly as defense minister in the Kohl administration, and Rainer Pitschas.[58] While the Constitutional Court had regarded the right to informational self-determination as an expression of, and as a means of promoting, the free development of the personality, Scholz and Pitschas gave this concept a peculiar turn by arguing that the realization of this goal depended on the prior success of the state in fending off threats to this right. In this way, they were able to derive from the welfarist mandate of the state and the postulated constitutional right to security an "independent state mandate to engage in precautionary information collection," which existed prior to and independent of the positive legal authorization of specific informational activities whose necessity privacy commissioners had read out of the census decision.[59] Moreover, they argued, not only were efforts to use privacy law to limit the informational activity of the police constitutionally flawed; it was also impossible to apply the principle in practice because the informational needs of the police were so diverse and constantly changing that "the legislator would be completely incapable of devising regulations of sufficient detail and comprehensiveness if he wanted, or were expected, to attempt to establish in advance concrete criteria or norms" for such surveillance.[60] This line of reasoning turned the right to informational self-determination on its head.

In the census decision, the Constitutional Court had ruled that citizens could be compelled to reveal their personal information only if the legislature specified how this information would be used and if it took precautions to ensure that the principle of *Amtshilfe* could not be invoked to use such information for purposes other than those for which it had originally been collected.[61] However, Scholz and Pitschas argued that the appeal to the final purpose principle to restrict the exchange of information that had been collected by the police rested on a different misreading. The Federal Privacy Protection Law had been widely interpreted to mean that, since the ministries, agencies, and departments that collectively made up the public administration represented functionally distinct entities, the exchange of information between them required explicit legal authorization. Scholz and Pitschas, however, argued that large parts of the public administration could be considered functional units within which information could be freely exchanged. They did not say just how these functional units were to be defined, and there was nothing in this line of reasoning that could prevent people from arguing that the entire public administration represented a single, unified informational entity. However, Scholz and Pitschas went only so far as to speak of the "functional identity of the security agencies,"[62] a claim that laid the theoretical foundation for the packet of security laws, which were analyzed in chapter 5.[63]

The Preliminary Draft and the Codification of the Precautionary Mandate

In March 1986, work was completed on a new version of the Preliminary Draft, which would become the basis for the reform of state police laws at the end of the decade.[64] The most important innovation of this March 1986 version was a more explicit formulation of the precautionary mandate. Beyond this, the Preliminary Draft consisted only of two dense, multipart articles. The first authorized the collection of personal information by the police, including its collection for precautionary purposes, while the second regulated the storage, use, and exchange of this information. However, the meaning of this precautionary mandate was anything but clear, and before the Preliminary Draft could become the model for state legislation, it would be necessary to clarify its meaning and determine whether, and to what extent, it was possible to regulate the new surveillance practices in ways that would be consistent with the right to informational self-determination and the rule of law once the classical mechanisms for limiting police authority had been weakened by the extension of police surveillance into the *Vorfeld*.

The March 1986 version of the Preliminary Draft began by stating that, as part of its charge to protect against dangers to public security and order, the police had to "take precautions for the prosecution of crime and to prevent crime (the preventive combatting of crime) as well as to make the necessary preparations to defend against future dangers (preparation for the defense against dangers)."[65] This opaque formulation made use of three separate words (*Vorsorge, Verhütung, Vorbeugung*) to denote the ways in which police activity was temporally displaced and conceived as an anticipated response to future events, whose occurrence was by definition less certain than that of concrete dangers, which were firmly anchored in both knowledge of present conditions and experiential rules that enabled a strong prognosis regarding the future occurrence of an event that would harm a specific legal interest. However, the "preventive combatting of crime," which was nowhere defined in the document, was a more general concept that subsumed both "taking precautions for the (future) prosecution of (future) crime" and the "prevention of crime." But even though taking precautions for the prosecution of crime represented an attempt to annex prosecutorial prerogatives for preventive purposes, and even though the prevention of crime represented an expansion of the police charge by displacing their action into the *Vorfeld* of concrete dangers, the official commentary and virtually every document issued by the interior ministry and police officials insisted that these activities did not expand police authority. They did so despite the fact that these activities were clearly directed against anticipated states of affairs, rather than concrete dangers, and that, by their nature, the new surveillance practices were more suited for aiding future prosecution than for preventing crime.[66]

The three components of this general charge must be examined separately. Preparations for the defense against future dangers had been included in the February 1985 draft under the ominous rubric of the "precautionary prevention of future dangers" (*Gefahrenvorsorge*). The term itself aroused concern because it appeared to open the door to the unlimited collection of information for purposes that were not clearly defined.[67] The March 1986 version clarified this to include the collection of the name and contact information for such persons as tow truck operators, physicians, civil defense officials, and the persons responsible for the operation of utilities, transportation systems, and industrial plants, as well as the information needed to prepare for typical, recurring dangers. In this form, the provision was relatively innocuous, though critics insisted that there was no valid reason why the Preliminary Draft—in a characteristic act of overkill—should have permitted the police to collect this information covertly or against the will of the concerned individuals.

The prevention (*Verhütung*) of crime encompassed actions taken in order to ensure that situations, where the threat of criminal activity was imminent and where the only option was the use of force by the police to halt actions that could no longer be forestalled, did not arise. Although the prevention of crime did not include primary prevention, it did include such activities as advising citizens regarding the best means of protecting themselves against different kinds of crime, compiling statistics, developing forensic tools, and stockpiling the various resources that would be needed to take effective action if an imminent danger were to present itself. But these preparatory measures also included collecting information that illuminated the criminal scene, its organizations, and its logistics, but that was not necessarily intended to be used to intervene in the course of events. This dimension of the prevention of crime overlapped with the task of taking precautions for the prosecution of crime and shared in the problems that it raised.

Taking precautions for the (future) prosecution of (future) crime was the most controversial element of the Preliminary Draft. Such activity was based on both the prognosis that serious crimes of one kind or another would be committed at some indeterminate point in the future and the assumption that these future crimes could be more effectively investigated and prosecuted if the police already possessed information regarding those persons who were likely to be involved in such acts. The idea of collecting information in advance of well-founded individual suspicion raised the questions of whether it was possible to lower the threshold of such surveillance enough to permit the police to effectively combat their *bêtes noires*, terrorism and organized crime, without opening the door to the kind of snooping—independent of all factual indications—that many people equated with the surveillance state, and whether the resulting gains in security against crime, which were presumed, but nowhere justified in detail, outweighed the resulting losses in security against arbitrary action by the state.[68] This provision was the focus of the harshest criticisms by justice ministry officials, who harbored "substantial reservations" regarding the inclusion of precautions for the prosecution of crime as part of the preventive charge of the police. "In contrast to the official commentary," Ministerialrat Stoltenberg insisted, "this is by no means simply a clarification of already existing police responsibilities, but an expansion of them .... The elimination of the condition that they can only act in case of concrete dangers would entail the abolition of the most important limitation of all on the activity of the police."[69]

The idea of taking precautions for the prosecution of crime rested on the intuitive claim that the police had always collected information on the criminal scene because, without being in a position to tap into some prior store of information, they would not know where to begin their investigation of new crimes. However, by the turn of the 1980s, the use of both the new surveillance practices to systematically collect information on persons who were not—or at least not yet—the object of well-founded individual suspicion and the new information and communication technologies to store, integrate, and disseminate this information had given this *Vorfeld* activity a new quality, which made it a far greater danger to privacy rights and civil liberties than had been the case as long as this information had been stored in the memory of individual policemen, the notebooks they kept, and the card files maintained at the local police station. In the words of Michael Kniesel (FDP, later SPD), the head of the Bonn police at the time and one of the authors of the official commentary on the Preliminary Draft, "It makes a fundamental difference whether one has to search for criminal records in the basement of a police headquarters or whether one can—with the aid of a computer and the Criminal Records Index—access all police headquarters from Flensburg to Konstanz."[70] Much of the debate over whether taking precautions for the prosecution of crime was encompassed by the preventive charge to the police fell into the gap between the commonsensical idea that the police had to be able to collect information in advance of actual offenses (and had always done so) and the new dangers posed by the systematic, computer-assisted collection of such *Vorfeld* information.[71]

Taking precautions for the (future) prosecution of (future) crime was the privileged function of what Stümper, Kniesel, and others called operative activity. Kniesel, who took a more differentiated position on the Preliminary Draft than virtually all other commentators, nevertheless spoke for many when he argued that the open collection of information and the reactive, defensive prosecution of discrete offenses had proven impotent in combatting organized crime, and he argued that the refusal to employ covert operative methods would be tantamount to giving up all hope of preventing or prosecuting victimless crimes and crimes that were likely to go unreported, as well as environmental offenses. It was necessary, he insisted, to adapt the surveillance methods employed by the police to the tactics employed by organized crime and terrorist groups, to the expanded temporal and spatial parameters of their activity, and to the new technologies that they employed.[72]

As we saw with Stümper, operative work sought to prevent crime by monitoring the criminal scene, exposing bases of operation, disrupting logistical infrastructures and distribution networks, minimizing the opportunities for the commission of specific kinds of crime, diminishing the profits therefrom, and generally forcing criminal groups to rein in their activity, shift their bases of operation, and devote their energy to maintaining their infrastructure. The ultimate goal was to hold criminal preparations in a perpetual state of disruptive abeyance. However, since the prosecution of street-level offenders seldom illuminated these deep criminal structures and the individuals who controlled them, it was almost by definition necessary to observe the contacts of persons who belonged to known or presumed criminal groups in hopes of generating the suspicion needed to commence formal investigations.[73]

Much of the literature argued that these preventive effects were ultimately attributable to the prosecution of the persons involved in these activities and that such a general deterrent effect could not justify the subsumption of such surveillance under the preventive charge to the police. Fingerprints and the information collected in the course of criminal investigations were the most important sources of leads for future investigations. To the extent that this information had been collected by the police in their capacity as investigatory agents for public prosecutors, this information remained, at least in theory, under the control of justice officials. However, one of the most important provisions of the Preliminary Draft would have given the police cojurisdiction over these materials and permitted them to retain information that would otherwise have had to be turned over to prosecutors and to use it for the preventive combatting of crime—even if the charges had been dropped or the person acquitted.[74] In addition, the covert surveillance practices regulated by the Preliminary Draft, including long-term observation, the use of informants and undercover agents, the use of "technical means" to record sound and images (especially within the protected space of the home), passive tracking, and computer matching, were more suited for identifying targets for more focused investigation and collecting information for future prosecutions than for directly preventing crime. For example, even though it was possible for undercover agents to provide information that might lead to arrests for specific offenses, doing so would endanger their cover and conflict with their ostensible mission to collect information on the ringleaders and logistical infrastructure of criminal organizations. Similarly, as we saw in chapter 8, the real purpose of passive tracking was less to collect information on the objects of such monitoring, who, by definition, were already known to police, than to identify their contact persons. The same could be said for negative matching, whose sole purpose was to generate suspicion.

The decision to claim that taking precautions for the prosecution of crime represented part of the preventive charge to the police was ultimately a political one taken by politicians and security officials who regarded the authority to collect information in advance of possible future offenses as essential to the maintenance of internal security. However, Kniesel argued that, to the extent that it was necessary to extend police surveillance into the *Vorfeld* of potential crime, it was more honest to do this by expanding the general charge to the police than by either adopting a looser construction of initial suspicion, which would preserve the letter of the Code of Criminal Procedure, while sacrificing some of its substance, or introducing into the Code the concept of the *Vorfeld*, which would contradict its basic logic and undermine the procedural protections that it offered.[75] And while critics argued that the information collected as part of the charge to take precautions for the future prosecution of crime primarily served prosecutorial purposes and only was used only secondarily to prevent crime, Kniesel parsed this overlap differently, arguing that it primarily served preventive purposes, but that it had a latent or "sleeping" repressive dimension that became manifest, for example, if the monitoring of criminal groups made it possible to file charges against specific individuals.[76]

Regardless of how one might interpret the new precautionary charge, the Preliminary Draft went on to codify the entire array of new surveillance practices developed in the 1970s. Justice ministry officials had criticized the February 1985 version because the extension of police authority appeared to permit the police to collect and store data on the basis of "mere suspicion." These reservations were compounded by the fact that neither the wording of the Preliminary Draft nor that of the official commentary were able to dispel their "substantial doubts" as to whether the proposal satisfied the principle of proportionality—a principle, they noted, that was becoming increasingly important as a mechanism for limiting police power as their investigative authority advanced further and further into the *Vorfeld* of concrete dangers.[77] These concerns were not dispelled by the March 1986 version.

Criticisms of both the provisions regulating police surveillance practices and those governing the subsequent exchange of information revolved around the all-important issue of whether it was possible to impose meaningful limits on surveillance, which was taking place increasingly far in advance of concrete dangers and well-founded individual suspicion. Not only did the Preliminary Draft grant the police the authority to collect personal information to protect against dangers; it also permitted them to collect information on persons against whom there were nothing more than mere "indications" that they might commit a crime in the future if the police judged that the information collected was necessary for the preventive combatting of crime. However, Ministerialrat Dr. Voth of the justice ministry warned that "the police should only be permitted to collect information if there is something more substantive than vague indications that a more or less specific crime is being prepared or at least planned. Indications that some kind of crime may be committed by some offender or another at some indefinite point in the future cannot justify the collection of personal information by the police."[78] On the other hand, while the February 1985 version had permitted the police to collect information for precautionary purposes on "other persons," justice ministry officials and the privacy commissioners praised the March 1986 version for replacing this broad category with the narrower and more precise term "contact or accompanying persons."[79]

The paragraph authorizing the use of covert methods was equally problematic. The sense that the Preliminary Draft failed to impose effective limits on precautionary surveillance was reinforced by the fact that it permitted such surveillance for a wide variety of crimes while failing to restrict the use of more intrusive, covert surveillance methods to the investigation of more serious offenses. It permitted the police to make use of covert means for the preventive combatting of crime if factual indications justified the assumption that the objects of such surveillance would commit one of approximately ninety serious crimes—and for the combatting of other offenses if there were factual indications that they would be committed professionally, habitually, or by criminal groups. Although this authority was nominally limited by the requirement that the intrusiveness of the surveillance measure not be disproportionate to the significance of the offense to be investigated, this provision still seemed to include a far greater spectrum of possible crime than it excluded, and Regierungsdirektorin Seibert suggested that whatever limitations may have been entailed by this explicit incorporation of the principle of proportionality were more than outweighed by the breadth of the offenses for which covert means could be employed.[80] The Preliminary Draft also authorized the use of passive tracking in ways that went far beyond current regulations with regard to both the persons against whom it could be used and the conditions under which it could be ordered.

The sections of the Preliminary Draft governing the storage and exchange of personal information also raised important questions. As we saw in part II, legislative authorization was necessary to define and delimit the specific purposes for which information could be collected. However, the relevant sections of the Preliminary Draft, which applied to information stored in both formatted and paper files, negated the final purpose principle for all intents and purposes. Both justice ministry officials and the privacy commissioners complained that the law, which permitted the police to store and process information if this were necessary for them to fulfill their responsibilities, treated the police as a unified, undifferentiated informational entity and thus ignored the fact that the information they held had been collected for different purposes and under different conditions.[81] The effect was to throw all of the information held by the police into a single pot and permit each piece to be used for any and all of the agency's responsibilities. The provision regulating the exchange of information among police agencies suffered from the same lack of differentiation and graduation. Justice ministry officials ultimately declared that this provision was so long, complex, and opaque that they could not determine what it actually meant, and the editors of the journal *Civil Liberties and Police* similarly despaired that, even after the most intense mental exertions, they could not think of a single instance where the exchange of information would be prohibited under the proposed regulations.[82]

In the end, opinion remained sharply divided regarding the desirableness and constitutionality of the precautionary surveillance codified by the Preliminary Draft. In her 1989 study, Edda Weßlau, who later served as an editor of *Kritische Justiz*, argued that the normative charge to preventively combat crime—especially by taking precautions for its prosecution—attenuated the connection between well-founded individual suspicion and the collection of information to such an extent that it could no longer guide police investigations or impose meaningful limits upon them. While much of the police literature spoke of the role of the new surveillance practices in concretizing those "indications" that did not meet the prevailing standard for opening a formal criminal investigation, Weßlau argued that, in the absence of normative limitations on their work, the exception tended to become the norm, and that precautionary surveillance tended to become a means for *generating* suspicion (*Verdachtsgewinnung*), rather than concretizing it. In practice, the absence of such limitations permitted precisely that kind of *Ausforschung*—investigations conducted independent of all initial, concrete suspicion—that critics saw as one of the defining features of the surveillance state.[83]

Although Kniesel had been involved in the drafting of the Preliminary Draft, he was less willing to see precautionary surveillance as the *sine qua non* of internal security and more sensitive than virtually any other police official to its impact on civil liberties. Since the concepts of security and prevention contained no intrinsic criteria by which these activities could be delimited, Kniesel warned that they opened the door to two complementary dangers. On the one hand, these ideas could justify "comprehensive and perfected prevention" along the lines of Herold's social sanitary project. On the other hand, the police could invoke the preventive mandate—much as Stümper had argued—to subordinate entire areas of social life to the quest for security through repression. Kniesel concluded that both the logic of prevention and the logic of repression pointed toward a "surveillance state of Orwellian proportions."[84] Ultimately, he insisted, like Baum, that the standard against which the activity of the police had to be measured should not be efficiency, but rather the rule of law.[85]

Kniesel also argued that a general mandate to surveil the population and the use of this information to generate suspicion represented foreign bodies in the police law of liberal societies, and he insisted that even the most basic privacy principles forbade "informational activity, which is directed against *all and sundry* and undertaken *without any criminalistic necessity*, in the *Vorfeld* of concrete dangers" (emphasis in original). The preventive combatting of crime, he argued, could only be made consistent with the rule of law if the police were required to use the new surveillance practices in a parsimonious manner and if the authorization of such activity were coupled with more effective procedural protections than those included in the Preliminary Draft. More specifically, he argued that precautionary surveillance had to be restricted to the prosecution of serious crimes and that it had to be predicated on factual indications that the objects of such surveillance were involved in specific criminal activities. Otherwise, he concluded, the preventive combatting of crime would amount to nothing more than surveillance "into the blue."[86]

Marion Albers took a different tack and arrived at different conclusions in her 2001 study of both the Preliminary Draft and the state police laws that had been reformed on the basis of this model. She argued that taking precautions for the (future) prosecution of (future) crime and for its prevention represented distinct, new responsibilities that could be neither lumped together under the preventive combatting of crime nor subsumed under the traditional charge to protect against concrete dangers; the Preliminary Draft itself and subsequent state laws, she concluded, had muddied the conceptual waters by attempting to do both. Both of these activities, Albers argued, were distinguished by the anticipatory displacement of the prognosis regarding a concrete danger or individual suspicion. However, she insisted that this did not necessarily entail the suspension or abandonment of the legal norms that had heretofore limited the scope of police activity. In contrast to Weßlau, Albers argued that these precautionary activities were not essentially unnormable and that the dense thicket of regulatory provisions found in the Preliminary Draft and subsequent legislation represented appropriate mechanisms for compensating for the weakening of traditional limitations on police authority resulting from this logical and temporal displacement. Albers concluded that the prevention of crime was not unconstitutional and that the constitutionality of taking precautions for the prosecution of crime—especially in the strong sense of generating suspicion—ultimately depended on whether concrete, individualized suspicion represented an inviolable constitutional minimum. In the end, she offered a differentiated assessment of the state police laws of the late 1980s and 1990s: "[A number of them] exhibit numerous constitutional deficits. Many of the individual provisions are constitutional or must be [considered constitutional only if they are] interpreted in a restricted sense. And many of them are in need of improvement. At the same time, though, many provisions must be considered successful formulations."[87]

But the most positive assessment of the Preliminary Draft came from state legislators, who accepted it as the basis for their legislative labors.

The Limits of Harmonization: The Reform of State Police Laws

Although the approval of the March 1986 version of the Preliminary Draft was the starting shot for the legislative race to reform state police laws, it was not immediately clear which path the runners would take.[88]

In the spring of 1988, the political fortunes of the Preliminary Draft were complicated by the completion, after eighteen months of work, of an FDP model draft for regulating the informational activity of the police.[89] The FDP draft was composed by a group headed by Hirsch and Justice Minister Hans A. Engelhard, and it went even further than the proposed 1985 revisions to the Hessian police law, which had been the first attempt to articulate a liberal alternative to the Preliminary Draft.[90] The FDP proposal rejected both the logic of total prevention, or what it called "precaution, planning and the active disposition of the environment for the purpose of social governance" (*Vorsorge, Planung und Sozialgestaltung*), and the logic of total repression—that is, the preventive combatting of crime—which the draft condemned as a logical and political monstrosity.[91] Instead, it held fast to the concept of concrete dangers as the only way of containing the precautionary mandate, which itself "contains no intrinsic limiting principle."[92]

Like the Hessian draft, the FDP proposal graduated the conditions under which various surveillance practices could be employed according to the intensity of the infringement on civil liberties they entailed, while the storage and exchange of this information were subjected to progressively more rigorous conditions. In contrast to the conservative idea of a constitutional right to "a life in security,"[93] the FDP argued that the best way to balance freedom and security was to limit the power of the police, ensure that police law adhered to the principle of proportionality, and make the process as transparent as possible. This last condition was secured by a number of notification requirements that the FDP believed were necessary for the concerned individuals to assert their rights, but that were seldom fulfilled, especially in investigations of terrorism or organized crime.[94]

Although the desire to craft a model law that would be acceptable to all of the states gave the Social Democrats a degree of leverage, differences among the parties regarding the conditions under which precautionary policing was authorized could not be overcome, and the March 1986 version included alternate conservative and Social Democratic versions of a dozen provisions.[95] In the spring of 1988, officials were still divided over whether to push ahead with yet another revision of the Preliminary Draft in a last-ditch effort to salvage the idea of a uniform police law. Until this point, state governments had refrained from moving ahead with the reform of their own police laws in the hope that the Social Democrats and the conservative parties could reach agreement on the alternative formulations that had been included in the Preliminary Draft and that the interior and justice ministries could overcome their differences over the scope of investigative authority to be granted to the police. However, from the very beginning, Engelhard had resisted the harmonization of the informational powers granted to the police by the Code of Criminal Procedure with the far more extensive authority contained in the Preliminary Draft, and the manifest failure to make any progress in this latter area meant that the Code of Criminal Procedure would not be revised in the foreseeable future. In the absence of such a prospect, it was inevitable that the states would more actively seek to reform their own police laws.[96] This finally led security officials to conclude that it made little sense to tilt yet again at the windmill of a uniform police law.[97]

As of 1985, only about half of the states had amended their police laws to bring them into alignment with the Model Draft. In 1986, Rhineland-Pfalz became the first state after the census decision to add information access and privacy provisions, which were closely modeled on the Preliminary Draft. However, between 1989 and 1994, all of the other states added such provisions, while in 1990 the soon to be former East Germany adopted a new police law that was modeled on the revised law of North Rhineland-Westphalia.[98] There were important differences among the reformed state laws. Some of them simply charged the police with protecting against dangers; others explicitly assigned the police responsibility for preparation for the defense against dangers and the prevention (*Verhütung*) of crime; and many, though not all, of these hewed closely to the Preliminary Draft in classifying these two forms of activity as elements of the larger task of the preventive combating of crime.[99] But regardless of their formulation of the general charge, they all authorized the preventive and precautionary practices set out in the Preliminary Draft.

Computer matching can be used to illustrate the range of alternatives open to the states in regulating these practices. In particular, there were five points where the matching could be given a more or less restrictive formulation: (1) could it be used for precautionary purposes or was it to be restricted to protecting against concrete dangers; (2) did the interest that was to be protected by such matching have to be as important as the protection of national security and life and limb, or could matching be used to prevent or prosecute less serious offenses; (3) could matching be used simply to make life easier for the police, or could it be used only if there were no other way for the police to carry out their responsibilities; (4) was the authority to order the measure to lie with the police, with elected officials, or with the judiciary; and (5) were the police to be permitted to make use of information that was discovered by chance during the process, but that was not directly related to the purpose for which the matching had originally been approved?

Although most states chose to permit the practice in order to prevent serious crime, they defined this in different ways, and they imposed different conditions on its use. Some permitted computer matching to protect against serious crime if there were factual indications of such a danger, and some imposed no additional material preconditions, while four states permitted matching only in case of a concrete danger. A half-dozen states stipulated that it could be used only on a subsidiary basis—that is, if it were not possible to protect against the stated danger in any other way. In most states, the decision to permit the police to seek access to external databases rested with elected officials, generally with the interior minister, while the remainder required judicial approval. Most states also specified that information obtained from such matching could be used only for the specific purpose for which the measure was authorized, though they sometimes allowed this information to be used either for purposes closely related to the original investigation or to prosecute one of a number of serious crimes, even if these were not related to the original offense.[100] This was important because the greater the extent to which the information collected could be used to prosecute crimes other than those for which the specific surveillance measure had been ordered, the more that such measures came to resemble instruments of a surveillance state. Such differences were probably inevitable in a federal system in which the states were governed by different parties at different times. Nevertheless, despite these differences, there remained a very strong family resemblance, and lamentations about the failure to harmonize the different state laws seem to be more the product of exaggerated expectations than the result of substantive differences.[101]

The debate over precautionary surveillance was one facet of the larger debate over the impact of prevention on the rule of law. As Constitutional Court justice Dieter Grimm argued at the time, modern societies cannot be governed exclusively by laws and norms because they have become so complex that it is impossible to anticipate, and thus legislatively authorize, all of the intermediate steps needed to attain a final policy goal. In such a situation, legislators are limited to enunciating general policy objectives, while the executive branch and the public administration, which are responsible for interpreting these policies and determining how they are to be applied in specific instances, operate in a normative space that is becoming increasingly attenuated. However, the absence of fully concretized legal norms makes it impossible to apply the principle of proportionality, limits the space for judicial review, and authorizes the expansion of precautionary action as far as necessary into the *Vorfeld* in order to combat every conceivable danger using whatever means are deemed most appropriate. The cumulative effect of this precautionary logic, Grimm concluded, has been to expand the remit of the administrative state to such an extent that the fundamental rights of the individual, which originally provided the positive rationale for state intervention into the social domain, could no longer function—as they had in the liberal era—as a final limit to state activity.[102]

This analysis precisely describes the development of criminal policy in the 1980s, when, as Weßlau argues, the attenuation—to the point of virtual disappearance—of the role of concrete dangers as the standard governing the informational activity of the police allowed the preventive combatting of crime and the preparation for the defense against dangers to become abstract norms, which the police could then flesh out on the basis of "indications," experience, and/or criminalistic hypotheses.[103] In this context, privacy protection law became the means by which the opponents of such precautionary surveillance attempted to impose limits and norms upon this otherwise unnormable activity.

In the past, the police had engaged in the anticipatory collection of criminal information, but they had only done so informally and in the shadow of liberal police law. However, in the 1970s and 1980s this form of surveillance became the flashpoint for conflict over the proper scope of state action as its activity underwent a massive expansion and systematization in response to the growing responsibilities of the interventionist state, which regarded prevention as the best, most rational, and most efficient way of combatting crime and other social problems, to the adoption of new information technologies, and to the emergence of new forms of crime. However, the informational demands of the police were expanding at the very moment when the census decision codified an antithetical logic based on the principles of informational self-determination, final purpose, and informational parsimony. In this context, the radicalization of the precautionary mandate interacted with the parallel radicalization of the liberal logic of informational parsimony to produce a dysfunctional, inflationary juridification of the informational activity of both the police and the civilian administration. The Preliminary Draft, as well as the other security and privacy laws approved in the second half of the 1980s, were characteristic products of this conjuncture.

The conception of internal security that informed the Preliminary Draft resembled nothing so much as that of Thomas Hobbes' *Leviathan* rearticulated in the language of the information society (or, to be more precise, of the information state), where privacy, rather than conscience, was the worm eating away at the core of the pacified, well-ordered polity. Here, the problems resulting from the inability to impose concrete norms on precautionary surveillance were compounded by the traumatic experiences of terrorism and organized crime. As Pitschas wrote in 2002, "The relationship between freedom and security has to be balanced anew because it is unclear what 'freedom' can mean in societies that are destabilized by terrorism, organized crime, the drug trade, and senseless violence. Here, the inherited understanding of the protection of freedom, which is based on the protection of fundamental rights against the state, encounters an entirely different reality."[104]

Such experiences encouraged politicians and security officials in the belief that security could only be attained if it were impossible for criminal intentions and actions to hide from the all-knowing eye of the state. In such a world, privacy and civil liberties would be swallowed without remainder by security and exist only provisionally and at the forbearance of the state. However, as Kniesel noted, the liberal constitutional state had been willing to function in a reactive, rather than in an anticipatory, mode and accept a degree of crime and insecurity because this was the price that had to be paid to preserve individual freedom, and he warned that the "paradigmatic preventive turn" that had taken place in both police and criminal law was coming to pose a threat to individual rights that was comparable to that posed by crime itself. "The state that aspires to realize the utopia of total security," he warned, "is, as a state of unfreedom, a police state."[105] In the debate over precautionary policing, privacy thus became the language through which the political problems entailed by the anticipatory foreclosure of the space of crime and freedom were theorized and their consequences contested.

Notes

1. "Programm für die Innere Sicherheit der Bundesrepublik Deutschland – Teil 1," supplement, *Gemeinsames Ministerialblatt* 31 (1972): 20.
2. Heiner Busch, "Hilfloser Datenschutz. Verrechtlichung, Individualisierung, Entpolitisierung," *CILIP* 85, no. 3 (2006): 3–9; Alfred Stümper, "Wie soll es denn weitergehen?" *Die Polizei* 78, no. 6 (1987): 159–63, who bemoaned (162) the fact that "the so-called 'security laws' are in principle privacy protection laws"; and Dieter Peitsch, "Die Informationsbeschaffung im neuen Polizeirecht," *ZRP* 25, no. 4 (1992): 127–30.
3. Although the new surveillance practices that were codified in the late 1980s were most often justified as a response to organized crime, they date almost without exception from the counterterrorism measures of the 1970s. The fact that Marion Albers, *Die Determination polizeilicher Tätigkeit in den Bereichen der Straftatenverhütung und der Verfolgungsvorsorge* (Duncker & Humblot, 2001), 181, n. 453, felt the need to ask whether this might be the case reflects the extent to which terrorism had been overlaid and, to a certain extent, repressed by organized crime as the central problem by which internal security had come to be defined, though she is inconsistent (100, 112, 202) as to the relative importance of terrorism and organized crime in this process. Edda Weßlau, *Vorfeldermittlungen. Probleme der Legalisierung "vorbeugender Verbrechensbekämpfung" aus strafprozeßrechtlicher Sicht* (Duncker & Humblot, 1989), 49–56, is clearer on both the origins of these surveillance practices and the reasons why they came to be associated with organized crime.

4. Michel Foucault, *The Birth of Biopolitics* (Palgrave, 2008); and Foucault, *Security, Territory, Population* (Palgrave, 2007).
5. Richard Ericson, *Crime in an Insecure World* (Polity, 2007), 24–31; and Giorgio Agamben, *State of Exception* (University of Chicago Press, 2005).
6. Claudia Aradau and Rens van Munster, *Politics of Catastrophe: Genealogies of the Unknown* (Routledge, 2011), 117–18.
7. Susanne Krasmann, "Der Präventionsstaat im Einvernehmen. Wie Sichtbarkeitsregime stillschweigend Akzeptanz produzieren," in "Sichtbarkeitsregime – Überwachung, Sicherheit und Privatheit im 21. Jahrhundert," special issue, *Leviathan* 25 (2010): 53–70; and Sven Opitz, "Zwischen Sicherheitsdispositiven und Securitization. Zur Analytik illiberaler Gouvernementalität," in *Gouvernementalität und Sicherheit*, ed. Patricia Purtschert et al. (Transkript Verlag, 2008), 201–28.
8. Erhard Denninger, "Prävention und Freiheit," in *Vom Rechtsstaat zum Präventionsstaat*, ed. Stefan Huster and Karsten Rudolph (Suhrkamp, 2008), 85–106, citation 94–95.
9. Shortly after taking office, Baum had brought the interior ministry departments responsible for the Federal Criminal Police and the Border Police together in a single division and offered Stümper the position as head of the new unit. Stümper, however, turned down the offer. "Über die Runden," *Der Spiegel*, 3 July 1978, 68–72.
10. Horst Herold, *Fahnden und Forschen. Perspektiven und künftige Schwerpunkte für den Einsatz elektronischer Datenverarbeitungsanlagen im Rahmen der Polizei* (IBM-Sonderdruck, 1966); and Herold, "Kybernetik und Polizei-Organisation," *Die Polizei* 61, no. 2 (1970): 33–37. On Herold, see Dieter Schenk, *Der Chef. Horst Herold und das BKA* (Spiegel-Buchverlag, 1998); Birgit Seiderer, "Horst Herold und das Nürnberger Modell (1966–1971). Eine Fallstudie zur Pionierzeit des polizeilichen EDV-Einsatzes in der Reformära der Bundesrepublik," *Mitteilungen des Vereins für Geschichte der Stadt Nürnberg* 91 (2004): 317–50; and Dorothea Hauser, *Baader und Herold. Beschreibung eines Kampfes* (Rororo, 1997).
11. "Herold gegen Alle. Gespräche mit dem Präsidenten des Bundeskriminalamtes," *Trans-Atlantik* 2 (November 1980), 29–40, citation 39.
12. Horst Herold, "Polizeiliche Informationsverarbeitung als Basis der Prävention," in *Prävention und Strafrecht. Tagungsberichte der Deutschen Kriminologischen Gesellschaft vom 4. Dezember 1976* (Kriminalistik-Verlag, 1977), 23–35, especially 30; and Herold, "Intensivierung der Verbrechensbekämpfung durch Einsatz elektronischer Datenverarbeitung – dargestellt am Beispiel eines Ballungsraumes," *Verbrechensbekämpfung heute und morgen. Arbeitstagung der bayerischen Kriminalpolizei* (1969), 130–75, especially 133.
13. Herold, *Fahnden und Forschen*, 9; Herold, "Künftige Einsatzformen der EDV und ihre Auswirkungen im Bereich der Polizei," *Kriminalistik* 28, no. 9 (1974): 385–92, especially 392; and Herold, "Gesellschaftlicher Wandel – Chance der Polizei?" *Die Polizei* 63, no. 5 (1972): 133–41, especially 134.
14. Herold, *Fahnden und Forschen*, 9.
15. Ibid., 9–11, 14; Herold, "Neue Wege kriminalpolizeilicher Verbrechensbekämpfung," in *Kriminologische Gegenwartsfragen*, vol. 9: *Vorträge bei der XV. Tagung der Gesellschaft für die gesamte Kriminologie*, ed. Hans Göppinger and Hermann Witter (Ferdinand Enke, 1970), 208–34, especially 211–12; Herold's inaugural address as president of the Federal Criminal Police (1971), cited in Seiderer, "Horst Herold," 348–49; and Herold, "Gesellschaftlicher Wandel – Chance der Polizei?," (1972), 134.
16. Herold, "Gesellschaftlicher Wandel – Chance der Polizei?" in *Grundlagen der Kriminalistik*, Bd. 11: *Kriminalstrategie und Kriminaltaktik*, ed. Herbert Schäfer (Steintor-Verlag, 1973), 13–35, citation 24.
17. Herold, "Neue Wege," 212–13.
18. Herold, "Gesellschaftlicher Wandel – Chance der Polizei?" (1972), 134, and (1973), 25; Herold, "Moderne Methoden der Verbrechensbekämpfung," *Bulletin*, 17 July 1974, 863–65; and "Herold gegen Alle," 36.

19. Herold, "Gesellschaftlicher Wandel – Chance der Polizei?" (1972), 134; Herold, "Gesellschaftlicher Wandel – Chance der Polizei?" (1973), citation 24; and *Polizei und Prävention*, 187. Or as Herold elsewhere argued, "Effective prevention demands the influencing of crime as it emerges at its very roots," "Möglichkeiten und Grenzen kriminalistisch-kriminologischer Forschung. Arbeitstagung an der Polizei-Führungsakademie Hiltrup vom 27. bis 29.11.1974," *Kriminalistik* 29, no. 2 (1975): 58–62, citation 61.
20. Alfred Stümper, "Prävention und Repression als überholte Unterscheidung?" *Kriminalistik* 29: no. 2 (1975), 49–53; and Stümper, "Die Wandlung der Polizei in Begriff und Aufgaben," *Kriminalistik* 34: no. 6 (1980), 242–45, especially 242. Stümper's work is glossed in Albers, *Die Determination polizeilicher Tätigkeit*, 108–16.
21. Alfred Stümper, "Probleme der Bekämpfung einer konspirativ vorgehenden, bandenmäßig organisierten Kriminalität," *Die Polizei* 73, no. 8 (1982): 229–31, citation 230.
22. Stümper, "Prävention und Repression als überholte Unterscheidung?" 52.
23. Stümper, "Probleme der Bekämpfung," 230; and Alfred Stümper, "Verbrechensbekämpfung im Umbruch und die operative Arbeit," *Kriminalistik* 31, no. 4 (1977): 150–55, especially 153.
24. Stümper, "Prävention und Repression als überholte Unterscheidung?" 53; and Stümper, "Probleme der Bekämpfung."
25. This view was made explicit in the preamble to the 1992 organized crime law, Drs. 12/989, 41.
26. Stümper, "Probleme der Bekämpfung," 230; and Albers, *Die Determination polizeilicher Tätigkeit*, 100–3. The Conference of Interior Ministers incorporated Stümper's ideas into their 1983 strategy document for combatting organized crime. See "Neue Methoden der Verbrechensbekämpfung. Bericht des vom Arbeitskreis II der Innenministerkonferenz eingesetzten ad hoc-Ausschusses," *CILIP* 17, no. 1 (1984): 76–86.
27. Eckart Conze, "Securitization – Gegenwartsdiagnose oder historischer Analyseansatz?" *GuG* 38 (2012): 453–67; Christopher Daase, "Die Historisierung der Sicherheit. Anmerkungen zur historischen Sicherheitsforschung aus politikwissenschaftlicher Sicht," *GuG* 38 (2012): 387–405, especially 388; and Daase, "National, Societal and Human Security: On the Transformation of Political Language," *Historical Social Research* 35 (2010): 24–39.
28. Stümper, "Zur Problematik der Verbrechensbekämpfung," 475.
29. Alfred Stümper, "Die Wandlung der Polizei in Begriff und Aufgaben," *Kriminalistik* 34, no. 6 (1980): 242–45, citation 242.
30. Alfred Stümper, "Wende im Lagebild Innere Sicherheit," *Die Polizei* 71, no. 10 (1980), 297–301, citation 299; and Stümper, "Sind Strategie und Taktik der Polizei noch zeitgemäß?" *Die Polizei* 72, no. 7 (1981): 197–203, citation 197.
31. Alfred Stümper, "Gedanken zur Schaffung einer Generaldirektion für die Innere Sicherheit (GdIS)," *"Kriminalistik* 33, no. 1 (1979): 2–5; and Stümper, "Wende im Lagebild Innere Sicherheit," 299.
32. Critics argued that Herold's social sanitary vision of the police harbored totalitarian tendencies. See Simitis's comments in Hessische Landesregierung, ed., *Informationsgesellschaft oder Überwachungsstaat. Strategien zur Wahrung der Freiheitsrechte im Computerzeitalter* (Opladen, 1986), I:313; and Eggert Schwan, "Droht der Überwachungsstaat?," *Leviathan* 12, no. 4 (1984): 560–77, especially 561.
33. Stefan Naas, *Die Entstehung des Preußischen Polizeiverwaltungsgesetzes von 1931* (Mohr Siebeck, 2003); and Hans-Harald Scupin, "Die Entwicklung des Polizeibegriffs und seine Verwendung in den neuen deutschen Polizeigesetzen," dissertation, Marburg, 1970.
34. Albers, *Die Determination polizeilicher Tätigkeit*, 19–26.
35. Gerd Heise and Reinhard Riegel, *Musterentwurf eines einheitlichen Polizeigesetzes mit Begründungen und Anmerkungen*, 2nd revised ed. (Richard Boorberg Verlag, 1978); *Sten. Ber.*, 8. Wahlperiode, 151. Sitzung (10 May 1979), 12124–34; "'Ich kann ja die Hand-

granate danebenwerfen,'" *Der Spiegel*, 2 August 1976, 29–33; and Albrecht Funk and Falco Werkentin, "Der Musterentwurf für ein einheitliches Polizeigesetz – ein Muster exekutiven Rechtsstaatsverständnisses," *KJ* 9 (1976): 407–22. On the drafting of the Model Draft, see the materials in BAK B141/64943-52 and StAH 136-1/461-67, 836, 2433. This approval had been delayed by three issues: the need to distinguish the preventive responsibilities of the police, which were to be regulated by police law, from their repressive, investigatory activities, which they carried out on behalf of justice officials and which were to be governed by the Code of Criminal Procedure; the bitter public debate over whether the police should be permitted to intentionally kill an offender, such as a kidnapper, if this were the only way to save the victim's life; and the question of whether machine guns and hand grenades should be included among the standard weaponry of the police. The questions relating to the first of these issues were delegated to a "harmonization commission," whose work stretched on for more than a decade without achieving the desired goal. Documents relating to the work of this group in the mid-1970s can be found in BAK B141/64955-65 and B106/83847, Bd. 3. Such harmonization was the key to avoiding the problems that would arise if the police had greater informational authority to combat dangers than to investigate crimes.

36. Reinhard Riegel, "Neueste Entwicklungstendenzen im Polizei- und Strafverfahrensrecht," *ZRP* 11, no. 1 (1978): 14–20, especially 14. On the precise scope of public security, see Albers, *Die Determination polizeilicher Tätigkeit*, 30–32.
37. Facts were distinguished from indications, which include speculations, hypothetical considerations or suppositions that are solely based on criminalistic experience independent from the facts in any specific instance. The reference in police law to "factual indications" was intended to convey the idea that presumptions or speculations alone were insufficient to justify police action and that there had to be some evidence connecting such general principles to the individual case at hand. The Code of Criminal Procedure established "sufficient factual indications" (*zureichende tatsächliche Anhaltspunkte*) as the threshold for opening a formal investigation, a formulation that emphasized that the indications present in the case at hand had to be sufficiently strong to justify the infringement on the rights of the concerned individual entailed by such an investigation.
38. Heise and Riegel, *Musterentwurf*, 46–51. The amendment to the Baden-Württemberg police law, which was approved before the final version of the Model Draft was adopted, went even further. It permitted the police to establish "control areas" encompassing entire streets or city districts in order to search for persons suspected of committing a number of particularly serious crimes; the police could then comb through the area and conduct identity checks on all persons found there. The authors of the Model Draft found this proposal constitutionally questionable. See IV/Heise to Staatssekretär, Betr.: Entwurf eines Gesetzes . . . Baden-Württemberg vom 11.6.1975, and Peter Müller to Burkhard Hirsch and Andreas von Schoeler, Betr.: Beratung Polizeigesetz . . . (19 February 1976), both in NRW NW 595/120; and *Gesetzblatt für Baden-Württemberg*, 1976, 228–30.
39. Weßlau, *Vorfeldermittlungen*, 294–99.
40. Wolfgang Hoffmann-Riem, "Abbau von Rechtsstaatlichkeit durch Neubau des Polizeirechts?" *JZ* 33 (1978): 335–39, citations 337–38; and Fritz Sydow, "Verbrechensbekämpfung nach neuem Recht," *ZRP* 10, no. 5 (1977): 119–25, who characterized (123) this provision as a "disconcerting (*befremdliche*) novelty." In contrast, the official commentary (Heise and Riegel, *Musterentwurf*, 50) declared it to be "undisputedly necessary," though without providing any explanation.
41. Heise and Riegel, *Musterentwurf*, 52–53, 15, 27. Although the act of fingerprinting itself often got lost in this debate, Hoffmann-Riem, "Abbau von Rechtsstaatlichkeit," 333–34, noted that the fingerprints taken under this provision could be retained indefinitely

because it permitted their retention until the original suspicion no longer existed—a condition that was seldom if ever met in practice. Even then, fingerprints were to be destroyed only on request, rather than automatically.

42. Sydow, "Verbrechensbekämpfung nach neuem Recht," 124–25; and Riegel, "Neueste Entwicklungstendenzen," 15–16, who noted that an early version of the Model Draft had proposed that the police be charged with "prosecuting" (*verfolgen*) crime, rather than with simply the subsidiary task of "investigating" (*erforschen*) it on behalf of prosecutors.
43. IV A 5/Staats, Betr.: 46. Konferenz der Justizminister und -senatoren, hier: Musterentwurf (1 October 1975), BAK B141/64946; and the justice ministry's response to the March 1976 version of the Model Draft, BMJ to BMI, Betr.: Musterentwurf . . . (14 April 1976), BAK B141/64952.
44. Reinhard Riegel, "Zu Stand und Entwicklungstendenzen des informationellen Befugnisrechts zur polizeilichen Aufgabenerfüllung: Licht, Schatten und Hoffnung," *DÖV* 43, no. 19 (1994): 814–21, especially 814.
45. Arbeitskreis Polizeirecht, *Alternativentwurf einheitlicher Polizeigesetze des Bundes und der Länder* (Luchterhand, 1979); and "Schatten voraus," *Der Spiegel*, 26 February 1979, 36–37.
46. Arbeitskreis Polizeirecht, *Alternativentwurf*, vii.
47. Ibid., viii–ix.
48. Ibid., 53–55.
49. Ibid., 113.
50. Ibid., 113–35.
51. Information über den Stand der Polizeigesetzgebung im Bund und in den Ländern (December 1978), NRW RW391/886; "Zum Stand der Verabschiedung des Musterentwurfs . . . ," *CILIP* 2, no. 1 (1979): 10; "Redaktionelle Stellungnahme zum Vorentwurf zur Änderung . . . ," *CILIP* 21, no. 2 (1985): 24–25; and "Zum Stand des Polizeirechts in der Bunderepublik," *CILIP* 22, no. 3 (1985): 72–73.
52. *Gesetzblatt der Freien Hansestadt Bremen* (11 April 1983), 141–56.
53. Niedersächsischer Minister des Innern to Arbeitsgemeinschaft der Innenministerien, Betr.: Musterentwurf (31 August 1978), and Krampol/Bayer. Staatsministerium des Innern to Arbeitsgemeinschaft der Innenministerien, Betr.: Musterentwurf (6 October 1978), both in StAH 136-1/2431. I have not been able to locate materials pertaining to the discussions to which Krampol refers.
54. IS 2/Werthebach to P I 5, Betr.: Erarbeitung bereichsspezifische Vorschriften . . . (11 September 1984), BAK B106/101408, Bd. 5; Niedersächsischer Minister des Innern to Innenminister/-senatoren, Betr.: Bereichsspezifische Datenschutzregelungen im Sicherheitssektor (25 October 1984), and Bundeskriminalamt to BMI, Betr.: Erarbeitung bereichsspezifischer Vorschriften . . . (20 November 1984), both in BAK B106/101408, Bd. 6.
55. Innenministerium Nordrhein-Westfalen, Formulierungsvorschläge: Entwurf zur Änderung des Musterentwurfs . . . (Stand: 10.8.1984), BAK B106/101408, Bd. 5; Innenministerium Nordrhein-Westfalen to Innenminister/-senatoren, Betr.: Entwurf von bereichsspezifischen Regelungen für die Datenerhebung und Datenverarbeitung im Bereich der Polizei (31 October 1984), and UAL P I/Reinhard Rupprecht to AL P I 5, Betr.: Besprechung von Vertretern der Innenministerien von CDU/CSU-regierten Ländern . . . am 30.10.1984, both in BAK B106/101408, Bd. 6; and Bereichsspezifische Regelungen für die Datenerhebung und -verarbeitung im Bereich der Polizei (Stand: 31.10.1984), BAK B106/122705, Bd. 7. The Vorentwurf zur Änderung des Musterentwurfs . . . (Stand: 8.2.1985) und Begründung are most easily accessible in *CILIP* 21, no. 2 (1985): 44–57.
56. IV A 6/Voth, Betr.: Entwurf zur Änderung des Musterentwurfs . . . (13 February 1985), BAK B141/123475; Anforderungen an Datenschutzregelungen im Polizeirecht. Beschluß der Konferenz der Datenschutzbeauftragten des Bundes und der Länder (24 January

1985), BAK B106/122705, Bd. 9; Leuze to Innenministerium Baden-Württemberg, Betr.: Vorentwurf zur Änderung des Musterentwurfs ... (29 August 1985), Berlin DSB: Musterentwurf; and Bundesbeauftragter für den Datenschutz to Bundesminister des Innern, Betr.: Vorentwurf zur Änderung ... (6 August 1985), BAK B141/123482.

57. Innenministerium Baden-Württemberg/Stümper to Innenminister Nordrhein-Westfalen, Betr.: Entwurf bereichsspezifischer Regelungen für die Datenerhebung und Datenverarbeitung im Bereich der Polizei (6 December 1984), and Niedersächsischer Minister des Innern, Ergebnisniederschrift über die Besprechung der Arbeitsgruppe der Abteilungsleiter am 27.11.1984, both in BAK B106/122705, Bd. 7.

58. Josef Isensee, *Das Grundrecht auf Sicherheit. Zu den Schutzpflichten des freiheitlichen Verfassungsstaates* (De Gruyter, 1983); Rupert Scholz and Rainer Pitschas, *Informationelle Selbstbestimmung und staatliche Informationsvorsorge* (Duncker & Humblot, 1984).

59. Scholz and Pitschas, *Informationelle Selbstbestimmung*, 104.

60. Ibid., 175.

61. Anforderungen an Datenschutzregelungen im Polizeirecht. Beschluß der Konferenz der Datenschutzbeauftragten des Bundes und der Länder (24 January 1985), BAK B106/122705, Bd. 9.

62. Scholz and Pitschas, *Informationelle Selbstbestimmung*, 188.

63. Their arguments were criticized at the time by Denninger, "Das Recht auf informationelle Selbstbestimmung und Innere Sicherheit," *KJ* 18, no. 3 (1985): 215–44; and Benda, "Das Recht des Bürgers auf informationelle Selbstbestimmung – Auswirkungen auf den Umgang mit persönlichen Daten bei den Sicherheitsbehörden. Vortrag im Rahmen der Vortragsveranstaltung des Niedersächsischen Ministers des Innern am 22.11.84 in Hannover," BAK B106/101408, Bd. 6.

64. Michael Kniesel and Jürgen Vahle, *VE ME PolG. Musterentwurf eines einheitlichen Polizeigesetzes in der Fassung des Vorentwurfs zur Änderung des ME PolG. Text und amtliche Begründung* (Kriminalistik-Verlag, 1990); the Preliminary Draft was reprinted in *CILIP* 24, no. 2 (1986): 75–86.

65. "Die Polizei hat im Rahmen dieser Aufgabe auch für die Verfolgung von Straftaten vorzusorgen und Straftaten zu verhüten (vorbeugended Bekämpfung von Straftaten) sowie Vorbereitungen zu treffen, um künftige Gefahren abwehren zu können (Vorbereitung auf die Gefahrenabwehr)."

66. Albers, *Die Determination polizeilicher Tätigkeit*, 118–20. Albers suggests that this formulation of the precautionary mandate represented a compromise between those who viewed precautionary activity as something entirely different from the traditional defense against (concrete) dangers and those who considered it to be one aspect of this charge.

67. Leuze to Innenministerium Baden-Württemberg, Betr.: Vorentwurf zur Änderung des Musterentwurfs ... (29 August 1985), Berlin DSB: Musterentwurf.

68. See, for example, BMI to BMJ, Betr.: Vorentwurf zur Änderung des Musterentwurfs ... (21 April 1987), BAK B141/123483, which claims that "true prevention (*Vorbeugung*) is without any doubt the most effective of all protective measures," but then notes the lack of any quantitative data to support the importance of taking precautions for the prevention of crime.

69. IV A 7/Ministerialrat Stoltenberg, Betr.: Vorentwurf zur Änderung des Musterentwurfs ... (27 May 1986), and—almost verbatim—IV A 6/Voth, Betr.: Vorentwurf zur Änderung des Musterentwurfs. Stellungnahme zum Vorentwurf ... (6 June 1986), both BAK B141/123482. The Stellungnahme des Deutscher Richterbunds zum Vorentwurf zur Ergänzung des Musterentwurfs ... (undated response to February 1985 version), BAK B106/122708, complained that the preventive combatting of crime failed to impose any limits whatsoever on police activity and argued that it was "misleading and dangerous" because it created the impression that the police possessed the authority to investigate crime independent of justice officials and the Criminal Code.

70. Michael Kniesel, "Neue Polizeigesetze contra StPO," *ZRP* 20, no. 11 (1987): 377–83, citation 381.
71. This gap runs right through Markus Möstl, "Die neue dogmatische Gestalt des Polizeirechts," *DVBl* 122, no. 10 (2007): 581–89, who argued that the collection of information in order to uncover dangers was part of the traditional charge to the police, that it should be understood as a supplement to the use of force to eliminate dangers, and that this *Vorfeld* activity could be regulated independently without undermining the use of concrete dangers as the organizing principle for the regulation of the use of force.
72. Michael Kniesel, "Vorbeugende Bekämpfung von Straftaten im neuen Polizeirecht – Gefahrenabwehr oder Strafverfolgung?" *ZRP* 22, no. 9 (1989): 329–32, citations 329.
73. Michael Kniesel, "Vorbeugende Bekämpfung von Straftaten im juristischen Meinungsstreit – eine unendliche Geschichte," *ZRP* 25, no. 5 (1992): 164–67, especially 165; and Michael Kniesel and Jürgen Vahle, "Zur Novellierung des nordrhein-westfälischen Polizeirechts," *DÖV* 43, no. 15 (1990): 646–51, especially 648. However, Weßlau, *Vorfeldermittlungen*, 320–25, argued that the "investigatory state of emergency" postulated by Stümper, Kniesel, and others was less a reality than a discursive construct, and she was less convinced that the proposed methods would yield the anticipated results.
74. See, for example, BMI to BMJ, Betr.: Vorentwurf zur Änderung des Musterentwurfs . . . (21 April 1987), BAK B141/123483.
75. Kniesel, "Vorbeugende Bekämpfung von Straftaten im juristischen Meinungsstreit," 166.
76. Kniesel, "Vorbeugende Bekämpfung von Straftaten im neuen Polizeirecht," 331–32.
77. IV A 6/Voth, Betr.: Entwurf zur Änderung des Musterentwurfs . . . (8 March 1985), BAK B141/123475.
78. IV A 6/Ministerialrat Dr. Voth, Entwurf zur Änderung des Musterentwurfs . . . (13 February 1985), BAK B141/123475; and IV A 6/Voth, Betr.: Vorentwurf zur Änderung des Musterentwurfs. Stellungnahme zum Vorentwurf . . . (6 June 1986), BAK B141/123482.
79. Bundesbeauftragter für den Datenschutz to Bundesminister des Innern, Betr.: Vorentwurf zur Änderung des Musterentwurfs . . . (6 August 1985), BAK B141/123482.
80. IV A 1/Regierungsdirektorin Seibert, Betr.: Vorentwurf zur Änderung des Musterentwurfs . . . (27 May 1986), BAK B141/123482.
81. IV A 1/Regierungsdirektorin Seibert, Betr.: Vorentwurf zur Änderung des Musterentwurfs . . . (27 May 1986), BAK B141/123482. The same point had been made in Anforderungen an Datenschutzregelungen im Polizeibereich. Beschluss der Konferenz der Datenschutzbeauftragten des Bundes und der Länder vom 24.1.1985, BAK B141/123480.
82. BMJ Stellungnahme zum Vorentwurf zur Änderung des Musterentwurfs . . . (June 1986), 25, BAK B141/123482; and "Redaktionelle Stellungnahme zum 'Vorentwurf . . . ,'" *CILIP* 21, no. 2 (1985): 21–43, citation 36–37.
83. Weßlau, *Vorfeldermittlungen*, 239, 280, 331–32. Heinz Wagner made a similar argument in both "Die Entwürfe zur Novellierung der Polizeigesetze, oder Die nicht normierenden Normen," *Demokratie und Recht* 17, no. 2 (1989): 165–76, and *Kommentar zum Polizeigesetz von Nordrhein-Westfalen und zum Musterentwurf eines einheitlichen Polizeigesetzes des Bundes und der Länder* (Luchterhand, 1987), especially 203–4.
84. Kniesel, "Neue Polizeigesetze contra StPO," 380; and Kniesel, "Vorbeugende Bekämpfung von Straftaten im juristischen Meinungsstreit," 164.
85. Michael Kniesel, "'Innere Sicherheit' und Grundgesetz," *ZRP* 29, no. 12 (1996): 482–89, especially 487–88.
86. Kniesel, "Neue Polizeigesetze contra StPO," 382; and Kniesel, "Vorbeugende Bekämpfung von Straftaten im juristischen Meinungsstreit," 166.
87. Albers, *Die Determination polizeilicher Tätigkeit*, 252ff., 347–49, citation 349.
88. In September 1987, the Working Group II police law committee was asked to simplify what the administration regarded as the excessively complex March 1986 version and

attempt to reconcile the differences between the conservative parties and the Social Democrats on key provisions. However, nothing came of this proposal. See P I 5/Schattenberg, Privatdienstschreiben von Herrn AL P to the senior police officials of the conservative states (17 August 1987), P I 5/Schattenberg, Informationsvermerk, Betr.: AK II-Sitzung am 17./18. September 1987 (September 9, 1987), and Stümper, Abteilungsinterne Notiz (21 September 1987), all in BAK B106/122709, Bd. 18.

89. Entwurf der Arbeitsgruppe Polizeirecht des Bundesfachaussschusses Innen und Recht der FDP zur Änderung des am 25.11.1977 von der Innenministerkonferenz beschlossenen Musterentwurfs and the Begründung (14 June 1988), in both HHStA Abt. 502/12487a and BAK B106/122710, Bd. 19; and Vorlage des Entwurfs der Arbeitsgruppe Polizeirecht . . . der FDP, BAK B106/122710, Bd. 19.

90. Gesetz zur Änderung des Hessischen Gesetzes über die öffentliche Sicherheit und Ordnung (HSOG), II. Entwurf (Stand: 30. September 1985), and Vorläufige Begründung (Stand: 15. August 1985), HHStA Abt. 502/12495a; and Synoptische Gegenüberstellung des Vorentwurfs . . . und des ersten Entwurfs . . . HSOG, HHStA Abt. 502/12504a. At the time, the state was governed by the country's first Social Democratic-Green coalition. However, the civil liberties activist Sebastian Cobler prepared a lengthy memorandum on behalf of the Hessian Greens in which he argued that the draft was tainted from beginning to end by the original sin of the preventive combatting of crime, which undermined the otherwise admirable formulation of the final purpose principle, and the party ultimately came out against the draft. See Hessischer Minister der Justiz to Hessian Minister des Innern, Betr.: Entwurf eines Gesetzes . . . (24 May 1985), and L I 3, Kabinettsache, Betr.: Gesetz zur Änderung . . . (13 September 1985), HHStA Abt. 502/12495b & a, respectively; and Cobler, Gutachten zu dem vom Hessischen Minister des Innern vorgelegten . . . Gesetzentwurf . . . (Stand: 30.9.1985) im Auftrag der Fraktion Die Grünen im Hessischen Landtag erstattet . . . (14 February 1986), HHStA Abt. 502/12504a.

91. Entwurf der Arbeitsgruppe Polizeirecht . . . Begründung, 12.

92. Vorlage des Entwurfs der Arbeitsgruppe Polizeirecht, 5.

93. P I 5 to conservative state interior ministers (29 September 1987), BAK B106/122709, Bd. 18.

94. Conservatives, Social Democrats, and left-wing civil libertarians all argued that, for better or worse, the FDP model draft did not hold consistently to these statements of principle.

95. At the same time that it approved the March 1986 version, the Conference of Interior Ministers also urged Interior Minister Zimmermann to push the justice ministry to revise the Code of Criminal Procedure to bring the investigatory powers that it granted to the police into alignment with the authority granted them by the Preliminary Draft. See P I 5/Kersten, Betr.: Vorentwurf zur Änderung . . . (4 March 1986), BAK B106/122707 and the materials in 122708.

96. The amendments to the Code contained in the 1992 Organized Crime Law gave the police the informational authority for repressive purposes that they had already been granted for preventive purposes by the police laws. Gesetz zur Bekämpfung des illegalen Rauschgifthandels und anderer Erscheinungsformen der Organisierten Kriminalität, *BGBl.*, 1992, 1302–12, Artikel 3.

97. P I 5/Schattenberg to Staatssekretär Neusel, Betr.: FDP-Entwurf . . (13 April 1988), P I 5/ Schattenberg, Betr.: Novellierung der StPO, hier: Besprechung des Arbeitsentwurfs . . . (April 18, 1988), and Zwischenbericht des ad hoc-Ausschusses "Recht der Polizei" des AK II zur Frage der Anpassung des Vorentwurfs . . . , all in BAK B106/122710, Bd. 19.

98. Volkmar Götz, *Allgemeines Polizei- und Ordnungsrecht*, 13. Aufl. (Vandenhoeck & Ruprecht, 2001), 33–39; Götz, "Die Entwicklung des allgemeinen Polizei- und Ordnungs-

rechts (1987 bis 1989)," *Neue Zeitschrift für Verwaltungsrecht* 9 (1990): 725–33; and "Polizeirecht der Länder. Zum Stand der Gesetzgebung," *CILIP* 31, no. 3 (1988): 105–8.
99. Albers, *Die Determination polizeilicher Tätigkeit*, 118–21, 180; and Reinhard Riegel, "Wesentliche Aspekte und Neuerungen im Polizeirecht der Länder," *Die Polizei* 89 (1998): 211–28.
100. Stefan Middel, *Innere Sicherheit und preventive Terrorismusbekämpfung* (Nomos, 2007), 96–208; Sönke Hilbrans, "Grundlage und Problematik der Rasterfahndung," in *Innere Sicherheit als Gefahr*, ed. Nils Leopold et. al. (Humanistische Union, 2003), 268–85; and Christoph Gusy, "Rasterfahndung nach Polizeirecht," *KritV* 85, no. 4 (2002): 474–90.
101. The conservative parties, however, had little truck for any of these limitations and qualifications, and one can get a sense of what their ideal vision of an amended police law would have looked like from the comments of Bavarian officials on the working draft of the informational provisions of the Code of Criminal Procedure, which was circulated by the justice ministry in the summer of 1986. See Arbeitsentwurf eines Gesetzes zur Regelung der rechtlichen Grundlagen für Fahndungsmaßnahmen, Fahndungshilfsmittel und für die Akteneinsicht im Strafverfahren (Stand: 31. Juli 1986), Berlin DSB Aktenzeichen 055-100; the materials in BAK B106/111085; Aktenvermerk: zum Arbeitsentwurf der BMJ zur Novellierung des StPO (undated), Bayer. Staatsministerium der Justiz, Leitlinien für Änderungen der Strafprozeßordnung . . . (10 December 1986), and I C 5/Honnacker, Informationsgespräch mit dem BDK (29 December 1986), all in BayHStA MInn/97094.
102. Dieter Grimm, "Der Wandel der Staatsaufgaben und die Krise des Rechtsstaats," "Verfassungsrechtiche Anmerkungen zum Thema Prävention," and "Die Zukunft der Verfassung," all in *Die Zukunft der Verfassung* (Suhrkamp, 1991), especially 432–37.
103. Weßlau, *Vorfeldermittlungen*, 328–32.
104. Rainer Pitschas, "Vom 'neuen Rechtsstaat': Freiheit in Sicherheit durch gesellschaftliche Verantwortungspartnerschaft für den inneren Frieden," in *Auf dem Weg in einen "neuen Rechtsstaat": Zur künftigen Architektur der inneren Sicherheit in Deutschland und Österreich*, ed. Rainer Pitschas and Harald Stolzlechner (Duncker & Humblot, 2004), 95–111, citation 108.
105. Kniesel, "'Innere Sicherheit' und Grundgesetz," 483, 487.

Conclusion

Privacy was no less important—and no less contested—at the end of the period under study here than it was at the beginning. However, in the interim the technologies and administrative practices that shaped the collection of personal information, as well as the specific ways in which this information was analyzed, understood, and used, had evolved substantially—and the political relevance of privacy had evolved along with them and has continued to do so since the turn of the millennium.

The logic of precautionary surveillance, the forms of informational power and social governance to which it gave rise, and the political questions that they raised are very different from those associated with integrated data processing, which had provided the catalyst for the articulation of the original privacy protection paradigm in the 1970s. To this extent, one can speak of a paradigm shift that applies not only to policing and internal security, but also to the broader use of personal information to govern the welfare state. It is, therefore, appropriate to conclude this study at the turn of the 1990s with the amendment of the Federal Privacy Protection Law and the simultaneous codification of precautionary surveillance by the revised state police laws, whose transgressive logic represented a direct challenge to the rule of law, the liberal economy of informational parsimony, and the privacy protection paradigm embodied in the Federal Privacy Protection Law.

The history told in the preceding pages has been a distinctly national one. However, although international law played virtually no role in the development of the country's privacy law during the period studied here, since the turn of the millennium human rights and EU privacy law have together had a greater impact on German privacy protection law than any other factors. The right to privacy that was enshrined in the 1950 European Convention on Human Rights regarded the family and the home as

---

Notes for this chapter begin on page 364.

the specific social location of the private. However, it was only after privacy had been reconceptualized in informational terms in West German national law that the right to informational privacy could be translated back to the regional level—in the form of a right to data protection—as a human right for the digital age. This depended on two developments. The first was the comparable reconceptualization of privacy in the national laws of the other states of Western Europe, the passage between the late 1970s and the mid-1990s of national privacy protection laws in these countries, and the parallel adoption of privacy regulations by the OECD (1980) and the Council of Europe (1981).[1] The second was the gradual expansion of the original right to privacy—which has emerged as the core of the European human rights regime that has evolved since the mid-1970s—to include data protection rights.[2]

The privacy regulations adopted by the OECD and the Council of Europe at the beginning of the 1980s failed to bring about the degree of harmonization of national data protection legislation that was needed to ensure the unimpeded transborder flow of personal information and promote the consolidation of a single market. The need for further EU action came together with the evolving continental human rights regime in the 1995 EU Data Protection Directive, whose objective was to "protect the fundamental rights and freedoms of natural persons, and in particular their right to privacy with respect to the processing of personal data,"[3] and then in the EU Charter of Fundamental Rights (2000/2009), which was the first such document to supplement the right to respect for private and family life with an independent right to the protection of personal data.[4] The 1995 Data Protection Directive required member states to bring their national data protection laws into alignment with the standards set down in the Directive. In Germany this was achieved through the 2001 amendment to the Federal Privacy Protection Law.[5] The privacy law was then amended three times in 2009 to address, among other things, issues that had been excluded from the 1990 reform, including credit reporting and scoring, workplace privacy, the "list privilege" regulating the use of personal data for advertising, and the use of personal information for market and public opinion research.[6]

These 2009 reforms marked the last hurrah of the national privacy protection tradition. In 2016, the EU adopted the General Data Protection Regulation. In contrast to the 1995 Directive, the 2016 Regulation was directly binding on the EU member states, and in 2017 the Bundestag made space for the EU Regulation by sweeping away the dense body of substantive law, whose history we have recounted here, and replacing it with a leaner privacy law that regulated organizational matters, the so-called "opening clauses" dealing with substantive issues—especially employment and labor law—that are to be regulated by national law, and those areas of data processing (primarily public security), which are explicitly exempted from EU law.[7] This was followed in 2019 by a second omnibus law, which amended the information access and privacy provisions of 154 separate laws to bring them into compliance with the EU Regulation.[8] However, Germany's national privacy protection law could be so easily replaced only because the new EU Regulation had itself taken account of the privacy laws of its member states, whose substantive provisions, if not necessarily their constitutional foundations, had increasingly come to resemble one another.

As we saw in chapter 5, by the 1980s privacy advocates were already growing concerned about the impact of microcomputers and the new media. Although these concerns became even more pressing with the growth of the internet and the spread of social media, since the early 2000s these concerns have been raised to a qualitatively new level by that cluster of computational, technological, infrastructural, and epistemological innovations known as Big Data, which is challenging in new ways the regulatory paradigm established in the age of the mainframe.

One of the central claims made by the proponents of Big Data is that the use of machine learning techniques to analyze large data sets can reveal patterns, correlations, and linkages that are invisible to other analytic methods and that cannot necessarily be expressed in the language of cause and effect. While consent means in principle consent for disclosure and use in clearly defined contexts, the unpredictable nature of these linkages makes it impossible to determine—at the moment of collection—how the information will ultimately be used or to assess the harms (or benefits) that may flow from the disclosure of any single piece of personal information, especially when these harms and benefits flow in a probabilistic manner from decisions made on the basis of aggregate data. In addition, the analysis of metadata and the combination of previously discrete data sets is allowing Big Data to radically expand the range of data that can be personally identifying. Big Data is also challenging consent by creating new ways to re-identify anonymized data. Moreover, even if individuals are not identifiable by name, they may still be addressable, and thus subject to consequential inferences, if they display a unique pattern or if their membership in a group can be inferred from anonymized information. In addition to all of these issues, not only is the use of advanced statistical methods to construct profiles for automated, predictive decision-making opaque to the point that it is impossible to speak of consent; such profiling often replicates any biases contained in the data used to train algorithms and may thus have disparate or discriminatory impact.[9]

However, European regulators have not stood by idly. The General Data Protection Regulation did more than just harmonize existing national laws. It also added new substantive provisions to respond to the specific challenges posed by Big Data, and going forward the task is to analyze the functioning of these new analytic methods and their enabling infrastructures, much as the earlier chapters of this book sought to thickly describe manual data and integrated electronic data processing systems, so as to better understand the ways in which Big Data, predictive analytics, and artificial intelligence are threatening dignity, self-determination, and the other values that are protected by the human right to privacy.

Since the turn of the century, privacy has become, in the words of *The Economist*, Europe's unofficial religion and the General Data Protection Regulation its unofficial holy text.[10] However, although this phrase appeared in a column that asked whether it would be possible to keep the privacy faith in the face of the public health challenges posed by the COVID-19 pandemic, only a few months later the European Court of Justice reaffirmed the importance of privacy in overturning the Privacy Shield agreement that permitted the transfer of personal data from the EU to the United States. In this case, the Court ruled that the transfer of personal information from the EU to the United States violated the rights to respect for family and private life and to the protection of personal data codified in the EU Charter of Fundamental Rights, because the failure to limit mass surveillance by the American intelligence agencies to the absolute minimum necessary, combined with the lack of effective legal recourse, meant that the rights of EU citizens could not be guaranteed a level of protection equivalent to that guaranteed by the General Data Protection Regulation.[11]

The problems raised by precautionary surveillance have been most acute in the security sector, where controversy has continued unabated. The codification of the new surveillance practices in the 1980s and 1990s created a situation in which a growing proportion of the informational activity of the police could not be understood as a response to concrete dangers, and in this domain debate has crystallized around the question of whether the diminished role of concrete dangers in defining, structuring, and delimiting the informational activity of the police has brought about the "end" or "dissolution" of classical liberal police law?[12]

Although the professional public is virtually unanimous in its belief that concrete dangers no longer represent the exclusive organizing principle for German police law, opinion is divided as to whether this is to be lamented, welcomed, or simply recognized.[13] But the real question is whether the cumulative effect of recent developments has simply been to erode or disorganize classical liberal police law or whether they have laid the basis for a new paradigm of police law to supplant the one that had taken shape across the preceding century. The most prominent proponent of the latter position is Rainer Pitschas, who has argued that police law should be reconceptualized as a form of "risk administration law" in which concrete danger is supplanted by the concepts of risk and precaution adapted from environmental and technical security law, that the established understanding of privacy in terms of strategic nonknowledge, which was developed in the liberal era to help tame Leviathan, should be abandoned, and that it is therefore necessary to develop a new "security culture" for the precautionary state.[14]

However, in a series of decisions over the past fifteen years, the Constitutional Court has pointed in a different direction. As we saw in chapter 9, the central problem in regulating precautionary surveillance was that of devising concrete norms that would ensure the proportionality of these measures by compensating for the less restrictive conditions under which they could be employed, the broader sphere of persons against whom they could be directed, and their greater prognostic uncertainty in comparison with classical liberal police law. In all of these cases, the Court has affirmed in principle the constitutionality of the precautionary surveillance practices under review, while at the same time ruling that the concrete provisions governing their use did not pass constitutional muster. For example, in its preventive telecommunications surveillance decision (2005), which reviewed the constitutionality of the Lower Saxony police law, the Court ruled that one of the pillars of the Preliminary Draft—taking precautions for the future prosecution of future crimes—fell within the competence of the justice system, not that of the police, and that the law was constitutionally unacceptable because the failure to define the extent to which potential threats must have assumed concrete form before they could become the object of police surveillance made it impossible to delimit the scope of such activity, for the courts to determine its legality, and for the citizens to foresee when they might become the objects of such surveillance.[15] The preventive computer matching decision (2006) reviewed the constitutionality of the North Rhineland-Westphalia law as it was used to search for possible Islamic "sleepers" after the 11 September 2001 attacks. The Court ruled that this measure, which was employed to surveil large populations and was not limited to persons for whom there were factual indications that they could be held individually responsible for the danger against which the practice was supposed to protect, would only be constitutional if it were used to protect against concrete dangers to important legal interests. A general state of danger, the Court maintained, did not justify its use for preventive purposes.[16]

Both the online search (2008) and the bulk collection of telephone and internet metadata (2010) decisions echoed this reasoning in ruling that the practices addressed in the two decisions would be constitutional only if they were employed to protect legal interests of overriding importance, such as a concrete danger to the life, limb, or freedom of a person, or to the security of the state, and if there were concrete indications that the person whose information was to be collected (online search) or whose information was to be made available to the police or prosecutors (telecommunications metadata) posed such a danger or had committed a correspondingly serious crime.[17] The last major appellate decision in this area involved the review of the 2009 amendment to the Federal Criminal Police Law, which had charged the agency with protecting against the dangers of international terrorism and authorized the use of a number of covert surveillance practices to achieve this goal. The 2016 ruling by the Constitutional Court affirmed the substance of the law, but concluded that numerous provisions of the law were unacceptable either because the conditions under which they could be employed were too broad or because the necessary procedural protections were missing.[18] In short, in all of these cases the Constitutional Court attempted to chart a path by which precautionary surveillance in advance of imminent dangers could be subjected to concrete norms and made consistent with the rule of law while barring their use to surveil individuals in the absence of at least a minimal degree of evidence that the specific persons posed a concrete danger.

The debate over precautionary surveillance shows no signs of subsiding. Against the background of the December 2016 attack on the Christmas market at Breitscheidplatz in Berlin, the Conference of Interior Ministers resolved in June 2017 to push for a new model police law to harmonize state legislation. Behind the rhetorical demand for uniform laws to guarantee a uniformly high level of security across the country, the proposed model law is yet again serving as a stalking horse for the expansion of precautionary surveillance. The interior ministers are considering a long list of possible measures, including giving the police the authority to use force in abstract threat situations (a measure that the courts have rejected in the past), introducing both indefinite preventive detention and expanded DNA testing for preventive purposes, expanding the scope of identity checks without probable cause, and codifying a number of new electronic surveillance practices, such as predictive policing, online searches, the interception of online communications before encryption, the monitoring of social media, the expanded use of both video surveillance and facial recognition technology, and the collection of both telecommunications metadata and mobile phone location data.

François Ewald's suggestion notwithstanding, we have not (yet) entered wholly and irrevocably into the "age of precaution."[19] In the polarized atmosphere of the late 1970s and 1980s, there was a tendency to regard every move beyond concrete dangers into the *Vorfeld* as an indicator of the country's drift toward an authoritarian surveillance state. However, in recent years such categorical opposition has given way to a more complex balancing of the proximity of the danger to be prevented, the potential harm ascribed to such future events, the intrusiveness of specific surveillance methods, and their perceived effectiveness in preventing dangers whose occurrence can only be explained in possibilistic terms. This represents a pragmatic middle strategy for governing the future—one that tacks between limiting police activity to combatting only those threats that grow organically and predictably out of the past and a Hobbesian information state, which regards security as a "super constitutional right" that trumps the individual freedoms that the liberal state is charged with protecting, authorizes the use of exceptional powers to seek out the unknown and the unknowable, and constantly runs the danger of degenerating into inefficient, disproportional, and arbitrary surveillance "into the blue."[20] However, the dangers of the informational leviathan are no less serious than those resulting from limiting the amount of information available to policy makers and the police. We are, therefore, on firmer ground if we continue to understand privacy protection law as the most important theoretical tool for ensuring that precautionary surveillance, which is often invoked for unsavory political purposes, but which may also be necessary for combatting the dangers of the modern world, is carried out in a manner that safeguards the rights of the citizenry against the power of an overweening state.

Notes

1. Gloria Gonzales Fuster, *The Emergence of Personal Data Protection as a Fundamental Right of the EU* (Springer, 2014).
2. Frédéric Sudre, *Droit européen et international des droits de l'homme* (PUF, 2019), 700-51; Marie-Thérèse Meulders-Klein, "L'irrésistible ascension de la 'vie privée' au sein des droits de l'homme," in *Le droit au respect de la vie privée au sens de la Convention européenne des droits de l'homme*, ed. Sudre (Nemesis Bruylant, 2005), 305-33; and, on the extension of privacy rights from the family to personal data, Gonzales Fuster, *The Emergence of Personal Data Protection*, 96-101.
3. Orla Lynskey, *The Foundations of EU Data Protection Law* (Oxford University Press, 2015), 46ff.; and Lynskey, "Deconstructing Data Protection: The 'Added-Value' of a Right to

Conclusion 365

Data Protection in the EU Legal Order," *International & Comparative Law Quarterly* 63, no. 3 (2014): 569-97.
4. Lynskey, *The Foundations of EU Data Protection Law*, 89-130; and Gonzales Fuster, *The Emergence of Personal Data Protection*, 163ff.
5. *BGBl.*, 2001, 904.
6. Ibid., 2009, 2254, 2814, and 2355.
7. Ibid., 2017, 2097-132; and Alexander Roßnagel, *Das neue Datenschutzrecht. Europäische Datenschutz-Grundverordnung und deutsche Datenschutzgesetze* (Nomos, 2018).
8. Zweites Gesetz zur Anpassung des Datenschutzrechts an die Verordnung (EU) 2016/679 und zur Umsetzung der Richtlinie (EU) 2016/680, *BGBl.*, 2019, 1626-718.
9. Shoshana Zuboff, *The Age of Surveillance Capitalism* (PublicAffairs, 2019); Julia Lane et al., eds., *Privacy, Big Data and the Public Good* (Cambridge University Press, 2014); Mireille Hildebrandt and Katja de Vries, eds., *Privacy, Due Process and the Computational Turn* (Routledge, 2013); Mireille Hildebrandt and Serge Gutwirth, eds., *Profiling the European Citizen* (Springer, 2008); Alessandro Mantelero, "Regulating Big Data: The Guidelines of the Council of Europe in the Context of the European Data Protection Framework," *Computer Law & Security Review* 33 (2017): 584–602; Kate Crawford and Jason Schultz, "Big Data and Due Process: Toward a Framework to Redress Predictive Privacy Harms," *Boston College Law Review* 55 (2014): 93–128; Solon Barocas and Andrew D. Selbst, "Big Data's Disparate Impact," *California Law Review* 104 (2016): 671–732; Mireille Hildebrandt, "Privacy as Protection of the Incomputable Self: From Agnostic to Agonistic Machine Learning," *Theoretical Inquires in Law* 20 (2019): 83–121; Tal Z. Zarsky, "Privacy and Manipulation in the Digital Age," *Theoretical Inquires in Law* 20 (2019): 157–88; Brett Aho and Roberta Duffield, "Beyond surveillance capitalism: Privacy, regulation and big data in Europe and China," *Economy & Society* 49, no. 2: 187–212 (https://doi.org/10.1080/03085147.2019.1690275); and the special theme of *Big Data & Society* 7, no. 1 (2020) on "Big Data and Surveillance: Hype, Commercial Logics and New Intimate Spheres."
10. "Privacy in a pandemic," *The Economist*, 23 April (https://www.economist.com/europe/2020/04/23/privacy-in-a-pandemic).
11. European Court of Justice, C-311/18 (http://curia.europa.eu/juris/liste.jsf?num=C-311/18).
12. Markus Möstl, "Die neue dogmatische Gestalt des Polizeirechts," *DVBl* 122, no. 10 (2007): 581-89; and Manfred Baldus, "Entgrenzungen des Sicherheitsrechts—Neue Polizeirechtsdogmatik?" *Die Verwaltung* 47, no. 1 (2014): 1-23.
13. In addition to Möstl and Baldus, see Reinhard Riegel, "Zu Stand und Entwicklungstendenzen des informationellen Befugnisrechts zur polizeilichen Aufgabenerfüllung: Licht, Schatten und Hoffnung," *DÖV* 43, no. 19 (1994): 814-21; Michael Kniesel, "'Innere Sicherheit' und Grundgesetz," *ZRP* 29, no. 12 (1996): 482-89, especially 482; Josef Aulehner, *Polizeiliche Gefahren- und Informationsvorsorge* (Duncker & Humblot, 1998); Hans-Heinrich Trute, "Die Erosion des klassischen Polizeirechts durch die polizeiliche Informationsvorsorge," in *Rechtsthorie und Rechtsdogmatik im Austausch*, ed. Wilfried Erbguth et al. (Duncker & Humblot, 1999), 402-28; Marion Albers, *Die Determination polizeilicher Tätigkeit in den Bereichen der Straftatenverhütung und der Verfolgungsvorsorge* (Duncker & Humblot, 2001), 209-15, 351, 368; Helmuth Schulze-Fielitz, "Nach dem 11. September: An den Leistungsgrenzen eines verfassungsstaatlichen Polizeirechts?," in *Recht im Pluralismus. Festschrift für Walter Schmitt Glaeser*, ed. Hans-Detlef Horn (Duncker & Humblot, 2003), 407-34; Friedrich Schoch, "Abschied vom Polizeirecht des liberalen Rechtsstaates. Vom Kreuzberg-Urteil des preussischen Oberverwaltungsgerichts zu den Terrorismusbekämpfungsgesetzen unserer Tage," *Der Staat* 43 (2004): 347-69; Stefan Middel, *Innere Sicherheit und preventive Terrorismusbekämpfung* (Nomos, 2007); Markus Thiel, *Die "Entgrenzung" der Gefahrenabwehr. Grundfragen von Freiheit und Sicherheit im Zeitalter der Globalisierung* (Mohr Siebeck, 2011); Byungwoog Park, *Wandel des klassi-*

schen Polizeirechts zum neuen Sicherheitsrecht (Berliner Wissenschafts-Verlag, 2013); and Bodo Pieroth et al., Polizei- und Ordnungsrecht, 8th ed. (Beck, 2014), 11-12, 19-21.
14. Rainer Pitschas, "Polizeirecht im kooperativen Staat. Der Schutz innerer Sicherheit zwischen Gefahrenabwehr und kriminalpräventiver Risikovorsorge," DÖV 55, no. 6 (2002): 221-31; Pitschas, "Kriminalistik durch Informationsvorsorge. Abschied vom klassischen Polizeirecht und Krise des traditionellen Datenschutzkonzepts," Kriminalistik 45, no. 12 (1991): 774-78; Pitschas, "Staatliches Management für Risikoinformation zwischen Recht auf informationelle Selbstbestimmung und gesetzlichem Kommunikationsvorbehalt," in Privatrecht im "Risikostaat," ed. Dieter Hart (Nomos, 1997), 215-63; and Pitschas, "Fortentwicklung des Polizeirechts und Legitimität des Staates," in Polizeirecht heute, ed. Ulrich Dautert (Schriftenreihe der Polizei-Führungsakademie no. 4, 1991), 7-31.
15. BVerfGE 113, 348 (367ff., 375-82).
16. BVerfGE115, 320 (320, 362-63).
17. BVerfGE 120, 274; 125, 260. Online searches (Online-Durchsuchungen) included the use of trojans, exploits, and other means to covertly access personal computers and information systems. The decision also enunciated a constitutional right to the "confidentiality and integrity of information technology systems" to compensate for the unavoidable risk that such practices would collect information pertaining to the absolutely protected core of the individual personality.
18. BVerfGE 141, 220.
19. Ewald, "The Return of Descartes's Malicious Demon: An Outline of a Philosophy of Precaution," in Embracing Risk: The Changing Culture of Insurance and Responsibility, ed. Tom Baker and Jonathan Simon (University of Chicago Press, 2002), 273-301, citation 299.
20. Manuel Bewarder and Thorsten Jungholt, "Friedrich erklärt Sicherheit zum 'Supergrundrecht,'" Die Welt, 16 July 2013.

Selected Bibliography

Agar, Jon. *The Government Machine: A Revolutionary History of the Computer*. MIT Press, 2003.
Aly, Götz, and Karl Heinz Roth. *The Nazi Census: Identification and Control in the Third Reich*. Temple University Press, 2004.
Albers, Marion. *Die Determination polizeilicher Tätigkeit in den Bereichen der Straftatenverhütung und der Verfolgungsvorsorge*. Duncker & Humblot, 2001.
———. *Informationelle Selbstbestimmung*. Nomos, 2005.
Aust, Stefan. *Der Baader Meinhof Komplex*, 2nd expanded edition. Hoffmann und Campe, 2007.
Barbas, Samantha. *Laws of Image: Privacy and Publicity in America*. Stanford University Press, 2015.
Bastian, Daniell. *Westdeutsches Polizeirecht unter alliierter Besatzung (1945–1955)*. Mohr Siebeck, 2010.
Baldus, Manfred. "Entgrenzungen des Sicherheitsrechts—Neue Polizeirechtsdogmatik?" *Die Verwaltung* 47, no. 1 (2014): 1–23.
Bauer, Susanne. "From Administrative Infrastructure to Biomedical Resource: Danish Population Registries, the 'Scandinavian Laboratory,' and the 'Epidemiologist's Dream.'" *Science in Context* 27, no. 2 (2014): 187–213.
Baumann, Imanuel. *Dem Verbrechen auf der Spur. Eine Geschichte der Kriminologie und Kriminalpolitik in Deutschland 1880 bis 1980*. Wallstein, 2006.
Baumann, Imanuel, Herbert Reinke, and Andrej Stephan, eds. *Schatten der Vergangenheit. Das Bundeskriminalamt und seine Gründungsgeneration in der frühen Bundesrepublik*. Luchterhand, 2011.
Beniger, James. *The Control Revolution: Technological and Economic Origins of the Information Society*. Harvard University Press, 1986.
Bennett, Colin. "In Defence of Privacy: The Concept and the Regime." *Surveillance & Society* 8, no. 4 (2011): 485–96 and the forum in this volume (497–516) on Bennett's essay.
———. *Regulating Privacy: Data Protection and Public Policy in Europe and the United States*. Cornell University Press, 1992.
Bennett, Colin, and David Lyon, eds. *Playing the Identity Card. Surveillance, Security and Identification in Global Perspective*. London, 2008.

Bergien, Rüdiger. "'Big Data' als Vision. Computereinführung und Organisationswandel in BKA und Staatssicherheit (1967–1989)." *Zeithistorische Forschungen* 14 (2017): 258–85.

———. "Programmieren mit dem Klassenfeind. Die Stasi, Siemens und der Transfer von EDV-Wissen im Kalten Krieg." *VfZ* 67, no. 1 (2019): 1–30.

———. "Südfrüchte im Stahlnetz. Der polizeiliche Zugriff auf nicht-polizeiliche Datenspeicher in der Bundesrepublik, 1967–1989." In *Wege in die digitale Gesellschaft. Computernutzung in der Bundesrepublik, 1955–1990*, edited by Frank Bösch, 39–63. Wallstein, 2018.

Betts, Paul. *Within Walls: Private Life in the German Democratic Republic*. Oxford University Press, 2010.

Boersma, Kees, Rosamunde van Brakel, Chiara Fonio, and Pieter Wagenaar, eds. *Histories of State Surveillance in Europe and Beyond*. Routledge, 2014.

Bösch, Frank. *Öffentliche Geheimnisse. Skandale, Politik und Medien in Deutschland und Großbritannien 1880–1914*. Oldenbourg, 2009.

Bösch, Frank, ed. *Wege in die digitale Gesellschaft. Computernutzung in der Bundesrepublik, 1955–1990*. Wallstein, 2018.

Boyne, Rob. "Post-Panopticism." *Economy and Society* 29, no. 2 (May 2000): 285–307.

Breckenridge, Keith. *Biometric State: The Global Politics of Identification and. Surveillance in South Africa, 1850 to the Present*. Cambridge University Press, 2014.

Breckenridge, Keith, and Simon Szreter, eds. *Registration and Recognition: Documenting the Person in World History*. Oxford, 2012.

Bull, Hans Peter. *Datenschutz, Informationsrecht und Rechtspolitik*. Duncker & Humblot, 2005.

———. *Informationelle Selbstbestimmung—Vision oder Illusion?* Mohr Siebeck, 2009.

———. "Neue Konzepte, neue Instrumente? Zur Datenschutz-Diskussion des Bremer Juristentages." *ZRP* 31, no. 8 (1998): 310–14.

———. *Sinn und Unsinn des Datenschutzes*. Mohr Siebeck, 2015.

Busch, Heiner, Albrecht Funk, Udo Kauß, Wolf-Dieter Narr, and Falco Werkentin. *Die Polizei in der Bundesrepublik*. Campus Verlag, 1985.

Canoy, Jose Raymund. *The Discreet Charm of the Police State: The Landpolizei and the Transformation of Bavaria, 1945–1965*. Brill, 2004.

Caplan, Jane, and John Torpey, eds. *Documenting Individual Identity: The Development of State Practices in the Modern World*. Princeton, 2001.

Cappello, Lawrence. *None of Your Damn Business. Privacy in the United States form the Gilded Age to the Digital Age*. University of Chicago Press, 2019.

Chandler, Alfred. *The Visible Hand: The Managerial Revolution in American Business*. Harvard University Press, 1977.

Clarke, Roger. "Information Technology and Dataveillance." *Communications of the ACM* 31, no. 5 (May 1988): 498–512.

Cohen, Deborah. *Family Secrets: Shame & Privacy in Modern Britain*. Oxford University Press, 2013.

Cohen, Julie. *Configuring the Networked Self: Law, Code, and the Play of Everyday Practice*. Yale University Press, 2012.

———. "What Privacy Is For." *Harvard Law Review* 126, no. 7 (May 2013): 1904–33.

Conze, Eckart. "Securitization—Gegenwartsdiagnose oder historischer Analyseansatz?" *GuG* 38 (2012): 453–67.

———. "Sicherheit als Kultur. Überlegungen zu einer 'modernen Politikgeschichte' der Bundesrepublik Deutschland." *VfZ* 53, no. 3 (2005): 357–80.

Daase, Christopher. "Die Historisierung der Sicherheit. Anmerkungen zur historischen Sicherheitsforschung aus politikwissenschaftlicher Sicht." *GuG* 38, no. 3 (September 2012): 387–405.

———. "National, Societal and Human Security: On the Transformation of Political Language." *Historical Social Research* 35 (2010): 24–39.

Dandeker, Christopher. *Surveillance, Power and Modernity: Bureaucracy and Discipline from 1700 to the Present Day.* Polity Press, 1990.

Deleuze, Gilles. "Postscript on the Societies of Control." *October* 59 (Winter 1992): 3–7.

Della Porta, Donatella. "Politische Gewalt und Terrorismus. Eine vergleichende und soziologische Perspektive." In *Terrorismus in der Bundesrepublik. Medien, Staat und Subkulturen in den 1970er Jahren*, edited by Klaus Weinhauer, Jörg Requate, and Heinz-Gerhard Haupt, 33–58. Campus Verlag, 2006.

Denninger, Erhard. "Prävention und Freiheit." In *Vom Rechtsstaat zum Präventionsstaat*, edited by Stefan Huster and Karsten Rudolph, 85–106. Suhrkamp, 2008.

Diebel, Martin. *"Die Stunde der Exekutive." Das Bundesinnenministerium und die Notstandsgesetze 1949–1968.* Wallstein, 2019.

———. "Planen für den Ausnahmezustand. Zivilverteidigung und Notstandsrecht." In *Hüter der Ordnung. Die Innenministerien in Bonn und Ost-Berlin nach dem Nationalsozialismus*, edited by Frank Bösch and Andreas Wirsching, 498–535. Wallstein, 2018.

Diewald-Kerkmann, Gisela. *Politische Denunziation im NS-Regime oder die kleine Macht der "Volksgenossen."* J. H. W. Dietz Nachfolger, 1995.

Eberle, Edward J. *Dignity and Liberty: Constitutional Visions in Germany and the United States.* Praeger, 2002.

Edwards, Paul. *The Closed World: Computers and the Politics of Discourse in Cold War America.* MIT Press, 1996.

Elmer, Greg. "A Diagram of Panoptic Surveillance." *New Media & Society* 5, no. 2 (2003): 231–47.

Ericson, Richard, and Kevin Haggerty. *Policing the Risk Society.* University of Toronto Press, 1997.

Ewald, François. "The Return of Descartes's Malicious Demon: An Outline of a Philosophy of Precaution." In *Embracing Risk: The Changing Culture of Insurance and Responsibility*, edited by Tom Baker and Jonathan Simon, 273–301. University of Chicago Press, 2002.

Fairchild, Amy, Ronald Bayer, and James Colgrove. *Searching Eyes: Privacy, the State, and Disease Surveillance in America.* University of California Press, 2007.

Fairfield, Joshua, and Christoph Engel. "Privacy as a Public Good." In *Privacy and Power: A Transatlantic Dialogue in the Shadow of the NSA-Affair*, edited by Russell A. Miller, 95–128. Cambridge University Press, 2017.

Figes, Orlando. *The Whisperers: Private Life in Stalin's Russia.* Penguin, 2008.

Fleischhack, Julia. *Eine Welt im Datenrausch. Computeranlagen und Datenmengen als gesellschaftliche Herausforderung in der Bundesrepublik Deutschland (1965–1975)*. Chronos, 2016.
Foucault, Michel. *The Birth of Biopolitics*. Palgrave, 2008.
———. *Discipline and Punish: The Birth of the Prison*. Vintage Books, 1979.
———. *Security, Territory, Population*. Palgrave, 2007.
Foschepoth, Josef. *Überwachtes Deutschland. Post- und Telefonüberwachung in der alten Bundesrepublik*. Vandenhoeck & Ruprecht, 2012.
Frohman, Larry. "Medical Surveillance and Medical Confidentiality in an Age of Transition: The Debate over Cancer Registration in West Germany." *Social History of Medicine* (forthcoming). https://doi.org/10.1093/shm/hkz067.
———. "Network Euphoria, Super-Information Systems, and the West German Plan for a National Database System." *German History* 38, no. 2 (2020): 311–37.
———. *Poor Relief and Welfare in Germany from the Reformation to World War I*. Cambridge University Press, 2008.
———. "Population Registration in Germany, 1842–1945: Information, Administrative Power, and State-Making in the Age of Paper." *Central European History* 53, no. 3 (2020): 503–32.
———. "Population Registration, Social Planning, and the Discourse on Privacy Protection in West Germany." *Journal of Modern History* 87, no. 2 (June 2015): 316–56.
———. "Redefining Medical Confidentiality in the Digital Era: Healthcare Reform and the West German Debate over the Use of Personal Medical Information in the 1980s." *Journal of the History of Medicine and Allied Sciences* 72, no. 4 (October 2017): 468–99.
Gandy, Oscar. *The Panoptic Sort: A Political Economy of Personal Information* (Westview Press, 1993.
Geyer, Martin. "Security and Risk: How We Have Learned to Live with Dystopian, Utopian, and Technocratic Diagnoses of Security since the 1970s." *Historia 396* 5, no. 1 (2015): 93–134.
Giddens, Anthony. *The Nation-State and Violence*. University of California Press, 1987.
Gilliom, John. "A Response to Bennett's 'In Defence of Privacy.'" *Surveillance & Society* 8, no. 4 (2011): 500–4.
Görtemaker, Manfred. *Geschichte der Bundesrepublik Deutschland*. C. H. Beck, 1999).
Grimm, Dieter. *Die Zukunft der Verfassung*. Suhrkamp, 1991.
Günther, Frieder. *Denken vom Staat her. Die bundesdeutsche Staatsrechtslehre zwischen Dezision und Integration 1949–1970*. Oldenbourg, 2004.
———. "Rechtsstaat, Justizstaat oder Verwaltungsstaat? Die Verfassungs- und Verwaltungspolitik." In *Hüter der Ordnung. Die Innenministerien in Bonn und Ost-Berlin nach dem Nationalsozialismus*, edited by Frank Bösch and Andreas Wirsching, 381–412. Wallstein, 2018.
Gugerli, David. *Wie die Welt in den Computer kam. Zur Entstehung digitaler Wirklichkeit*. S. Fischer, 2018,
Haggerty, Kevin. "Tear Down the Walls: On Demolishing the Panopticon." In *Theorizing Surveillance: The Panopticon and Beyond*, edited by David Lyon, 23–45. Willan Publishing, 2006.

Haggerty, Kevin, and Richard Ericson. "The Surveillant Assemblage." *British Journal of Sociology* 51, no. 4 (December 2000): 605–22.

Hannah, Matthew. *Dark Territory in the Information Age: Learning from the West German Census Controversies of the 1980s*. Ashgate, 2010.

Hanshew, Karrin. "Beyond Friend or Foe? Terrorism, Counterterrorism and a (Transnational) Gesellschaftsgeschichte of the 1970s." *GuG* 42 (2016): 377–403.

———. *Terror and Democracy in West Germany*. Cambridge University Press, 2012.

Harvey, Elizabeth, Johannes Hürter, Maiken Umbach, and Andreas Wirsching, eds. *Privacy and Private Life in Nazi Germany*. Cambridge University Press, 2019.

Hempel, Leon, Susanne Krasmann, and Ulrich Bröckling. "Sichtbarkeitsregime: Eine Einleitung." In "Sichtbarkeitsregime—Überwachung, Sicherheit und Privatheit im 21. Jahrhundert," special issue, *Leviathan* 25: (2010): 7–24.

Hert, Paul de, and Serge Gutwirth. "Privacy, Data Protection and Law Enforcement: Opacity of the Individual and Transparency of Power." In *Privacy and the Criminal Law*, edited by Erik Claes, Serge Gutwirth, and Anthony Duff, 61–104. Intersentia, 2006.

Higgs, Edward. *The Information State in England*. Palgrave, 2004.

Hof, Tobias. *Staat und Terrorismus in Italien 1969–1982*. Oldenbourg, 2011.

Hürter, Johannes. "Anti-Terrorismus-Politik. Ein deutsch-italienischer Vergleich, 1969–1982." *VfZ* 57, no. 3 (2009): 329–48.

Hürter, Johannes, ed. *Terrorismusbekämpfung in Westeuropa. Demokratie und Sicherheit in den 1970er und 1980er Jahren*. De Gruyter, 2015.

Hughes, Kirsty. "The Social Value of Privacy, the Right of Privacy to Society and Human Rights Discourse." In *Social Dimensions of Privacy*, edited by Beate Roessler and Dorota Mokrosinska, 225–43. Cambridge University Press, 2015.

Igo, Sarah. *The Known Citizen: A History of Privacy in Modern America*. Harvard University Press, 2018.

Jaeger, Alexandra. *Auf der Suche nach "Verfassungsfeinden." Der Radikalenbeschluss in Hamburg 1971–1987*. Wallstein, 2019.

Kaack, Heino. "Die Liberalen." In *Die zweite Republik. 25 Jahre Bundesrepublik Deutschland—eine Bilanz*, edited by Richard Löwenthal and Hans-Peter Schwarz, 408–32. Seewald Verlag, 1974.

Kammerer, Dietmar. *Bilder der Überwachung*. Suhrkamp, 2008.

Kasper, Thomas. "'Licht im Rentendunkel': Die Computerisierung des Sozialstaats in Bundesrepublik und DDR." Dissertation, Leibniz-Zentrum, University of Potsdam, 2018.

Koenen, Gerd. *Das rote Jahrzehnt. Unsere kleine deutsche Kulturrevolution, 1967–1977*. Kiepenheuer & Witsch, 2001.

Krasmann, Susanne. "Der Präventionsstaat im Einvernehmen. Wie Sichtbarkeitsregime stillschweigend Akzeptanz produzieren." In "Sichtbarkeitsregime—Überwachung, Sicherheit und Privatheit im 21. Jahrhundert," special issue, *Leviathan* 25 (2010): 53–70.

Kraushaar, Wolfgang, ed. *Die RAF und der linke Terrorismus*, 2 Bde. HIS Verlag, 2006

Ladeur, Karl-Heinz. "Das Recht auf informationelle Selbstbestimmung: Eine juristische Fehlkonstruktion." *DÖV* 62, no. 2 (January 2009): 45–55.

Lammert, Markus. *Der neue Terrorismus. Terrorismusbekämpfung in Frankreich in den 1980er Jahren*. De Gruyter, 2017.
Lauer, Josh. *Creditworthy: A History of Consumer Surveillance and Financial Identity in America*. Columbia University Press, 2017.
Leendertz, Ariane. "Das Komplexitätssyndrom. Gesellschaftliche 'Komplexität' als intellektuelle und politische Herausforderung." In *Die neue Wirklichkeit. Semantische Neuvermessungen und Politik set den 1970er Jahren*, edited by Leendertz and Wencke Meteling, 93–131. Campus Verlag, 2016.
Loveman, Mara. "The Modern State and the Primitive Accumulation of Symbolic Power." *American Journal of Sociology* 110, no. 6 (May 2005): 1651–83.
Lyon, David. *The Electronic Eye: The Rise of Surveillance Society*. Polity, 1994.
———. *Identifying Citizens: ID Cards as Surveillance*. Cambridge, 2009.
———. "Situating Surveillance: History, Technology, Culture." In *Histories of State Surveillance in Europe and Beyond*, edited by Kees Boersma, Rosamunde van Brakel, Chiara Gonio, and Pieter Wagenaar, 32–46. Routledge, 2014.
———. *Surveillance Society: Monitoring Everyday Life*. Open University Press, 2001.
Lyon, David, ed. *Surveillance as Social Sorting: Privacy, Risk and Automated Discrimination*. Routledge, 2002.
Marx, Gary. "What's New about the 'New Surveillance'? Classifying for Change and Continuity." *Surveillance & Society* 1, no. 1 (2002): 9–29.
———. *Windows into the Soul: Surveillance and Society in an Age of High Technology*. University of Chicago Press, 2016.
März, Michael. *Linker Protest nach dem Deutschen Herbst*. Transkript Verlag, 2012.
Mangold, Hannes. *Fahndung nach dem Raster. Informationsverarbeitung bei der bundesdeutschen Kriminalpolizei, 1965–1984*. Chronos, 2017.
Manton, Kevin. *Population Registers and Privacy in Britain, 1936–1984*. Palgrave, 2019.
Markovits, Andrei, and Philip Gorski. *The German Left: Red, Green and Beyond*. Oxford University Press, 1993.
Mayer-Schönberger, Viktor. "Generational Development of Data Protection in Europe." In *Technology and Privacy: The New Landscape*, edited by Philip Agre and Marc Rotenberg, 219–41. MIT Press, 1997.
Mende, Silke. *"Nicht rechts, nicht links, sondern vorn." Eine Geschichte der Gründungsgrünen*. Oldenbourg, 2011.
Mergel, Thomas. "Zeit des Streits. Die siebziger Jahre in der Bundesrepublik als eine Periode des Konflikts." In *Geschichte denken. Perspektiven auf die Geschichtsschreibung heute*, edited by Michael Wildt, 224–43. Vandenhoek & Ruprecht, 2014.
Metzler, Gabriele. *Konzeptionen politischen Handelns von Adenauer bis Brandt. Politische Planung in der pluralistischen Gesellschaft*. Schöningh, 2005.
Middel, Stefan. *Innere Sicherheit und preventive Terrorismusbekämpfung*. Nomos, 2007.
Moeller, Robert G. *Protecting Motherhood: Women and the Family in the Politics of Postwar West Germany*. University of California Press, 1996.
Möstl, Markus. "Die neue dogmatische Gestalt des Polizeirechts." *DVBl* 122, no. 10 (2007): 581–89.

Moses, Dirk. *German Intellectuals and the Nazi Past*. Cambridge University Press, 2007.
Moyn, Samuel. "Personalism, Community, and the Origins of Human Rights." In *Human Rights in the Twentieth Century*, edited by Stefan-Ludwig Hoffmann, 85–106. Cambridge University Press, 2011.
Naas, Stefan. *Die Entstehung des Preußischen Polizeiverwaltungsgesetzes von 1931*. Mohr Siebeck, 2003.
Nissenbaum, Helen. "Contextual Integrity Up and Down the Data Food Chain." *Theoretical Inquiries in Law* 20 (2019): 221–56.
———. *Privacy in Context: Technology, Policy, and the Integrity of Social Life*. Stanford University Press, 2010.
Noethen, Stefan. *Alte Kameraden und neue Kollegen. Polizei in Nordrhein-Westfalen 1945–1953*. Klartext, 2003.
Noiriel, Gérard. "The Identification of the Citizen: The Birth of Republican Civil Status in France." In *Documenting Individual Identity: The Development of State Practices in the Modern World*, edited by Jane Caplan and John Torpey, 28–48. Princeton, 2001.
Nolte, Paul. "Öffentlichkeit und Privatheit: Deutschland im 20. Jahrhundert." *Merkur* 686 (June 2006): 499–512.
Nützenadel, Alexander. *Stunde der Ökonomen. Wissenschaft, Politik und Expertenkultur in der Bundesrepublik, 1949–1974*. Vandenhoeck & Ruprecht, 2005.
Oberloskamp, Eva. *Codename TREVI. Terrorismusbekämpfung und die Anfänge einer europäischen Innenpolitik in den 1970er Jahren*. De Gruyter, 2017.
Opitz, Sven. "Zwischen Sicherheitsdispositiven und Securitization. Zur Analytik illiberaler Gouvernementalität." In *Gouvernementalität und Sicherheit*, edited by Patricia Purtschert, Katrin Meyer, and Yves Winter, 201–28. Transkript Verlag, 2008.
Park, Byungwoog. *Wandel des klassischen Polizeirechts zum neuen Sicherheitsrecht*. Berliner Wissenschafts-Verlag, 2013.
Perry, Joe. "Healthy for Family Life: Television, Masculinity, and Domestic Modernity during West Germany's Miracle Years." *German History* 25, no. 4 (2007): 560–95.
Piazza, Pierre. *Histoire de la carte nationale d'identité*. Odile Jacob, 2004.
Posner, Richard. "The Right of Privacy." *Georgia Law Review* 12, no. 3 (Spring 1978): 393–422.
Post, Robert. "The Social Foundations of Privacy: Community and Self in the Common Law Tort." *California Law Review* 77 (1989): 957–1010.
Poster, Mark. *The Mode of Information: Poststructuralism and Social Context*. University of Chicago Press, 1990.
Pratt, Walter. *Privacy in Britain*. Bucknell University Press, 1979.
Regan, Priscilla. *Legislating Privacy: Technology, Social Values, and Public Policy*. University of North Carolina Press, 1995.
———. "Privacy and the Common Good: Revisited." In *Social Dimensions of Privacy*, edited by Beate Roessler and Dorota Mokrosinska, 50–70. Cambridge University Press, 2015.
Reichardt, Sven. *Authentizität und Gemeinschaft. Linksalternatives Leben in den siebziger und frühen achtziger Jahren*. Suhrkamp, 2014.

Requate, Jörg. *Der Kampf um die Demokratisierung der Justiz*. Campus, 2008.
Richards, Neil. "The Dangers of Surveillance." *Harvard Law Review* 126, no. 7 (2013): 1934–65.
——. "Reviewing *The Digital Person*: Privacy and Technology in the Information Age." *Georgetown Law Journal* 94 (2006): 1087–140.
Rigoll, Dominik. "Kampf um die innere Sicherheit: Schutz des Staates oder der Demokratie?" In *Hüter der Ordnung. Die Innenministerien in Bonn und Ost-Berlin nach dem Nationalsozialismus*, edited by Frank Bösch and Andreas Wirsching, 454–97. Wallstein, 2018.
——. *Staatsschutz in Westdeutschland. Von der Entnazifizierung zur Extremistenabwehr*. Wallstein, 2013.
Robins, Kevin, and Frank Webster. *Times of the Technoculture: From the Information Society to the Virtual Life*. Routledge, 1999.
Rössler, Beate. *The Value of Privacy*. Polity, 2004,
Roßnagel, Alexander. *Das neue Datenschutzrecht. Europäische Datenschutz-Grundverordnung und deutsche Datenschutzgesetze*. Nomos, 2018.
Ruck, Michael. "Ein kurzer Sommer der konkreten Utopie: Zur westdeutschen Planungsgeschichte der langen 60er Jahre." In *Dynamische Zeiten. Die 60er Jahre in den beiden deutschen Gesellschaften*, edited by Axel Schildt, 362–401. Hamburg, 2000.
Rule, James. *Private Lives and Public Surveillance: Social Control in the Computer Age*. Schocken, 1974.
Sachse, Carola. *Der Hausarbeitstag. Gerechtigkeit und Gleichberechtigung in Ost und West, 1939–1994*. Wallstein, 2002.
Scheiper, Stephan. *Innere Sicherheit. Politische Anti-Terror-Konzept in der Bundesrepublik Deutschland während der 1970er Jahre*. Schöningh, 2010.
Schenk, Dieter. *Der Chef. Horst Herold und das BKA*. Spiegel-Buchverlag, 1998.
Schmitt, Martin, Julia Erdogan, Thomas Kasper, and Janine Funke. "Digitalgeschichte Deutschlands. Ein Forschungsbericht." *Technikgeschichte* 83, no. 1 (2016): 33–70.
Schoch, Friedrich. "Abschied vom Polizeirecht des liberalen Rechtsstaates. Vom Kreuzberg-Urteil des preussischen Oberverwaltungsgerichts zu den Terrorismusbekämpfungsgesetzen unserer Tage." *Der Staat* 43 (2004): 347–69.
Schulte, Philipp H. *Terrorismus und Anti-Terrorismus-Gesetzgebung: Eine rechtssoziologische Analyse*. Waxmann, 2008.
Schulz, Frauke. *"Im Zweifel für die Freiheit": Aufstieg und Fall des Seiteneinsteigers Werner Maihofer in der FDP*. Ibidem, 2011.
Schulz, Sarah. *Die freiheitliche demokratische Grundordnung. Ergebnis und Folgen eines historisch-politischen Prozesses*. Velbrück, 2019.
Schulze-Fielitz, Helmuth. "Nach dem 11. September: An den Leistungsgrenzen eines verfassungsstaatlichen Polizierechts?" In *Recht im Pluralismus. Festschrift für Walter Schmitt Glaeser*, edited by Hans-Detlef Horn, 407–34. Duncker & Humblot, 2003.
Schwartz, Paul. "The Computer in German and American Constitutional Law: Towards an American Right of Informational Self-Determination." *American Journal of Comparative Law* 37, no. 4. (Autumn, 1989): 675–701.

Schwartz, Paul, and Karl-Nikolaus Peifer. "Prosser's *Privacy* and the German Right of Personality: Are Four Privacy Torts Better than One Unitary Concept?" *California Law Review* 98 (2010): 1925–87.
Scott, James. *Seeing Like a State*. Yale University Press, 1998.
Scrivano, Paolo. "Signs of Americanization in Italian Domestic Life: Italy's Postwar Conversion to Consumerism." *Journal of Contemporary History* 40, no. 2 (2005): 317–40.
Seefried, Elke. *Zukünfte. Aufstieg und Krise der Zukunftsforschung, 1945–1980*. De Gruyter, 2015.
Seefried, Elke, and Dierk Hoffmann, eds. *Plan und Planung. Deutsch-deutsche Vorgriffe auf die Zukunft*. De Gruyter 2018.
Seiderer, Birgit. "Horst Herold und das Nürnberger Modell (1966–1971). Eine Fallstudie zur Pionierzeit des polizeilichen EDV-Einsatzes in der Reformära der Bundesrepublik." *Mitteilungen des Vereins für Geschichte der Stadt Nürnberg* 91 (2004): 317–50.
Shearer, David. "Elements Near and Alien: Passportization, Policing, and Identity in the Stalinist State, 1932–1952." *JMH* 76 (2004): 835–81.
Simon, Bart. "The Return of Panopticism: Supervision, Subjection and the New Surveillance." *Surveillance & Society* 3, no. 1 (2005): 1–20.
Solove, Daniel J. "Privacy and Power: Computer Databases and Metaphors for Information Privacy." *Stanford Law Review* 53, no. 6 (July 2001): 1393–462.
———. "Privacy Self-Management and the Consent Dilemma." *Harvard Law Review* 126 (2013): 1880–903.
———. *Understanding Privacy*. Harvard University Press, 2008.
Stalder, Felix. "Privacy Is Not the Antidote to Surveillance." *Surveillance & Society* 1, no. 1 (2002): 120–24.
Süß, Winfried. "'Wer aber denkt für das Ganze?' Aufstieg und Fall der ressortübergreifenden Planung im Bundeskanzleramt." In *Demokratisierung und gesellschaftlicher Aufbruch. Die sechziger Jahre als Wendezeit der Bundesrepublik*, edited by Matthias Frese, Julia Paulus, and Karl Teppe, 349–77. Schöningh, 2003.
Tantner, Anton. *Ordnung der Häuser, Beschreibung der Seelen. Hausnummerierung und Seelenkonskription in der Habsburgermonarchie*. StudienVerlag, 2007.
Terhoeven, Petra. *Die Rote Armee Fraktion*. C. H. Beck, 2017.
———. "Im Ausnahmezustand. Die Bundesrepublik während des 'roten Jahrzehnts' (1967–1977)." In *Ausnahmezustände. Entgrenzungen und Regulierungen in Europa während des Kalten Krieges*, edited by Cornelia Rauh and Dirk Schumann, 67–91. Wallstein, 2015.
Thiel, Markus. *Die "Entgrenzung" der Gefahrenabwehr. Grundfragen von Freiheit und Sicherheit im Zeitalter der Globalisierung*. Mohr Siebeck, 2011.
Torpey, John. *The Invention of the Passport: Surveillance, Citizenship and the State*. Cambridge University Press, 2000.
Trute, Hans-Heinrich. "Die Erosion des klassischen Polizeirechts durch die polizeiliche Informationsvorsorge." In *Rechtstheorie und Rechtsdogmatik im Austausch*, edited by Wilfried Erbguth, Friedrich Müller, and Volker Neumann, 402–28. Duncker & Humblot, 1999.

Varon, Jeremy. *Bringing the War Home: The Weather Underground, the Red Army Faction, and Revolutionary Violence in the Sixties and Seventies.* University of California Press, 2004.
Wagner, Patrick. *Volksgemeinschaft ohne Verbrecher.* Christians, 1996.
Webster, Frank. *Theories of the Information Society*, 2nd ed. Routledge, 2002.
Wegener, Jens. "Order and Chaos: The CIA's HYDRA Database and the Dawn of the Information Age." *Journal of Intelligence History* 19, no. 1 (2020): 77–91.
Wehner, Christoph. *Die Versicherung der Atomgefahr. Risikopolitik, Sicherheitsproduktion und Expertise in der Bundesrepublik Deutschland und den USA, 1945–1986.* Wallstein, 2017.
Weinhauer, Klaus. *Die Schutzpolizei in der Bundesrepublik zwischen Bürgerkrieg und innerer Sicherheit. Die turbulenten sechziger Jahre.* Schöningh, 2003.
———. "Staatsmacht ohne Grenzen? Innere Sicherheit, 'Terrorismus'-Bekämpfung und die bundesdeutsche Gesellschaft der 1970er Jahre." In *Rationalitäten der Gewalt. Staatliche Neuordnungen vom 19. bis zum 21. Jahrhundert*, edited by Susanne Krasmann and Jürgen Martschukat, 215–38. Transkript, 2015.
———. "Terrorismus in der Bundesrepublik der Siebzigerjahre. Aspekte einer Sozial- und Kulturgeschichte der Inneren Sicherheit." *AfS* 44 (2004): 219–42.
Weinreb, Alice. *Modern Hungers: Food and Power in Twentieth-Century Germany.* Oxford University Press, 2017.
Weßlau, Edda. *Vorfeldermittlungen. Probleme der Legalisierung "vorbeugender Verbrechensbekämpfung" aus strafprozessrechtlicher Sicht.* Duncker & Humblot, 1989.
Wetzell, Richard. *Inventing the Criminal: A History of Criminology, 1880–1945.* University of North Carolina Press, 2001.
Whitman, James Q. "The Two Western Cultures of Privacy: Dignity versus Liberty." *Yale Law Journal* 113 (2004): 1151–221.
Wirsching, Andreas. *Abschied vom Provisorium, 1982–1990.* Deutsche Verlags-Anstalt, 2006.
Wood, David Murakami. "Beyond the Panopticon? Foucault and Surveillance Studies." In *Space, Knowledge and Power: Foucault and Geography*, edited by Jeremy Crampton and Stuart Elden, 245–63. Ashgate, 2007.
Wright, Alex. *Cataloging the World: Paul Otlet and the Birth of the Information Age.* Oxford University Press, 2014.
Wunschik, Tobias. *Baader-Meinhofs Kinder. Die zweite Generation der RAF.* Westdeutscher Verlag, 1997.
Zaiotti, Ruben. *Cultures of Border Control: Schengen and the Evolution of European Frontiers.* University of Chicago Press, 2011.
Zuboff, Shoshana. *The Age of Surveillance Capitalism.* PublicAffairs, 2019.
———. "Big Other: Surveillance Capitalism and the Prospects of an Information Civilization." *Journal of Information Technology* 30 (2015): 75–89.

Index

Action Plan for the Modernization and Intensification of Crime Prevention, 238, 239
Adenauer, Konrad, 9, 212, 214
administrative power, 5, 8, 19, 20, 22, 38, 39, 40, 44, 59, 87, 110, 209, 223–32, 243. *See also* informational power
    Anthony Giddens on, 4, 5, 6, 110
    role of privacy in theorizing and contesting, 6, 13, 22, 40, 64
advertising, targeted marketing, junk mail, 60, 114, 118, 125, 132n65, 196, 199, 200, 359
Agar, Jon, 38
Albers, Marion, 177, 344
alibi controls, 288
Alternative Draft for a Uniform Police Law for Federal and State Government, 332, 333
Aly, Götz, 136, 141
Amtshilfe, 86, 91, 125, 152, 166, 183, 335
Appel, Roland, 158
Aradau, Claudia, 325
Arendt, Hannah, 83
Auernhammer, Herbert, 14, 109, 115, 118
automobility
    increasing, 235
    securitization of, 19, 253–57, 260. *See also* Federal Motor Vehicle Bureau

Baader, Andreas, 216, 218, 219, 221, 260, 277, 278, 285, 286, 296, 297, 300
Badura, Peter, 151
Bangemann, Martin, 194
Baudrillard, Jean, 88
Baum, Gerhart, 15, 56, 127, 303, 305, 306
    appointment as interior minister, 12, 20, 306
    and limitation of state surveillance, 192, 193, 194, 266, 285, 306, 343
    tensions with Herold, 309
Baumann, Reinhold, 183, 187, 257
    concern about national ID card, 265
Benda, Ernst, 14, 58, 90, 91, 98, 188, 233, 234
    dysfunctional dissemination of information and the destruction of the private sphere, 91, 149, 201n5
Beniger, James, 2, 5
Bentham, Jeremy, 23
Bergien, Rüdiger, 252
Big Data. *See* Privacy: Big Data
Birkelbach, Willi, 115, 119
Boeden, Gerhard, 283, 288
Boge, Heinrich, 273, 309, 314
Bölsche, Jochen, 313
borders, space, and place—securitization of, 257–60, 267. *See also* population registration: hotel registration requirement
    INPOL and the intensified surveillance of borders and internal state space, 258, 259
    normalization of space, 259
    and the privacy issues raised by, 252, 253, 255, 256, 257, 274
    terrorist strategies and the importance of border controls, 258
    use of mobile terminals, 258
Börner, Holger, 147
Bourdieu, Pierre, 39
Brandeis, Louis, 81, 83

Brandt, Willy, 11, 12
Bresse, Klaus, 65, 66
Brunnstein, Klaus, 148
Buback, Siegfried, 221, 255
Bull, Hans Peter, 13, 126, 150, 186, 187, 189, 198, 255, 256, 272, 299, 301, 307, 308, 309
    appointment as federal privacy commissioner, 123
    criticism of census decision, 201n6, 201n15
    criticism of surveillance state discourse, 295, 313
    and the goals of privacy protection law, 126
    moderate position on census, 147, 149, 150
    on national ID card, 264
    on passive tracking, 295
    relationship with Herold, 307
    warning about mixing statistical and administrative data, 139

census boycotts (1983/87), 8, 15, 135–69. *See also* census decision
    access to partly anonymized census data, 139, 140
    applicability of final purpose principle to census data, 151–53
    arguments before Constitutional Court, 148–53
    assessment of boycott success, 158–60
    census data and the government of the welfare state, 151, 159, 160, 161, 162
    census forms, 140, 141
    census law, 16, 135–40, 154
    and de-anonymization of census data, 140, 148
    debate over door-to-door count, 136, 137, 152, 160–62, 168
    debate over the legitimacy of the boycotts, 146, 147
    disenchantment with politics, 166, 167
    imagery, 144, 164
    and informational needs of local government, 140
    interpretation by Marxist groups, 144
    and memory politics, 15, 136, 141
    normalizing power of census data as focus of protests, 15, 136, 142, 143
    obligation to work as census taker, 146
    as privacy-based social movement, 137, 157
    protest rhetoric, 136–38, 143
    refusal of Constitutional Court to hear legal challenges to 1987 census law, 137, 158
    registration of protesters in police information systems, 155
    registry comparison, 137–39, 147, 149, 153
    Schummellinie, 156, 157
    state efforts to suppress boycotts, 16, 145, 146, 154, 155
    suspicion regarding banality of questions, 141
    temporary injunction (1983), 149, 150
    transition to registry-based censuses, 168
census decision, 8, 58, 127, 135, 177–90, 313, 314, 335
    abstract juxtaposition of individual and society, 97, 98, 182
    administration reaction to, 184
    applicability of decision to all uses of personal information, 181
    chilling effect of surveillance and informational asymmetry, 181, 201n8
    constitutional role of privacy commissioners, 183, 184
    constitutionality of census, 16, 153, 160, 184
    construction of privacy as individual right, 16, 17, 177–79, 182, 183
    criticisms of Court's reasoning, 16, 177, 182–83
    and electronic data processing, 180, 182
    and failure to roll back state and private surveillance, 199
    and final purpose principle, 151, 152, 183
    impact of informational asymmetry and uncertainty on self-determination, 180
    and national ID card law, 262, 264, 265
    privacy as precondition for democratic process, 181

prohibition of
  Vorratsdatenspeicherung, 183,
  201n17
protection of census data against de-
  anonymization, 184
and revision of federal and state
  information laws, 16, 178, 323
social nature of man and limits on
  informational self-determination,
  182
transparency rights, 183
undertheorized communicative
  dimension, 17, 82, 180, 182
Central Aliens Registry
  (Ausländerzentralregister), 229, 258,
  267
Central Persons Index (Zentraler
  Personenindex), 268, 271–73
Chandler, Alfred, 2, 5
Christian Democratic Union (CDU), 9, 12,
  15, 53, 59, 60, 64, 96, 178, 213, 266
  views on privacy and security, 17,
    178, 185, 193
Christian Social Union (CSU), 9, 12, 15, 150
civil registration, 37, 43
Clemens, Joachim, 266
Code of Administrative Procedure, 16,
  132n59, 187
Code of Criminal Procedure, 16, 235, 295,
  330, 331, 332, 340, 345, 346, 351–52n35,
  356n95
Cohen, Julie, 90
  critique of individualist conception
    of privacy, 25, 26
communes (*Wohngemeinschaften*), 53,
  170n11, 287, 320n88
communism, 9, 155, 212, 213, 214, 216
computer matching (*Rasterfahndung*), 289,
  299–301, 323, 346, 347
  and non-existence of harmless data,
    300
computers, computerization, 2, 7, 8, 19, 23,
  61, 149, 227, 229, 252, 360
  and the information revolution in
    government, 55, 61, 66
  mainframes, 3, 189
  personal computers, 189
  systems analysis, 231, 232, 233, 238
concrete danger, 144, 283, 284, 295, 326,
  331, 337, 341, 343, 345, 346, 347, 363,
  364. *See also* police law: general charge;
  precautionary surveillance: and the

extension of surveillance into the *Vorfeld*
  of concrete dangers and well-founded
  individual suspicion
  versus general state of danger, 362
  versus risk, 362
  and well-founded individual
    suspicion as historical threshold
    for police action, 20, 21, 283, 323,
    324, 328, 330–32, 338, 344, 361
Conference of State and Federal Interior
  Ministers, 229, 232, 235, 239, 259, 271,
  288, 290, 308, 334, 363
  approval (and subsequent
    revocation) of counterterrorism
    measures, 287, 288, 290, 305
  as central body for the coordination
    of domestic policy, 228
  controversy over adequacy of
    Conference authorization of
    surveillance measures, 307, 323
  decision to construct INPOL, 19, 239,
    243, 252, 270, 305
  plan for harmonization of state
    police laws, 324
  and Preliminary Draft, 334
Conference of State and Federal Privacy
  Commissioners, 123
Constitutional Court
  (Bundesverfassungsgericht) decisions
  ban of Communist Party, 213
  bulk collection of telephone
    and internet metadata
    (*Vorratsdatenspeicherung*), 362, 363
  census. *See* census decision
  clandestine tape recording, 93
  divorce papers, 94
  drug addiction counseling, 94
  Elfes, 79
  Eppler, 96, 180
  Federal Criminal Police Law, 363
  Investment Assistance, 82, 96–97
  Lebach, 95, 96
  medical records, 94
  microcensus, 79, 80, 85, 92, 93, 148,
    149, 151, 153
  preventive computer matching, 362
  Saroya, 95
  temporary injunction blocking 1983
    census, 16
consumer credit (reporting), 52, 84, 87,
  104n44, 114, 119, 121, 196, 359. *See also*
  Schufa

contact persons, 260, 299, 302, 340, 341
Conze, Eckart, 213
counterterrorism, 18, 20, 218, 221, 253, 282, 286, 287, 290, 297, 300, 302, 305, 333. *See also* Federal Criminal Police (Bundeskriminalamt): centralization of counterterrorism authority; police, policing
Crime/Criminal Database, 242, 267, 270, 271, 273, 274. *See also* INPOL
   abandonment of, 271, 273
   conceptual difficulties with project, 270
Criminal Records Index (Kriminalaktennachweis, KAN), 242, 272, 274, 338. *See also* INPOL
Croissant, Klaus, 296

Dammann, Ulrich, 14, 64, 87, 88
data doubles, 2, 87, 164, 263, 264
databases, 10, 11, 23, 45, 50, 59, 60, 85, 111, 112, 115, 118, 142, 235, 251, 258, 262, 265, 267, 268, 274, 290, 299, 307, 311, 347
   and representation, 2, 24, 86–88, 177
Deleuze, Gilles, 23, 24, 88
Denninger, Erhard, 326, 332
Dickopf, Paul, 227, 233, 234, 236, 238
Ditfurth, Jutta, 141
division of informational powers, 86, 265
domestic affairs committee (Bundestag), 54, 255, 266, 299, 306
   and national ID card law, 266
   June 1989 hearings on privacy and security laws, 195
   May1974 hearings on privacy and population registration laws, 121
   national ID card law, 261
   November 1972 hearing on the Federal Privcy Protection Law, 114–20
   securitization of automobility, 254
Domestic Intelligence Agency (Bundesamt für Verfassungsschutz), 17, 178, 190–94, 197–99, 285, 298, 313
   conflict with Federal Criminal Police over authority to engage in precautionary surveillance, 298
   founding of agency, 214
   information exchange with the police and separation rule, 191, 192, 198, 214. *See also* Informational Collaboration Law

   proportionality of surveillance practices, 190, 197
   support of police in surveillance of radical milieu, 288
   surveillance and the final purpose principle, 190, 191, 197
   transparency rights and proposed exceptions for security agencies, 189, 196, 198
Dreising, Wolf von, 41, 44
Drenkmann, Günter von, 219
Dutschke, Rudi, 217

Economist, The, 361
Egloff, Willi, 100
electronic (integrated) data processing, 2, 8, 9, 64, 67, 111, 177, 209, 233, 241
   as catalyst for privacy protection law, 61–67, 358
   impact on public administration, 86
   integration or transparency effect, 10, 11, 12, 61, 64, 180
   and loss of control over information, 11, 40, 65, 66, 80, 94, 96, 149
   one-time principle, 62, 63
   and violation of the principles of privacy law, 64, 120
Elektronisches Entgeltnachweis (ELENA), 60
Emergency Laws, 214, 215, 216, 244n16
Engelhard, Hans A., 345
Ensslin, Gudrun, 216, 218, 221
Enzensberger, Hans Magnus, 311, 312
Eppler, Erhard, 96
Erb, Ulrike, 163, 164, 166
Erhard, Benno, 122
Erhard, Ludwig, 9, 10, 12
Ericson, Richard, 23
Erkelenz, Gabriele, 120, 125
Ermisch, Günter, 299, 300, 301
European Conference for Domestic Security (TREVI Conference), 258
European Convention on Human Rights, 358
European privacy law, 359, 361
   convergence with human rights law, 359
Ewald, François, 364

fair information practices, 14, 67, 109
Federal Border Police (Bundesgrenzschutz), 190, 191, 214, 215, 219, 239, 258

Index 381

Federal Central Crime Register
  (Bundeszentralregister), 251
Federal Court of Justice
  Schacht (Letter to the Editor)
    decision, 92
Federal Criminal Police
  (Bundeskriminalamt), 6, 17, 20, 190,
  209–50, 268, 273, 298, 299, 304, 313
  agency founding and
    responsibilities, 191, 213, 222, 223
  authorizing law and its amendment,
    223, 238, 239, 240, 288, 305, 363
  as central coordinating office for the
    country's police, 239
  and centralization of
    counterterrorism authority, 19,
    20, 210, 238, 284–89, 297, 302, 309
  computerization of. *See* INPOL;
    police, policing
  counterterrorism division, 239, 288
  development of a stand-alone
    computer system for the agency,
    232–38
  fingerprint files, 222, 226–28, 236,
    237, 253. *See also* fingerprints,
    fingerprinting
  Five-Year Plan to Increase the
    Effectiveness of the Federal
    Criminal Police, 234
  hunt for Schleyer, 301–3
  impact of manual data processing
    on agency effectiveness, 19, 209,
    222–27
  information exchange with
    intelligence agencies and the
    separation rule, 191, 310
  interior ministry audit (Faude
    report), 224–27, 233, 241, 306, 307
  manpower, 225, 316n24
  professional or habitual criminals
    and growing workload of, 223,
    224
  Protective Services Division
    (Sicherungsgruppe), 239, 253,
    285, 288
  and question of preventive authority,
    288, 295, 305
  SoKo Baader-Meinhof, 218, 285, 286,
    288
  subsidiary role of, 210, 222, 239, 240
  wanted persons and stolen objects
    files, 226, 233, 236

Federal Motor Vehicle Bureau, 251, 256, 257
  Central Vehicle Information System
    (ZEVIS), 186, 251, 253, 254, 255,
    273, 274
  debate over access to ZEVIS
    information, 255–57
  integration of ZEVIS and INPOL,
    229, 253, 267
  vehicular surveillance, 255
  ZEVIS as national address book, 256,
    276n16
  ZEVIS law as typical product of
    post-census decision conjuncture,
    256, 257
Federal Privacy Protection Law
  (Bundesdatenschutzgesetz), 3, 8, 10,
  11, 12, 14, 16, 20, 26, 40, 50, 54, 55, 56,
  67, 101, 108–27, 177, 178, 179, 185, 186,
  200, 261, 284, 294, 302, 332, 333. *See also*
  privacy
  amendment of, 15, 16, 124–27, 177,
    186–90, 194–96, 359, 360
  complexity and opaqueness of
    privacy law, 198, 199, 200
  compliance mechanisms, 113, 119,
    121
  conflict between SPD and FDP over
    purpose of federal privacy law,
    125–27
  consent as basis for information
    processing, 111, 196
  conservative efforts to limit authority
    of federal privacy commissioner,
    186–87, 195, 196
  debate over extension of law to
    collection of information, 115,
    116, 187, 196
  debate over extension of law to
    paper files, 115, 121, 131n50, 185,
    187, 188, 195, 196, 333, 342
  definition of *Datenschutz*, 112
  disputed priority of privacy and
    access rights, 109, 111
  elastic clauses, 15, 109, 120, 123, 126,
    166
  formatted files and scope of law, 14,
    112, 114, 188, 195, 196
  harmonization of German law with
    EU privacy law, 359, 360
  impact of new technologies on
    regulatory paradigm of law, 189,
    360

impossibility of defining privacy harms in the abstract, 14, 112, 117
and informational infringement (*Informationseingriff*), 54, 124, 323
informational privacy as theoretical foundation of law, 109
and the informational unity of the state, 86, 117, 118, 335
juridification of informational activity, 14, 126, 198, 199, 305, 324, 334, 348
legitimate privacy interests of the individual, 49, 111, 112, 120, 125
linkage of privacy and population registration laws, 17, 55, 111, 184–87, 178
linkage of privacy and security laws, 184–87, 189. *See also* Omnibus Bill
nature of the harms against which the law was to protect, 114
and need for formal legislative authorization of data processing, 54, 60, 124, 182, 183, 199, 290, 307, 323, 334, 335
and the negotiation of socially adequate norms, 14, 24, 25, 108, 120, 200
personal versus factual or commercial information, 116, 117, 118, 119
precautionary surveillance and challenge to original privacy protection paradigm, 358
regulation of information exchange in the public administration, 13, 67, 112, 113, 117–22, 152, 187, 196
regulation of information processing in the private sector, 112, 113, 114, 118, 119, 121, 125, 196. *See also* advertising, targeted marketing, junk mail
significance of the law, 198–200, 252, 274, 294
and state privacy laws, 122, 123, 194
structure of law, 112, 113, 114
tension between general principles and anticipated domain-specific privacy legislation, 110, 120
transparency provisions, 109, 113, 121
transparency rights and proposed exemption of security agencies, 113, 188, 189, 196

Fiedler, Herbert, 14, 90, 198
fingerprints, fingerprinting, 42, 69n18, 236, 242, 261, 271, 331, 333, 339. *See also* Federal Criminal Police (Bundeskriminalamt): fingerprint files
Foreign Intelligence Agency (Bundesnachrichtendienst), 191
Foucault, Michel, 1, 23, 324, 325
Frankfurter Allgemeine Zeitung, 52, 62, 146, 150
Frankfurter Rundschau, 150
Free Democratic Party (FDP), 9, 17, 53, 59, 60, 124, 127, 148, 178, 179, 189, 190, 191, 200, 210, 215, 257, 265, 274
  alternative version of Preliminary Draft, 344, 345
  break with SPD over economic policy, 15
  call for constitutional right to *Datenschutz*, 125
  criticism of Informational Collaboration Law, 194
  influence on privacy and security legislation, 17, 196, 197, 200, 266
  linkage of privacy and security laws, 178, 184–87
  views on privacy, security, and surveillance, 17, 185, 190, 192, 193, 194, 257. *See also* Baum, Gerhart
freedom of information, 13, 118, 166, 188

Gaserow, Vera, 150
General Data Protection Regulation, 7, 359, 361
Genscher, Hans-Dietrich, 12, 48, 109, 110, 111, 115, 211, 239, 241, 252, 285, 302, 306, 310
  electronic data processing and modernization of the public administration, 12, 111, 118, 123
  views on privacy, 49, 50, 111
German Association for Privacy Protection, 123
German Autumn, 56, 221, 274, 282, 301–3
Gestapo, 7, 141, 144, 266
Giddens, Anthony, 4, 5, 6, 110
Grass, Günter, 147
Greens
  attitudes toward information technology, 164, 165, 166
  census boycotts and civil disobedience, 137, 145, 157

critique of statistical governance, 16, 135, 137, 154, 159, 160–65, 169
differences over boycott strategy, 156, 157
proposals for reform of privacy protection law, 166
and leadership of census boycotts, 137, 154, 156
Grimm, Dieter, 347
Guidelines for the Pursuit of Politically Motivated Violent Offenders, 287

Haag, Siegfried, 295, 296
Habermas, Jürgen, 83, 164
Hadeler, Heinz, 256
Haggerty, Kevin, 23
Hanshew, Karrin, 222
Heißler, Rolf, 300
Helbing, Monika, 260
Hellenbroich, Heribert, 314
Hennis, Wilhelm, 83
Herold, Horst, 6, 19, 143, 209, 210, 211, 227, 232, 237, 238, 241, 242, 243, 257, 267, 268, 269, 270, 273, 283, 285, 286, 289, 294, 295, 296, 298, 299, 301, 302, 305, 307, 309, 310, 312, 326–29
  1966 plan for national criminal information system, 230, 231, 232
  appointment as president of the Federal Criminal Police, 210, 211, 238
  and criminal geography, 268, 269
  critique of informational hierarchies, 211, 269
  and cybernetics, 20, 211, 252, 268, 269, 270, 327
  and the design of INPOL, 241, 242, 243
  fahnden und finden/fahnden und forschen, 326
  forced from office, 309
  information question, 6, 26
  information, computers, and the search for natural laws of crime and deviance, 144, 211, 230, 231, 232, 327
  master plan for combatting terrorism, 254, 287, 289, 290, 291, 292, 293
  social sanitary mission of the police as liberal governmentality, 21, 144, 312, 326–28, 343

as target of census protests, 143, 144, 327
tensions with Baum, 309
and the unique importance of passive tracking, 294
Hesse
  commissioner model, 66, 67
  data processing and privacy laws, 40, 63–67
Heußner, Hermann, 201
Hirsch, Burkhard, 191, 194, 313, 334
Höcherl, Hermann, 305
Hoffmann-Riem, Wolfgang, 199, 331, 332
Hölder, Egon, 44, 162
homosexuals, homosexuality, 53
  and privacy concerns, 106n66, 144, 171n27
Honnacker, Heinz, 193, 199
Hubmann, Heinrich, 92

IBM, 267, 275n7
Igo, Sarah, 23
indications, 191, 200, 330, 341, 343, 348
  distinction between facts, indications, factual indications, and sufficient factual indications, 352n37
  factual (*tatsächliche Anhaltspunkte*), 197, 200, 295, 330, 333, 338, 341, 342, 343, 346, 362, 363
  sufficient factual (zureichende tatsächliche Anhaltspunkte), 296
information. *See also* personal information (data)
  access rights, 13, 81, 101, 108, 109, 110, 116, 324, 334, 346, 360
  determination of the meaning of information by pragmatic interests that shape its collection and encoding, 4, 5, 24, 86, 87, 160, 162, 163
  as a distinct policy concern, 10
  information question, 6, 15, 66
information law, 98–101, 100, 101, 123, 126, 177, 200
information processing regime, 126, 188
information society, 1, 2, 4, 5, 26, 108, 161, 162, 314
information state, 29n18
  and the informational recasting of Hobbes' *Leviathan*, 348, 364
Informational Collaboration Law, 185, 186, 190, 194

FDP hostility toward, 191
informational power (social power generated by control of information), 1, 3, 4, 5, 7, 8, 13, 14, 15, 17, 37, 38, 67, 80, 85, 99, 100, 101, 118, 126, 169, 183, 310, 358
   and limits of individualist conception of privacy, 3, 22, 23, 26, 36
   normalizing, disciplinary power of, 15, 141–45
   role of privacy in theorizing and contesting, 5, 6, 13, 22, 40, 64, 80, 85, 89, 90, 97, 98
informational privacy, 22, 359
   and American privacy law, 81
   as counterconcept to data integration, 3, 6, 10, 11, 61–67, 108, 109
   as response to limitations of private sphere, 3, 4, 22, 82, 98, 109
   versus spatial and decisional privacy, 4, 95, 98
informational self-determination (right to), 8, 92, 94, 95, 96, 109, 166, 177–84, 186, 188, 189, 193, 197, 201n12, 336. *See also* census decision; privacy
   construction of privacy as individual right, 16, 17, 177–79, 182, 183
   problems specifying concrete harms, 14, 109, 126
   as remedy for loss of control over personal information, 12, 13, 40, 96, 179
   right to determine how one is represented by others, 87, 93, 94, 95, 96, 97
   as strand of personality rights, 16, 91, 135
inmate surveillance, 288–90, 323
INPOL, 10, 19, 257, 259, 267, 270. *See also* Crime/Criminal Database; INPOL-new; PIOS
   architecture, 19, 233, 240–43, 267, 269, 305
   automation and the formalization of tacit knowledge, 101, 234, 245, 284
   automation of modus operandi system, 234, 253, 270
   build out, 19, 252, 253
   data integration and the elimination of redundant files, 229, 230, 257
   decision to construct, 19, 51, 239, 243, 252, 270, 305
   and government at a distance, 19, 257, 273
   initial plans, 227–32
   integration with civilian databases, 19, 243, 251
   and policing of borders, 258
   privacy issues, 19, 252, 306, 307, 308
   relation between state and national criminal information systems, 210, 243
   wanted persons and stolen objects systems, 234, 242, 252, 253
INPOL-new, 19, 20, 252, 267–74, 305
   and the democratization of police information, 269, 270
   privacy concerns raised by component systems, 271, 272, 273, 274
   and transformation of police into a cybernetic system, 268, 269, 270
internal security, 157, 163, 178, 192, 210, 211–22, 238, 239, 306, 324, 340, 343, 358
   and balance between security and civil liberties, 18, 244n16, 213, 217
   Cold War origins, 18
   communism as hinge between internal and external security, 214
   directed primarily against the left, 18, 213
   end of postwar internal security regime, 22, 285, 301
   and legacy of Hobbes, 348
   as mirror image of privacy, 20, 284
   Social Democrats and the welfarist reconfiguration of internal security, 18, 210, 215
Isensee, Josef, 335

June 2 Movement, 216, 219

Kaleth, Hans, 209
Kamlah, Ruprecht, 52, 54
Karl, Helmut, 238
Kauß, Udo, 60
Kerbs, Diethart, 52, 53
K-Groups, 216
Kiefer, Anselm, 167
Kienbaum Consultants, 241, 242, 243
Kiesinger, Kurt, 9, 10, 11
Kinkel, Klaus, 194

Index 385

Klein, Joachim, 295
Kniesel, Michael, 338, 339, 340, 343, 349
Kohl, Helmut, 15, 16, 135
Kolleck, Bernd, 162
Kommunale Gemeinschaftsstelle für Verwaltungsvereinfachung, 42, 45, 54
Koselleck, Reinhard, 83
KpS Guidelines, 298, 333
    and competence of privacy commissioners to assess compliance with privacy law, 187, 308, 309
    and culling of police files, 271, 308
Krampol, Karl, 334
Kreuzberg decision, 330

Ladeur, Karl-Heinz, 177
Laufs, Paul, 178, 266
Leithäuser, Eva, 151
Lenk, Klaus, 85
Leuze, Ruth, 14
Lindenberg, Udo, 59
Lorenz, Peter, 219, 286, 287, 296
Lottmann-Bückler, Annerose, 260
Lotze, Werner, 302
Loveman, Mara, 39
Luhmann, Niklas, 98
Lutterbeck, Bernd, 188
Lyon, David, 66

Mahler, Horst, 216
Maihofer, Werner, 12, 258, 262, 267, 271, 288, 301, 302, 303, 304, 305, 310, 324, 329
    and logics of total prevention and repression, 311, 312, 314, 324, 329, 345
    resignation, 12, 306
Mallmann, Otto, 14, 83, 84, 89, 98, 99, 100
Marx, Karl, 53, 326, 327
Meinhof, Ulrike, 216, 218, 221
Meins, Holger, 219, 286
microcensus, 16, 101, 160, 162, 168.
    See also Constitutional Court (Bundesverfassungsgericht) decisions: microcensus
militant democracy, 211, 212
    Weimar experience and response to terrorism, 217
Military Counterintelligence Agency (Militärischer Abschirmdienst), 186, 191
Mirbach, Gunther von, 148
Möcklinghoff, Egbert, 333

Model Draft for a Uniform Police Law for Federal and State Government, 324, 330–34, 346
    decision not to regulate precautionary surveillance, 333, 334
    and expansion of police surveillance authority, 324, 330, 331
    formulation of general charge, 330–31. *See also* police law reform and harmonization of state police laws, 333
    regulation of "standard measures" regarding the use of force, 330
Mückenberger, Ulrich, 139
Müller, Paul J., 88, 89, 90
Munster, Rens van, 325

Narr, Wolf-Dieter, 159
National Crime Reporting System, 222–25, 242, 283
    concept of perseverence, 223
    modus operandi system, 223, 224. *See also* INPOL: automation of modus operandi system
    and professional or habitual criminal, 222, 223, 283, 325
national ID card, 44, 51, 56, 60, 61, 192, 252, 266
    access to registry information, 56, 252, 257, 265, 266, 274
    concern about use of serial number as ersatz national ID number, 56, 58, 261, 262, 265, 266
    convenience of, 265, 266
    data shadows, 262–64
    earlier identification documents, 39, 261
    forgery and alteration of cards by RAF, 254, 260
    and government at a distance, 267
    ID card law, 186, 190, 193, 260, 261, 262, 265
    linkage to security laws, 186, 265
    machine readability, 261, 262, 265, 313
    police monitoring of *Ausweisverlierer*, 260
    privacy concerns raised by, 261, 262, 265
    and the securitization of automobility, 255, 260

and the securitization of identity,
  260–67
 social movement directed against ID
  card, 262–64
 state monopoly over the legitimate
  means of identification, 44, 45
national ID number, 10, 51, 55, 56, 59
 attitude of state and local
  government toward, 42, 43, 45
 Bundestag rejection of, 40, 55, 122
 concern about privacy implications
  of, 52, 53, 54, 55
 initial public attitude toward, 49
 and introduction of electronic data
  processing, 38–59, 62
 recent revival of idea, 73n76
 responsibility for issuing, 43, 47
 and unambiguous identification of
  individuals, 39, 43, 44
 use in other countries, 49, 50
National Security Agency (United States),
  307
national wanted persons day
  (Bundesfahndungstag), 234, 235
National Working Group of Critical Police
  Officers, 312, 313
Nazi Germany, 9, 18, 41, 141
 association of census takers with
  block wardens, 140
 memory of and postwar privacy
  thought, 6, 7, 15, 83, 136, 141
 population registration, 39
 reintegration of former Nazis under
  Adenauer, 212
 unexpiated complicity of older
  generation, 216
Neusel, Hans, 194
New Left, 210, 216
 and the Federal Republic as latently
  fascist polity, 282
 and the "long march through the
  institutions," 217
new police surveillance practices, 21, 282–
  301, 323. See also Federal Criminal Police
  (Bundeskriminalamt); INPOL; computer
  matching; inmate surveillance;
  passive tracking; PIOS; precautionary
  surveillance
 as building blocks of precautionary
  surveillance regime, 284
 distinguishing characteristics, 283, 284
 limitations of, 285, 297, 303, 304, 314

privacy concerns relating to, 290, 294,
  295, 297, 298, 299, 301
Nissenbaum, Helen, 24, 89
Noelle-Neumann, Elisabeth, 162

Omnibus Bill, 194, 195, 256, 266. See
  also Domestic Intelligence Agency;
  Federal Privacy Protection Law
  (Bundesdatenschutzgesetz); Federal
  Motor Vehicle Bureau; Informational
  Collaboration Law; national ID card: ID
  card law
 April 1986 hearings on, 189
 as strategy for reform of security and
  privacy laws, 184, 186, 187
Orwell, George, 23, 61, 65, 141, 143, 217,
  311, 313, 343
Osswald, Albert, 64, 65, 66, 67

passive tracking (beobachtende Fahndung),
  253, 288, 289, 290–97, 299, 302, 308, 323,
  333, 340, 342
 approval by Working Group II, 291
 and privacy implications of, 294,
  295, 296
 and question of concrete danger as
  threshold for surveillance, 295, 296
 status as preventive or repressive
  measure, 294–96
personal information (data), 8, 11, 26, 37, 60,
  81, 108, 148, 178
 definition, 4
 the Federal Privacy Protection law
  and debate over the scope of, 116,
  117, 118, 119
 and the governance of the welfare
  state, 3, 20, 49, 54, 91, 137, 358
 as medium for social governance, 3,
  4, 5, 29n18, 16
 politics of, 6, 169
 as steering medium, 2, 3, 65
 surveillance by means of records and
  personal information, 2, 28n10
personality profiles, 14, 52, 87, 90, 143, 184,
  263, 311. See also privacy
 and the predetermination of
  individual development, 93, 99,
  100
 definition of, 104n44
personality rights, 85, 88, 91, 92, 98, 135,
  193, 200. See also informational self-
  determination (right to)

Index 387

absolutely protected core and its
  jurisprudential irrelevance, 82,
  93, 94
and American privacy law, 81
and clash of fundamental rights, 108,
  109, 187, 188
conflicting rights of self and other,
  96, 97
and dignitarian injuries, 11, 80, 81,
  82, 93, 97, 99, 180, 181
limited by social obligations, 82
PIOS, 267, 268, 289, 290, 297–99, 303, 308,
  323
  as central repository for
    counterterrorism surveillance,
    253, 288, 293, 296
  and conflict between police
    and intelligence agencies
    over authority to engage in
    precautionary surveillance, 298,
    299
  and lowering of threshold for police
    surveillance, 297, 298, 299
  meaning of acronym, 279n71, 297
  search capacity of, 297, 317n48
  and surveillance of "other persons,"
    298, 299, 318n52
  and the visibility of criminal
    complexes, 297
Pitschas, Rainer, 335, 336, 348, 362
planning, 9, 10, 11, 136, 141
  data integration and modeling
    of interdependencies across
    functional domains, 65
  and privacy, 54, 64, 65, 66, 117
  role of census data, 141, 160, 161
  state information and planning
    systems, 40, 44, 58, 63, 64, 65, 66,
    148
  US National Data Center, 75n89
Podlech, Adalbert, 13, 98, 117, 148, 152, 200,
  332
  definition of surveillance state, 310
  personality rights and privacy, 90, 96,
    97, 98, 151, 180
  shift of privacy framework from
    individual to systemic level, 101
police, policing, 5, 8, 10, 12, 16, 17, 19,
  20, 26, 39, 52, 143, 193, 211, 214, 215,
  219. See also Federal Criminal Police
  (Bundeskriminalamt); INPOL; new
  police surveillance practices

creation of riot police, 214
declining clearance rate in 1960s,
  234, 235
disenchantment with and
  Thermidorean reaction against
  police surveillance regime, 21,
  285, 302, 305, 306, 309, 310
early history of police informatics,
  209, 210, 211, 228
expansion of surveillance capacity,
  15, 200, 282
imposition of privacy law on the
  police, 306–10
information as alpha and omega of
  police work, 209
use of covert methods, 287, 310, 323,
  332, 337, 339, 340, 341, 342, 363
police law, 16, 17, 21, 185, 190, 323–49. See
  also Model Draft for a Uniform Police
  Law for Federal and State Government;
  Preliminary Draft for the Amendment
  of the Model Draft for a Uniform Police
  Law
  general charge, 18, 295, 323, 330, 331,
    332, 333, 337, 340, 344, 346
  liberal police law, 20, 21, 284, 285,
    311, 314, 323, 325, 348, 361, 362
Ponto, Jürgen, 221, 283
population registration, 8, 10, 11, 16, 26,
  37–61, 235, 252, 262
  backward reporting system, 44
  as catalyst for the politicization of
    privacy, 10, 40, 50, 61–67
  and the expansion of state
    surveillance capacity, 44, 45
  Federal Population Registration Law,
    40, 47, 54, 55, 56, 57, 59, 67, 108,
    110, 111, 120
  hotel registration requirement, 55,
    56, 259, 260, 303
  impact on popular culture, 59
  and national population information
    system, 10, 39, 45, 46
  Population Registration Framework
    Law, 40, 56–60, 260
  and privacy concerns, 49–58, 61, 111
  programmatic commitment to
    information exchange, 47, 55, 57
  public access to registry information,
    51
  Reich Population Registration
    Ordinance, 39, 40

security aspects of, 39, 40, 45, 51, 52, 55, 56
as source of state power, 38, 39
and transparency of population, 37, 38, 58, 60
Poster, Mark, 88
precautionary surveillance, 323–49, 358, 361–64. *See also* Herold, Horst; Preliminary Draft for the Amendment of the Model Draft for a Uniform Police Law; Stümper, Alfred
   as antithesis of ordinary crime and perseverant modus operandi, 325
   and challenge to liberal police law, 21, 285, 314, 361, 362
   challenge to original privacy protection paradigm, 358
   conservative rationale for, 334–35
   definition of, 325
   and the extension of surveillance into the *Vorfeld* of concrete dangers and well-founded individual suspicion, 20, 21, 284, 288, 324, 326, 328, 332, 336, 338–41, 343, 347
   further expansion of in response to December 2016 attack on Breitscheidplatz, 363
   and the governance of the welfare state, 20, 347, 348
   and increasing uncertainty of prognosis, 295, 362
   and internal security, 324, 343
   and modes of governmentality, 21, 324, 328, 329
   qualified endorsement by Constitutional Court, 362
   transgressive logic of, 21, 22, 324, 325, 326, 358
Preliminary Draft for the Amendment of the Model Draft for a Uniform Police Law, 326, 331, 336–44, 362. *See also* precautionary surveillance
   as characteristic product of the post-census decision conjuncture, 348
   and the codification of new surveillance practices, 323, 339, 340, 341, 346
   FDP alternative version, 344, 345
   formulation of precautionary mandate, 336

   harmonization of police law and Code of Criminal Procedure, 345, 346, 351–52n36
   negation of final purpose principle, 342
   preparations for the defense against future dangers, 336, 337
   preventive combatting of crime, 331
   controversy over preventive or repressive nature, 339, 340, 341
   debate over subsumption under general charge, 336, 337
   inconsistent adoption in state police laws, 346
   precautions for the (future) prosecution of (future) crime, 336, 337, 338, 339, 340, 362
   prevention (Verhütung) of crime, 336, 337
   terrorism, organized crime, and the rationale for, 338–39
   reform and harmonization of state police laws, 344, 345, 347
   and transformation of police law into information privacy and access law, 324
privacy. *See also* administrative power; Federal Privacy Protection Law (Bundesdatenschutzgesetz); informational power; informational self-determination (right to); personality profiles
   analysis of context as precondition for the determination of privacy and access rights, 13, 80, 89, 90, 99, 100, 101, 117, 126, 152, 182
   and Big Data, 360, 361
   and consumer protection, 110
   as counterconcept to data integration, 40, 61, 64
   and defense of norms and the rule of law against precautionary surveillance, 21, 324, 348, 349, 358
   and final purpose principle, 67, 87, 89, 151, 183, 188, 190, 191, 192, 193, 197, 199, 257, 335
   in healthcare field, 17
   and human rights, 358, 359
   individualist conception of, 3, 13, 16, 17, 22, 25, 80, 98, 177, 178, 179, 182, 183

Index 389

informational parsimony, 21, 40, 88, 324, 348, 358
as mirror image of internal security, 20, 178, 284
politicization of, 3, 6. *See also* population registration: as catalyst for the politicization of privacy
privacy advocates, 13, 14, 178
privacy protection as social movement, 6, 13, 59, 110
as a reflexive, communicative relationship, 5, 13, 22, 80, 97, 98, 99, 152, 153
as role-specific disclosure, 12, 13, 26, 88–91, 99
secondary use of information, 61, 62, 65, 88, 114, 149, 153, 183, 310
strands or dimensions of, 4
technological change forcing renegotiation of socially acceptable information exchange, 19, 33, 256, 274, 339
theories of, 22–26
versus data protection, 22, 29n15
privacy commissioners, 17, 61, 67, 123, 149, 154, 179, 189, 190, 195, 197, 204n55, 261, 265, 272, 273, 301, 314, 334, 335, 341, 342
census decision and constitutional role of, 183, 184
common cause with FDP, 17, 179, 185, 190, 257
Conference of State and Federal Privacy Commissioners, 123
conflict with security officials over competence of, 308, 309
conservative criticisms of, 119, 186, 187, 199
private sphere, 23, 50, 54, 66, 79, 83, 84, 89, 90, 91, 93, 94, 95, 96, 117, 126, 148, 153, 168, 177. *See also* informational privacy
disappearance of social preconditions of, 83, 84, 85, 86, 88
and the public sphere (society), 25, 80, 83
as response to totalitarianism, 83
and shift to informational self-determination as basis for postwar privacy theory, 22, 24, 80, 152

theoretical limitations of concept, 4, 79, 80, 82, 92, 109
unusable as basis for privacy protection legislation, 79, 92
Program for the Internal Security of the Federal Republic of Germany, 239
Proll, Astrid, 218
Proll, Thorwald, 218
Prosser, William, 81
Proudhon, Pierre-Joseph, 1
public administration, 9
computerization of, 8, 9, 62, 63. *See also* national ID number
as unified informational entity, 86

Quetelet, Adolphe, 327

radical milieu
as source of logistical support and recruitment, 282, 283
logistical imperatives of life in the underground as the basis for mapping, 289, 290
police efforts to map, 20, 282–314
Radicals Resolution, 53, 155, 217, 239, 285
contribution to surveillance state debate, 310
Raspe, Jan-Carl, 219, 286
Rasterfahndung. *See* computer matching
Red Army Faction (RAF), 216, 217, 218, 219, 221, 239, 245, 254, 259, 260, 278, 283, 285, 290, 296, 300, 302, 371. *See also* Schleyer, Hanns Martin: kidnapping
founding and history, 216–21
inmate surveillance and identification of supporters, 290
May Offensive, 51, 218, 286
relationship to supporters and sympathizers, 282, 283, 287
second generation, 219, 296
trial of, 219, 296
Regan, Priscilla, 25
Revolutionary Cells, 216, 295
Riegel, Reinhard, 14
Robinson lists, 125
Rommel, Manfred, 147
Roth, Karl Heinz, 136, 141
Rouette, Leo, 233, 234, 237, 238
Rule, James, 2, 5, 8

Schäuble, Wolfgang, 195

Schelsky, Helmut, 83
Schenk, Dieter, 289, 297
Schilly, Otto, 156
Schleyer, Hanns Martin, 140, 221, 255, 261, 285, 301, 302, 303, 305, 306, 309
  kidnapping, 221, 260, 301–3
Schmidt, Helmut, 12, 124, 286, 305, 306
Scholz, Rupert, 335, 336
Schomerus, Rudolf, 125, 126, 199
Schröder, Friedrich-Christian, 146
Schufa, 118, 119, 124
Schwan, Eggert, 14
Scott, James, 5, 37
security, 17, 20, 21, 143, 178, 191, 192, 193, 251, 264, 308, 312, 325, 326, 329, 338, 343, 349
  constitutional right to, 193, 335, 345, 364
  internal. *See* internal security
  public, 18, 188, 330, 331, 332
  quest for total security as source of unfreedom, 312, 313
Seibert, Regierungsdirektorin, 342
Seifert, Jürgen, 264
separation rule. *See* Domestic Intelligence Agency (Bundesamt für Verfassungsschutz); Federal Criminal Police (Bundeskriminalamt)
Siemens, 62, 253, 267, 275n7
Simitis, Spiros, 13, 84, 85, 87, 89, 90, 98, 99, 115, 116, 118, 119, 120, 142, 149, 151, 152, 184, 187, 189, 190, 199
  analysis of context as precondition for determination of privacy and access rights, 89, 152
  and disappearance of private sphere, 84, 85, 117
  information collection as a strategic process, 87, 89
  normalizing power of information processing, 85, 100, 142
  privacy as calculated nonknowledge, 89
  rejection of individualist understanding of privacy rights, 99, 152
  and strong reading of census decision, 199
  warning about mixing statistical and administrative data, 139
Social Democratic Party (SPD), 11, 15, 59, 124, 178, 213, 215, 216
  and grand coalition, 9, 215
  retreat from earlier reservations regarding state power, 222
  and social-liberal coalition, 11, 15, 200, 210, 285
  support for the modernization of the police, 200
  understanding of crime as social problem, 210
Social Insurance Code
  and domain-specific privacy provisions, 57
social insurance funds, 43
  computerization of, 10
  police access to files, 141, 235, 236, 257, 300
Socialist Patients Collective, 216, 219
Society for Legal and Administrative Informatics, 123
Society for Privacy Protection and Data Security, 123
Söhnlein, Horst, 218
Solove, Daniel, 82
Spiegel, Der, 52, 122, 123, 147, 158
  Big Brother going electronic, 311
  criticism of police surveillance regime, 303, 304
  national ID card as admission ticket to the surveillance state, 264
  "The Steel Net Is Being Drawn over Us," 308
  on surveillance state, 311, 313
Spranger, Carl-Dieter, 150
Staak, Werner, 215, 305
Stadler-Euler, Maja, 148, 149, 151
Staeck, Klaus, 164
Steinke, Wolfgang, 254
Steinmüller, Wilhelm, 13, 86, 92, 100, 110, 120, 149, 166, 188, 310
Stern, 308
Ströbele, Hans-Christian, 156, 266
Stümper, Alfred, 308, 326, 328, 329, 334, 339, 343
surveillance. *See also* information; police; policing; population registration; precautionary surveillance; privacy; surveillance state
  approaches to the study of, 1, 2
  definition, 4, 28n10, 28n12
  observational, 23, 28n10, 311, 323
  as power or control, 5

Index

private sector as moving force behind development of, 29n18
routinization and bureaucratization of the collection of personal information, 4, 6, 22, 23, 83, 84
surveillant assemblages, 23
surveillance state (*Überwachungsstaat, Sicherheitsstaat*), 21, 66, 136, 142, 168, 192, 217, 260, 295, 297, 302, 309–14, 329, 338, 343, 347, 364
    as attempt to conceptualize the erosion of liberal police law, 285, 311
    definition, 310, 321n106
    as discourse of the civil libertarian left, 310
    information and its bureaucratic processing as basis of state power, 310
    limitations imposed by technology and conflicts of interest, 254
    moderate views on issue, 313
    national ID card as the final stone in the edifice of, 262
    police articulation of positive vision of logic of total repression, 314, 324, 328–29
    reactions to discourse by security officials, 314

Tanneberger, Stephan Maria, 157
Taz, 150
terrorism, 10, 15, 19, 137, 218, 284, 338. *See also* counterterrorism; Federal Criminal Police (Bundeskriminalamt); Red Army Faction (RAF)
    causes of radicalization, 216, 282
    distinction between hard core, supporters, and sympathizers, 282
    and limits of modus operandi analysis, 283
    major terrorist groups, 216
    number of persons involved, 216
    shift in Social Democratic attitudes toward, 286, 287
    unexceptionality of West German policy toward, 221, 222

urban guerilla tactics, 216, 218

Varon, Jeremy, 216
Volmer, Ludger, 266

Waffenschmidt, Horst, 147
Wagner, Rolf-Clemens, 300
Warren, Samuel, 81, 83
Weinhauer, Klaus, 18
welfare state, 9, 108, 117, 311
    census data and the governance of, 151, 159, 160, 161, 162
    personal information and the governance of, 3, 20, 49, 54, 83, 84, 91, 137, 358
    precautionary surveillance and the governance of, 20, 347, 348
Werckmeister, Georg, 100
Weßlau, Edda, 344, 348
    criticism of Preliminary Draft, 342, 343
Weyer, Willi, 227
Wild, Gisela, 148, 149, 151
Working Group II, 228, 229, 291
    electronic data processing commission, 229, 232, 237
Working Group Kripo, 228, 237, 273
    electronics subcommission, 234

Younger Committee, 67, 68n9

Zapf, Wolfgang, 161, 162
Zeit, Die, 150
    criticism of census boycott, 159
    criticism of informational collaboration law, 194
    criticism of registry-based census, 176n121
    limitation of police surveillance as precondition for freedom, 307
ZEVIS. *See* Federal Motor Vehicle Bureau
Zimmermann, Friedrich, 15, 16, 127, 147, 151, 159, 166, 194, 195, 196, 198, 262, 313
    support for national ID card, 264
    understanding of privacy rights, 178
Zinn, Georg August, 64

www.ingramcontent.com/pod-product-compliance
Lightning Source LLC
Chambersburg PA
CBHW071329080526
44587CB00017B/2780